Handbook of
Career Counseling
Theory and Practice

Handbook of Career Counseling Theory and Practice

WITHDRAWN

Mark L. Savickas
W. Bruce Walsh, Editors

Davies-Black Publishing
Palo Alto, California

Published by Davies-Black Publishing, an imprint of Consulting Psychologists Press, Inc., 3803 East Bayshore Road, Palo Alto, California 94303; 800-624-1765

Special discounts on bulk quantities of Davies-Black books are available to corporations, professional associations, and other organizations. For details, contact the Director of Book Sales at Davies-Black Publishing, 3803 East Bayshore Road, Palo Alto, California 94303; 650-691-9123; Fax 650-988-0673.

03 02 01   10 9 8 7 6 5 4 3
Printed in the United States of America

Credits appear on page 439, which constitute a continuation of the copyright page.

Library of Congress Cataloging-in-Publication Data
    Handbook of career counseling theory and practice: /
Mark L. Savickas and W. Bruce Walsh, editors.
      p.   cm.
    Includes bibliographical references and index.
    ISBN 0-89106-080-4
    1. Vocational guidance   I. Savickas, Mark.   II. Walsh, W. Bruce.
HF5381.H1332   1996
158.6—dc20
                                              95-44470
                                                CIP

FIRST EDITION
First printing, 1996

Contents

Introduction

Toward Convergence Between Career Theory and Practice

Mark L. Savickas
Northeastern Ohio Universities College of Medicine

W. Bruce Walsh
Ohio State University

CHANGES ATTRIBUTED TO the move to postindustrial society, the information age, postmodern culture, and a global economy have prompted escalating debate about the utility of contemporary theories of vocational behavior for the practice of career intervention (Richardson, 1993, 1994; Savickas, 1993, 1994; Tinsley, 1994). The schism between career theory and practice has a long history of generating discussion between academics and practitioners. Currently, these discussions resemble heated debates that are widening the schism. Unfortunately, the schism has reached the point where Polkinghorne (1992) concluded that counseling psychology now has two sciences: a science of theory and research performed by academicians and a science of practice.

A series of studies has confirmed the belief that theory is little used by practitioners (Morrow-Bradley & Elliott, 1986; Polkinghorne, 1992). Practitioners need knowledge of how to produce beneficial results in clients. They get it from experience with clients, oral tradition, and emerging research about the process of psychotherapy, not from theory and research.

In accord with the growing disenchantment among practitioners, some researchers have also challenged the usefulness of career theory for the practice of career counseling. For example, Fitzgerald and Betz (1994, p. 103) have recently written about the "general lack of utility of major career theories to large segments of the population." They account for this shortcoming by explaining that (a) the concept of career development may not be a meaningful concept in the lives of the majority of the population, (b) research on career theories examines the smallest segment of the population, and (c) theories do not systematically attend to the role of structural and cultural factors in conditioning individual vocational behavior.

The degree to which practitioners find career theories useful in their work became of particular interest to vocational psychologists during a conference on "Convergence Between Theories of Career Choice and Development" conducted in April 1992 by the Vocational Behavior and Career Intervention Special Interest Group in the Counseling Psychology Division of the American Psychological Association (Vocational SIG). During this conference, a heated debate occurred on the rift between theory and practice. Part of this debate can be read in a book that emerged from the conference, *Convergence in Career Development Theories* (Savickas & Lent, 1994). To respond to the debate and advance our thinking on the issue, in May 1994 the Vocational SIG conducted a conference entitled "Toward the Convergence of Career Theory and Practice." This handbook was inspired by that conference.

In general, this handbook addresses two pivotal questions. The first question asks whether practice can ever inform theory. Practitioners are frustrated by the hierarchy implicit in the theory versus practice dichotomy. Practitioners know that theory is "practice at distance" and that theory takes meaning from and advances practice. The second question asks why vocational psychologists have not produced an explicit theory of career counseling. A career counseling theory can overlap with a theory of vocational behavior or career development, yet a career counseling theory really should concentrate on the relationship and communication dimensions of the interaction between clients and counselors. Both questions, passionately articulated, address the transaction between practice and theory as well as how this transaction can be eased.

In constructing the handbook and writing its chapters, the contributing authors shared the goal of advancing the integration of career theory and practice as well as easing transactions between practitioners and researchers. As a result, this handbook provides a comprehensive treatment of the interface between practice and theory. The six chapters discuss the interface itself by analyzing the disparate cultures of researchers and practitioners and the transactional problems that arise when representatives of the two cultures meet to agree upon and work toward a common goal, namely, fostering career development. The remaining chapters each deal with how the integration of practice and theory can be enhanced. The chapter authors have focused on how to foster career development in clients, that is, *career counseling theory*, rather than descriptions and explanations of vocational behavior, that is, *career development theory*. This handbook presents three new theories of career counseling, six chapters on how to more effectively use the major career development theories in constructing career interventions, and three chapters about how practitioners can use technical eclecticism to orchestrate the translation of the major career development theories into a unified practice of career intervention. In addition, it offers eight chapters on innovations in career assessment and counseling. These groups of chapters, which each approach theory-practice integration from a different vantage point, are organized coherently into five sections of the handbook.

PART 1: PUTTING CAREER THEORY INTO PRACTICE

The chapters in the opening section of this handbook address the general issue of converging theory and practice and reducing the rift between theorists and practitioners. In considering these issues, the authors draw on their personal experiences in constructing and researching theory as well as translating theory into practice and practice into theory. The authors thoughtfully comment on the existence of the rift between practice and theory, carefully analyze the causes of the rift, and suggest creative remedies that might serve to narrow the gap between the two areas. In particular, John L. Holland and Edwin L. Herr closely examine the rift between theory and practice and draw different conclusions about the current situation. Lenore W. Harmon explains that not only is there a gap between theory and practice but there is also a rapidly widening gap between contemporary counseling models, methods, and materials and the diverse situations and complex problems presented by contemporary clients. Consuelo Arbona asserts that the theory-practice rift is irrelevant to the worklives of ethnic and racial minorities who live in poverty. Arbona's contention dramatically advances Harmon's argument concerning a practice-reality gap. John D. Krumboltz and Margaretha S. Lucas seek to reduce the rift by advocating, respectively, a new learning theory for career counseling and methods for building cohesiveness between practitioners and researchers.

PART 2: MAKING CAREER COUNSELING THEORY MORE USEFUL

The chapters in the handbook's second section examine how major counseling theories are useful in career intervention, how counseling theory influences the practice of career intervention, future directions in making counseling theory more practical, and how counseling theories have adapted to feedback from practitioners. Whereas the chapters in the first section address the issue at hand at a general level of analysis, the chapters in this second section deal with the issue from the particular perspectives of several distinct theoretical models for career intervention. The theoretical perspectives selected for inclusion were meant to represent the career counseling models and methods that are both widely used and of longstanding importance to the field. Jane L. Swanson, from the perspective of trait-and-factor theory, asserts that the theory is the practice. Writing from the person-centered perspective, Ellen B. Lent wonders if it is a specious indictment to claim that theory has failed practice. Judy M. Chartrand uses the social learning perspective to offer a new sociocognitive counseling model that explicitly attends to linking career theory to practice. David A. Jepsen, adopting the developmental perspective, considers four forms of rhetoric and their effectiveness in translating developmental theory into practice. Beverly J. Vandiver and Sharon L. Bowman adapt L. Gottfredson's (1981) theory of occupational aspirations to facilitate the theory-practice translation. Itamar Gati proposes that computerized career guidance systems can act as laboratories for researchers who aim to reduce the gap between theory and practice. Mark L. Savickas closes the section with a chapter that describes a conceptual framework for systematically linking theories to the practice of career assessment and intervention.

PART 3: INNOVATIONS
IN CAREER ASSESSMENT

Career assessment measures and techniques are often cited as a primary means of translating theory into practice. Accordingly, the chapters in the third section of the handbook examine criticisms of and new directions for the practice of career assessment as well as the use of assessment instruments during career counseling. Gary D. Gottfredson suggests that theory and practice linkages could be strengthened by a schematic map that shows counselors and researchers how to better use existing segments of career theories to address specific practice problems. John O. Crites illustrates a systematic approach to ensuring a theory-practice linkage in describing the construction, development, and use of his *Career Mastery Inventory*. Fred H. Borgen and Lenore W. Harmon use the 1994 *Strong Interest Inventory*™ to illustrate how practice and research can lead to new theoretical models of interests and personality. W. Bruce Walsh emphasizes a research agenda for fostering theory-practice integration that uses as focal points recent innovations in assessment such as idiographic measurement, the Big Five, and practical intelligence. Linda Mezdylo Subich recommends that breaking the "uniformity myth" will advance theory-practice integration by focusing the attention of counselors on the uniqueness of the individual and the particulars of his or her worldview and social context. Rosie Phillips Bingham and Connie M. Ward describe three new assessment instruments that alert counselors to issues of gender and race as they translate theories into practice. Naomi M. Meara candidly discusses the chapters on assessment in this section, emphasizing the need to increase the sensitivity and specificity of assessment procedures to multiple worldviews and diverse cultures.

PART 4: INNOVATIONS
IN CAREER COUNSELING

The chapters in the fourth section of the handbook focus on criticisms of and new directions for contemporary theory and practice of career intervention. In particular, the authors offer specific suggestions for healing the rift between practice and theory. Frederick T. L. Leong identifies boundaries, cultures, and complexity as problems that separate career theory from practice and then recommends that researchers and practitioners remain in contact with each other in order to communicate and collaborate. Mary Sue Richardson recommends that career counseling be reconceptualized as counseling/psychotherapy with a specialty in work, jobs, and career. Richard A. Young and Lasislav Valach propose that postmodern philosophy of science has produced new career theories that explicitly address the convergence of career theory and practice. Audrey Collin discusses the three chapters in this section by considering how the relationships among theorists, practitioners, and clients affect the nature of practice and then presents a model for "reflective practice" of career intervention.

PART 5: CLOSING COMMENTS

The concluding section contains three chapters that summarize and reflect on the prior chapters. Samuel H. Osipow argues that contemporary career theory was not designed to provide operational procedures to use in career intervention and, thus, he wonders if counselors expect too much from career theory. He encourages practitioners to be more active in theory construction and more willing to communicate and collaborate with researchers in turning theory into practice. Roger A. Myers concludes that the convergence between theory and practice is a problem of considerable import, one that is likely to persist into the foreseeable future. He implies that the main contribution of the handbook has been to reveal the varying levels of concern about the rift between career practice and theory and to examine varying explanations of the rift's origin and possible resolution. Walsh and Savickas conclude the handbook by highlighting the recommendations made by the contributors to the handbook for better integrating career practice and theory.

CONCLUSION

Given the schism between career theory and practice, efforts must be made to provide forums in which theorists and practitioners communicate directly with each other and encourage close listening to the diverse frames of reference and overall goals espoused by practitioners and theorists.

The authors in this handbook have been selected to represent diverse views on the rift between theory and practice. As you read their chapters, note how each author answers the five central questions that structure this handbook:

- How can career theories be renovated to address the majority of individuals in society?

- How can practice inform theory?

- What are the best prospects for building clearer connections between practice and theory?

- How can we increase the cohesiveness between practitioners and researchers?

- What type of research can produce knowledge that is useful to practitioners in realistically addressing the complexities presented by diverse clients in various clinical situations?

These questions beg for clarification before the field of career counseling can progress beyond its current achievements.

REFERENCES

Fitzgerald, L. F., & Betz, N. E. (1994). In M. L. Savikas & R. W. Lent (Eds.), *Convergence in career development theories: Implications for science and practice* (pp. 103–117). Palo Alto, CA: Davies-Black Publishing.

Gottfredson, L. S. (1981). Circumscription and compromise: A developmental theory of occupational aspirations. *Journal of Counseling Psychology, 28,* 545–579.

Morrow-Bradley, C., & Elliott, R. (1986). Utilization of psychotherapy research by practicing psychotherapists. *American Psychologist, 41,* 188–197.

Polkinghorne, D. E. (1992). Postmodern epistemology of practice. In S. Kvale (Ed.), *Psychology and postmodernism* (pp. 146–165). London: Sage.

Richardson, M. S. (1993). Work in people's lives: A location for counseling psychologists. *Journal of Counseling Psychology, 40,* 425–433.

Richardson, M. S. (1994). Pros and cons of a new location: Reply to Savickas (1994) and Tinsley (1994). *Journal of Counseling Psychology, 41,* 112–114.

Savickas, M. L. (1993). Career counseling in the postmodern era. *Journal of Cognitive Psychotherapy: An International Quarterly, 7,* 205–215.

Savickas, M. L. (1994). Vocational psychology in the postmodern era: Comment on Richardson (1993). *Journal of Counseling Psychology, 41,* 105–107.

Savickas, M. L., & Lent, R. W. (1994). *Convergence in career development theories: Implications for science and practice.* Palo Alto, CA: Davies-Black Publishing.

Tinsley, H. E. A. (1994). Construct your reality and show us its benefits: Comment on Richardson (1993). *Journal of Counseling Psychology, 41,* 108–111.

PART ONE

PUTTING CAREER
THEORY INTO PRACTICE

THE SIX CHAPTERS in this first section of the handbook focus on the issues of converging theory and practice, reducing the rift between practitioners and theorists, and improving academic training in the practical use of theory. The section opens with a chapter by Holland, who first assesses the current status of the rift between researchers and practitioners and then offers his suggestions for improving the situation. Holland cogently observes that the American Counseling Association and the American Psychological Association, particularly its Counseling Psychology Division with its Vocational Behavior and Career Intervention Special Interest Group, have become minor players in career practice. He wisely concludes that academia can no longer lead career practice but that theorists and researchers can become more sensitive and intelligent participants. The remedies that he would have us consider emphasize ideas for better communication and suggestions for fruitful exchange between theorists and practitioners, including specific ideas for how to accomplish this through modifying career journals and conventions. Holland further advises career counselors and theorists to be careful about supporting the goals of postmodern philosophy as it pertains to career theory. He reminds readers about the contributions of logical positivism and the continued vitality of traditional person-environment fit models for career choice and adjustment. He advises that person-environment fit models still provide practitioners with helpful theories and useful products and, although presented as "universal theories," they may be modified to comprehend unique career problems as well as the general concerns shared by special populations in an era of great economic, social, and political change.

In Chapter 2, Herr describes the societal trends that are reshaping the possibility structures and the access mechanisms available to workers. These changes demand revision of theory and affect the vision of the practitioners who use it. He persuasively asserts that, on close reading, the often-repeated critique of a disjunction between theory and practice may be a myth or, at least, an overstatement. To support this assertion, he documents three categories of explicit attempts to integrate theory and practice. Given the current split between practitioners and theorists/researchers, he suggests that the "myth" seems to be based in issues surrounding the language systems used. Theory is described in abstract words and concepts, whereas practice is described in the concrete particularities of individual cases. Ideas to address the assumed split in theory and practice require more extensive and direct collaboration on theory building and research by teams of theorists and practitioners. Not unlike Holland, Herr argues that theorists must be in fuller dialogue with practitioners to overcome their conceptual and language differences. Additional suggestions include the recommendation that in revising theories to be more relevant to practice, researchers should emphasize the context of work and career development by focusing on the family, community, and institutions, not just on individuals. Herr also encourages the formation of teams of theorists and practitioners who can collaborate to devise a matrix for translating what we know about careers into practice knowledge that is relevant for particular types of clients. He also implies that this matrix guide further elaboration of segmental theories and that for now at least, career scholars forsake the pursuit of unified theory.

In Chapter 3, Harmon explains that in addition to the gap between theory and practice, there is a gap between counselors' knowledge and skills when compared to the complex problems faced by their clients. She refers to this second gap as existing between counseling practices and the reality of clients' diverse situations and complex problems. This practice-reality disjunction seems to be caused by rapid changes in society and the world of work. Societal changes, as we move to a postindustrial era, are rapidly outstripping available counseling models, methods, and materials. Harmon addresses these problems by first proposing some practical ideas about how both theorists and practitioners can reduce the gap between theory and practice. She then makes suggestions about how the gap between practice and reality can be closed through changes in how counselors are trained and in the way that they choose to work.

In Chapter 4, Arbona counters the assumption that theory should guide practice with the assertion that practitioners' experience should also be considered a knowledge base for guiding practice. Accordingly, she encourages counselors to draw on their own experiences and view the "self" as an important instrument in the counseling process. Arbona also points out that career theory, at its best, will always be insufficient to completely guide practice. For example, to be most helpful to clients who are exploring career options, counselors need to provide current knowledge about both the labor market and the link between training and specific occupations. After concluding that there are inherent limits on the degree to which career theory can guide practice, Arbona illustrates this conclusion by discussing the career development needs and concerns of individuals of various ethnic and minority groups who live in poverty. For many of these individuals, work is not a salient life role. Thus, the question of how career theory can better guide career intervention for them is a specious question. Rather than access to better career interventions, these individuals need improved educational and academic opportunities. Given these resources, their resulting educational and academic achievement will make the work role more central in their lives, thereby increasing the relevance of existing career theories.

In Chapter 5, Krumboltz first examines the limitations in the classic model of trait-and-factor counseling, including the static view of individuals, inattention to emotions, and an emphasis on occupational choice rather than the implementation of a choice. He further argues that jobs are changing from stable occupations to team-performed tasks. He then offers a new theory of career counseling that addresses these deficiencies. The goals of his new learning theory of career counseling are to foster the learning of skills, interests, beliefs, values, work habits, and personal qualities that enable a client to create a satisfying life in a changing work environment. The task for career counselors is to promote learning. What follows is a formal presentation of this new theory of career counseling, along with a practical discussion of counseling techniques. Krumboltz concludes the chapter by identifying the major benefits of the new theory as (a) encouraging career counselors to use assessment instruments to stimulate new learning, (b) prompting increased use of educational interventions, (c) endorsing learning outcomes as criteria for counseling success, and (d) diminishing the distinctions between career and personal counseling.

In the final chapter in this section, Lucas explains why many career counselors ignore career theories and the research that tests them. When counselors encounter difficulties in counseling process, they rarely, if ever, consult professional journals because the research projects described in the journals have been designed and executed by academicians and tend to lack direct relevance to what actually occurs in a career counseling session. The research answers theoretical questions but does not address the questions practitioners ask in their offices. Following her analysis of the theory-practice split, Lucas suggests how to increase the clinical relevance of career research and strengthen the natural relationship that exists between practitioners and researchers by means of a "practitioner-scientist" model. In this discussion, she uses Holland's Social and Investigative personality types to consider practical ways to prompt practitioners to convert their clinical questions into research projects. As a second way to bridge the gulf, she suggests that instead of describing individual cases or elaborating universally applicable theories, practitioner-scientists and scientist-practitioners should develop models or minitheories to guide treatment protocols for frequently encountered career problems in specific populations.

CHAPTER ONE

Integrating Career Theory and Practice

The Current Situation and Some Potential Remedies

John L. Holland
Professor Emeritus, Johns Hopkins University

I HAVE HAD many difficulties in preparing this chapter—actually, more difficulties than ever before. I found it hard to find any relevant facts, but it was easy to find many divergent opinions about the current status of career practice and theory and their explicit use of one another. The proposed remedies often appear one-sided, such as fix theories, yet little is said about fixing practitioners. If you consider our attitudes and resources, many proposed solutions are grossly impractical, uninformed, and unrealistic. To make matters worse, we are in an era of great economic, social, and political change in which multiple good causes, instant entrepreneurs, and special interest groups bash one another, so useful communication has become a rare activity.

Because I am old, I have two additional problems. I am supposed to be above the pettiness and bias of my past competitive life and engaged in helping younger colleagues. I find this expectation hard to meet from time to time. In addition, next year, at 75, my faculties, according to the American Psychological Society Committee on Vitality for Life (1993), are likely to drop precipitously, so I am trying to finish my important projects this year. Fortunately, I started voice lessons last year before I got this bad news. I am not worried about my piano lessons, because it is clear that you can get better with practice even after you enter a nursing home.

At any rate, I finally concluded that the most useful thing I could do would be to begin a clarification of the theory-practice problem and to propose some potential remedies. The reader is invited to amend my attempt or to reject these ideas and propose more useful solutions.

1

CURRENT CAREER PRACTICE

I will begin with an attempt to characterize the current state of career practice. This controversial characterization will include my evaluation of the strengths and weaknesses of these diverse services and an assessment of the barriers to achieving better practice. Then I will give current research and theory the same treatment. Finally, I will propose some ideas for stimulating more productive practitioner-research or theorist interactions.

There are two major groups that provide career assistance—one group emphasizes individual work and the other emphasizes group work. The first group of practitioners works one-to-one in a wide range of settings. Their experience and training ranges from no relevant qualifications except ambition, to an appropriate degree supplemented by a good internship and a long tenure as a career practitioner. They work in a wide range of settings, including colleges, businesses, government agencies, and individual practices.

The second group of practitioners focuses more on group methods than on one-to-one counseling to cope with large populations. They include people who run career and placement centers in colleges, plan and operate career guidance programs in high schools, or provide outplacement services and career development programs in businesses or government agencies. These workers depend heavily on such things as workshops, training materials, occupational information centers, self-help inventories and modules, computers, peer group assistants, and volunteers.

This diverse collection of the trained, untrained, and ambitious is trying to meet the vocational assistance needs among people of all ages. They are so numerous and successful that they—practitioners of all kinds—are now the major players in this field. The National Career Development Association in the American Counseling Association, the Counseling Psychology Division with its Vocational Special Interest Group in the American Psychological Association, and academic research and theory have become *minor* players in career practice. Whatever you may think, practitioners are more attuned to the needs of our diverse populations than any other professional group.

Strengths

Although most practice goes unevaluated in any formal way, what evidence we do have is usually positive. In addition, there are a number of career centers that serve students and adults in creative ways. There are also some successful plans for developing and managing school guidance programs that are beginning to have some impact. The work of solo practitioners is rarely evaluated except by insurance companies, but everyone should read Jan Birk's (1994) presidential address to the Counseling Psychology Division, which provides a pioneering account of the creative development of a rural practice with its work and nonwork activities.

Deficiencies and Problems

The great strengths of practitioners have been accompanied by some deficiencies and environmental problems. I don't know how prevalent these are or even if anyone else has the same perceptions. I should amend this belief. Actually, I know two people who agree with me. At any rate, I offer these speculations for your evaluation.

First, I wonder if some career counselors are getting good diagnostic and counseling training. I usually read a few of the responses in the "Getting Down to Cases" section of the *Career Development Quarterly*. The responses to a case vignette by experienced counselors often ignore the content of the cases and proceed to demonstrate the fertility of their imaginations. I think this journal section could become, with some judicious editing, a superior Rorschach. I have seen the same imaginative work demonstrated when Ph.D.'s were asked in a workshop to interpret a simple interest profile.

Second, many career workers are addicted to a single treatment—one-to-one counseling—rather than employing a variety of treatments. Yes, Oliver and Spokane (1988) report that one-to-one is more effective per hour than group activities, but educational and group methods are the only way we will be able to fill the need for service in middle- and low-income groups.

Third, an unknown proportion of counselors seem to exhibit one or more reading problems. I know that they do not read test manuals. For instance, an old *Self-Directed Search* manual had a gross error in a key to test a reader's knowledge of the manual. No one ever wrote to the publisher to point out this error. I suggested that the publisher pay people $100 for each documented error they could find as a way to increase readership. He only looked pained.

A few critics and reviewers appear to exhibit minor dyslexic problems. I am sympathetic because I too have a minor dyslexic disorder that I have passed on to my son. In a recent review, a former editor and good fellow cites my evaluation of the evidence about "congruency" in 1985 to mean that I had given up on this idea. I have not. My evaluation of the quality of the evidence and the usefulness of the theoretical constructs are independent of one another. Another critic admitted that he had never read my theory but felt comfortable that his evaluation had merit. Surely, there must be a rule that people must read publications they evaluate.

I also wonder about the scientific training of some practitioners. Some appear unable to discriminate opinion and theoretical fantasy from generally acceptable kinds of evidence. Perhaps a consumers union is needed for the practice and research literature. Parenthetically, responsibility for these alleged problems should be shared with editors, trainers, researchers, and theorists who have their own collection of deficiencies.

Finally, I am distressed by the occasional insensitivity to a client's vocational aspirations. Some counselors don't appear to listen to a client's goals and proceed instead to confront or administer treatments designed to change a person's aspirations without getting informed consent or understanding.

Along with some personal weaknesses, practitioners are confronted with many environmental barriers. These include journals that are usually not receptive to qualitative accounts of practitioner casework and speculation. If practioners are part of a large organization, they usually lack the power and status to get needed resources or resist cockeyed administrative changes. Solo practitioners must maintain caseloads to support themselves; this makes convention going and reading a luxury, isolating them from other practitioners and the vocational literature or any other literature. In any event, reading about the current philosophical wars or research that has no useful findings is low on a practitioner's agenda, if it is there at all.

CURRENT THEORY AND RESEARCH

The explosion of career services is now matched by an explosion in theorizing and research. A wide range of books and articles is devoted to research and speculation about the work experience of adults and the special career issues confronting women and many other groups. The theorizing ranges from a few acute insights to lists of assumptions about work that have been tested with some evidence, as opposed to the author's enthusiasm. These speculations are also characterized by their isolation from one another as well as any potentially supportive literature.

The theorizing often starts from ground zero. This tendency is not all bad. Paying close attention to conventional wisdom or, in this case, relevant theory may blind you to useful ideas. I find it helpful and reassuring to rummage through this literature because I occasionally find something useful. It is like going to a yard sale—you rarely strike gold.

I expect this great range of speculative activity to have some beneficial effects. It may stimulate some desirable theoretical revision in old theories or stimulate new theories. I would also expect that practitioners would find some of this work immediately helpful because it implies new and promising ways of looking at client problems.

Strengths

Despite the proliferation of recent speculation, the old person-environment fit theories exhibit a continuing dominance and strength in research and usage. The Minnesota duo (Dawis & Lofquist, 1984) continue to revise their theory and stimulate new work. I continue to revise my own delusional system, although very slowly. For example, Gary Gottfredson's chapter (this volume) describes the *Career Attitudes and Strategies Inventory* (Holland & Gottfredson, 1994) that grew out of an attempt to insert belief theory into my typology.

I attribute the dominance of person-environment fit theories to their focus on two major issues in a person's aspiration and work histories. What kind of work will bring happiness? Can I perform it well? These questions apply to choices or decisions at any age, including what to do in one's golden years.

In contrast, the questions raised by both developmental and learning theories of worker problems focus on questions that interest practitioners more than clients. These interpretations are supported by the popularity of the inventories of vocational interests and job satisfaction and the relative unpopularity of developmental or decision-making inventories. In short, the multiple questions about work are not equally attractive or relevant to clients. When they seek counseling, clients do not show up asking for maturity inventories or wanting to know the implications of their life stage.

Weaknesses

Most theories go largely unexplored by any formal testing. Most evaluation occurs in the usage of inventories and scales designed to measure theoretical constructs. Usage is an important yet ambiguous criterion because it is occasionally contaminated with the cultlike activities of true believers and entrepreneurs.

The dominant theories have received mixed research support—some ideas receive strong and explicit support; other ideas receive only weak support or none at all. The content of criticism varies from year to year. At different times, critics have claimed that person-environment theories have neglected the processes of change and development over the life span and have been seen as unhelpful for women and the poor. Currently, the popular criticism is that congruency is dead.

The less prominent speculations—developmental and learning theories—attract some research attention, but they rarely come up with a big robust finding. Until recently, a major obstacle for these theories has been the lack of instrumentation for applying their constructs in practice and research. If they are to measure change, some assessment devices are needed that will work from adolescence through old age.

Controversy and Misunderstanding

The development of career theory has been accompanied by much misunderstanding of how theories should be constructed and revised. Of special importance, psychologists—but not philosophers—fail to recognize how controversial any theoretical undertaking is. Put another way, no particular philosophy of science comes with a guarantee.

Ironically, the dominant and successful vocational theories exhibit the influence of old-fashioned logical positivism, with its concern for clear definitions and some semblance of a logical structure. These theories continue to provide helpful theory and products for career counselors.

In recent years, critics have argued that we would make more rapid or desirable progress if we adopted a postmodernist stance, did much more qualitative research, revised inventories so men and women would look alike, and revise theories so they could respond to almost any question. Let me take these requests one at a time.

First, different theories are developed to answer different questions. Also, different theories focus on different facets of career development. Consequently, different theories have differential patterns of strengths and weaknesses. For instance, developmental and learning theories focus on the processes entailed in vocational behaviors, but they have much less to say about the organization of career knowledge. Person-environment (P-E) fit theories focus on the organization of knowledge, but they have much less to say about the processes of development and learning. In short, all theories are incomplete formulations that will never be adept at answering everyone's questions. At the same time, many authors are revising theories to clarify statements, to increase the scope of questions they can respond to, and to do anything else that appears appropriate and possible.

Second, some questions about women's choices and work histories have been answered via P-E theory and its related research. The large-scale studies of women's work histories show the same predictable patterns that men's histories do when successive jobs are classified in a six-category system (Gottfredson, 1977).

In addition, the positive effects of the *Self-Directed Search* (Holland, Fritzsche, & Powell, 1994), a P-E inventory, are similar for men and women. Twenty experiments report positive outcomes for men and women as well as for some high-risk groups. Despite their hype, inventories using balanced scales or norms have no special effects or advantages for women. The three experiments assessing the effects of taking the *Uniact,* the *Strong Interest Inventory,* or the *Kuder Occupational Interest Survey* reported no special outcomes.

Third, the plea for qualitative research appears old hat and redundant. Everyone—career counselors, researchers, theorists, and educators—engages in informal speculation and observation about career activities and problems. Some people disguise their experiences as theories; others share their speculations with friends or no one at all.

Fourth, the calls for a new philosophy of science or a postmodern stance assume that a correct philosophy of science would stimulate the knowledge we need. Now we are being asked to take a ride on the cruise ship Postmodern, whose captains cannot agree on a course because they cannot construct a single map.

Philosophy aside, our scientific problems have more mundane origins. For instance, the Vocational Special Interest Group in the Counseling Psychology Division numbers about 200 people. A review indicates that about 180 do little or no research. The remaining 20 include 15 people who do an occasional research piece, while only 4 or 5 are very active researchers. It takes man and woman power to do research. Research also requires money; grant funds for career research have always been rare. Most researchers have funded their work by stealing time and materials from other projects or sponsors.

I conclude that to study work, you need a substantial workforce. If you go through the Counseling Psychology Division roster, and similar rosters of sympathetic organizations, you will reach a similar conclusion.

There are many environmental influences that interfere with vocational research and theory. They include psychology departments that emphasize little bitsy experiments and deprecate applied work. Incidentally, we could capitalize on their current focus by going cognitive. After all, we listen a lot to people's *thinking* about their work. The influence of academia also includes writing for an audience that has only a selective interest in practical problems. In our case, researching and writing about how to listen carefully to one person at a time is encouraged, but the study of sloppy group methods has low status.

MORE PRODUCTIVE PRACTITIONER-RESEARCH-THEORIST EXCHANGES

I come now to the constructive part of my chapter. I see many things we could do to improve the quality and productivity of the exchanges—social and intellectual—between practitioners and researchers. These include some revisions of our theories and research efforts, practice activities, and communications. Some changes look easy; others look farfetched, if not impossible. My suggestions also assume that my diagnosis has some validity. You may disagree. I should add that I assume that the scientist-practitioner model is a myth for most of us. Most people exemplify one model much more than the other.

As you know, there is a growing literature on practitioner-researcher problems, but no consensus on the origins of the alleged rift or the solutions. Some writers attribute our mutual alienation to logical positivism and recommend constructivism and practice-based knowledge as solutions. I don't believe these intellectual wars have any value for improving the quality of our work; they are too far away from our daily practice and research activities. Instead, I believe we could make some rapid revisions in how we communicate with one another, as well as some changes in how we engage in practice and research, that would foster more constructive interactions.

Communications

Our communications could be improved in several ways. Some journals serve mainly as outlets for researchers, and in recent years they have become addicted to theory, limited experiments, tiny pieces of large problems, and occasional good causes that their editors advocate. This work exemplifies one important scientific tradition, but in our case this orientation focuses on one-to-one treatments and crowds out more global and sloppier work about career practice and group interventions. We have also moved from using simple data analytic techniques that most people understand to using hyperanalytical statistics that only a sophisticated few can comprehend. This compels many of us to find a math tutor to help us grasp any main findings. Often, there are none.

One remedy would be to establish a few practitioner sections or forums in journals that would be devoted to ideas and insights about career practice, research, and theory. Here practitioners only would write for practitioners and career researchers. No data analyses or qualitative shenanigans would be allowed.

Another remedy would be to reduce our focused editorial power. Journals are dominated by conservative beliefs about research, so there is little risk taking. These conservative biases are accentuated because authors see the same club of people no matter where they turn. In short, focused editorial power limits the range of acceptable research within a single journal, and, because editors and consulting editors serve on multiple journals, authors have trouble finding a fresh second opinion. As you know, to cry too much about rejections is a sign of low status. I have converted low status to high status by claiming that I have more rejections than most people have acceptances. At any rate, my remedy for openness is to ask everyone to serve only a single journal. As usual, this suggestion has received a mixed reaction.

Some changes in our convention formats might also help. The poster sessions have been a step in the right direction. The meet-the-author sessions have been helpful for some people. Why not try to explore some related formats, such as small defined groups composed of equal numbers of practitioners and researchers? To ensure commitment, perhaps participants would have to register. The half-and-half formula is intended to reduce the one-sided interactions of the meet-the-author or "old-person" formats. The American Educational Research Association has studied its convention communication problems and considered some revisions that we might want to emulate. In our case, new formats might also include distinguished practitioners interacting with small groups. These focus groups might be assigned special topics or left to create their own.

Whatever we try, it should involve more face-to-face discussions. My recent conversations with practitioners have been helpful in getting a more accurate picture of their daily work problems and of their use of research and theory. The written accounts of our interactions are not good substitutes for a little oral communication that can often resolve some misunderstandings or at least clarify what the disagreement or problem is.

Research and Theory

In research, a *redistribution* of effort might be more useful to practitioners of all kinds. This redistribution would include the following:

- Less evaluation of graduate student training and institutional and personal rankings, and fewer counseling process studies and studies of a single sex
- More evaluation (experimental and clinical) of career interventions of all kinds
- More reports of new interventions and comparative studies of the effects of old and new interventions, as well as the effects of professional and nonprofessional practitioners

Society is interested in outcomes, not processes or our chronic complaints about identity, professional status, ethics, and training.

Academics and researchers should focus more on those topics that will make a difference in the great sea of practice. These shifts would capitalize on our talents and on our old and strong research base. Our one-to-one research is in direct competition with clinical psychology, social work, and psychiatry. In contrast, more career-intervention research, especially the study of group interventions, would benefit those practitioners who have to cope with hordes of high school and college students as well as displaced workers, employed adults, and retirees. Even if short-term therapy could be reduced to effective five-minute career counseling, the vast need would never be met. Although academia can no longer lead career practice, we can become more sensitive and intelligent participants. It is time to give up our myopic academic stance.

What to do about current theories of career development presents multiple alternatives and ambiguities. The theories of Dawis and Lofquist (1984) and of Holland (1985) follow universal models or a one-size-fits-all-groups approach. The research suggests that these theories work well for most groups, but some people, including some well-educated middle-class White women, disagree. Theoretical revisions usually consist of minor adjustments to the basic theory. For instance, I tried in 1985 to show how a typology could be used to explain why some women become homemakers and others become careerists (Holland, 1985, p. 31). In contrast, some authors advocate special theories for women, African Americans, and Hispanics, but most writing has focused on speculations about women's work experience.

Gutek and Larwood (1987) provide a helpful summary of the complaints about universal theories ("Men's Theories of CD"). They also propose that a desirable theory for women would cope with five major concerns: career preparation; opportunities; the influence of marriage, pregnancy, and children; timing; and age. They also rough out a bare-bones theory. These speculations represent the most comprehensive, succinct, and readable attempt to define what a women's career development theory should explain.

Like most theories for a single group, they seek answers to questions that universal theories do not ask or cannot cope with. My hypothesis about working in or out of the home might be helpful for understanding interrupted work patterns but not timing. I would favor asking women direct questions about pregnancy, marriage, and timing and forget about a theoretical explanation. Theories of interpersonal relations appear more appropriate here than career theory.

At this time, the most useful strategy might be to elaborate these theories so they could be tried out in research and practice. Another strategy would be to explore universal theories for their ability to cope with these new questions.

Another strategy would be to explore Sedlacek's (1994, in press) groundbreaking ideas for the development of assessment measures for diverse populations. He has clarified the issues that affect assessment with diverse populations and has outlined some practical ideas for developing scales or inventories that would be more appropriate and valid for minority groups than traditional measures.

Practice Renewal

The sins of research and theory are not responsible for all the deficiencies in career practice. Like academics, practitioners tend to settle into a few routine activities. Career practice also needs a renewal program beyond the occasional workshop or certified training modules. Several possibilities appear promising. They include the following:

- Performing simple surveys of existing services for their popularity, effectiveness, and need

- Exploring whether or not you have a complete cafeteria of services or only one service

- Solo practitioners considering partnerships that support group treatments

These ideas are an attempt to express that we need to consider modest to radical restructuring of services.

Many practitioners, in and out of businesses or educational institutions, have done all these things, but many have not benefitted from a good self-study.

Finally, more convention attendance and reading might be helpful. It is true that the returns from attendance are slim, but conventions are often the only place where one can discover something new and useful.

SO WHAT?

I don't have a big windup for my ideas, yet I do want to express my hidden agenda and some concerns that I have about our collective future.

I want to confess that I set out to offend as many people as possible so that I would never be invited to write another chapter! At the same time, I hoped to stimulate your creative and critical faculties as you read the research, intellectual, and political agendas in the chapters that follow.

REFERENCES

American Psychological Society Committee on Vitality for Life. (1993, December). Human capital initiative. [Special issue]. *American Psychological Society Observer,* Report No. 2, 8–24.

Birk, J. M. (1994). Country roads: Counseling psychology's rural initiative. *The Counseling Psychologist, 22,* 183–196.

Dawis, R. V., & Lofquist, L. H. (1984). *A psychological theory of work adjustment.* Minneapolis: University of Minnesota.

Gottfredson, G. D. (1977). Career stability and redirection in adulthood. *Journal of Applied Psychology, 62,* 436–435.

Gutek, B., & Larwood, L. (1987). *Women's career development.* Newbury Park, CA: Sage.

Holland, J. L. (1985). *Making vocational choices.* Englewood Cliffs, NJ: Prentice Hall.

Holland, J. L., Fritzsche, B. A., & Powell, Amy B. (1994). *Technical manual for the Self-Directed Search.* Odessa, FL: Psychological Assessment Resources.

Holland, J. L., & Gottfredson, G. D. (1994). *The career attitudes and strategies inventory.* Odessa, FL: Psychological Assessment Resources.

Oliver, L. W., & Spokane, A. R. (1988). Career-intervention outcome: What contributes client gain? *Journal of Counseling Psychology, 35,* 447–462.

Sedlacek, W. E. (1994). Issues in advancing diversity through assessment. *Journal of Counseling and Development, 72,* 549–553.

Sedlacek, W. E. (in press). An empirical method of determining nontraditional group status. *Measurement and Evaluation in Counseling and Development.*

CHAPTER TWO

Toward the Convergence of Career Theory and Practice

Mythology, Issues, and Possibilities

Edwin L. Herr
Pennsylvania State University

FOR ALL OF the criticisms and the promises inherent in the notion of the convergence of career theory and practice, both researchers and practitioners are encountering a new set of realities that will affect both the formulation and testing of theory and its implementation. Although it is not possible to address such matters in depth here, let me cite only a few of the trends that will affect the modification of existing theory and the processes of new theory construction, as well as the vision and the tools by which practitioners discharge their professional responsibilities.

In an abbreviated litany, they include the following realities:

- *The globalization of the workforce*. The increased cross-national mobility of the workforce and the problems of insufficient information and loss of cultural identity will require career counselors to enlarge the paradigms and boundaries of the meaning and practice of career counseling.

- *A growing global labor surplus*. Counselors will need to change their orientations with many clients from the choice of jobs or education or career patterns to the choice of activities, volunteer or otherwise (as Denmark is now considering), for those persons who may never be employed or reemployed.

- *Organizational transformations in the workplace.* New models of personnel development, not just of personnel management, are being created, eliminating much of middle management and many white-collar jobs. Workforces are being downsized to reduce permanent overhead costs and to incorporate newer forms of advanced technology, increasing overall productivity-cost ratios. In the process, there are changes in the nature of career ladders, work cultures, and worker-management interaction. Such conditions are stimulating increased attention to human resource development, including incorporation of the skills of counseling psychologists who have expertise in vocational psychology and career counseling and who understand the language and culture of the workplace and the classes of employee problems that occur in the work context.

- *The rise of a contingent workforce in the United States and around the world.* Temporary employees have special skills that are purchased for limited periods of time; they do not have long-term institutional identification or stable health and pension benefits as part of their career. These circumstances may contribute to redefining career patterns as we have come to think of them, as well as herald the need for a new theory of work and its role in human identity.

- *The rising importance of the knowledge worker and of literacy, numeracy, communication, and computer literacy skills as prerequisites for employability and lifelong learning in many of the emerging occupations and in the primary labor market.* Although intellectual and academic skills have always been implicit aspects of career theory, the rising expectations for workers to have the educational skills, problem-solving and higher-order thinking skills inherent in work as a learning activity will, in the future, make such skills an explicit part of career theory.

- *The growing awareness of linkages between positive or negative career experiences and mental health, self-esteem, purposefulness, physical well-being, the ability to support and maintain a family, and the perception that one has life options and can practice an internal locus of control.* Many of these connections have been reinforced as researchers have probed the psychology of unemployment and its emotional, physiological, and behavioral results. These hold implications for new paradigms that integrate personal and career counseling and treat unemployment (as well as underemployment), not simply as individual economic problems but also as major mental health issues worthy of comprehensive programs of intervention, including counseling.

- *The recent appearance of new government policy and legislation on the school-to-work transition and work-based learning that address the problems of work-bound youth.* These youths have been identified as the "forgotten half," the noncollege-bound, the alienated, the disconnected, or the at-risk, depending on which subset of this large population one addresses. In essence, these analyses have suggested that for perhaps 50% of our adolescent population, there are no transition services available between the time they leave high school and the time they enter and adjust to employment. These young people are often cut adrift psychologically as they try to convert their aspirations into actualities, however clear or vague they may be. It is likely that in the 21st century there will be major attention given to the interaction between the career-relevant processes of schooling, transition, and induction into work and the need for differential treatment approaches that will take into account the uniqueness as well as the connection between each of these three stages.

■ *The demographic trends related to new entrants to the workforce between now and 2005 or beyond: primarily women, people of color, and immigrants.* The development of career counseling models for such people that is related to their entrance, adjustment to, and mobility in work will stimulate far more attention to the impact of cultural diversity on career behavior and on cross-cultural interventions in that behavior.

The perspectives listed hereinabove do not exhaust the many possibilities that could be cited. As the world's economic and political systems are being dramatically transformed, so are the possibility structures and the access mechanisms available to those whom career theory must address and practitioners must assist. These circumstances will stimulate theories of work, career behavior, and career interventions that go far beyond implied theories of task characteristics and worker attributes, such as those defined in the *Dictionary of Occupational Titles*. These work theories will include perspectives that integrate task characteristics and worker attributes within parameters that reflect the context of work, the dynamics of the labor market, and a more complete application of the meaning of motivational and dispositional attributes as the mediators of skill, ability, and knowledge.

These examples signal that as comprehensive shifts in economic and sociopolitical dynamics occur and modify the contexts in which human identity and work behavior are negotiated and as, for example, knowledge bases about the cognitive sciences continue to expand, our critiques of career theory and practice must incorporate new realities. One of the ultimate truths that must be factored into our discussions about these matters is that researchers and practitioners, and those whose lives are the content for both theory and practice, are, to some degree, captives of the historical period in which they were trained or began their research, as well as by the prevalent social, psychological, economic, or gender assumptions that prevailed when their theory was originally constructed. But such social, political, and economic contexts do not remain static. As a result, one of the problems in keeping theory and practice congruent, or reciprocal in their effects on each other, is that both are figuratively chasing moving targets. Dynamic behavioral possibilities or expectations and shifting work contexts increase the multiprobabilistic nature of the factors influencing career behavior and the patterns of response that occur. Thus, theories of career behavior, particularly comprehensive ones, must also be open, evolving, and incomplete.

Such time-related factors in theory construction and content may also be the cross-generational nexus for reports that many counseling psychology students or practitioners are not particularly interested in career theory or career counseling (Fitzgerald & Osipow, 1986; Goldschmidt, Tipton, & Wiggins, 1981). Their views of reality and social dynamics may be different from those emphasized in the theoretical models conceived by an older generation of theorists or researchers. Not seeing the conditions or populations of current import in their worldview reflected in theoretical emphases may be a factor that causes the younger practitioner or student of counseling psychology to dismiss career theory and practice as too narrowly defined or too abstract or too removed from the emotional or psychological content that they believe is important to them and their contemporaries. Embedded in these concerns may be the possibility that insufficient attention is given in training and in model building to the history of theory development and practice. Such situations may not adequately present how these models have evolved and changed as new knowledge bases, interdisciplinary insights, and interpretations of social and economic trends have influenced both theory and practice. In response, it may also be necessary to find new methods to help reduce the time, energy, and resources that the testing and implementation of new career theory and practice have historically taken to respond more rapidly to contemporary needs and conditions.

Such perspectives support the need for the following conditions to occur. If there is to be a convergence of career theory and practice in the future, both must be more fully contextualized (Vondracek, Lerner, & Schulenberg, 1986), more attentive to the characteristics of the environments in which work is chosen and performed, more focused on the obstacles, barriers, and messages that differentiate rather than unify the career behavior of subpopulations of clients, and more perceptive about the reality that individual development does not occur in a vacuum. Instead, it occurs within multiple contexts—school, family, community, society, historical periods—that may be in conflict about the messages sent to individuals, the options made available to them, the quality of the information, reinforcements, and support systems provided. In this sense, the future of career theory and practice and their convergence may also depend on greater attention to the importance of the explanatory power of general systems theory as the various parts of the individual's environments are understood in their interactive effects on behavior.

A final prefatory perspective here is that while it is desirable for career theory and practice to converge, each of these bodies of knowledge is, at least to some extent, guided by a different set of realities. Career theories must first describe the structure of behavior, how it changes across time or longitudinally, factors in its continuity or discontinuity, the mechanisms by which it is learned or modified, assumptions on which predictions about its future course rest, and the classification and integration of disparate facts and observations that need to be organized into a coherent set of principles or statements about the nature of behavior as it is and as it might be. Such theory construction can be rather narrowly targeted or comprehensive in its sweep. In any case, however, any particular career theory is a lens that is shaped to some degree by the primary discipline of the theorist— economics, differential or developmental psychology, sociology, anthropology, political science—and by his or her personal experience as it is focused on some phenomenon to be better understood and elaborated. It is a particular way of comprehending and interpreting reality as it is shaped by the tools and vision of the observer. Also, although there are many formal statements about what should constitute a "good" theory and how theories should be compared that I will not visit here, there is the further matter that career theory is first a theory of behavior rather than of intervention (Savickas, 1993). In essence, career theory primarily elaborates the targets for intervention rather than provides a theory of intervention itself. As I will suggest in the next section, in historical terms, the major career theorists also have recommended specific interventions or systems of interventions that are congruent with the theoretical assumptions they advocate. However, in an attempt to sharpen the point, the content of theories of behavior and the theories of intervention, while hopefully overlapping, tend to be different. Career theories deal principally with the options for behavior or choice available in a society, how these are structured or learned, their unfolding expression over time, the factors that affect time-related development, and the influences or tasks required in decision points that are critical to the demonstration of effective behavior. Theories of intervention deal principally with what and how change is produced in career behavior, and under what conditions, for whom, and how it can be accelerated or learned. In addition to responding to the target behaviors, influences, and tasks or decision points where intervention is most likely to be necessary or effective as these are suggested by career theory, theories of intervention are also bound by issues of ethics, statements of governmental policy or legislative mandate, and the availability of emerging technology (e.g., assessment instruments, computer-mediated career guidance systems, and psychoeducational models counseling strategies) in ways that career theories are not.

MYTHS RELATED TO CONVERGENCE OF CAREER THEORY AND PRACTICE

Given these prefatory observations concerning the complexities that attend the construction of career theory and practice, it is important to acknowledge that one of the persistent myths that is embodied in the professional literature, and often in the "oral culture" of counselors, is that formal theory is not relevant to what counselors do; it does not speak to their day-to-day activities because it does not speak to the idiosyncratic experience of individual clients (Jepsen, 1984). Career theory and career practice are frequently seen as separate because career theorists do not inform practitioners how to use their theories. But a close reading of the evolution of the major career theories seems to suggest otherwise. Depending on how comprehensively one reads the published works of the major career theorists and the people whose theories are now beginning to extend or refine the earlier career theories, there is typically a discussion of what interventions arise from or would be appropriate to operationalize or intervene in the descriptions of behavior encompassed by that theory. Some theorists have primarily developed assessment instruments to be used by counselors with whatever counseling approach they espouse; some theorists have constructed both assessment instruments and techniques compatible with their theories; and others have recommended counseling techniques that would be compatible with their career theories. I wish to cite three examples of attempts to facilitate the integration of career theory and practice— those of Holland, Super, and Krumboltz. There are many other approaches that could be cited as well.

Holland's Integration of Theory and Practice

Holland's classic theory of types of persons, work environments, and the interactions between persons and environments has provided counselors major constructs that enable them to (a) organize the massive data available about people and jobs (Weinrach, 1984); (b) recognize that the choice of an occupation is an expression of personality and not a random event (Holland, 1982); (c) classify work personalities as one or a combination of six types—Realistic, Investigative, Artistic, Social, Enterprising, or Conventional (RIASEC); (d) pursue the probability that people search for environments that will let them exercise their skills and abilities, express their attitudes and values, and take on agreeable problems and roles; and (e) recognize that a person's behavior is determined by an interaction between personality and environment (Holland, 1973, 1985).

To emphasize the interactive character of the person-situation correspondence in which people function in the workplace, Holland has classified work environments into six categories analogous to the six personal orientation typologies. Holland also makes more explicit than do most of his contemporary theorists that occupations are ways of life and that work environments reflect the characteristics of those inhabiting them rather than being only sets of isolated work functions or skills.

To facilitate the utility of his career theory and the assessment of its major constructs, Holland has, in the tradition of differential psychology, provided several tools to assist the practitioner to validate and use the insights and research findings that have constituted the knowledge base that has accrued from his work. These tools take several forms. One form is the use of assessment instruments such as the *Vocational Preference Inventory, My Vocational Situation*, and the *Self-Directed Search*. Another is the use of his theoretical framework, RIASEC, as the organizing and interpretive structure for the most recent iterations of the *Strong Interest Inventory* and its use as the conceptual structure for some informational components of the DISCOVER computer-mediated career guidance system. Finally, Holland's three-letter coding system of the major personality types is used as a way of organizing educational (e.g., Harrington, Feller, & O'Shea, 1993) and occupational information, both as reported in such sources as a *Dictionary of Holland Occupational Codes* (Gottfredson, Holland, & Ogawa, 1982) and as a mechanism by which to access and organize information found in such U.S. Department of Labor publications as the *Dictionary of Occupational Titles* and the *Guide for Occupational Exploration* (Jones, 1980) or to analyze work histories and develop occupational exploration plans for clients. In addition to these explicit efforts to integrate his career theory and practice, Holland's work has continued to stimulate wide-ranging empirical work and syntheses of the rapidly growing body of research studies spawned by his efforts (more than 450 studies in 1990) to validate and refine his theoretical constructs and their meaning (e.g., Gottfredson & Holland, 1990; Gottfredson, Jones, & Holland, 1993; Holland, Gottfredson, & Baker, 1990; Meier, 1989; Rounds, Davison, & Dawis, 1979; Spokane, 1985; Ward & Walsh, 1981).

Super's Integration of Theory and Practice

A second example comes from a primarily developmental, rather than a differential psychological or structural-interactive, perspective. Super has, like Holland, provided a variety of methods by which to integrate his career theory with counseling practice. His approach integrates the interaction of personal and environmental variables in the unfolding of career patterns or career development across time. He has made explicit the intimacy of career development and personal development in his construction of career life stages or maxicycles and in the minicycles of substages and developmental tasks, as well as the behavior pertinent to each as they mark major periods of transition across the life span from birth to retirement and beyond. Within such longitudinal parameters, Super emphasized the career development process as one of compromise and synthesis in which his primary construct—the development and implementation of the self-concept—operates. The basic theme is that individuals, as socialized organizers of their own experiences, choose occupations that allow them to function in a role consistent with a self-concept, and that the latter conception is a function of their developmental history. Super has labeled his approach differential–developmental–social–phenomenological psychology (Super, 1969) to indicate the confluence of knowledge bases that he has synthesized and ordered. He indicated that what he has contributed is a "segmental theory, a loosely unified set of theories dealing with specific aspects of career development taken from developmental, differential, social, and phenomenological psychology and held together by self-concept or personal-construct theory (1984) and by learning theory" (1990). His is not a single-choice matching approach but rather a longitudinal developmental approach. For example, Super (1990) depicted a career as

> the life course of a person encountering a series of developmental tasks and attempting to handle them in such a way as to become the kind of person he or she wants to become. With a changing self and changing situations, the matching process is never really completed. (pp. 225–226)

He provided terms such as *career maturity* and *career adaptability* to define the affective and cognitive variables related to the individual's readiness to cope with developmental tasks in different life stages.

As Super's work evolved, he and his students and other researchers have provided a large body of research, including the Career Pattern Study, a longitudinal study of more than 100 men from the time they were in ninth grade until they were well into adulthood, 35 years of age and beyond, that has yielded positive to mixed evidence about some of his propositions. This body of research, for example, has identified the behaviors characteristic of career maturity at various life stages, the elements of decision-making models, and the recycling of tasks at periods of career transition and floundering (e.g., Blustein, 1988; Fretz & Leong, 1982; Herr, Weitz, Good, & McCloskey, 1981; Jepsen & Prediger, 1981).

With particular respect to the integration of career theory and practice, from the beginning of his conceptual work, Super has constructed assessment instruments and counseling models that have been based on his career theory. His assessment instruments have included the *Career Development Inventory*, the *Adult Career Concerns Inventory*, the *Work Values Inventory*, and, more recently, the *Values Inventory*, the *Salience Inventory*, and the *Career Rainbow*. Each of these instruments attempts to describe or measure individual career behavior in ways that are useful in defining goals for counseling and explicating one's maturity or levels of career planfulness, knowledge, and attitudes about career choice, intrinsic and extrinsic life-career values, and the relative importance to the client of five major life roles: student, worker, homemaker, leisurite, and citizen. Crites' work as a career theorist (e.g., Crites, 1969) and as a theorist of career counseling (Crites, 1981) deserves separate treatment in its own right. But for our purposes, it is appropriate to note that his widely used instrument, the *Career Maturity Inventory*, was designed to assess the elements that Super originally described under the rubric of vocational maturity (Crites, 1974), and recent research has shown that its construct validity is supported by Super's career theory (Luzzo, 1993).

In addition to the assessment instruments developed from his career theory, Super's concepts of career development have served as the framework for career education programs in the United States (Herr & Cramer, 1992) and abroad (Watanabe & Herr, 1993; Watts, Super, & Kidd, 1981). Further, Super's developmental model has provided a frame of reference that can accommodate and be modified or refined by the theories of others. One excellent example is Sharf's (1992) analysis of how Linda Gottfredson's developmental theory of occupational aspirations has relevance for several of Super's concepts. For example, Gottfredson's theory expands Super's idea of self-concept and his early views about the seven career patterns of women that are primarily shaped by how women deal with marriage and homemaking. But his theory does not directly address gender issues or the major roles played by sex bias, sex roles, and prestige in shaping the choices of women. Gottfredson uses these central concepts as she activates the processes of circumscription and compromise. *Circumscription* refers to the idea that various factors limit career choice at different ages—for example, gender will influence occupational preferences from the age of six years and up, whereas social background or prestige will affect occupational preferences from the age of nine years and up. *Compromise* refers to the necessity for a person to modify career choices due to limiting environmental factors such as a competitive job market and to the likelihood that the earlier a factor, for example, sex type, becomes important in shaping occupational preference, the less likely it is that the individual will compromise on that variable. Gottfredson's (1981) theoretical compatibility with Super's work is seen in her statement that her theory

> accepts the fundamental importance of self-concept in vocational development, that people seek jobs compatible with their images of themselves. Social class, intelligence, and sex are seen as important determinants of both self-concept and the types of compromises people must make. (p. 546)

Finally, Super has frequently focused on the relationship of his career theory and career counseling as a process. For example, in his classic work, *The Psychology of Careers,* Super (1957) stated the following:

> It is important that the student, client or patient put his self-concept into words early in the counseling process . . .to clarify his actual role and his role aspirations; he needs to do it for the counselor, so that the counselor may understand the nature of the vocational problem confronting him.

Super recommended that such roles be implemented by alternating nondirective and directive methods by which the client and the counselor could engage in exploration, self-concept portrayal, clarification of feelings, reality testing, and the formulation of possible actions to be chosen and implemented.

Much more recently, Super developed what has come to be called the C-DAC model, which integrates (a) concepts from his career theory; (b) the use of the instruments he has authored to assess work salience, values, and career maturity or adaptability; and (c) the *Strong Interest Inventory*, into a career counseling process (Neville & Super, 1986; Super, Osborne, Walsh, Brown, & Niles, 1992) that can vary in the sequence of instruments and concepts pursued, depending on the client's needs. These needs could include, for example, the need to understand the client's readiness for career decision making and the client's need to confirm or identify an occupational choice (Niles & Usher, 1993).

Krumboltz's Integration of Theory and Practice

The third example of a comprehensive and historical major theoretical approach is that of the social learning approach to career decision making that has evolved though various iterations since the early 1970s from the work of Krumboltz, L. Mitchell, A. Mitchell, Jones, and Gelatt. This approach has its origins in general learning theory, as proposed by Bandura (1982), with its roots in reinforcement theory and classical behaviorism, and has in its recent applications encompassed cognitive behavioral theory. Basic to this approach is the assumption that "individual personalities and behavioral repertoires that persons possess arise primarily from their unique experiences rather than from innate developmental or psychic processes. The learning experiences consist of contact with and cognitive analysis of positively and negatively reinforcing events" (Mitchell & Krumboltz, 1984, p. 235). Krumboltz and his associates have called attention to four major categories of influences and to three types of outcomes. The influences include the following:

- Genetic endowment and special abilities
- Environmental conditions and events
- Learning experiences, such as *Instrumental Learning Experiences* (ILEs), in which antecedents—covert and overt—behavioral responses, and consequences are present; and *Associative Learning Experiences* (ALEs), in which the learner pairs a previously neutral situation with some emotionally positive or negative reaction (observational learning and classical conditioning are examples)
- Task approach skills (e.g., problem-solving skills, work habits, mental sets)

These four types of influences and their interactions lead to such outcomes as

- *Self-Observation Generalizations* (SOGs)—overt or covert statements evaluating one's own actual or vicarious performance in relation to learned standards
- *Task Approach Skills* (TASs)—cognitive and performance activities and emotional predispositions for coping with the environment, interpreting it, and making covert or overt predictions about future events (e.g., value clarifying, goal setting, information seeking, planning)
- *Actions*—entry behaviors that indicate overt steps in career progression (e.g., applying for a job or changing a college major)

Within a decision theory frame of reference, then, this model suggests that becoming a particular kind of worker or student is not simply a function of preference or choice but rather is "influenced by complex environmental (e.g., economic) factors, many of which are beyond the control of any single individual" (Krumboltz, Mitchell, & Gelatt, 1975, p. 75). The theoretical concepts of Krumboltz and his associates over the past two decades have spawned a large number of empirical studies, which in turn have provided support for many of the hypotheses generated by a social learning theory of career decision making. Such studies have also provided insight into a variety of possible career interventions that link career theory and practice, including the use of reinforcement and modeling with different media in group and individual settings.

Depending on when and which aspect of the theory are considered, there are a variety of techniques that counselors can use in relation to a social learning theory of career decision making. Indeed, some of these precede the formal theory and are reflected in the work in behavioral counseling that Krumboltz and his students did in the 1960s. For example, Ryan and Krumboltz (1964) reported that systematically reinforcing decision and deliberation statements of students in counseling did increase the rate of deliberation and decision statements significantly and that this reinforced behavior generalized to noncounseling settings. In 1964, Krumboltz and Thoresen (Krumboltz, 1964) randomly assigned 192 eleventh-grade pupils to individual and group counseling settings in which the following four procedures were used by counselors: (a) reinforcement of verbal information-seeking behavior, (b) presentations of a tape-recorded model interview followed by reinforcement counseling, (c) presentation of film or filmstrip plus discussion as a control procedure, and (d) inactive control. The findings were: (a) the model-reinforcement and reinforcement counseling provided more external information seeking than the control procedure; (b) with a male model, model reinforcement counseling surpassed reinforcement counseling for males but not for females; and (c) group and individual settings were about equally effective on the average, but interactions were found to be affected by counselor variables, schools, set of subjects, and treatments.

Moving to the present, among the many practical applications of Krumboltz's recent work is that which deals with the private rules of decision making and how these can be influenced by irrational beliefs (1983). Krumboltz has identified several types of problems that can arise from faulty self-observation generalizations or inaccurate interpretation of environmental conditions. Krumboltz contends that some of the beliefs and private rules in career decision making relate to the fact that making decisions is a painful process that involves at least four causes of stress: threat to self-esteem, surprise, deadlines, and absence of allocated time for decision making. Within such perspectives, Krumboltz contends that there are methods for identifying and acting on the irrational beliefs, stresses, and private rules that he describes. Among them are such direct connections between his career theory and career practices as the following possibilities: assessment of the content of the client's self-observation and worldview generalizations and the processes by which they arose, structured interviews, thought listing, in vivo self-monitoring, imagery, career decision-making simulations, reconstruction of prior events, use of cognitive restructuring techniques to help alter dysfunctional or inaccurate beliefs and generalizations, use of computerized guidance systems to provide and reinforce problem-solving tasks, teaching belief-testing processes, analyzing task approach skills and teaching those in deficit (Mitchell & Krumboltz, 1990), and the use of the *Career Beliefs Inventory* (Krumboltz, 1988) to identify presuppositions that block individuals from achieving their career goals.

It is worth noting that the roots of the social learning approach of Krumboltz and his colleagues in Bandura's work is also the genesis of the large body of work on self-efficacy, the expectations or beliefs that one can perform a given behavior. Self-efficacy theory and, to a lesser degree, outcome expectancies, have become explanatory systems for many career-related behaviors, stress reactions, phobias, social skills, coping behaviors, achievement, sports performance, mathematics performance, choice of college major, academic performance, career entry behaviors, and others (e.g., Bandura, 1982; Betz & Hackett, 1981, 1983, 1986; Campbell & Hackett, 1986; Hackett, 1985; Lent & Hackett, 1987). Many of these studies, which essentially test the validity and application of a general theory of learning for career behavior, have made recommendations for interventions by which to strengthen self-efficacy expectations.

Let me acknowledge that, in addition to the three I have cited, there are many other researchers/theorists whose work in integrating theory and research related to career behavior should be identified. Many of them have made major contributions to both theory and practice, to the development of assessment tools, or to the construction of new or refined theoretical perspectives. They include Blustein (1988, 1989); Brown and Brooks (1984, 1990, 1991); Dawis and Lofquist (1978); Osipow (1983, 1990); Osipow, Carney, Winer, Yanico, and Koschir (1976); Savickas (1984, 1993); Savickas, Stilling, and Schwartz (1984); Spokane (1991); and Vondracek, Lerner, and Schulenberg (1986).

ISSUES IN INTEGRATING CAREER THEORY AND PRACTICE

The examples cited herein of the integration of theory and practice lead to a basic question: If the lack of the integration of career theory and practice is a myth, at least at the level of conceptualization of the interaction of these two bodies of knowledge, what is the problem? Why do we continue to read and hear that there are not bridges between career theory and practice and that, at best, career theory is irrelevant to career practice? Although there are many possible explanations, one of the sets of observations that I find particularly useful is the analysis of Jepsen (1984). Drawing on the earlier insights of Borow (1982) and Osipow (1983), Jepsen argued that the application of career theory to practice is essentially a problem of translating theory into the explicit terms useful to practicing counselors. He has identified two forms of translations as problematic: One has to do with translating theoretical ideas into practical actions; the second has to do with translating "everyday career behavior into theoretical concept systems" (p. 135). Jepsen (1984) suggested that, with regard to translating theory into practice,

> Although counselors perform many tasks, two stand out as generalizable to most career guidance practices (Crites, 1981). The first is problem *identification*.... This process is also called "diagnosis'" or "needs assessment." The second task is *intervention design,* the process of designing or adopting interventions to reach the client's goals. (p. 136)

Jepsen (1984) goes on to contend that

> [t]hese two tasks require deliberate thinking involving ideas about the structures and dynamics of career behavior,...assessments of client status...instrument selection which presupposes some state of theory about the behaviors observed,...the logical connections between them, and their sequence. (p. 137)

To revert from Jepsen's insights to my personal language system, there are several fundamental issues that underlie the matter of the integration or convergence of career theory and practice. One is the need for career theory to be seen as the seedbed for hypotheses for explanations of clients' presenting problems that can help counselors to understand, interpret, or classify the client's current choice dilemmas, anxieties, or conflicts. There have been various taxonomies of career problems as they appear to various theorists for 50 years or more, but these taxonomies are not comprehensive, current, or, perhaps, even used by most practitioners. Although the content of the three career theories previously mentioned are important and sometimes overlapping explanatory systems of career behaviors (and their likely labels of the etiology of career behavior are to some degree reflected in the content of existing taxonomies of career presenting problems), the constructs of these three career theories are not systematically or comprehensively included in any taxonomic structure that I am aware of. To extend the point, there is no DSM IV of career behavior. Maybe there should not be, but such a classification system can provide a compilation of the empirical evidence and the speculation that shapes a profession's interpretation of its relevant behavioral content and the interventions found to be useful in providing change in it. We have a large and rich literature describing career behavior, but our efforts to catalogue what we know, to assess the comparability of career theories as explanatory systems for problem identification, goal setting, program planning, and problem solving for practitioner use are still primitive. Nevertheless, there are some examples of formative steps in that direction (e.g., Brown & Brooks, 1984, 1990; Herr & Cramer, 1992).

Part of the problem of integrating theory and practice is also the language system used. Most career theorists are academics, not full-time practitioners, and the range of populations we are likely to serve is narrower than the range of populations that seeks to learn from our theories. Thus, our writing is frequently at a level of abstraction and lacking certitude, which causes practitioners to dismiss much of what we write as irrelevant. They want more assurance about the etiology of presenting problems, about the interventions that are likely to work, and about the actual linkage between scientists and practitioners, provided in a language form that is comfortable and understandable in relation to the goal-setting and problem-setting functions in which counselors and clients engage.

But there is another problem of language that also relates to the matter of integrating career theory and practice. It is definitional and it sometimes obscures the outcomes that should be expected from interventions or indeed from career theories themselves. For example, when we use the term *career,* are we talking about job, occupations, career patterns across time, or all of them? Similarly, when we use *career guidance, career counseling,* or *career education,* do we mean that these are interchangeable terms or discrete categories of interventions? I sometimes read of counselors "doing career development." Does that mean that career development is an intervention or the behavioral target of interventions? Because I am at least as guilty as anyone else of using these terms with less precision than they deserve, I raise the issue because the semantics of theory and practice affect what practitioners receive from theory and their likely understanding of the implications theory holds for interventions. When our unit of concern is how one forges a career pattern over time rather than choosing a job or an occupation within a restricted time perspective, by using the same descriptive language for each activity, we tend to homogenize events and processes that are different in content and in the differential treatment issues that need to be addressed.

These issues also need to be seen in terms of population and contexts. For example, it is logical to assume that the particular set of activities and outcomes descriptive of a developmental approach to career guidance when provided for an affluent, suburban upper elementary school population should differ from the activities and outcomes of a developmental approach to career guidance used with a disadvantaged adult population in a community agency. But how should these two delivery systems differ? What does career theory provide us to help with such conceptualization and planning? I think career theories can help with such issues, but they are frequently not translated in the form or the level of specificity that practitioners find helpful in the more concrete realities with which they deal on a daily basis.

Solving these perceived dilemmas is not easy, but, at a minimum, solutions will require much more extensive and direct collaboration on theory building and research by teams of theorists and practitioners. Career theorists must be in fuller dialogue with practitioners about the problems they experience in the settings and with the populations they serve. In this sense, theory construction must increasingly be directed to understanding and explaining the behaviors, problems, and contexts related to the career concerns of specific populations. This point further suggests that samples of convenience—for example, sophomore students in Psychology 102 getting extra credit for participating in a study—are inadequate to understand the problems of school leavers, noncollege-bound populations, immigrant populations, persons of color, and women who are not college students. We need more naturalistic studies that take place in the contexts and tell the stories of people who live their lives in circumstances that differ from those experienced by middle-class and educated populations.

Although there are studies that suggest that some of our existing career theories are relevant to groups outside of middle-class or male populations, there are still tendencies to overgeneralize what we know about career behavior to population groups about whom we have little direct research. Also there continues to be a tendency to try to refine and extend our current career theories rather than construct new theories that are much more attentive to the barriers, obstacles, and contextual constraints—racism, sexism, ageism—that are of primary significance to many persons of color, women, persons with disabilities, and persons of alternative sexual orientation to whom practice needs to be directed and relevant.

Another issue that potentially divides theory and practice has to do with the availability of measures of theoretical constructs that comprehensively assess the constructs that career theories incorporate. As suggested earlier in this chapter, there is a growing inventory of assessment instruments that have evolved directly from career theory. However, it is not clear, and probably unlikely, that the existing instruments measure the major constructs of each theory comprehensively. Although there were several important content analyses in the 1970s (e.g., Westbrook, 1974) of career development instruments that existed then, the content analyses of existing assessment instruments are less than complete today. To the degree that such a condition exists, it also limits the intervention outcomes likely to be measured or that it is possible to measure. As a major part of this problem, Osipow (1983), among other observers, has criticized many career theories because the terms used are not easily converted into concrete observable behavior. Research data on a limited set of theoretical outcomes, on samples of convenience, or on intervention outcomes at one point in time and not across time restricts feedback to theorists about necessary refinements in career theories and diminishes the utility of theory for practice and, in the larger sense, the integration of career theory and practice. Although important, such an analysis of the status of research as related to each of the extant career theories deserves much more comprehensive analysis than is possible within the scope of this chapter.

Comparative and Emerging Views on Issues Separating Career Theory and Practice

Within the context of the issues that separate career theory and practice, it is useful to briefly revisit what other earlier commentators have described as the problems of existing career theories and assess how these problems have changed, if at all. Both Crites (1969) and Borow (1982), from their vantage points of the time, suggested that career theories could be criticized because of the limited scope of career behaviors that were included in any given career theory. In essence, extant theories were seen as more akin to segments or fragments of theory rather than comprehensive and integrated theories. They were also concerned about the methodological problems related to theory construction and, in particular, the tendency of most extant career theories to engage in description, not prediction. It might be noted here that the lack of attention to cause and effect relationships between prior developmental experience and subsequent behavior is paralleled by our existing body of research on the intervention side. For example, given the propensity to do research on career behavior or interventions at a specific point in time, we frequently cannot explain why a particular dependent variable was chosen as the outcome to be sought from career counseling or another form of career intervention or how it is connected to career theory. Thus, our research data gives us insufficient help in understanding the relationship between the achievement of an intervention outcome at a particular point in time (e.g., a mature orientation to decision making, a use of exploratory resources, or accurate self-estimates) and subsequent outcomes (e.g., work adjustment, job satisfaction, occupational mobility). Such a condition is associated with the third criticism of Borow and Crites, the problem of practical applications of career theory in counseling and in other interventions. We have previously addressed this issue from several perspectives and found that there is substantial work to be done to help integrate career theory and practice.

Savickas (1989) has suggested that "although we know that career interventions generally have positive effects...now we need to determine which interventions, with whom, and under what circumstances" (p. 102). Indeed, little can be said about the likely effects of different types of career guidance, career counseling, or other career interventions in relation to specific categories of individual problems or needs (Tinsley & Heesacker, 1984) or attribute-by-treatment interactions that examine the notion that the outcomes of career intervention are a function of the interaction of client attributes with the treatments they receive (Fretz, 1981). The reality seems to be that regardless of how direct the connection to a specific career theory, the weight of evidence of aggregated studies, whether through meta-analysis or other techniques, suggests that career education (Baker & Popowicz, 1983), career counseling (Holland, Magoon, & Spokane, 1981; Oliver & Spokane, 1988; Spokane & Oliver, 1983), and career guidance (Herr, 1986) do yield positive results and that the general efficacy of such interventions is no longer in question (Rounds & Tinsley, 1984). The explanations of which career interventions, for whom, and under what conditions is less clear. More research is needed that links client goals to treatment using the scaling of goal attainment (Cytrynbaum, Ginath, Birdwell, & Brandt, 1979), or to diagnostic procedures or taxonomic classifications of career behaviors, and to the long-term effects of particular career interventions on subsequent behaviors.

Certainly, one of the major emerging issues that will likely affect the convergence of career theory and practice relates to whether the construction of career theory continues to rest primarily on psychological assumptions about the primacy of individual action or on dynamic and interactional sociological, anthropological, organizational, or economic perspectives that put people into contexts that shape or restrict individual action and create barriers and obstacles that must be understood and surmounted. Such views give particular attention to the specific features of the context within which the individual is developing and with which she or he is engaged in adaptive interchanges (Vondracek, 1990). To the degree that such views become more fully embedded in career theory, they stimulate the development of interventions that are targeted not only to the individual but also to the family, the community, institutional settings, and social policy. Both from the perspective of career theory and practice, it is important to know the effects of situational variables—family history, home community, socioeconomic status, race, ethnicity, gender—on career development and on the interventions appropriate to people experiencing different combinations of such contextual effects.

Gottfredson (1990) has addressed several areas that are necessary in future applications and research using Holland's theory of careers. In my view, his observations are relevant beyond the work of Holland and include in abridged form such perspectives as the following. According to Gottfredson, among other possibilities he cites, we need the following:

- A range of practical treatments for people who need different levels and types of treatment.

- More evidence about such basic items as the effects of providing different amounts and modes of information.

- *Experimental* tests of diagnostic ideas linking identity, barriers, and topological assessments to *levels* and *varieties* of assistance. (p. 4)

Possibilities for Increasing Convergence of Career Theory and Practice

I have already suggested some possibilities for increasing the convergence of career theory and practice. I will conclude by adding several additional possibilities.

First, existing career theories should be seen as complementary ways of knowing, not competing and fully developed alternative explanations of the same behavioral set or population. There are major voids in the knowledge necessary about women, minorities, and other groups in the society whose career behavior has been particularly affected by the magnitude of social, political, and economic changes of the past quarter century, but if one takes an aggregate view of existing career theory and research, there are tentative sets of constructs and propositions that can be used to explain different patterns of career behavior for a range of subpopulations and to design differential interventions or systems of interventions (Herr & Cramer, 1992). However, such existing configurations deserve experimental treatments by goal and by client attributes that are comprehensively done and meticulously described by behavioral outcome and by the intervention process involved.

Second, we must seek to convert what we know from the already excellent work of many researchers and research synthesizers (e.g., Holland, Magoon, & Spokane, 1981; Spokane, 1991; Spokane & Oliver, 1983) into a matrix that is accessible by behavioral outcome or presenting problem, by client type, by setting, and by intervention. Such a matrix needs to be seen primarily as a translation of what we know and its practical relevance rather than why we know it and its theoretical significance.

Third, we must seek more collaboration between theorists, researchers, and practitioners as joint members of research teams focused particularly on enlarging our understanding of career behavior as reinforced or hindered in specific settings and as it is lived by specific populations. It is in such possibilities that quantitative and qualitative research methods can be combined to test our theoretical predictions and expand available descriptions of the richness of the settings, cultures, and contexts that mediate our theoretical predictions and affect the implementation and perceived viability of interventions.

Fourth, we need to forgo, for the immediate future, the implicit assumption of the possibility of creating one omnibus career theory. Instead, we must concentrate on increasing the number of segmented theories that focus more directly on the specific forms of obstacles, barriers, reinforcements, received messages, and other variables affecting the career behavior of women, ethnic minorities, persons with disabilities, and persons of alternative sexual orientations, by level of education, socioeconomic level, and other indexes. The results of such studies need to be compared to constructs already validated in existing career theory. They need to be incorporated into new and complementary theories of career behavior in cases where available theoretical conceptualization does not adequately describe the career behavior of particular subpopulations, integrate existing knowledge, or guide future research and intervention. It seems appropriate to recommend that prior to the construction of new, segmented theories, an intense effort should be focused on obtaining the perspectives afforded by qualitative research methods as the basis for formulating new or refined theoretical assumptions and intervention strategies and subsequently validating these through experimental methods. In collaborative research teams of theorists, researchers, and practitioners, the latter group of professionals could provide the major energy to do the ethnographic and other qualitative analyses important to expanded perspectives on the career experiences of women and culturally different groups, and on the contexts and social realities within which career behavior is stimulated and shaped for these populations. Of importance in such perspectives, I believe, is a need to examine the trends away from primary reliance on positivist to naturalist research methodologies, including the rise of constructivist approaches in which both the researcher and subject are intimately involved in framing the important questions, interpreting the reality of the subject, and understanding the individual's construction of personal meaning and social reality and the socialization processes that led to such behavioral outcomes (Guba, 1990). Although I am probably stretching the point somewhat, such approaches can also enhance the understanding of the phenomena involved in developmental-contextual approaches to career development (Vondrocek, 1990).

Fifth, increased attention needs to be given to shifting paradigms of career counseling and of other career interventions (Brown & Brooks, 1991; Herr & Cramer, 1992; Rounds & Tinsley, 1984; Spokane, 1991). Some questions to consider are the following: For whom and under what conditions do career counseling and personal counseling essentially fuse? What are the conceptual sources for the apparent expansion of forms of career intervention? Are these tied to career theory or are they coming from atheoretical or other conceptual frames of reference? To what degree and for whom does one type of intervention substitute for another form of intervention? What are the cost-benefit ratios of using various types of career interventions (e.g., individual or group, or computer mediated)?

Finally, some implications about the training of counseling psychologists and other counselors in career work need to be examined in depth. Why do these students choose counseling psychology as a profession but deny the importance of career theory and practice as the roots of this discipline? Is the teaching they receive limited in its portrayal of the convergence of career theory and practice, the importance of work choice and adjustment in human identity, the range of problems (including those defined as major mental health problems) associated with unsuccessful or ineffective access to the labor force and premature termination of an employed role, the emerging stimuli for expanding paradigms of career work to meet the challenges of the international economy, the changing work organizations and possibility structures in this nation and abroad, and the globalization and mobility of the world's workforce? Are these students not being provided the hands-on and clinical opportunities to work with populations for whom jagged occupational histories, unemployment, and underemployment are realities that have prompted negative physiological, behavioral, and emotional outcomes? What are the characteristics of training models where counseling psychology students are committed to career work and are considered by intern sites and employers as competent and effective?

CONCLUSION

This analysis focused on the assumption in career psychology and counseling that career theory and practice are not integrated. The concept of myth was used to suggest that there are clear demonstrations of how three major career theories have integrated practice by the development and the advocacy of assessments and counseling techniques that facilitate the use of theoretical constructs in working with clients. Although such attempts to integrate career theory and practice are evident in the professional literature, there are other issues that need to be addressed to facilitate the integration of theory and practice. They include awareness that major aspects of such integration include the translation of concepts between theorists and practitioners, the range of population concerns and the specificity of language used in theory, and the comprehensiveness of available assessment instruments in incorporating theoretical constructs. Several possibilities were offered for addressing such issues and for furthering the search for more effective integration of career theory and practice.

REFERENCES

Baker, S. B., & Popowicz, C. L. (1983). Meta-analysis as a strategy for evaluating effects of career education interventions. *Vocational Guidance Quarterly, 31*, 178–186.

Bandura, A. (1982). Self-efficacy mechanism in human agency. *American Psychologist, 37*, 122–147.

Betz, N. E., & Hackett, G. (1981). The relationship of career-related self-efficacy expectations to perceived career options in college women and men. *Journal of Counseling Psychology, 28*, 399–410.

Betz, N. E., & Hackett, G. (1983). The relationship of mathematics self-efficacy expectations to the selection of science-based college majors. *Journal of Vocational Behavior, 23,* 329–345.

Betz, N. E., & Hackett, G. (1986). Applications of self-efficacy theory to understanding career choice behavior. *Journal of Social and Clinical Psychology, 4,* 279–289.

Blustein, D. L. (1988). A canonical analysis of career choice crystallization and vocational maturity. *Journal of Counseling Psychology, 35,* 294–297.

Blustein, D. L. (1989). The role of goal instability and career self-efficacy in the career exploration process. *Journal of Vocational Behavior, 35,* 194–203.

Borow, H. (1982). Career development theory and instrumental outcomes of career guidance: A critique. In J. D. Krumboltz & D. A. Harnel (Eds.), *Assessing career development.* Palo Alto, CA: Mayfield.

Brown, D., & Brooks, L. (1984). *Career choice and development. Applying contemporary theories to practice.* San Francisco: Jossey-Bass.

Brown, D., & Brooks, L. (1990). *Career choice and development: Applying contemporary theories to practice* (2d ed.). San Francisco: Jossey-Bass.

Brown, D., & Brooks, L. (1991). *Career counseling techniques.* Boston: Allyn & Bacon.

Campbell, N. K., & Hackett, G. (1986). The effects of mathematics task performances on math self-efficacy and task interest. *Journal of Vocational Behavior, 28,* 149–162.

Crites, J. O. (1969). *Vocational Psychology.* New York: McGraw-Hill.

Crites, J. O. (1981). *Career counseling: Models, methods, and materials.* New York: McGraw-Hill.

Cytrynbaum, S., Ginath, Y., Birdwell, J., & Brandt, C. (1979). Goal attainment scaling. *Evaluation Quarterly, 3,* 5–40.

Dawis, R. V., & Lofquist, L. H. (1978). A note on the dynamics of work adjustment. *Journal of Vocational Behavior, 12,* 76–79.

Fitzgerald, L. F., & Osipow, S. H. (1986). An occupational analysis of counseling psychology: How special is the specialty? *American Psychologist, 41,* 535–544.

Fretz, B. R. (1981). Evaluating the effectiveness of career interventions. *Journal of Counseling Psychology, 28*(1), 77–90.

Fretz, B. R., & Leong, F. T. L. (1982). Career development status as predictor of career intervention outcomes. *Journal of Counseling Psychology, 29,* 388–393.

Goldschmidt, M., Tipton, R. M., & Wiggins, C. (1981). Professional identity of counseling psychologists. *Journal of Counseling Psychology, 28,* 158–167.

Gottfredson, G. D. (1981). Circumscription and compromise: A developmental theory of occupational ascriptions. *Journal of Counseling Psychology, 28,* 545–579.

Gottfredson, G. D. (1990, August). Applications and research using Holland's theory of careers: Where we would like to be and suggestions for getting there. In *Applications and research using Holland's theory of careers: Some evaluation.* Symposium conducted at the annual meeting of the American Psychological Association, Boston.

Gottfredson, G. D., Holland, J. L., & Ogawa, D. K. (1982). *Dictionary of Holland occupational codes.* Palo Alto, CA: Consulting Psychologists Press.

Gottfredson, G. D., & Holland, J. L. (1990). A longitudinal test of the influence of congruence: Job satisfaction, competency utilization, and counterproductive behavior. *Journal of Counseling Psychology, 37,* 389–398.

Gottfredson, G. D., Jones, E. M., & Holland, J. L. (1993). Personality and vocational interests: The relation of Holland's six interest dimensions to five robust dimensions of personality. *Journal of Counseling Psychology, 40,* 518–529.

Guba, E. (1990). Subjectivity and objectivity. In E. W. Eisner & A. Peskkin (Eds.), *Qualitative inquiry in education. The continuing debate* (pp. 74–91). New York: Teachers College Press.

Hackett, G. (1985). The role of mathematics self-efficacy in the choice of math-related majors of college women and men: A path analysis. *Journal of Counseling Psychology, 32,* 47–56.

Harrington, T. F., Feller, R., & O'Shea, A. J. (1993). Four methods to determine RIASEC codes for college majors and a comparison of its rates. *Career Development Quarterly, 41,* 383–392.

Herr, E. L. (1986). *Why counseling?* (2d ed.). Alexandria, VA: AACD Press.

Herr, E. L., & Cramer, S. H. (1992). *Career guidance and counseling through the lifespan: Systematic approaches.* New York: HarperCollins.

Herr, E. L., Weitz, A., Good, R., & McCloskey, G. (1981). *Research on the effects of secondary school curricular and personal characteristics upon postsecondary educational and occupational patterns.* (NIE-G-80-0027). University Park, PA: University Park.

Holland, J. L. (1973). *Making vocational choices: A theory of careers.* Englewood Cliffs, NJ: Prentice Hall.

Holland, J. L. (1982). *Some implications of career theory for adult development and aging.* Paper presented at the annual meeting of the American Psychological Association, Washington, DC

Holland, J. L. (1985). *Making vocational choices: A theory of vocational personalities and work environments,* (2d ed.). Englewood Cliffs, NJ: Prentice-Hall.

Holland, J. L., Gottfredson, G., & Baker, H. G. (1990). Validity of vocational aspirations and interest inventories: Extended, replicated, and reinterpreted. *Journal of Counseling Psychology, 22,* 411–412.

Holland, J. L., Magoon, T. M., & Spokane, A. R. (1981). Counseling psychology: Career interventions, research, and theory. *Annual Review of Psychology, 32,* 279–300.

Jepsen, D. A. (1984). Relationship between career development theory and practice. In N. C. Gysbers and Associates (Eds.), *Designing careers: Counseling to enhance education, work, and leisure* (pp. 135–159). San Francisco: Jossey-Bass.

Jepsen, D. A., & Prediger, D. J. (1981). Dimensions of adolescent career development: A multi-instrument analysis. *Journal of Vocational Behavior, 19,* 350–368.

Jones, L. K. (1980). Holland's typology and the new guide for occupational exploration: Bridging the gap. *Vocational Guidance Quarterly, 29*(1), 70–75.

Krumboltz, J. D. (1964). The effect of behavioral counseling in groups and individual settings on information-seeking behavior. *Journal of Counseling Psychology, 11,* 324–333.

Krumboltz, J. D. (1983). *Private rules in career decision making.* Columbus, OH: National Center for Research in Vocational Education.

Krumboltz, J. D. (1988). *The Career Beliefs Inventory.* Palo Alto, CA: Consulting Psychologists Press.

Krumboltz, J. D., Mitchell, A., & Gelatt, H. B. (1975). Applications of social learning theory of career selection. *Focus on Guidance, 8,* 1–16.

Lent, R. W., & Hackett, G. (1987). Career self-efficacy: Empirical status and future directions. *Journal of Vocational Behavior, 30,* 347–382.

Luzzo, D. A. (1993). A multi-trait, multi-method analysis of three career development measures. *Career Development Quarterly, 41,* 367–374.

Meier, E. L. (1989). Integrative elaboration of the congruence theory. *Journal of Vocational Behavior, 35,* 219–230.

Mitchell, L., & Krumboltz, J. D. (1990). Social learning approach to career decision making: Krumboltz's theory. In D. Brown & L. Brooks (Eds.), *Career choice and development: Applying contemporary theories to practice* (2d ed., pp. 145–196). San Francisco: Jossey-Bass.

Nevill, D., & Super, D. E. (1986). *The Values Scale: Theory, application, and research manual.* (Research Edition). Palo Alto, CA: Consulting Psychologists Press.

Niles, S. G., & Usher, C. H. (1993). Applying the career development assessment and counseling model to the case of Rosie. *Career Development Quarterly, 42,* 61–66.

Oliver, L. W., & Spokane, A. R. (1988). Career-intervention outcome: What contributes to client gain? *Journal of Counseling Psychology, 35,* 447–462.

Osipow, S. H. (1983). *Theories of career development* (3d ed.). Englewood Cliffs, NJ: Prentice Hall.

Osipow, S. H. (1990). Convergence in theories of career choice and development: Review and prospect. *Journal of Vocational Behavior, 36,* 122–131.

Osipow, S. H., Carney, C. G., Winer, J. L., Yanico, B. J., & Koschier, M. (1976). *Career Decision Scale.* Columbus, OH: Marathon Press.

Rounds, J. B., Jr., Davison, M. L., & Dawis, R. V. (1979). The fit between Strong-Campbell Interest Inventory general occupation themes and Holland's hexogonal model. *Journal of Vocational Behavior, 15,* 303–315.

Rounds, J. B., Jr., & Tinsley, H. E. A. (1984). Diagnosis and treatment of vocational problems. In S. Brown & R. Lent (Eds.), *Handbook of Counseling Psychology* (pp. 137–177). New York: Wiley.

Ryan, T., & Krumboltz, J. D. (1964). Effect of planned reinforcement counseling on client decision-making behavior. *Journal of Counseling Psychology, 11,* 315–323.

Savickas, M. L. (1984). Career maturity: The construct and its appraisal. *Vocational Guidance Quarterly, 32,* 222–231.

Savickas, M. L. (1989). Annual review: Practice and research in career counseling and development. *Career Development Quarterly, 38,* 100–134.Savickas, M. L. (1993). Career counseling in the postmodern era. *Journal of Cognitive Psychotherapy: An International Quarterly, 7,* 205–215.

Savickas, M. L., Stilling, S. M., & Schwartz, S. (1984). Time perspective in vocational maturity and career decision making. *Journal of Vocational Behavior, 25,* 258–269.

Sharf, R. S. (1992). *Applying career development theory to counseling.* Pacific Grove, CA: Brooks/Cole.

Spokane, A. R. (1985). A review of research on person-environment congruence in Holland's theory of careers. *Journal of Vocational Behavior, 26,* 306–343.

Spokane, A. R. (1991). *Career intervention.* Englewood Cliffs, NJ: Prentice Hall.

Spokane, A. R., & Oliver, L. W. (1983). The outcomes of vocational intervention (pp. 99–136). In S. H. Osipow & W. B. Walsh (Eds.), *Handbook of Vocational Psychology* (Vol. 2). Hillsdale, NJ: Erlbaum.

Super, D. E. (1969). Vocational development theory: Persons, positions, and processes. *The Counseling Psychologist, 1,* 2–9.

Super, D. E. (1984). Career and life development. In D. Brown & L. Brooks (Eds.), *Career choice and development. Applying contemporary approaches to practice* (pp. 192–239). San Francisco: Jossey-Bass.

Super, D. E. (1990). A life-span, life-space approach to career development. In D. Brown & L. Brooks (Eds.), *Career choice and development: Applying contemporary theories to practice* (pp. 197–261). San Francisco: Jossey-Bass.

Super, D. E. (1994). A life-span, life-space perspective on convergence. In M. Savickas & R. W. Lent (Eds.), *Convergence in career development theories: Implications for science and practice* (pp. 63–74). Palo Alto, CA: Davies-Black Publishing.

Super, D. E., Osborne, W. L., Walsh, D. J., Brown, S. D., & Niles, S. G. (1992). Developmental career assessment and counseling: The C-DAC model. *Journal of Counseling and Development, 71,* 74–79.

Tinsley, H. E. A., & Heesacker, M. (1984). Vocational behavior and career development: A review. *Journal of Vocational Behavior, 25,* 139–190.

U.S. Department of Labor. (1991). *Dictionary of Occupational Titles* (4th ed.). Washington, DC: Author.

Vondracek, F. W. (1990). A developmental-contextual approach to career development research. In R. A. Young & W. A. Borgen (Eds.), *Methodological approaches to the study of career* (pp. 37–56). New York: Praeger.

Voncracek, F. W., Lerner, R. M., & Schulenberg, J. E. (1986). *Career development: A life-span approach.* Hillsdale, NJ: Erlbaum.

Ward, C. M., & Walsh, W. B. (1981). Concurrent validity of Holland's theory for non-college degreed Black women. *Journal of Vocational Behavior, 18,* 356–361.

Watanabe, A. M., & Herr, E. L. (1993). Career development issues among Japanese work groups. *Journal of Career Development, 20,* 61–72.

Watts, A. G., Super, D. E., & Kidd, J. M. (1981). *Career Development in Britain.* Cambridge, UK: Hobson's Press.

Weinrach, S. G. (1984). Determinants of vocational choice: Holland's theory. In D. Brown & L. Brooks (Eds.), *Career choice and development: Applying contemporary theories to practice* (pp. 61–93). San Francisco: Jossey-Bass.

Westbrook, B. W. (1974). Content analysis of six career development tests. *Measurement and Evaluation on Guidance, 7*(3), 172–180.

CHAPTER THREE

A Moving Target

The Widening Gap
Between Theory and Practice

Lenore W. Harmon
University of Illinois at Urbana-Champaign

T HE FACT THAT our discussion in this handbook centers on integrating theory and practice implies that there is a gap between the two. This chapter concentrates on defining the nature of that gap and discussing what we might do about it.

When daily headlines proclaim corporate plans to lay off thousands of workers in the name of downsizing or retrenchment, it is increasingly clear that the concept of change must be incorporated in any definition of *career* in today's society. No longer can workers, no matter what their level of education or experience, expect to have the same job for life. For the most part, our theories have been developed from the implicit assumption that career development proceeds toward a choice of career or a career path that is relatively stable and predictable and controlled by the individual. However, the clients we see today can no longer afford to make such naive assumptions. They need to plan for change because the world of work is itself changing.

THE ORIGIN OF THE GAP

Changes in the World of Work

Robert Reich (1991, Chaps. 14–16), the current U.S. Secretary of Labor, has characterized the types of jobs available in our society in a way that differs somewhat from the categories used by psychologists or sociologists. The three categories he uses are symbolic-analytical services, routine production services, and in-person services. *Symbolic-analytical services* involve identifying and solving problems and planning, whereas *routine production services* and *in-person services* both involve simple and repetitive tasks. The latter two differ mainly in that in-person services involve more personal contact and social skills than routine production services. These categories are functional and refer to the processes used in the world of work, although we can infer that symbolic-analytic services involve manipulating ideas or data, whereas routine production services involve manipulating things or data; and in-person services involve dealing with people. Whereas symbolic-analytical occupations tend to be valued highly and rewarded accordingly, routine and in-person services do not.

Reich noted that several factors are affecting the kinds of jobs that are available today. Routine operations are going to the cheapest labor pool, often outside the United States. For example, many goods we use today can be produced more cheaply in Mexico or Southeast Asia. In-person services are becoming increasingly automated. The job of long-distance telephone operator—one I held as a college student—for example, has been almost completely eliminated by technology that allows people to dial their own long-distance calls, including conference calls involving people in several states. Personal service jobs, except those that cannot be automated, seem to be on the decline and jobs in symbolic analytical services are going to those who can manipulate information most efficiently.

The relationship between employer and employee has also changed. Organizations such as the Ford Motor Company and the Pullman Railroad Coach Company, which took a paternalistic view of their workers early in this century, are difficult to find today. Now the relationship between employer and employee is based on bottom-line profit. Workers are often hired for the duration of a specific project without the expectation of long-term employment. For example, the skills needed to develop a product may not be needed once that product is developed, so the employer and employee will part company once the development is complete, with the employer going on to new and different projects and the employee looking for similar projects in a different company.

Neither career theory nor practice has developed to meet this rapidly changing situation in which forces outside the individual may be much more influential in determining the worker's opportunities in the world of work than ever before.

Changes in Career Counseling

As practitioners, our rate of change is not commensurate with the rate of change in society, although we have made scientific advances. In the theoretical realm, the recognition that the concept of self-efficacy has important implications for career behavior (Hackett & Betz, 1981) was a major theoretical advance. However, applications of self-efficacy theory to career counseling have been slow to materialize. Recognition that family relationships and the separation/individuation issues faced by young people are related to the career development of young adults is also a major theoretical step forward (Blustein, Walbridge, Friedlander, & Palladino, 1991). However, the implications are very difficult to incorporate in practice, as are any findings with implications for family life and child rearing.

In the practical realm, it is not that we do not wish to change, but that the problems our clients face are very complex. The fact that counselors have recognized a need to understand and deal with clients from different cultures (Fouad & Bingham, 1995; Sue & Sue, 1990), with sexual harassment in the workplace (Fitzgerald, 1993), and with unemployment (Mallinckrodt & Fretz, 1988; Schlossberg & Leibowitz, 1980) suggests that we are willing to change. However, it is not clear what we can do to help people who are not prepared to enter a world of work that requires high-level skills and an ability to keep up with changing trends and technologies.

THE NATURE OF THE GAP

So what is the nature of the gap that concerns us? Actually, we confront two gaps: the gap between theory and practice, and the gap between the knowledge and skill levels of counselors and the reality of the enormous problems of today's worker. Our theory and practice are not always well integrated on the one hand, but on the other hand, even when they are, they fall far short of providing useful answers to increasingly complex questions. In fact, the lack of integration of theory and practice (or the gap between them) may be a partial result of the complexity of the issues we face in practice.

As a child, I was taught to shoot by my father, who was a sportsman. I wasn't very good at it, yet I learned some basic things: It is much more difficult to hit a moving target than a stationary one; it is more difficult to hit a distant target than a close one; and the marksman or markswoman must assume a stationary position for maximum accuracy. I see the task of integrating theory and practice in a way that addresses the problems of our contemporary clients as analogous to trying to hit a distant and moving target while advancing ourselves, but at a rate more slowly than the target. As we attempt to integrate theory and practice, the problems our clients face are increasingly difficult. There is a gap between theory and practice, as indicated earlier. There is an even larger gap between what we know and what we need to know, and it is that gap that seems to be widening most rapidly. We are truly in a difficult position. We can either stop trying to make a difference or find ways to continue our efforts.

Because we are in no better position than our clients to control the economy in which we function, we need to find ways to help individuals deal with change. We must all find ways to increase our comfort with the fact that the world of work is changing more rapidly than ever before and to increase our sense of control of our own lives and destinies within an increasingly complex social and economic environment.

CHANGES TO THEORY AND PRACTICE

Theory

Developing and disseminating theories is a time-consuming and expensive enterprise. Theory building is almost always tied to practical problems, but by the nature of the enterprise, the scientist working to expand theory often deals with small details related to the larger picture faced by the practitioner and the client. It may be worthwhile to attempt to develop some guidelines for theory development in the face of rapid change. Theory builders might consider the following guidelines:

- Work inductively from the problems of practice and remain grounded in the problems of practice when expanding theories.

- Define career achievement in individualistic ways that make some type of achievement attainable for everyone. This may require alterations to our usual definitions of achievement to reduce their dependence on external variables such as promotion and prestige. The concepts that are used as dependent variables should be relevant to individuals or small classes of individuals.

- Acknowledge that there may be fewer extrinsic satisfactions in work for most people than there have been in the past and address ways of helping workers find intrinsic satisfactions, even in routine production and service jobs.

- Recognize that the most difficult career-related problems in our society are (a) indecisiveness, *not* indecision, on which we most often focus; (b) lack of hope—when one does not expect to get a job, one will not put forth much effort to attain it; (c) lack of imagination about how to attain satisfactions from work—expecting an experience to be aversive can become a self-fulfilling prophecy; and (d) lack of courage and skill to change the workplace into something that would be more satisfying.

- Be aware of the overlap between career counseling and personal counseling.

- Recognize the relationship between the effectiveness of career interventions and the preparedness of the targeted population to profit from them. I would argue with Spokane (1991), who seems to believe that there is little or no overlap between career and personal interventions. Personal interventions might be crucial to preparing an individual to profit from a career intervention and, in my estimation, might overlap with career intervention.

- Acknowledge that many career-related problems are beyond the control of clients and that many clients have multiple problems that are beyond their control.

In summary, the ideal theory would recognize that the toughest career problems are rooted in the personal, often developmental, problems of self-definition and a sense of personal control.

Practice

To remain relevant in a changing society, the practitioner must change more quickly than theory, always moving beyond what is known to explore the new problems posed to the client by society. This is where the target shooting analogy applies to the two types of gaps between theory and practice defined earlier. Although both the scientist and the practitioner are changing, the nature of their respective duties requires that the practitioner move more quickly than theory can move to keep up with the changing situation in the world in which clients live. Nevertheless, the reality of clients' lives changes more quickly than practice. So we have three elements, all moving at different rates with widening gaps between any two of them. Unfortunately, it seems that the situation in the world is always moving most quickly. Our theory and practice must change more rapidly to catch up if our effectiveness in dealing with clients is to keep pace with change or narrow the important gap between our practical skills and the reality of the problems our clients face.

Practitioners succeed or fail not just on the basis of their theoretical knowledge but on the basis of their ability to go beyond what is known and proven. They must apply theories to new and untried situations. They must use intuition to develop hunches where there is no theory to guide them. It may be worthwhile to attempt to develop some guidelines for practice in the face of rapid change. Such guidelines for practitioners might include the following:

- Use of theory to the extent that it applies to the problems that clients present
- Recognition that theory will usually lag behind practice, requiring courage, creativity, and intuition in developing ways to deal with the problems that clients present
- Awareness of change in society, anticipating it rather than letting it be a surprise
- Recognition of the responsibilities to (a) communicate innovations to other practitioners; (b) validate the effectiveness of innovations, or work with scientists who will do so; and (c) consider the theoretical implications of innovations and attempt to integrate them theoretically, or work with scientists who will do so

In summary, practitioners should be seen, by others and by themselves, as both the leaders in theoretical developments and as the most important element in theory development, as well as bold innovators in practice.

CLOSING THE GAP

Training Professionals Devoted to Change

As noted above, I believe that practitioners are the key to closing the gap between practice and the realities of the world of work. Nevertheless, we often train counseling psychologists as though we expected all of them, and certainly the best of them, to become scientists. At a recent social gathering of the faculty and students of a well-respected counseling psychology program, the students staged a skit featuring a "Geraldo"-like panel on the topic of "Practitioner Personality Disorder." The message to the faculty, delivered through humor, was that they are made to feel deviant and even "sick" if they are interested in practice. The first step in training professionals devoted to change might be to train psychologists who are proud to be practitioners faced with the challenges of changing realities.

To tie research more closely to practice, we might develop ways to get students to think about the theoretical implications of their practice. If scientists and practitioners were trained to think of practice as the basis for theoretical innovation and development, our science might begin to move more quickly toward explaining the realities of our clients' lives.

We might also make efforts to find ways to make evaluating interventions, especially those with theoretical implications, more feasible as graduate student research. This is clearly not easy to do. Such research is time consuming, risky, and requires an incredible amount of cooperation with busy practitioners. It is no wonder that we often encourage graduate students to do quicker and easier research instead.

These training strategies might help to close the gap between theory and practice and between practice and reality.

Working as a Counseling Psychologist: Two Strategies

Recognizing that counseling psychologists can be among either the symbolic analysts of Reich's system or the routine service providers leads us to the conclusion that symbolic analysts are more likely to find ways to close the gaps between theory and practice and between practice and the realities of the world of work than are routine service providers. This suggests two strategies. I call them the *traditional* strategy and the *risky and restless* strategy.

The traditional (and modal) strategy is characterized by the following attitudes and goals on the part of the psychologist: (a) Find a job and keep it until you get a better one in terms of promotional opportunities, prestige, and money; (b) select a workplace with some security in terms of funding so that you can stay as long as you want; (c) select a workplace where you deal with clients who are like you and have relatively manageable problems, both in content and number; and (d) do research that earns you recognition.

Although these goals and attitudes are not unimportant, they may not lead us to close the two types of gaps I have identified. They rest on assumptions about stability that may be less tenable than they were previously, due to reductions in both health care and educational funding. Those secure positions where one works with clients similar to oneself may be more and more difficult to find in the future.

The risky and restless strategy is characterized by the following goals and attitudes on the part of the psychologist: (a) Find a job with the expectation that you will either lose funding or burn out within a few years; (b) recognize that the challenges of dealing with different populations and problems can be exciting and intellectually and emotionally challenging; (c) do research and develop theories based on the kind of clients you are seeing in your current position and plan interventions and evaluate them to determine if they are effective; and (d) plan to be unemployed every once in a while during periods of transition and develop ways to cope with such transitions—both financially and emotionally.

This risky and restless strategy rests on assumptions that:

- Change is exciting and manageable.
- Instability is not irresponsibility.
- Society will find ways to provide health care and other benefits to people who pursue this track.

Note that the risky and restless strategy is the same kind of strategy that is being forced on many people in all types and levels of careers in our society. If we lived this strategy, we might understand our career counseling clients better and be better able to formulate theories based on our experience with them. We might actually quicken our pace to match more closely the pace of our changing society as well as enhance our understanding and our ability to help. Clearly, the gaps between theory and practice and between practice and reality would be reduced. It would seem to be in the best interests of our clients and our profession if they were.

In this chapter, I have argued that the gap between career theory and practice has its origin in changes in the world of work and career counseling, the former being relatively fast and the latter being relatively slow. I believe that there are actually two gaps that confront us, one between theory and practice and one between the knowledge and skill level of counselors and the realities of the complex problems clients face. The problems of closing these gaps are increased by the fact that theory moves more slowly than practice and practice moves more slowly than the realities of the workplace. Finally, I have argued that closing the gaps may require a rather risky strategy in which practice moves beyond theory while informing it and practitioners become more like their own clients in experiencing the uncertainties of the world of work.

REFERENCES

Blustein, D., Walbridge, M., Friedlander, M., & Palladino, D. (1991). Contributions of psychological separation and parental attachment to the career development process. *Journal of Counseling Psychology, 38*, 39–50.

Fitzgerald, L. F. (1993). *The last great open secret: Sexual harassment of women in the workplace and academia.* Washington, DC: Federation of Behavioral, Psychological, and Cognitive Sciences.

Fouad, N. A., & Bingham, R. P. (1995). Career counseling with racial/ethnic minorities. In W. B. Walsh & S. H. Osipow (Eds.), *Handbook of vocational psychology* (2d ed., pp. 331–366). Hillsdale, NJ: Erlbaum.

Hackett, G., & Betz, N. E. (1981). A self-efficacy approach to the career development of women. *Journal of Vocational Behavior, 18,* 326–339.

Mallinckrodt, B., & Fretz, B. R. (1988). Social support and the impact of job loss on older professionals. *Journal of Counseling Psychology, 35,* 281–286.

Reich, R. (1991). *The work of nations.* New York: Vintage Books.

Schlossberg, N. K., & Leibowitz, Z. (1980). Organizational support systems as buffers to job loss. *Journal of Vocational Behavior, 17,* 204–217.

Spokane, A. R. (1991). *Career Intervention.* Englewood Cliffs, NJ: Prentice Hall.

Sue, D. W., & Sue, D. (1990). *Counseling the culturally different: Theory and practice* (2d ed.). New York: Wiley.

CHAPTER FOUR

Career Theory and Practice in a Multicultural Context

Consuelo Arbona
University of Houston

THIS CHAPTER EXAMINES the applicability of career theory to ethnic and racial minority populations, with particular emphasis on Hispanics. I will first discuss three assumptions that I have regarding the relations among career theory, research, and practice in general. Then I will propose that the question of how to integrate career theory and practice as it pertains to large segments of the U.S. population may be a specious question.

THE RELATIONSHIP BETWEEN THEORY, RESEARCH, AND PRACTICE

The ultimate test of career theory's usefulness lies in its contribution to practice. One of my assumptions is that theory and research can guide practice in a variety of ways that are not limited to providing prescriptions for specific interventions (Cohen, Sargent, & Sechrest, 1986). Theory also contributes to practice by providing a framework from which counselors may derive working hypothesis about clients' issues. However, these working hypotheses are likely to be influenced by both conceptual maps and experiential knowledge structures (Hoshmand, 1991).

In a survey of the utilization of psychotherapy research by practicing psycho-therapists (Morrow-Bradley & Elliot, 1986), the majority of the respondents reported that they gained their most useful information from their experience with clients. This makes sense, and I believe that most career counselors would also report greater gains from their own experience than from theory or research findings. Regardless of the applicability of theory and research to counseling, it is the actual encounters with clients that provide that third dimension in which knowledge from various sources is integrated and made one's own. It follows, then, that, as Hoshmand (1991) has proposed, practitioners could contribute to the scientific endeavors of the profession—in theory formulation and testing—through the knowledge derived in their practice. However, in the scientist-practitioner model, formal research is considered the primary scientific activity, and the possible contributions of practitioners to the knowledge base of the profession are not usually recognized (Hoshmand, 1991).

Consistent with this view, my second assumption is that the relationship among theory, research, and practice is one of reciprocal determinism (Bandura, 1986) in which the arrows of influence are bidirectional among the three components. However, in counseling psychology research training, which is dominated by positivistic science, we tend to emphasize the notion that theory should guide research, which in turn should guide practice in a linear, unidirectional fashion. Furthermore, research training within the positivistic tradition emphasizes the learning of techniques and procedural standards in experimentation while not paying much attention to the training of the researcher as a conceptualizing and human instrument (Hoshmand, 1991, 1994). In clinical training, in contrast, the use of the self as an important instrument in the counseling process is emphasized.

Hoshmand (1991) has proposed that training in the use of the self-as-instrument in both research and counseling practice would reduce the perceived discontinuity between the scientific and applied aspects of the profession. In her model, clinical inquiry—that is the process by which the practitioner derives knowledge during practice—is treated as a scientific activity and counseling practice is used as a context for scientific training. In addition to teaching how to conduct formal research, such training emphasizes the development of attitudes, skills, and qualities of mind that are essential to all investigative activities and acts of knowing in human inquiry.

Hoshmand (1994) has described a practice-oriented approach to research supervision that emphasizes the application of clinical thinking and practice-oriented methods to inquiry. For example, students are encouraged to frame research questions based on problems encountered in practice and not just from the research or theoretical literature. Students are also encouraged to use investigative methods closely aligned with the skills that they have developed as practitioners. As she suggests, however, this approach tends to coincide more with the social constructivist approach to science than with the positivistic, hypothetic-deductive research tradition.

My third assumption is that to be effective, career counselors need to know more than career theory and intervention-related research. To be most helpful to clients who are exploring careers, counselors need to have current knowledge of the labor market and understand the relationship between training and specific occupations. I believe this is an area where the gulf between career theory and career practice is most evident.

A situation arose in the conference that inspired this book that illustrates this point. A participant asked how theory could guide career counseling with a middle-aged, displaced, blue-collar worker who did not believe his skills could be useful in other areas of work. One of the panelists responded that career learning theory would guide the counselor to communicate to the client that she would help him explore and learn about areas in which he could use his skills and that together they would be able to find a way. Although I believe that adopting this stance, as suggested by the learning model for career counseling, is appropriate, I do not believe it is sufficient. The counselor also needs to have some ideas regarding how this worker's skills relate to other occupations that may be available to him. In other words, she needs to have a sense of what might be possible for a person in such circumstances in the labor market, without necessarily having "the answer" for the client. This knowledge is not part of career theories content, and theoreticians do not need to deal with this level of specificity. However, counselors working with clients do. Therefore, knowledge of theories is not enough to guide counselors in their work with clients, because knowledge regarding specific training and employment paths are beyond the scope of theory formulation.

In summary, sustaining my three assumptions is the notion that there are inherent limits to the applicability of career theory to practice. On the one hand, counselors need factual information related to the world of work. On the other hand, as practitioners, we must build the bridge between theory and practice in the process of working with clients. We need to open channels of communication to allow the knowledge garnered during practice to come back to enrich our theories. It is likely that learning how to use ourselves as instruments in both research and practice will facilitate discovering such paths. With these ideas in mind, I will next discuss the applicability of career theory to ethnic minorities, particularly Hispanic Americans.

CAREER THEORY AND HISPANICS

In this section I will concentrate on Hispanics for two reasons. First, it is the group with which I am most knowledgeable. Second, I believe that we need to identify the specific elements of each minority group's experience that contribute to the proposed relationship among race, ethnicity, culture, and career development variables (Betancourt & Lopez, 1993). Only then will we be able to determine if there is sufficient overlap across groups to warrant talking about the career development process of ethnic minorities as a group.

Statements noting how current career theories are not relevant for Hispanics and other ethnic and minority groups abound in the counseling literature. The lack of theory regarding the career development of minorities is a well-recognized problem with which counselors have not been able to grapple. As a consequence, no theoretical formulations have emerged to fill this identified void. This state of affairs may be due, at least in part, to the fact that counselors may be actually asking the wrong questions.

When I started thinking about this chapter, the following question came to my mind: Do I believe that counseling theories are adequate to guide career counseling practice for the various Hispanic groups? My answer to this question was a qualified yes. Current theories are useful in guiding the career choice process of specific Hispanic subgroups, particularly:

■ Middle- and upper-class individuals of all races

■ Adolescents of at least average academic achievement, regardless of socioeconomic status or race, for whom the student and worker role is salient

■ Adults with higher education, regardless of race or socioeconomic status of their family of origin

Though not perfect or complete, existing theories offer a good enough or adequate framework to help clients from these populations deal with issues of career choice. Two recent books support this contention: Brown and Brooks' (1991) *Career Counseling Techniques* and Spokane's (1991) *Career Interventions*. However, an issue implicit in my answer is that the crucial dimension in determining the applicability of career theories to the career choice process of Hispanics is not race or ethnicity but *educational development* and *academic achievement*. These factors are, of course, intimately related to socioeconomic background.

Educational Achievement and Career Choice

Educational attainment constitutes the bedrock of career development and choice, regardless of an individual's race, ethnicity, or socioeconomic background. I concur with Betz (1994) when she says that "education creates options, while lack of education closes them; without options the concept of choice itself has no real meaning" (p. 27). In a similar vein, Fitzgerald and Betz (1994) and Richardson (1993) have suggested that the concept of career has meaning only for individuals who have access to educational opportunities that lead to stable and meaningful occupational opportunities that allow for progressive movement over time. This is true regardless of a person's race, ethnicity, or socioeconomic status.

The nature of the relationship between educational achievement and career development has led me to conclude that the often-posed question—What do we need to do to make career theories useful in guiding practice with Hispanics?—may be the wrong question to ask. This question emphasizes issues of ethnicity and culture in relation to career development and choice. However, issues of race, ethnicity, and culture relate to the career choice process of an individual only when that individual is in a position of making a choice.

Hispanic youth are overrepresented among the nation's school dropouts (U.S. Bureau of the Census, 1991). It is well known that dropouts and students who graduate illiterate face an unstable work life limited to menial and often temporary jobs in the secondary labor market. Because school dropouts tend to have very few occupational choices, the question as we have framed it—What do we need to do to make career theories useful in guiding the career choice process with Hispanics?—pertains only to a relatively small segment of the Hispanic population: those who, because of exceptional qualities or social class extraction, are able to achieve academically.

When one examines closely the educational experiences of low-income children, it seems as though there is a conspiracy (Arbona, 1994). Low-income, uneducated parents lack the resources, educational and financial, to provide their children with a learning-rich environment or to monitor their learning experiences at school. In turn, these children have access to inadequate schools and academic programs that do not compensate for their lack of early learning experiences at home (Arbona, 1994; Brantlinger, 1993). So the cycle continues: Poor, uneducated children follow their parents' footsteps in the labor market and in the social class structure.

It seems, then, that a more useful question for a large proportion of the Hispanic population may be, What does the career counseling field—its theories, research, and practice—have to offer to individuals who are born and raised in low-income, uneducated households? Although a large percentage of children and youth in poverty belong to ethnic and racial minority groups, including Hispanics, many of them, in fact thousands of them, are White (Dryfoos, 1991). In this regard, uneducated, poor Whites and Hispanics have in common the fact that career counseling theory, research, and practice offer them little help. In my view, the apparently insurmountable challenge that ethnic and racial minorities pose to the career counseling field is not caused by differences in culture, race, or ethnicity but rather by poverty and its concomitant lack of education—issues that the counseling profession has not really dealt with.

Career Development and Social Class

I believe that we need to reformulate our questions regarding the relationship between ethnic/racial group membership and career development, paying closer attention to issues of social class and access to education. Quantitative studies suggest that Hispanic college students and graduates may not be all that different from their White counterparts regarding career-related variables. For example, Luzzo (1992) reported that Hispanic college students were similar to their White counterparts in terms of career decision-making attitudes and skills and congruence between assessed interests and occupational aspirations. In a study with African-American, Mexican-American, and White college freshmen, Arbona and Novy (1991) reported more gender than ethnic differences in career aspirations and expectations. Research with college graduates suggest that Mexican Americans tend to be similar to their White counterparts in terms of attitudes toward work (Isonio & Garza, 1987; Raines, 1988), career strategies, and expectations (Penley, Gould, De la Vina, & Murphy, 1989), as well as in their need for achievement and career progression behaviors (Gould, 1980, 1982). Finally, researchers have consistently reported that Holland's hexagonal model of career interests is valid for Hispanic students, and inventories based on Holland's scales seem appropriate for assessing the career interests of these students (Arbona, 1990).

Similarly, a few recent qualitative studies (Bullington, 1993; Bullington & Arbona, 1994; Carspecken & Cordeiro,1995; Cordeiro & Carspecken, 1993) suggest that low-income, Hispanic, college-bound high school students (Mexican Americans in Texas and Puerto Ricans and Dominicans in New York City) are similar to their mainstream counterparts in various aspects of career development. In terms of career maturity, these students seem to be engaged in the vocational tasks that mark the exploratory stage of career development that is appropriate for their age as suggested by Super's (1990) theory. These students also show planfulness and realism of career choice, which are indicators of career maturity. In terms of values, they ascribe to mainstream views that define success in terms of individual attainment and material rewards. Furthermore, they have an instrumental view of education: They believe that a college education is the passport that will lead them to a good job, moving out of the "barrio" and joining the White middle-class lifestyle.

This is not to suggest that issues related to race and ethnicity are unimportant among educated and noneducated Hispanics. They are, although quantitative studies that compare Hispanic and Anglos in terms of predetermined career-related variables are unlikely to allow for these issues to emerge. The qualitative studies mentioned before, however, suggest that successful Hispanic students are painfully aware of the negative ways in which Hispanics are often characterized.

Social Class, Careers, and Ethnic Identity Development

In defining who they are, Hispanic students often feel the need to distance themselves from both the majority-held negative views of Hispanics as well as their own negative views of their ethnic group. For them, achieving is an identity issue. On the one hand, they believe (or hope) that their success will prove the negative stereotypes wrong. On the other hand, what motivates them is to move away from what they see as prevalent in their culture of origin—in their words, "I don't want to be uneducated with 10 kids running around the house" or "I don't what to see myself barefoot and pregnant" (Cordeiro & Carspecken, 1993)—and move toward the successful world out there, which in their minds seems to be White and middle class. It appears that in the construction of their sense of self as Hispanics, issues of social class and ethnicity are intertwined; and, while they are able to articulate what they want to move away from, it is not as clear what they think they will become: Hispanic middle class is not a category with which they are familiar.

In terms of career theory, these qualitative studies suggest that for low-income, academically successful Hispanic students, developing a sense of ethnic identity constitutes an additional developmental task, as compared to their middle-class White counterparts that they need to contend with as they make educational and career decisions. This notion coincides with the research of Phinney and her colleagues that shows that exploration of ethnic identity issues is much more salient among minority adolescents and young adults, particularly African Americans and Mexican Americans, than among their majority counterparts (Phinney, 1989; Phinney & Alipuria, 1990; Phinney & Tarver, 1989).

Research with African Americans also supports this proposition. Studies have found that, although Levinson's model of adult development fits the experiences of African-American males from various professions and social classes, it did not account for the influence of race in their lives (Thomas & Alderfer, 1989). For these men, coming to terms with their sense of self as African Americans (ethnic/racial identity) and dealing with the implications of race in their lives be-came a task in itself.

These findings imply that understanding the nature of ethnic and racial identity formation and how it relates to career choice and career decision making needs further exploration. I think it is possible to do so in the context of current theories of career development and identity development. (For a discussion of these issues, see Arbona, 1995; Helms & Piper, 1994.) This is one example of how existing theories may be expanded to include experiences unique to the career development of Hispanics, similar to the way some career theories have been expanded to include issues that are salient to women, particularly middle-class or educated women (Walsh & Osipow, 1994).

Now, I wonder, is it also possible to expand our theories to apply to poor, uneducated Hispanics, or do we need to develop new theories that might comprehend the life experiences of these groups? Or, as Fitzgerald and Betz (1994) have suggested, should we recognize the limitations of our theories and accept that the notion of work and careers may not be psychologically central to the lives of many individuals?

CONCLUSIONS

In my view, attending to the needs of poor, uneducated Hispanic children and youth requires more than expanding our existing theories of career development. It may require, as Richardson (1993) has proposed, that we move from the study of careers to the study of work in people's lives so that we include in our domain work at all levels of education and prestige. Or it may require that we shift our attention from career choice to cognitive and academic development.

In an extensive review of prevention programs with at-risk children and adolescents, Dryfoos (1990) concluded that the acquisition of basic academic skills is a necessary precondition for the prevention of other negative behaviors such as substance abuse, delinquency, and teen pregnancy. Furthermore, she concluded that to prevent academic failure and other negative behaviors in at-risk children, programs need to include two components: (a) individual attention from a responsible, caring adult who is able to provide support and advocacy to one or more children and (b) comprehensive services that change the social environment in which the children and youth are raised and educated. No small task!

I believe that only when our Hispanic children become academically successful adolescents and adults will our career theories and interventions be useful in guiding them in their educational and occupational choices. In the meantime, we are faced with this question: Should we expand the scope of our efforts to include low-income groups? Or, as Fitzgerald and Betz (1994) have suggested, should we recognize the limitations of our theories and direct our efforts to those with the socioeconomic or educational resources to make work and career a central aspect of their sense of self?

SUMMARY

In this chapter, I have proposed that existing career theories provide practitioners with a useful framework from which they can help clients who have access to educational resources make decisions about which educational and work paths to follow. However, I also propose that knowledge and use of career theory is not sufficient to help these clients make informed choices. To be most helpful, career counselors also need to have current knowledge of the labor market and the relationship between training and specific occupations.

For the most part, empirical findings suggest that existing theories, although incomplete, are also useful in guiding the career choice process among middle-class Hispanics and Hispanics of at least average academic achievement for whom the student and worker role is salient, regardless of socioeconomic status. To be most pertinent to Hispanics and other ethnic minority groups, however, career theories need to be expanded to examine experiences unique to the lives and career development experiences of these groups, such as ethnic and racial identity.

Existing theories have little to offer clients who do not have access to educational resources. Because school dropouts have very few occupational choices, theories of career development that emphasize the choice process do not really pertain to the large number of Hispanic youngsters who drop out of school every year. In my view, to facilitate the career development process of poor, uneducated Hispanic children and youth, counselors first need to attend to their cognitive and academic development needs and provide support and advocacy for their social/emotional needs. Simply expanding current theories or developing new ones will not suffice.

REFERENCES

Arbona, C. (1990). Career counseling research with Hispanics: A review of the literature. *The Counseling Psychologist, 18,* 300–323.

Arbona, C. (1994). *First generation college students: A review of needs and effective interventions.* Houston: Decision Information Resources.

Arbona, C. (1995). Theory and research on racial and ethnic minorities: Hispanic Americans. In F. Leong (Ed.), *Career development and vocational behavior of racial and ethnic minorities.* Hillsdale, NJ: Erlbaum.

Arbona, C., & Novy, D. M. (1991). Career aspirations and expectations among black, Mexican American, and white college students. *Career Development Quarterly, 39,* 231–239.

Bandura, A. (1986). *Social foundations of thought and action: A social cognitive theory.* Englewood Cliffs, NJ: Prentice Hall.

Betancourt, H., & Lopez, R. (1993). The study of culture, ethnicity, and race in American psychology. *American Psychologist, 48,* 629–637.

Betz, N. E. (1994). Basic issues and concepts in career counseling for women. In W. B. Walsh & S. H. Osipow (Eds.), *Career counseling for women* (pp. 1–41). Hillsdale, NJ: Erlbaum.

Brantlinger, E. A. (1993). *The politics of social class in secondary school: Views of affluent and impoverished youth.* New York: Teachers College Press.

Brown, D., & Brooks, L. (1991). *Career counseling techniques.* Boston: Allyn & Bacon.

Bullington, R. L., (1993). *Constructions of parental influence on the career development of Hispanic adolescents.* Unpublished doctoral dissertation, University of Houston.

Bullington, R. L., & Arbona, C. (1994). *An exploration of the career development tasks of Mexican-American youth.* Manuscript submitted for publication.

Carspecken, P. F., & Cordeiro, P. (1995). Being, doing, and becoming: The identities of successful Hispanic students. *Qualitative Inquiry, 1,* 87–109.

Cohen, L. H., Sargent, M. M., & Sechrest, L. B. (1986). Use of psychotherapy research by professional psychologists. *American Psychologist, 41,* 198–206.

Cordeiro, P. A., & Carspecken, P. F. (1993). How a minority of the minority succeed. *International Journal of Qualitative Studies in Education, 6,* 277–290.

Dryfoos, J. G. (1990). *Adolescents at risk: Prevalence and prevention.* New York: Oxford University Press.

Dryfoos, J. C. (1991). Adolescents at risk: A summation of work in the field: Programs and policies. *Journal of Adolescent Health, 12,* 630–637.

Fitzgerald, L. F., & Betz, N. E. (1994). Career development in cultural context: The role of gender, race, class, and sexual orientation. In M. L. Savickas & R. Lent (Eds.), *Convergence in career development theories: Implications for science and practice* (pp. 103–108). Palo Alto, CA: Davies-Black Publishing.

Gould, S. (1980). Need for achievement, career mobility, and the Mexican-American college graduate. *Journal of Vocational Behavior, 16,* 73–82.

Gould, S. (1982). Correlates of career progression among Mexican-American college graduates. *Journal of Vocational Behavior, 20,* 93–110.

Helms, J. E., & Piper, R. E. (1994). Implications of racial identity theory for vocational psychology. *Journal of Vocational Behavior, 44,* 124–138.

Hoshmand, L. T. (1991). Clinical inquiry as scientific training. *The Counseling Psychologist, 19,* 431–453.

Hoshmand, L. T. (1994). Supervision of pre-doctoral graduate research: A practice-oriented approach. *The Counseling Psychologist, 22,* 147–161.

Isonio, S. A., & Garza, R. T. (1987). Protestant work ethic endorsement among Anglo Americans, Chicanos, and Mexicans: A comparison of factor structures. *Hispanic Journal of Behavioral Sciences, 9,* 413–425.

Luzzo, D. A. (1992). Ethnic group and social class differences in college students' career development. *Career Development Quarterly, 41,* 161–173.

Morrow-Bradley, C., & Elliot, R. (1986). Utilization of psychotherapy research by practicing psychotherapists. *American Psychologist, 41,* 188–197.

Penley, L. E., Gould, S., De la Vina, L., & Murphy, K. (1989). An early career focused study of Hispanic college graduates in business. *Hispanic Journal of Behavioral Sciences, 11,* 360–380.

Phinney, J. S. (1989). Stages of ethnic identity development in minority group adolescents. *Journal of Early Adolescence, 9,* 34–49.

Phinney, J. S., & Alipuria, L. L. (1990). Ethnic identity in college students from four ethnic groups. *Journal of Adolescence, 13,* 171–183.

Phinney, J. S., & Tarver, S. (1989). Ethnic identity search and commitment in black and white eighth graders. *Journal of Early Adolescence, 3,* 265–277.

Raines, R. T. (1988). The Mexican-American women and work: Intergenerational perspective of comparative ethnic groups. In M. B. Melville (Ed.), *Mexicans at work in the United States.* (Mexican American Studies Monograph No. 5). Houston: University of Houston, Mexican American Studies Program.

Richardson, M. S. (1993). Work in people's lives: A location for counseling psychologists. *Journal of Counseling Psychology, 40,* 425–433.

Spokane, A. R. (1991). *Career intervention.* Englewood Cliffs, NJ: Prentice Hall.

Super, D. E. (1990). A life-span, life-space approach to career development. In D. Brown & L . Brooks (Eds.), *Career choice and development* (pp. 197–261). San Francisco: Jossey-Bass.

Thomas, D. A., & Alderfer, C. P. (1989). The influence of race on career dynamics: Theory and research on minority career experiences. In M. B. Arthur, D. T. Hall, & B. S. Lawrence (Eds.), *Handbook of Career Theory* (pp. 133–158). New York: Cambridge University Press.

U.S. Bureau of the Census. (1991). *The Hispanic population in the United States: March 1991.* (Current Population Report, No. 455). Washington, DC: U.S. Government Printing Office.

Walsh, W. B., & Osipow, S. H. (1994). *Career counseling for women.* Hillsdale, NJ: Erlbaum.

CHAPTER FIVE

A Learning Theory
of Career Counseling

John D. Krumboltz
Stanford University

THIS HANDBOOK IS dedicated to the proposition that we must heal the rift between career theory and practice. Career theories have been largely irrelevant to practice because they have focused on career development, not counselor intervention. What better way to heal that rift than to propose a theory that prescribes practical counselor interventions?

A theory of career counseling differs from a theory of career development. Career development theory explains why people follow a particular career path. However, it does not explain what a career counselor can do to help people shape their own career paths. We have many alternative theories of career development (Osipow, 1983), and some have said that we have no theory of career counseling.

Actually, we do have a theory of career counseling that has exerted a dominant influence on the behavior of career counselors and clients for close to a century. We now call it trait-and-factor theory. This theory prescribed what counselors needed to do. Its purpose was to match workers to occupations. It had its origins at the beginning of the 20th century and was first articulated by Frank Parsons (1909). Trait-and-factor theory grew out of a need to fill the industrial labor force with people able and willing to perform specific types of tasks. The proper functioning of the industrial system required a stable workforce. Job turnover was expensive. Dissatisfied workers would leave jobs after expensive training programs, so it was important to find a way to channel people into occupations that they would find satisfying or at least tolerable. Once an individual found such a suitable occupation, the normal expectation was that she or he would remain in it for a lifetime.

To match individuals with occupations, Parsons (1909) proposed a three-step model: (a) Know the individual's characteristics, (b) know the occupational requirements, and (c) exercise "true reasoning" to match the individual to the occupation. The simplicity and directness of the theory led to its wide adoption and continuing applicability to the present time. Its assumptions are so pervasive that almost every career counselor uses trait-and-factor theory to some extent, although many do so without awareness and even with denial.

Thousands of psychometric tests were developed to assess individuals' characteristics. Elaborate classification schemes and rating systems were established to define the requirements of different occupations, and profiles, charts, and, more recently, computers have been employed to facilitate the matchmaking.

Trait-and-factor theory is still useful for part of what career counselors do, but the problems we face now are far larger than the problems trait-and-factor theory was designed to address.

PURPOSES TO BE SERVED BY A CAREER COUNSELING THEORY

The purpose of a theory is to help us understand a complex domain so that we can take more useful and intelligent actions. A theory enables us to step back from the nitty-gritty details and see the big picture. A good theory is a simplified representation of reality, identifying relationships among the most crucial characteristics and ignoring the rest. Elsewhere I have likened a theory to a map (Krumboltz, 1991b, 1994). A good theory should be a useful representation of some parts of reality, just as a map needs to represent those parts of the topography that will be useful to the map reader. Both a map and a theory deliberately oversimplify reality but still enable their respective users to answer a multitude of specific questions.

A good theory may provide a rationale for already-existing career counseling practices. A new theory does not necessarily invalidate prior counseling practices. On the contrary, it may justify them. There are many creative, talented, and energetic career counselors who are effectively helping their clients solve a variety of complex problems. They use a multitude of techniques that may have been derived from other theories or from practical experience. A new theory capitalizes on the best of current practices and provides a rationale for why they work. It may also suggest some new ideas. Ideally, it provides support and justification for the best practices, stimulates the creation of new techniques, and suggests criteria for evaluating outcomes. Krumboltz (1994) suggested that a career counseling theory should be accurate, responsible, comprehensive, integrative, and adaptive. Let us consider how some of these criteria are related to the needs of modern society.

People Need to Expand Their Capabilities and Interests, Not Base Decisions on Existing Characteristics Only

People taking an interest inventory, for example, are asked whether they like, dislike, or are indifferent to hundreds of tasks, occupational titles, and hobbies.

Most people have had no direct experience with the vast majority of the activities represented on the inventory. Yet they must answer all, or virtually all, of the items or risk having their results declared invalid. There is no way for them to reply, "I don't know yet," "I haven't tried that yet," or "I'd like to learn more about that before I answer."

Thus, interest inventories tend to channel people into fields related to expressed interests that are based on limited past experience. Although the intent of interest inventories is to open up new possibilities, the very structure of the inventories discourages development of new interests. Trait-and-factor theory puts emphasis on closing out competing alternatives to focus in on the one occupation that comes closest to matching interests based on past experiences. Those who want to explore new activities, hobbies, and occupations get virtually no encouragement from the standard way in which interest inventories are constructed and interpreted.

People Need to Prepare for Changing Work Tasks, Not Assume That Occupations Will Remain Stable

Matching an individual to an occupation requires that the occupation have a common and stable set of duties and expectations. At one time, this requirement was quite reasonable. The industrial age needed large numbers of workers in distinct occupational categories such as welders, bookkeepers, and linotype operators. All the workers within each category performed virtually identical tasks that required very similar skills and interests.

The modern age is changing the old order. Workers are increasingly being expected to accomplish whatever work needs to be accomplished, not merely to fulfill a written job description. Workers are members of teams that are expected to cooperate in producing a product or providing a needed service (Peters, 1992). The skills needed by the team can vary over time as the project progresses. The practice of outsourcing brings in temporary contract workers who can contribute their particular expertise before moving on to other projects.

The entire concept of a "job" may become obsolete (Bridges, 1994). There will still be unending work that needs to be done, but the rigid task specification and resulting turf protection brought about by job descriptions inhibits people from performing work as quickly and efficiently as international competition demands. Employees will not only need to create new products and services for the marketplace, they will also need to market themselves within their own organizations.

Such a radical restructuring of the workplace has already created, and will increasingly create, disruptions of expectations and severe stress (Barker, 1992; Beckhard & Pritchard, 1992; Handy, 1989; Land & Jarman, 1992; Ray & Rinzler, 1993). To adapt constructively to these changes, workers will need to learn new skills and attitudes and learn to cope with a new set of insecurities (Senge, 1990). Self-development will constitute the new work ethic for the 21st century (Maccoby, 1981). Bridges (1994) puts it this way:

Workers without a clear development strategy will be workers without much of a future. For they will not be able to provide continually upgraded and redesigned services that better meet the customer/client's emerging needs. (p. 10)

Career counselors will have an opportunity to play a major role in helping individuals learn how to cope with the need for new skills and the associated stresses. Individuals who believe they need not improve themselves may need to be confronted with the new realities in a way that will motivate and inspire constructive adaptations. Career counselors can be in the forefront of a movement to help individuals and organizations adapt constructively to the changing workplace. If career counselors see their job as merely matching individuals to existing occupations, they will rapidly become obsolete because stable occupations as we have known them are on the way out.

People Need to Be Empowered to Take Action, Not Merely to Be Given a Diagnosis

Clients need help in taking effective action. The task of finding a suitable niche in the world of work is a long process of trial and error. It is understandable that clients procrastinate and develop zeteophobia, the fear of exploring future possibilities, when facing the overwhelming prospect ahead (Krumboltz, 1993). Trait-and-factor theory must take much of the blame for this inaction because there is nothing in the theory that states that clients need to take any action. When career counselors apply trait-and-factor theory, they collect information about the client, make occupational information available, and then either recommend or encourage the client to state the best possible match. The job is then complete, according to classic trait-and-factor theory. The occupational match is the end product.

Clients, however, even if they buy into the occupational match, are left hanging with important unanswered questions: "How would it feel to work in that occupation?"; "How would my family react?"; "How do I prepare for entry into this occupation?"; "How do I acquire an actual job?"; "What if I don't like it?"; "What do I do next?"; and "I'm afraid of asking questions—how can I get over my fear?"

Career counselors know that clients have these questions, and they need to provide some information resources for clients to use. But clients are expected to use them independently. Career counselors do not generally see it as part of their role to follow up with clients, check on the answers, suggest additional questions, and provide emotional support for direct personal explorations of opportunities. Some counselors do engage in these activities, but they do so because they are caring people, not because trait-and-factor theory directs them to.

Career Counselors Need to Deal with All Career Problems, Not Just Occupational Selection

Trait-and-factor theory would have us believe that occupational matching is the only task of career counselors. Although it is clearly one of the tasks, there are many other career problems faced by clients. As Krumboltz (1993) has observed, some of the other concerns include the following:

Locus of Control: Who is in charge of my career?

Career Obstacles: How can I hope to achieve my career goals when I face so many obstacles?

Job Search Knowledge: How do I go about finding the kind of job I think I would like?

Job Search Motivation: How can I keep looking for a job in the face of real and potential rejection?

Job Relationships: How can I learn to get along with my boss and co-workers?

Job Burnout: What should I do when I am no longer satisfied with my present job?

Occupational Advancement: How can I become more successful in my career?

Retirement Planning: How can I arrange a satisfactory transition to my retirement years? (p. 144)

These other problem domains require a wide range of counselor interventions. Each of them is laden with emotional content. Retirement planning, for example, according to Krumboltz (1993), "is not a simple case of learning some new hobbies. Giving up one's work environment requires a profound shift in values and relationships. It can pose emotional problems just as severe as those triggered by divorce" (pp. 144–145).

These additional concerns would involve career counselors in most of the roles of other counselors. Indeed, the integration of career and personal counseling is long overdue (Krumboltz, 1993; Richardson, 1993).

Career counseling is sometimes seen as a diminishing concern of neophyte counselors. It is perceived as boring and uninteresting. The reason for this perception is that the simple three-step process of trait-and-factor theory makes career counseling seem dull. The theory subjects clients to, as Crites (1981) put it, "three interviews and a cloud of dust." The cloud of dust is the lack of closure after the diagnosis has been delivered.

Career counseling is, in fact, the most complex, fascinating, and important form of counseling. It only seems less so because we have implicitly adopted a theory that represents it as a simplistic process. It is time to describe career counseling as the complex, fascinating, and crucially important task that it is.

CAREER COUNSELING FROM A LEARNING PERSPECTIVE

Career counseling is the most complex type of counseling because the counselor must possess all the skills of other counselors and, in addition, know employment trends, methods of preparing for various work roles, career assessment techniques, and methods for changing work-related behavior, emotions, and cognitions.

The social learning theory of career decision making (SLTCDM), proposed by Krumboltz (1979), was a career development theory that described how an uncountable number of learning experiences combine to shape each person's career path. People with differing genetic characteristics are exposed to infinitely varied learning opportunities (or lack thereof) as a result of the social, cultural, and economic circumstances that exist at the time and place where they live. The consequences of these learning experiences are synthesized by each individual into *self-observation generalizations* and *task approach skills,* which guide each person's thinking about appropriate career decisions and actions.

The SLTCDM provided a coherent explanation of a person's career path after it occurred, but it was an insufficient guide to practicing career counselors who wanted to know what they could do now to help people who were troubled with a variety of career-related concerns.

The proposed learning theory of career counseling builds on the SLTCDM, explains why we need a new theory, and outlines the goals, assessment strategies, and interventions that career counselors can use to promote healthy career development.

The SLTCDM attributed occupational choices to a lifelong sequence of learning experiences unique to each individual. Learning experiences were classified as either instrumental or associative. Instrumental learning occurs from the consequences of a behavior. A child who is taken to a dance class, for example, and receives attention, praise, and satisfaction from performing well-coordinated dance steps will generate a more positive self-observation generalization about dancing than will a child who is not reinforced in this way. The child learns from the consequences of his or her own performance.

Associative learning experiences occur from observing others. Attending dance recitals, listening to dancers describe their work, and reading about the lives of famous dancers are a few of the ways a person can generate interest, or disinterest, in the occupation of dance.

As a result of being born into one particular family setting, individuals are exposed to a limited variety of learning opportunities. The social, cultural, economic, geographic, and political circumstances that surround us make available quite different opportunities for different individuals. People form their self-observation generalizations and task-approach skills from a limited set of possible experiences. Each person sees a small range of possibilities because each person has been exposed to only a relatively few opportunities. Furthermore, the consequences of learning differ widely, too. For equal performance, some children receive generous praise and support, whereas others suffer abuse and degradation.

Hence, when people become confused about their career and seek help from a career counselor, the counselor would see their confusion as a natural consequence of the learning experiences that they have had. Current levels of skills and interests, blocking beliefs, contradictory values, poor work habits, and inhibited personality patterns need not necessarily be the basis for choosing an occupation. Rather, they are the basis for designing new learning experiences.

The Goal of Career Counseling

The goal of career counseling is to facilitate the learning of skills, interests, beliefs, values, work habits, and personal qualities that enable each client to create a satisfying life within a constantly changing work environment.

The task of career counselors is to promote client learning. Thus, career counselors can be seen as coaches, educators, and mentors—not simply matchmakers.

Skills, interests, beliefs, values, work habits, and personal qualities are all subject to change as a result of subsequent learning experiences. Their present status as revealed by various assessment instruments is seen as the beginning point for new learning, not merely the basis for a diagnosis.

The reason for all this learning activity is to promote clients' abilities to create satisfying lives for themselves. The components of a satisfying life will vary widely for different clients. They may include successful accomplishment in some endeavor, harmonious family relationships, intriguing hobbies, religious activities, or environmental protection work. An important part of the counseling process is to help clients define the elements of a satisfying life and instill in them the idea that this definition is subject to continual change. Naturally, no counselor can guarantee a client's "success" in achieving a satisfying life. Yet the counselor can help clients learn qualities that increase the probability of success.

Note that the work environment is assumed to be constantly changing. A pattern of behavior that produced success 10 years ago may no longer be adequate or even relevant. Occupations are changing. The career counselor must be able to challenge clients' outmoded concepts and help them see how better to adapt to changing conditions in the workplace.

The Role of Assessment[*]

Career assessment instruments summarize some part of what clients have already learned. The test results can be used in two ways: (a) to make inferences about how clients might match certain educational or occupational environments and (b) to suggest promising new learning experiences. Almost all the efforts of career counselors have been directed toward the matchmaking use. Tremendous advantages may accrue from expanding the role of career assessment instruments to advance subsequent learning.

Career assessment instruments themselves do not prescribe learning experiences. Rather, they can serve as a framework for the counselor and client to use collaboratively to identify preferences, skills, and beliefs that the client has learned and to suggest additional preferences, skills, and beliefs that the client might want to learn in the future. Then the counselor can use educational interventions to help the client learn more effective career problem-solving strategies.

---

[*]This section draws substantially on concepts presented in "Career Assessment as a Learning Tool," by J. D. Krumboltz and M. A. Jackson, 1993, *Journal of Career Assessment*.

Counselors can use assessment results to help clients further define and integrate key themes, patterns, and conflicts relevant to their current career concerns. Thus, they create assessments of what clients have learned about their career problems and collect mounting evidence about what they now need to learn to move toward their career goals. Let us see how the assessment process might be applied in five traditional career domains.

Skills.   Skill assessments are often interpreted as aptitudes, virtually unchangeable predispositions to perform at a defined level of proficiency. Little effort has been devoted to using tests to define targets for new learning. Part of the problem is that tests typically yield norm-referenced, not criterion-referenced, scores. Thus, clients are informed of a percent of the population they exceed, not what they need to learn next. Part of the problem is that test manuals do not provide information about how one might improve performance. Indeed, considerable effort is expended in discouraging people from receiving coaching about how they can score higher. Part of the problem is due to the implicit assumption in trait-and-factor theory that the counselor should know the individual's characteristics, not change them.

But times are changing. The *Scholastic Aptitude Test* has now become the *Scholastic Assessment Test*. More criterion-referenced tests are on the market. Preparing applicants for entrance examinations constitutes a growing market. Counselors can use skill tests as ways of pinpointing specific new learning goals. Limited skills can be seen as a temporary state. Skill tests no longer need to be used merely to restrict people from aspiring to certain occupations.

Interests.   For years we have assumed that current interests are a good basis for choosing future occupations, and there is a considerable body of evidence to suggest that this assumption has some merit. However, we have not taken advantage of the fact that interests continue to be learned. A number of people in recent years have developed a fascination with computers, for example. How many other interests might be developed, given appropriate social and environmental opportunities?

Counselors can use interest inventories to do more than merely assess the degree to which interests have been learned. They can also use interest inventories to help clients identify interest areas they may want to develop in the future. Many clients have limited interests because they have had relatively little opportunity to learn about alternative activities. It is hard to be interested in something one has never tried. Counselors could take a proactive stand in encouraging clients to try out new activities to determine whether new interests can be identified.

What about the argument that vocational interests may have a genetic component? Several twin studies have indicated that approximately 30 to 50% of interest score variance can be attributed to heritability (Betsworth et al., 1994; Lykken, Bouchard, McGue, & Tellegen, 1993). Does the presence of a genetic contribution diminish the possibility of helping people learn new interests? Even if 50% of the variance is due to heredity, another 50% is still subject to environmental influences. The studies have clustered interests into categories (e.g., adventurous) and compute the heritability coefficients for categories, not specific activities. Thus, a person might have a genetic predisposition to prefer adventurous activities but, at the same time, may never have thought to explore specific activities within the category such as law enforcement work or sky diving. Learning new interests within categories, as well as between categories, could open up broad new vistas for clients.

Lykken, Bouchard, McGue, and Tellegen (1993), whose study indicated that about 50% of interest variance was associated with genetic variation, state that "interests are learned traits.... A rational, cooperative subject will not express interest in, say, team sports if he or she has never participated in such sports and does not know what they are" (p. 656).

Beliefs.   Career beliefs may be held fervently because of limited learning opportunities. It is logically impossible for someone to know that something is false and still believe it. On the emotional level, however, beliefs can contradict facts. One of the most frequent comments made by witnesses to shocking events is "I couldn't believe it!"

Almost everyone develops false or misleading career beliefs sometime during their lives. These beliefs can prohibit people from taking appropriate action to solve their own problems. People can easily become entrapped by their own assumptions.

Some people are so afraid of failing, for example, that they will never apply for a job that requires talent, even though they may be better qualified than those who eventually get the job. Counselors can help such people examine their assumptions and reconsider their options and the possible consequences of them. For counselors to merely accept stated beliefs and assumptions as givens would seriously limit client options. Counselors can use assessment instruments to identify beliefs that need changing as well as confirm facilitative beliefs (Krumboltz, 1991a).

Values.   Values are generally assumed to be stable and unassailable, but values change. Many people have made radical changes in their values: Priests have become agnostics, agnostics have become priests. Less radical changes in values are even more common. People learn to be more accepting of views contrary to their own. People learn to share their ideas and possessions more generously. Changing values about environmental protection, for example, may affect a worker's attitude toward an employer who is polluting the atmosphere. Conflicting values need to be examined.

The events that contribute to shaping value changes may not be well understood, but they certainly occur. "We need not have to visit the Wizard of Oz to develop more wisdom, more compassion, or more courage. A trip to a learning-oriented counselor may be sufficient" (Krumboltz & Jackson, 1993, p. 396).

Personality.   Personality tests have been used to identify existing personality types and preferences, but virtually no effort has been devoted to helping people change their personality styles and strategies. For example, there may be people who have introverted preferences because of a lack of social experience and/or unrealistic beliefs about their own social skills. They may well want to change their current preference to make themselves more suitable for certain types of tasks. Some introverts may want to become more extroverted. Likewise, some thinking types may want to develop their feeling capacity.

Personality characteristics need not be conceptualized as permanent traits. Personality characteristics are acquired through learning to a large degree (a genetic contribution, if any, notwithstanding). Because learning experiences occur throughout life, a possibility exists for new personality preferences to be learned. Counselors could help their clients realize that old personality patterns need not dictate their future but that new patterns can be learned. Learning experiences could then be designed accordingly.

INTERVENTION METHODS

If counselors keep in mind that the goal is to facilitate useful learning by clients, then any ethical intervention that fosters such learning can be part of counselors' repertoires. Although a sharp distinction cannot always be drawn, interventions may be classified as either (a) developmental and preventive or (b) targeted and remedial. The following merely illustrate the range of possible interventions.

Developmental and Preventive Interventions

Because work plays such a large role in the lives of almost everyone, preparation for it pervades every activity. Learning math skills, reading, drawing pictures, dancing, playing games, and conversing with friends can all be seen as part of the process of acquiring the skills and personal qualities that will shape a career path. At the same time, more specific activities can be included to educate people about career possibilities.

Career Education.   During the 1970s, under the leadership of Sidney Marland and Kenneth Hoyt, career education was a national priority. The rationale was that career education could be "infused" through the regular curriculum. Thus, English teachers were expected to point out how literary skills would be useful in various careers, and math teachers were to emphasize the occupational value of mathematical reasoning. Teachers were asked to modify their curricula to incorporate the career implications of the subject areas they taught. Given gradually decreasing financial support, most could not, or would not, sustain the effort required for this infusion of activity.

Counselors, already overburdened by multiple demands, were generally not given the sufficient time and resources to coordinate career education activities. Some people devised brilliant programs and implemented them for several years. Many students benefitted from their efforts (Hoyt & High, 1982). But in any given school, no one was responsible for implementing a career education program. No one's career was at stake. There was no political constituency to campaign for needed funds. As Magnum (1993) has described the political demise of career education, "there were no funds to purchase allegiance" (p. 9).

Career education was, and still is, a powerful idea. The politics of making it work are complex, and great ideas do not necessarily receive funding. Political winds shift, and now career education is less visible, though it has not disappeared. Career education activities continue, but without the federal funds to support a concerted effort (Hoyt, 1993).

School-to-Work Initiative. The problems career education was intended to solve are still with us. A School-to-Work Transition Act was signed into law in 1994 that would enable high school students to continue their learning while they gained work experience. Its goals were to:

- Transform American workplaces into learning components of the education and youth training system by encouraging employers to provide structured work-based learning experiences to high school students

- Improve the knowledge and skills of youth and motivate them to stay in school and work hard by integrating academic and occupational learning, integrating school-based and work-based learning, and building linkages between secondary and postsecondary education

- Promote career exploration and counseling in order to help students identify their career interests and goals

Whatever future legislation produces, it is clear that concern over the career preparation of young people continues. Further, it is clear that the provision of learning experiences is seen as the route toward solving the problems. The specifics will change, but helping people learn desirable career-relevant skills and characteristics will continue to be an important national goal.

We may need to reinvent career education under a new name. Maybe this time we will do it better. Regardless of what we do, people are struggling to make sense of their lives, to find ways to contribute, live in harmony with their environment, and create satisfying lives for themselves. Counselors can help if they see their task as designing learning experiences for everyone who needs them.

Job Club Programs. The power of the group to support proactive job search behavior was capitalized on brilliantly by Azrin and Besalel (1980). They developed, implemented, and conducted research on the Job Club, a rigorous set of job-seeking procedures that counselors can use to help groups of students find jobs. They reported a 90% success rate compared to a 28% to 60% success rate for control groups. More recent work continues to support the efficacy of this approach (Elksnin & Elksnin, 1991; Stidham & Remley, 1992).

The strong learning orientation is evident in the following Azrin and Besalel quotation (1980):

> The behavioral emphasis on learning...presumes that intensive training can give unsuccessful clients the skills that will make them successful. Therefore, behavioral job counseling in the Job Club excludes no one as being inherently inept or unemployable.... Learning is greatly facilitated by structured modeling and imitation. (p. 108)

Study Materials. A multitude of learning resources are available. A magnificent array of books, magazine articles, films, videotapes, audiotapes, and CD-ROMs provide ample opportunities for people of all ages to educate themselves if they choose to use the materials. The National Geographic Society has produced a series of 10 videotapes for early elementary school students titled *Your Town* to acquaint children with occupations in institutions such as hospitals, libraries, police stations, and post offices. For adolescents, Danish et al. (1992) have created a training program to help young people develop healthy life skills and learn how to accomplish their goals. At the adult level, the everpopular *What Color Is Your Parachute?* (Bolles, 1994) provides creative job-seeking ideas. Every year, new and revised materials are produced to satisfy career learning needs.

Simulations. Simulated environments have been used extensively to teach important skills under relatively low-stress conditions. For example, flight simulators are being used to train both military and civilian pilots. Instructors can deliberately program emergency situations of various types to see whether their trainees can handle them adequately. If the trainee makes a mistake and "crashes," no harm is done. The mistake can be identified and remedial instruction can be provided.

In career counseling, simulations have been used to teach students about the consequences of making life decisions (Varenhorst, 1968, 1973), to test the adequacy of various decision-making models (Krumboltz, Scherba, Hamel, & Mitchell, 1982), and to give students a sample of working at various occupations (Krumboltz, 1970). Students often find planning the future onerous, overwhelming, and fear provoking. They are expected to identify some occupation to which they aspire when they have no experience in any occupations. A chance to solve problems in a variety of different occupations would give students a partially realistic experience in each occupation. If the simulated occupational experiences were sufficiently well designed, students would be excited by some of the opportunities presented and might be motivated to explore the future possibilities with more enthusiasm. Career counselors would need to have some structured learning materials available to provide these simulated occupational experiences.

Tailored and Remedial Interventions

Some individuals need help specifically tailored to their situation. The techniques that follow are examples of interventions that counselors could use to help individuals or a small group engage in learning to solve particular problems. Although distinctions between cognitive and behavioral techniques are not great, examples of each category will be provided.

Cognitive Interventions. Cognitive interventions rely heavily on verbal understanding and insight. Much of our understanding of these interventions is due to the pioneering work of Bandura (1971), Beck (1976), Ellis (1962), and Meichenbaum (1977). Noer (1993) has identified the severe emotional consequences of layoffs and corporate downsizing on employees and their families and has suggested some helpful cognitive approaches.

Goal clarification. Counseling is based on an implicit or explicit agreement between client and counselor about what is to be accomplished and what roles each is to play. An essential early step in counseling is to reach a mutual understanding so that the client and counselor can work cooperatively toward the same outcome. Clients often come to counselors with unrealistic expectations—for example, "Give me a test that will tell me what I should do." It is important to expose implicit assumptions so that they can be corrected early in the counseling process.

Some people define their own problems in ways that make it impossible to solve them. This is the "I should have decided yesterday how I'm going to spend the rest of my life" issue. Although the counselor may empathize with the feelings of panic such a goal would engender, the counselor would not want to accept such a goal as a target for counseling. The initial step is to defuse the anxiety. One procedure is to comment on how helpful it is that the client's plans are open. Open-mindedness can be seen as a virtue. Although they might feel better if they had a decision already made, clients should feel that they have not foreclosed options with a premature choice and can still explore several possibilities.

The counselor can also point out that it is not necessary to plan the rest of one's life—it may be quite sufficient to decide what to try next. Planning after that point can depend on how the client evaluates the initial experience. The client needs to be given permission to take the necessary time to plan the next step. Then the initially massive problem can be broken down into a series of manageable ministeps. The client then might be able to state a new goal: "I want to plan the next step in my career."

Cognitive restructuring. Reframing involves seeing a problem from another viewpoint. For example, a problem can be seen either as a situation requiring avoidance and escape or as a situation to be mastered. Counselors can help their clients see problems in a new light and thereby change their ways of dealing with them. Sampson, Peterson, Lenz, & Reardon (1992) and Hampl (1986) have described how conceptual structures influence career problem solving and how clients' new insights can be generalized to other situations. In a sample of college undergraduates, it appeared quite clear that cognitive structures were associated with methods of making decisions, career exploration behaviors, and career planning (Neimeyer, Nevill, Probert, & Fukuyama, 1985).

Mitchell and Krumboltz (1987) experimentally compared a cognitive restructuring intervention with the teaching of decision skills. A no-treatment control group was also included. The cognitive restructuring treatment proved most effective in reducing anxiety and promoting career exploration. The college undergraduates also reported more satisfaction in applying the cognitive skills they had learned. Similar evidence of effectiveness was provided by Taves, Hutchinson, and Freeman (1992) in using a cognitive instruction program to teach job interview skills to learning-disabled high school students.

Let us consider a concrete example. A client has been employed in a small retail store for five years when the position of buyer becomes available. Although the client would like the promotion, she feels she cannot ask for it.

If the boss thinks I'm the best person for the buyer job, he will ask me to do it. If not, he will ask someone else.

Perhaps there is something you could do to help.

I don't know what I could do.

Let's look at the problem from your boss' viewpoint. What kind of a person would he like to be a buyer?

Someone who knows what customers will buy, someone who can negotiate good prices.

Would you qualify?

Oh yes, I know I could do the job.

Does your boss know you could do the job?

Probably not.

Then let's talk about what you can do to persuade your boss that you are the best person for the job.

I don't like to brag about myself.

Do you like to tell the truth about yourself?

Yes, but it doesn't feel right to be too forward.

Perhaps you would be doing your boss a favor by letting him know your qualifications and your interest in the position.

But I've always been taught not to be presumptuous or pushy.

And you seem to really enjoy being helpful to others.

Yes, actually, I could be more helpful to the store in the buyer position than in my current position.

So now our task is to figure out the best way for you to convince him that the store would benefit from your promotion to buyer.

Yeah, what can I do?

The blocking belief here was that the client assumed that no action was needed to obtain the promotion. The client and counselor may still need to figure out exactly what actions would be best, but the crucial commitment to take some action has been obtained from the client.

The counselor obtained that commitment by tailoring the discussion to coincide with the client's existing values, not by confronting them directly. The counselor appealed to the values of telling the truth and helping others, not self-aggrandizement. When the counselor reframed the problem in terms of the client's fundamental values, the client could see a rationale for taking action.

Countering a troublesome belief. Some troublesome beliefs are simple misunderstandings or faulty facts. They can be countered with statements of fact. If Terry believes "I'm not tall enough to be a police officer," when, in fact, Terry is tall enough, the belief is a problem only if Terry is eliminating law enforcement as a career possibility because of that belief. If Terry had no interest in becoming a police officer under any circumstances, it would be a dubious use of time to disabuse Terry of that misconception. However, suppose Terry, who is 5 feet 7 inches, does want to be a police officer and believes that to qualify one must be at least 5 feet 8 inches. A simple statement that not all police departments have a height requirement could open up a whole world of opportunities for Terry.

Nevo (1987) described counters to 10 beliefs. Countering a deeply ingrained belief requires more than logic. It requires consistent reinforcement. Many people have grown up in environments where negative messages predominate. They are repeatedly addressed by insulting names such as "Dummy" or "Clumsy." They are told, "You never do anything right" or "You couldn't fight your way out of a paper bag." Contrary to the proverb about sticks and stones, words can hurt; and the repetition of hurtful words creates a belief in their accuracy. To counter negative beliefs, the counselor can use positive supporting words: "You are strong," "You can do it," and "You are making progress." The message must be genuine, and it needs reiteration. The client can also learn to reiterate the positive messages. Some people use tape recorders so that they can listen to their positive messages. Johnson and Silva (1990) presented a case study illustrating the use of confrontation and cognitive restructuring in career counseling. Occasionally, a well-timed silence can stimulate the reexamination of assumptions.

Cognitive rehearsal. Clients can be taught to rehearse positive verbal statements about themselves to replace the negative verbal statements that were drilled into their heads from earlier experiences.

We also have evidence that people tend to prefer interacting with others who verify their own self-concepts. Thus, people with positive self-concepts prefer evaluators who give them positive strokes, and those with negative self-concepts prefer evaluators who give them negative criticism.

A counselor can acknowledge that tendency to a client: "You may find it hard to hear when I tell you that you are capable. You are not used to hearing words like that. But you are capable and I want you to learn to be able to say so yourself."

Clients can be taught to label their behavior, not themselves. When a client says, "I made a fool of myself," the counselor can say, "You felt foolish, but you made just one mistake." Clients can practice saying, "I goofed," but not "I'm goofy."

Narrative analysis. Each client has a unique story to tell. Counselors can use client narratives to identify themes in a client's life (Jepsen, 1993; Leahy, 1991; Savickas, 1991). Reviewing recurring themes can give clients a sense of meaning about their lives.

With a learning perspective, a counselor can do more. Clients can be helped to see that they are the authors of their own narratives, not the protagonists or victims in someone else's novel. They need not continue to follow the same themes that have guided them thus far in life. If they choose, they can change the plot. As Savickas (1993) puts it, "Instead of positioning clients as recipients of pre-defined services such as occupational information and interest inventory interpretation, career counselors are affirming clients as agents interpreting their needs and shaping their lives out of a range of possibilities" (p. 211).

Exploration bibliotherapy. Counselors can encourage clients to explore actively career options they are considering through reading biographies, interviewing people about their work, observing people at work, or working parttime or as volunteers.

Behavioral Interventions. Behavioral interventions, while using words and verbal understandings, rely on practice and experiential exercises. Recognition of the importance of instrumental behavior and its consequences is due in large part to the theoretical and experimental work of B. F. Skinner (1953), although many others have added substantial applications subsequently.

Role-playing. We tend to adopt beliefs that are consistent with our own behavior. If you want someone to adopt a different belief, you may want to get that person to act in a way that is consistent with the new belief. Role-playing is an ideal way to get people to try out new behaviors in a safe environment.

Research in social psychology demonstrates rather convincingly that improvisational role-playing of behavior inconsistent with one's previous behavior is an effective mechanism for change (McGuire, 1985, cited in Zimbardo & Leippe, 1991).

Desensitization. Career counseling has primarily been conceptualized as an intellectual exercise, whereas personal counseling was generally seen to involve treatment of emotional concerns such as phobias. The existence of phobias in career counseling has been totally overlooked.

Career decisions are crucial to human happiness. A career affects the way one spends most of one's waking day. It can affect the kind of people with whom one socializes, and it affects the choice of a marriage partner, vacation plans, neighbors, and retirement possibilities. With so much riding on career decisions, one might expect people to be eager to spend time mapping out the best possible decisions for themselves.

In fact, career planning is often avoided until the last possible moment. Many college seniors arrive at a counselor's door in a panic, wanting to know what do with the rest of their lives. Their zeteophobia needs to be treated with the same effort and care with which a counselor would treat any other phobia. The emotional concomitants of career planning are a central part of the counselor's responsibility.

Successful treatments for other phobias demonstrate conclusively that facing feared situations directly and learning to cope with the panic reactions is the quickest and most effective way of overcoming the phobia. Avoiding the feared situation seldom works. Young people are sheltered from having to make important decisions about structuring their lives until they graduate. The educational system is a "codependent" in that it enables them to avoid difficult career decisions. Then, suddenly, they are turned loose with little skill and a strong case of zeteophobia. Treatment would logically involve gradually increasing exposure to career exploration tasks, but research will be needed to test alternative approaches. The treatment of zeteophobia by career counselors would involve them in the emotional concerns of their clients and would tend to minimize differences between career and personal counseling.

Using paradoxical intention to discover disconfirming evidence. *Paradoxical intention* is a technique that asks clients to engage in an extreme form of the very behaviors that constitute the problem. For example, clients complaining of insomnia may be asked to stay awake all night and take hourly notes on their condition. A couple with a sexual dysfunction are absolutely forbidden to engage in sexual intercourse but are given a homework assignment of caressing each other's bodies. Athanasou (1984) has proposed that paradoxical intention be used with unemployed clients to exaggerate the anxiety associated with their unemployment status in an effort to help them overcome their passivity and take some constructive actions.

Although it must be used cautiously, the same general approach can be adapted to selected cases of career counseling in school settings. One eighth grader resisted efforts to get him engaged in career exploration. He said he hated to work and requested a job where he wouldn't have to do anything but watch other people work. The career counselor, instead of confronting his unrealistic desire, encouraged him to read up on jobs that required observation such as inspectors, lifeguards, and TV directors. Intrigued by the idea that he might actually find a job requiring "no work," the young man entered the school's career center and began to work.

Transmitting metamessages. In human communication, words are important, but the metamessage behind those words is even more important. We sometimes make fun of small talk, but small talk plays a vital role in the metamessages it sends. Small talk about the weather conveys the metamessage, "I think you are a person worth talking to." Career counselors can help clients see that their words and body language communicate a rich array of messages, far more than a literal interpretation of the words would indicate.

Using humor for perspective. Nevo (1986) has advocated that career counselors use a sense of humor in dealing with the serious problems they confront. Although most uses of humor need to be spontaneous recognitions of the absurdities of life, some advance planning can be useful. Nevo mentioned the work of Katz (1959), who used cartoons to clarify career issues.

Investigating assumptions to discover disconfirming evidence. The counselor cannot know whether a given belief is accurate or not, but the counselor can encourage some exploration if the client's belief appears to be impeding progress. Corbishley and Yost (1989) have advocated a collaborative approach in which the counselor and client examine the relationships among the client's beliefs, negative feelings, and behavior.

A related method involves the collection of evidence necessary to confirm or disconfirm a blocking belief. Krumboltz (1991a) described a college student who majored in premed under the mistaken belief that he had to please his father. The counselor encouraged frank communication between father and son, which revealed that the father was merely trying to support what he assumed to be his son's ambition.

EVALUATION

A learning theory approach to career counseling requires a radical revision in the criteria used to measure success. Two of the most popular ways in which career counseling success has been measured in research studies are by (a) detecting a reduction in *indecision* and (b) measuring an increase in *congruence* between stated occupational goals and measured characteristics.

Open-Mindedness Is Preferable to Indecision

Indecision is a problem for advocates of trait-and-factor theory. The third step in that theory, matching an individual to an occupation, cannot be completed until the individual declares a decision about the proper match.

Under a learning theory of career counseling, indecision is seen as a necessary and desirable quality to motivate learning activities. It is understandable that people are undecided, given the immense number of choices and the unforeseeable future. Indecision is the most logical and sensible response. Labeling the state as *open-mindedness* rather than indecision also helps (Krumboltz, 1992).

Creativity Is Preferable to Congruence

Measures of congruence are based on the fact that a substantial portion (not necessarily a majority) of people employed in a given occupation share some similar characteristics. Thus, clients with those characteristics who choose the designated occupation are said to be congruent and represent a successful outcome. Clients with the same characteristics who choose a quite different occupation are incongruent and must be tallied as career counseling failures. The congruency criterion overlooks the fact that people with quite different characteristics are also successful in the occupation. It overlooks the fact that the research on the occupation occurred some time ago and that occupations are changing. It overlooks the possibility that some fresh eyes and creative approaches can make a major contribution to an occupation. Heterogeneity, not homogeneity, within occupations is now more highly valued. Congruence is no longer a sufficient criterion for measuring the success of career counseling.

Relevant Learning Activities

More relevant criteria will include measures of the ways that clients are expanding their capabilities, diversifying their interests, finding new ways to express their preferences, reexamining their fundamental assumptions, and developing flexibility to handle a wider variety of tasks. Clients need to experiment with possibilities; they need to explore; and they need to learn, try, and experiment.

Tentative decisions to try out an alternative may be useful. Everyone does not need to make a "career decision." In fact, few people do. A decision implies a commitment to stick to a particular course of action through thick and thin. Many people begin law school, for example, and then drop out after discovering it is not for them. They should not feel like failures for abandoning a stated goal. They should feel like explorers who have successfully eliminated one small area where no gold is buried. They might better rejoice in having gained some new friends and picked up some useful knowledge. Giving people permission to explore and make tentative tryouts will stimulate more learning than insisting that people overcome their indecisiveness, and it will reduce feelings of guilt and failure in the process.

People want to know if they are making progress. Methods are needed to provide feedback to both clients and counselors. If the goal of counseling is to produce learning that leads to the creation of a more satisfying life, criteria might include both process and product outcomes. Process outcomes would consist of measures of the effort that clients have exerted to achieve their goals. Some such outcomes have been termed career exploratory behavior or information-seeking behavior (Krumboltz & Schroeder, 1965; Krumboltz & Thoresen, 1964).

The more immediate product outcomes of career counseling would be desired changes in a client's skills, interests, beliefs, values, work habits, or personal qualities. Evidence that any of these changes has occurred can be assessed psychometrically or anecdotally. More distant product outcomes might include subjective measures of satisfaction. Because each client may have a different goal, the ultimate test is the extent to which each client makes progress toward his or her own goals.

ETHNIC AND GENDER SENSITIVITY

The basic principles of this theory would apply equally well to people of different ethnic groups, gender, religion, sexual orientation, and nationality. People acquire their culture by learning, and new learning experiences enable them to adapt to changing circumstances.

However, the specifics could vary radically. The specific learning goals might well be quite different for people from different cultures. Preferred methods for learning could differ, and assessment devices would need to be adapted to the language and customs of each cultural group. Even though average differences between groups might be observed on any of these measures, individual differences within groups will still exist. Counselors work with individuals, not group means, so sensitivity to the needs of each individual is crucial to success in counseling.

The exact ways in which specific groups might tend to prefer certain goals and react to various assessments and interventions provide rich opportunities for research studies. Some preliminary evidence is already available, pointing to the usefulness of cognitive-behavioral learning strategies with women in making decisions about marriage, motherhood, and career (Stringer-Moore, 1981); dealing with employment dissatisfaction (Keller, Glauber, & Snyder, 1983); and managing conflicts within dual-career families (Elman & Gilbert, 1984). The approach also seems to be effective in helping at-risk youth manage their anger in career-related environments (Freeman, Hutchinson, & MacWilliam, 1992).

PRACTICAL IMPLICATIONS FOR CAREER COUNSELORS

What difference will a learning theory of career counseling make to practicing career counselors? For some it will merely reinforce and justify what they are already doing. For others it may reorient their thinking and practices in important ways.

Use of Assessment Instruments to Stimulate New Learning

In addition to using assessment instruments to match currently existing client characteristics with current and prior job descriptions, career counselors using a learning framework will use assessment instruments to identify possible new skills the clients might learn, explore additional interests that might be cultivated, challenge the usefulness of old beliefs, expand interpersonal competencies, and explore how clients can contribute their expanding talents to the marketplace while creating more satisfying lives for themselves.

Use of More Educational Interventions

Any ethical and effective method of promoting client learning can be used. Learning outcomes are not confined to facts about the self and occupational information. New attitudes, revised beliefs, improved skills, more consistent values, better work habits, and a wider array of personality characteristics all become targets for learning.

Learning Outcomes as Criteria of Success

Career counselors reduce the time they spend worrying whether their clients have *decided* and focus more on what their clients are *learning*. Criterion measures will include assessment of attempts to learn, new behaviors, revised thoughts, and more comfortable emotional reactions. Whether a career choice is congruent with expressed interests becomes just one of many possible outcomes, not necessarily the goal of career counseling.

Integrating Career and Personal Counseling

Helping clients create more satisfying lives for themselves is a general goal shared by many helping professionals. Career counselors will no longer be simple matchmakers but will instead generate learning experiences for their clients that involve a wide array of personal as well as career issues. The competencies of career counselors will need to equal and exceed the competencies of other types of counselors.

PRACTICAL IMPLICATIONS FOR THE CAREER DEVELOPMENT PROFESSION

The practical implications for the profession are profound. Career counselors rank low on the prestige pecking order because their work is seen as simplistic. Expanding the scope of the profession by incorporating learning theory may also elevate it in the eyes of onlookers as well as career counselors themselves.

The Task of Career Counseling Becomes a National Priority

National leaders constantly discuss the importance of the school-to-work transition in education. Conceiving of career counseling as a learning experience positions it as one of the central educational goals of the nation. It is no longer merely a matchmaking service, a frill for those who ought to have been able to figure out a good match by themselves. The economic welfare of the nation depends on its citizens learning career-relevant skills and characteristics and learning to adapt to a constantly changing work environment. As Kiechel (1994) puts it, "the key to success, perhaps even to survival, in the new world is…lifelong learning" (p. 69).

Career Counselors Assume Leadership

A task of this magnitude needs strong leadership. The efforts of many individuals need to be coordinated. Large sums of money need to be appropriated to support research and development activities as well as intervention activities. The creative imagination and practical leadership skills of the profession will be challenged by undertaking this large and critical task.

Counseling Becomes a Central Educational Mission

Counselor training is viewed by some people in schools of education as an expensive frill. Critics argue that we should not be training "therapists." Under a learning theory, counseling becomes central to the educational enterprise. Counselors are educators. They arrange learning experiences just as teachers arrange learning experiences. The students may be called clients, but they are learners. The learning goals may be individually targeted in counseling, but in schools, teachers are often called upon to generate individualized educational plans for certain students. Ideally, all of education would be tailored to the needs of individuals. Grouping students by age levels is a method of economizing—all members of the same age cohort do not have the same educational needs, even though they are sometimes treated as if they do. Counselors can be seen as educators responsible for individually tailoring learning experiences to accomplish cognitive, emotional, and behavioral goals.

The Prestige and Attractiveness of Career Counseling Increase

Career counseling is generally thought to be one of the lower-prestige forms of counseling. Less training is required to perform it. It is thought to be boring in contrast to personal counseling, which deals with such interesting topics as interpersonal relationships, sexual dysfunction, and agoraphobia. Trait-and-factor theory is largely responsible for this state of affairs. The simple three-step model is boring. Matching individuals to occupations can be done quite efficiently by a machine. Emotional issues are easily ignored.

Under a learning theory, the whole life of each client is subject to thoughtful consideration. What new learnings would enable this client to create a more satisfying life? How could those learning experiences be designed and implemented? How do these learnings mesh with family values, community norms, and national priorities? How can we measure how successful our interventions have been with each client? Engaging in these challenging educational tasks could never be seen as boring. The job would challenge the best talents. Career counselors would need to know more than any other type of counselor. They would need the skills of other counselors and more besides—information about the workplace, employment trends, career assessments, and interventions. Only the best could become career counselors.

QUESTIONS AND CONCERNS

When this theory was discussed with colleagues, several themes appeared. Here are some typical questions and my responses to them.

Q: Some of my clients only want to know what occupation they should enter. Isn't it OK to work with them on the goal they state?

A: Of course it's OK. You and your client can work toward any goal you both want. You could and should use all the tools of the profession to help your clients. You may want to be aware of two things, however: (a) Your clients will not be making just one occupational decision in their lives; you may want to teach them in a manner that will enable them to remember the process so that they can make future decisions without your help and (b) when they do arrive at the name of an occupation they say they want to enter, don't assume that your job is finished. They still have to do all the hard work of making their aspiration a reality. They will need a knowledgeable and supportive counselor all the more during their attempts to implement a decision.

Q: I already use all the principles and interventions you advocate. Why do I need another theory?

A: You probably don't, unless you are occasionally asked why you do what you do. Now you can simply answer that you are implementing a learning theory of career counseling.

Q: I don't think I am qualified to use some of the interventions you describe. I have not had any training or experience in using them. What should I do?

A: Don't use any procedure if you are incompetent to use it. Everyone who uses the procedure had to do so a first time. They learned how to do it, so can you. Attend workshops, go to professional meetings, take courses, acquire a mentor, read the professional literature. Learning is valuable for counselors as well as clients.

Q: I don't really want to learn a set of new techniques. I'm quite happy the way I am. If my clients need some service I don't provide, why can't I just refer them to someone competent to provide that service?

A: You can refer them. You don't have to do anything you don't want to do. However, you may want to ask yourself, "Am I doing what's best for my clients?" and "Am I doing what's best for me?"

Q: Aren't we going to be invading the turf of other professionals if we start talking about marital issues or phobia treatments?

A: Our goal should be to provide the best possible service to our clientele. Thinking about their career and personal concerns at the same time will probably make sense to them and be most helpful. There is so much learning that needs to occur that there should be plenty of work for everyone.

REFERENCES

Athanasou, J. A. (1984). *A paradoxical intention: A brief description of a cognitive behaviour therapy approach and its potential for counselling.* (ERIC Document Reproduction Service No. ED 279 920).

Azrin, N. H., & Besalel, V. A. (1980). *Job club counselor's manual*. Baltimore: University Park Press.

Bandura, A. (1971). *Social learning theory*. Morristown, NJ: General Learning Press.

Barker, J. (1992). *Future edge: Discovering the new paradigms of success*. New York: William Morrow.

Beck, A. T. (1976). *Cognitive therapy and the emotional disorders*. New York: International Universities Press.

Beckhard, R., & Pritchard, W. (1992). *Changing the essence*. San Francisco: Jossey-Bass.

Betsworth, D. G., Bouchard, T. J., Jr., Cooper, C. R., Grotevant, H. D., Hansen, J. C., Scarr, S., & Weinberg, R. A. (1994). *Journal of Vocational Behavior, 44*, 263–278.

Bolles, R. N. (1994). *What color is your parachute?* Berkeley, CA: Ten Speed Press.

Bridges, W. (1994). *Job Shift: How to prosper in a workforce without jobs*. Reading, MA: Addison-Wesley.

Corbishley, M. A., & Yost, E. B. (1989). Assessment and treatment of dysfunctional cognitions in career counseling. *Career Planning and Adult Development Journal, 5*, 20–26.

Crites, J. O. (1981). *Career counseling: Models, methods, and materials*. New York: McGraw-Hill.

Danish, S. J., Mash, J. M., Howard, C. W., Curl, S. J., Meyer, A. L., Owens, S., & Kendall, K. (1992). *Going for the goal: Leader manual*. Richmond: Virginia Commonwealth University, Department of Psychology.

Elksnin, L. K., & Elksnin, N. (1991). The school counselor as job search facilitator: Increasing employment of handicapped students through job clubs. *School Counselor, 38*, 215–220.

Ellis, A. (1962). *Reason and emotion in psychotherapy*. New York: Stuart.

Elman, M. R., & Gilbert, L. A. (1984). Coping strategies for role conflict in married professional women with children. *Family Relations, 33*, 317–327.

Freeman, J. G., Hutchinson, N. L., & MacWilliam, E. (1992). *Anger management for at-risk youth*. Paper presented at the annual meeting of the National Consultation on Vocational Counselling, Ottawa, Canada. (ERIC Document Reproduction Service No. ED 341 945).

Hampl, S. P. (1986). Cognitive-behavioral intervention strategies for adult career counseling. *New Directions for Continuing Education, 32*, 15–31.

Handy, C. B. (1989). *The age of unreason*. Boston: Harvard Business School Press.

Hoyt, K. B. (1993). Collaboration: The key to success in private sector/education system relationships. *Youth Policy, 15*(6–7), 11–15.

Hoyt, K. B., & High, S. (1982). Career education. In H. Mitzel (Ed.), *Encyclopedia of educational research* (pp. 231–241). New York: Free Press.

Jepsen, D. A. (1993). *Career as a story: Applications to career counseling practice*. Paper presented at the annual meeting of the American Counseling Association, Atlanta.

Johnson, R. W., & Silva, S. (1990). Confronting a career myth: The case of Rhonda. *Career Development Quarterly, 38*, 204–207.

Katz, M. R. (1959). *You: Today and tomorrow* (3d ed.). Princeton, NJ: Educational Testing Service, Cooperative Tests and Services.

Keller, K. E., Glauber, D., & Snyder, J. (1983). Beliefs-focused and skills-focused employment interventions for women. *Journal of Employment Counseling, 20*, 163–168.

Kiechel, Walter, III. (1994, April 14). A manager's career in the new economy. *Fortune*.

Krumboltz, J. D. (1970). Job experience kits. *Personnel and Guidance Journal, 49*, 233.

Krumboltz, J. D. (1979). A social learning theory of career decision making. Revised and reprinted in A. M. Mitchell, G. B. Jones, & J. D. Krumboltz (Eds.), *Social learning and career decision making* (pp. 19–49). Cranston, RI: Carroll Press.

Krumboltz, J. D. (1991a). *Manual for the Career Beliefs Inventory*. Palo Alto, CA: Consulting Psychologists Press.

Krumboltz, J. D. (1991b). The 1990 Leona Tyler Award Address: Brilliant insights— Platitudes that bear repeating. *The Counseling Psychologist, 19*, 298–315.

Krumboltz, J. D. (1992). The wisdom of indecision. *Journal of Vocational Behavior, 41*, 239–244.

Krumboltz, J. D. (1993). Integrating career and personal counseling. *Career Development Quarterly, 42*, 143–148.

Krumboltz, J. D. (1994). Improving career development theory from a social learning perspective. In M. L. Savickas & R. W. Lent (Eds.), *Convergence in career development theories: Implications for science and practice* (pp. 9–31). Palo Alto, CA: Davies-Black Publishing.

Krumboltz, J. D., & Jackson, M. A. (1993). Career assessment as a learning tool. *Journal of Career Assessment, 1*, 393–409.

Krumboltz, J. D., & Schroeder, W. W. (1965). Promoting career planning through reinforcement. *Personnel and Guidance Journal, 44*, 19–26.

Krumboltz, J. D., Scherba, D. S., Hamel, D. A., & Mitchell, L. K. (1982). Effect of training in rational decision making on the quality of simulated career decisions. *Journal of Counseling Psychology, 29*, 618–625.

Krumboltz, J. D., & Thoresen, C. E. (1964). The effect of behavioral counseling in group and individual settings on information-seeking behavior. *Journal of Counseling Psychology, 11*, 324–333.

Land, G., & Jarman, B. (1992). *Breakpoint and beyond*. Champaign, IL: Harper Business.

Leahy, R. (1991). Scripts in cognitive therapy: The systematic perspective. *Journal of Cognitive Psychotherapy: An International Quarterly, 5*, 291–304.

Lykken, D. T., Bouchard, T. J., Jr., McGue, M., & Tellegen, A. (1993). Heritability of interests: A twin study. *Journal of Applied Psychology, 78*, 649–661.

Maccoby, M. (1981). *The leader: A new face for American management*. New York: Simon & Schuster.

Magnum, S. L. (1993). Career education: An opportunity lost. *Youth Policy, 15*(6–7), 6–10.

Meichenbaum, D. H. (1977). *Cognitive-behavior modification: An integrative approach*. New York: Plenum Press.

McGuire, W. J. (1985). Attitudes and attitude change. In G. Lindzey & E. Aronson (Eds.), *Handbook of social psychology: Volume II* (3d ed., pp. 233–346). New York: Random House.

Mitchell, L. K., & Krumboltz, J. D. (1987). The effects of cognitive restructuring and decision-making training on career indecision. *Journal of Counseling and Development, 66*, 171–174.

Neimeyer, G. J., Nevill, D. D., Probert, B., & Fukuyama, M. (1985). Cognitive structures in vocational development. *Journal of Vocational Behavior, 27*, 191–201.

Nevo, O. (1986). Uses of humor in career counseling. *Vocational Guidance Quarterly, 34*, 188–196.

Nevo, O. (1987). Irrational expectations in career counseling and their confronting arguments. *Career Development Quarterly, 35*, 239–250.

Noer, D. M. (1993). *Healing the wounds.* San Francisco: Jossey-Bass.

Osipow, S. H. (1983). *Theories of career development* (3d ed.). Englewood Cliffs, NJ: Prentice Hall.

Parsons, F. (1909). *Choosing a vocation.* New York: Houghton Mifflin.

Peters, T. (1992). *Liberation management: Necessary disorganization for the nanosecond nineties.* New York: Knopf.

Plomin, R., DeFries, J. C., & Loehlin, J. C. (1977). Genotype-environment interaction and correlation in the analysis of human behavior. *Psychological Bulletin, 84,* 309–322.

Ray, M., & Rinzler, A. (Eds.). (1993). *The new paradigm in business.* New York: J. P. Tarcher/Perigree.

Richardson, M. S. (1993). Work in people's lives: A location for counseling psychologists. *Journal of Counseling Psychology, 40,* 425–433.

Sampson, J. P., Jr., Peterson, G. W., Lenz, J. G., & Reardon, R. C. (1992). A cognitive approach to career services: Translating concepts into practice. *Career Development Quarterly, 41,* 67–74.

Savickas, M. (1991). *Career as story: Explorations using the narrative paradigm.* Paper presented at the conference of the International Association for Educational and Vocational Guidance, Lisbon, Portugal.

Savickas, M. (1993). Career counseling in the postmodern era. *Journal of Cognitive Psychotherapy: An International Quarterly, 7,* 205–215.

Scarr, S., & McCartney, K. (1983). How people make their own environments: A theory of genotype-environment effects. *Child Development, 54,* 424–435.

Senge, P. (1990). *The fifth discipline.* New York: Doubleday/Currency.

Skinner, B. F. (1953). *Science and human behavior.* New York: Macmillan.

Stidham, H. H., & Remley, T. P., Jr. (1992). Job club methodology applied in a workfare setting. *Journal of Employment Counseling, 29,* 69–76.

Stringer-Moore, D. M. (1981). *Uses of assertiveness training for women in midlife crises.* Paper presented at the annual convention of the American Psychological Association, Los Angeles. (ERIC Document Reproduction Service No. ED 211 917).

Taves, R. A. H., Hutchinson, N. L., & Freeman, J. G. (1992). The effect of cognitive instruction in the development of employment interview skills in adolescents with learning disabilities. *Canadian Journal of Counselling, 26,* 87–95.

Varenhorst, B. B. (1968). Innovative tool for group counseling: The life career game. *The School Counselor, 5,* 357–362.

Varenhorst, B. B. (1973). Game theory, simulation and group counseling. In J. Vriend & W. Dyer (Eds.), *Counseling effectively in groups,* pp. 226–233. Englewood Cliffs, NJ: Educational Technology Publications.

Zimbardo, P. G., & Leippe, M. R. (1991). *The psychology of attitude change and social influence.* New York: McGraw-Hill.

CHAPTER SIX

Building Cohesiveness Between Practitioners and Researchers

A Practitioner-Scientist Model

Margaretha S. Lucas
University of Maryland, College Park

RESEARCH IN OUR journals tends to answer many questions but few that are asked by practitioners in their offices (Goldman, 1977; Howard, 1985; Polkinghorne, 1983). Most research published in counseling and career counseling journals such as *Career Development Quarterly, Journal of Counseling and Development, Journal of Counseling Psychology,* and the *Journal of Vocational Behavior* has not been designed with the counseling situation in mind. Articles may cover such topics as applying and extending the Holland (1985) theory, dual-career couples' job satisfaction, alignment of family and work roles, career issues of gay men, vocational assessment for multicultural clients, and enhancement of a sense of agency; yet professional counselors seeking consultation on complex situations presented in their offices would learn little of practical value from such articles. For the client who struggles with transition from high school to college, for problems of career indecision related to lack of motivation, possibly linked to fear of failure, and for those clients dealing with parental expectations that conflict with their own interests, the journals offer few suggestions. Even the more practical "In the Field" and "On the Campus" sections in the *Journal of Counseling and Development* and the *Journal of College Student Development* tend to primarily cover descriptions for programs and workshops, including those for older students, emergency services, or orientation programming for minority students, and include little about specific counseling situations. Articles that describe research on such topics as the use of the repertory grid in career counseling or mapping the nomological network of career self-efficacy, or even those linking personal issues with career problems, such as the integration of sexual orientation in career counseling or psychological distress and counseling duration, shed little light on career problems confronted in the office. Few of them suggest ways to accomplish successful treatment in particular situations. In my experience, practitioners rarely use journal articles as reference sources, and for good reason. Counselors insist on relevance and journals do not provide it. The adequacy of research in terms of its relevance to counselors has not improved much since Krumboltz (1966) stated many years ago, "What we need to know is which procedures and techniques, when used to accomplish what kinds of behavior change, are most effective with what kinds of clients when applied by what kind of counselor" (p. 22).

A NATURAL INTERDEPENDENCE BETWEEN SCIENTISTS AND PRACTITIONERS

Research questions and the results of testing them do not come into existence through armchair reflection or divine inspiration. They emerge, ironically, from experience and observation by scientists and practitioners. Assumptions based on observation are tested empirically, and reformulated and modified accordingly, reflecting an interdependence between researchers and practitioners. For example, there is no question that career counselors need theory and research to help guide them in their practice. Common career counseling tasks such as interpretation of test results, career information giving, and referrals to job descriptions are based on theory building and testing of large groups of people for reliability and validity of generalized principles. The best example is John Holland's (1985) theory that people make career decisions based on how well they know themselves and work activities. Theory with concomitant research to test it is intended to focus practice situations and questions. If theory and its resulting research questions are well articulated, they can provide help in understanding the *why* of the efforts and in steering practitioner activity accordingly. Global observations by practitioners regarding positive outcomes of treatment (e.g., the importance of empathy and "readiness for counseling") have allowed scientists to design studies testing specific factors that contribute to successful outcome. In turn, scientists ask practitioners to test these factors, which then, in turn, refines theory. To the extent that practice is based on objective scientific findings and scientifically sound theories, and to the extent that research is clinically meaningful—derived from practitioners' conveyed questions, insights, and experience—better science (research and theory) is conducted and more informed treatment is practiced.

ROLES TO BE PLAYED BY SCIENTISTS
AND PRACTITIONERS

It is clear that both the scientist and the practitioner play decisive roles in advancing the field of counseling and career counseling, but it is also clear that neither have been as helpful as they could be. Those who do research in career development tend to design hypotheses that have, at best, only an indirect link with counseling situations. For example, knowing that participation, commitment, and values expectations (career salience) in home-family roles contribute significantly to self-esteem in adolescent offenders enriches Super's (1980) life-span career development theory and teaches the understanding of the importance of career roles for particular young people. However, attention to such career dimensions does not automatically translate into ways to build higher self-esteem, and, in the office, the importance of a person's work values still needs to be determined in context. The other side of the coin, of course, is that few practitioners do research, as has been documented over the years by many researchers (Barlow, 1981; Gelso, 1994; Shinn, 1987). Even research that would be considered relevant by practitioners, such as investigations that examine effective strategies in circumscribed situations, is rarely undertaken by practitioners. Gelso (1994) suggested that the most effective way to increase the scientific productivity of counseling psychologists would be to change their graduate training environment. Holland (1986) viewed personality traits as the main factor contributing to the low research productivity of students and faculty attracted to counseling psychology. According to him, it is primarily individuals who are categorized as social (i.e., service oriented) that enter counseling psychology.

DEVELOPING
A PRACTITIONER–SCIENTIST MODEL

The following suggestions are intended to increase clinical relevance of career research and strengthen the natural relationship that exists between the practitioner and the researcher by means of a practitioner-scientist model. A paradigm to promote research activities by counselors, however, requires first and foremost an environment of personal and administrative support in the form of weekly time that is set aside for counselors to meet and develop research ideas. Counselors need assistance in data collection, analyses, and word processing, but they also need professional development opportunities to create a sequence of training events, including workshops in professional writing, consultation with statisticians, and research design by experts trained in social sciences research. Even more important, encouraging research activity among the reluctant requires creating an atmosphere of collegial trust and involvement that allows disclosure of positive and negative experiences in the research process. To view rejection of a manuscript as a challenge, not as a reflection of one's worth as a researcher, is pivotal in building a research program.

When a supportive environment is in place, one of the easier and less intimidating ways to start on the road to research is by reading and discussing "In the Field," "On the Campus," and "Getting Down to Cases" articles in counseling journals. Counseling center directors can stimulate such activity by providing counselors with one or two hours a week, possibly spent over lunch, in which they get together in small or large groups to encourage professional development. In these study groups, articles describing such topics as workshops on how to enhance minority students' career self-efficacy and integrative career assessment for adult learners can be discussed. These articles can form a stimulus for counselors to create their own innovative programs or suggest ways for them to write up already existing projects. Articles that report client cases, specific outreach programs for particular populations, or how-to articles that describe, for example, the development of a career consultation liaison with the honors student program on campus allow practitioners to organize their thoughts and develop writing skills.

Getting one's feet wet this way, with proper environmental support, may lead to the formation of research teams in an agency. The social type of researcher, especially, may enjoy brainstorming with colleagues on types of problems the agency's services face and how they could be addressed by research. Questions regarding underutilization of career services by particular populations, duplication of services with other agencies on campus, and possible ways to complement other agencies such as a career center might be explored by the practitioner-researcher and supported by the agency's administration. As another example, an agency may want to study the effectiveness of its career services by tabulating the frequency of no-shows for its career services after intake; a next step might be to address potential differential no-show patterns between computer- and counselor-guided career services. Members of the research team might explore whether client type (e.g., freshman/senior, high/low vocational identity) affects persistence in counseling. The research can be conducted either quantitatively or qualitatively, with a number of subjects or as a single case study. In any of these research endeavors, it is of crucial importance to keep the research project small, circumscribed, and, preferably, part of a larger research program, such as a service delivery evaluation project, to help maintain focus and interest.

For the more investigative type of practitioner, theoretical research might be more appropriate. She or he might find equally interested colleagues in the agency, brave it alone, or seek collaboration with colleagues in the academic department. It is unfortunate and ironic that, after identical training in graduate school, counseling psychologists who choose an academic career seem to develop into a species different from those who become practitioners. To promote relevant research, collegial involvement in which both the academic and the practitioner return to their scientist-practitioner roots and offer their unique goals and skills may prove the most fruitful. Academic psychologists might explore with practitioners ways to conduct research in an agency that allows integration of counseling experiences with findings from research literature. Similarly, practitioners who heavily engage in counseling typically are skilled observers and can develop clinically relevant hypotheses for research. Questions regarding individual change, how well a client from a particular culture fits a theoretical model, what types of defense mechanisms allow for constructive career decision making, and how issues such as dependency, counterdependency, lack of motivation, or cross-cultural familial relationships relate to successfully completed treatment anchor research questions and strategies in practice. Using many observation points provided by practitioners allows explanations of phenomena to move from the particular to the general, carrying with them the implication of predictability of situations they are explaining. Consequently, such empirical generalizations abstracted from concrete cases help conceptualize treatment and process issues, resulting in informed theory building. As such, practitioners' participation in research, in whatever form it may take, can provide the missing link needed for providing studies necessary to advance the field. Theoretical research, then, whether quantitative, qualitative, survey based or process based, will not be dismissed as obscure, ambiguous, and extraneous, but viewed as a transformation of counselors' reality that brings new insights and perspectives that can be tested. A scientist-practitioner or a practitioner-scientist engagement allows both parties' unique contributions to converge while maintaining their integrity. It can potentially advance the field by describing individual cases linked to generalized theories or developing models or minitheories guiding treatment protocols for frequently encountered career problems in specific populations.

THE BENEFITS OF RESEARCH PARTICIPATION BY PRACTITIONERS

Finally, as active participants and consumers of research, practitioners learn to think of alternate hypotheses to explain clinical observations, because, like everyone else, they tend to attend to information that confirms their existing beliefs and discount information that is contrary to their existing beliefs (Slusher & Anderson, 1989). A case in point is the history of career guidance for women, which has reflected, until recently, society's constraining messages about the appropriate career goals for women. Career counselors mirrored society's stereotypes and were unable to process information provided by women seeking career services in an objective manner. Although our current research methodology cannot address fully the nature of the career counseling process, practitioners' involvement in research helps them refine their own counseling hypotheses. Recognizing one's own biases and thinking more objectively functions as a crucial and possibly only means of checking on one's work. Carl Rogers (1955) was very aware of the danger of counselor bias. In 1955, he observed that he could "deceive myself in regard to my creatively formed subjective hunches" about a client (p. 275). He believed that the scientific method, as a way of thinking, led him to "check the subjective feelings or hunch or hypothesis of a person with the objective fact" (p. 275). His hope for the future was that "each researcher would be a practitioner in some field and each practitioner would be doing some research" (Heppner, Rogers, & Lee, 1984, p. 19).

CONCLUSION

The relationship among theory, research, and practice can be viewed as interdependent and triangular based. Thus, scientific research is designed, in part, to provide answers to practitioners' pressing questions regarding specific clients' effective career decision making. Research also functions, however, as a vehicle to organize observations and facts into a logical framework of theory that explains behavior in a more general way. As such, theory guides research by establishing relations and conditions among events that help practitioners and researchers understand phenomena. To the practitioner-scientist model, practitioners provide a crucial link by thinking about applied problems they encounter in their offices and processing this information as scientists. Subjecting their thinking to empirical tests as well as contemplating new ideas from the research literature encourages systematic and thoughtful analyses of experiences and judicious application of the knowledge and attitudes gained from such analyses.

REFERENCES

Barlow, D. H. (1981). On the relation of clinical research to clinical practice: Current issues, new directions. *Journal of Consulting and Clinical Psychology, 49,* 147–155.

Dorn, F. J. (1985). *Publishing for professional development.* Muncie, IN: Accelerated Development, Inc.

Gelso, C. J. (1994). On the making of a scientist-practitioner: A theory of research training in professional psychology. *Professional Psychology: Research and Practice, 24,* 468–476.

Goldman, L. (1977). Toward more meaningful research. *Personnel and Guidance Journal, 55,* 565–368.

Heppner, P. P., Rogers, M. E., & Lee, L. A. (1984). Carl Rogers: Reflections on his life. *Journal of Counseling and Development, 63,* 14–20.

Holland, J. L. (1985). *Making vocational choices: A theory of vocational personalities and work environments.* Englewood Cliffs, NJ: Prentice Hall.

Holland, J. L. (1986). Student selection, training, and research performance. *The Counseling Psychologist, 14,* 121–126.

Howard, G. S. (1985). Can research in human sciences become more relevant to practice? *Journal of Counseling and Development, 63,* 539–545.

Krumboltz, J. (1966). *Revolution in counseling.* Boston: Houghton Mifflin.

Rogers, C. R. (1955). Persons or science? A philosophical question. *American Psychologist, 10,* 267–278.

Polkinghorne, D. (1983). *Methodology for the human sciences: Systems of inquiry.* Albany: State University of New York.

Shinn, M. R. (1987). Research by practicing school psychologists: The need for fuel for the lamp. *Professional School Psychology, 2,* 235–243.

Slusher, M. P., & Anderson, C. A. (1989). Belief perseverance and self-defeating behavior. In R. Curtis (Ed.), *Self-defeating behaviors: Experimental research, clinical impressions, and practical implications* (pp. 11–40). New York: Plenum.

Super, D. (1980). A life-span, life-space approach to career development. *Journal of Vocational Behavior, 16,* 282–298.

PART TWO

MAKING CAREER COUNSELING THEORY MORE USEFUL

THE SEVEN CHAPTERS in this section of the handbook concentrate on the usefulness of major counseling theories in career intervention and avenues for making them even more useful. Swanson's chapter opens this section by examining the first theoretical approach to career counseling, namely, the trait-and-factor model. She traces the evolution of trait-and-factor counseling into person-environment fit theory as an eminent example of the dynamic interaction between practice and theory. After tracing the numerous contributions of the individual differences tradition in trait-and-factor counseling and person-environment theory, Swanson counters the critics of "directive" counseling. Furthermore, she suggests that unwarranted criticism of the newly evolving *person-environment counseling* model has forestalled opportunities for greater integration between career theory and practice and has hindered communication between career practitioners and researchers. She concludes by identifying future directions for the further development of person-environment counseling and the more complete integration of theory with practice.

Writing from the person-centered perspective first articulated by Carl Rogers, in Chapter 8, Lent describes the basic tenets of this orientation to psychotherapy and explains how they can be useful in career counseling and in reducing the theory-practice divide. She argues that blurring the boundaries that separate different types of career intervention along the continuum from information giving to psychotherapy can result in a specious indictment of theory failing practice. She supports this argument with a case that illustrates some of the advantages of a person-centered approach to career counseling. In closing, Lent addresses implications for practice and science in the coming years and urges practitioners to appreciate the advantages inherent in a person-centered approach to career counseling as they encounter a postmodern world and address the needs of diverse clients.

In Chapter 9, Chartrand addresses how the social cognitive theory of career development articulated by Lent, Hackett, and Brown can be more effectively linked to practice. She begins by differentiating theories of vocational development from models for career counseling by examining their distinct purposes and language and then illustrating the differences with a case study. After examining the importance of the theory-practice transaction, she presents a new counseling model that originates with explicit attention to how a particular career theory can be linked to counseling practice. The new model extends the theories of social cognitive career development and of interpersonal styles into the counseling domain as Chartrand weaves them together with research on the counseling process to produce a new "sociocognitive-interactional" model for career counseling. She describes the model's two stages of assessment and intervention and then illustrates each with a case study.

In Chapter 10, Jepsen addresses the theory-practice rift from the perspective of developmental psychology. To answer questions about the relationships between career theory and practice, especially from the developmental camp, he analyzes theory as argument. In so doing, he considers four forms of rhetoric—logic, facts, metaphors, and stories—as they pertain to Super's career development theory. He suggests that the four forms communicate to practitioners at differential levels of effectiveness. He then shows, by use of four examples, how developmental career theory has directly influenced practice and provides two examples of how practice might influence theory. He contends that the theorist's knowledge of groups and the practitioner's understanding of individuals separates the counselor from the theorist. He concludes by suggesting "back-translation" as a means of furthering the dialogue between theory and practice. Moreover, he suggests that metaphor and story, as forms of rhetoric, have great potential to narrow the theory-practice gulf. According to Jepsen, stories and metaphors can enhance dialogue between theorists and practitioners, especially if they are willing to deal with storied cases, intervention goals, and qualitative data.

Vandiver and Bowman use their chapter to propose a revision to Gottfredson's theory of occupational aspirations that results in a better translation of the theory into practice. They begin by reviewing Gottfredson's theory about circumscription and compromise in the development of occupational aspirations, along with criticisms of the theory. They use the criticisms and accumulated research to reconceptualize and expand Gottfredson's theory. Their expanded theoretical statement incorporates the construct of self-schemas, that is, hypothetical cognitive structures for perceiving, organizing, processing, and using information. They apply this schematic reconceptualization of the processes of circumscription and compromise to the practice of career counseling. The schematic perspective they use explicitly links Gottfredson's theory and its revision to the everyday practice of career counseling.

In 1986, Tony Watts suggested that computer-assisted career guidance systems (CACGS) can act as change agents in stimulating improvements in career counseling theory and practice. In Chapter 12, Gati agrees with Watts, yet goes a step further.

Gati argues that CACGS can act as laboratories for researchers who aim to reduce the gap between career theory and practice. Next, he illustrates how resolving problems and dilemmas in designing CACGS can actually further the integration of decision theory with the practice of career intervention. He then shows how practice can drive the improvement of theory with an example. The next step in improving CACGS requires that the user's dialogue with the computer be evaluated during the session itself. The technology exists to evaluate dialogue quality, but career counseling theory is silent about what characterizes optimal dialogue and feedback. Until theory and research evolve in this direction, advances in practice will be stalled or guided by clinical experience. In short, questions about the design and development of CACGSs provide a critical test of counselors' ability to transform theory into practice because such a transformation requires operationalizing the concepts of a theory and designing practical procedures that implement the concepts.

In the final chapter in this section, Savickas presents a framework that eases the exchange between career theory and practice. The framework was designed to systematize and enhance the interaction between theory and practice in the daily work of practitioners who assess and counsel diverse clients with career concerns. The framework provides a single, unified schema that counselors can use to (a) assess client career concerns, (b) identify the career theory that best comprehends those concerns, (c) select inventories and tests designed to measure and clarify those concerns, and (d) apply intervention strategies devised to resolve those concerns. The chapter includes a discussion about how the framework can be used to prompt work toward a science of career counseling that is grounded in case studies and will result in micropractices designed to resolve particular problems for specific populations of clients.

CHAPTER SEVEN

The Theory *Is* the Practice

Trait-and-Factor/Person-Environment Fit Counseling

Jane L. Swanson
Southern Illinois University at Carbondale

In the wise choice of a vocation there are three broad factors: (1) a clear understanding of yourself, your aptitudes, abilities, interests, ambitions, resources, limitations, and their causes; (2) a knowledge of the requirements and conditions of success, advantages and disadvantages, compensation, opportunities, and prospects in different lines of work; (3) true reasoning on the relations of these two groups of facts. Every young person needs help on all three of these points.

(Parsons, 1989, p. 5)

T HESE OFTEN-CITED words reflect the origin of career counseling. As an active participant in the social reform movement of his time, Parsons was motivated by his own life experience to provide vocational guidance to young adults who were struggling with the enormous social, political, and economic changes occurring in the United States at the turn of the century. The significance of Parsons' work is clearly acknowledged, yet other important influences preceded him, such as the work of Munsterberg and Richards (Crites, 1969). The ideas articulated by Parsons were implemented by subsequent pioneers in vocational psychology, such as Donald G. Paterson, John G. Darley, and Beatrice J. Dvorak at the Minnesota Employment Stabilization Research Institute (MESRI) and Harry Kitson and Edward L. Thorndike at Columbia University (Crites, 1969; Super, 1983).

Parsons' (1989) work, originally published in 1909, served as the cornerstone of trait-and-factor counseling, as articulated in the prolific writing of E. G. Williamson (1939). Other forces converged to shape how trait-and-factor counseling was practiced, such as the emerging psychometric movement, the development of interest and ability tests, and the impetus that World Wars I and II created for the assessment and classification of recruits and for the readjustment of returning post-war veterans (Whiteley, 1984). Trait-and-factor counseling thus was born out of pragmatic and pressing needs and offered solutions to the real-world problems of occupational choice and adjustment, particularly in difficult economic times. The result was a wealth of tools, resources, and techniques comprising an "eminently usable method of vocational counseling" (Super, 1983, p. 29).

For many years, the trait-and-factor approach was the sole method of career counseling. The emergence of the client-centered therapy in the 1950s, heralded by the publication of Carl Rogers' (1942) book, *Counseling and Psychotherapy,* led to a decline in career counseling in general and to trait-and-factor counseling in particular (Crites, 1981). However, trait-and-factor ideas are enjoying a recent resurgence. In the current reincarnation, what traditionally has been known as *trait-and-factor counseling* has evolved into *person-environment fit counseling* (Chartrand, 1991; Lofquist & Dawis, 1991; Rounds & Tracey, 1990). This evolution demonstrates the interplay of theory and practice that has characterized trait-and-factor counseling: Changes in theory have responded to recognition of the complexity of what constitutes career counseling and career choice. The evolution of the trait-and-factor approach into the person-environment fit approach reflects the maturation of an applied perspective into an integrated blend of theory and practice.

The fundamental premise guiding this chapter is that trait-and-factor counseling, both historically and in its present form, is a superb example of how theory and practice can be successfully interwoven—that is, for trait-and-factor counseling, the theory is the practice. Two points will be used to illustrate this premise. First, trait-and-factor ideas are alive and well, despite the enormous amount of change in society and in the structure of occupations that has occurred since their inception. Second, the overarching framework of person-environment fit theory (the contemporary form of trait-and-factor counseling) offers a great deal of theoretical and practical flexibility, the potential of which is underdeveloped and unrealized (Rounds & Tracey, 1990). These two points will be discussed in the next two sections, followed by a consideration of future directions for the convergence of theory and practice in person-environment fit counseling.

First, however, a brief discussion of terminology is necessary. Recent authors have suggested that the term trait-and-factor is anachronistic and should be replaced by person-environment fit (Chartrand, 1991; Rounds & Tracey, 1990). Admittedly, trait-and-factor is outdated, particularly in light of the theoretical and applied advances that have resulted in the person-environment fit perspective, and the continued use of this term may contribute to the perception that trait-and-factor counseling has nothing to offer counselors or clients in the 1990s and beyond. For the purposes of this chapter, trait-and-factor is used when discussing the initial formulations of the approach and in highlighting the historical connection, whereas person-environment fit is used when discussing more contemporary formulations.

Rather than a simple exercise in semantics, however, the terminology clearly supports the main premise of the chapter. Our common lexicon reveals that the phrase *trait-and-factor* is most frequently linked with counseling, whereas the phrase *person-environment* fit is more likely to occur with theory, suggesting precisely what will be argued in the remainder of this chapter: that the evolution of trait-and-factor into person-environment fit exemplifies a dynamic interaction of theory and practice. On the one hand, trait-and-factor was initially designed to be an approach to career *counseling,* and the trait-and-factor approach has been characterized as atheoretical (Crites, 1981; Williamson & Biggs, 1979). Person-environment fit theory, on the other hand, is a more comprehensive term that reflects both its historical roots in trait-and-factor ideas as well as the focus on advancing our theoretical understanding of vocational behavior and career psychology. In other words, "trait-and-factor" is, or was, a method of career counseling; person-environment fit is a more broadly defined theory of vocational behavior that incorporates trait-and-factor ideas.

THE CONTINUED UTILITY
OF TRAIT-AND-FACTOR COUNSELING

The first indication that trait-and-factor counseling exemplifies the convergence of theory and practice is that trait-and-factor ideas continue to hold both heuristic and practical value. The basic tenet underlying trait-and-factor counseling is that people differ in their traits and jobs differ in their requirements; if traits of people and requirements of jobs can be isolated and measured, then one can match people and jobs (Hewer, 1963). Extensions of these principles can be seen in assumptions of contemporary person-environment fit theories (Chartrand, 1991; Rounds & Tracey, 1990). In this section, the initial accounts of trait-and-factor counseling will be discussed, followed by an examination of the criticism of and support for trait-and-factor counseling, and, finally, a description of the evolution of trait-and-factor counseling into person-environment fit counseling.

Initial Formulations of Trait-and-Factor Counseling

As noted earlier, the foundations of trait-and-factor counseling can be found in the work of Parsons (1989) and Williamson (1939). According to Spokane and Glickman (1994), Parsons himself laid the foundations not only for the trait-and-factor approach but also for its blend of theory and practice:

> Parsons provided the first clear statements about the clinical science of career intervention. Practice and theory formed a seamless amalgam to Parsons. He used scientific principles in his practice and expected his clients to use them in their thinking as well. He was a true scientist practitioner. (p. 299)

In addition to the three principles cited earlier—knowledge of oneself, knowledge of the world of work, and "true reasoning"—Parsons also discussed other principles underlying the practice of vocational guidance that continue to be evident in our current views of career counseling (Jones, 1994). For example, Parsons emphasized that choosing a vocation was more important than securing a job. Further, he stated that "no person may decide for another what occupation he should choose" but that an individual could benefit from expert advice and information related to the decision (Parsons, 1989, p. 4). Finally, Parsons discussed the counselor's role in giving accurate feedback to clients regarding their strengths and weaknesses and encouraged the counselor to convey such feedback with "utmost frankness and kindliness in a friendly effort to enable the applicant to see himself exactly as others see him, and correct whatever deficits may stand in the way of his advancement" (Parsons, 1989, p. 23).

Williamson and Darley's (1937) formulation of trait-and-factor counseling used a case history method reminiscent of Parsons' approach. Williamson and Darley (1937) conceptualized counseling as comprising a six-step process—analysis, synthesis, diagnosis, prognosis, counseling, and follow-up—in which the first four steps were "the province of the professional" (Rounds & Tracey, 1990, p. 4). Williamson, like Parsons, emphasized rational, analytical problem solving in which information is gathered, alternatives are generated, and an optimal choice is selected. Further, the foundation of trait-and-factor counseling was differential diagnosis, and Williamson (1939) defined four categories of concerns related to career decision making: no choice, uncertain choice, unwise choice, and discrepancy between interests and aptitudes.

Finally, according to Rounds and Tracey (1990), Williamson's major contribution was the role of tests and actuarial methods in career counseling. Although Parsons laid the groundwork for career assessment through the use of a comprehensive interview protocol, the inclusion of formal assessment into career counseling awaited the development of assessment tools and psychometric techniques that emerged during the period following World War I (Zytowski & Swanson, 1994).

Building on these initial works, the trait-and-factor approach was modified considerably in subsequent years, most notably by Williamson and his colleagues (Williamson, 1965a, 1965b; Williamson & Biggs, 1979). Williamson and Biggs (1979) described four stages in the development of trait-and-factor counseling, which they characterized as focusing on (a) developing ways to measure individuals' attributes to predict educational and vocational success, (b) developing models for the counseling process and expanding differential diagnosis to include "a variety of client adjustment problems beyond educational and vocational ones" (Williamson & Biggs, 1979, p. 92), (c) refining conceptualizations of traits and outcome criteria via application of factor analytic techniques, and (d) examining the philosophical and theoretical aspects of the approach in response to criticisms of its directive nature. The descriptions of these four stages document the dynamic, changing character of trait-and-factor counseling, and, further, demonstrate the interplay between theory and practice that has characterized trait-and-factor counseling since its inception.

Evaluation of Trait-and-Factor Counseling

During the past 30 years, many writers have proclaimed the trait-and-factor approach to be outdated and in decline (Crites, 1981; Krumboltz, 1994; Osipow, 1983; Yost & Corbishley, 1987). One of the most frequently cited critics has been Crites (1981):

> [A]s practiced by too many Trait-and-Factor counselors who have not updated the model...and methods..., this approach has gone into an incipient decline. It has devolved into what has been caricatured as "three interviews and a cloud of dust""... At best, this widespread oversimplification of Trait-and-Factor career counseling provides the client with a mass of test information, which is frequently forgotten or distorted.... At worst, it completely ignores the psychological realities of decision making that lead to indecision and unrealism in career choice...and it fails to foster those more general competencies, for example, self-management, which are the essence of true Trait-and-Factor career counseling. (pp. 49, 52)

Crites' (1981) "three interviews and a cloud of dust" characterization of the practice of outdated trait-and-factor counseling has been frequently repeated and seems to have led to a rejection of the theory by many individuals for reasons not wholly accurate. Ironically, although Crites' view often is interpreted as a condemnation of trait-and-factor counseling, he clearly stated that the approach is problematic *when counselors apply its outdated version,* as demonstrated by the less frequently cited statement that immediately preceded the quote cited earlier: "In the hands of its highly competent and enlightened originators who are still practicing, it is most likely as viable today as it was in the past" (Crites, 1981, p. 49).

Paradoxically, at least in terms of the purpose of this volume, it may be important to separate the theoretical model from its counseling application to fully appreciate the contributions that trait-and-factor counseling has to offer. For example, Rounds and Tracey (1990) noted that the criticisms of Williamson's early techniques as directive and advice giving needed to be separated from evaluation of trait-and-factor theory. These original techniques were developed and promulgated at a time when the reigning therapeutic paradigm also was directive; the field of counseling had not yet experienced the complete paradigmatic shift led by Carl Rogers. Rogers' approach, considered heretical when initially introduced, proposed that the counselor-client relationship was the vehicle for therapeutic change, deemphasizing the role of the counselor as an expert (Raskin & Rogers, 1989). This paradigm shift clearly had implications for the practice of trait-and-factor career counseling (Bordin, 1949), which was criticized as being overly directive. However, the application of trait-and-factor theory does not require the use of directive or advice-giving counselor techniques, nor is there evidence to suggest that counselors applying contemporary person-environment fit approaches have retained the directive techniques advocated during the earlier days of trait-and-factor counseling.

Further, both the techniques and the theory have changed substantially since the 1930s and 1940s, yet some of the most ardent critics do not seem to acknowledge these changes. As indicated earlier, Williamson himself continued to modify and refine the trait-and-factor approach, and contemporary person-environment fit approaches, such as those of Holland (1992) and of Dawis and Lofquist (1984), are notable for their attention to continued theoretical and applied developments. Some of the most troubling criticism has been recently articulated by Krumboltz (1994), who asserted that trait-and-factor counseling prompted counseling psychologists' negative opinions of career counseling. Krumboltz (1994) then claimed that trait-and-factor counseling

> oversimplifies the complexities of helping people with a wide range of career problems. Trait-and-factor theories lead us to overlook crucial anomalies, to short circuit our responsibilities, to leave our clientele underserved, and to convey to our colleagues a false image that our task is boring, unskilled, and irrelevant to more essential educational endeavors. (p. 15)

Krumboltz's (1994) denunciation of trait-and-factor theory and practice illustrates Spokane's (1994) characterization of trait-oriented career psychologists as "bruised from years of unfair and inaccurate criticism" (p. 120). This type of criticism denigrates practitioners who are competently delivering career counseling to scores of clients, without avoiding their responsibilities or underserving clients. Moreover, this criticism may serve to further alienate the various theoretical positions from one another, as well as the theorists from the practitioners.

Three factors seem to underlie the critique of trait-and-factor theory: (a) misreading or misrepresenting the theoretical and applied concepts, as discussed by Rounds and Tracey (1990) and Spokane (1994), (b) ignoring the historical and social context surrounding the initial theoretical statements, and (c) not acknowledging the significant changes that have occurred since the initial formulations of trait-and-factor counseling. These three factors have led to a regrettable situation in which trait-and-factor/person-environment fit concepts are discarded by many theorists and practitioners as outdated or limited in their utility. What is ironic is that any rift that exists between theory and practice does not seem to occur *within* the person-environment fit approach but, rather, in practitioners turning away from person-environment fit theory because of the misrepresentation that has occurred.

In contrast to the critics of trait-and-factor theory, other recent writers (Brown, 1984; Chartrand, 1991; Rounds & Tracey, 1990) have built a case for the health and vitality of trait-and-factor concepts. Rounds and Tracey (1990) argued that "reports of the death of trait-and-factor counseling have been greatly exaggerated, that much of the current criticism is poorly thought out and weak in form" (p. 6). Further, they argued for the continued utility of trait-and-factor theory, as evidenced in current person-environment fit theories. Brown (1984) commented that "those counselors who followed the three-interviews-and-a-cloud-of-dust approach never really understood the approach, for Williamson never advocated a test-and-tell approach or a simplified approach." He concluded that "no theory or approach has yet been developed that has satisfactorily replaced trait-oriented thinking, whether the concern be work adjustment, career counseling, or personnel selection" (pp. 14–15).

The early influence of trait-and-factor theory appears to be undisputed, although some authors, most notably Krumboltz (1994), have contended that the influence was negative in valence. However, in spite of protests to the contrary, trait-and-factor thinking *continues* to deeply permeate our view of career choice and career counseling. Whatever one's theoretical orientation, the constructs articulated by theorists such as Holland (1992), Dawis and Lofquist (1984), and even Parsons (1989) and Williamson (1939) enter into how we conceptualize career psychology. Contemporary person-environment fit theories are the direct descendants of Parsons and Williamson and continue to provide the philosophical underpinning, if not the explicit structure, for career counseling.

For example, in the counseling psychology doctoral training program at Southern Illinois University, students take a course in counseling skills and a course in vocational psychology theories, then begin their practicum at the university career services agency. They are not indoctrinated into particular theoretical views of career counseling, nor are they given a formulaic way to conduct career counseling with their clients. In fact, they likely have absorbed much of the previously cited criticism about the trait-and-factor perspective and rarely cite trait-and-factor or person-environment fit as the theoretical orientation guiding their work with clients. Yet students consistently use trait-and-factor/person-environment fit terms to describe what they are doing with clients: They conceptualize career counseling as the classic Parsonian three-step process, in which they assist the client in (a) gaining knowledge about her or himself, (b) gathering information about the world of work, and (c) determining how these two bodies of knowledge intersect in a career choice. This observation suggests that the ideas expressed in person-environment fit theories provide something quite central or essential to our understanding of career choice and development; as Zytowski and Borgen (1983) have noted, "the central Parsonian assumption...approaches the stature of a paradigm" (p. 8).

Evolution of Trait-and-Factor into Person-Environment Fit

Rounds and Tracey (1990) stated that "Williamson's formulations about vocational counseling are as viable today as they were in the 1930s—when, that is, they are articulated with current psychotherapy and counseling theory" (p. 1). This statement carries an important message: It acknowledges that a theory need not be—in fact, ought not be—discarded merely because the historical and social context surrounding the theory's development has changed. Moreover, this statement implies that the valuable components of a theory can be augmented and strengthened with the addition of current theoretical or empirical knowledge.

Without a doubt, the trait-and-factor approach has changed over the years. As noted earlier, Williamson and Biggs (1979) described four stages in the development of trait-and-factor counseling; yet, as they forecasted, "the definitive history of trait-and-factor counseling has yet to be written" (p. 91). The emergence of contemporary person-environment fit approaches can be viewed as the next logical step in the ongoing evolution of trait-and-factor counseling rather than as a discontinuous development or a rejection of its historical roots.

Rounds and Tracey (1990) identified several changes that occurred as trait-and-factor counseling developed, particularly as it evolved into person-environment fit counseling. First, although still primarily rational in nature, it involves both cognitive and affective processes. Second, clinical information and qualitative methods are used to complement more traditional types of assessment information. Third, it relies less on the direct methods of advising and teaching as a form of counselor influence. Additional changes include the central idea that person-environment fit is a reciprocal ongoing process and that the client learns the person-environment fit model as a basis for present and future problem solving and decision making. Moreover, the client is conceptualized as an active agent in the counseling process, including the decision to use assessment and the selection of specific assessment instruments.

Three central assumptions underlie contemporary person-environment fit theories (Chartrand, 1991; Rounds and Tracey, 1990). First, "individuals seek out and create environments...that provide and/or allow for behavioral trait manifestation" (Rounds & Tracey, 1990, p. 18), that is, environments that are consistent or congruent with an individual's characteristics. Second, the degree of fit between person and environment is related to important outcomes, for both the person and the environment, and greater fit leads to better outcomes. Third, the process of person-environment fit is reciprocal: The individual shapes the environment and the environment shapes the individual.

Thus, the trait-and-factor approach is neither stagnant nor extinct, as some of its critics would imply. The continued vitality of trait-and-factor ideas is evidenced in their transformation into person-environment fit theories. Although the trait-and-factor approach has changed significantly as it developed into person-environment fit, direct derivatives of the original principles developed by Parsons and Williamson can be seen in assumptions of contemporary person-environment fit theories.

OVERARCHING FRAMEWORK
WITH THEORETICAL AND PRACTICAL FLEXIBILITY

A second indication that trait-and-factor/person-environment fit counseling exemplifies the convergence of theory and practice is that person-environment fit theories offer a great deal of unrecognized flexibility for both theory and practice.

Person-environment fit theories, rather than limiting the career counseling practitioner (as critics suggest), provide an organizing framework that allows for
the integration of diverse issues that clients bring to counseling. To examine this
argument, the section will begin with an attempt to separate fact from stereotype
in terms of trait-and-factor/person-environment fit counseling, followed by a
discussion of how person-environment fit theories provide both flexibility and
adaptability.

In evaluating the status of trait-and-factor/person-environment fit counseling, it
is important to remember the influence of historical and social contexts, throughout
its development as well as now. Trait-and-factor counseling originated from an
applied perspective with a focus on immediate, real-world problems in a context of
a Depression-era mentality. Further, the clients were predominantly White males—
as were the counselors—and the occupational structure was less complex and
generally required less training for initial job entry. A final contextual feature was
that counselors were functioning primarily as test givers and interpreters due to
restrictions on what was considered within the realm of their professional responsibilities (Rounds & Tracey, 1990). The recognition of a theory's context is critical
for future interchange between theory and practice because context is, by definition,
dynamic: Attention to context demands that we recognize when the context has
changed and that we respond accordingly. Clearly, then, trait-and-factor/person-
environment fit theory has evolved substantially, yet needs further theoretical
refinement to continue to be viable in current and future contexts.

As discussed earlier, examination of the criticisms of the trait-and-factor/
person-environment fit approach suggests that it is not the theory itself that has been
criticized but rather its application. Critics who wrote in the 1980s and 1990s
seemed to react to techniques of trait-and-factor counseling that were remnants of
a much earlier time. Granted, some counselors may still apply trait-and-factor
techniques as they were originally advocated by Williamson (1939); however, these
techniques are more accurately considered vestiges of an earlier era rather than the
defining characteristic of contemporary person-environment fit counseling.

Separating Fact from Stereotype

The stereotypic view of trait-and-factor counseling portrayed by its critics suggests
that the focus of career counseling is quite circumscribed. Krumboltz (1994)
actively proposed this view: "Trait-and-factor theory enables us to answer only a
small fraction of the questions brought to career counselors" (p. 15); however, his
example of a "fictitious dyed-in-the-wool trait-and-factor counselor" is a misrepresentation of contemporary person-environment fit counseling. For example, in a
fictitious counseling session, Krumboltz presented a counselor who claims to be
unable to help a client plan for retirement unless the client intends to find a new job.
This view of trait-and-factor/person-environment fit counseling is unnecessarily
narrow and oversimplified. *Environment* is more broadly defined than simply the

immediate environment of a specific job. Although Krumboltz acknowledged that his view was exaggerated, this picture seems to purposely ignite strong negative reactions where they are unwarranted. Further, Krumboltz (1994) argued that trait-and-factor theories

> do not help us understand the emotional and skill acquisition tasks required for a job search, they do not inform us about overcoming job-related phobias, they do not address problems associated with handling sexual harassment, job burnout, the constantly changing employment environment, dual career families, or retirement planning. (p. 16)

Contrary to Krumboltz's statement, person-environment fit theories clearly address these types of problems. An unequivocal example is the theory of work adjustment (TWA), recently expanded to person-environment correspondence (PEC) theory, which is derived from trait-and-factor theory (Dawis & Lofquist, 1984, 1993; Lofquist & Dawis, 1991). An important concept in PEC theory is that of salient environments, which acknowledges the multiplicity of environments and roles that an individual occupies. The salience of the various environments to an individual guides the priority that she or he places on different person-environment correspondences. Further, the salience of an environment is neither an absolute nor a static property but should be viewed relative to other environments with greater or lesser salience and likely to change over time. The concept of salient environments allows a full consideration of issues related to job search and adjustment, unfavorable or changing working conditions, balancing dual-career and work-nonwork demands, job or career change, and retirement. Although person-environment fit theories never defined environment as narrowly as Krumboltz (1994) implied, PEC theory explicitly acknowledges the broad range of environments with which an individual interacts.

In addition, there are other occurrences of stereotypic portrayals of trait-and-factor/person-environment fit counseling. Chartrand (1991) noted that a number of questionable interpretations exist regarding trait-and-factor counseling, such as the idea that occupational choice is an event, that jobs are inhabited by a single type of person, and that there is one correct goal for every career decision maker. These interpretations do not accurately reflect the assumptions of trait-and-factor counseling, and they obscure the value of trait-and-factor ideas.

It is puzzling that trait-and-factor/person-environment fit approaches have generated so much negative reaction. As Rounds and Tracey (1990) asked, "What is it about this approach that provokes ire and contention but no theoretical progress?" (p. 37). Presumably, no one would argue that we ignore "good fit" in career choice or in career counseling, nor would they disagree that accurate perceptions of oneself and potential environments can enhance career decision making. The problem with trait-and-factor/person-environment fit counseling seems to lie in the erroneous perception that it must be delivered in a particular, inflexible manner and that, by definition, it *must* ignore other variables that constitute the context of a client's life.

For example, there is nothing in the trait-and-factor approach that limits career counseling to "three sessions and a cloud of dust"; in fact, Crites' often-cited quotation was described by him as being a caricature (although he believed it a frequent occurrence) of the original formulation of trait-and-factor counseling. As a criticism of trait-and-factor counseling, it ignores the role of historical and social contexts. In practice, the mechanical application of trait-and-factor career counseling may have been more likely to occur when the need for career assistance was the most pressing, such as for job placement in the postwar years. However, trait-and-factor/person-environment fit theory also is consonant with the relative luxury of greater time and less economic pressure that typifies many of the settings in which career counseling services are delivered, allowing the possibility of as many counseling sessions as it takes for the counselor and client to identify the issues, integrate relevant assessment information, and arrive at a decision or plan of action.

Thus, the view of trait-and-factor/person-environment fit counseling as narrowly circumscribed is neither fair nor accurate. Person-environment fit theories provide precisely the kind of flexible framework for counseling that allows for the inclusion of a myriad of factors influencing career-related exploration, decision making, and adjustment. Perhaps the task awaiting trait-and-factor–oriented theorists is to explicitly demonstrate such flexibility. As Rounds and Tracey (1990) wrote, "trait-and-factor counseling remains without a significant body of proponents interested in reaping its possible empirical and theoretical rewards as an object of study" (p. 37). The time has come to supplant heated criticism with constructive efforts to refine the theoretical constructs and explicitly connect theory with practice.

Developing the Flexibility of Person-Environment Theories

In contrast to previous authors who have focused on the limitations of the theories, I contend that trait-and-factor/person-environment fit theories provide a solid theoretical framework that can subsume all other practice orientations; as Crites (1981) commented, the three components of Parsons' formulation must be addressed by all theoretical approaches to career counseling. Indeed, the influence of the theory is apparent in many other theoretical approaches.

I further suggest that we do not need new theories of career counseling; our available theories are quite adequate, although they are in need of some updating or further explication. What we need instead is more attention to the rapprochement between existing theory and practice, to the drawing of explicit linkages that apparently are not as evident as would be optimal. Spokane and Glickman (1994) identified the twin themes that have always existed within vocational psychology: (a) theories that describe career choice and adjustment and (b) models that suggest how to assist clients in making career choices. Person-environment fit theories can address both of these issues (Rounds & Tracey, 1990).

Trait-and-factor/person-environment fit counseling always has been firmly rooted in differential psychology, with a focus on the identification and measurement of individual differences. The commitment to individual differences, as argued by Dawis (1992, 1994), implies a great flexibility in person-environment fit theories by suggesting that individuals also vary in measurable ways on many other career-relevant background dimensions, such as family background, developmental stages, personality traits, and career choice process dimensions such as career maturity, indecision, self-efficacy. One of the greatest strengths and contributions of the trait-and-factor theoretical lineage is that it influenced and took advantage of the burgeoning technology of the psychometric movement, and formal career assessment continues to occupy a central role in person-environment fit theories. Moreover, recent conceptualizations of career assessment include an expanded set of relevant variables (Betz, 1992) as well as methods of assessment (Goldman, 1990; Healy, 1990).

Further, an additional contribution of the individual differences approach is the focus on describing and predicting how demonstrated differences in individual attributes relate to important outcome criteria, such as occupational success and satisfaction, thus providing an explicit, empirical foundation for what occurs in career counseling. Finally, attention to cultural diversity in career choice and career counseling is also consonant with the philosophical stance that the individual differences approach lends to person-environment fit theories.

FUTURE DIRECTIONS FOR THE CONVERGENCE OF THEORY AND PRACTICE

Over the years, applications of trait-and-factor counseling have responded to the changing needs of clients, yet these changes have not always been incorporated back into the theoretical statements. However, as argued earlier, the theory and its application offer a great deal of adaptability to adjust to changing social and economic circumstances.

Perhaps the most immediate need for theoretical revision is the clear and explicit inclusion of variables such as gender, race, and ethnicity. In spite of the fact that career counseling has been steeped in the tradition of individual differences, some of these fundamental individual differences variables often have been overlooked (Betz, 1992; Swanson & Bowman, 1994). Yet they are absolutely critical given the diversity of clients who request career assistance. The basic framework of trait-and-factor theory can be augmented with the addition of contextual variables in a systematic way. For example, recent writers have suggested that Holland's (1992) theory might be modified to better account for observed ethnic/racial and gender differences in the structure of interests (Hansen, 1992; Swanson, 1992).

Fitzgerald and Betz (1994) suggested a framework that acknowledges structural and cultural factors in considering the applicability of career theories. They defined *structural factors* as characteristics of society or an organization that "limit access to or opportunities in the occupational and/or organizational environment" (p. 107), such as discrimination or poverty. They define *cultural factors* as "beliefs and attitudes commonly found among group members...[that] serve as self-perpetuating barriers to the individual" (p. 107). Further, they noted that

> each of these factors has been found to affect vocational behavior in important, systematic, and predictable ways, yet each is generally ignored by the major theories of such behavior, a situation that limits their power for understanding much of the population. (p. 107)

Fitzgerald and Betz (1994) encouraged the examination of the applicability of theories to groups that have been historically overlooked by examining the applicability of specific theories, using individual differences and structural or cultural factors as moderator variables, and analyzing the influence of structural and cultural factors in the conceptualization and measurement of important variables in career theories. Fitzgerald and Betz (1994) have provided an excellent direction to proceed in systematically examining and revising person-environment fit theories to more effectively address issues of cultural diversity. As an example, Fitzgerald and Rounds (1994) analyzed the theory of work adjustment and suggested ways that it might be expanded to address issues of work and family interface and sexual harassment.

A second direction in which both theory and practice can be modified is in the realm of process variables in career counseling. Process variables generally have been ignored in career counseling (Swanson, 1995) but perhaps more so in traditional trait-and-factor approaches. Further, process variables may need extra attention in contemporary person-environment fit theories due to the "bad press" that the counselor-client relationship has received from critics of trait-and-factor approaches. Paradoxically, process issues may be well suited to an application of person-environment fit concepts, as recommended by Rounds and Tracey (1990). Although trait-and-factor counseling has been repeatedly criticized because of inattention to the counselor-client relationship—or, perhaps more accurately, because of the directive nature of the relationship—it also offers a useful strategy for examining the therapeutic relationship through the concept of person-environment correspondence.

Finally, person-environment fit theories offer a useful framework for addressing the kind of questions that require attention in the theory and practice of career counseling. For example, the question asked by Williamson and Bordin (1941) continues to be pertinent: "What counseling techniques (and conditions) will produce what types of results with what types of students?"

SUMMARY

The premise of this chapter is that trait-and-factor/person-environment fit counseling is an exemplary case of the convergence of theory and practice, as is illustrated by the continued value of its ideas and by the flexibility and adaptability it offers to both the theory and practice of career counseling. Further connections between theory and practice may be promoted through attention to overlooked individual difference variables, such as gender, race, and ethnicity, and counseling process variables.

REFERENCES

Betz, N. E. (1992). Career assessment: A review of critical issues. In S. D. Brown & R. W. Lent (Eds.), *Handbook of counseling psychology* (2d ed., pp. 453–484). New York: Wiley.

Bordin, E. S. (1949). Counseling points of view, non-directive and others. In E. G. Williamson (Ed.), *Trends in student personnel work*. Minneapolis: University of Minnesota Press.

Brown, D. (1984). Trait and factor theory. In D. Brown, L. Brooks, & Associates (Eds.), *Career choice and development* (pp. 8–30). San Francisco: Jossey-Bass.

Chartrand, J. M. (1991). The evolution of trait-and-factor career counseling: The person X environment fit approach. *Journal of Counseling and Development, 69,* 518–524.

Crites, J. O. (1969). *Vocational psychology*. New York: McGraw-Hill.

Crites, J. O. (1981). *Career counseling: Models, methods, and materials*. New York: McGraw-Hill.

Dawis, R. V. (1992). The individual differences tradition in counseling psychology. *Journal of Counseling Psychology, 39,* 7–19.

Dawis, R. V. (1994). The theory of work adjustment as convergent theory. In M. L. Savickas & R. W. Lent (Eds.), *Convergence in career development theories: Implications for science and practice* (pp. 33–43). Palo Alto, CA: Davies-Black Publishing.

Dawis, R. V., & Lofquist, L. H. (1984). *A psychological theory of work adjustment: An individual differences model and its applications*. Minneapolis: University of Minnesota Press.

Dawis, R. V., & Lofquist, L. H. (1993). Rejoinder: From TWA to PEC. *Journal of Vocational Behavior, 43,* 113–121.

Fitzgerald, L. F., & Betz, N. E. (1994). Career development in cultural context: The role of gender, race, class, and sexual orientation. In M. L. Savickas & R. W. Lent (Eds.), *Convergence in career development theories: Implications for science and practice* (pp. 103–177). Palo Alto, CA: Davies-Black Publishing.

Fitzgerald, L. F., & Rounds, J. B. (1994). Women and work: Theory encounters reality. In W. B. Walsh & S. H. Osipow (Eds.), *Career counseling for women* (pp. 327–353). Hillsdale, NJ: Erlbaum.

Goldman, L. (1990). Qualitative assessment. *The Counseling Psychologist, 18,* 205–213.

Hansen, J. C. (1992). Does enough evidence exist to modify Holland's theory to accommodate the individual differences of diverse populations? *Journal of Vocational Behavior, 40,* 188–193.

Healy, C. C. (1990). Reforming career appraisals to meet the needs of clients in the 1990s. *The Counseling Psychologist, 18,* 214–226.

Hewer, V. H. (1963). What do theories of vocational choice mean to a counselor? *Journal of Counseling Psychology, 10,* 118–125.

Holland, J. L. (1992). *Making vocational choices* (2d ed.). Odessa, FL: Psychological Assessment Resources.

Jones, L. K. (1994). Frank Parsons' contribution to career counseling. *Journal of Career Development, 20*(3), 287–294.

Krumboltz, J. D. (1994). Improving career development theory from a social learning perspective. In M. L. Savickas & R. W. Lent (Eds.), *Convergence in career development theories: Implications for science and practice* (pp. 9–31). Palo Alto, CA: Davies-Black Publishing.

Lofquist, L. H., & Dawis, R. V. (1991). *Essentials of person-environment-correspondence counseling.* Minneapolis: University of Minnesota Press.

Osipow, S. H. (1983). *Theories of career development* (3d ed.). Englewood Cliffs, NJ: Prentice Hall.

Parsons, F. (1989). *Choosing a vocation.* Garrett Park, MD: Garrett Park Press. (Original work published 1909)

Raskin, N. J., & Rogers, C. R. (1989). Person-centered therapy. In R. J. Corsini & D. Wedding (Eds.), *Current psychotherapies* (4th ed., pp. 155–194). Itasca, IL: F. E. Peacock.

Rogers, C. R. (1942). *Counseling and psychotherapy.* Boston: Houghton Mifflin.

Rounds, J. B., & Tracey, T. J. (1990). From trait-and-factor to person-environment fit counseling: Theory and process. In W. B. Walsh & S. H. Osipow (Eds.), *Career counseling: Contemporary topics in vocational psychology* (pp. 1–44). Hillsdale, NJ: Erlbaum.

Spokane, A. R. (1994). The resolution of incongruence and the dynamics of person-environment fit. In M. L. Savickas & R. W. Lent (Eds.), *Convergence in career development theories: Implications for science and practice* (pp. 119–137). Palo Alto, CA: Davies-Black Publishing.

Spokane, A. R., & Glickman, I. T. (1994). Light, information, inspiration, cooperation: Origins of the clinical science of career intervention. *Journal of Career Development, 20*(3), 295–304.

Super, D. E. (1983). The history and development of vocational psychology: A personal perspective. In W. B. Walsh & S. H. Osipow (Eds.), *Handbook of vocational psychology* (Vol. 1, pp. 5–37). Hillsdale, NJ: Erlbaum.

Swanson, J. L. (1992). Rejoinder: In search of structural validity. *Journal of Vocational Behavior, 40,* 229–238.

Swanson, J. L. (1995). The process and outcome of career counseling. In W. B. Walsh & S. H. Osipow (Eds.), *Handbook of vocational psychology* (2d ed., pp. 217–259). Hillsdale, NJ: Erlbaum.

Swanson, J. L., & Bowman, S. (1994). Career assessment with African-American clients. *Journal of Career Assessment, 2,* 210–225.

Whiteley, J. M. (1984). A historical perspective on the development of counseling psychology as a profession. In S. D. Brown & R. W. Lent (Eds.), *Handbook of counseling psychology* (pp. 3–55). New York: Wiley.

Williamson, E. G. (1939). *How to counsel students: A manual of techniques for clinical counselors.* New York: McGraw-Hill.

Williamson, E. G. (1965a). *Vocational counseling.* New York: McGraw-Hill.

Williamson, E. G. (1965b). Vocational counseling: Trait-factor theory. In B. Stefflre (Ed.), *Theories of counseling* (pp. 193–214). New York: McGraw-Hill.

Williamson, E. G., & Biggs, D. A. (1979). Trait-and-factor theory and individual differences. In H. M. Burks, Jr., & B. Stefflre (Eds.), *Theories of counseling* (3d ed., pp. 91–131). New York: McGraw-Hill.

Williamson, E. G., & Bordin, E. S. (1941). A statistical evaluation of clinical counseling. *Educational and Psychological Measurement, 1,* 117–132.

Williamson, E. G., & Darley, J. G. (1937). *Student personnel work.* New York: McGraw-Hill.

Yost, E. B., & Corbishley, M. A. (1987). *Career counseling: A psychological approach.* San Francisco: Jossey-Bass.

Zytowski, D. G., & Borgen, F. H. (1983). Assessment. In W. B. Walsh & S. H. Osipow (Eds.), *Handbook of vocational psychology* (Vol. 2, pp. 5–40). Hillsdale, NJ: Erlbaum.

Zytowski, D. G., & Swanson, J. L. (1994). Parsons' contribution to career assessment. *Journal of Career Development, 20,* 305–310.

CHAPTER EIGHT

The Person Focus in Career Theory and Practice

Ellen B. Lent
University of Maryland, College Park

HOW DOES ANY theoretical formulation contribute to wise practice? A theoretical formulation can offer a better lens through which to view the phenomenon in question as well as provide understandable, testable hypotheses. It can also suggest methods for assessing the theory's utility and it can offer a framework for systematic application. How does wise practice inform theory development? It informs it by providing data for assessing the theory's utility, enhancing understanding of single samples of a multiple reality, producing information to refine and revise theoretical propositions, and testing axioms and hypotheses in vivo. Both theory and practice contribute to advancing the field by producing *practice knowledge*, earned by theoreticians, practitioners, and researchers in their work.

Our challenge is continuing development of practice knowledge in the career counseling arena, without which separations between practice and knowledge remain. There must be new ways for theory and practice to inform one another. Attention must be paid to changing paradigms and alternate ways of knowing that affect study and practice.

When theory and practice do not mingle, the science, the scientists, the intervention specialists, and the targets of scientific intervention all suffer. The tendency to "go with what we know" must be countered by embracing new knowledge and new theories that can enrich our work. The sheer challenge of gathering new data and reporting new observations is tremendous; projects such as this handbook attempt to distill recent developments and make change easier for vocational and career specialists to contemplate.

This chapter addresses the topic of person-centered theory and practice, focusing on career issues. I will describe the major tenets of person-centered theory and its application in the career domain. I will also explore current confusion about defining career theory and applying it to practice. Next, I will evaluate a case study from three different theoretical perspectives, showing the added value of a person-centered conceptualization. Then, I will discuss the usefulness and applicability of person-centered theory more broadly in the context of career research and theory; arguing that person-centered theory is the most effective stance from which to conceptualize career issues. Finally, I will outline implications for both practice and science, with an eye toward the changing nature of clients and the science-practice environment.

PERSON-CENTERED APPROACH

As explicated by Rogers and colleagues (Raskin & Rogers, 1989; Rogers, 1942, 1961, 1979), as well as by others (Boy & Pine, 1990; Bozarth & Fisher, 1990; Patterson, 1974), the person-centered view of personality change through psychotherapy has as its ultimate goal the self-actualization of the individual. Self-actualization represents the fullest expression of the individual's potential and capacities, separate from social expectations or culture-bound definitions of normality (Patterson, 1974). The individual's inherent desire to live in relation to others is acknowledged so that the intrapersonal and the interpersonal coexist as frameworks for growth. The dynamic nature of self-actualization informs the view of person-centered theory; therefore, people are always in development, and there is no final point in life at which experiencing ends. Humans naturally move toward self-actualization, so Patterson concludes that it is a goal of therapy as well as a basic motive of life.

Distress, or emotional disturbance, is characterized by being deprived of emotional support by oneself and others, having one's perceptions distorted by unfilled needs, being closed to certain experiences, and lacking in self-understanding and self-acceptance. It is considered the opposite of being spontaneous, creative, independent, and compassionate (Patterson, 1974, p. 40).

Person-centered therapy provides a special arena for clients in distress to approach full functioning, or self-actualization. If clients can move toward self-actualization, they are free to pursue intermediate goals, such as making suitable career decisions. At the outset, therapists provide interpersonal conditions in which clients can perceive and move toward their goals: The conditions in-clude empathic understanding, respect, and genuineness. Further, the therapist displays important behaviors such as specificity, confrontation, self-disclosure, and immediacy. (See Bozarth and Fisher, 1990, for a full discussion of these concepts.)

After the initial counseling relationship is firmly established, therapeutic movement toward client-identified goals can proceed. The presenting issues of clients may change or deepen. The therapist may offer a variety of interventions, based in a thorough awareness of the client's worldview and respectful of the client's ability to move toward a higher level of functioning. Clients retain the power to define and remediate their problems. Boy and Pine (1990) observe that in this phase, counselors must guard against an authoritarian stance in which power is not shared equally with clients.

The outcome of successful person-centered counseling includes an increasing balance between interpersonal, vocational, spiritual, and recreational activities that energize persons to reach their highest functioning. Psychological stability and an ongoing commitment to experience life fully evolve from this balance among the four therapeutic activities (Boy & Pine, 1990).

Career Application

How does the person-centered approach address career and vocational concerns? An initial answer is that, given the development of facilitative interpersonal relationships and the power to decide on appropriate interventions, clients will move closer to the ultimate goal of self-actualization and be freer to pursue intermediate career goals while overcoming external constraints to the best of their ability.

Another description of this process is offered by Bozarth and Fisher (1990):

> Person-centered career counseling is a relationship between a counselor and a client, arising from the client's career concerns, which creates a psychological climate in which the client can evolve a personal identity, decide the vocational goal that is fulfillment of that identity, determine a planned route to that goal, and implement that plan. The person-centered career counselor relates with genuineness, unconditional positive regard, and empathy; the locus of control for decisions remains with the client out of the counselor's trust in the self-actualizing tendency of the individual. The focus in person-centered career counseling is that of attitudes and beliefs that foster the natural actualizing process rather than on techniques and goals. (p. 54)

The assessment and counseling process provides a positive, low-risk environment in which clients can express with increasing freedom their hopes, needs, and perceived barriers to reaching their goals. This approach offers a holistic view of clients' concerns, minimizing assumptions about what clients need and how success will be measured.

In the process of counseling, structured assessments can play a role in assisting clients with self-understanding. For instance, Miller (1988) modified the *Adjective Checklist* (Gough, 1960) into subgroups representing the six Holland types to use with clients in exploring their values and interests. A variety of vocational card sort techniques are used in client assessment and exploration (Slaney & MacKinnon-Slaney, 1990). The *Strong Interest Inventory* (1994) is often used to introduce clients to the Holland typology and allow comparison of their interest patterns to those of other working women and men. With more impaired clients, intellectual, neuropsychological, and personality testing can provide important perspectives to aid them in setting and reaching goals.

As Watkins (1993) stated, psychological and career assessment is most correctly applied within the person-centered tradition when clients initiate it. He cited Rogers' view that testing initiated by the therapist communicates a message inimical to a person-centered approach; that is, the counselor is the expert and will choose to use tools not in the client's possession to extract information and transfer it back to the client for his or her benefit. This approach removes clients from the decision-making position necessary to advance therapeutic goals.

Person-centered career counseling seeks to support and celebrate clients' efforts to set their own goals in the area of work and career and to assist them in balancing those goals with their needs in other life theaters and roles. This process should support healthy changes in clients' behaviors, thoughts, and attitudes in the career area and, potentially, in other aspects of living.

Confusion in Definition and Application

It is important that thinkers and practitioners of every persuasion not be lured into a blurring of boundaries among types of career interventions. As Patterson (1974) has stated, there is a continuum of psychological helping relationships anchored by information giving on one end and counseling/psychotherapy on the other. *Career interventions*, according to Spokane (1991), can embrace a great variety of activities; however, it is objectionable to state that counseling theories fail career practice if they do not incorporate the entire continuum.

It is unrealistic to demand that personality and counseling theory incorporate all career interventions, including information sharing and other data-based events. Career counselors who are focusing on the client need not possess specific knowledge about career and job market issues that they pass on to their clients in the counseling process (e.g., Bozarth & Fisher, 1990). Others (e.g., Brown & Brooks, 1991; Spokane, 1991) imply that all career counselors must provide this information and be knowledgeable about specific external factors, such as job market and occupational structure information. In addition, Spokane (1991) takes person-centered theory to task for ignoring environmental and social constraints on career decision making.

These requirements are puzzling. Why is the reality of the labor market any different from the reality of substance abuse or socioeconomic status? Why must any counseling theory attend to occupational data or labor market conditions more thoroughly than any other environmental variable that affects individuals who are in distress? Counseling and personality theories are not required to help theorists or practitioners develop extensive knowledge of the 12 steps of the Alcoholics Anonymous program or methods for obtaining public assistance. It is only required that the theory accurately conceptualizes, and that the practitioner accurately understands, the client's need, addresses that need in counseling, and correctly guides the client to appropriate sources of information outside of the counseling setting.

There may be a number of external barriers facing career clients, just as is the case with clients who have other presenting issues. These challenges may be spelled out in a theory of personality development, yet it is not a fatal flaw if they are absent. Current welfare regulations provide more assistance for teenage mothers who leave their parents' home than for those who remain at home; this could be an important barrier to a client who wants and needs the emotional support of her parents. There are substance abuse prevention programs based on both spiritual and secular conceptions of recovery; this might represent an important factor in a client's choice of program and potential for positive treatment outcome. Practitioners of various theoretical schools do not look to theory for guidance in the details that such issues present.

If theories or interventions actually ignore external barriers to personality change and improvement, they deserve criticism and need revision. If, however, person-centered theorists and practitioners incorporate awareness of such barriers and make allowances for their effect on client outcome, that should be satisfactory. If one approaches career theory and practice from the perspective that the client is in no distress and is thinking and acting without blind spots or other conflicts, then information exchange and other intellectually focused interventions should be appropriate. If, however, one finds that there are unspoken issues interfering with the stated career problem, then available personality and counseling theory have plenty to offer.

If a person-centered assessment finds no indication of emotional distress, an intervention other than counseling might be appropriate. There certainly can be reasons other than emotional disturbance in which clients seeking career assistance could be in distress, including lack of education and training, discrimination, or lack of access to information.

Some career-oriented interventions risk premature diagnosis and premature slotting of clients' presumed goals into categories that are defined by the client's initial statement or addressed by specific techniques. Person-centered assessment and treatment avoids that risk by asking the client to begin defining the problem and to join with the therapist in discussing intermediate goals. If clients need information, education, or other assistance, then the counselor can point them in the appropriate direction outside of the counseling relationship. The assumption is that fully functioning clients will mobilize the information they need. If the person's perceptions are distorted by lack of self-understanding or other emotional barriers that prevent full functioning, then person-centered counseling is the appropriate intervention.

Case Study

Probably the most important contribution of person-centered theory is in the initial career assessment process. This can be illustrated with a case study. This case was originally presented by Hartung (1992) and was discussed from three different theoretical perspectives. Later, the case (Hartung, 1993) and the discussions (Lent, 1993; Niles & Usher, 1993; Powers & Griffith, 1993) appeared in the *Career Development Quarterly*. This case illustrates the possible limitations of directive, nonperson-centered approaches.

A 35-year-old single White female with an A average appealed to a community college counseling center to assist her with indecision about choosing a health-related major. She completed interest and vocational maturity testing, which showed average scores on the Holland (1985) themes of Realistic, Investigative, and Social; a very high level of career decision-making ability; and a lack of knowledge about health-related fields. She had many years of experience in clerical positions, including one in a hospital emergency room.

The case was discussed from developmental, Adlerian, and person-centered perspectives. In the developmental conceptualization, the client's issues were taken at face value, and career-based explanations and recommendations were offered. The Adlerian authors put much effort into reading between the lines, yet failed to allow the client's initial presentation to truly inform their recommendations.

A *directive* intervention approach that emphasizes paper-and-pencil assessment, data gathering, and occupational information might reduce or eliminate the client's willingness to present affect-laden material. Characteristic of the directive approach is the statement in Niles and Usher's (1993) case discussion: that "an initial focus of career counseling with her must arouse her interest in career planning" (p. 65). This statement represents the view that the counselor knows best what the client needs. This approach might signal to the client that she is not in charge of the intervention and could lead to premature termination or some other treatment failure.

It also ignores the discrepancy between the client's stated problem and her presentation during the interview and assessment, perhaps because developmental career practice does not dictate specific evaluation for distorted perceptions or other subtle indicators of emotional distress.

For different reasons, the Adlerian interpretation of this case misses the hidden issue (Powers & Griffith, 1993). There is an assumption of normative social reasons for individual reactions present here that muffles the uniqueness of the client's presentation and misses the opportunity to search for explanations of discrepant impressions in the initial presentation. For instance, the authors interpret her fear that male partners would hurry her into sexual contact as a reaction to her father's presumed aggressiveness in this arena with her mother.

The person-centered approach (Lent, 1993) identified puzzling inconsistencies in the initial presentation and recommended open-ended follow-up assessment to rule out a "traumatic or invasive experience related to sexuality" (p. 68). As it turned out, this client had recently survived a rape and had not presented this information in the intake, allowing it to surface much later in the course of treatment (Hartung, personal communication, 1992). This traumatic event had a significant effect on the client's approach to career issues, something that was missed by the other two case discussions. After this information surfaced, the client developed more awareness and was less constricted; she was better able to mobilize her resources and began moving toward completion of a degree in a health-related field.

THE MERITS OF THE PERSON-CENTERED APPROACH

If the initial assessment approach to the career client were the same as to any other— that is, a respectful attempt to see the world the way the client sees it—the chances for successful outcomes might increase. Such an approach helps avoid the "temptations of power and certainty" (Amundson, Stewart, & Valentine, 1993) that can lead to client dissatisfaction and premature termination. It requires the therapist to address the client as a unique individual and express immediate reactions to the client's presentation, using confrontation and self-disclosure.

It is proposed that a two-tiered approach to career problems, based in person-centered theory, should occur:

- First, complete a person-centered intake to gather information and to screen for discrepancies and other indications of distress. Extend the assessment phase for clients who present such indications.

- Second, refer unambiguous information seekers to career guidance technologies, classes, or workshops, and others to individual or group counseling, based on the outcome of the assessment. Using Patterson's (1974) continuum of psychological helping relationships, the client may fit into the information-giving location, which is highly cognitive, or the counseling/psychotherapy location, which is highly affective, or the client might require a combination of interventions.

Career technologies or interventions are analogous to Alcoholics Anonymous: They are aids or programs to which clients can be referred for psychoeducational and self-enhancement reasons. They are located closer to the information end of the helping continuum.

As noted in Spokane (1991), dropout from group or individual career intervention occurs most often when client anxiety level is high. Clients with anxiety or other distress should be identified during assessment so that their needs can be fully met in the appropriate career intervention. It is important to observe anxiety level during assessment and treatment and to make efforts to manage the anxiety and retain the client's level of hope. This type of treatment is closer to the affective, or counseling, end of the continuum.

Oliver and Spokane (1988), summarizing their meta-analysis of career interventions, made two recommendations that are well addressed by person-centered theory and practice: First, improve diagnosis so that objectives of treatment can be accurately stated and the intervention's effectiveness can be adequately judged; and second, reduce premature terminations to keep clients in treatment long enough to achieve the best outcome possible. In the first instance, diagnosis can be improved if the assessor avoids a technique-based evaluation of the presenting concern. In the second, clients are likely to remain involved in the intervention, provided they believe that their needs have been fully understood and are being adequately addressed and that they perceive some improvement in the distress or discomfort that prompted their request for assistance.

Implications for Practice and Science in the Next Century

The contemporary issues of increasingly diverse person factors and social conditions provide an important context for the present discussion. The ongoing change to a multicultural society and workforce and its implications for career counseling is well addressed by Savickas (1993). This article indirectly makes an excellent case for the person-centered approach and its usefulness in the future of career practice.

In age, gender, disability status, sexual orientation, and ethnicity, people who seek career services will be increasingly diverse as American society proceeds toward the 21st century. Clients at different stages of self-development, with more established stereotypes, more life experience, and, possibly, more advanced levels of distress will seek services. If they are seen in college counseling settings along with younger students, counselors might be tempted to approach them in the same way as they would a younger person, risking inaccurate diagnosis and conceptualization.

If a nontraditional worker is seen in a private practice or work setting, the counselor may mistakenly approach this person as though she or he were a traditional worker, ignoring questions about how the person experiences his or her work life, whether she or he has faced discrimination, and other significant issues. For both settings, a thorough person-centered assessment, combined with a vocational history written by the client (see Spokane, 1991, for an example), should help avoid inaccurate diagnoses and recommendations.

Other concerns relating to the usefulness of career counseling that Savickas (1993) raises are also elegantly addressed by person-centered theory. Describing the waning modern zeitgeist in career intervention, Savickas suggested that up until now, the following has occurred: Career counselors have neglected relationship factors in favor of delivering information; off-the-shelf techniques have predominated over clients' self-direction; counselors have stayed in the expert role and avoided the person-in-relation role; and the person-environment fit concept has taken precedence over more individual, agentic approaches to finding meaning in work. The superordinate goal of self-actualization is well suited to all the postmodern factors cited here. It is, as Savickas would say, a "useful perspective."

Another emerging issue with implications for vocational science and practice is the cafeteria of alternate research paradigms (Hoshmand, 1989), including discovery-oriented psychotherapy research (Mahrer, 1988). Person-centered theory in the career domain can be enhanced through such research methods and can inform research through its phenomenological view of the person and the environment.

For example, Hoshmand (1989) cites two introductory steps in phenomenological research: bracketing and individual reflection. The former procedure involves identifying and then putting aside one's personal biases and assumptions about the research topic; the latter involves becoming connected to one's personal experience with the topic under study (for instance, researchers reflecting on career decisions in their own history prior to gathering data on career clients). These processes resemble efforts made in the person-centered therapy context—that is, valuing and accepting the client's unique worldview and providing appropriate affective self-disclosures. Skill development and transfer between science and practice could benefit both activities.

A second of many examples comes from discovery-oriented psychotherapy research (Mahrer, 1988). One research approach described involves discovering connections among conditions, operations, and consequences in psychotherapy. This process requires researchers to avoid specifying unitary hypotheses in advance. For instance, researchers might ask, When a therapist provides empathy and positive valuing (*condition*) and the client perceives those qualities without distortion (*operation*), what are the consequences, including greater client self-acceptance? Gathering data to answer this question relies on tapes of counseling sessions, which can then be evaluated for various consequences. Theory suggests likely outcomes but does not drive the data gathering or interpretation.

Similarly, in person-centered career counseling, expectations about the nature of career clients do not determine the initial assessment and data gathering. Career inventories are not automatically administered, and the client is first perceived as a whole person with multiple strengths and challenges.

Finally, the six innovations in career counseling described by Savickas (1993) are reviewed below and linked to concepts of person-centered theory. These innovations are currently taking place to some degree, and they are supported and enhanced by person-centered theory and practice.

No More Experts.   Therapists never were the "experts" in the person-centered perspective. They provide an accepting and genuine relationship in which clients can grow and express themselves more fully.

Enable Rather Than Fit.   The ubiquitous principle of congruence or fit, Savickas says, obstructs a view of clients as diverse and unique within a multicultural society. He suggests, and person-centered theory supports, an approach to career clients that encourages and rewards personal uniqueness. This perspective reduces the power of the job description or career path and emphasizes instead the talents and interests of the person.

Rewrite the Grand Narrative.   This refers to expanding the focus in career counseling to include nonwork activities such as family and social life, spirituality, and leisure pursuits. Further, counselors will help clients determine how their work role relates to their other roles. This is already reflected in the work of many career theorists and researchers; it is directly addressed by Boy and Pine (1990).

Career Is Personal. The artificial dichotomy between career and personal coun-seling, Savickas predicts, will fade. The useful focus on how clients make meaning from all parts of their lives will drive the change, and objective descriptions of the labor market and individual interests will not crowd out more personal evaluations of one's role in the world of work. This concept is enthusiastically shared by person-centered views of personality development and change.

Career Development Theory Is Not Counseling Theory. Vocational theories, Savickas argues, do not inform counselors how to work with individual clients. He encourages counselors to search for meanings with clients that can evolve into new theories of how people construct their vocational world. Person-centered interven-tions need not be placed into a category of empty subjectivity in this regard; instead, they can be construed as the best methods for encouraging clients to create meanings relevant to career and other areas of life.

Stories Rather Than Scores. Comprehensive career counseling, according to Savickas, shifts the focus from a client's objectively obtained scores on interest or ability testing toward a phenomenological narration of the person's vocational life. Quantified comparisons to norm groups are less of interest than the person's unique view of reality and decision making. This view is consistent with the person-centered approach, because the client is empowered to define and direct his or her own treatment. The counselor attempts to assimilate the client's world and to experience it the way the client does as much as possible. This stance is necessary for the subjectivity that Savickas (1993) recommends.

So, how can person-centered theory be more useful to career practitioners? There are at least four ways: First, person-centered theory provides the strongest protec-tion against inaccurate diagnosis and incorrect application of special technologies by defining the assessment phase as crucial in understanding the client's worldview. Second, it clarifies at which point on the psychological helping continuum a particular intervention lies by separating vocational information and guidance from experiential counseling or therapy. Third, it answers the call for an emphasis on perspective taking that characterizes the diverse population that continues to request career services. Fourth, it is consistent with various methods of hypothesis testing and data gathering, so that practitioners can more comfortably take on the researcher role in their everyday work.

The person-centered approach is also consistent with a spontaneous, personal stance in psychological endeavor. Practitioners who are aware of striving for their own actualization can model openness and free functioning with their clients. Their personal efforts can inform their professional work. As Patterson (1974) states, "counselors must be more concerned about *being someone* with the client than in *doing something*" to the client (p. 116). According to Savickas (1993), we must "appreciate multiple perspectives and emphasize our relationship to each other" (p. 208). This is rooted firmly in the person-centered tradition.

CONCLUSION

Theories are valuable only when users continue to choose them to explore, test, apply, and expand their work. Practice is effective only when users incorporate new discoveries and concepts into their repertoire of application and inquiry. It is my hope that this discussion has demonstrated the benefits of the person-centered approach and will encourage theorists and practitioners to think of person-centered theory as useful—and even essential—to the future of career counseling and other interventions. The special features of the person-centered approach in supporting convergence between the scientist and the practitioner in each of us, and between career theory and practice, are noteworthy as our field develops a more holistic perspective of individuals and their career behaviors.

REFERENCES

Amundson, J., Stewart, K., & Valentine, L. (1993). Temptations of power and certainty. *Journal of Marital and Family Therapy, 19,* 111–123.

Boy, A. V., & Pine, G. J. (1990). *A person-centered foundation for counseling and psychotherapy.* Springfield, IL: Charles C. Thomas.

Bozarth, J. D., & Fisher, R. (1990). Person-centered career counseling. In W. B. Walsh & S. H. Osipow (Eds.), *Career counseling: Contemporary topics in vocational psychology* (pp. 45–78). Hillsdale, NJ: Erlbaum.

Brown, D., & Brooks, L. (1991). *Career counseling techniques.* Boston: Allyn & Bacon.

Gough, H. G. (1960). The Adjective Check List as a personality assessment research technique. *Psychological Reports, 6,* 107–122.

Hartung, P. J. (1992, April). *Settling for second best: A career counseling case.* Symposium presented at the meeting of the Great Lakes Regional Conference for Counseling Psychology, East Lansing, Michigan.

Hartung, P. J. (1993). Balancing work and love: The case of Rosie. *Career Development Quarterly, 42,* 56–60.

Holland, J. L. (1985). *Making vocational choices: A theory of vocational personalities and work environments* (2d ed.). Englewood Cliffs, NJ: Prentice Hall.

Hoshmand, L. T. (1989). Alternate research paradigms: A review and teaching proposal. *The Counseling Psychologist, 17,* 3–79.

Lent, E. B. (1993). Reading between the lines. *Career Development Quarterly, 42,* 66–69.

Mahrer, A. R. (1988). Discovery-oriented psychotherapy research: Rationale, aims, and methods. *American Psychologist, 43,* 694–702.

Miller, M. J. (1988). A client-centered career counseling assessment method. *Person-Centered Review, 3,* 195–212.

Niles, S. G., & Usher, C. H. (1993). Applying the C-DAC model. *Career Development Quarterly, 42,* 61–66.

Oliver, L. W., & Spokane, A. R. (1988). Career-intervention outcome: What contributes to client gain? *Journal of Counseling Psychology, 35,* 447–462.

Patterson, C. H. (1974). *Relationship counseling and psychotherapy.* New York: Harper & Row.

Powers, R. L., & Griffith, J. (1993). An Adlerian response. *Career Development Quarterly, 42,* 69–75.

Raskin, N. J., & Rogers, C. R. (1989). Person-centered therapy. In R. J. Corsini & D. Wedding (Eds.), *Current psychotherapies* (pp. 155–194). Itasca, MN: F. E. Peacock.

Rogers, C. R. (1942). *Counseling and psychotherapy.* Boston: Houghton Mifflin.

Rogers, C. R. (1961). *On becoming a person.* Boston: Houghton Mifflin.

Rogers, C. R. (1979). *Client-centered therapy.* Boston: Houghton Mifflin.

Rogers, C. R. (1986). Client-centered approach to therapy. In I. L. Kutash & A. Wolf (Eds.), *Psychotherapist's casebook: Theory and technique in practice* (pp. 2–15). San Francisco: Jossey-Bass.

Savickas, M. L. (1991). The meaning of work and love: Career issues and interventions. *Career Development Quarterly, 39,* 317–324.

Savickas, M. L. (1993). Career counseling in the postmodern era. *Journal of Cognitive Psychotherapy, 7,* 205–215.

Slaney, R. B., & MacKinnon-Slaney, F. (1990). The use of vocational card sorts in career counseling. In C. E. Watkins, Jr., & V. L. Campbell (Eds.), *Testing in counseling practice* (pp. 317–371). Hillsdale, NJ: Erlbaum.

Spokane, A. R. (1991). *Career intervention.* Englewood Cliffs, NJ: Prentice Hall.

Strong Interest Inventory. (1994). Palo Alto, CA: Consulting Psychologists Press.

Watkins, C. E., Jr. (1993). Person-centered theory and the contemporary practice of psychological testing. *Counselling Psychology Quarterly, 6,* 59–67.

CHAPTER NINE

Linking Theory with Practice

A Sociocognitive Interactional Model for Career Counseling

Judy M. Chartrand
Virginia Commonwealth University

A SIMPLE QUESTION can be a lightning rod that draws strong reactions, engenders reflection, and leads to new insights. Eysenck's blunt affront to the practice of psychotherapy was a provocative question, which spurred research and acted as an important conduit for progress. The same function is served by the question of whether we need separate theories to explain career development and career counseling. This question is a common thread that runs through lively discussions on personal versus career counseling (e.g., Hackett, 1993; Subich, 1993) and the gap between science and practice. In this chapter, I respond to this pivotal question by briefly noting the different purposes served by theories of career development and models for career counseling. Then I present an example of theory-practice transaction using a social cognitive framework.

THEORIES AND MODELS

A theory can be differentiated from a model. The former is a heuristic, judged by the canons of science, that typically explains an unfolding process, whereas the latter is a descriptive guide, often for change, and is judged by pragmatic outcomes. The purpose of vocational theories is to explain human behavior, including career development and adjustment, ideally within a socioeconomic context. The major vocational theories differ in terms of abstraction (molecular to molar), foci across developmental time line (Dawis, 1994), and, in some cases, epistemic assumptions.

In general, the major theories (Dawis & Lofquist, 1984; Gottfredson, 1981; Holland, 1985; Krumboltz, Mitchell, & Jones, 1976; Super, 1990) have done a fairly good job of mapping out theoretic networks that explain vocational behavior (cf. Borgen, 1991; Hackett & Lent, 1992). However, these theories do not answer many of the questions that arise in counseling practice, nor were they intended for that purpose. Theories of career development were not developed to address how clients view their problems or how they view counseling. They do not explain timing and intensity of interventions, emotional and cognitive reactions clients have to their career problems, interpersonal dynamics between counselor and client, and the unique benefits of different intervention modalities.

In addition to different purposes, theories and models use different language. All of the major vocational theories have been tested and evaluated from a logical positivist paradigm using criteria such as quality of operational definition, testability, and generalizability. Although these criteria are vital, translating them into practice can leave practitioners at a loss for how to deal with specific clients. The scientific goal of explaining behavior is sometimes several steps removed from the applied goal of changing behavior. In practice, counselors seek to address specific client problems, whereas, with theory, they seek to explain universal behavior. The point of interest can be very different. For example, in positivist-driven research, an individual might be an outlier—a statistical deviate—and that is of no major concern in theory development. In counseling practice, that individual might be the client.

The purpose of career counseling models is to describe activities and processes used to assist people in their career development and/or to resolve their career difficulties. Applied researchers, practitioners, and clients use pragmatic standards to evaluate models of career counseling, with the primary criterion being effectiveness. Unfortunately, there are few available models to guide career assessment and intervention (Hackett, 1993). Of those that do exist, the best weave together knowledge of vocational theory, career interventions, and psychotherapy process (e.g., Spokane, 1991). It is evident that theories of vocational development and adjustment are critical in career counseling, but they are only one part of a career counseling model. A recent case study illustrates this point. Heppner and Hendricks (1995) presented both process and outcome results of two career clients, one identified as being career undecided and the other as career indecisive. Results indicated that career counseling was more successful for the undecided than the indecisive client, with the former reporting greater gains in career decidedness and vocational choice clarity than the latter. The undecided client found counseling moderately to greatly helpful, whereas the indecisive client found counseling to be neutral to slightly helpful. The undecided client-counselor dyad were in greater agreement on the most helpful events in counseling and counselor intent-client outcome than were the indecisive client-counselor dyad. For the indecisive counselor-client pair, changes from worst to best session all related to greater counselor attention to interpersonal aspects of the relationship. The relationship was important to both the undecided and the indecisive client, but the working alliance was stronger for the undecided client.

This case study depicts the intricacies of career counseling, including the importance of diagnostic conceptualization and interpersonal processes, in addition to an understanding of career development. Counselors do not need separate *theories* of career development and career counseling. They need to develop career counseling *models* that integrate theories of vocational development and adjustment with knowledge of counseling process. Counselors need theory-practice transaction. Subsequent sections illustrate theory-practice transaction using a social cognitive theory of career development (Lent et al., 1994) and a scheme that addresses counseling process issues. The model, which is sociocognitive and interactional, emphasizes cognitive processes yet includes cognitive-affective-behavioral sequences and interpersonal dynamics. The theory of career development is introduced first, followed by the proposed model.

SOCIAL COGNITIVE THEORY OF CAREER DEVELOPMENT

The social cognitive theory of career development (Lent et al., 1994) attempts to explain the development of career and academic interests, the career choice process, and performance outcomes. The theory is based on the assumption of triadic reciprocality (Bandura, 1986), which posits the bidirectional influence of personal attributes, environmental factors, and overt behavior. To illustrate a portion of the theory, the career/academic choice process is presented in Figure 1. The process begins with the prediction that person inputs (e.g., gender, predispositions) and contextual affordances are bicausally related and that both predict learning experiences. In turn, learning experiences predict self-efficacy and outcome expectations. These key variables sequentially predict interests, choice goals, choice actions, and performance and attainments. Contextual influences that occur at a point in time closer to the choice behavior also predict choice goals and actions and moderate the interest-choice goal and the choice goal–choice action relationship.

Essentially, the social cognitive theory of career development offers practitioners a developmental perspective that explicitly includes mechanistic constructs and both person and environmental factors. Explicit acknowledgment of person inputs and contextual affordance is particularly important because of the diversity of people and their experiences. Although the theory is recent and has not been fully tested, it rests on a solid empirical foundation, namely, social cognitive theory. It is also quite conducive to counseling because major constructs (e.g., interests) can easily be examined using popular assessment instruments. Interesting examples of how this theory can be applied in career change counseling with college educated women has been presented (Brown & Lent, 1994). The social cognitive theory of career development can be incorporated into a sociocognitive interactional career

124

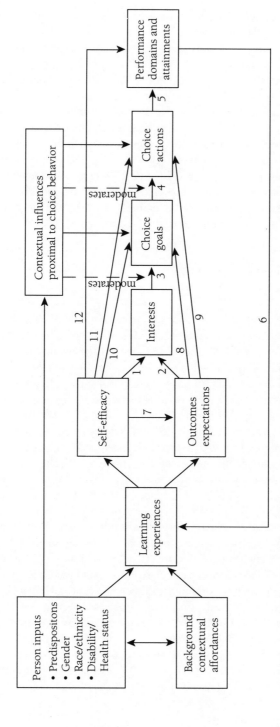

FIGURE 1   Sociocognitive Model of Person, Contextual, and Experiential Factors Affecting Career-Related Choice Behavior

counseling model that describes social cognitive and interactional processes. The social cognitive component addresses the "what to focus on" and the interactional component addresses the "how to" within a counseling context. Before presenting the model, each component is described.

Sociocognitive Component

Sociocognitive processes can be used to explain individual differences in readiness to process and use information gained in counseling. They represent the framework for accessing content in career counseling, and, as such, several underlying assumptions need to be introduced. One assumption is that sociocognitive processes are hierarchically structured. Core cognitive constructs, or metacognitions, are tacit organizational principles that are central to cognitive organization, and they contain beliefs that pertain to a fundamental sense of self. Core constructs are useful for understanding thematic unity among thoughts, feelings, and behavior (Kelley 1955; Mahoney, 1982; Meichenbaum & Gilmore, 1984). A second assumption is that core constructs shape lower-level or peripheral constructs. A related assumption is that peripheral cognitive constructs are less central to self and can be modified without serious modification of core constructs. In contrast, efforts to change core constructs often result in anxiety and, therefore, efforts to reduce anxiety (Safran, Vallis, Segal, & Shaw, 1986).

These assumptions have direct implications for counseling practice. In career counseling, it is important to understand clients' core and peripheral construct systems and to assess both levels. In addition, intervening at a peripheral construct level will not result in long-lasting effects if peripheral beliefs diverge from core beliefs. Career-relevant cognitions may involve core cognitions, peripheral cognitions, or both. In career counseling, a conceptual model that includes both tiers is useful so that counselors can ascertain whether career cognitions are core or peripheral. The potential distinction between *metacognitions,* which are core constructs that pertain to a fundamental sense of self, and *career-specific cognitions,* which may include peripheral or core cognitions, is illustrated in Figure 2. This conceptual model draws heavily from therapy-oriented cognitive (e.g., Safran et al., 1986) and social problem-solving models (Nezu & D'Zurilla, 1989) and attempts to integrate these models with a social cognitive theory of career development (Lent et al., 1994). The proposed model includes interlinked metacognitive-affective–behavioral response styles that represent the interactive relation among thought, feeling, and behavior patterns. This set can be thought of as orienting responses that include general and relatively stable reactions and responses that are based on past development and reinforcement history (Nezu & D'Zurilla, 1989).

Although metacognitive content will be unique for each individual, certain cognitive themes, affective reactions, and behavioral response modes are common. Themes of love and competence underlie many dysfunctional beliefs. Individuals who base their self-worth on love and respect from others tend to be interpersonally

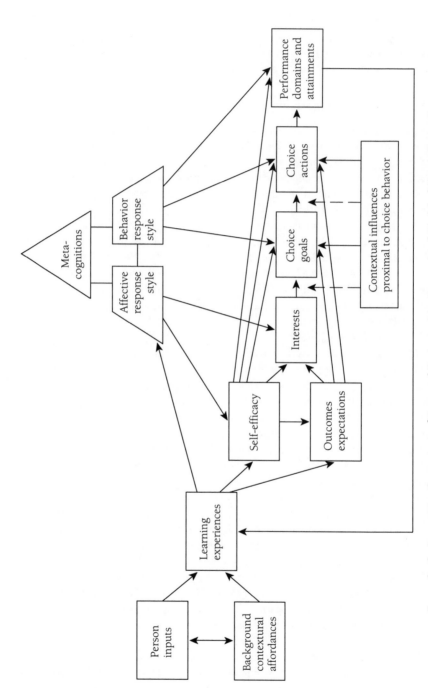

FIGURE 2   Sociocognitive Component of Proposed Sociocognitive Interactional Model of Career Counseling

Note. Broken arrows illustrate the impact of moderation.

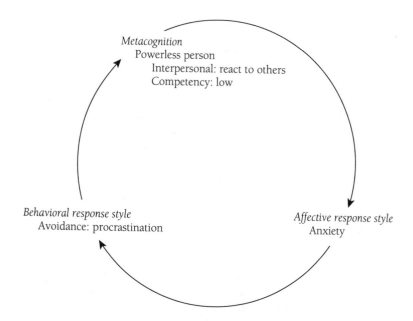

Metacognition
Powerless person
Interpersonal: react to others
Competency: low

Behavioral response style
Avoidance: procrastination

Affective response style
Anxiety

FIGURE 3   Metacognitive-Affective-Behavioral Response Styles:
An Example of an Interactive Cycle

oriented, and those who base their self-worth on competence tend to be achievement oriented (Safran et al., 1986). With respect to behavioral style, approach-avoidance tendencies represent a major dimension for differentiating problem-solving responses (D'Zurilla & Nezu, 1990). Finally, with respect to affective style, positive and negative affectivity are two primary affective dimensions, with depression representing low positive affectivity and anxiety representing high negative affectivity (Watson & Tellegen, 1985). These categories offer one possible framework for organizing assessments of metacognitive-affective-behavioral response styles.

The metacognitive-affective-behavioral response styles are not simply structures but can also be conceived in terms of an interactive cycle. A client example is used in Figure 3 to depict one possible sequence, cognitive-affective-behavioral. This client sought career counseling because her job was being phased out and she wanted a new career, but she was having difficulty developing and executing career plans. She frequently looked to others for affirmation and perceived herself as having little competence, which collectively suggested self-perceptions of being impotent. At a metacognitive level, she thought of herself as powerless when faced with choices or problems, and this view fed into an anxious response style. In turn, her anxiety contributed to an avoidant and procrastinating response pattern, which, ultimately, reinforced her perceptions of herself as powerless.

Interactional Component

Interpersonal factors, such as a client's interpersonal style and counselor-client interactions, are critical in career counseling. Yet, interpersonal functioning has been a neglected area in career assessment literature, relative to interests, values, and abilities (Chartrand & Bertok, 1993). There are several reasons for paying closer attention to interpersonal style in the career development and counseling literatures. First, interpersonal functioning is becoming more important in successful work adjustment as the workplace increasingly emphasizes working in teams and success through cooperation (Savickas, 1993). In this instance, interpersonal functioning refers to individual interactional style. A second reason for focusing on interpersonal functioning is that the interpersonal process is a key ingredient in effective treatment (Gelso & Carter, 1994) and in successful career counseling (e.g., Heppner & Hendricks, 1995). In this instance, interpersonal functioning refers to dynamic interactions between counselor and client. In the previous example, the client was interpersonally passive, and her style inhibited her efforts to negotiate a job faze out and initiate job interviews. Essentially, it affected her career development. In counseling, she was also deferential, and her style shaped counselor-client interactions and the counseling process. To maintain an assertive balance within the relationship, the counselor responded with a supportive yet relatively nondirective style.

An assumption in this proposed sociocognitive interactional model is that cognitive mediation occurs between counselor intent and client reaction to intervention (Martin, 1987). Maintaining correspondence between counselor-client behaviors and cognitions is important for successful therapy. Therefore, counselors need to understand clients' cognitive mediation processes and respond accordingly. Counselors' interpersonal awareness—monitoring subtle shifts in communication via personal reactions and observing nonverbal behaviors—facilitates this process. It is important to remember that the process of confronting and challenging core beliefs generates anxiety. A career counselor's intent might be to provide career information that is related to the client's goals for counseling. However, if this information challenges core cognitions, it is likely to create anxiety and not be processed (Safran, 1984). In this situation, counselor intention and client reaction are too divergent, and adjustments are needed to move to an optimal range of correspondence. Adjustments are likely to involve counselor movement toward client reactions. Thus, the counselor may want to respond to the client's anxiety. From an interactional perspective, the essence of good counseling is being aware of and responsive to clients' core cognitive, affective, and behavioral reactions.

A SOCIOCOGNITIVE INTERACTIONAL COUNSELING MODEL

The beginning phases of counseling typically involve the counselor gathering information and developing rapport. Then the counselor helps the client; or, in a group format, clients frame (organize) or reframe vocational self-concept and/or identify obstacles to career development. The third phase involves client information synthesis, implementation actions, and termination activities (Spokane, 1991). The interpersonal process between counselor and client(s) is likely to change over phases of counseling (Strong, Walsh, Corcoran, & Hoyt, 1992; Tracey, 1993). Career counseling tends to be goal directed, and the interpersonal process is likely to change as the goals of counseling change. The proposed model components and processes are described using a case study and an assessment and intervention framework.

Assessment

In career counseling (e.g., Kirschner, Hoffman, & Hill, 1994), counselor information gathering and support are used to foster relationship building and problem assessment. In the beginning phase of counseling, information gathering involves assessment of metacognitive-affective-behavioral response styles, in addition to standard career information (e.g., work history). It is necessary to engage in vertical and horizontal exploration of cognitive processes to determine core cognitive processes and related affective and behavioral response styles. This can be accomplished by assessing automatic thoughts and dysfunctional beliefs.

A case example of a college student who sought career counseling provides a concrete example of sociocognitive assessment. Cheryl, a college junior, came to a counseling center because of career indecision. She was a premed major yet reported ambivalence about a career in medicine. Her academic records indicated that she was an excellent student who had the ability to pursue any career. Horizontal exploration of her cognitions suggested that she saw herself as competent and capable across situations, especially within the academic and career areas. She enjoyed science and thought that becoming a physician offered many benefits. The family domain elicited "hot" cognitions. When talking about career and family plans, she emphasized that she wanted it to be different from her family of origin. Her father, who was a physician, was often absent, and she remembered that when he was at home, he was pushing achievement and had a controlling style. In general, her affective style was modulated, and she typically approached problems in a direct fashion.

A shift to a vertical exploration of her cognitions suggested the following metacognitions. If she moved into medicine, which she enjoyed, she would be like her father—hard driving, domineering, controlling, and unavailable to her family. This belief, which she had not previously articulated, was negative and inconsistent with her fundamental self-view. When she began to think about being a physician, she was aware of mild dysphoria and reported a lack of enthusiasm for her classes but could not identify the reason for her dissatisfaction. Although she continued to do well in the classroom, she missed a registration deadline because she was un sure about her career goals, which is what prompted her to seek counseling. A diagram of the sociocognitive component of the model using

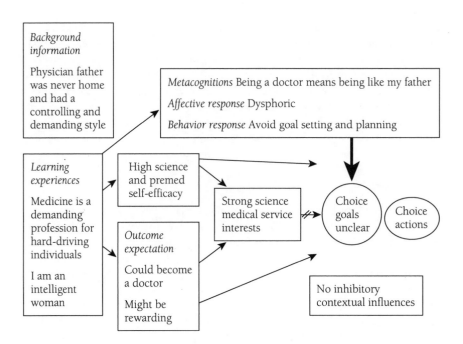

FIGURE 4   Sociocognitive Component of the Sociocognitive Interactional Model
for Career Counseling: A Case Example

the interview and psychometric information provided by Cheryl is presented in
Figure 4.

Intervention

The middle phase of counseling often involves developing a vocational schema or
identifying obstacles to career development (Spokane, 1991). The goal is to help the
client acquire new information or change existing attitudes; however, discrepancies
between counselor intentions and client reactions may arise as the counselor and
client move toward change (Strong et al., 1992). Counselor intentions are likely to
focus on feelings, insight, or challenges to facilitate change (Kirschner, Hoffman, &
Hill, 1994). The optimal intensity and content of counselor intentions for particular
clients can be anticipated from assessing their metacognitive structure. For some
clients, it is necessary to move back and forth between career cognitions and
metacognitive-affective-behavioral responses (see Figure 4).

During the initial part of the intervention phase, Cheryl was able to identify her
desire for a professional career and a family. Her interests suggested that she was

similar to people in the medical field, and her self-efficacy in this area was quite high. She saw no apparent external barriers to a career in medicine.

However, in the face of accumulating self-report information that she would fit into the medical field, she remained undecided about her career goals. The intervention then shifted to an articulation of her metacognitions, the metacognitive-affective-behavioral response cycle, and how these related to her difficulty in determining her career goals. By discussing her ambivalence—on the one hand, liking the medical field, but on the other, being afraid of becoming like her father—she was able to identify her metacognitions and become aware of her metacognitive-affective-behavioral response cycle. Acquiring an understanding of this sequence involved several adjustments in the interpersonal process. An excerpt from a session, presented below, illustrates how the counselor had to move from dealing with peripheral career cognitions to working at a metacognitive level. Initial attempts to provide career information were not successful and required an assessment of the client's cognitive mediation (i.e., what she had processed). The career information proved to be peripheral to the client's metacognitive belief that she didn't want to be like her father. Once this belief was identified, she began to describe her affective and behavioral response pattern. By the end of counseling (10 sessions), Cheryl reported renewed interest in her science classes and comfort with her decision to apply to medical school. Following is a dialogue illustrating the interactional process during cognitive intervention. Intentions and reactions occurring during the dialogue appear in parentheses:

Not all physicians are like your father. You could have a very different lifestyle.
(Change attitudes about lifestyle of physician; provide career information).

Yeah, that's true. (Client looks away.)

You agreed with me, but I noticed that you looked away. I was wondering about your reaction to what I said.
(Assess cognitive mediation [what client had processed].)

Well, it makes sense, but he was never home and I'm afraid that would happen to me. I don't want to be like that.
(Client had not processed information because career information was peripheral and inconsistent with metacognition about self as a physician [i.e., don't be like Dad].)

So, every time you think about going to med school you think, I'm going to be just like my Dad—not there for my family—and I don't want to be like him.
(Identify and focus on metacognition.)

Yeah, it's depressing. I don't want that life. I don't know, I still study and do well, but it becomes a chore.
(Client begins to express affective-behavioral response cycle. Her ambitions frighten her.)

SUMMARY

The question of whether we need separate theories of career counseling and development has been refocused to whether we need to integrate career theory and practice. A qualified answer to this question is yes, in a complementary fashion. Theories of career development and adjustment are created to explain vocational behavior and models of career counseling are created to guide practice. Each serves a very different purpose, and consolidation would ignore this critical difference. A more viable option is the development of career counseling models that incorporate and complement theories of career development.

The proposed sociocognitive interactional model is an initial effort to complement a social cognitive theory of career development. The sociocognitive component addresses the counseling content, and the interpersonal component addresses interpersonal functioning, both in terms of individual style and the dynamic counseling process. Metacognitive-affective-response styles and sequences are used to understand clients' reactions to career problems. Intervention involves identifying and challenging these response cycles in relation to the career problem. Cognitive mediation is viewed as a key mechanism for understanding client reactions to counselor interventions. Interpersonal cues are used to determine when to access client cognitive mediation processes and how to maintain correspondence between counselor intention and client reactions.

Ideally, the sociocognitive interactional model will stimulate further thought and refinements and encourage counseling process and outcome research. After 40-plus years of vocational research, we have several venerable theories of career development and adjustment and a new theory that holds hope for advancement. We also have a good sense of the overall effectiveness of career interventions (Oliver & Spokane, 1988). Unfortunately, we know relatively little about the career counseling process, and there are few models to guide research efforts. One hopes these limitations in our knowledge base will be short lived and the question of whether we need separate theories of career development and career counseling will become dated. Theory-practice transaction is a promising answer to the convergence question.

REFERENCES

Bandura, A. (1986). *Social foundations of thought and action: A social cognitive theory*. Englewood Cliffs, NJ: Prentice Hall.

Borgen, F. H. (1991). Megatrends and milestones in vocational behavior: A 20-year counseling psychology retrospective. *Journal of Vocational Behavior, 39,* 263–290.

Brown, S. D., & Lent, R. W. (1994). A sociocognitive framework for understanding and promoting career development. In M. V. Abreu, E. R. Santos, & M. P. Paixao (Eds.), *Counseling theory, research, and practice*. Coimbra, Portugal: Luso-American Foundation for Development and Cooperation.

Chartrand, J. M., & Bertok, R .L. (1993). The evolution of trait-and-factor career counseling: A person-environment fit approach. *Journal of Career Assessment, 1,* 323–340.

Dawis, R. V. (1994). The theory of work adjustment as convergence theory. In M. L. Savickas & R. W. Lent (Eds.), *Convergence in career development theories: Implications for science and practice* (pp. 33–44). Palo Alto, CA: Davies-Black Publishing.

Dawis, R. V., & Lofquist, L. (1984). *A psychological theory of work adjustment.* Minneapolis: University of Minnesota Press.

D'Zurilla, T. J., & Nezu, A. M. (1990). Development and preliminary evaluation of the Social Problem-Solving Inventory. *Psychological Assessment, 2,* 156–163.

Gelso, C. J., & Carter, J. A. (1994). Components of the psychotherapy relationship: Their interaction and unfolding during treatment. *Journal of Counseling Psychology, 41,* 296–306.

Gottfredson, L. (1981). Circumscription and compromise: A developmental theory of occupational aspirations. *Journal of Counseling Psychology, 28,* 545–579.

Hackett, G. (1993). Career counseling and psychotherapy: False dichotomies and recommended remedies. *Journal of Career Assessment, 1,* 105–117.

Hackett, G., & Lent, R. D. (1992). Theoretical advances and current inquiry in career psychology. In S. D. Brown & R. W. Lent (Eds.), *Handbook of counseling psychology* (2d ed., pp. 419–451). New York: Wiley.

Heppner, M. J., & Hendricks, F. (1995). A process and outcome study examining career indecision and indecisiveness. *Journal of Counseling and Development, 73,* 426–437.

Holland, J. L. (1985). *Making vocational choices: A theory of vocational personalities and work environments* (2d ed.). Englewood Cliffs, NJ: Prentice Hall.

Kelley, G. A. (1955). *The psychology of personal constructs.* New York: Norton.

Kirschner, T., Hoffman, M. A., & Hill, C. E. (1994). Case study of the process and outcome of career counseling. *Journal of Counseling Psychology, 41,* 216–226.

Krumboltz, J., Mitchell, A., & Jones, G. (1976). A social learning theory of career selection. *The Counseling Psychologist, 6,* 71–81.

Lent, R. W., Brown, S. D., & Hackett, G. (1994). Toward a unifying social cognitive theory of career and academic interest, choice, and performance. *Journal of Vocational Behavior, 45,* 79–122.

Mahoney, M. J. (1982). Psychotherapy and human change processes. In *Psychotherapy research and behavior change* (Vol. 1). Washington, DC: American Psychological Association.

Martin, J. (1987). *Cognitive-instructional counseling.* Ontario, Canada: Althouse Press.

Meichenbaum, D., & Gilmore, B. (1984). The nature of unconscious processes: A cognitive-behavioral perspective. In K. S. Bowers & D. Meichenbaum (Eds.), *The unconscious reconsidered* (pp. 273–298). New York: Wiley.

Nezu, A. M., & D'Zurilla, T. J. (1989). Social problem solving and negative affective conditions. In P. Kendall & D. Watson (Eds.), *Anxiety and depression: Distinctive and overlapping features* (pp. 285–315). San Diego: Academic Press.

Oliver, L. W., & Spokane, A. R. (1988). Career counseling outcome: What contributes to client gain? *Journal of Counseling Psychology, 35,* 447–462.

Safran, J. D. (1984). Assessing the cognitive-interpersonal cycle. *Cognitive Therapy and Research, 8,* 333–348.

Safran, J. D., Vallis, T. M., Segal, Z. V., & Shaw, B. F. (1986). Assessment of core cognitive process in cognitive therapy. *Cognitive Therapy and Research, 10,* 509–526.

Savickas, M. L. (1993). Career counseling in the postmodern era. *Journal of Cognitive Psychotherapy: An International Quarterly, 7,* 205–215.

Spokane, A. R. (1991). *Career intervention.* Englewood Cliffs, NJ: Prentice-Hall.

Strong, S. R., Walsh, J. A., Corcoran, J. L., & Hoyt, W. T. (1992). Social psychology and counseling psychology: The history, products, and promise of an interface. *Journal of Counseling Psychology, 39,* 139–158.

Subich, L. (1993). How personal is career counseling? [Special issue]. *Career Development Quarterly, 42,* 129–191.

Super, D. E. (1990). A life-span, life-space approach to career development. In D. Brown, L. Brooks, & Associates (Eds.), *Career choice and development* (pp. 197–261). San Francisco: Jossey-Bass.

Tracey, T. J. (1993). An interpersonal stage model of the therapeutic process. *Journal of Counseling Psychology, 40,* 396–409.

Watson, D., & Tellegen, A. (1985). Toward a consensual structure of mood. *Psychological Bulletin, 98,* 219–235.

CHAPTER TEN

Relationships Between Developmental Career Counseling Theory and Practice

David A. Jepsen
University of Iowa

THIS CHAPTER ADDRESSES four questions about the relationship between developmental career counseling theory and practices:

- What is the nature of the relationship between career counseling theory and career counseling practice?
- How has developmental career counseling theory influenced career counseling practices?
- How have career counseling practices influenced developmental career counseling theory?
- What are the prospects for future theorizing and practices?

Although the theory-practice relationship is important to *all* career theories and related practices, I will restrict this chapter to illustrations and references from developmental theory and counseling and especially to the work of Donald E. Super. By assessing how the theory-practice relationship functions so that we can avoid misapplication and prepare for special opportunities, I hope to provide "preventive maintenance" for developmental career counseling.

Examination of theory-practice relationship requires some conceptual definitions and boundaries. Developmental theorists share common beliefs about human development that are not necessarily shared by other theorists. Developmentalist assumptions about careers have been explained thoroughly elsewhere (e.g., Beilin, 1955; Jepsen, 1990; Vondracek, Lerner, & Schulenberg, 1986); an abbreviated list of assumptions is given here: (a) Development is a self-constructive process; (b) a person's activity has both structure and function; (c) a person functions as a unified system; and (d) new subsystems of action emerge from old subsystems of action but in different forms.

Although career *development* theory essentially achieves intellectual goals, career *counseling* theory is also constructed to help achieve social values. Career development theory is constructed to explain the natural phenomena of human careers. Career counseling theory, in contrast, explains the phenomena that influence socially valued career outcomes such as success and satisfaction in work roles. Counseling theory contains proposals for *action within a specified social context,* such as the dyadic or small-group therapeutic relationship. Super's (1990) segmental models contained propositions for both a career development theory explaining careers (e.g., choice and adjustment go through stages) and counseling interventions (e.g., development can be "guided" in certain ways).

Because counseling theory invokes social as well as intellectual values, it is disseminated to a unique, socially conscious audience composed of a broad community of helping professionals. This community includes career counselors and others who perform diverse roles such as policy makers, administrators, social scientists, psychologists, teachers, and counselors of all specialties. They all share, or at least claim to share, the broadly construed value of improved quality of careers across the general population.

Career counseling *practice* addresses real-world problem solving, including the tasks of problem identification and intervention construction (Jepsen, 1984). Career counselors constitute a heterogeneous group who work in many settings. This group includes developmental career counselors who justify their work based on strong beliefs about human development. These beliefs include the following: (a) Careers unfold and change across a life span; (b) early actions affect later ones; (c) different career-related problems are experienced at different ages or stages; and (d) different interventions are appropriate at different ages or stages and for different problems. Among career counselors, developmentalists constitute a subset who practice what Super (1983) called "truly developmental counseling."

THEORY-PRACTICE RELATIONSHIP

The craft of understanding and influencing others' careers, which is the essence of "truly developmental" career counseling, presents formidable challenges to theorists and practitioners. A career, whether a particular person's career or generalizations across many careers, is a fundamentally more complex phenomenon than the people who observe it. I have adapted Hofstede's (1984) arguments about the intangible nature of constructs in the social sciences to support this assertion. Social scientists study phenomena that exhibit a higher level of complexity than do physical scientists, who have a greater likelihood of consensus among scholars (and technical practitioners) about definitions and measures of the subject matter.

Hofstede argues, based on a General Hierarchy of Systems (Von Bertalanffy, 1968), that social scientists study systems at the level called "human organizations and society," making the complexity overwhelming as compared to physics and biology. A social scientist is a member of the "person" system located on the hierarchy at a level that is less complex than his or her subject. Social scientists can never completely grasp what goes on at the level of social systems, and their individual perceptions will never be exactly the same as their colleagues', which prevents consensus on definitions and measures. As a result, social scientists employ models or analogues from simpler systems to represent more complex phenomena.

Because careers occur within human organizations and society, all career theorists are subject to the social scientists' constraints: (a) There is no such thing as complete objectivity about careers; (b) more than one view is accepted as valid; (c) because we will always be subjective, we must try to be "intersubjective" by pooling and integrating a variety of necessarily subjective perspectives from different observers; and (d) reciprocal communication among observers of careers is essential to understand and influence people's careers. My purpose is to discuss the developmental perspective on career counseling, one of the necessarily subjective viewpoints within the reciprocal communication network and the community of helping professionals.

Theory as Argument

Theory is used to persuade and influence others to adopt a particular interpretive explanation of the subject at hand. A career theory is a special form of rhetoric or argument designed to advance and defend a particular, and necessarily subjective, perspective on the human career. (My view of theory is indebted to McCloskey's [1990, 1994] application of rhetorical analysis to economic theory.) Each recorded theory, such as the early chapters in Brown and Brooks (1990), becomes a text from which readers, including career counselors, make and exchange interpretations and applications. When convergence conferences are organized, theorists attempt to arrive at intersubjective views (e.g., Savickas & Lent, 1994).

Career theories contain at least four distinctive rhetorical forms: (a) logic, (b) facts, (c) metaphors, and (d) stories, as is presumed in all rhetoric since Aristotle. The structure of an argument is expected to follow the rules of logic and often includes premises, either a priori assumptions or propositions established elsewhere, and conclusions achieved through syllogisms and other deductive methods. Facts and data are assembled and used to make inferences that strengthen the premises in the logical structure. Metaphors are used to communicate the theory through verbal, visual, and mathematical symbols as well as analogues or models. Stories are used to explain theory through narrative accounts of key events in career.

Donald E. Super (1953) advanced 10 propositions that served as the first formal argument for his own necessarily subjective perspective on the human career. The propositions are a set of conclusions rather than premises. Since the appearance of first arguments, there have been revisions (Super, 1990; Super & Bachrach, 1957), counter arguments (Holland, 1969; LoCoscio, 1964; O'Hara, 1969), rebuttals (Super, 1969), and discussions about pooling and integrating observations (Super, 1994). The latest version of the propositions appears in Super (1990).

Super used all the rhetorical forms when constructing and revising his developmental theory of careers and its application to career counseling. The quality of his logic and supporting facts is the usual basis for formal analysis and evaluation of theory texts. Super's developmental theory has been evaluated several times (Brown & Brooks, 1990; Crites, 1969; Osipow, 1983) against such criteria as logical consistency and empirical support. Facts introduced as parts of a theoretical argument, usually as premises in the overall syllogism, are evaluated against rules of evidence. Traditionally, these rules have been derived from empiricist philosophy. A frequent reference in the social sciences is Ernest Nagel's (1971) *The Structure of Science*. Recently, other voices reflecting other epistemologies have been raised in an exciting debate about what constitutes an adequate relationship between theory and data (Chow, 1993; Gergen, 1991).

Over the last 40 years, new facts have often contributed to revision of Super's theoretical arguments. Early findings from the Career Pattern Study supported his 1953 propositions that "choice and adjustment [is] a continuous process [that] may be summed up in a series of life stages" (Super, 1953, p. 189). For example, his data showed that ninth-grade boys were involved in *exploration* of occupations rather than *decisions* about them (Super, 1960). However, a longitudinal study of the same participants as adult men assessed the frequency of exploration in adulthood (Phillips, 1982a, 1982b) and resulted in a small, but significant, revision in the statement of this proposition: "A small (mini) cycle takes place in transitions from one stage to the next" (Super, 1990, p. 206). There are more particulars, of course, but suffice it to say Phillips' new facts, integrated with facts gathered by others, provided a strong counterexample to the 1953 theoretical proposition, thus challenging the logic and eventually leading to an amplified proposition.

Metaphors have a different effect than logic or facts because (a) metaphors are more easily retained in memory and (b) metaphors are able to penetrate the emotion surrounding prejudices and biases. Super's most recent theory summary (1994) includes no less than four figures, each depicting an analogue for a "segment" of his theory. The stair-step metaphor (Super, 1990; Tiedeman, 1961) is an example of a familiar drawing symbolizing both the complex concept of *stages,* as distinct discontinuous segments of an extended process, and the dramatic stage-to-stage *transitions.* The figure has undoubtedly aided in advancing the career model as a contrast to the long-standing occupational model, a contrast I will discuss later. Super also used a rainbow metaphor to represent the idea of multiple social roles enacted over the life span. His rainbow has contributed greatly to a broadened understanding of the career model and probably to the application of role theory in career counseling research and practice. These metaphors are immensely effective in communicating key concepts, yet unfortunately their literal simplicity often fails to capture the whole weight of the theoretical argument. For example, the stair steps—recently converted to ladder (Super, 1994)—represent the boundaries of stages but may overstate the abruptness in transitions, as Jepsen and Grove (1981) have shown with data representing Tiedeman's career decision stages. A series of rising and falling curves that look like a mountain range was presented as an improved, although still limited, metaphor.

Effective examples of story are used in Super's arguments to demonstrate observable manifestations of abstract ideas. The early stories (Super, 1957b) usually supported arguments explaining the nature of careers. In his recent work (Super, 1983, 1990; Super, Osborne, Walsh, Brown, & Niles, 1992), cases illustrate the unique nature of developmental career counseling. The narrative account of J. C. (Super, 1990) is especially effective because it begins and concludes with client-counselor contact rather than a chronological life history. Practicing counselors and educators are more likely to comprehend and apply theories supported by storied cases because the argument is made using familiar content. Like other forms of argument, some stories are more effective than others, a point to which I will return in the final section of this chapter.

Practitioners as Consumers

I turn now to the role of practicing career counselors, who make up one of several professional helper groups with a special interest in reading the text of career counseling theory and thus can be thought of as "consuming" theoretical arguments.[1] Counselors find ideas in theories, and, through experience informed by experimentation, shape them into intellectual tools for improving their work with clients. At a literal level, practicing counselors read articles and listen to speeches about theoretical explanations of careers and career counseling and decide which explanation is best suited to their circumstances. Career counselors are most noticeable as consumers when they purchase tangible products copyrighted by theorists, such as inventories or kits. The practitioner may find it is difficult to separate the product from the theory and thus is perceived to be consuming theory through purchasing products.

DEVELOPMENTAL THEORISTS' CONTRIBUTIONS TO PRACTICE

Developmental theorists, particularly Super, have made many notable contributions to the craft and practice of career counseling. Space limitations necessitate presentation of four only.[2] These four contributions were selected because they are

---

[1] I assume that theorists and counselors are distinguishable groups. The scientist-practitioner role championed in applied psychology specialties deliberately blurs the differences, but I interpret the hyphen as denoting a functional distinction.

linked to observable changes, sometimes evolutionary changes, in everyday career counseling practices. Three of the four were advanced in the 1950s and today seem like slogans or clichés; at the time of their introduction, they proposed significant alterations in everyday career counseling practice.

The career model. Super (1953) proposed the idea that occupational choice was a lengthy process and challenged the accepted view that career counseling should focus on the single act of choosing an occupation. This complex concept, called *the career model* as opposed to the dominant *occupational model* of the time (Super, 1957a, 1961), was Super's major contribution to career counseling practice (Jepsen, 1994; Phillips & Blustein, 1994). Several observations probably led Super to state a proposition that emphasized process: data about frequent changes in choices, most obviously during adolescence, and reasoning (logic) that other related psychological functions—for example, cognitive processes—developed over the first 18 to 21 years of life.[3]

Super's proposition called for modifications in assessment practices. Career assessments gradually changed focus from trait psychographs to career patterns, that is, graphs of activities over time (Super, 1954b) and estimates of contemporary career maturity illustrated by Super and Overstreet (1960). Developmental counselors focus on clients' histories of performances, preferences, reasons for preferences, and the exploratory experiences associated with competing preferences. Counselor interpretations of assessment data changed from a function analogous to actuaries to a function similar to historians or biographers. Super advocated supplementing the practice of interpreting clients' traits and making probabilistic predictions by applying an historical-developmental analysis for recurring themes and underlying trends and then projecting the themes/trends into the future by extrapolation. This perspective contributed to dramatic changes in career counseling actions.

Career stages. The traditional temporal portrait of career in the first half of this century visualized a dichotomous change from a child's nonworking activity to an adult's working activity—his or her occupied time or occupation. The counselor intervened at the point of choice, that is, at the point the individual was choosing the particular occupation. Other choices were essentially matters of changing jobs within an occupation or, occasionally, changing occupations. Super's (1953) developmental theory included the proposition that the process of choice and adjustment was continuous and "may be summed up in a series of life stages." His argument was based on the work of Charlotte Buehler (1933), who observed that

---

[2]The interested reader should consult the Festschrift issue honoring Super's work in the September 1994 issue of the *Career Development Quarterly*. It contains eight articles, each analyzing a concept from his theory—for example, work values, self-concept, and career patterns—and contemporary applications to career counseling.

[3]A logical extension of this developmental process argument, since modified, was Crites' (1974) hypothesis that choice processes are a monotonic function of age.

the life span is divisible into five stages depicting qualitatively different activities dominating each stage.[4] Super (1953) also postulated that development through the life stages can be guided and proposed two broad strategies: facilitating maturation of abilities and interests and aiding in reality testing.

The idea of life stages has different meaning for different career theorists (Jepsen, 1974). Nonetheless, it has affected practices by cautioning against the oversimplification of assisting children and youth by treating them as miniature adults seeking entry into occupations. School guidance programs have begun to encourage students to explore several occupations rather than to converge on a few alternatives. The National Occupational Information Coordinating Committee (NOICC) National Guidelines for Career Development (NOICC, undated), which suggest different career development goals for children, adolescents, and adults, is a widely disseminated contemporary application of a developmental concept championed by Super.

Self-concept. During the first half of the century, careers were often viewed from the perspective of the social system, for example, the nation or the organization. Assisting people with choices was considered part of the solution to national and societal problems, such as integrating immigrants and youth into the job market or transforming World War I and World War II civilian inductees into an effective military force and later reintegrating discharged military personnel (many of whom were coping with disabling injuries) into the postwar civilian workforce. Indeed, some of the most popular career counseling tools, such as differential aptitude tests and courses on occupational requirements and trends, were adapted from national programs for selection and allocation. Super (1954a) called this viewpoint the *manpower view.*

Super's now-familiar proposition that the process of vocational development is essentially that of developing and implementing a self-concept (Super, 1953) challenged the accepted manpower view of career guidance and led to greater attention to the subjective, personal perspective of the chooser in the choice process. Super's writings on career counseling coincided with the rise in popularity of client-centered therapy (Rogers, 1951) and developmental school guidance (Matthewson, 1949), so simple direct effects are not suggested. Consequently, developmental career counselors encouraged clients to view themselves as actors guided by their own purposes, rather than as pawns moved about by directors from the state or the system or the economy or "the way it has always been." Counselor's interpretations focused on a person's view of him or herself and the person's perceived opportunities rather than on test-based trait views and corresponding economic descriptions of occupations.

Super suggested specific interventions to enhance self-concepts. Another of his original propositions stated that the process of compromise between self-concept

---

[4]Super retained Buehler's names for the stages, which has aggravated, among others, people aged 65 and over, who resent the portrayal of their careers as "in decline."

and reality is one of *role-playing* (Super, 1953). Many contemporary developmental counselors use some version of role-playing when clients are working on compromise processes. They help clients gather and process information through career biographies, information interviews, and other techniques designed to obtain the individual worker's perspective on occupations and employing organizations. Guided fantasy and role-playing in the counseling interview have become popular career counseling techniques (Brown & Brooks, 1991).

The job role as social role. As a developmental theorist, Super (1980) initiated the integration of social role theory into career development theory. He called attention to the idea that job roles are reciprocally related to other roles such as family (son/daughter, spouse, parent), leisure, learner (student), and citizen (community service) roles. With the notable exception of the psychodynamic theorists, career development theories at midcentury viewed jobs in isolation from other roles, and this seemed to be the accepted view in career counseling practices. The idea that a job is interrelated to other roles has illuminated and given names to persistent client problems such as role conflict, role overload, and role complementarity.

The concept of *role salience,* the relative importance people attach to roles, has been introduced to practicing counselors through the use of the career rainbow and the standardized *Saliency Inventory* (Nevill & Super, 1986). Super demonstrated how to incorporate work salience, work values, and career maturity into an assessment of readiness to make career decisions. Assessment of interrole relationships (Brown & Brooks, 1991) has become an accepted technique in developmental career counseling.

Summary

Super's arguments for a developmental perspective on the human career have, over the years, made significant contributions to career counseling practices. Some ideas from developmental theory have been absorbed into everyday practices (career as sequence of jobs), others were tried and revised (stages as patterned behaviors at fixed times), and others remain largely untried and unfinished (career patterns). Tangible evidence of influence is also found in areas of assessment that I have not elaborated here. Practicing counselors continue to consume career maturity or career development inventories, values inventories, and role-salience inventories.

Practitioner's assumption systems have also been influenced by the developmentalist viewpoint. Super's early arguments created a dynamic tension among career theorists. The dialectic about basic assumptions and beliefs has also influenced daily career counseling practices, as the following examples illustrate:

- Super's phenomenological premises led to considerations of the objective-subjective (idiographic vs. nomothetic) continuum in assessment.

- Super's arguments for including social role expectations as a force in choosing an occupation challenged the accepted view that enduring traits are the primary (or exclusive, all other things being equal) forces.

■ Super's distinction between an allocation ("manpower") perspective versus a socialization perspective directly concerned practitioners and their employers.

None of these debates are resolved—indeed, they may be reduced to instances in which "more than one view is acceptable as valid"—but the major challenges were often initiated by Super.

Developmental arguments, including those of Blocher and Seigal (1981) and Vondracek, Lerner, and Schulenberg (1986), as well as Super, have set the stage for contemporary consideration of a social construction view, as opposed to a physical reality view, of such considerations as gender, race, social class, sexual preference, and disability in career development (see Richardson's [1993] arguments). There is a great deal of theoretical work to be done on these issues.

CONTRIBUTIONS OF PRACTICE TO THEORY

The contributions of career counseling practice to career counseling theory are less obvious. I will describe two contributions and then address the question of why there are so few.

The recent emphasis in developmental career counseling on client's observable, transferable job-related skills seems to have its origins in the practice of skill identification techniques rather than theory. Crystal and Bolles' (1974) extensive discussion of skill identification rationale and procedures was born out of the necessity of providing assistance to aeronautical engineers left without jobs in the early 1970s. Skill identification practice has been refined and incorporated into a repertoire of career counseling techniques (e.g., Brown & Brooks, 1991). I was unable to identify an integration of skill identification into Super's (1953) early proposition that guided development involves facilitating the maturation of abilities and reality testing of self-concepts. A similar case could be made for the Job Club "movement" (e.g., Azrin & Besalel, 1982; Azrin, Flores, & Kaplan, 1975), which emanated from practitioners' efforts to place individuals with disabilities or who were receiving public assistance into competitive employment.[5] Although there is no direct evidence of influence on theory, especially developmental theory, both the practices of skill identification and Job Clubs have the potential to embellish Super's (1953) developmental counseling propositions about facilitating maturation of aptitudes and role-playing in real-life activities, respectively. Readers may think of other examples, but I conclude that it is difficult to find evidence of counseling theory being influenced by practice. I suspect counseling theorists could supply several tales about practitioners' suggestions.

---

[5] Job Club initially used operant conditioning but later emphasized social role-playing.

The Metaphor of Two Clubs

Because reciprocal communication among observers is critical to understanding and interventions, why is there such limited evidence of reciprocity? I shift from an historical analysis to an examination of contemporary relationships between theorists and practitioners as the source of limited reciprocal influence. I speculate that counseling theorists and practicing counselors have been organized into separate groups like separate subcultures or clubs. I'll indulge the reader in a little amateur ethnography and assemble data to make a case in support of this notion.

Career theorists are a small group because membership is restricted to those recognized for having written formal treatises explaining human careers. The small number of chapters in Brown and Brooks' (1990) compendium on theories of career choice and development gives a sense of the small numbers. The group expands from time to time to include researchers, critics, and other text readers. Before the early 1980s, career theorists formed an almost exclusively White male club. Fortunately, this has changed in recent years, but there is still ample room for expansion. Another boundary seems to be discipline; some have said it is an academic psychologist's club although that too is changing, as the *Handbook of Career Theory,* edited by Arthur, Hall, and Lawrence (1989), clearly demonstrates.

Career theorists generally share a commitment to an empirical philosophy of science and seek truth through evidence and reason. They appear to admire mid-20th-century heroes such as psychologists Paterson, Thorndike, and Terman and methodologists such as Spearman, Strong, and Guilford. They meet periodically—several times a year it seems—at conventions and conferences such as the one that inspired this handbook. They perform informal rituals by preparing papers to meet style requirements and offering criticism that follows set procedures and courtesies.

Many career counselors work in organizations devoted to everyday practice in education and human services. Others work for large organizations such as Fortune 500 companies or the federal government, including the military. Career counselor groups are loosely knit but distinguishable from other clubs of academic advisers, family therapists, job analysts, placement specialists, and so on. They are a relatively large group when taken as a whole, but membership boundaries are continually in dispute, so it is hard to determine the group's actual size.

They believe in experience as the shortest and surest avenue to understanding careers and prefer inductive approaches to understanding social systems. Their heroes come from authoritative wisdom nurtured by experience. They admire Richard Bolles and Howard Figler and counselors and personnel workers who have real-world, hands-on experiences. They also have heroes in the field of therapy such as Albert Ellis or Carl Rogers. I am amazed at how few of them recognize the achievements of the theorists' club. Their informal rituals include exchanging techniques such as paper-and-pencil instruments and kits or strategies and tactics that they find useful in working face-to-face with clients or students.

Of course, the clubhouse analogy breaks down in the details, and the generalities have exceptions. My point is simply that the two groups are separated in many ways and that, while a few people spend time with both groups, different discussions and activities occur within each group.

Language

The problems of reciprocal communication between the two clubs lie in part with the language customarily employed by each. Theorists talk about constructs, models, paradigms, propositions, theorems, hypotheses, data, predictions, error, and so on. If I called Donald Super or Fred Vondracek, our conversation would undoubtedly be sprinkled with some of these words. If I called Dan Zioberek, who works as a career counselor in our local community college, or Bonnie Malone, who is a career counselor in private practice, our conversation would include a discussion about problems, materials, information, interpretations, and the like.

The language of each club reflects their particular view of career development reality. Practitioners look at people one or two at a time; the unit of interest is the individual. The theorist looks at people in general; the unit of interest is the population. The practitioner, committed to the welfare of a client, tries to *understand* the individual. The career theorist, committed to a clearer perspective about human nature, strives for a deepened *knowledge* about the population. Career counseling theorists are committed to broadening knowledge about interventions, generalizable across people. Carl Jung's (1958) distinction between a doctor's understanding and a scientist's knowledge bears repeating:

> I can only approach the task of *understanding* [an individual human being] with a free and open mind, whereas *knowledge* of man [sic] or insight into human character, presupposes all sorts of knowledge about mankind [sic] in general. (p. 18)

Translation from theoretical language to the language of practice—changing Super's words into words that career counselors use—sometimes requires constructing definitions that fit the practitioner's experiences. A few years ago, I (Jepsen, 1989) made an attempt to translate the theoretical construct *developmental task* for a Canadian practitioner audience by inventing a new term, *intermittent powerful messages,* to describe "aspects of a general expectation to take the actions necessary to enter productive work roles" (p. 10). If the translation was successful, practitioners should be able to incorporate the language into everyday explanations. Ineffective translations of the developmental task concept used in practice abound and often contain the same words, such as *development,* or an equally abstract term, such as *maturation,* to define the theoretical construct.

Back-translations from practical to theoretical language—changing career counselors' words into those useful to the theorist—likewise require the careful selection of terms. An example comes from my 15 years as faculty supervisor of an undergraduate class in career planning intended for career-undecided college students. During that time, I had direct or indirect contact with more than 3,500 students. I listened to teaching assistants describe interactions with students, examined students' written projects, course evaluations, and surveys, observed student reactions to speakers and each other, and occasionally taught a section myself. As a result, I built a reservoir of college students' accounts about parental and peer pressures to make choices, instances of experiencing developmental tasks or intermittent powerful messages. In an attempt to capture college students' collective experiences, I invented a tale about grandma's query at a family gathering when she asked for all to hear: "What are you going to *do* when you leave the university?" Intermittent? Probably. Powerful messages? Definitely! The tale seems effective in affirming, if not specifying, the meaning of a career developmental task as experienced by college students.

Ineffective back-translation occurs when labels with a pejorative edge are used to describe client experiences. An example is the use of terms, sometimes taken from theoretical language, such as *career immaturity* or *unrealistic choices* or *floundering* to describe particular clients' behaviors—especially without proper qualifying explanations.

Rhetoric

Looking beyond the language problems, the rhetoric between theorist and practitioner is seldom symmetrical; the rhetoric of each serves different purposes and takes different forms. Theorists' arguments purport to explain systematic, generalizable career phenomena and influences on careers. Practitioners often form arguments for purposes of understanding anomalies in their caseload, trying to comprehend the puzzling client problem or unravel the reasons why their usual interventions seem ineffective for a difficult-to-understand client problem.

The two groups use contrasting rhetorical forms that may contribute to the ineffective communication. The essential elements in theorists' arguments are *logic* and *data*. For example, more than 40 years ago, Eli Ginzberg (1952) attempted to account for patterned behavioral changes over time from the nonworking child to the young adult entering an occupation. He assembled social science data available at that time into a logical format and argued for a new explanation of the phenomena he called occupational choice processes.

Practitioners, on the other hand, often use stories and metaphors to describe the problems in their work. The case reports in the *Career Development Quarterly* over the past few years offer a wide range of examples of counselors' rhetoric. Most effective published counseling cases represent anomalies or exceptions to modal career development through which the counselor-author argues for attention to a particular pattern within the career. For example, I chose the Case of Sal for the first case in the *Quarterly,* a story from my own counseling experiences (Jepsen, 1986), because Sal presented a fascinating combination of simultaneous changes in family and employment while learning new skills and strategies to cope with a handicapping condition.

Practitioners are much more likely to understand theorists when they hear stories and metaphors. For example, Super's rainbow metaphor has contributed greatly to the general understanding and the application of role theory in career counseling practice. Indeed, the metaphor was converted into a paper-and-pencil activity for clients. Super used several counseling cases (Super, 1983; Super, Osborne, Walsh, Brown, & Niles, 1992) to demonstrate applications of selected ideas from developmental theory. Because they are easily translated into symbols representing day-to-day counseling activities, these metaphors and cases constitute the arguments through which career counselors are more likely to comprehend the underlying ideas.

Less clear is how theorists incorporate the practitioner's stories and occasional metaphors into their work. Perhaps the most public examples of theory revision are in the writings of Eli Ginzberg (1972), who reversed his assumptions about the processes involved in occupational choices, and H. B. Gelatt (1962, 1989), who made dramatic changes in some important assumptions about career decision-making processes.

NEW DIRECTIONS

I have suggested that the gulf between theorists and practitioners is like a separation into two clubs. The two groups employ different languages and rhetoric forms that make mutual understandings difficult. The metaphors of clubs, language, and rhetoric not only aid in understanding the reciprocal communication necessary for progress in human services but, by extrapolation, should also assist in constructing promising new directions in the dialogue between theory and practice. Four new directions are suggested:

Convert developmental theories to a story form to facilitate applications in practice. I offer an example of such a story called "The Story of a Developing Career in a Strange Land" (see Appendix). The analogies are obvious to those who regularly study the text of developmental theory. But there is sufficient ambiguity in the story to allow unfamiliar readers to make their own connections to experience without the details of logic and data. Such stories can be validated with practicing counselors, who will undoubtedly offer modifications and elaborations. Is the plot sufficiently universal? Are the characters strong? Is the setting convincing? Their revisions will engage them in applying a theory to thinking about their day-to-day practices.

Construct more career counseling cases. Counseling theorists can follow a disciplined form approximating the system and order of developmental counseling theory. The cases should focus primarily on counseling rather than development, although the client's development will unfold through the counseling story. The case of J. C. (Super, 1990) may provide a good start. The effectiveness of the cases will be in illustrating the propositions from theory while maintaining the context of the case subject. Alternatively, theorists and practitioners can engage in career counseling demonstrations—much as we see in family therapy work—to dramatize the counseling theory. Such a proposed activity might have positive effects on both the theorist's ideas and the practicing counselor's actions.

Utilize qualitative data. Career counselors should capitalize on qualitative or naturalistic methods to collect data about their experiences to theorists. Practitioners have access to extraordinarily complex and seemingly unique data that may be more coherently presented through methods such as ethnography or narrative analysis rather than questionnaires, tests, and inventories. Reed, Patton, and Gold (1993) offer a promising example with their conversation analysis of vocational interest interpretation sessions.

Share practical goals. Career counselors should provide developmental theorists with statements about the goals and intended outcomes that accurately represent their practices. Some editing of material addressed to the practitioner's public may be needed, but theorists should benefit from practitioners' parsimonious statements about their intentions. For example, a career counselor's beliefs about careers, career problems, and solution processes should be an important reference for counseling theory revisions.

CONCLUSIONS

A theorist-practitioner dialogue is part of a communication network among necessarily subjective views about the nature of human careers and how careers can be enriched through constructive interventions. Each participant in the network has a different perspective, assumed to be valid in its own right. Therefore, discussions such as those appearing in this handbook strive for intersubjective agreement as the basis for policy and practices.

Theory, including career counseling theory, is communicated as an argument. Written theory serves as a text from which readers, including practitioners, make interpretations and applications. Developmental theorists, especially Donald Super, use all four forms of rhetoric: logic, facts, metaphors, and stories. His text was shown to have dramatically influenced career counseling practices and assumptions. Evidence is ambiguous about practitioners influencing theory text. The reciprocal communication between developmental career theory and counseling practice was likened to two clubs with different purposes, languages, and rhetoric.

A theory-practice dialogue in the service of client needs may be enriched through several proposed activities: (a) converting theoretical constructs into metaphors and theoretical propositions into story form, (b) operationalizing counseling theory through *counseling* cases, (c) using qualitative/naturalistic methods to capture counseling experiences with its many subtleties and nuances, and (d) explicating practicing counselors' statements about their intended effects. These promising activities are suggested in the spirit of making theory more useful to practice.

I leave one final thought. After thorough examination of Super's theoretical texts for a comprehensive chapter on developmental counseling (Jepsen, 1990), I concluded that Super's work, accumulated across all its segments, provides rich material rewarding a patient text interpreter with fresh insights about contemporary problems in career counseling. I encourage practitioners to partake.

REFERENCES

Arthur, M. B., Hall, D. T., & Lawrence, B. S. (1989). *Handbook of career theory*. New York: Cambridge University Press.

Azrin, N. H., & Besalel, V. (1982). *Finding a job*. Berkeley, CA: Ten Speed Press.

Azrin, N. H., Flores, T., & Kaplan, S. J. (1975). Job Finding Club: A group-assisted program for obtaining employment. *Behavior Research and Therapy, 13*, 17–27.

Beilin, H. (1955). The application of general developmental principles to the vocational area. *Journal of Counseling Psychology, 2*, 53–57.

Blocher, D. H., & Seigal, R. (1981). Toward a cognitive developmental theory of leisure and work. *The Counseling Psychologist, 9*, 33–44.

Brown, D., & Brooks, L. (Eds.). (1990). *Career choice and development*. San Francisco: Jossey-Bass.

Brown, D., & Brooks, L. (1991). *Career counseling techniques*. Boston: Allyn & Bacon.

Buehler, C. (1933). *Der menschliche Lebenslauf als psychologisches Problem [The human course of life as a psychological problem]*. Leipzig, Germany: S. Hirzel.

Chow, S. L. (1993). Acceptance of a theory: Justification or rhetoric? *Journal for the Theory of Social Behaviour, 22*, 447–474.

Crites, J. O. (1969). *Vocational psychology*. New York: McGraw-Hill.

Crystal, J. C., & Bolles, R. N. (1974). *Where do I go from here with my life?* New York: Seabury Press.

Gelatt, H. B. (1962). Decision making: A conceptual frame of reference for counseling. *Journal of Counseling Psychology, 9*, 240–245.

Gelatt, H. B. (1989). Positive uncertainty: A new decision-making framework for counseling. *Journal of Counseling Psychology, 36*, 252–256.

Gergen, K. J. (1991). Emerging challenges for theory and psychology. *Theory & Psychology, 1*, 1–13.

Ginzberg, E. (1952). Toward a theory of occupational choice. *Personnel and Guidance Journal, 30*, 491–494.

Ginzberg, E. (1972). Toward a theory of occupational choice: A restatement. *Vocational Guidance Quarterly, 20*, 169–176.

Hofstede, G. (1984). *Culture's consequences: International differences in work-related values* (Abridged ed.). Beverly Hills, CA: Sage.

Holland, J. L. (1969). A critical analysis. *The Counseling Psychologist, 1*, 15–16.

Jepsen, D. A. (1974). The stage construct in career development. *Counseling and Values, 18*, 124–131.

Jepsen, D. A. (1984). Relationship between career development theory and practice. In N. C. Gysbers (Ed.), *Designing careers: Counseling to enhance education, work, and leisure* (pp. 135–159). San Francisco: Jossey-Bass.

Jepsen, D. A. (1986). Case of Sal. *Career Development Quarterly, 35,* 69–70.

Jepsen, D. A. (1989). Antecedent events to adolescent career decision processes. *Guidance and Counseling, 4,* 5–14.

Jepsen, D. A. (1990). Developmental career counseling. In W. B. Walsh & S. H. Osipow (Eds.), *Career counseling: Contemporary topics in vocational psychology.* Hillsdale, NJ: Erlbaum.

Jepsen, D. A. (1994). The thematic-extrapolation method: Incorporating career patterns into career counseling. *Career Development Quarterly, 43,* 43–53.

Jepsen, D. A., & Grove, W. M. (1981). Stage order and dominance in adolescent decision-making processes: An empirical test of the Tiedeman-O'Hara paradigm. *Journal of Vocational Behavior, 18,* 237–251.

Jung, C. G. (1958). *The undiscovered self.* New York: Mentor.

LoCoscio, R. (1964). Delayed and impaired vocational development: A neglected aspect of vocational development theory. *Personnel and Guidance Journal, 42,* 885–887.

Matthewson, R. H. (1949). *Guidance policy and practice.* New York: Harper & Row.

McCloskey, D. N. (1990). *If you're so smart: The narrative of economic expertise.* Chicago: University of Chicago Press.

McCloskey, D. N. (1994). *Knowledge and persuasion in economics.* New York: Cambridge University Press.

Nagel, E. (1971). *The structure of science.* New York: Harcourt, Brace & World.

National Occupational Information Coordinating Committee. (Undated). *The National Career Development Guidelines.* Washington, DC: Author

Nevill, D. D., & Super, D. E. (1986). *The Salience Inventory.* Palo Alto, CA: Consulting Psychologists Press.

O'Hara, R. P. (1969). Comments on Super's papers. *The Counseling Psychologist, 1,* 29–31.

Osipow, S. H. (1983). *Theories of career development* (3d ed.). Englewood Cliffs, NJ: Prentice Hall.

Phillips, S. D. (1982a). Career exploration in adulthood. *Journal of Vocational Behavior, 20,* 129–140.

Phillips, S. D. (1982b). The development of career choices: The relationship between patterns of commitment and career outcomes in adulthood. *Journal of Vocational Behavior, 20,* 141–152.

Phillips, S. D., & Blustein, D. L. (1994). Readiness for career choices: Planning, exploring, and deciding. *Career Development Quarterly, 43,* 63–73.

Reed, J. R., Patton, M. J., & Gold, P. B. (1993). Effects of turn-taking sequences in vocational test interpretation interviews. *Journal of Counseling Psychology, 40,* 144–155.

Richardson, M. S. (1993). Work in people's lives: A location for counseling psychologists. *Journal of Counseling Psychology, 40,* 425–533.

Rogers, C. R. (1951). *Client-centered therapy: Its current practice, implications, and theory.* Boston: Houghton Mifflin.

Savickas, M. L., & Lent, R. W. (1994). *Convergence in career development theories: Implications for science and practice.* Palo Alto, CA: Davies-Black Publishing.

Super, D. E. (1953). A theory of vocational development. *American Psychologist, 8,* 185–190.

Super, D. E. (1954a). Guidance: Manpower utilization or human development? *Personnel and Guidance Journal, 33,* 8–14.

Super, D. E. (1954b). Career patterns as a basis for vocational counseling. *Journal of Counseling Psychology, 1,* 12–20.

Super, D. E. (1957a). The preliminary appraisal in vocational counseling. *Personnel and Guidance Journal, 396*, 154–161.

Super, D. E. (1957b). *The psychology of careers.* New York: Harper.

Super, D. E. (1960). The critical ninth grade: Vocational choice or vocational exploration? *Personnel and Guidance Journal, 39*, 107–109.

Super, D. E. (1961). Some unresolved issues in vocational development research. *Personnel and Guidance Journal, 40*, 11–14.

Super, D. E. (1969). Some comments on the comments. *The Counseling Psychologist, 1*, 35–36.

Super, D. E. (1980). A life-span, life-space approach to career development. *Journal of Vocational Behavior, 16*, 282–298.

Super, D. E. (1983). Assessment in career guidance: Toward truly developmental counseling. *Journal of Counseling and Development, 63*, 555–562.

Super, D. E. (1990). A life-span, life-space approach to career development. In D. Brown & L. Brooks (Eds.), *Career choice and development* (pp. 197–261). San Francisco: Jossey-Bass.

Super, D. E. (1994). A lifespan, lifespace perspective on convergence. In M. L. Savikas & R. W. Lent (Eds.), *Convergence in career development theories: Implications for science and practice.* Palo Alto, CA: Davies-Black Publishing.

Super, D. E., Osborne, W. L., Walsh, D. J., Brown. S. D., & Niles, S. G. (1992). Developmental career assessment and counseling: The C-DAC model. *Journal of Counseling and Development, 71*, 74–80.

Super, D. E., & Bachrach, P. B. (1957). *Scientific careers and vocational development theory.* New York: Teachers College Press.

Super, D. E., & Overstreet, P. L. (1960). *The vocational maturity of ninth grade boys.* New York: Teachers College Press.

Tiedeman, D. V. (1961). Decision and vocational development: A paradigm and its implications. *Personnel and Guidance Journal, 40*, 15–20.

Von Bertalanffy, L. (1968). *General system theory: Foundations, development, applications.* New York: Braziller.

Vondracek, F. W., Lerner, R. M., & Schulenberg, J. E. (1986). *Career development: A life-span developmental approach.* Hillsdale, NJ: Erlbaum.

APPENDIX: THE STORY OF A DEVELOPING CAREER IN A STRANGE LAND

Once upon a time, a child entered into a strange world seeking to share precious gifts and find something very important to do. The gifts were of two kinds: Some were brightly colored fabric patches draped over the child's body and others were seeds carried in special pouches. The patches remained with the child throughout the duration of the child's time in the strange world and all would know the bright colors.

The child carried two seed pouches, but the essence of the seeds was not apparent to either the child or the world's inhabitants. (The inhabitants of this strange world quarreled a lot about how many seeds were in each pouch and what names to give them.) The seeds grew in accordance with the nutrients added to the pouches. At first, the inhabitants allocated the nutrients, but the child soon realized where the nutrients were stored and later discovered one of the potent nutrients was labeled "education, formal."

The child periodically encountered adventures in the strange world. Some were pranks contrived by the inhabitants seemingly to test the resilience of the child; some emanated from the powerful forces of nature. The most exciting adventures occurred when the child was finding clues in the search for the important thing to do. These adventures always left memories that did not go away.

As time went on, the colorful fabric patches seemed to function like passes permitting entry to the games and rituals that engaged the inhabitants. It soon became clear to the child that the patches were connected to the important thing to do.

After many years, the child entered adolescence and began to ponder about the patches, the seeds (which now had produced vines), the memories, and finding the important thing to do. As the pondering continued, the adolescent discovered a new voice and used it to compose stories about the patches, vines, memories, and thing to do. The adolescent told versions of the story to some of the inhabitants but rarely had the opportunity to tell the whole story.

Inhabitants called "social scientists" listened to the stories but could not agree about what they were hearing. These social scientists were pleasant enough when they were alone, but they quarreled with each other about the adolescents' patches, vines, memories, and stories. One group studied the patches and made pronounce-ments about their colors and size. Another group examined the pouches, seeds, nutrients, and resulting vines and spoke out about how aspects of each were responsible for the vine's length, strength, and color. Still a third group noted the adolescent's memories and guessed about the adventures that created them. These social scientists showed little interest in the important thing to do, instead referring the protagonist's questions to another group of inhabitants called "humanists."

The adolescent, now approaching young adulthood, thought the social scientists used a lot of big words and argued a lot. Nevertheless, the young adult reluctantly left the social scientists feeling enlightened about the nature of the patches, vines, memories, and stories but still unsure about the important thing to do.

The young adult happened onto a much larger group of inhabitants in the world that still seemed strange. This group, which had no obvious name, talked in hushed tones and used the mantra of "Mm-hmm" frequently and exhibited an annoying habit of repeating what they had just heard. The young adult entered the group and noticed a rise in temperature, which made the seeds restless and the patches less troublesome.

A nameless guru stepped out from the group, motioned to a quiet spot and, through a ritualistic conversation, seemed to draw out more of the young adult's stories than even the teller had heard before. But more exciting to the youth, the tales kept surfacing about the search for the very important thing to do. Ever since the storyteller had arrived in the strange land, all the inhabitants had been shouting "Find the important thing to do," but the guru had an uncanny way of getting it all out.

After they finished talking, the guru slipped back into the disorganized group and the young adult never saw the guru again. (The guru's group was so disorganized that the young adult later learned they couldn't agree on a name, though they all responded to "helper.") The young adult's memory of the talks was blurred, but the vines had a growth spurt, the story segments were not so bothersome, and even the inhabitants' treatment of the patches was more manageable for a few days.

As for the important thing to do, well that seemed to be what our protagonist had been doing all along, constructing and telling pieces of stories to whomever would listen, but it was mostly for himself to hear and understand. The child-now-adult lived on after these events, though not always happily, for the world was strange to the end. The protagonist savored some measure of contentment and serenity in the stories made richer by the warm rituals of the guru and the enlightenment of the social scientists.

CHAPTER ELEVEN

A Schematic Reconceptualization and Application of Gottfredson's Model

Beverly J. Vandiver
Pennsylvania State University

Sharon L. Bowman
Ball State University

RECENTLY, IT HAS been recommended that vocational theories incorporate a cognitive perspective as a better way to explain the process of career development and choice (Hackett, Lent, & Brown, 1991). Linda Gottfredson's (1981) vocational theory provides a framework for the application of a cognitive perspective in redefining the integration of process and content issues of career development and choice (Gati & Winer, 1987). Gottfredson's present theory, however, has been criticized as being too rigid in its assumptions of a specific linear sequence that may actually be more variable (Pryor & Taylor, 1989). This chapter also includes the criticism leveled at Gottfredson's work to reconceptualize and expand the theory. In doing so, it uses the construct of self-schema to better link Gottfredson's model of career development to the actual process of career counseling. The chapter also includes applications of the new model to career counseling and concludes with a case illustration highlighting how the model can be used in career assessment and counseling.

GOTTFREDSON'S CIRCUMSCRIPTION-COMPROMISE MODEL

According to Gottfredson (1981), *a vocational self-concept*—how individuals view themselves in the development, selection, and implementation of a career—arises from the overall self-concept. The development of a vocational self-concept begins early in life and is defined through four developmental *orientations*. The four orientations are size and power, sex role, social valuation, and unique self. As individuals complete each orientation, they begin to narrow their vocational options. This funneling process, known as *circumscription*, leads to a set of occupational alternatives called the *social space*, from which the career choice is made. The four orientations describe the development of cognitive capacities, the evolution of self-concept, and the changing orientation to work as individuals age from three years to adulthood. Factors such as sex, socioeconomic status, intelligence, interests, abilities, and values vary in importance across orientations. According to Gottfredson, all children proceed through the orientations in the prescribed order; intelligence level, however, may moderate the speed of progression.

The first orientation is to size and power (ages three to five); children engage in dichotomous thinking such as big-little and good-bad. From this orientation, children learn that adults have the power, which is partially defined through having an occupation. Children then imagine themselves as powerful by pretending to have occupations themselves.

The second orientation is to sex role (ages six to eight); at this time, children begin to grasp the concept of sex roles or the idea that society prescribes a certain acceptable set of behaviors for each sex. Children learn sex roles from their parents, yet they also gain insight from their peers, older adults, and the media. Some parents may try to instill quite broad sex roles in their children, forgetting that children are exposed to many other viewpoints. Children begin this orientation process with external cues and end it with an internal belief system. Gottfredson noted that sex type stabilizes during this orientation and remains stable throughout the rest of one's life. Therefore, sex type is the first boundary through which occupational preferences (social space) are circumscribed. In essence, children circumscribe or narrow their occupational aspirations based on their view of the social rules about sex roles; any occupations that are perceived as available only for the opposite sex are removed from further consideration.

The third orientation is to social valuation (ages nine to thirteen), as children begin to delineate levels of social class and prestige for themselves and for occupations. During this orientation, children identify their effort lines, the maximum amount of effort they are willing to exert to obtain a particular occupation. Effort, therefore, is a key aspect in defining social space within this orientation. The more effort an individual exerts, the higher the prestige level of the occupation and vice versa. As children circumscribe their occupational aspirations, those occupations that are perceived as below a minimum level of prestige are removed from further consideration. Thus, prestige is the second boundary through which occupational alternatives (social space) are narrowed.

The final orientation in the circumscription of occupational choices is to the internal, unique self (ages 14 and over). From this orientation, selection of an occupation is based on the individual's abilities and interests; an individual's personal identity is reflected in the vocational realm, and actual experience in the occupational world further defines an individual's self-concept. The field of work or interest is the final boundary through which occupational alternatives are narrowed.

The path of some individuals through this process results in selection of an "ideal" occupation, whereas others find that barriers such as changes in the workplace and their personal life force them to reassess their occupational aspirations. For the group that must reassess their aspirations, compromises are made to accommodate personal goals and vocational realities. The process of compromise requires broadening the range of occupational possibilities when a suitable occupation cannot be identified in the existing social space. It is important to understand that compromise does not occur if adequate options are available; individuals do not consider new options unless forced to do so after exhausting the social space. Gottfredson (1981) stated that the compromise process occurs in an orderly fashion back through the orientations.

Vocational interest is the first boundary compromised in the search for an accessible job. According to Gottfredson (1981), individuals can find other suitable outlets to express their interests (e.g., leisure activities). If broadening the area of vocational interests does not result in a suitable occupation, prestige level is the next thing compromised. An individual's self-concept of sex type is considered to be the most strongly protected aspect of the self and will only be sacrificed as a last resort.

RESEARCH STATUS OF GOTTFREDSON'S MODEL

Research on Gottfredson's (1981) theory has been sparse. To date, it has yielded mixed support for the concepts of circumscription and compromise. The existence of the key dimensions of sex type, prestige, and interest have been supported, but they do not follow the prescribed plan. The research on the circumscription process (Henderson, Hesketh, & Tuffin, 1988; Lapan & Jingeleski, 1992; Leung & Harmon, 1990) demonstrated that circumscription does not occur at the specified age ranges proposed by Gottfredson. Children narrowed their career options by sex type but did so earlier (Henderson et al., 1988) or later than Gottfredson had indicated (Leung & Harmon, 1990). The time of circumscription for prestige was also found to vary; children either narrowed their career options by prestige at the hypothesized age range (Henderson et al., 1988) or continued to examine the prestige level of careers into adolescence, which would overlap with the orientation to unique self (Leung & Harmon, 1990). Thus, Gottfredson's conceptualization of circumscription has received mixed support.

A second group of studies (Hannah & Kahn, 1989; Hesketh, Durant, & Pryor, 1990a; Hesketh, Elmslie, & Kaldor, 1990b; Holt, 1989; Leung & Plake, 1990; Pryor & Taylor, 1986; Taylor & Pryor, 1985) tested the compromise process using either two or all three of the proposed dimensions. These studies have provided only partial support for the compromise process, suggesting that its occurrence did not match the proposed sequence (i.e., career interest was not always sacrificed first, prestige was not always sacrificed second, and sex type was not always sacrificed last). As a result, these studies have concluded that the compromise process may be more complex than what Gottfredson hypothesized. The compromise process may be moderated by a number of variables, including age, sex, sex-role attitudes, socioeconomic status, and interest area (Holt, 1989; Leung & Plake, 1990; Pryor & Taylor, 1986).

There are two plausible explanations for the mixed support for Gottfredson's theory. First, the mixed empirical support may be due to the methodologies employed. A variety of measures and methodologies, including forced-choice (Holt, 1989; Leung & Plake, 1990), card sort (Holt, 1989), fuzzy graphic rating scales (Hesketh et al., 1990a), hypothetical career options (Taylor & Pryor, 1985), and policy-capturing procedure (Hesketh et al., 1990b), have been used to test the circumscription and compromise process. These methodologies have each yielded different findings. As a result, it is impossible to distinguish between the artifacts of the measures and the true nature of the findings. More accurate and valid measures or methodologies may need to be developed and employed if researchers are to accurately test the model.

Second, a more complex process may underlie circumscription and compromise. Although the measurement of the circumscription and compromise processes may need to be improved, the available research (e.g., Hesketh et al., 1990a; Holt, 1989; Taylor & Pryor, 1985) supports the need for theory revision. A revision of Gottfredson's theory is required to explain the mixed findings. In essence, Gottfredson's model does not explain or resolve the findings in which the dimensions of sex type, prestige, and interest were compromised in various sequences. Gottfredson's model of circumscription and compromise appears to be static and does not account for individual differences in the circumscription and compromise process. Several researchers (e.g., Bodden & James, 1976; Gati, 1986; Neimeyer & Metzler, 1987) have suggested that a process-oriented theory utilizing schema may be better able to account for individual differences in the salience of the factors considered most important in career decision making.

AN OVERVIEW OF SCHEMA

Schema are hypothetical cognitive structures that help in perceiving, organizing, processing, and utilizing information (Fiske & Taylor, 1991). Schema provide a framework allowing people to identify and attend to stimuli that are important to them while ignoring the rest. People use a number of well-defined schema for processing information and making sense out of their world. For example, most people have a well-defined schema of mother, father, and boss so that they can easily incorporate new information about any one of these roles into the respective schema. By encoding and storing information schematically, it is easier to recall information more readily than information stored loosely in memory. Each person is considered to utilize schema in a relatively stable manner in processing and understanding; yet, how information is interpreted and what schema are created are reflective of individual differences.

Self-schema represent one of the unique cognitive differences among people. Self-schema are "cognitive generalizations about the self, derived from past experiences, that organize and guide the processing of self-related information" (Markus, 1977, p.64). Self-schema consist of those aspects of a person's behavior that are the most important to that person; not everything a person does is part of the self-schema (Markus, 1977). Basic pieces of information make up the core of an individual's self-schema; this includes name, representations of the physical appearance, and representations of relationships with significant people such as parents, spouse, or partner. Individual differences are based on unique self-schema features such as the self-schema of an athlete versus a nonathlete. Trait concepts—for example, shy or outgoing—can also be part of a person's self-schema. In essence, the elements that comprise self-schema vary from person to person; therefore, information is processed differently by everyone.

Early evidence (Markus, 1977; Rogers, Kuiper, & Kirker, 1977) for self-schema established the viability of the construct as well as the general methodology to measure it. One study (Markus, 1977) found that the trait dimension of independence versus dependence was an important element in many people's self-schema. Based on how they rated themselves, either high on independence or high on dependence, participants were classified as possessing either a schema for independence or dependence or as aschematic (those with neither schema). Weeks later, when asked to respond to a list of self-descriptive adjectives, those participants with a schema for dependence responded more quickly to the dependence-related adjectives but took longer to respond to the independence-related adjectives. The independence-schema participants showed the opposite pattern. Those without a schema for the two traits showed no difference in making these judgments for either of the types of words. These findings demonstrated that people process information more rapidly when they have a strong cognitive structure that is related to that specific information.

Researchers have provided a considerable amount of evidence in support of the self-schema model in a number of areas such as body weight (Markus, Hamill, & Sentis, 1987), clinical depression (Dance & Kuiper, 1987; Derry & Kuiper, 1981; Kuiper & Derry, 1982), and race (Smith & Lewis, 1985).

Pertinent to Gottfredson's career model and the reconceptualization of it is the concept of gender schema. Unlike other types of schema, its existence has not been widely accepted and has generated numerous studies and debate. Three models of gender schema have been proposed. Bem (1981) asserted that individuals who are either highly masculine or feminine are sex-typed and process information in terms of gender. In contrast, Markus, Crane, Bernstein, and Siladi (1982) countered Bem's view with the self-schema gender theory, in which individuals are believed to construct an elaborate self-schema about their gender. Those sex-typed for specific gender attributes will have a stronger self-schema of either masculinity or femininity, not just a general gender schema. Androgynous people are considered to be schematic for both feminine and masculine attributes. In essence, individual differences dictate the kind of self-schema people have about their gender. Spence and her colleagues (Spence, 1985; Spence & Helmreich, 1978; Spence & Sawin, 1985) have proposed that gender schema is more complex and that the construct is multifaceted. Gender-linked qualities and behaviors are not necessarily correlated to one another, and when such a relationship exists, other reasons besides gender may be moderating the linkage between gender and behavior. In general, there are multiple and complex factors underlying the specific gender schema that people acquire and manifest.

Studies have supported Bem's model (Bem, 1981; Frable & Bem, 1985; Larsen & Seidman, 1986), Markus' model (Markus et al., 1982; Payne, Connor & Colletti, 1987; Skitka & Maslach, 1990), and Spence's model (Edwards & Spence, 1987; Hungerford & Sobolew-Shubin, 1987). Although the conceptual basis of gender schema theory and the methodology used to measure it (Deaux, Kite, & Lewis, 1985) have been questioned, the overall research indicates that gender schema is a plausible construct. The pertinent issue becomes which model best describes gender schema and whether it is applicable in understanding and reconceptualizing Gottfredson's concept of sex type. Each of the gender-schema model are plausible and reflect ways people may develop and utilize gender schema in interacting in the world. These gender-schema models are also plausible in explaining the mixed results found for the sex-type orientation during the compromise process. Besides the role gender schema may play in understanding the sex-type orientation of Gottfredson's career model, the self-schema construct serves an equally useful function in providing a broader and more dynamic and flexible framework in explaining how individuals develop a vocational self-concept and also make career decisions.

A SCHEMATIC RECONCEPTUALIZATION OF GOTTFREDSON'S THEORY

The Process of Circumscription

The process and sequence of circumscription is not questioned in this reconceptualization. What is at issue, instead, is the respective weight given each orientation in the circumscription process. Gottfredson defines the orientation to sex type as the most important aspect in the process of selecting an occupation. Prestige and interest have less weight, as determined by their sequence in the circumscription process. These orientations serve to define more narrowly one's occupational preferences. In contrast, this schematic model of circumscription suggests that a person's experiences and interpretations determine the degree of importance each orientation has in shaping a vocational self-concept. Although the development of sex type may occur earlier in life than social valuation (prestige) or interest, it may not necessarily carry more weight in the circumscription process than prestige or interest. Rather, an individual is either schematic or aschematic for each of these orientations separately. Based on a person's experiences and inter-pretations of them, a self-schema is developed for sex type. The person may be any one of the following: (a) schematic for sex-type in general, (b) schematic for either masculine or feminine traits, (c) schematic for both sex-typed traits, or (d) aschematic for sex-type traits. Future experiences and the interpretations of them will determine the importance of sex type in the person's developing self-concept.

As a person enters the orientation of social valuation (prestige), the same process will occur. A person's experiences and interpretation of them will determine whether the person is schematic or aschematic for prestige. A separate self-schema for prestige will develop in addition to the distinct self-schema for sex type. Now the degree of importance of prestige is weighted in relation to the degree of importance of sex type. The social space and the zone of alternatives are now defined by these two orientations. How that social space and zone of alternatives are defined is determined by how each of these two orientations have been weighted. Again, sex type may not be the defining dimension; prestige could be more of an influence on the person's vocational self-concept.

During the final orientation of unique self (interest), a person will either develop a self-schema for interest or be aschematic for interest. During adolescence and young adulthood, many individuals are unsure of what they are good at as well as what interests them. Their experiences and the interpretations of them will determine the development of an interest self-schema. The interest self-schema is separate and distinct from the sex-type and prestige self-schema. Although these orientations may have separate self-schema, there now exists an interacting process among the three dimensions based on the continued interpretations of a person's experiences. At this point, vocational interest may be valued as more important than sex type or prestige. Or it is possible that the prestige of a particular occupation may be more important than interest or sex type. Yet again, sex type may be the primary dimension in the narrowing of occupational choices.

In essence, each person's circumscription process is unique and can best be understood as paralleling the individual weighting process of a multiple regression formula. The importance of one dimension may vary, depending on what other dimensions have developed, as well as how they are weighted, given the unique experiences of each person.

Childhood experiences and interpretations of those experiences will determine the degree of importance each orientation has to vocational development. The shape and function of an hourglass best characterize the schematic circumscription process. The top of the hourglass represents information taken in cognitively and emotionally by an individual. As this information is interpreted by the individual, it is weighted in degree of importance and deposited in a self-schema for that particular experience or event. As time goes by, new information of a similar topic may be taken in, and its interpretation may dramatically change that specific self-schema. The same goes for the development and change of other self-schema.

For instance, a female child may first learn and experience a narrow view of sex role for females. Yet her career aspirations, abilities, and interests may be broader than what has traditionally been defined as appropriate for females. This additional information, and how she interprets it, may significantly change the weight given to her sex-type orientation. The weighting accorded to her career aspirations and abilities and interests will alter the value she may give to her sex-type orientation. Thus, new experiences and their interpretations may precipitate one of two possibilities; either the self-schema will remain the same or it will change. Given the fact that life and experiences as well as interpretations of them are not static but dynamic, a person's self-schema is constantly changing. As a result, it is only logical to consider the changing nature of a person's vocational self-schema. Sex-type orientation may be learned early in life, but a person's experiences and the cognitive interpretation may change these original self-schemas of sex type. The same goes for the orientation to social valuation. What experiences and their interpretations determine the aspirations of a certain prestige level for an individual? Do new experiences and events alter the importance of a person's prestige level? Finally, as a person begins to develop interests, abilities, and talents, this level of orientation to unique self may alter the importance of sex type and prestige. Or it is possible that the importance of prestige level may alter the importance of interests and abilities.

Many children may follow not only the hypothesized sequence but also share a fairly common schema of sex type, prestige, and interest. Although socialization experiences are uniquely based on cultural and familial background, most children are exposed to the socialization stereotypes of the larger culture. For example, according to stereotypes, nurses are female, whereas firefighters are male. Yet within this broader social framework, some girls may aspire to be firefighters and some boys may want to be nurses. From this perspective, an individual's circumscribed social space would reflect the relative importance of sex type, prestige, and interest. For example, if many of the individual's role models work in sex-typed occupations, then the individual may become schematic for sex type. Another individual may be schematic for prestige; the status of the occupation may override the interests or sex type of the occupation. The individual's unique vocational self-schema would be the primary deciding factor in the circumscription process, not the order of the development of the orientation. That unique schema pattern would, in turn, affect the compromise process.

The Compromise Process

The compromise process can also be reconceptualized to explain the conflicting literature on Gottfredson's original model. What is most important to an individual's vocational self-concept or career schema? The order of compromise would depend on the unique self-schema pattern circumscribed. A man who is schematic for interest would not compromise his interest goals but may be willing to sacrifice prestige as well as sex type in order to meet his interest goals. Examples of persistence in following one's dreams (interests), regardless of circumstances, are legend (the "starving artist" or "struggling actor" who won't give up the dream); they may not be career schematic for sex type or prestige as are many other people. In contrast, there are other people who decide to give up their interest goals in order to achieve more money or status. Consider, for example, people in management who stay in it for the money or status. They may have the necessary ability for their work but not any particular interest in it. They may be more schematic for financial reward than their jobs or career. Some people may be schematic for all three dimensions and refuse to compromise interest, sex type, or prestige. These people may only pursue one kind of career and nothing else. There are also people who are aschematic for all three dimensions who may wander from career to career, either because they are unsure of their interests and the importance of sex type or status, or influenced by other factors but not by these three dimensions.

In general, the circumscription and compromise process appear to be part of a larger self-schema of a person's self/personality. Therefore, the compromise process is unique for each person in terms of what sequence will occur. How important each of these dimensions have been to a person in the development of a vocational self-concept and career will determine to what degree a person will compromise each of these dimensions.

In summary, this schematic reconceptualization of Gottfredson's theory can explain the mixed support for the circumscription and compromise processes. Different sequences of the compromise process of the three dimensions may reflect the unique individual differences of the participants' vocational self-schema. Although this schematic model of the circumscription and compromise processes is only hypothetical until it can be systematically tested, an initial step in this direction is to examine its use in clinical application. A schematic approach to career counseling fits with the idea of working with the individual.

APPLICATION OF THE CAREER SCHEMA MODEL TO CAREER COUNSELING

The application of a schematic model of Gottfredson's theory in career counseling must begin where all other models of counseling begin, namely, with assessment. In this case, an assessment of the client's vocational self-concept is based on the constructs of the self-schema and the orientations to sex type, prestige, and interest. Usually, the primary focus of career counseling has been to assess the client's career interests and to intervene in a psychoeducational manner (Manuele-Adkins, 1992). Only recently have other issues, such as sex role, sexual orientation, and race been considered pertinent enough to be addressed in career counseling (Bowman, 1993; Elliot, 1993).

From a schematic perspective, information is gathered to assess the client's general and vocational self-concept. Similar to other forms of clinical assessment, this information can be collected by interview and paper-and-pencil measures. Nurius (1986) suggested a functional analysis of the specific self-schema primarily used by the client. Although this process is the prototype of a behavioral functional analysis, the primary difference is that how a person thinks about him or herself is equally important as how those thoughts are exhibited behaviorally. In addition, it is important to consider the context of the self-schema. By specifying the context, it may be possible to identify clients' beliefs and expectations about themselves as well as their hopes and fears. Another assessment procedure suggested by Nurius (1986) was to have clients focus on their perception of actuality and possibility. The perception of actuality addresses clients' present perception of who they are, whereas the perception of possibility examines clients' hopes and fears about themselves and the likelihood of their fruition.

In summary, an assessment of a person's general self-concept can be conducted by collecting information about how the person views the self in various contexts, identifying the belief system and hopes and fears.

In gathering information about the salience of the orientations of Gottfredson's theory, it would be helpful to have a multicultural focus. Contextualizing clients on nonpsychological variables that may have an enormous influence on their self-concept and psychological state ensures that a thorough assessment has been made of their general functioning and current vocational status. Are the dimensions of sex type and prestige playing a vital role in the circumscription process? What is the client adamant about not giving up if the ideal occupation is not available or readily accessible?

Once an assessment has been made of the person's self-concept and specific self-schema have been identified, counseling can take into account how career fits within the self-concept and what aspects are important or unimportant. By focusing on the cognitive processes, career counseling becomes more than just a review of the person's career interests and options. The integration of the additional information gathered about the person's self-schema and orientations to sex type, prestige, and interests broadens what the person will get out of the counseling process. If the client is schematic for particular nonpsychological variables, it would be useful to explore what those variables mean to him or her and the possible influence they may have on career development and choice. Experiential directives can be provided to help facilitate the client's examination and possible alteration of self-schema, depending on whether the self-schema are too broad or narrow. The following case illustration highlights how a new model for career choice can be utilized in career assessment and counseling.

DAVID: A CASE ILLUSTRATION

David, an 18-year-old, single, White male, was referred to the counseling center by his academic adviser. He had stopped attending classes in midsemester and did not return to them for five to six weeks. He commented, "I don't know why I do the things that I do...something is holding me back." Despite his lack of attendance, he continued to take his exams by cramming the night before and had primarily a C average. During his absence from classes, he reported either staying in bed or sitting in his room asking himself the question, What am I doing? On the problem checklist, David rated concerns about assertiveness and values and beliefs as high. His college major and career goals were rated as low concerns or causing him no problems at all. He reported a similar experience of giving up when he was a senior in high school and believed it was due to experiencing a lot of pressure from his parents, especially from his father, to be successful and to prepare himself to take over the family business. His school adviser referred him to a counselor, and he expressed that he felt that the counselor had helped him "get his life into shape."

Inquiry into his family background revealed that David is the only son and the older of two children as well as the firstgeneration college student. His 17-year-old sister is in her senior year of high school and does not appear to be under the same kind of pressures from parents. Both parents are in their late 40s; his father is in charge of the family laundry and drycleaning business. His mother takes care of the books for the business. The family business has been in existence for generations, dating back to the "old country." Because David is the only son, he is expected to take over the business. As a result, he feels trapped into pursuing a major that will help him run the business successfully. He says he doesn't really like college but feels he needs it in order to be successful in life. Although he wants to explore other career options, he says he must follow in his father's footsteps and feels he has no other options.

An assessment based on a schema-focused approach (Nurius, 1986; Young, 1990) indicated that David is either aschematic for a vocational self-concept or that his career schema has been suppressed due to the overwhelming pressures he has perceived or internalized from his parents. Although he appears to have undergone the three levels of orientation—sex type, prestige, and interests—it is not readily apparent what his career schema is. For all appearances, and based on parental expectations, he has circumscribed to a traditionally male-oriented career (business). His career choices have been narrowed as a result of pursuing college. Although he may not be schematic for college, he is schematic for prestige. He noted that he doesn't like college, but he believes he needs it in order to be successful. He appears to be schematic for a career based on parental expectations but not based on his own interests. Either he has suppressed his own career interests or is aschematic and, as a result, it is easier for him to take on the career schema of his parents. In summary, David appears to be experiencing depression and is immobilized due to the perceived or real imposition his parents have placed on his career development and choice.

Treatment would involve a combination of career and personal counseling. More assessment needs to be made of the client's general self-concept in relation to his vocational self-concept. What kind of schema does the client have of himself in general? In addition, a functional analysis needs to be made of the client's belief system. He sees no options for his life. In the same vein, his hopes and fears need to be fully explored. He appears to be immersed in a sense of hopelessness, and his fears appear to be what immobilize him. He fears being trapped into a career he doesn't want and fears the unknown he faces if he doesn't keep the career presented to him by his parents. Finally, the circumscription and compromise processes need to be separated for him; he has not allowed himself to examine what he really likes, based on interests, prestige, and sex type. A career inventory might provide a foundation for him to explore different career interests. It will need to be emphasized that exploration doesn't mean that he has to narrow his options so quickly. It will be necessary to encourage him to look at what he is schematic for and see these as being in a zone of alternatives. Dealing with the problems of the client's compromise process can be addressed once it is clear what career schema the client possesses. The goal will be to undo the compromise process for him because he has perceived his parents' expectations as the barrier to explore his own interests. This will entail examining his worse fears (barriers/obstacles), such as that of his parents disowning him if he doesn't compromise his own career schema. Also, it will be necessary to encourage the client not to swing the other way and ignore examining possible options he has within the family business.

SUMMARY

Gottfredson's vocational theory of circumscription and compromise provides another perspective from which to understand how career development and choice occur. Interests and abilities are not the only factors: By contextualizing the process of career development and choice, it is possible to see what nonpsychological aspects are also salient. A schematic reconceptualization of Gottfredson's career theory provides more flexibility in understanding how the dimensions of sex type, prestige, and interest interact to explain the unique career choice and compromises each individual makes. This reconceptualization also improves the link between Gottfredson's theory and the actual process of career counseling. This new model of counseling for career choice may enhance career counseling by providing a framework in which counselors can incorporate a broader base of information as they assess and counsel clients.

REFERENCES

Bem, S. L. (1981). Gender schema theory: A cognitive account of sex typing. *Psychological Review, 88,* 354–364.

Bodden, J. L., & James, L. E. (1976). Influence of occupation information giving on cognitive complexity. *Journal of Counseling Psychology, 23,* 280–282.

Bowman, S. L. (1993). Career intervention strategies for ethnic minorities. *Career Development Quarterly, 42,* 14–25.

Dance, K. A., & Kuiper, N. A. (1987). Self-schemata, social roles, and a self-worth contingency model of depression. *Motivation and Emotion, 11,* 251–268.

Deaux, K., Kite, M. E., & Lewis, L. L. (1985). Clustering and gender schemata: An uncertain link. *Personality and Social Psychology Bulletin, 11,* 387–397.

Derry, P. A., & Kuiper, N. A. (1981). Schematic processing and self-reference in clinical depression. *Journal of Abnormal Psychology, 90,* 286–297.

Edwards, V., & Spence, J. T. (1987). Gender-related traits, stereotypes, and schemata. *Journal of Personality and Social Psychology, 33,* 146–154.

Elliot, J. E. (1993). Career development with lesbian and gay clients. *Career Development Quarterly, 41,* 210–225.

Fiske, S. T., & Taylor, S. (1991). *Social cognition* (2d ed.). New York: McGraw-Hill.

Frable, D. E. S., & Bem, S. L. (1985). If you are gender schematic, all members of the opposite sex look alike. *Journal of Personality and Social Psychology, 45,* 459–468.

Gati, I. (1986). Making career decisions: A sequential elimination approach. *Journal of Counseling Psychology, 33,* 408–417.

Gati, I., & Winer, D. (1987). The relationship between vocational interests and the location of an ideal occupation in the individual's perceived occupational structure. *Journal of Vocational Behavior, 30,* 295–308.

Gottfredson, L. S. (1981). Circumscription and compromise: A developmental theory of occupational aspirations [Monograph]. *Journal of Counseling Psychology, 28,* 545–579.

Hackett, G., Lent, R. W., & Greenhaus, J. H. (1991). Advances in vocational theory and research: A 20-year retrospective. *Journal of Vocational Behavior, 38,* 3–38.

Hannah, J. S., & Kahn, S. E. (1989). The relationship of socioeconomic status and gender to the occupational choices of Grade 12 students. *Journal of Vocational Behavior, 34,* 161–178.

Henderson, S., Hesketh, B., & Tuffin, K. (1988). A test of Gottfredson's theory of circumscription. *Journal of Vocational Behavior, 32,* 37–48.

Hesketh, B., Durant, C., & Pryor, R. (1990a). Career compromises: A test of Gottfredson's (1981) theory using a policy-capturing procedure. *Journal of Vocational Behavior, 36,* 97–108.

Hesketh, B., Elmslie, S., & Kaldor, W. (1990b). Career compromise: An alternative account to Gottfredson's theory. *Journal of Counseling Psychology, 37,* 49–56.

Holt, P. (1989). Differential effect of status and interest in the process of compromise. *Journal of Counseling Psychology, 36,* 42–47.

Hungerford, J. K., & Sobolew-Shubin, A. P. (1987). Sex-role identity, gender, identity, and self-schemata. *Psychology of Women Quarterly, 11,* 1–10.

Kuiper, N. A., & Derry, P. A. (1982). Depression and nondepressed content self-reference in mild depressives. *Journal of Personality, 50,* 67–79.

Lapan, R. T., & Jingeleski, J. (1992). Circumscribing vocational aspirations in junior high school. *Journal of Counseling Psychology, 39,* 81–90.

Larsen, R. J., & Seidman, E. (1986). Gender schema theory and sex role inventories: Some conceptual and psychometric considerations. *Journal of Personality and Social Psychology, 50,* 205–211.

Leung, S. A., & Harmon, L. W. (1990). Individual and sex differences in the zone of acceptable alternatives. *Journal of Counseling Psychology, 37,* 153–159.

Leung. S. A., & Plake, B. S. (1990). A choice dilemma approach for examining the relative importance of sex type and prestige preferences in the process of career choice compromise. *Journal of Counseling Psychology, 37,* 399–406.

Manuele-Adkins, C. (1992). Career counseling is personal counseling. *Career Development Quarterly, 40*, 313–323.

Markus, H. (1977). Self-schemata and processing information about the self. *Journal of Personality and Social Psychology, 35*, 63–78.

Markus, H., Crane, M., Bernstein, S., & Siladi, M. (1982). Self-schema and gender. *Journal of Personality and Social Psychology, 42*, 38–50.

Markus, H., Hamill, R., & Sentis, K. P. (1987). Thinking fat: Self-schema for body weight and the processing of weight relevant information. *Journal of Applied Social Psychology, 17*, 50–71.

Neimeyer, G. J., & Metzler, A. (1987). The development of vocational schema. *Journal of Vocational Behavior, 30*, 16–32.

Nurius, P. S. (1986). Reappraisal of the self-concept and implications for counseling. *Journal of Counseling Psychology, 33*, 429–438.

Payne, T. J., Conner, J. M., & Coletti, G. (1987). Gender-based schematic processing: An empirical investigation and reevaluation. *Journal of Personality and Social Psychology, 52*, 937–945.

Pryor, R. G. L., & Taylor, N. B. (1986). What would I do if I couldn't do what I wanted to do? Investigating career compromise strategies. *Australian Psychologist, 21*, 363–376.

Pryor, R. G. L., & Taylor, N. B. (1989). Circumscription and compromise: Some problems and possibilities. *Australian Psychologist, 24*, 101–113.

Rogers, T. B., Kuiper, R. A., & Kirker, W. S. (1977). Self-reference and the encoding of personal information. *Journal of Personality and Social Psychology, 35*, 677–688.

Skitka, L. J., & Maslach, C. (1990). Gender roles and the categorization of gender-relevant behavior. *Sex Roles, 22*, 133–150.

Smith, R., & Lewis, R. (1985). Race as a self-schema affecting recall in black children. *Journal of Black Psychology, 12*, 15–29.

Spence, J. T. (1985). Gender identity and implications for concepts of masculinity and femininity. In T. B. Sonderegger (Ed.), *Nebraska Symposium on Motivation: Psychology and gender* (Vol. 32, pp. 59–96). Lincoln: University of Nebraska Press.

Spence, J. T., & Helmreich, R. I. (1978). *Masculinity and femininity: Their psychological dimensions, correlates and antecedents.* Austin: University of Texas Press.

Spence, J. T., & Sawin, L. L. (1985). Images of masculinity and femininity: A reconceptualization. In V. O'Leary, R. Unger, & B. Wallston (Eds.), *Sex, gender and social psychology* (pp. 35–66). Hillsdale, NJ: Erlbaum.

Swanson, J. L. (1992). Review: Vocational behavior, 1989–1991: Life-span career development and reciprocal interaction of work and nonwork. *Journal of Vocational Behavior, 41*, 101–161.

Taylor, N. B., & Pryor, R. G. L. (1985). Exploring the process of compromise in career decision making. *Journal of Vocational Behavior, 27*, 171–190.

Young, J. E. (1990). *Cognitive therapy for personality disorders: A schema-focused approach.* Sarasota, FL: Professional Resource Exchange.

CHAPTER TWELVE

Computer-Assisted Career Counseling
Challenges and Prospects

Itamar Gati
The Hebrew University of Jerusalem

CAREER COUNSELING IS one of the central issues in career development theory (Osipow, 1983, 1987; Savickas & Lent, 1994). One of the aims of career counseling is to facilitate the career decision-making process of individuals who face critical transition points. Indeed, career counseling can be viewed as a type of decision counseling (Jungermann & Schutz, 1992), with the goal of helping clients make better career decisions (Phillips, 1992). Computer-assisted career guidance systems (CACGSs) were developed as additional tools to help individuals better cope with decision making during transitions (Katz, 1993; Rayman, 1990; Sampson et al., 1990). Today CACGSs are used independently by individuals as well as by clients as an adjunct to their personal counseling.

Watts (1986) discussed three possible functions of CACGSs. They may serve, first, as a tool for career counselors; second, as a substitute for career counselors; and third, as a change agent that provokes change and stimulates improvements in career counseling theory and practice. It is this third role of CACGSs that provides the rationale for this chapter. Specifically, developing a CACGS requires translating the concepts of the theory underlying the system and the relations among these concepts into well-defined variables and systematic procedures. Thus, the introduction of CACGSs creates a novel and unique opportunity to examine a variety of career theories and test our ability to put them into practice. However, despite the potential of CACGSs, these systems have not received the attention they deserve in the field of counseling psychology.

In this chapter, I will address the challenge of integrating theory and practice in career decision making by focusing on CACGSs as representatives of innovative practical theory-based interventions. I will begin by reviewing career decision making from a decision–theoretic viewpoint. Then, the potential role of CACGSs as facilitators of the career decision-making process will be reviewed, and problems and dilemmas concerning CACGSs will be discussed. Next, I will describe some features of a specific CACGS designed to deal with these dilemmas and problems. I will then discuss a critical component that is still rare in the typical CACGS, namely, online (i.e., real time) quality control of an individual's dialogue with the computerized system. Finally, I will summarize three studies that demonstrate the fruitful interplay and constructive integration of theory and practice in CACGS and discuss the implications for career counselors.

DECISION THEORY
AND CAREER DECISION MAKING

Cognitive approaches play an increasing role in understanding the processes involved in career counseling (Brown, 1990; Neimeyer, 1988; Osipow, 1987; Walsh & Osipow, 1988). In this section, I briefly review the major components of career decision-making theory, highlighting some key elements that are crucial for applying it to career choices. For a comprehensive review of the decision-making perspective on career choices, the reader may consult Brown (1990), Jepsen and Dilley (1974), Mitchell and Krumboltz (1984), Phillips (1994), and Walsh and Osipow (1988). Like other types of decision making, career decision making has the following features: (a) There is an individual who has to make a decision; (b) there are a number of alternatives to select from; and (c) the decision maker has certain aspects or criteria that can be used to compare and evaluate the various alternatives in order to locate the most preferred one.

In addition to these characteristics, which are common to all decisions, career decisions also have certain unique features. First, the number of potential alternatives is often relatively large (e.g., the number of occupations, majors, and colleges available for students or the number of potential employers a recent graduate might consider). Second, there is an extensive amount of information available (e.g., in the *Dictionary of Occupational Titles, Occupational Outlook Handbook*, and occupational information libraries) on each alternative. One of the factors that contributes to this flood of information is the within-occupational variance that characterizes most occupations (Gati, 1986; Katz, 1993; Matarazzo, 1986; Meir & Yaari, 1988; Super, 1953). Third, a large number of aspects, criteria, and attributes (e.g., length of training, degree of independence, type of relationship with people) are required to adequately characterize occupations and the individual's preferences in a detailed and meaningful way (Gati, Garty, & Fassa, 1996; Katz, 1993; Lofquist & Dawis, 1978).

Because of these features of career decisions, counselors cannot adopt decision theory as is but should adapt it to the unique features of career decisions (Gati, 1986). For example, considering the vast amount of information on the one hand

and the cognitive and material constraints of the individual (Pitz & Harren, 1980) on the other, it seems that counselors ought to give up the unattainable goal of making the optimal decision using the normative, compensatory model (Pitz & Harren, 1980; Zakay & Barak, 1984). Instead, counselors may consider adopting the notion of *bounded rationality* (Simon, 1957), which refers to aiming at the realistic goal of making a "good enough" or "satisfying" decision (Phillips, 1994).

Furthermore, because it is impractical to explore all alternatives in depth, career decisions are typically characterized by the intermediate, practically unavoidable step of identifying a relatively small set of "promising" alternatives (Montgomery, 1989) on which the individual can collect comprehensive information (Gati, Fassa, & Houminer, 1995). This intermediate stage must be carried out carefully to minimize the possibility of discarding potentially suitable alternatives because any alternative that was not identified as "promising" at this stage will be ignored and will not receive further attention.

The complexity of the career decision-making process, which results from these characteristics, creates the need for guidance during the process itself (Gati, 1986; Gati, Fassa, & Houminer, 1995; Katz, 1966, 1993; Pitz & Harren, 1980). Traditionally, it was exclusively career counselors who provided the required guidance. Lately, as the potential of computers has been recognized, CACGSs have been developed to provide an additional way to meet this need.

COMPUTER-ASSISTED CAREER GUIDANCE SYSTEMS

CACGSs differ among themselves in many respects, including in aspects such as their scope, content, structure, style, procedures, and rationale (Katz & Shatkin, 1983); but the basic distinction is between career information and career guidance systems. The potential of computers to provide information was recognized quite early in the development of CACGSs (Harris-Bolsbey, 1984; Katz, 1993; Rayman, 1990; Sampson, 1983; Taylor, 1988). Computers can hold a large amount of information, which may easily be updated. In the context of career decisions, where the number of alternatives is very large and there are frequent changes in the characteristics of many occupations, this feature of computers seems especially beneficial. Later, the potential role of computers as providers of some guidance was also recognized (Harris-Bowlsbey, 1984, 1991; Katz, 1993; Katz & Shatkin, 1983; Rayman, 1990; Sampson, 1983; Taylor, 1988). Specifically, computerized systems can facilitate the career decision making of individuals by providing them with a general framework and leading them through the process step by step.

Today, computers are easily accessible, many people are familiar with them, and most people no longer regard them as alien. Furthermore, these systems also have the important advantage of allowing privacy, which is desired by some clients when dealing with their personal preferences. The large number of people who use

CACGSs each year (Niles & Garis, 1990), as part of the face-to-face counseling process as well as independent of it, provide evidence that these systems satisfy a widespread need.

Dilemmas and Problems

CACGSs are, however, more complex than they may first appear and deserve more critical attention than they typically receive (Gati, 1995; Johnston, Buescher, & Heppner, 1988; Katz, 1984). System developers face certain problems and dilemmas (although, unfortunately, they often ignore them), many of which stem from the unique characteristics of career decisions reviewed above. In this section, relying on the viewpoint of decision theory, I briefly review 12 problems and dilemmas that relate to three issues: (a) the occupational database, (b) the decision-making process, and (c) conducting an effective computerized dialogue. These problems and dilemmas may be more or less relevant to any particular CACGS, depending on its unique characteristics. A more elaborate discussion of nine of these problems may be found in Gati (1995).

Occupational Database. The occupational database is the heart of both career information and career guidance systems. This database contains the information about the occupational, or educational, alternatives, including the characteristic level(s) for each criterion or aspect in the different occupations. This information permits a structured search for occupational alternatives compatible with the preferred occupational characteristics selected by the user. The following are two problems relating to the issue of the occupational database.

The apparent precision of the data versus its unique "soft" character. Computer-based systems have an image of being faultless and precise (Sampson, 1986) because they usually include well-defined (i.e., numerical or categorical) data that create an impression of precision (Anastasi, 1992). However, in most CACGSs, a significant part of the database consists of "soft" information, whose selection, processing, and presentation is based on expert judgments (Gati, 1990a; Katz, 1993) because no objective indices are available (e.g., how to characterize occupations for degree of independence or degree of variety). It may be claimed that, for some aspects, objective data, which is not based on human judgment (e.g., income, length of training), is accessible. However, even such objective data (e.g., an income of $25,000) has a different subjective meaning for each individual: First, it does not take into account a number of relevant factors (e.g., taxes, family size, and the income of a spouse); and, second, it is perceived differently by each individual based on his or her unique point of view. Thus, despite its image of precision, the data included in CACGSs is subject to unintentional biases, has less than perfect reliability and validity, and is given unique, subjective meaning by each individual.

Dealing with within-occupational variance. Because of the limited information processing and storage capacity of both CACGSs and their users, the information characterizing an occupation has to be summarized in order for it to be useful.

However, measures of central tendency do not reflect the within-occupational variance that is an inherent characteristic of occupations; this variance is important because it reflects the fact that different people can engage in the same occupation (Super, 1953; Zytowski & Hay, 1984). The question then is how to inform clients about this within-occupational variance without significantly increasing the amount of information presented.

Career Decision-Making Process. In spite of the differences between CACGSs, certain characteristics of the career decision-making process are represented in most systems. The following five problems deal with the career decision-making process.

Eliciting aspirations while encouraging compromise. To identify promising alternatives that are compatible with an individual's preferences, the individual's aspirations have to be explicated. However, because the combination of all the desirable characteristics in one occupation (i.e., the ideal occupation) is usually unattainable in the real world, most career decisions involve compromises (Gati, 1993; Gottfredson, 1981; Leung & Harmon, 1990). The problem is how to elicit both aspirations and compromises without confusing or frustrating the client.

Increasing or decreasing the number of alternatives considered. The number of alternatives each client considers at the beginning of the career decision-making process varies. Some consider only a single alternative or two, without being aware of other alternatives that are perhaps more compatible; such a restricted range of alternatives may result in poorer decisions (Phillips, 1992). Others consider many alternatives, often vaguely defined, which cannot all be explored in depth. The question is, therefore, Should the system aim at increasing or decreasing this initial set of alternatives?

How should abilities and skills be taken into account? By using available objective ability scores (e.g., *General Aptitude Test Battery*) as implied, for example, by Gottfredson's (1986) *Occupational Aptitude Pattern Map*, the system may eliminate many occupations without sufficient justification. One reason for this is that the reliability of these scores is far from perfect. Another reason is that the relevance of certain abilities to future success in the world of work is only partial: There are no well-defined minimal or maximal cutoff thresholds for being engaged in particular occupations or for success or "satisfactoriness" in them (Dawis & Lofquist, 1984). Eliciting self-estimates of aptitudes and skills, which is another way to take abilities into account, has the serious disadvantage of being subject to biases (Lunneborg, 1982). Thus, the dilemma is how to consider this important factor yet circumvent these problems.

To rank or not to rank? Ranking the occupations according to their degree of compatibility to the individual appeals to most clients because it makes it easier for them to choose one (Brown, 1990; Mitchell & Krumboltz, 1984). However, a rank ordering creates three significant problems: First, it may unintentionally restrict clients from carrying out "free" exploration in the next stage; second, it may be invalid because not all the potentially relevant aspects are included in the search; and third, it transfers the responsibility for the decision to the CACGS.

Should there be a single list or multiple lists of promising alternatives?   One approach, employed by a number of CACGSs, is to generate several different lists during the search for "promising" alternatives, basing each list on a different type of criterion (e.g., aptitudes, interests, values). This approach is rather detailed and enables one to focus on the alternatives that are suitable with regard to specific aspects. However, it may confuse the client, particularly when different alternatives appear in the different lists. Another approach is to provide a single list of promising alternatives based on all aspects relevant to the client. The disadvantage of the single-list approach, at least when it is used in a search in which all aspects are considered simultaneously, is that often no alternative matches the client's preferences in all aspects. Consequently, clients may end up with no occupations on their list.

Conducting an Effective Dialogue.   Because the interaction between a career counselor and a deliberating counselee is unique in its complexity and involves various ways of communicating, it cannot be completely replaced by a dialogue between a computer and a deliberating individual. Nevertheless, today's software permits quite a flexible dialogue that can adapt itself to different counselees and still be effective for each of them. The challenge is how to design an effective CACGS without pretending or imposing the illusion during the dialogue that the computer is, in fact, a counselor. The five problems that follow deal with designing an effective computerized dialogue.

Dealing with uncertainty.   Individuals prefer to avoid uncertainty (Tversky & Kahneman, 1981), and hence there is an expectation that the dialogue will eliminate the uncertainties involved in making the decision. Indeed, the discomfort of uncertainty seems to be one of the chief motivations for seeking out career counseling (B. Benyamin, personal communication, December 25, 1994). Yet, uncertainty is inherent in most career decisions because both the individual and the occupational world constantly change (Brown, 1990; Gelatt, 1989). There are uncertainties about the future state of the world, including such issues as the probability of realizing the promising alternatives (Gati, 1990b), whether the individuals will succeed and be satisfied in the chosen occupation, and what their future preferences will be. Furthermore, the individual's preferences are often "fuzzy" or not well defined (Gati, 1986, 1995; Hesketh, Pryor, & Gleitzman, 1989).

Sophistication versus simplicity.   Because career decision making is a complex process (Katz, 1979, 1993; Phillips, 1994), a CACGS aimed at facilitating this process must necessarily be sophisticated. However, notions related to decision theory and its applications (e.g., decision support system, sensitivity analysis) may confuse and even intimidate the novice client. Thus, the question is how to design a complex and sophisticated system that will nevertheless allow the client to conduct a simple and direct dialogue.

The amount of relevant information.   Although there is a very large amount of potentially relevant occupational information, the limitations on human information processing (Pitz & Harren, 1980) dictate that only part of it can be processed during a dialogue with a CACGS. Providing too much information is therefore ineffective, as it results in partial processing and poor retention of the information. Providing insufficient information, however, may impair the decision-making process and its outcomes.

Flexible versus constrained dialogue. One facet of interactivity in a CACGS is the degree of control the clients have over the dialogue—specifically, their influence on the set and the sequence of modules used (Katz & Shatkin, 1983). As in a museum, there are typically two ways to explore the modules of a CACGS: free, unconstrained exploration or a single, imposed path that everyone must follow. A disadvantage of the latter is that it may appear to restrict the user's freedom, but it does have the advantage of allowing a more efficient and often also more effective dialogue.

How to provide a truly individualized dialogue in a computerized system. Each individual is unique and deserves special feedback tailored to his or her responses. As in face-to-face career counseling, a flexible and truly personalized dialogue seems desirable. However, CACGSs are preprogrammed without any knowledge of each potential user. The challenge, then, is to design the dialogue to be flexible so that it provides the optimal degree of help to the maximal number of clients.

POSSIBLE PRACTICAL SOLUTIONS

Making Better Career Decisions

One CACGS that implements many of the desirable features of such systems (Katz, 1984) and allows dealing with the problems and dilemmas herein is called Making Better Career Decisions (MBCD; Gati, 1990c). I will begin by introducing this system and then highlight the ways it deals with each problem and dilemma.

MBCD aims, in particular, to facilitate the search for a limited-sized set of promising alternatives compatible with the individual's preferences and hence are worth further exploration (i.e., the prescreening stage; Beach & Potter, 1992). The system accomplishes this by using the sequential-elimination approach (Gati, 1986; Gati, Fassa, & Houminer, 1995). Figure 1 summarizes the major steps involved in this process.

The dialogue is divided into distinct steps that correspond to distinct components of the career decision-making process. For example, to avoid confounding, the importance of aspects and the within-aspect preferences are elicited separately. This separation is desirable because high importance does not necessarily imply a preference for one of the extreme levels (e.g., length of training may be highly important to a client because of a preference for a two-year period of training, no more and no less). Accordingly, the dialogue begins by asking the clients to rate on a seven-point scale the degree of importance they attribute to each of the aspects

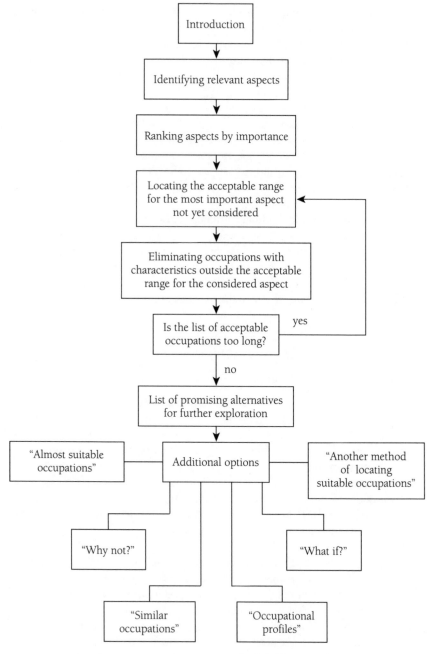

FIGURE 1   A Schematic Diagram of a Structured Search for Promising Alternatives

included in MBCD. These aspects were identified by career counselors and clients as relevant to career decision making (Gati, Garty, & Fassa, 1996; Sampson et al., 1990). Next, the clients are asked to rank a subset of about 10 aspects that they rated as important, from the most important to the least important.

Then the sequential search begins: Starting with the most important aspect specified, clients are asked to report their within-aspect preferences in each aspect, along five ordered levels. (For example, for the aspect *degree of variety*: 1 = little variety, 2 = below average variety, 3 = average variety, 4 = above average variety, and 5 = high variety). For each of the aspects, clients are asked to indicate first the most preferred level in that aspect (the optimal level) and then additional levels that they are willing to compromise on (acceptable levels).

Following the importance rating of the aspects, the clients report their preferences in each of the aspects, and the system eliminates the incompatible occupational alternatives from their list. In this way, as the client progresses along the aspects, the list is gradually reduced in size. After each aspect is considered, detailed feedback is offered (e.g., the number of alternatives eliminated because of the last aspect, and, if requested, which alternatives have been eliminated and which retained). In addition, online recommendations are given when necessary. (For example, when relatively many alternatives have been eliminated because of the client's preferences in a particular aspect, the client may be advised to consider compromising more in this aspect.) The dialogue is flexible and allows the client to change responses at any phase (e.g., as a result of the feedback). This process is terminated when the client's list of compatible occupations is reduced to a manageable set of seven alternatives or fewer (Miller, 1956).

At the end of the sequential-elimination process, the client is offered six additional options. Their purpose is to decrease the chances of discarding a potentially suitable alternative. The following options are offered:

- "Almost suitable occupations"—for locating alternatives that were eliminated because of only a slight mismatch in one aspect
- "Another method of locating suitable occupations"—for conducting another search for suitable alternatives using a compensatory model (e.g., Katz, 1966; Zakay & Barak, 1984) that locates alternatives that appear attractive overall, even though one or more of their characteristics may be incompatible with the user's preferences
- "Why not?"—for identifying why a certain alternative (out of those identified as overall attractive, using the compensatory search or any other alternative considered attractive by the user) was found incompatible in the sequential search
- "What if"—for exploring how the set of promising alternatives would change if the client's preferences were different

■ "Similar occupations"—for identifying alternatives similar in their characteristics to a certain desirable alternative (which, for example, may seem unattainable)

■ "Occupational profiles"—for obtaining a concise description of an occupation in all aspects included in the system

Finally, the client is provided with a brief printed summary of the dialogue. A complete printed record of the dialogue is available for the counselor.

The Solutions Adopted in MBCD to Deal with the Dilemmas and Problems

The following are 12 solutions offered by MBCD to deal with the 12 problems and dilemmas presented previously.

Occupational Database Solutions.
The apparent precision of the data versus its unique "soft" character. In MBCD, subjectivity is highlighted instead of being covered up. First, in order to decrease the illusion of precision and objectivity, five qualitative verbal labels that imply subjectivity (e.g., very high, above average, average, below average, low) are used to denote the within-aspect levels, rather than quantitative values. Second, the user is explicitly informed before and during the dialogue, as well as in the printed summary, about the role of expert judgment in the construction of the database.

Addressing within-occupational variance. The alternatives included in MBCD's database have a range of characteristic levels in each aspect, reflecting the variations within them. Promising alternatives are located by matching this range with the range of levels the client regards as acceptable. This prevents eliminating alternatives just because their typical level does not match the individual's preferences. As long as the alternative has the potential to satisfy the client's preferences, it is not eliminated from the list. Furthermore, the information on the range of characteristic levels is made explicit to the clients for those alternatives about which they have requested more detailed information (i.e., using the option of "Occupational profiles").

Decision-Making Solutions.
Eliciting aspirations while encouraging compromise. The client's within-aspect preferences are elicited in two stages during the dialogue with MBCD. First, clients are asked to report the optimal level, reflecting their aspirations in that aspect. Then they are given the option to indicate additional acceptable levels, reflecting their readiness to compromise (Gati, 1993). Distinguishing between the two stages decreases the chances of confusion or frustration and guides clients to clarify their preferences more analytically.

Increasing or decreasing the number of alternatives considered. The dialogue is flexible and tailors itself to the unique characteristics of the individual:

It helps decrease the number of alternatives when this number is too large and to increase the number of alternatives when the number is too small. Specifically, the sequential search ends when the client's list of compatible occupations is reduced to a manageable set of seven alternatives or fewer (Miller, 1956). This permits presenting each client with a small set of promising alternatives (reduced in size for those who did not have specific options and increased in size for those who considered only one or two alternatives). The client can then focus on this set of promising alternatives for in-depth exploration.

How should abilities and skills be taken into account? Considering abilities, aptitudes, and skills is important. However, the best way to do this is not necessarily obvious. Assuming that the motivation to fake rarely exists with respect to preferences, MBCD helps clients consider their abilities and skills by eliciting preferences for using abilities (instead of self-assessment, which is more prone to biases). Thus, only alternatives that coincide with abilities that the clients want to use remain on their list of promising alternatives.

To rank or not to rank? Because of the problems associated with ranking, MBCD presents each client with a limited-sized set of promising alternatives organized in alphabetical order without ranking. The client is encouraged to collect additional information outside the system before arriving at a rank order or choosing one particular alternative as the most suitable. Because the set of promising alternatives is limited in size, the task of in-depth exploration is realizable. This information makes it possible to compare and contrast the alternatives in all potentially important considerations. In fact, the system computes the value of each alternative for each user, and this information may be used for research purposes. But because of its potential disadvantages, it is not accessible to the client.

Should there be a single list or multiple lists of promising alternatives? The main list of promising alternatives includes the set of alternatives identified as compatible with the clients' preferences in those aspects most important to them, using the sequential search; as this list is based on many aspects, it is typically coherent. Yet clients can ask for another list that contains a set of suitable occupations located by a compensatory-model search. This list is based on the overall attractiveness of the various alternatives, using all aspects included in the system. Alternatives that are included in both lists, and hence may be regarded as the most promising, are highlighted. Clients are also encouraged to explore those occupations that appear on only one of the lists, using the "Why not?" option.

Effective Dialogue Solutions.

Dealing with uncertainty. Uncertainty cannot and should not be eliminated, yet its negative consequences can and should be reduced. To do this, MBCD first provides clients with a systematic framework to guide them through the career decision-making process, thereby reducing the discomfort resulting from uncertainty. Second, preferences are elicited in terms of a range of acceptable levels, which includes the optimal level, in order to reduce the impact of the uncertainty about present as well as future preferences on the list of alternatives identified as promising (Gati, 1986, 1995; Hesketh, Pryor, & Gleitzman, 1989). Third, utilizing a range of levels to characterize occupations makes it possible to reduce the influence of possible future changes in the characteristics of occupations on their compatibility with the client's preferences (Gati, 1986).

Sophistication versus simplicity. To make the dialogue direct and friendly, complex concepts are translated into simplified concepts that can easily be comprehended by the users (e.g., "Almost suitable occupations" and "Why not?" options are used instead of "sensitivity analysis"). In addition, most of the sophistication is hidden. For example, the list of "Similar occupations" the clients receive depends on their unique importance ratings of the aspects, giving higher weights to those aspects that are important to them. However, to avoid distraction and confusion, the clients are not told that the system is using their unique importance ranking to construct this list.

The amount of relevant information. To direct the clients to relevant information and facilitate its processing, MBCD separates the career decision-making process into distinct stages. First, the system guides the clients in locating and considering a subset of the aspects that are most important to them. The system then helps them locate a small set of promising alternatives that they can focus on for further exploration. In this way, the client can avoid the cognitive overload of exploring too many alternatives in depth. In addition, the concisely structured information about each occupation on which the search for promising alternatives is based can be obtained using the option of "Occupational profile." Finally, a six-to eight-page printout summarizing the dialogue is provided to remind the clients of their inputs and the course and results of the dialogue.

Flexible versus constrained dialogue. MBCD's dialogue begins with a fixed order of modules corresponding to the stages derived from the sequential-elimination model. This allows the client to focus on preferences rather than on how to use the system. Then, after locating a small set of promising alternatives, the clients are encouraged to explore each of the additional options (see Figure 1) in whatever sequence they choose. However, the sequence of the various additional options as they are presented on the computer monitor is not haphazard; rather, the options are displayed in a theoretically motivated sequence ("Almost compatible alternatives," "Compensatory search," "Why not," "What if," "Similar occupations," and "Occupational profile").

How to provide a truly individualized dialogue in a computerized system. As a partial answer to this challenge, the dialogue in MBCD is continuously monitored. As stated, detailed feedback is provided at each step of the search, and online recommendations are given when necessary. If, for example, too few aspects were taken into account before the end of the sequential search and there are too many occupations on the list of promising alternatives, it is recommended to the client that additional aspects be considered, even if they are less important. Clients can then change their responses accordingly.

Indeed, providing individualized feedback seems essential if one wants to turn computers from information systems into guidance systems. There are indications that certain components of counseling can be successfully computerized (e.g., interpreting the responses in an interest inventory; Gati, 1987; Gati & Blumberg, 1991). In the next section, I will elaborate on one of the most important facets of counseling—evaluating the dialogue's quality and providing the individual with truly individualized feedback.

Assessing the Quality of the Dialogue

Experienced counselors are usually able to monitor the quality of their interaction with their clients and judge whether the counseling process and its results are satisfactory. A parallel quality control should be applied to the computerized dialogue. However, except for rare cases, the dialogue between the client and the CACGS occurs without the presence of the counselor, so such an evaluation of quality can be carried out by the counselor only after the encounter with the CACGS ends. Furthermore, in many cases even such delayed quality control is not available for various reasons: No printed summary of the dialogue is available and the client cannot recall the dialogue accurately; the printout obtained at the end of the dialogue is inefficient because it is too long and unorganized; there is insufficient time during the session with the counselor; the counselor is unfamiliar with the CACGS; and so on. In any case, monitoring the dialogue after the encounter with the CACGS has ended has only limited value because it does not allow the clients to utilize the feedback during the dialogue and to change their responses accordingly if they want to. Thus, it seems not only desirable but also essential to incorporate a quality control module into CACGSs in order to monitor the dialogue in real time and provide the client with immediate individualized feedback. Indeed, I believe that with an appropriate theoretical framework, CACGSs can provide such feedback, which is an essential component of counseling.

The evaluation of the dialogue's quality can be based on three types of data: (a) the client's inputs, (b) the course of the dialogue, and (c) the dialogue's outcome. Specifically, criteria that define quality have to be developed for each of these components, based on theoretical considerations and corresponding empirical findings. Such criteria should indicate what characterizes the optimal state of affairs and what appears undesirable and what, hence, requires appropriate feedback. However, the search for these criteria highlights the difficulties encountered in the transformation of theory into practice: Do we have a theory that explicates what constitutes optimal input? What is the optimal course of a client-CACGS dialogue? What are the desirable outcomes of the dialogue? Do we have relevant empirical findings on these theoretical questions?

In this section, I propose several criteria that demonstrate the kind of quality control I believe can be incorporated into CACGSs. Note that these are general proposals; the specific criteria necessarily depend on the particular CACGS considered—its theoretical rationale and its unique features.

Evaluating the Inputs.   The first set of criteria can be applied to the client' inputs, which include the relative importance they attribute to the various aspects and their within-aspect preferences and aptitudes. I suggest four possible criteria for this component. The first criterion is the compatibility or similarity between the client's preferences in related aspects (i.e., aspects that typically co-occur in occupations and co-vary in individuals' preferences). Lack of compatibility can indicate that the client's preferences are inconsistent, unreliable, and not consolidated. For example, preference for a low level of personal responsibility and a high level of authoritative-ness seem incompatible and may indicate that the client's preferences have not yet been sufficiently consolidated.

Second, the degree of variance in the client's responses can be evaluated in such things as the relative importance attributed to the aspects, in the location of the optimal levels relative to other levels (e.g., their extremity), and in the number of acceptable levels in each aspect. A repeated pattern of responses across the various aspects (e.g., selecting the middle level as the optimal in all aspects) can indicate lack of differentiation (e.g., Neimeyer, 1988), again reflecting insufficient consolidation.

Third, the client's readiness to compromise may be examined. If the client is willing to make large compromises in most aspects, the list of promising alternatives will include too many alternatives (instead of only a few to focus on for future exploration). In contrast, if the client is not willing to compromise at all, the search for compatible alternatives will end very quickly, taking into account only a few aspects. Both types of extremes are undesirable and require appropriate feedback.

Fourth, incompatibility between preferences and related aptitudes (e.g., prefer-ring the realistic or technology field but reporting low technical aptitude) also deserves attention.

Evaluating the Course of the Dialogue.   A second set of criteria can be applied to the course of the dialogue between the user and the CACGS. These criteria should determine whether the dialogue reflects a systematic and constructive career decision-making process as indicated by effective utilization of the CACGS. The following three criteria appear important. First, one should note how many and which modules of the system were used. A very short dialogue that makes use of only a few of the available modules may indicate a shallow, superficial decision-making process. Second, the sequence of modules used should be considered. Different sequences of the same set of modules reflect different qualities of the dialogue because the sequence indicates the clients' understanding and awareness of the course of the dialogue and their progress in the decision-making process. Third, the client's willingness to follow the system's recommendations and make the advised changes can also be of interest. Ignoring all recommendations may indicate rigidity and lack of willingness to accept professional advice and may result in a less than optimal dialogue. Following all advice, in contrast, may indicate dependency.

Evaluating the Dialogue's Outcome.   The third set of criteria can be applied to the results of the dialogue (e.g., the set of alternatives identified as suitable for the individual). Providing feedback during the dialogue reduces the chance of problematic outcomes. Still, problematic and conflicting outcomes may appear anyway (e.g., in cases where the client disregards previous feedback). I suggest two criteria for this facet. The first is the number of alternatives included in the client's list at the end of the search. A list of four to seven promising alternatives seems desirable because it constitutes a set that is small enough to be further explored (Gati, Fassa, & Houminer, 1995) yet large enough to allow exploration without too narrow a focus. A list that contains only one or two alternatives may limit the clients, whereas a list of more than 10 may confuse them. Second, the degree of heterogeneity among the compatible alternatives should also be considered. Heterogeneity, which means that the set of alternatives includes dissimilar occupations (Gati, 1985), may sometimes indicate that the client's preferences are not consolidated or that very few aspects were used in the search.

Feedback can be provided during the dialogue with the CACGS for each of these three sets of criteria. For example, in the relevant cases, the client may receive feedback such as "You are advised to consider compromising more because the number of alternatives compatible with your preferences is decreasing too fast"; "You did not use the module of 'Almost Compatible Alternatives'; you are advised to use it before ending your dialogue"; or "Your list of compatible occupations includes occupations from different fields and is not focused enough. You are advised to see a career counselor to help you verify that this list is indeed the most compatible with your preferences."

THE INTERRELATIONS BETWEEN THEORY, RESEARCH, AND PRACTICE

Three Examples of Relevant Research

As demonstrated, questions about the design and development of CACGSs provide a critical test of counselors' and system developers' ability to transform theory into practice. Specifically, such a transformation requires operationalizing the theory's concepts and designing practical procedures based on the relationships among these concepts. However, the interrelationship between theory and practice also has another facet. Specifically, CACGSs can serve as an important means for testing the theories underlying them as well as answering other theoretical questions. For instance, the information included in the occupational database and the monitored dialogues of clients with the system are unique and novel data, and analyzing them may contribute to our understanding of the processes involved in career decision making. In this section, I will describe three types of studies that utilize the potential of CACGSs for providing these new kinds of data.

The Relationships Between the Relative Importance of Aspects and the Individual's Willingness to Compromise. As mentioned, in MBCD, the importance of the aspects and the within-aspect preferences are elicited separately. This permits us to examine the relationship between the relative importance of an aspect and the client's willingness to compromise on that aspect, as reflected in the client's within-aspect preferences. Recall that in the sequential-elimination approach (Gati, 1986; see Figure 1), the search for career alternatives compatible with the individual's preferences begins with the most important aspect, continues to the aspect second in importance, and so on. This sequence is based on the assumption that the client is less willing to compromise on the more important aspects and more willing to do so on the less important ones (Gati, 1993). Hence, only few, if any, alternatives will be eliminated due to preferences in aspects of low importance. This assumption was tested and supported by Gati, Shenhav, and Givon (1993), who used the monitored dialogues of clients with MBCD as well as data collected by questionnaires. In this study, the client's willingness to compromise was defined by the number of within-aspect levels the individual was willing to consider in each aspect, where a larger number of levels indicated a greater willingness to compromise. It was found, as hypothesized, that the number of acceptable levels was smaller in the more important aspects than in the less important ones.

The Structure of Aspects.   One of the questions faced by developers of CACGS is which set of aspects to include in the system. Theoretically, a large number of aspects is desirable. This is the case because the variety of aspects permits a more refined and sensitive search for compatible alternatives. However, if the number of aspects is too large, it may confuse the client and render the career decision-making process too long and cumbersome. Thus, all CACGSs have to limit the set of included aspects in some way, and the question is then which aspects to include. A recent study by Gati, Givon, Meyer, and Fassa (1995) demonstrated one way of investigating this question using the data available in a CACGS. In this study, the relationship among the aspects was examined using two aspect structures: One was derived from career clients' preferences as reported during their dialogue with MBCD, whereas the other was derived from the occupational database of MBCD, which was constructed using career counselors' ratings of occupations. Comparing the structures revealed that some pairs of aspects are close to each other in both structures (e.g., working in the field of "Arts & Entertainment" and using "Artistic ability" or working in the field of "Business" and being engaged in "Negotiation"). This proximity indicated that these pairs of aspects received a similar pattern of preferences across subjects and similar ratings across occupations and hence that they are similar in meaning. This covariation in preferences and co-occurrence in occupations indicates a partial overlap and suggests that the two aspects can be combined into one. This study may also have theoretical implications for the relationship between interests and abilities (e.g., Barak, Librowsky, & Shiloh, 1989; Barak, Shiloh, & Haushner, 1992), as the observed pattern of proximities seems to indicate a dependence between the two.

The Implicit Decision Strategies Used by Career Clients.   There are two general families of decision-making models: compensatory models (e.g., multiattribute utility and expected utility) and noncompensatory models (e.g., sequential elimination and satisficing). Gati and Tikotzki (1989) analyzed the monitored dialogues of clients with a computerized occupational information system as a basis for answering the question of which strategies are more frequently used by individuals—compensatory or noncompensatory. The findings revealed that fewer than 4% of the subjects searched for information in a manner compatible with a compensatory model (i.e., collecting comprehensive information on all options), whereas all the others used a noncompensatory search (i.e., focusing on only some alternatives while disregarding others), at least in part of the dialogue. Furthermore, as could be expected, the tendency to rely on a noncompensatory search increased when more career alternatives were considered. These findings, which were observed in a system in which the dialogue was not constrained in any way, are compatible with those of Lichtenberg, Shaffer, and Aranchtingi (1993), who used an experimental design, and can be interpreted as supporting the descriptive validity of the sequential-elimination approach.

Relevance for Career Counselors

The increased trend toward using CACGSs in career counseling has important implications for counselors' work. Specifically, many career counselors incorporate the use of CACGSs into the counseling process and make the computerized dialogue an integral part of their interaction with their clients. For example, before directing their clients to use a CACGS, the counselor can discuss their expectations, highlighting common misperceptions about computerized systems. After the completion of the dialogue with the CACGS, the counselor can help the clients benefit more from the dialogue by discussing, integrating, and interpreting the feedback and the information received during the dialogue. Moreover, by reviewing the printout of the dialogue, counselors can learn more about their clients (e.g., consolidation and consistency of reported preferences, willingness to compromise, and decision-making style) and identify inconsistencies with their own impressions from previous sessions. Some of these characteristics can then be brought to the clients' attention in order to increase their self-understanding and awareness.

Thus, while CACGSs can replace some of the counselors' traditional roles (e.g., assessing vocational interests, eliciting preferences, identifying promising alternatives, and providing information), they also allow them to devote more time to their other roles as counselors. These other roles include providing refined judgments and sensitive evaluations, as in identifying preferences that are unrealistic for the client, dealing with dilemmas that result from conflicting preferences, coping with the influence of significant others, restructuring the decision, reframing the compromises involved to reduce their negative consequences (Gati, 1995), and exploring ways to increase the prospects of realizing an attractive alternative.

In addition to the changes that may occur in their work as a result of the incorporation of CACGSs into the counseling process, counselors can benefit from the familiarity with the rationale underlying CACGSs. Indeed, I believe that the interplay between theory and practice in CACGS can benefit not only career decision-making theory and CACGSs but also face-to-face career counseling. First, decision theory (e.g., Brown, 1990; Gati, 1986; Katz, 1993) and information-processing theory (e g., Peterson, Sampson, & Reardon, 1991; Pitz & Harren, 1980) may be considered as additional potential theoretical frameworks for guiding career counseling practice. Second, many of the dilemmas and problems involved in using CACGSs are also encountered daily by counselors, and some of the suggestions for dealing with them may be applicable to face-to-face counseling as well. These include: (a) the need to acknowledge that all career-related information may be subject to unintentional selection and presentation biases; (b) the need to elicit both aspirations and compromises; (c) the need to cope with the uncertainty involved; (d) the need to provide only the relevant information; and (e) the need to evaluate the quality of the counseling process in real time.

In turn, the developers of CACGSs should utilize the practical knowledge of people who work with clients daily because their direct experience can provide unique insights. For example, the notion of *fuzzy logic* (e.g., Hesketh, Pryor, & Gleitzman, 1989), which refers to processes based on heuristics and approximations and often characterizes the way counselors work with their clients, may be beneficial if implemented into CACGSs. Furthermore, counselors can help improve available systems by constructively criticizing them (Katz, 1984) and, if possible, participating in the development teams along with theoreticians.

SUMMARY

Based on decision theory, I reviewed 12 problems and dilemmas related to the development of CACGSs. Some of these problems concern the occupational database (e.g., the apparent precision of the data versus its unique "soft" character; dealing with within-occupational variance); others are related to the career decision-making process itself (e.g., how should abilities and skills be taken into account; to rank or not to rank); and still others concern the effectiveness of the dialogue (e.g., sophistication versus simplicity or flexible versus constrained dialogue). I then described MBCD, a specific CACGS that implements many of what I believe to be desirable or at least satisfactory solutions to these problems and dilemmas. Next, I discussed the need for designing a quality control module to monitor the dialogue in real time and provide the client with immediate individualized feedback. In contrast to Katz (1984), who discussed the issue of the quality of CACGSs in general (e.g., accuracy of the information, theoretical basis), the focus of this chapter was on the quality of individuals' career decision making, as expressed in their dialogue with the computerized system. I suggested that the evaluation of the dialogue's quality should be based on three sets of criteria that correspond to three types of data: the client's inputs, the course of the dialogue, and the dialogue's outcomes.

Obviously, no computer can provide the human qualities of a counselor. For example, no computer can replace the face-to-face personalized contact and the human support that counselors provide. Similarly, a computer cannot help clients resolve their conflicts between incompatible preferences or deal with the influences of significant others, nor can they help clients acknowledge and accept their weaknesses and disabilities. Indeed, Katz (1984) proposed that the question of interest is not whether a computer-assisted career guidance system can replace counselors (for which the answer is obviously no) but rather, What are the desirable characteristics of a system of this sort that can be considered as "doing no harm" and can thus be distributed unrestrictedly? I believe that the preferred way to answer this question is by dealing explicitly with the problems and dilemmas discussed in this chapter and particularly by incorporating a quality control module into CACGSs. Such a quality control module should direct clients to personal counseling if their particular problems cannot be dealt with appropriately by the CACGS.

CACGSs' role as a change agent, provoking changes and stimulating improvements, provided the rationale for this chapter. I demonstrated here that the development of CACGSs raises many important theoretical questions. For example, what should the relationship between aspirations and compromise be? How should uncertainty be dealt with? What constitutes an ideal career decision-making process? Only after we have well-defined answers to these questions can we translate them into practical procedures. Furthermore, once CACGSs are incorporated into the counseling practice, they can be used as additional means for testing various theoretical conceptualizations. The monitored dialogues of clients, as well as the occupational information stored in the CACGS' database, have already proven themselves as fruitful sources of data that can contribute to a better understanding of the career decision-making and career counseling processes. This constructive interplay between career counseling theory and practice in the context of CACGSs can, I believe, benefit not only theoreticians and researchers but also practitioners and their clients.

I would like to thank Naomi Fassa, Martin Katz, and Jim Sampson for valuable discussions and Reuma Benziman, Beni Benyamin, Naomi Goldblum, Shoshana Helman, Dafna Houminer, Elchanan Meir, Ofra Nevo, Sam Osipow, Shoshana Shiloh, and Dan Zakay for their comments on a previous draft of this chapter. The preparation of this chapter was supported by a grant from the Higher Education Board, Department of Education, Israel.

REFERENCES

Anastasi, A. (1992). Tests and assessment: What counselors should know about the use and interpretation of psychological tests. *Journal of Counseling and Development, 70,* 610–615.

Barak, A., Librowsky, I., & Shiloh, S. (1989). Cognitive determinants of interests: An extension of a theoretical model and initial empirical examinations. *Journal of Vocational Behavior, 34,* 318–334.

Barak, A., Shiloh, S., & Haushner, O. (1992). Modification of interests through cognitive restructuring: Test of a theoretical model in preschool children. *Journal of Counseling Psychology, 39,* 490–497.

Beach, L. R., & Potter, R. E. (1992). The pre-choice screening of options. *Acta Psychologica, 81,* 115–126.

Brown, D. (1990). Models of career decision making. In D. Brown, L. Brooks, & Associates (Eds.), *Career choice and development* (2d ed., pp. 395–421). San Francisco: Jossey-Bass.

Dawis, R., & Lofquist, L. (1984). *A psychological theory of work adjustment.* Minneapolis: University of Minnesota Press.

Gati, I. (1985). Description of alternative measures of the concepts of vocational interest: Crystallization, congruence, and coherence. *Journal of Vocational Behavior, 27,* 37–55.

Gati, I. (1986). Making career decisions: A sequential elimination approach. *Journal of Counseling Psychology, 33,* 408–417.

Gati, I. (1987). Description and validation of a procedure for the interpretation of an interest inventory score profile. *Journal of Counseling Psychology, 34,* 141–148.

Gati, I. (1990a). The contribution of differential feature-cost analysis to the evaluation of computer-assisted career guidance system. *Journal of Career Development, 17,* 119–128.

Gati, I. (1990b). Why, when, and how to take into account the uncertainty involved in career decisions. *Journal of Counseling Psychology, 37,* 277–280.

Gati, I. (1990c). *Making Better Career Decisions (MBCD): A computer-assisted career decision making system.* Department of Psychology, The Hebrew University of Jerusalem.

Gati, I. (1993). Career compromises. *Journal of Counseling Psychology, 40,* 416–424.

Gati, I. (1995). *Framings of career compromises and their implications.* Unpublished manuscript, Department of Psychology, The Hebrew University of Jerusalem,

Gati, I. (1995). Computer-assisted career counseling: Dilemmas, problems and possible solutions. *Journal of Counseling and Development, 73,* 51–56.

Gati, I., & Blumberg, D. (1991). Computer versus counselor interpretation of interest inventories: The case of the Self-Directed Search. *Journal of Counseling Psychology, 38,* 350–366.

Gati, I., Fassa, N., & Houminer, D. (1995). Applying decision theory to career counseling practice: The sequential elimination approach. *Career Development Quarterly, 43,* 211–220.

Gati, I., Garty, Y., & Fassa, N. (1996). Using career-related aspects to assess person-environment fit. *Journal of Counseling Psychology, 63.*

Gati, I., Givon, M., Meyer, Y., & Fassa, N. (1995). *The structure of occupational aspects: A comparison between the perceptions of career counselees and career counselors.* Unpublished manuscript, Department of Psychology, The Hebrew University of Jerusalem.

Gati, I., Shenhav, M., & Givon, M. (1993). Processes involved in career preferences and compromises. *Journal of Counseling Psychology, 40,* 53–64.

Gati, I., & Tikotzki, Y. (1989). Strategies for the collection and processing of occupational information in making career decisions. *Journal of Counseling Psychology, 36,* 430–439.

Gelatt, H. B. (1989). Positive uncertainty: A new decision-making framework for counseling. *Journal of Counseling Psychology, 36,* 252–256.

Gottfredson, L. S. (1981). Circumscription and compromise: A developmental theory of occupational aspirations. *Journal of Counseling Psychology, 28,* 545–579.

Gottfredson, L. S. (1986). Occupational aptitude patterns map: Development and implications for a theory of job aptitude requirements [Monograph]. *Journal of Vocational Behavior, 29,* 254–291.

Harris-Bowlsbey, J. (1984). The computer and career development. *Journal of Career Development, 63,* 145–148.

Harris-Bowlsbey, J. (1991). *The respective roles of the counselor and the computer in the career development process.* Paper presented at the International Association of Educational and Vocational Guidance Conference, Lisbon, Portugal.

Hesketh, B., Pryor, R., & Gleitzman, M. (1989). Fuzzy logic: Towards measuring Gottfredson's concept of occupational social space. *Journal of Counseling Psychology, 36,* 103–109.

Jepsen, D. A., & Dilley, J. S. (1974). Vocational decision-making models: A review and comparative analysis. *Review of Educational Research, 44,* 331–349.

Johnston, J. A., Buescher, K. L., & Heppner, M. J. (1988). Computerized career information and guidance systems: Caveat emptor. *Journal of Counseling and Development, 67,* 39–41.

Jungermann, H., & Schutz, H. (1992). Personal decision counseling: Counselors without clients? *Applied Psychology: An International Review, 41,* 185–200.

Katz, M. R. (1966). A model for guidance for career decision making. *Vocational Guidance Quarterly, 15,* 2–10.

Katz, M. R. (1979). Assessment of career decision making: Process and outcome. In A. M. Mitchell, G. B., Jones, & J. D. Krumboltz (Eds.), *Social learning and career decision making* (pp. 81–100). Cranston, RI: Carroll Press.

Katz, M. R. (1984). Computer-assisted guidance: A walkthrough with running comments. *Journal of Counseling and Development, 63,* 153–157.

Katz, M. R. (1993). *Computer-assisted career decision making.* Hillsdale, NJ: Erlbaum.

Katz, M. R., & Shatkin, L. (1983). Characteristics of computer-assisted guidance. *The Counseling Psychologist, 11*(4), 15–31.

Leung, S. A., & Harmon, L. W. (1990). Individual and sex differences in the zone of acceptable alternatives. *Journal of Counseling Psychology, 37,* 153–159.

Lichtenberg, J. W., Shaffer, M., & Arachtingi, B. M. (1993). Expected utility and sequential elimination models of career decision making. *Journal of Vocational Behavior, 42,* 237–252.

Lofquist, L. H., & Dawis, R. V. (1978). Values as secondary to needs in the theory of work adjustment. *Journal of Vocational Behavior, 12,* 12–19.

Lunneborg, C. E. (1982). Systematic biases in brief self-ratings of vocational qualifications. *Journal of Vocational Behavior, 20,* 255–275.

Matarazzo, J. D. (1986). Computerized clinical psychological test interpretations: Unvalidated plus all mean no sigma. *American Psychologist, 41,* 14–24.

Meir, E. I., & Yaari, Y. (1988). The relationship between congruent specialty choice within occupation and satisfaction. *Journal of Vocational Behavior, 33,* 99–117.

Miller, G. A. (1956). The magical number seven, plus or minus two: Some limits on our capacity for processing information. *Psychological Review, 63,* 81–97.

Mitchell, L. K., & Krumboltz, J. D. (1984). Research on human decision making: Implications for career decision making and counseling. In S. D. Brown & R. W. Lent (Eds.), *Handbook of counseling psychology* (pp. 238–282). New York: Wiley.

Montgomery, H. (1989). From cognition to action: The search for dominance in decision making. In H. Montgomery & O. Svenson (Eds.), *Process and structure in human decision making* (pp. 23–49). New York: Wiley.

Neimeyer, G. J. (1988). Cognitive integration and differentiation in vocational behavior. *The Counseling Psychologist, 16,* 440–475.

Niles, S., & Garis, J. W. (1990). The effects of a career planning course and a computer-assisted career guidance program (SIGI PLUS) on undecided university students. *Journal of Career Development, 16,* 237–248.

Osipow, S. H. (1983). *Theories of career development* (3d ed.). Englewood Cliffs, NJ: Prentice Hall.

Osipow, S. H. (1987). Counseling psychology: Theory, research, and practice in career counseling. *Annual Review of Psychology, 38,* 257–278.

Peterson, G. W., Sampson, J. P., & Reardon, R. C. (1991). *Career development and services: A cognitive approach.* Pacific Grove, CA: Brooks/Cole.

Phillips, S. D. (1992). Career counseling: Choice and implementation. In S. D. Brown & R. W. Lent (Eds.), *Handbook of counseling psychology* (2d ed., pp. 513–547). New York: Wiley.

Phillips, S. D. (1994). Choice and change: Convergence from the decision-making perspective. In M. L. Savickas & R. W. Lent (Eds.), *Convergence in career development theories: Implications for science and practice* (pp. 155–163). Palo Alto, CA: Davies-Black Publishing.

Pitz, G. F., & Harren, V. A. (1980). An analysis of career decision making from the point of view of information processing and decision theory. *Journal of Vocational Behavior, 16,* 320–346.

Rayman, J. R. (1990). Computers and career counseling. In W. B. Walsh & S. H. Osipow (Eds.), *Career counseling: Contemporary topics in vocational psychology* (pp. 225–262). Hillsdale, NJ: Erlbaum.

Sampson, J. P., Jr. (1983). An integrated approach to computer applications in counseling psychology. *The Counseling Psychologist, 11,* 65–74.

Sampson, J. P., Jr. (1986). The use of computer-assisted instruction in support of psychotherapeutic processes. *Computer in Human Behavior, 2,* 1–9.

Sampson, J. P., Jr., Reardon, R. C., Humphrey, J. K., Peterson, G. W., Evans, M. A., & Domkowski, D. (1990). A differential feature-cost analysis of nine computer-assisted career guidance systems. *Journal of Career Development, 17,* 81–112.

Savickas, M. L., & Lent, R. W. (Eds.). (1994). *Convergence in career development theories: Implications for Science and Practice.* Palo Alto, CA: Davies-Black Publishing.

Simon, H. A. (1957). *Models of man: Social and rational.* New York: Wiley.

Super, D. E. (1953). A theory of vocational development. *American Psychologist, 8,* 185–190.

Taylor, K. M. (1988). Advances in career-planning systems. In W. B. Walsh & S. H. Osipow (Eds.), *Career decision making* (pp. 137–211). Hillsdale, NJ: Erlbaum.

Tversky, A., & Kahneman, D. (1981). The framing of decisions and the psychology of choice. *Science, 211,* 453–458.

Walsh, W. B., & Osipow, S. H. (Eds.). (1988). *Career decision making.* Hillsdale, NJ: Erlbaum.

Watts, A. G. (1986). The role of the computer in career guidance. *International Journal for the Advancement of Counseling, 9,* 145–158.

Zakay, D., & Barak, A. (1984). Meaning and career decision making. *Journal of Vocational Behavior, 24,* 1–14.

Zytowski, D. G., & Hay, R. (1984). Do birds of a feather flock together? A test of the similarities within and the differences between five occupations. *Journal of Vocational Behavior, 24,* 242–248.

CHAPTER THIRTEEN

A Framework for Linking Career Theory and Practice

Mark L. Savickas
Northeastern Ohio Universities College of Medicine

THIS CHAPTER DESCRIBES a framework designed to strengthen the connection between theory and practice as well as to ease the transaction between researchers and counselors. Before describing the framework, the chapter presents the rationale for the framework and a personal story about how it evolved. The initial part of the chapter also considers why counselors and researchers might benefit from schema that coordinate the application of theory to practice. The middle section of the chapter describes a framework that systematically organizes the association among career theories, problems presented by clients, and career services. The chapter then concludes with a discussion of how the framework might stimulate and facilitate research on career intervention and advance a science of practice.

RECIPROCITIES BETWEEN THEORY AND PRACTICE

In everyday life, the world presents itself to individuals as problems to be solved. This statement is doubly true in the consulting room where a counselor faces the problem of how to best address a client's problem. In working as problem-solving consultants, counselors encounter daily the professional problem of deciding which theory and intervention to use with which clients. For example, when clients seek help in choosing a college major, counselors may address that concern by using the trait-and-factor model and its associated methods and materials. In this instance, the model may sufficiently address the problem. However, all too often, a client's problem does not align with available career theories as well as it does in this example. A counselor's favorite theory may not address some problems or only partially address them. Career theories do not comprehensively address all the problems that clients present because career theorists designed their models to be partial, or, to use Super's (1969, pp. 8–9) word, *segmental*. Career theorists specify which problems they seek to address and then construct a theory to comprehend those problems. For example, Super (1990) used developmental theory and longitudinal methods to study intrapersonal differences in career decision-making processes at two or more points in time, whereas Holland (1985) used person-environment fit theory and cross-sectional methods to study interpersonal differences in personality traits between two or more individuals. Neither Super nor Holland ignored the time or trait dimensions in vocational behavior; rather they each emphasized one over the other.

Theorists not only devise their conceptual models to address circumscribed problems, they also select a particular epistemology and a disciplinary stance that shapes what they can know about those problems. Consequently, even when theories address the same problem, theories are not univocal. Because theorists view the problem from different standpoints, they see distinct aspects of the problem and thus prescribe interventions targeted for the aspect that their viewpoint accentuates. Thus, problems in making a career choice can be conceptualized from the perspective of career maturity, career decision making, and vocational identity. Each of these perspectives on the choice problem stems from different epistemologies and disciplines. For example, viewing choice problems as immaturity follows from a developmental psychology perspective and leads to educational interventions that foster more adaptive attitudes and competencies for career choice. In contrast, viewing choice problems as decision-making difficulties follows from an adjustment psychology perspective and leads to interventions that reduce anxiety or conflict prompted by the choices under consideration. Viewing choice problems as identity issues follows from a personality psychology perspective and leads to psychosocial interventions that foster personal development. Of course, taking all three perspectives on the choice problem deepens the counselor's understanding of the client's situation and leads to more comprehensive and effective intervention.

Theorists' preferences for epistemic and disciplinary stances shape how they address the question, What can we know about a problem? Few counselors are concerned with this knowledge question. Instead, counselors concentrate on a different question, namely, What should the client do about the problem? The answer to the theorists' knowledge question rests in abstract principles and objective knowledge. The answer to the counselor's action question rests in subjective understanding of a unique client in a particular situation. Of course, whenever possible, counselors use objective knowledge and theory to conceptualize the client's subjective experience. However, all too often, theory only addresses part of the client's complex problem. Thus, to fully understand each client and what to do to assist that client, counselors must draw from their own experience and practical knowledge. Whereas theory can be partial, practice must be holistic.

Clients who present career problems cannot isolate their career problems from their other life issues. This leads to the question addressed by Gottfredson in this volume. How do counselors apply theories that are partial and simple to clients who are whole and complex?

LINKING CAREER THEORY AND PRACTICE: THE PRIVATE LOGIC OF COUNSELORS

In general, the most salient issue at the center of the theory-practice nexus seems to focus on how counselors decide what to do. Particular questions that stem from this issue include the following: Which theories do counselors use with whom? How do counselors turn objective theory into subjective understanding? Which techniques work best with which clients? How can counselors communicate practice knowledge to theorists?

Such questions are best studied by working with counselors who have an extensive repertoire of theory-based techniques and vary the interventions they use to suit client needs and styles. By this, I mean to exclude counselors who rely on one theory and its associated techniques. These "unitheoretical" counselors commit themselves to a singular perspective rooted in one theoretical model. For example, at the beginning of my career, I adhered to the trait-and-factor model and assigned a standard battery of tests to all new career clients before meeting with them for the first time. Counseling then consisted of a session in which I interpreted the test results, followed by a second session in which the client would make choices and plans. Counselors who adhere to a single perspective make no choices about which techniques to employ with a new client because each client receives the same basic service. This approach is not taken just by adherents to the trait-and-factor model. I have seen some career counselors rigidly use the singular perspective associated with person-centered, social cognitive, and Adlerian counseling models and methods.

Answers to questions concerning theory-practice linkages might be better directed to counselors who take multiple perspectives on clients' presenting problems. These counselors use technical eclecticism as they draw on several career theories to conceptualize a career case and possess a diverse repertoire of intervention techniques associated with different theories. When these counselors encounter a new client, they match their available theories and techniques to the needs of that client. In effect, these counselors answer, for each new client, a critical question first stated by Williamson and Bordin (1941): "What counseling techniques (and conditions) will produce what types of results with what types of students?" (p. 8). I have often wondered what private rules these counselors follow in choosing which procedures to use with whom. Studying how practitioners apply theory seems to be a high priority for those who wish to better coordinate theory and practice, to the enrichment of both.

The next section of this chapter offers one response to the question of how counselors decide what to do with each client. I try to answer the question by presenting a framework that links career theories, client problems, and counseling interventions. The framework emerged from 20 years of counseling experience and conversations with colleagues. It seeks to bridge the current gap between theory and practice in a useful, commonsense manner. Metaphorically, I view the framework as a toolbox that organizes the most common career problems and relevant career interventions in discrete compartments bounded by separate career theories. I hope the framework will be useful to practitioners in guiding and increasing the application of theoretical models, methods, and materials.

HOW THE FRAMEWORK EMERGED

My practice has always informed my understanding of existing theory. My first interest in theory came from desperation. When I was completing my training as a school psychologist, the director of the university's counseling center offered me a position as a counselor. In reporting to work for the first time, I entered the counseling center behind a student who asked the receptionist for an appointment to discuss his career. The director joined us in the foyer, said hello to the student, and then said to me, "Here is your first appointment." As a school psychology trainee, I knew nothing about career intervention. The director quickly taught me how to do trait-and-factor guidance. He was a past master of the model and its methods. I tried to emulate his counseling style and strategies. Half of the time, I seemed to succeed. In those instances, my clients were happy and referred their friends to me. However, half the time I failed. Thus, in striving to improve, I did what Holland (this volume) often suggests—I read a book. The book was *Vocational Psychology: The Study of Vocational Behavior and Development* by John Crites (1969). It taught me about the content and process of vocational development and instructed me in the effort to develop career choice readiness by helping clients to learn and use attitudes and competencies for planning, exploring, and deciding. These methods helped with clients who had previously remained undecided or unrealistic after completing trait-and-factor guidance with me. My work improved. Now I was useful to two-thirds of my clients, or even three-fourths, in a good week. Nevertheless, I was still frustrated. I wondered why my attempts to develop career choice readiness worked so well with some clients yet were ineffective with other clients. How could I help clients who were indecisive, not just undecided, prepare to decide?

In my search for an answer, I looked to psychodynamic theory. Ed Watkins (1984) and David Blustein and his associates (Blustein, Devenis, & Kidney, 1989) taught me about the psychodynamics of career development and the importance of identity and life scripts. The work of Audrey Collin and Richard Young (1986) and

David Jepsen (1992) on action theory, hermeneutics, and the narrative paradigm taught me how individuals construct their identities and write their scripts. Again, my work improved. It got even better when I learned about null environments, contextual affordances, and cultural embeddedness from Nancy Betz (1989), Arnold Spokane (1991), and Fred Vondracek (1990).

So that was my journey: from objective vocational guidance to developmental career education to subjective career counseling to enabling a client to cope with the opportunity structure and cultural barriers. Toward the end, I finally understood what a prominent colleague meant when she told me the shocking news that she no longer did career counseling. Instead, each of her clients receives brief therapy that includes attention to career concerns embedded in the constellation of their life roles.

During my journey, I never realized that I was a fanatic. I had become a fan of each new theory that I learned. As I traveled on my long journey toward becoming a useful career counselor, I had become increasingly theory-rich and action-poor. How could I turn my empirical knowledge and interpretive understanding loose in a consulting room? I eventually figured out that my infatuation with each new theory that I learned had, in succession, trapped me in a singular perspective provided by the standpoint of that theory.

In the end, I returned to what my colleague had said about brief therapy. Brief therapy requires that a counselor adopt multiple perspectives from which to view a client's career concerns and respond with a technical eclecticism that matches client needs with appropriate interventions. In other words, I sought to learn to use theories and their associated techniques as they were meant to be used. Each theory addresses a circumscribed problem; trying to apply it outside of its range of convenience frustrates both the client and the counselor.

To orchestrate the theories and techniques in a manner that eases the theory-practice exchange, I designed a framework for career services. The framework makes me more systematic in applying technical eclecticism as well as allows me to understand how each client whom I counsel teaches me something about theory and teaches my theories something about practice. I have used the framework as a matrix, such as the one suggested by Herr (this volume), to connect my practice-knowledge to the career development needs expressed by particular types of clients. I believe that the framework responds, at least in part, to Gottfredson's (this volume) suggestion that we strengthen the linkages between theory and practice by drawing a schematic map that shows how to better use segments of existing career theories to address specific practical problems. Eventually, the framework may lead to systematic protocols of micropractices for particular populations as suggested by Lucas (this volume). For now, the framework forces me to consider each client from the multiple perspectives of the object, the subject, the context, and their reciprocal interaction. The framework sometimes even helps me to navigate the troubled waters of the scientist–practitioner stream in professional psychology.

A FRAMEWORK FOR CAREER SERVICES

In simple terms, the framework for career services adapts Wagner's (1971) theory of structural analysis of personality to the domain of vocational psychology. Wagner constructed structural analysis as a practical means to relate psychodynamic personality theory to the clinical use of intelligence tests, projective techniques, and personality inventories.

Wagner's theory of structural analysis uses three basic constructs to map personality: *facade self, introspective self,* and *drives.* Developmentally, the facade self emerges first, in response to environmental stimuli, as a means of adapting to social demands. The facade self, simply stated, consists of behavioral tendencies and problem-solving skills. It reacts to the environment and maintains reality contact. The introspective self develops later when "the individual takes cognizance of his [or her] own functioning, achieves a sense of identity, and formulates a subjective set of ideals, goals, and self-appraisals" (Wagner, 1971, p. 424). The introspective self, simply stated, consists of self-concept and ideals. It provides for internal living and enlarges the sense of identity in the facade self. In the structural model, drives press on both the facade and introspective selves.

The facade and introspective units of structural analysis correspond to the objective and subjective perspectives. The facade is rational, analytic, and empirical. In contrast to the facade's logical functioning, the introspective self is psychological. It is the domain of complex purposes, consciousness, and agency. Counselors operationally define the facade with *scores* from objective measures such as interest inventories and understand the introspective self with *stories* from projective techniques or biographical narratives. Whereas the facade is logical and the introspective self is psychological, the environment is sociological. Individuals are always situated in some community; they act and feel relative to the situations in which they find themselves. The internal dialogues between the facade and introspective selves is a process dimension that consists of intrapersonal "self-talk." The other process dimension model in structural analysis is the interpersonal reciprocal interaction between the facade self and the community.

The structural analysis model, translated into the language of the vocational realm, organizes the multiple perspectives from which the practitioner might view a career client and helps the counselor to assess where, in the welter of complex stimuli presented by the client, the most useful intervention might be aimed.

Figure 1 shows the simple translation of the schemata into the language of worklife. The environment is portrayed as life roles and can be discussed in the language of Super's (1990) life-career rainbow model and construct of role salience. The facade is a vocational self that can be operationally defined by Holland's (1985) RIASEC adjustive orientations and behavioral repertoires. Viewing traits as unitary adaptive mechanisms also locates them in the facade self. The introspective self can be understood using Hughes' (1958) construct of subjective career and linguistically explained and operationally defined with variables such as "Adler's life-style"

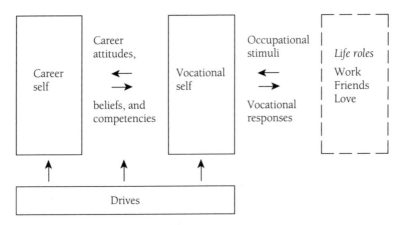

FIGURE 1   A Framework for Converging Career Theories

From "Convergence Prompts Theory Renovation, Research Unification, and Practice Coherence," by M. L. Savickas, 1994, in *Convergence in Career Development Theories*, M. L. Savickas & R. W. Lent, Eds. (p. 251), Palo Alto, CA: Davies-Black Publishing. Reprinted with permission.

(Watkins, 1984), Cochran's (1991) "narrative knowledge," Super's (1954) "career patterns," and Super's (1963) "self-concept." Drives have been largely ignored in vocational theory, with the notable exception of Bordin's (1990) important work and measures such as the *Vocational Apperception Test* (Ammons, Butler, & Herzog, 1950) and card sorts (Slaney & MacKinnon-Slaney, 1990).

The process dimensions in the framework can be comprehended using Krumboltz's (1979) social learning theory. For example, the interaction between the vocational self and environment lends itself to stimulus-response language and to Bandura's (1978) ideas about reciprocal determinism. The self-reflective structure called *career* engages in self-observation generalizations and can be operationally defined with the *Career Maturity Inventory* (Crites, 1978), *Career Beliefs Inventory* (Krumboltz, 1988), and *Career Development Inventory* (Super, Thompson, Lindeman, Joordan, & Myers, 1981).

CONTENT OF THE FRAMEWORK: PROBLEMS AND INTERVENTIONS

Each segment of the framework can be delineated by the types of problem and interventions it houses. A review of career decision-making scales and career maturity inventories identifies distinct types of problems that can be located at different places in the framework. The framework portrayed in Figure 2 shows six types of career questions that clients ask. The illustration links a particular career intervention to each question. The six types of career services are occupational

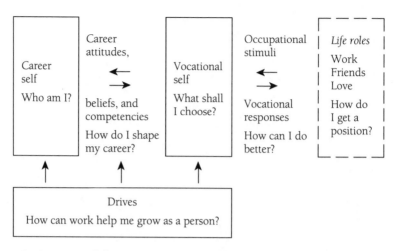

FIGURE 2   A Framework for Career Assessment and Intervention

Adapted from "Convergence Prompts Theory Renovation, Research Unification, and Practice Coherence," by M. L. Savickas, 1994, in *Convergence in Career Development Theories*, M. L. Savickas & R. W. Lent, Eds. (p. 253), Palo Alto, CA: Davies-Black Publishing. Reprinted with permission.

placement, vocational *guidance*, career *counseling*, career *education*, career *therapy*, and position *coaching*. The following six sections explain, for each segment in the framework, the explicit question, implicit problem, relevant theory, and pertinent intervention.

Occupational Placement Addresses Problems in Starting a Career

How do I get a job? Clients ask this question when they know the occupation in which they want to work and seek help in securing a job in that occupation. This question and the problems inherent in it are located in the "Life roles" segment of the framework because they concern the world of work and behavior in it. Individuals who have made a choice and committed themselves to implementing it benefit from assistance in planning and achieving the chosen position. Placement interventions emphasize skill training and concentrate on helping clients gather information, write résumés, network, search for opportunities, and prepare for interviews. Placement interventions may be directed to reduce job search anxiety, increase assertiveness, counter mistaken beliefs, encourage exploratory behavior, increase social skills, and refine self-presentation behavior. Placement need not deal only with occupations; it can also concentrate on helping clients secure an educational position such as a seat in graduate, professional, or technical school. Relevant theoretical models and placement methods are described in Herr, Rayman, and Garis (1993), Shingleton and Fitzpatrick (1985), and Stevens (1973).

Vocational Guidance Addresses Problems in Making Career Choices

What shall I choose? Clients ask this question when they possess a clear vocational identity and want help in translating that identity into occupational alternatives. This question and the problems inherent in it are located in the "Vocational self" segment of the framework because they concern the individual's coping repertoire. Individuals who can clearly articulate their vocational identity benefit from assistance in translating that identity into matching occupations. Starishevsky and Matlin's (1963) article about translating self-talk into occupation talk captures the essence of the guidance as a translation service. Guidance interventions emphasize translation of self-concepts into congruent occupations and concentrate on helping clients identify and explore possible matches between the self-concept and jobs. Guidance helps clients to articulate their vocational identities by discussing interests and abilities. It also increases the number of fitting options that the individual explores. Guidance interventions include administering and interpreting interest inventories and ability tests, providing educational and vocational information, prompting exploratory behavior, and identifying career fields for consideration. Relevant theoretical models and guidance methods are described by Holland (1985), Katz (1993), Lofquist and Dawis (1991), and Swanson (this volume).

Career Counseling Addresses Problems in Self-Conception

Who am I? Clients ask this question when they cannot yet articulate their self-concepts and want help in exploring who they are and what life goals they should pursue. This question and the problems inherent in it are located in the "Career self" segment of the framework because they deal with self-awareness and values. Individuals who cannot yet recognize and label the themes in their lives benefit from assistance in reflecting on patterns in their life stories. Career counseling interventions emphasize self-exploration and concentrate on helping clients to clarify their values and examine existential issues. The interventions include self-exploration and values clarification techniques that concentrate on heightening self-awareness and increasing self-esteem. The interventions prompt clients to elaborate their self-concepts through introspection. Relevant theoretical models and counseling methods are described by Brown and Brooks (1991), Lent (this volume), Savickas (1989), and Super (1954).

Career Education Addresses Problems in Developing a Career

How do I shape my career? Clients ask this question when they are disoriented and confused about their careers and want help in understanding and dealing with vocational developmental tasks. This question and the problems inherent in it are located in the arrows between the "Career self" and "Vocational self" segments of the framework shown in Figure 2 because they deal with career attitudes, beliefs, and competencies. Individuals who live in the moment without regard to imposing their own will on the future benefit from assistance in learning how to shape their destinies. Educational interventions emphasize self-control and concentrate on helping clients to develop adaptive attitudes toward and competencies for designing and managing their own careers. Career education interventions strengthen agentic attitudes, self-efficacy beliefs, and decision-making competencies. The actual interventions rely on deliberate psychological education and developmental counseling techniques that orient individuals to developmental tasks and foster the attitudes and competencies that lead to task mastery. Relevant theoretical models and career education methods are described by Blocher (1974), Hoyt (1975), Ivey (1986), and Super (1974).

Career Therapy Addresses Personal Problems

How can work help me grow as a person? Clients ask this question when they experience significant problems in formulating an integrated and coherent self-concept and want help to overcome barriers and thwart conditions that frustrate gratification of needs. This question and the problems inherent in it are located in the "Drives" segment of the framework because they deal with the need to feel more secure. Individuals who have been discouraged by their life experiences benefit from assistance in modifying their prototypical reactions to situations. Career therapy works best with clients whose excessive indecisiveness, anxiety, and conflicts thwart their efforts to form a coherent self-concept and adaptive lifestyle. Therapeutic interventions help clients to work through traumatic experiences, increase their sense of self-worth, and cope with problematic situations and significant others. Relevant theoretical models and career therapy methods are described by Blustein (1987), Blustein and Spengler (1995), Meara and Patton (1994), Richardson (this volume), and Subich (1993).

Position Coaching Addresses Problems of Adaptation

How can I do better? Clients ask this question when they encounter problems in meeting the demands of the educational or vocational position that they occupy. This question and its inherent problems are located in the arrows between the "Vocational self" and "Life roles" because they deal with adaptation to life roles. Individuals who want to increase their success in and satisfaction with their work roles benefit from assistance in strategizing how to get ahead and get along. Position coaching interventions emphasize adaptations that improve the fit between the self and position by helping clients deal with the organizational culture, position requirements, and co-workers. Coaching assists these individuals to clarify the problem, identify pertinent attitudes and behaviors that address the problem, and then rehearse and implement these new attitudes and behaviors. Relevant theoretical models and position coaching methods are described by Carden (1990), Crites (this volume), Dix and Savickas (1995), Hall (1987), Lofquist and Dawis (1969), and Savickas (1991).

APPLICATION OF THE FRAMEWORK

In performing an intake interview with a new client, I use the framework to systematically assess the client's career problem and consider what the client might do about it. Assessment differs from measurement. Career tests and inventories gather data with which to measure client traits that contribute to the presenting problem. The results of measurement locate the client on a normal distribution of people who vary on the trait being measured. In this manner, tests and inventories generally provide objective details about the problem. In contrast, assessment reveals the problem itself because assessment focuses on problem identification and problem solving. The point is that assessment of a problem should generally precede measurement of a problem. Before administering career inventories and tests, counselors should assess the problem about which they want to collect in-depth data, then administer the specific inventories and tests that measure that problem.

My assessment of a client's problem involves a short series of branching decisions. I begin with the main branch of determining whether the client is ready for vocational guidance or not. Functionally, this branching decision forces me to concentrate on the individual's vocational identity. If clients can state their interests, abilities, values, and life goals, then they are ready to translate that vocational identity into occupational possibilities. If they have a diffused or confused sense of vocational identity, then I turn my attention to understanding why they cannot coherently articulate their life themes and central projects.

After the primary branching decision, a secondary branching decision is made. If the primary decision was to concentrate on the causes of a diffuse identity, then the counselor must assess whether identity formation is thwarted by problems in (a) self-conception and meaning making, (b) delayed development of career coping attitudes and competencies, or (c) motivational distortions. In approaching this secondary branching decision, the counselor addresses issues of self-concept and values by asking clients to answer the Who am I? question and to tell stories about how their problem started. If their responses are appropriately coherent, consistent, and complex, the counselor concentrates attention on the maturity of attitudes and competencies for career choice and adaptation (i.e., the arrows between the "Career self" and "Vocational self" in Figure 2). If their responses are fragmented, disjointed, and simplistic, then the counselor explores the issue of anxiety and conflict ("Drives" segment of the model) to see if career therapy must deal with motivational distortions before proceeding to career counseling about self-concept issues. If the motivation problem seems to require motivation management, then the counselor can deal with the indecisiveness, anxiety, and conflict by using career therapy techniques. However, if the motivation problem seems to require motivation modification, then psychotherapy may be indicated. Assessing the problem as career misconceptions, self-concept development, or motivational distortion implicitly prescribes certain categories of intervention as noted herein. The counselor can use career education to change beliefs, career counseling to clarify self-concept, or career therapy to manage motivation.

If the primary branching decision was that the client possesses a clear and stable vocational identity, the issue now is one of person-environment fit. Accordingly, the secondary branching decision focuses on identifying the client's current problem in implementing the vocational identity in the social environment. In approaching this secondary branching decision, the counselor addresses issues of environmental demands and social situation by asking clients to answer the question, How am I doing in my current position? Client responses generally reveal whether they are encountering problems of educational/vocational choice, transition, or establishment. If their responses indicate that they want to stay in their current school or work position, then the counselor examines issues of how clients can do better (e.g., stabilize, consolidate, advance, maintain) in the position that they already occupy. If their responses indicate that they wish to change positions, then the counselor must determine whether they have chosen a new position. If they have not, then the counselor assesses what they can do to explore and choose a new position. If their responses indicate that they have already chosen a new position, then the counselor assesses what they will do to secure that position. Assessing the problem as choosing a new position, securing a new position, or improving performance in the current position implicitly prescribes certain categories of intervention as noted herein. The counselor can use guidance to predict fit, placement techniques to secure fit, or coaching techniques to improve fit.

Having identified the problem, the counselor can begin to conceptualize it by selecting a theory that speaks directly to the client's problem. That theory will almost automatically indicate general intervention strategies that address the problem. To devise a specific treatment plan, at this point, the counselor can assign tests and inventories to gather measurement data about the specific problem to be addressed. Each theory uses particular inventories and tests to operationally define the problems it addresses. Gathering measurements and more information about the client's problem is typically quite useful in formulating a specific treatment plan. For example, if the problem seems to be one of career attitudes, beliefs, and competencies, then the counselor might measure the problem by assigning inventories such as the *Career Development Inventory* (Super, Thompson, Lindeman, Joordan, & Myers, 1981), the *Career Maturity Inventory* (Crites, 1978), and the *Career Beliefs Inventory* (Krumboltz, 1988). If the problem seems to be one of choosing a fitting position, then the counselor might measure dimensions of fit by assigning the *Self-Directed Search* (Holland, 1985) or the *Strong Interest Inventory* (Harmon, Hansen, Borgen, & Hammer, 1994). In short, each theory uses distinct measurement tools

to clarify the problem. Thus, counselors are well advised to use measures constructed to operationally define the theory that they employ to conceptualize a
client's problem.

APPLYING PRACTICE TO THEORY

The model for career services presented in this chapter eases the exchange between
career theory and practice. The framework was designed to systematize and
enhance the interaction between theory and practice in the daily work of practitioners who assess and counsel diverse clients presenting career concerns. It provides
a single, unified schema that counselors can use to (a) assess client career concerns,
(b) identify the career theory that best comprehends those concerns, (c) select
inventories and tests designed to measure and clarify those concerns, and (d) apply
intervention strategies devised to resolve those concerns.

Because the framework organizes various theoretical perspectives on assessment
and intervention, the framework may be useful in addressing Williamson
and Bordin's (1941, p. 8) question: "What counseling techniques (and conditions)
will produce what types of results with what types of students?" Counselors
could systematically address this question using the framework and then incorporate the resulting practice knowledge back into segments of the framework. The
goal would be to use the framework to map career problems (Gottfredson,
this volume; Herr, this volume) and then develop protocols for effective intervention with particular populations. This effort might coalesce into validated
micropractices that coincide with major segments of the framework. In this manner, the framework for applying career theory to practice may be used to apply
practice to theory.

Lucas (this volume) speaks to this process of applying practice to theory when
she suggests that counselors systematically collect case studies linked to major
career theories and then use the cases to develop counseling models or minitheories
that specify "treatment protocols for frequently encountered career problems in
specific populations." To develop this practice knowledge, counselors and theorists
might begin with practice particulars, not theoretical abstractions. They could
follow Lucas' suggestion to use case studies as units of knowledge production. Case
studies allow career researchers to isolate change mechanisms specific to a precise
technique in a particular dyad (Kirschner, Hoffman, & Hill, 1994). By examining
a similar series of clinical cases, counselors and researchers could identify need-to-
know concepts and basic science issues. These theoretical issues could be addressed, one hopes, ignoring traditional theoretical and disciplinary boundaries, by
formulating micropractice (theory-based strategies) protocols for particular populations. The resulting micropractice could then be placed in the appropriate
segments of the framework. Such an approach would continue to use science as the
cornerstone of theory and practice, but it would begin with issues generated from

clinical cases, use multiple epistemic perspectives to examine the issues, and validate micropractices that resolve the issues for particular populations. Beginning research with clinical cases would allow counselors to return to their roots in the philosophies of pragmatism and functionalism as well as use social constructionism to broaden their epistemic perspectives beyond the vantage point of logical positivism (Savickas, 1995). For example, case study research from a constructivist perspective might use Cochran's (1990) "dramaturgical phenomenology" to identify and frame basic issues. Cochran has suggested that researchers and practitioners could construct a common narrative from the study of a group of individuals who have experienced a single career phenomenon such as indecision. The resulting narrative would certainly identify important issues and themes and possibly suggest micropractices that address them.

This clinical case approach to building a science of career intervention would also elaborate the meaning of existing career theories. Counselors create the meaning of a theory and its best beliefs when they use a theory with particular sets of clients. The use of a theory shows, or makes visible through application, the strengths and weaknesses of that theory. In particular, application of a theory reveals its oversights and flaws. In addressing these omissions, as they must do when they assist clients with complex problems, counselors elaborate and improve the theory. What counselors do when they practice shapes what researchers can know because activity structures meaning.

One example of work on micropractices and applying practice to theory is the research conducted in the late 1970s by Osipow and his colleagues. They devised a typology of career clients based on actual cases seen by Osipow while working as a counselor at Pennsylvania State University and a professor at Ohio State University. After reflecting on clients' presenting problems, Osipow and his colleagues were able to operationally define a typology of undecided students (particular populations, to use Lucas' term) and then conceptualize highly pertinent interventions (minitheories) for each type (Osipow, Winer, Koschier, & Yanico, 1975). Through this grounded research, they were able to produce a popular assessment instrument, the *Career Decision Scale* (CDS; Osipow, Carney, Winer, Yanico, & Koschier, 1976), that is quite useful in career counseling and has prompted a great deal of research on matching clients to interventions. Interestingly, in the context of this book, researchers and theorists, but not counselors, have repeatedly criticized the CDS for its atheoretical origins, complex items, and puzzling factor structure (cf. Slaney, 1988). Theory is partial, practice is holistic. The use of *inclusive types* in the CDS items was an excellent way to systematically reflect the wholism, complexity, and particularity that comprises practice. Critics of the CDS sometimes miss this point when they assert that the CDS should meet the criteria established for measures of *isolated traits* (Savickas & Jarjoura, 1991). These criteria decontextualize traits from situations to form generalizable, abstract principles of behavior. Clearly, following Lucas' suggestion about how to apply career counseling practice to theory requires more case study research such as that conducted by Osipow and his colleagues.

CONCLUSION

The career field is currently on the brink of a battle between theory and practice. Such battles can escalate into wars, as we have seen in the competition between the American Psychological Association and the American Psychological Society. To avoid a similar misdirection of energy and resources by vocational psychologists and career counselors, we must stop choosing between theory and practice and begin the search for a higher synthesis. The tension between theory and practice is precisely the starting point for such a synthesis, a synthesis that could result in a science of career intervention that integrates practice knowledge with theoretical models and research findings. Sooner or later, the field must link questions rooted in theory, such as What can we know? and How can we know it? with questions rooted in practice, such as What should we do? How do we know that it works? and Can we do it better? Starting to address these questions as a group by using schemas such as the framework presented in this chapter may lead to a science of practice.

Career counselors, theorists, and researchers must work together to meet the enormous challenge of bridging the gap between objective knowledge and subjective understanding to make possible a science of career intervention. It is a substantial challenge to create a systematic science of intervention, especially one that benefits clients. Nevertheless, this is precisely the challenge that practitioners and researchers must meet if they are to advance the field beyond its present accomplishments and refurbish vocational psychology and career counseling for the 21st century.

REFERENCES

Ammons, R. B., Butler, M. N., & Herzog, S. A. (1950). A projective test for vocational research and guidance at the college level. *Journal of Applied Psychology, 34,* 198–205.

Bandura, A. (1978). The self-system in reciprocal determinism. *American Psychologist, 33,* 344–358.

Betz, N. E. (1989). Implications of the null environment hypothesis for women's career development and for counseling psychology. *Journal of Counseling Psychology, 17,* 136–144.

Blocher, D. (1974). *Developmental counseling* (2d ed.). New York: Ronald Press.

Blustein, D. (1987). Integrating career counseling and psychotherapy: A comprehensive treatment strategy. *Psychotherapy, 24,* 794–799.

Blustein, D., Devenis, L., & Kidney, B. (1989). Relationship between identity formation process and career development. *Journal of Counseling Psychology, 36,* 196–202.

Blustein, D. L., & Spengler, P. M. (1995). Personal adjustment: Career counseling and psychotherapy. In W. B. Walsh & S. H. Osipow (Eds.), *Handbook of Vocational Psychology* (2d ed., pp. 295–329). Hillsdale, NJ: Erlbaum.

Bordin, E. (1990). Psychodynamic models of career choice and satisfaction. In D. Brown & L. Brooks (Eds.), *Career choice and development: Applying contemporary theories to practice* (2d ed., pp. 102–144). San Francisco: Jossey-Bass.

Brown, D., & Brooks, L. (1991). *Techniques of career counseling.* Boston: Allyn & Bacon.

Carden, A. (1990). Mentoring and adult career development. *The Counseling Psychologist, 18,* 275–299.

Cochran, L. (1990). Narrative as a paradigm for career research. In R. A. Young & W. A. Borgen (Eds.), *Methodological approaches to the study of career* (pp. 71–86). New York: Praeger.

Cochran, L. (1991). *Life-shaping decisions.* New York: Peter Lang.

Collin, A., & Young, R. (1986). New directions for theories of career. *Human Relations, 19,* 837–853.

Crites, J. (1969). *Vocational psychology: The study of vocational behavior and development.* New York: McGraw-Hill.

Crites, J. (1978). *The Career Maturity Inventory.* Monterey, CA: CTB/McGraw-Hill.

Dix, J. E., & Savickas, M. L. (1995). Establishing a career: Developmental tasks and coping responses. *Journal of Vocational Behavior, 47,* 93–107.

Hall, D. T. (Ed.). (1987). *Career development in organizations.* San Francisco: Jossey-Bass.

Harmon, L. W., Hansen, J. C., Borgen, F. H., & Hammer, A. L. (1994). *Applications and technical guide for the Strong Interest Inventory.* Palo Alto, CA: Consulting Psychologists Press.

Herr, E. L., Rayman, J. R., & Garis, J. W. (1993). *Handbook for the college and university career center.* Westport, CT: Greenwood Press.

Holland, J. (1985). *Making vocational choices: A theory of vocational personalities and work environments* (2d ed.). Odessa, FL: Psychological Assessment Resources, Inc.

Hoyt, K. B. (1975). *Career education: Contributions to an evolving concept.* Salt Lake City, UT: Olympus.

Hughes, E. (1958). *Men and their work.* Glencoe, IL: Free Press.

Ivey, A. (1986). *Developmental therapy: Theory into practice.* San Francisco: Jossey-Bass.

Jepsen, D. (1992, March). Understanding careers as stories. In M. Savickas (Chair), *Career as story.* Symposium conducted at the annual meeting of the American Association for Counseling and Development, Baltimore.

Katz, M. R. (1993). *Computer-assisted career decision making: The guide in the machine.* Hillsdale, NJ: Erlbaum.

Kirschner, T., Hoffman, M. A., & Hill, C. E. (1994). Case study of the process and outcome of career counseling. *Journal of Counseling Psychology, 41,* 216–226.

Krumboltz, J. (1979). A social learning theory of career decision making. Revised and reprinted in A. Mitchell, G. Jones, & J. Krumboltz (Eds.), *Social learning and career decision making* (pp. 19–49). Cranston, RI: Carroll Press.

Krumboltz, J. (1988). *The Career Beliefs Inventory.* Palo Alto, CA: Consulting Psychologists Press.

Lofquist, L., & Dawis, R. (1969). *Adjustment to work: A psychological view of man's problems in a work-oriented society.* New York: Appleton-Century-Crofts.

Lofquist, L. & Dawis, R. (1991). *Essentials of person-environment correspondence counseling.* Minneapolis: University of Minnesota Press.

Meara, N. M., & Patton, M. J. (1994). Contribution of the working alliance in the practice of career counseling. *Career Development Quarterly, 43,* 161–178.

Osipow, S. H., Carney, C. G., Winer, J. L., Yanico, B., & Koschier, M. (1976). *The Career Decision Scale.* (3d ed.). Columbus, OH: Marathon Consulting & Press.

Osipow, S. H., Winer, J. L., Koschier, M., & Yanico, B. (1975). A modular approach to self-counseling for vocational indecision using audio-cassettes. In L. Simpson (Ed.), *Audiovisual media in career development*. Bethlehem, PA: College Placement Council.

Savickas, M. L. (1989). Career-style assessment and counseling. In T. Sweeney (Ed.), *Adlerian counseling: A practical approach for a new decade* (3d ed., pp. 289–320). Muncie, IN: Accelerated Development Press.

Savickas, M. L. (1991). The meaning of work and love: Career issues and interventions. *Career Development Quarterly, 39,* 315–324.

Savickas, M. L. (1995). Current theoretical issues in vocational psychology: Convergence, divergence, and schism. In W. B. Walsh & S. H. Osipow (Eds.), *Handbook of vocational psychology* (2d ed., pp. 1–34). Hillsdale, NJ: Erlbaum.

Savickas, M. L., & Jarjoura, D. (1991). The Career Decision Scale as a type indicator. *Journal of Counseling Psychology, 38,* 85–90.

Shingleton, J. D., & Fitzpatrick, E. B. (1985). *Dynamics of placement: How to develop a successful career planning and placement program*. Bethlehem, PA: College Placement Council Foundation.

Slaney, R. B. (1988). The assessment of career decision making. In W. B. Walsh & S. H. Osipow (Eds.), *Career decision making* (pp. 33–76). Hillsdale, NJ: Erlbaum.

Slaney, R. B., & MacKinnon-Slaney, F. (1990). The use of vocational card sorts in career counseling. In C. E. Watkins, Jr., & V. L. Campbell (Eds.), *Testing in Counseling Practice*. Hillsdale, NJ: Erlbaum.

Spokane, A. (1991). *Career intervention*. Englewood Cliffs, NJ: Prentice Hall.

Starishevsky, R., & Matlin, N. (1963). A model for the translation of self-concepts into vocational terms. In D. Super, R. Starishevsky, N. Matlin, & J. Joordan, *Career development: Self-concept theory* (pp. 33–41). New York: College Entrance Examination Board.

Stevens, N. B. (1973). Job-seeking behavior: A segment of vocational development. *Journal of Vocational Behavior 3,* 209–219.

Subich, L. (Ed.). (1993). How personal is career counseling? [Special issue]. *Career Development Quarterly, 42* (2).

Super, D. E. (1954). Career patterns as a basis for vocational counseling. *Journal of Counseling Psychology, 1,* 12–20.

Super, D. E. (1963). Toward making self-concept theory operational. In D. Super, R. Starishevsky, N. Matlin, & J. Joordan, *Career development: Self-concept theory* (pp. 17–32). New York: College Entrance Examination Board.

Super, D. E. (1969). Vocational development theory. *Counseling Psychologist, 1,* 2–30.

Super, D. E. (Ed.). (1974). *Measuring vocational maturity for counseling and evaluation*. Washington, DC: National Career Development Association.

Super, D. E. (1990). A life-span, life-space approach to career development. In D. Brown & L. Brooks (Eds.), *Career choice and development: Applying contemporary theories to practice* (2d ed., pp. 197–261). San Francisco: Jossey-Bass.

Super, D. E., Thompson, A. S., Lindeman, R. H., Joordan, J., & Myers, R. A. (1981). *Career Development Inventory*. Palo Alto, CA: Consulting Psychologist Press.

Vondracek, F. (1990). A developmental-contextual approach to career development research. In R. Young & W. Borgen (Eds.), *Methodological approaches to the study of career* (pp. 37–56). New York: Praeger.

Wagner, E. (1971). Structural analysis: A theory of personality based on projective techniques. *Journal of Personality Assessment, 35,* 422–435.

Watkins, C., Jr. (1984). The Individual Psychology of Alfred Adler: Toward an Adlerian vocational theory. *Journal of Vocational Behavior, 24,* 27–48.

Williamson, E. G., & Bordin, E. S. (1941). The evaluation of vocational and educational counseling: A critique of the methodology of experiments. *Educational and Psychological Measurement, 1,* 5–24.

PART THREE

INNOVATIONS IN CAREER ASSESSMENT

THE SEVEN CHAPTERS in Part 3 deal with criticisms of and new directions for the contemporary practice of career assessment and the use of assessment instruments during career counseling. In the section's opening chapter, Gary Gottfredson approaches the repair of the theory-practice gap by suggesting that the linkages could be strengthened by a schematic map that shows both counselors and researchers how to better use existing segments of career theories to address specific practical problems. He uses the chapter to provide an initial map for just this purpose. He begins by building a convincing case that a fruitful approach to the practice of counseling may be to use applicable partial theories to gain the best grip on a particular problem. In essence, he advises counselors to use theories to comprehend problems for which the theories were originally addressed. He cogently argues that to be useful, scientific statements must be simple, while concluding that no simple theory can address every problem. To organize how counselors might selectively use partial theories tailored for specific problems, Gottfredson offers a "general purpose framework" that illustrates the relationship of multiple subtheories to several core vocational problems. The framework rests on five main ideas, that is, career status, satisfaction, attainment, direction of activity, and work performance, and is bolstered by four secondary concepts, that is, environmental competence, personal resources, life circumstances, and congruence. The presentation of the framework is followed by a "map" showing how multiple partial theories can fit together into a "comprehensive model of career status." Next, Gottfredson explains how many elements in the career status model can be operationally defined by existing vocational assessment techniques, inventories, and tests. Nevertheless, the model reveals elements for which counselors lack measures. To begin to fill these gaps, Gottfredson and Holland (1991) have constructed the *Position Classification Inventory* to assess person-job match, and, more recently, Holland and Gottfredson (1994) have developed the *Career Attitudes and Strategies Inventory* to assess directly some previously neglected features of the career status model such as geographic barriers and interpersonal abuse. The chapter advances the field toward the goal of mapping the full range of theories into career problems or issues so that it will be possible for practitioners and researchers to select those segmental theories most suited to a particular problem at hand.

In Chapter 15, Crites illustrates the process by which research links theory to practice with a discussion of the construction, development, and use of his *Career Mastery Inventory*. Crites first analyzes the link between career theory and practice focusing on the theory-language and data-language used in the philosophy of science. He explains four basic modes for articulating the relationship between theory-language and data-language: model, deductive, functional, and inductive. To articulate the theory-language link to data-language in each mode requires research, whether it be quantitative or qualitative. The research, when systematically programmed, proceeds from surveys to discover relevant variables, technique research to construct and develop measures for the identified variables, theoretical research to test hypotheses about these variables, and, finally, applied research to determine which courses of action practitioners might take in regard to situations and clients whose concerns include these variables. Crites then illustrates a program of research—from survey to applied—that formulated and developed the construct of career mastery and eventually produced a research-based measure and practical counseling interventions.

In Chapter 16, which focuses on innovations in interest measurement, Borgen and Harmon provide an example of how practice informs theory. E. K. Strong, Jr., eschewed theory, preferring to develop his interest inventories by persistent empirical work. The resulting inventories have an illustrious history of being extremely useful to clients and their counselors. Based on the empirical data available from interest measurement, theorists have constructed models, such as Holland's RIASEC types, that explain how interests express personality. These personality theories enhance the usefulness of interest assessment and interpretation in counseling practice. The 1994 *Strong Interest Inventory* (*Strong*) strengthens the theoretical links between personality and interests by explicitly attending to personality by way of four Personality Style Scales. These scales measure preferences for and comfort with broad styles of living. Counselors can use the scales to help clients explore their strategies for learning, working, and playing as well as to contribute additional clinical insights regarding relationships between dimensions of personality and interests. The addition of the Personal Style Scales to the *Strong* continues the inventory's tradition of practice-theory linkages grounded in both rigorous empiricism and clinical insight.

In Chapter 17, Walsh addresses the perceived gap between career theory and practice by examining it from each side of the divide. First, he addresses the question, What research agenda can produce knowledge that is useful to practitioners and translates career theory into practice? He answers the question by encouraging research that uses the idiographic model, involves the Big Five personality dimensions, and emphasizes practical intelligence. He then looks at the theory-practice gap from the practice side of the divide in addressing a second question: What practice agenda would facilitate the translation of practice into theory? Walsh answers this question simply—work on a model of career counseling, a model distinct from theories of career development. He lists seven desidirata, inspired by work in the psychotherapy literature that deals with a unified theory of therapeutic process, for such a career counseling model.

Chapter 18 seeks to improve the translation of theory into practice by examining the uniformity myth that is implicit within career assessment models, measures, and materials, especially those that manifest ethnocentric and masculinist biases. Subich invites readers to more fully integrate an appreciation of individual uniqueness into the practice of career assessment. She asks counselors to identify and reject assessment inventories and tests that assume the cultural homogeneity of clients. She endorses previous calls for reform of career assessment in emphasizing that counselors collaborate with clients, empower clients to actively shape their careers, explicitly attend to clients' contextual situations, and follow through with clients to help them implement their plans. Subich explains the relevance of treatises on feminism and multicultural counseling to the reformation of career assessment. She illustrates her points with an analysis of problems in the use of the *Strong* with culturally diverse groups. In considering future directions, she recommends attention be focused on developing measures of contextual barriers and degree of acculturation, especially measures such as sentence completions, card sorts, and work samples that use qualitative procedures and emphasize idiographic interpretation.

In Chapter 19, Bingham and Ward seek to sensitize counselors to issues of gender and race as they apply career development theory to the practice of career intervention. Toward this end, they describe three instruments that they constructed and developed to help counselors adapt intervention strategies to be more appropriate in counseling with ethnic minority women. The *Multicultural Career Counseling Checklist* sensitizes counselors to issues of ethnic/racial identity and addresses topics such as the client's worldview, history, local sociopolitical issues, and stereotypes. The *Career Counseling Checklist* assesses the client's knowledge about the world of work, client self-confidence, and influences on the client, including age, race, gender, and disability. The *Decision Tree* helps counselors to determine whether to emphasize personal or career concerns with a client and the initial steps they might take to ensure that the client receives the most effective service. Then, Phillips, Bingham and Ward describe a "culturally appropriate career counseling model" that guides counselors to be more inclusive and considerate of worldviews that differ from their own. They conclude the chapter with a case study that illustrates the use of the checklists and each of the seven steps in the culturally sensitive model for career counseling.

In the final chapter in this section, Meara comments on the prior six chapters in this section. She sets the stage by offering a clear point of view with which to consider the chapters and reminds counselors that the assessment procedures and measuring instruments of career assessment must be more sensitive to the needs of women and non-Anglos and take into account the environments in which these clients find themselves, environments that may not be optimal for their personal and vocational development. Even in trying to become more sensitive to worldviews and diverse cultures, our models and materials still implicitly prefer a future orientation and a rational style of decision making. Yet a future orientation and preference for rational decision making may not be the strategies used by our clients. For clients who do not share our values and assumption about life, the model and methods may have little usefulness. To begin to address this situation, we need to make explicit our assumptions (tell clients that we think preparing for the future is critical), train individuals to be planful and prudent (future oriented), and influence public policy to help create meaningful futures for clients whom society has disenfranchised and marginalized. From the perspective at this vantage point, Meara candidly evaluates the contributions of the prior chapters.

CHAPTER FOURTEEN

Some Direct Measures of Career Status

Putting Multiple Theories into Practice

Gary D. Gottfredson
Gottfredson Associates

Practitioners and scientists are concerned with theories to explain the major features of a person's career behavior and current status. It is not realistic to expect a single theory to be useful for all vocational problems. Taken together, however, the range of vocational theory should be broad enough to include the common influences on careers that most people encounter.

In this chapter, I will describe some career problems that theory should explain, show that multiple theories deal with different aspects of these problems, and illustrate how measures of career status from different perspectives can be applied to the assessment of different aspects of career problems and career adjustment. This assemblage of partial theories is useful to the extent that each partial theory (a) has validity, that is, it corresponds with evidence, (b) makes understanding and communication easier rather than more complicated, (c) does not contradict other partial theories utilized, (d) suggests ways to help people with their careers, and (e) can be put to work through useful measurement tools.

WHAT REQUIRES UNDERSTANDING OR EXPLANATION?

The focus of this discussion is on the general, persistent features of career status, not on the short-term or evanescent states experienced from time to time. Put another way, I am concerned with questions such as, Is a person typically satisfied and successful? and What explains persistent patterns of career achievement, choice, and satisfaction?

A list of important outcomes that should be addressed by vocational theory and some common psychological tasks associated with each outcome follow:

- *Typical level of work satisfaction.* The psychologist's task is to identify ways that a person or organization might promote job satisfaction or avoid undermining it.

- *Level of occupational attainment.* The psychologist's task is to identify how higher levels of occupational prestige or income might be attained or how a person's level of attainment might be understood.

- *Direction of activity or the area in which satisfaction and achievement are pursued—often called choice.* The psychologist's tasks are to understand how career choices come about and to help individuals consider alternatives that they are likely to find satisfying and in which they will likely be successful. Psychologists are also asked to find ways to influence the distribution of choices for groups of people or within an organization. For example, a comprehensive understanding of the determinants of vocational choice will be useful in designing interventions to increase the numbers of women or minorities entering scientific fields.

- *Level of typical performance within a position or work environment.* The psychologist's task is to identify ways to improve the performance of a worker or a group of workers.

- *Stability and quality of vocational adjustment—the extent to which predictable work and career arrangements meet the economic and psychological needs of the individual.* The psychologist's tasks include assessing vocational adjustment and identifying ways a person making a difficult vocational adjustment (unemployment, frequent unemployment, insufficiently dependable income, handicapping conditions, low vocational identity) might achieve more stability.

COMMON COUNSELING PERSPECTIVES

Differential Psychology

The dominant perspective used by counseling psychologists is person-job matching. This perspective is represented by Holland's (1985, 1992) theory, the theory of work adjustment (TWA; Dawis & Lofquist, 1984), and Schneider's (1987) attraction-selection-attrition (ASA) theory.

Holland's Congruence Theory.   Individuals enter and persist in occupations that are congruent with their personality types. Satisfaction results from congruence between vocational personality type and environmental type. Other vocational outcomes are direct products of personality type or environmental type. That is, people tend to behave in ways characteristic of the types they resemble, and environments elicit and sustain the behaviors they reward. Holland's theory explains choice or field of work, and it explains satisfaction as a product of person-job congruence.

TWA Correspondence Theory.   Satisfaction results from a correspondence of personal needs and job reinforcers; satisfactoriness (supervisor's appraisal) results from a correspondence of personal abilities and job requirements. TWA explains persistence, satisfaction, and stability of vocational adjustment by reference to correspondence of worker needs and abilities on the one hand and job reinforcers and requirements on the other.

ASA Theory.   People are attracted to organizations that have inhabitants who resemble them, are selected into organizations on the basis of their similarity to decision makers, and leave the organization if they do not match. ASA theory explains choice or direction and attrition from organizations.

The dominant perspective, which may be called modern differentialism, is bolstered by the availability of a variety of job analysis tools (Harvey, 1991)[1] and by a variety of reasonably established assessment, selection, and placement techniques (Guion, 1991) and validity generalization results (Schmitt, Ones, & Hunter, 1992).

Career Development

A secondary perspective that influences many counselors is Super's (1990) developmental view. Career status or appropriate career tasks are functions of the developmental stage. If a person is a student, his or her career issues are determined by that position on a life "rainbow." Developments are based on earlier progress, but people are also said to revisit or continue to be concerned with multiple stage-related roles. Others who adopt a developmental perspective (Vondracek, Lerner, & Schulenberg, 1986) call attention to the multiple contexts in which development occurs and favor complex rather than simple explanations.

Most contributors from this perspective do not concretely address the matters identified above as requiring explanation; or, when they do, they shift to ideas drawn from the differentialist tradition (Super, Osborne, Walsh, & Brown, 1992). For these reasons, and because simple, operationalized theory is still a useful aim of science and practice, the developmental perspective will not be not discussed further here. Developmental contextualism does, however, provide a litany of potential influences on careers and has amply demonstrated its utility for generating post hoc insight.

---

[1]Harvey provides a useful overview, but consult his chapter with caution, taking care to distinguish opinion from evidence and persuasive argument.

THEORIES FROM OTHER FIELDS

Multiple theoretical perspectives are helpful in fleshing out the full range of influences on career status. These perspectives are drawn from industrial organizational, personality-social, and clinical psychology, as well as sociology. A brief summary of several theoretical perspectives from other subfields of psychology or sociology is presented in Table 1, along with the more common counseling perspectives.

The Porter and Lawler (1968) and the Locke and Latham (1990a, 1990b) theories were designed to suggest ways to alter organizational arrangements to increase performance and satisfaction. These useful and well-researched perspectives also have some implications for understanding performance and satisfaction in counseling. So far, tests of the counseling implications of these theories have not been reported, although they are well supported in research by industrial and organizational psychologists.

Porter and Lawler direct attention to the clarity of expectations for performance, resources and skills for performance, and the uncertain links among effort, reward, perceived equity, and expected consequences of effort. Locke and Latham's goal-setting theory adds an emphasis on cognitive and self-regulatory functions of goal setting, putting into practical theory the psychological insights derived from work by Deci and Ryan (1985), Dweck (1986), Howard and Conway (1986), Keisler (1971), and others. Goal selection, commitment, and the powerful influences of these processes on behavior cannot be overlooked in the explanation of career behavior.

The Krumboltz, Mitchell, and Jones (1976) social learning theory of career development (SLT) translates social learning ideas (Bandura, 1977) into career terms. It provides a way of describing and understanding the origins of learned generalizations about the self and career-related options. This perspective suggests a search for influences of personal developmental history on *self-observation generalizations* (SOGs) and choices. It may be particularly useful for understanding or identifying idiosyncratic influences because it does not incorporate a taxonomy of learning histories or choices. The SLT perspective is useful for suggesting new experiences that can improve upon unfortunate learning experiences to make alternative choices possible for individuals.

The sociocognitive process theory (SCT) described by Lent and Hackett (1994) and Lent, Brown, and Hackett (1994) imports more recent developments from SLT (Bandura, 1986) into vocational psychology. It deserves special comment because it has become a topic of many recent contributions to the counseling psychology literature.

The SCT described by these counseling psychologists deals with the development of interest and choice and specific areas of performance. It emphasizes situation-specific behavior and events over which individuals exercise control. It appears to discount evidence of the stability and predictive value of ability: "Social

TABLE 1 Multiple Partial Theories of Career Status

Theory	Explains	Explanatory Mechanism
Holland (1985)	Entry and persistence in different kinds of work, types of behavior displayed, satisfaction	People's behavior is predictable from a knowledge of the personality types they most resemble; environments elicit and sustain particular behaviors they value and reward; and people seek congruent environments; environments recruit and retain congruent people; and congruence promotes satisfaction.
Dawis & Lofquist (1984)	Satisfaction, satisfactoriness, and tenure	Correspondence between individual's needs and an environment's reinforcers leads to satisfaction; correspondence between an individual's abilities and an environment's requirements leads to satisfactoriness and satisfaction; and satisfactoriness leads to tenure.
Schneider (1987)	Entry and persistence in organizational environments	People are attracted to organizations with inhabitants like themselves; people who are dissimilar to others in an organization leave it.
Porter & Lawler (1968)	Job satisfaction and performance: direction, intensity, and maintenance of behavior of workers within an organization	A chain with multiple weak links connects personal characteristics, work conditions and arrangements, reinforcement properties of the job, and expectations with satisfaction and performance. Satisfaction is explained by perceived equitable and valued rewards for effort expended.
Locke & Latham (1990a, 1990b)	How organizational arrangements can be altered to increase satisfaction and improve performance	Goal acceptance and feedback influence satisfaction and performance in a perspective that complements Porter and Lawler's. To the extent that the explanatory variables in the Porter-Lawler and Locke-Latham theories are stable over time, they may explain general satisfaction and stability of work adjustment.
Krumboltz, Mitchell, & Jones (1976), Bandura (1977)	How career-related choices are made	Social learning explains choices by reference to learned generalizations about self and occupational possibilities.

TABLE 1   Multiple Partial Theories of Career Status (continued)

Theory	Explains	Explanatory Mechanism
Bandura (1986), Lent & Hackett (1994)	Interest development, choice, and performance	Situation-specific beliefs about the self are influenced by learning; people make choices and set goals in conformity with their expectations for efficacy.
Eberhardt & Muchinsky (1982), Mumford & Owens (1982), Neiner & Owens (1985)	How personal histories are associated with occupational destinations	Personal histories can be classified and associated with subsequent occupational destinations; complements social learning theory.
Sewell, Haller, & Portes (1969), L. Gottfredson (1981)	Level of occupational attainment	Ascribed characteristics, social influences, aspirations, and ability explain the level of occupational attainment.
Price & Mueller (1986)	Job satisfaction and turnover	Job satisfaction is a function of routinization (−), concentration of power (−), communication, social integration, pay, degree to which rewards and punishments are related to performance, opportunity for promotion, quantitative work overload (−), and worker "professionalism."
Hackman & Oldham (1975)	Job satisfaction	Job satisfaction is a function of job meaningfulness (skill variety, task identity, task significance), autonomy, and feedback.
Caplan et al. (1975), Osipow & Spokane (1984), Lazarus (1993), Fitzgerald et al. (in press)	Responses to stressors (strain and adjustment)	Stress and adjustment are a function of environmental stressors, the coping resources of the individual, and the significance of events as appraised by the person. Stressors are functions of organization and job context.
Weitz (1952), Staw & Ross (1985)	Job satisfaction	Job satisfaction is partly determined by a disposition to be satisfied or happy.

cognitive theory views ability as a dynamic rather than a fixed attribute" (Lent & Hackett, 1994, p. 96). Direct influences of ability on performance are deemphasized. In contrast, this account of SCT emphasizes self-efficacy expectations that are "seen as a dynamic set of self-beliefs that are specific to particular performance domains" (Lent et al., 1994, p. 83).

This perspective implies the hopeful possibility that if individuals can construe themselves as efficacious in a particular area, they can be expected to make choices in conformance with that expectation, with concomitant performance conse- quences. Because people's self-estimates appear to have substantial validity (Westbrook, Buck, Wynne, & Sanford, 1994), this application appears most promising in the case of an objective mismatch of specific efficacy expectations and an individual's potential (i.e., incorrect expectations). Self-efficacy expectations deserve the attention this perspective has prompted. Research applying generalizability theory (Cronbach, Gleser, Nanda, & Rajaratnam, 1972) would be useful in revealing the extent to which the operational measures for self-efficacy used in research on SCT are empirically more labile than are the conventional measures of self-confidence, self-assessed competencies, and interests they have been introduced to supplement.[2] The distinction among these related constructs as operationalized requires clarification with more persuasive evidence.

SCT shares with goal-setting theory a useful emphasis on goals and on the manipulability of behavior. Both perspectives deserve experimental tests in career interventions. Tests that are abundant in industrial and organizational contexts (Locke & Latham, 1990a) and short-term educational experiments (e.g., Schunk & Swartz, 1993) have yet to appear in the counseling literature for SCT. By providing demonstrations of the content and nature of learning experiences that can shape self-efficacy expectations, and thus interests and choices, SCT could become as powerful as the Porter-Lawler and goal-setting theories in suggesting interventions to alter career-related outcomes. The raw material is in Bandura's (1986) foundation and is reflected in explications for counselors (Lent, Brown, & Hackett, 1994). These applications demonstrated in other contexts require research and develop- ment in career development contexts.

The research on biographical antecedents of occupational field selection by Eberhardt and Muchinsky (1982), Mumford and Owens (1982), and Neiner and Owens (1985) complement SLT by showing how personal histories can be classified and associated with subsequent occupational destinations. Although the biographi- cal research does not appear to have generated practical applications in career intervention more advanced than the Individual Counseling Record (Paterson, Gerken, & Hahn, 1953), it may have applications in designing or suggesting experiences that would alter the distribution of ultimate career destinations for young people. For example, special programs to provide more opportunities in high school or college that are typical of persons who eventually become scientists might produce a few more scientists—especially if the individuals exposed to these programs showed

---

[2]Whereas those who develop scales are often at pains to demonstrate that their measures show stability over time, SCT clearly implies that measures of self-efficacy should be labile. One part of demonstrating construct validity for such measures would entail showing that they are, in fact, manipulable or show less stability over time than similar measures thought to be more traitlike.

Investigative interests. Additional potential uses of biographical research and assessment are suggested by Morrison (1994) and Tenopyr (1994).

Sociological theories of occupational destination (Otto & Haller, 1979; Sewell, Haller, & Portes, 1969; L. Gottfredson, 1981) use ascribed characteristics, social influences, individual effort, and ability to explain level of occupational attainment and the distribution of labor in society. These theories seek to explain the distribution of people and groups to occupations (attainment). Most sociological perspectives direct attention to the influence of privilege and the differential social influence and resources available to different individuals, and they emphasize occupational level (attainment) and associated status or prestige as the primary measure of a job or a career.

A distinct sociological theory of satisfaction that has benefited from considerable research is Price and Mueller's (1986) satisfaction-turnover model. This perspective meshes well with psychological theories developed by Porter and Lawler (1968) and Hackman and Oldham (1975). These perspectives emphasize the importance of features of the work (significance, variety, feedback) for satisfaction.

Osipow and Spokane (1984) have introduced ideas drawn from the study of stress, strain, and coping (Caplan et al., 1975; Lazarus, Averill, & Opton, 1974) to suggest a model in which perceived (but presumably more or less objective) stress produces the personal experience of one or more kind of strain, influenced by the pattern of coping resources utilized by the individual. A related theoretical perspective (Caplan et al., 1975) gives more prominence to personality traits and discrepancies between desired and actual levels of potential stressors than do Osipow and Spokane. And Lazarus (1993) has recently suggested a cognitive-motivational-relational perspective in which a stress reaction (strain) is determined not just by the stressor but also by its significance as appraised by the person. These perspectives are useful in understanding adjustment in the presence of stressors. Caplan et al. (1975) and Osipow and Spokane (1984) provide career-relevant measures; House and Rizzo (1972) reveal stressors due to role conflict and ambiguity; and Lazarus reminds us that responses to stressors depend upon the cognitive-emotional processes of the person experiencing them.

A similar perspective for explaining the consequences of sexual harassment (one specific stressor) has been offered by Fitzgerald, Hulin, and Drasgow (in press). This model explains harassment as a function of organizational and job context and the vocational and psychological outcomes of harassment as influenced by personal vulnerability and response style.

Finally, the commonplace observation (Weitz, 1952) that some people seem to be happy with most situations while others are chronic gripers has generated recent research (Staw & Ross, 1985) that has led to the recognition that job satisfaction is at least partly determined by a disposition to be satisfied. Some people may have enduring personality dispositions that doom them to lives of dissatisfaction. Neither counseling psychologists nor their clients should spend too much time searching for the roots of this kind of unhappiness in assessments of person-job mismatch; nor should this be regarded as an easily treatable thinking error.

DIFFERENT PROBLEMS CALL
FOR DIFFERENT EXPLANATIONS

Each of the foregoing theories appears useful for understanding some problems. Of these, the Locke and Latham theory provides the clearest guidance for an organization wishing to improve specific aspects of work performance or to design a satisfying work arrangement given the workers available. The Porter-Lawler model is also useful for this purpose. Goal-setting theory, in particular, suggests the importance of goal acceptance in directing and sustaining behavior.

The SLT perspective, combined with Beck's (1976) cognitive approach to therapy, provides the most direct guidance for helping a person who is hobbled by self-limiting beliefs (presumably the result of an unfortunate learning history). The account of SLT by Krumboltz et al. helps us recognize *circumscription* (L. Gottfredson, 1981) as a possible result of a self-limiting SOG, and cognitive therapy may help clients remove unhelpful self-imposed barriers.

SCT suggests situation-specific learning interventions and direct attempts to manipulate aspects of self-beliefs. If efficacy expectations are labile and specific, multiple specific interventions may have to be repeated on many occasions to produce lasting benefits. Like goal-setting theory, it suggests goal-setting interventions.

TWA deals with the problem of unstable work histories. TWA seems open-ended, at least in principle. By adding new variables to address specific vocational problems, TWA might be applied in a flexible fashion. For example, new variables could be added as reinforcers or demands, although in practice new reinforcers are rarely added.

Holland's theory communicates organized information relating person characteristics to occupational environments. It also summarizes much information about regularities in individual differences.

ASA emphasizes how groups may become homogeneous and inhospitable to individuals dissimilar to the typical member (highlighting some of the unfortunate consequences of homogeneity).

A fruitful approach to the practice of counseling may be to use applicable partial theories to gain the best grip on particular problems. Different theories are expected to be most efficient for the problems they were created to address.

Complaints About Theory

Fitzgerald and Betz (1994) were concerned that individuals occupied by economic survival seldom find their way into studies reported in the *Journal of Counseling Psychology* (JCP) and the *Journal of Vocational Behavior* (JVB) and state, as a consequence, "we know almost nothing about the career choice process in the majority of the population" (p. 106). To some extent, this concern reflects a failure to discover or use relevant research; it overlooks connections between a problem and research by industrial psychologists or labor economists.

Research on reasonably representative samples has sometimes been published in JVB and JCP. In an earlier report on the distribution of people's aspirations and available employment according to census data (G. Gottfredson, Holland, & L. Gottfredson, 1975), we showed that some people will have to be employed in incongruent jobs because the distribution of employment available does not match the distribution of people's aspirations. In particular, many more women have been employed in Conventional jobs in Holland's classification than aspire to those jobs, illustrating how the theory explains some career dissatisfactions of women. This work illustrates the applicability of typological theory to some career problems of women.

An important evaluation of a program to help the unemployed obtain employment (Azrin, Philip, Thienes-Hontos, & Besalel, 1981) was reported in JVB. Similarly, results on career development from Project Talent (McLaughlin & Tiedeman, 1974), published in JVB, support the usefulness of occupational classifications in a reasonably representative sample.

Fitzgerald and Betz (1994) are surely correct that JVB and JCP are not prime repositories for research on the hard-core unemployed. But just because research is not reported in specific counseling journals does not mean that a population is not a concern of work published in *Journal of Human Resources, Journal of Applied Psychology, Human Relations, Personnel Psychology,* and elsewhere. Data from the National Longitudinal Studies (Parnes, Miljus, Spitz, & Associates, 1970, and subsequent reports) have usually been summarized in technical reports rather than journals. Research from more recent national samples are often reported in sociology journals. Much useful material from the sociological and industrial and organizational psychology literature appears underutilized by counselors.

Many counseling psychologists are isolated because they work in universities and university counseling centers, and it is not surprising that when they do research, they involve the groups with whom they most often come into contact. This handicap is less severe in industrial psychology and labor economics.[3]

Harmon (1994) observed that theories usually involve just a few dimensions and that such explanations must be only partial. This observation identifies two key features of theories: To be useful scientific statements, they must be simple; but no simple theory can address every problem. Some complaints about theories are, in reality, complaints that a given theory was not constructed for a problem with which the critic is concerned.

---

[3]In fairness, it should be observed that researchers studying noncollege populations do not usually reach out to counseling psychologists by publishing their work in the *Journal of Counseling Psychology*. For example, I did not offer my work on consistency of Holland code and employment stability for a sample of male urban parolees (Gottfredson & Lipstein, 1975) to JCP. In that research, *California Psychological Inventory* Socialization scores and biographical data on extensiveness of criminal record were more important than race and more efficient than consistency in predicting employment stability— illustrating the usefulness of theoretical perspectives suited to the problem at hand.

INTERIM SUMMARY: JUDICIOUS CHOICE OF THEORY

By identifying the scope and limitations of different theories—and by selecting theories matched to the problem requiring explanation—we may efficiently address many phenomena. Put another way, if the full range of theories is mapped into problems or issues, it may be possible for practitioners and researchers to select those segmental theories most suited to the particular problem at hand. In contrast, seductive theorizing that fails to cope in a parsimonious and useful way with major career problems can distract the practitioner from more useful formulations. Similarly, there is no value in incorporating redundant ideas, constructs empirically indistinguishable from others, or ideas lacking in validity.

A GENERAL PURPOSE THEORY

In this section, I will provide a general purpose framework that uses subtheories as specific engines for specific problems. As a starting point, this theory serves as a reminder that vocational outcomes are functions of both persons and environments. The influences of person-environment interactions are of secondary importance. I will state the organizing theoretical framework succinctly, usually not referring to its roots in the specific theoretical perspectives outlined above or in related research.

Main Ideas

The following main ideas explain vocational adjustment, work satisfaction, level of attainment, career choice and persistence, and work performance.

Career Status. Vocational adjustment (performance, satisfaction, economic stability, and vocational identity) is a function of personality (ability, agreeableness, neuroticism, conscientiousness) and the work environment (rewards and aversive features such as pay, work meaningfulness, autonomy, and information about performance versus quantitative work overload, inequity, or interpersonal abuse).

Satisfaction. Other things being equal, typical level of work satisfaction is determined by the following:

- *The individual's general potential for positive affect (agreeableness).* People who are disposed to be happy or satisfied in most aspects of their experience are also most likely to be satisfied in their work.

- *The typical availability of rewards in the work environment.* A simplifying assumption is that everyone finds money rewarding. Rewards and punishments include the interpersonal, monetary or concrete, and intrinsic or abstract benefits of effort in an environment.

■ *The absence of uncontrollable punishment in the environment.* Typological differences notwithstanding, everyone is presumed to find the absence of resources for task performance, obstacles to accomplishment of tasks, and thwarting of goal-directed effort to be frustrating or punishing. To some degree, everyone will find physical discomfort, tedium, and the expenditure of sustained physical effort disagreeable.

Attainment.   Other things being equal, the level of career attainment is a function of (a) parental educational and economic resources, (b) parental intelligence and other personal characteristics,[4] (c) individual personality[5] (ability, commitment, self-discipline), (d) encouragement by others, (e) absence of life situations that thwart attainment (pregnancy occurring at an early age, incarceration or expulsion from school, the necessity of leaving school to earn money).

Choice.   Other things being equal, the direction of activity is determined by (a) individuals' efforts to obtain work that is congruent with their interests, (b) the differential competition for work of different categories (i.e., the ratio of workers desiring work of that kind and the available jobs), and (c) the availability of work of the desired kind at the desired level of attainment.

Performance.   Other things being equal, the quality of a person's work performance is a function of the following personal influences: general ability, work involvement or commitment (including goal acceptance), self-control and conscientiousness, and requisite knowledge or skill to do the work; and the following environmental influences: tools or resources required to do the work, clear indication of what should be done, clear goals, feedback on performance, and rewards and punishments contingent on performance.

Secondary Concepts

A number of secondary concepts or influences on career behavior that are based on the main ideas spelled out earlier are also well documented by research or appear unlikely to be false on the basis of rational analysis. These are spelled out next.

Environmental Competence.   Competent environments are defined as environments (organizations, settings) that (a) produce high performance from inhabitants, (b) are successful in recruiting high-performing and likable people, and (c) satisfy those who inhabit them. Other things being equal, the following propositions explain environmental competence.

---

[4]Sociological models of occupational attainment omit parental intelligence. This is an obvious misspecification of the models. The evidence for the intergenerational transmission of intelligence and personality is compelling (Rowe, 1994), and it is unbecoming and unscientific of sociologists or psychologists to ignore these influences or to feel uncomfortable about including them in explanations.

[5]I have treated abilities as one aspect of personality—traits on which people differ.

- *Environmental structuring.* Environments that (a) signal what behavior is needed, (b) track individual performance so that consequences can be provided, and (c) dispense rewards and punishments contingent on performance produce better performance.

- *Selectivity.* Environments that recruit persons with requisite talents and personal characteristics (because, for example, they have good selection ratios; attract able, resourceful, happy people; use sound selection procedures; have good reputations) produce better performance and more satisfaction.

- *Equity.* Work environments that dispense rewards in a manner that is equitable, consistent, and related to effort or performance produce more satisfaction.

Personal Resources.   Psychological health (emotional stability vs. neuroticism), skill development, dominance, and risk-taking and personal construals (self-confidence vs. cognitive obstacles composed of self-limiting beliefs or expectations) affect satisfaction, performance, vocational identity, and other aspects of vocational adjustment because these resources determine the coping strategies an individual most often employs. Some people avoid destructive, ineffective, or debilitating outcomes and create beneficial or productive arrangements; others fall prey to multiple traps. Individuals also differ in their tendency to interpret interpersonal events as hostile, threatening, helpful, or friendly—leading to different reactions to similar events. Among these personal influences are (a)the general coping capacity of the individual—the individual's general level of psychological adjustment versus neuroticism (career worries is one facet of neuroticism); (b) skill development; (c) dominant style; (d) risk-taking style; (e) perceived geographical barriers; (f) other perceptual or cognitive styles; and (g) other self-limiting beliefs (vs. general self-confidence or specific positive expectations).

Life Circumstances.   The special life circumstances of individuals also influence their vocational behavior. Many individuals do not have the responsibility of caring for dependents or accommodating to the desires of significant others, but such responsibility is a major influence on others. Many individuals do not have special obstacles such as addictions, criminal records, or physical handicaps that make some career objectives difficult to attain or maintain, but those obstacles are usually major influences on the careers of those who experience them. The following circumstances tend to thwart career satisfaction, performance, and attainment.

- *Family responsibility.* The assumption of a burdensome family role is a source of strain for individuals who are also pursuing careers. Individuals differ in the extent to which they enact family responsibilities. Some workers have no dependents; others abandon them. Adolescents and adults of any age may be deeply involved with family commitments.

■ *Career obstacles.* Some career obstacles may affect a large number of individuals. Some people cope effectively with these obstacles, whereas others find them disabling. Among these difficulties are appearance, physical limitations, race or ethnic identification, sex, sexual orientation, age, legal or immigration status, religion, lack of self-confidence, lack of money, lack of connections or social support, a criminal record, smoking, alcohol, or other drug abuse, health problems, emotional problems, and credit difficulties.

Congruence.   Other things being equal, people experience more satisfaction in environments where the mix of reinforcers matches their salient personal characteristics, that is, their interests and specific skills or abilities.

HOW PARTIAL THEORIES FIT TOGETHER

The framework sketched above is too complex to be a practical guide to every career intervention and every attempt to assess career status or problems. One need only consider the long—but still incomplete—assessment program spelled out by Super et al. (1992) to see how considering all influences on a career would quickly make assessment and intervention impractical. Practicing counselors and clinicians will have to identify the partial theories that are most likely to provide valuable insights for clients with particular individual problems—or for groups they assist in specific settings.

A map showing how influences derived from multiple partial theories fit together is shown in Figure 1. For example, TWA and Holland's theories involve the boxes for personality, job, person-job congruence, and career status. They focus most directly upon the congruence box. In contrast, the contributions of Hackman and Oldham (1974, 1975), Porter and Lawler (1968), and Locke and Latham (1990a, 1990b) involve mostly the variables located in the box for job—and they deal with performance and satisfaction within job. Much sociological work focuses on the variables labeled as exogenous influences or life circumstances in Figure 1. The personnel selection literature in industrial psychology focuses mostly on personality (including ability) and career status (including satisfaction and performance).

MEASUREMENT FOR IMPLEMENTING
THEORY IN PRACTICE

The selective use of partial theories tailored for specific vocational problems requires sound measures of the theoretical constructs that can be practically applied. In this last section, I discuss translating vocational theory into measures for practice and the evaluation of vocational interventions.

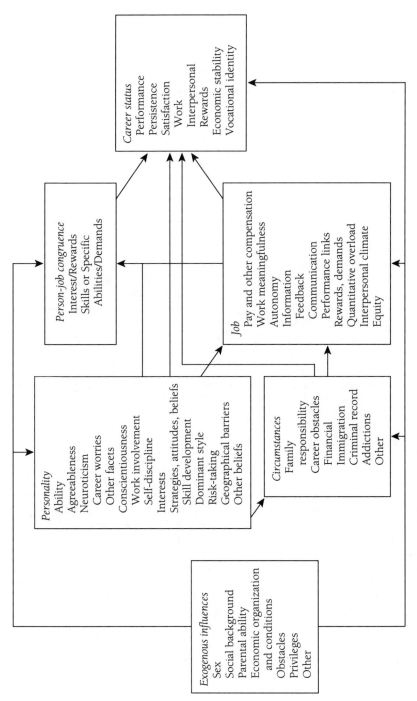

FIGURE 1   An Organizing Framework for Career Theory

TABLE 2   Illustrations of Potential Measurement Operations
for a Comprehensive Model of Career Status

Exogenous Influences

- Self-reported sex
- Reports of parental education or income; prestige scores for reported occupation (Nam & Terrie, 1988; Temme, 1975; Treiman, 1977)
- Parents' ability test scores
- Economic indicators for social areas (dominant industry, employment rates, labor market mechanisms operating, unionization, etc.)
- Assessment of cultural regularities: ethnic stereotypes, legal impediments, racism, elitism, sexism
- Presence of tax credits for employing persons from targeted areas, earmarked scholarships, and so on
- Others

Personality

- General and specific ability tests (e.g., *Armed Services Vocational Aptitude Battery,* U.S. Department of Defense, 1994; *General Aptitude Test Battery,* Hartigan & Wigdor, 1989; *Wonderlic Personnel Test,* Anonymous, 1992)
- Broad personality inventories (e.g., NEO-FFI, NEO-PI, Costa & McCrae, 1992; *Hogan Personality Inventory,* Hogan, 1986)
- Special purpose personality inventories (e.g., *Employee Assistance Program Inventory,* Anton & Reed, 1994)
- Interest inventories (e.g., *Self-Directed Search,* Holland, Fritzsche, & Powell, 1994; *Vocational Preference Inventory,* Holland, 1985; *Strong Interest Inventory,* Hansen, 1992; *Campbell Interest and Skill Survey,* Campbell, Hyne, & Nilsen, 1992) and related instruments (*Minnesota Importance Questionnaire,* Gay, Weiss, Hendel, Dawis, & Lofquist, 1971)
- Attitude, belief, or style measures (e.g., *Career Attitudes and Strategies Inventory* (CASI) Work Involvement, Dominant Style, Skill Development, or Risk-Taking Style scales (Holland & Gottfredson, 1994); job involvement scales (Lodahl & Kejner, 1965; Paullay, Alliger, & Stone-Romero, 1994); other assessments of attitudinal or cognitive barriers or obstacles (e.g., *Career Beliefs Inventory,* Krumboltz, 1991; *My Vocational Situation,* Holland, Daiger, & Power, 1980); and coping style or preference inventories (e.g., *Assessment of Daily Experience,* Stone & Neale, 1984; *Personal Resources Questionnaire,* Osipow & Spokane, 1987)

Circumstances

- Family involvement or roles (e.g., CASI Family Commitment scale, Holland & Gottfredson, 1994; scales from or derived from the *Quality of Employment Survey,* Quinn & Staines, 1979; Higgins, Duxbury, & Irving, 1992)
- *CASI Career Obstacles Checklist* (Holland & Gottfredson, 1994)
- *Employee Assistance Program Inventory* Marital Problems and Family Problems scales (Anton & Reed, 1994)
- Other self-report, interview, or archival data on financial, criminal, and medical problems (e.g., *Michigan Alcoholism Screening Test,* Selzer Zinokur, & von Rooijen, 1975; *Addiction Severity Index,* McLellan et al., 1985; *Salient Factor Score,* Hoffman & Beck, 1976; *Symptom Checklist-90-R,* Derogatis & Lazarus, 1994)

TABLE 2   Illustrations of Potential Measurement Operations
for a Comprehensive Model of Career Status (continued)

Job

- Company records or self-reports of pay and other elements of compensation
- Structured job analysis data related to job complexity and other aspects of the work (*Position Analysis Questionnaire*, Mecham, McCormick, & Jeanneret, 1977; *Common Metric Questionnaire*, Harvey, 1993; *Fleishman Job Analysis Survey*, Fleishman & Reilly, 1992; *Functional Job Analysis Scales*, Fine, 1989)
- *Job Diagnostic Survey* assessments of skill variety, task identity, task significance, autonomy, and feedback (Hackman & Oldham, 1974)
- Organizational climate surveys (e.g., Morale scale of the *Effective School Battery*, Gottfredson, 1984; *Organizational Assessment Inventory*, Van de Ven & Ferry, 1980; *Campbell Organizational Survey*, Campbell, 1994)
- Assessments of role conflict, job ambiguity, communication (e.g., Breaugh & Colihan, 1994; Rizzo, House, & Lirtzman, 1970)
- *Position Classification Inventory* (to assess RIASEC), Gottfredson & Holland, 1991
- CASI Interpersonal Abuse scale (Holland & Gottfredson, 1994), *Effective School Battery* Personal Security scale (Gottfredson, 1984)

Person-Job Congruence

- Congruence index between *Position Classification Inventory* (Gottfredson & Holland, 1991) code for job and *Self-Directed Search* (Holland, Fritzsche, & Powell, 1994) code for person
- Congruence index between *Dictionary of Holland Occupational Titles* (Gottfredson & Holland, 1989) code and *Vocational Preference Inventory* (Holland, 1985) code for person
- Correspondence assessed using theory of work adjustment methods (Dawis & Lofquist, 1984)
- Match between tested aptitudes and aptitude range of successful workers

Career Status

- Supervisor ratings (e.g., Minnesota Satisfactoriness scales, Dawis & Lofquist, 1984)
- Occupational attainment level (e.g., prestige or socioeconomic level, Nam & Terrie, 1988; Temme, 1975; Treiman, 1977)
- General job satisfaction measures (CASI Job Satisfaction scale, Holland & Gottfredson, 1994; *Job Satisfaction Blank No. 5*, Hoppock, 1935; *Minnesota Satisfaction Questionnaire,* Weiss, Dawis, England, & Lofquist, 1967)
- Specific job satisfaction measures (*Job Descriptive Index*, Smith, Kendall, & Hulin, 1985)
- Vocational identity (*My Vocational Situation* Vocational Identity scale, Holland, Daiger, & Power, 1980)

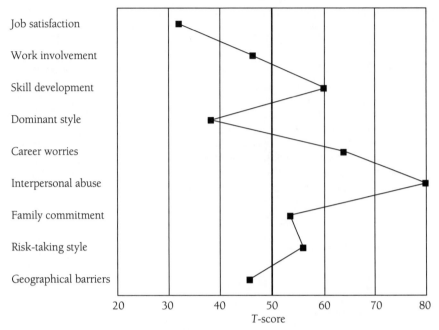

FIGURE 2 *Career Attitudes and Strategies Inventory* (CASI) Profile
for a Harassed Worker

A comprehensive discussion of measurement cannot be accomplished here, but I have sketched the array of possibilities in Table 2. The specific instruments cited illustrate but certainly do not exhaust the possibilities. For example, Tenopyr (1994) has suggested parallels between biodata factors and personality factors measured by the inventories explicitly cited. This is a plausible suggestion, especially because many personality inventory items and biodata inventory items are nearly indistinguishable.

For some variables, much useful research and development is already complete. For other variables, most of the work remains to be done. In recent years, John Holland and I have been working to devise measuring devices to fill some of the gaps. Until we developed the *Position Classification Inventory* (Gottfredson & Holland, 1991), only indirect methods of assessing person-job match were possible because we lacked direct measures of specific jobs in terms of Holland's environmental classification. Taken together, the portions of the general framework covered by Holland's theory and measured by the *Self-Directed Search*, the *Position Classification Inventory*, and the hexagonal calculus focus only on interests, job rewards and demands, and congruence. Figure 1 makes clear how much ground is left uncovered by these tools and why we always say that they should be used together with other information.

Most recently, Holland and I have extended our research on constructs outside of the person–job matching tradition in order to meet some additional practical assessment needs. We developed the *Career Attitudes and Strategies Inventory* (CASI; Holland & Gottfredson, 1994) to assesses directly some neglected features of career status. Figure 2 shows a profile of measures from our new inventory. This profile is for a woman who has extremely low job satisfaction and who reports a great deal of interpersonal abuse at work. The utility of such an assessment is immediately apparent. It suggests that a detailed analysis of person-job congruence or career development stage would not only be unnecessary but also rude. Unless there is compelling information to suggest otherwise, a counselor should get on with helping the individual achieve a satisfactory resolution for the interpersonal abuse. Suggestions raised by many partial theories can temporarily be ignored.

By using constructs from multiple partial theories, the general purpose framework described here reveals the limitations of any single partial theory. The general theory and associated measures suggested in Table 2 should help counselors match partial theories and measures to specific career problems.

SUMMARY

I have provided a short list of important career problems for which vocational theory is useful in practice. I asserted that the core career theories most often discussed by counseling psychologists are useful for coping with these problems but that they represent only a part of a broader range of useful research and theory. I provided a theoretical framework for illustrating the relation of multiple partial theories to several core vocational problems. Finally, I showed how partial theories and associated measures are useful in different parts of the overall framework for career psychology.

I am grateful for the editorial counsel of Denise C. Gottfredson and John L. Holland and for comments from Robert W. Lent on an earlier version of this chapter.

REFERENCES

Anonymous. (1992). *Wonderlic Personnel Test and Scholastic Level Exam user's manual.* Libertyville, IL: Wonderlic Personnel Test.

Anton, W. D., & Reed, J. R. (1994). *Employee Assistance Program Inventory professional manual.* Odessa, FL: Psychological Assessment Resources.

Azrin, N. H., Philip, R. A., Thienes-Hontos, P., & Besalel, V. (1981). Follow-up on welfare benefits received by job club clients. *Journal of Vocational Behavior, 18,* 253–254.

Bandura, A. (1977). *Social learning theory.* Englewood Cliffs, NJ: Prentice Hall.

Bandura, A. (1986). *Social foundations of thought and action: A social cognitive theory.* Englewood Cliffs, NJ: Prentice Hall.

Beck, A. T. (1976). Cognitive therapy and emotional disorders. New York: International Universities Press.

Breaugh, J. A., & Colihan, J. P. (1994). Measuring facets of job ambiguity: Construct validity evidence. Journal of Applied Psychology, 79, 191–202.

Campbell, D. P. (1994). Campbell Organizational Survey. Minneapolis: National Computer Systems.

Campbell, D. P., Hyne, S. A., & Nilsen, D. L. (1992). Manual for the Campbell Interest and Skill Survey. Minneapolis: National Computer Systems.

Caplan, R. D., Cobb, S., French, J. R. P., Jr., Van Harrison, R., & Pinneau, S. R., Jr. (1975). Job demands and worker health: Main effects and occupational differences (NIOSH 75-160). Washington, DC: U.S. Government Printing Office.

Costa, P. T., Jr., & McCrae, R. R. (1992). Revised NEO Personality Inventory and NEO Five-Factor Inventory: Professional manual. Odessa, FL: Psychological Assessment Resources.

Cronbach, L. J., Gleser, G. C., Nanda, H., & Rajaratnam, N. (1972). The dependability of behavioral measurements: Theory of generalizability for scores and profiles. New York: Wiley.

Dawis, R., & Lofquist, L. (1984). A psychological theory of work adjustment. Minneapolis: University of Minnesota Press.

Deci, E. L., & Ryan, R. M. (1985). Intrinsic motivation and self-determination in human behavior. New York: Plenum.

Derogatus, L. R., & Lazarus, L. (1994). SCL-90-R, Brief Symptom Inventory, and matching clinical rating scales. In M. E. Maruish (Ed.), The use of psychological testing for treatment planning and outcome assessment (pp. 217–248). Hillsdale, NJ: Erlbaum.

Dweck, C. S. (1986). Motivational processes affecting learning. American Psychologist, 41, 1040–1048.

Eberhardt, B. J., & Muchinsky, P. M. (1982). Biodata determinants of vocational typology: An integration of two paradigms. Journal of Applied Psychology, 67, 714–727.

Fine, S. A. (1989). Functional job analysis scales: A desk aid (Rev. ed.). Milwaukee, WI: Sidney A. Fine Associates.

Fitzgerald, L. F., & Betz, N. E. (1994). Career development in cultural context: The role of gender, race, class, and sexual orientation. In M. L. Savickas & R. W. Lent (Eds.), Convergence in career development theories: Implications for science and practice (pp. 103–117). Palo Alto, CA: Davies-Black Publishing.

Fitzgerald, L. F., Hulin, C. L., & Drasgow, F. (in press). The antecedents and consequences of sexual harassment in organizations: An integrated model. In G. Keita & S. Sauter (Eds.), Job stress 2000: Emergent issues. Washington, DC: American Psychological Association.

Fleishman, E. A., & Reilly, M. E. (1992). Fleishman Job Analysis Survey Administrator's guide. Palo Alto, CA: Consulting Psychologists Press.

Gay, E. G., Weiss, J. J., Hendel, D. D., Dawis, R. V., & Lofquist, L. H. (1971). Manual for the Minnesota Importance Questionnaire (Bulletin 54). Minneapolis: University of Minnesota, Industrial Relations Center.

Gottfredson, G. D. (1984). Effective School Battery user's manual. Odessa, FL: Psychological Assessment Resources.

Gottfredson, G. D., & Holland, J. L. (1989). Dictionary of Holland occupational codes (2d ed.). Odessa, FL: Psychological Assessment Resources.

Gottfredson, G. D., & Holland, J. L. (1991). *Position Classification Inventory: Professional manual.* Odessa, FL: Psychological Assessment Resources.

Gottfredson, G. D., Holland, J. L., & Gottfredson, L. S. (1975). The relation of vocational aspirations and assessments to employment reality. *Journal of Vocational Behavior, 7,* 135–148.

Gottfredson, G. D., & Lipstein, D. J. (1975). Using personal characteristics to predict parolee and probationer employment stability. *Journal of Applied Psychology, 60,* 644–648.

Gottfredson, L. S. (1981). Circumscription and compromise: A developmental theory of occupational aspirations. *Journal of Counseling Psychology, 28,* 545–579.

Guion, R. M. (1991). Personnel assessment, selection, and placement . In M. D. Dunnette & L. M. Hough (Eds.), *Handbook of industrial and organizational psychology* (2d ed., Vol. 2, pp. 327–398)). Palo Alto, CA: Davies-Black Publishing.

Hackman, J. R., & Oldham, G. R. (1974). *The job diagnostic survey: An instrument for the diagnosis of jobs and the evaluation of job redesign projects* (Tech. Rept. No. 4). New Haven, CT: Yale University, Department of Administrative Sciences.

Hackman, J. R., & Oldham, G. R. (1975). Development of the Job Diagnostic Survey. *Journal of Applied Psychology, 60,* 159–170.

Hansen, J. C. (1992). *User's guide for the Strong Interest Inventory.* Palo Alto, CA: Consulting Psychologists Press.

Harmon, L. W. (1994). Frustrations, daydreams, and realities of theoretical convergence. In M. L. Savickas & R. W. Lent (Eds.), *Convergence in career development theories: Implications for science and practice* (pp. 225–234). Palo Alto, CA: Davies-Black Publishing.

Hartigan, J. A., & Wigdor, A. K. (Eds.). (1989). *Fairness in employment testing: Validity generalization, minority issues, and the General Aptitude Test Battery.* Washington, DC: National Academy Press.

Harvey, R. J. (1991). Job analysis. In M. D. Dunnette & L. M. Hough (Eds.), *Handbook of industrial and organizational psychology* (2d ed., Vol. 2). Palo Alto, CA: Davies-Black Publishing.

Harvey, R. J. (1993). *The development of the Common Metric Questionnaire (CMQ)* [Research Monograph]. San Antonio, TX: Psychological Corporation.

Higgins, C. A., Duxbury, L. E., & Irving, R. H. (1992). Work-family conflict in the dual-career family. *Organizational Behavior and Human Decision Processes, 51,* 51–75.

Hoffman, P. B., & Beck, J. L. (1976). Salient factor score validation—a 1972 release cohort. *Journal of Criminal Justice, 4,* 69–76.

Hogan, R. (1986). *Hogan Personality Inventory manual.* Minneapolis: National Computer Systems.

Holland, J. L. (1985). *Manual for the Vocational Preference Inventory.* Odessa, FL: Psychological Assessment Resources.

Holland, J. L. (1992). *Making vocational choices: A theory of vocational personalities and work environments.* Odessa, FL: Psychological Assessment Resources. (Original work published 1985)

Holland, J. L., Daiger, D., & Power, P. (1980). Some diagnostic scales for research in decision making and personality: Identity, information, and barriers. *Journal of Personality and Social Psychology, 39,* 1191–1200.

Holland, J. L., Fritzsche, B. A., & Powell, A. B. (1994). *Self-Directed Search technical manual.* Odessa, FL: Psychological Assessment Resources.

Holland, J. L., & Gottfredson, G. D. (1994). *Career Attitudes and Strategies Inventory: An inventory for understanding adult careers.* Odessa, FL: Psychological Assessment Resources.

Hoppock, R. (1935). *Job satisfaction.* New York: Harper.

House, R. J., & Rizzo, J. R. (1972). Role conflict and ambiguity as critical variables in a model of organizational behavior. *Organizational Behavior and Human Performance, 7,* 467–505.

Howard, G. S., & Conway, C. G. (1986). Can there be an empirical science of volitional action? *American Psychologist, 41,* 1241–1251.

Keisler, C. A. (1971). *The psychology of commitment.* New York: Academic Press.

Krumboltz, J. (1991). *Career beliefs inventory.* Palo Alto, CA: Consulting Psychologists Press.

Krumboltz, J., Mitchell, A., & Jones, G. (1976). A social learning theory of career selection. *Counseling Psychologist, 6,* 71–81.

Lazarus, R. S. (1993). From psychological stress to the emotions: A history of changing outlooks. *Annual Review of Psychology, 44,* 1–21.

Lazarus, R. S., Averill, J. R., & Opton, E. M., Jr. (1974). The psychology of coping: Issues of research and assessment. In G. V. Coehlo, D. A. Hamburg, & J. E. Adams (Eds.), *Coping and adaptation* (pp. 249–315). New York: Basic.

Lent, R. W., Brown, S. D., & Hackett, G. (1994). Toward a unifying social cognitive theory of career and academic interest, choice, and performance. *Journal of Vocational Behavior, 45,* 79–122.

Lent, R. W., & Hackett, G. (1994). Sociocognitive mechanisms of personal agency in career development: Pantheoretical prospects. In M. L. Savickas & R. W. Lent (Eds.), *Convergence in career development theories.* Palo Alto, CA: Davies-Black Publishing.

Locke, E. A., & Latham, G. P. (1990a). *A theory of goal-setting and task performance.* Englewood Cliffs, NJ: Prentice Hall.

Locke, E. A., & Latham, G. P. (1990b). Work motivation and satisfaction: Light at the end of the tunnel. *Psychological Science, 1,* 240–246.

Lodahl, T. M., & Kejner, M. (1965). The definition and measurement of job involvement. *Journal of Applied Psychology, 49,* 24–33.

McLaughlin, D. H., & Tiedeman, D. V. (1974). Eleven-year career ability and change as reflected in Project Talent data through the Flanagan, Holland, and Roe occupational classifications systems. *Journal of Vocational Behavior, 5,* 177–196.

McLellan, A. T., Luborsky, L., Cacciola, J., Griffith, J., McGahan, P., & O'Brien, C. P. (1985). *Guide to the Addiction Severity Index* (ADM 85-1419). Washington, DC: U.S. Government Printing Office.

Mecham, R. C., McCormick, E. J., & Jeanneret, P. R. (1977). *Position Analysis Questionnaire technical manual.* West Lafayette, IN: University Book Store.

Morrison, R. F. (1994). Biodata applications in career development research. In G. S. Stokes, M. D. Mumford, & W. A. Owens (Eds.), *Biodata handbook: Theory, research, and use of biographical information in selection and performance prediction.* Palo Alto, CA: Davies-Black Publishing.

Mumford, M. D., & Owens, W. A. (1982). Life history and vocational interests. *Journal of Vocational Behavior, 21,* 330–348.

Nam, C. B., & Terrie, E. W. (1988). *1980-based Nam-Powers occupational status scores (WPS 88-48).* Tallahassee, FL: Florida State University, Center for the Study of Population.

Neiner, A. G., & Owens, W. A. (1985). Using biodata to predict job choice among college graduates. *Journal of Applied Psychology, 70,* 127–136.

Osipow, S. H., & Spokane, A. R. (1984). Measuring occupational stress, strain, and coping. *Applied Social Psychology Annual, 5,* 67–83.

Osipow, S. H., & Spokane, A. R. (1987). *Occupational Stress Inventory manual, research version.* Odessa, FL: Psychological Assessment Resources.

Otto, L. B., & Haller, A. O. (1979). Evidence for a social psychological view of the status attainment process: Four studies compared. *Social Forces, 57,* 887–914.

Parnes, H. S., Miljus, R. C., Spitz, R. S., & Associates (1970). Career thresholds: A longitudinal study of the educational and labor market experiences of male youth (Vol. 1). *Manpower Research Monograph* (No. 16). Washington, DC: U.S. Government Printing Office.

Paterson, D. G., Gerken, C. d'A., & Hahn, M. E. (1953). *Revised Minnesota Occupational Ratings Scales.* Minneapolis: University of Minnesota Press.

Paullay, I. M., Alliger, G. M., & Stone-Romero, E. F. (1994). Construct validation of two instruments designed to measure involvement and work centrality. *Journal of Applied Psychology, 79,* 224–228.

Porter, L. W., & Lawler, E. E., III. (1968). *Managerial attitudes and performance.* Homewood, IL: Irwin-Dorsey.

Price, J. L., & Mueller, C. W. (1986). *Absenteeism and turnover among hospital employees.* Greenwich, CT: JAI Press.

Quinn, R., & Staines, G. (1979). *The 1977 Quality of Employment Survey.* Ann Arbor, MI: Survey Research Center.

Rizzo, J. R., House, R. J., & Lirtzman, S. I. (1970). Role conflict and ambiguity in complex organizations. *Administrative Science Quarterly, 15,* 150–163.

Rowe, D. C. (1994). *The limits of family influence: Genes, experience, and behavior.* New York: Guilford Press.

Schmitt, F. L., Ones, D. S., & Hunter, J. E. (1992). Personnel selection. *Annual Review of Psychology, 43,* 627–670.

Schneider, B. (1987). The people make the place. *Personnel Psychology, 40,* 437–454.

Selzer, M. L., Zinokur, A., & von Rooijen, L. (1975). A self-administered short Michigan Alcoholism Screening Test (SMAST). *Journal of Studies on Alcohol, 36,* 117–126.

Sewell, W. H., Haller, H. O., & Portes, A. (1969). The educational and early occupational attainment process. *American Sociological Review, 34,* 82–92.

Schunk, D. H., & Swartz, C. W. (1993). Goals and progress feedback: Effects on self-efficacy and writing achievement. *Contemporary Educational Psychology, 18,* 337–354.

Smith, P. C., Kendall, L. M., & Hulin, C. L. (1985). *The Job Descriptive Index* (Rev. ed.). Bowling Green, OH: Bowling Green State University, Department of Psychology.

Staw, B. M., & Ross, J. V. (1985). Stability in the midst of change: A dispositional approach. *Journal of Applied Psychology, 70,* 469–480.

Stone, A. A., & Neale, J. M. (1984). New measure of daily coping: Development and preliminary results. *Journal of Personality and Social Psychology, 46,* 892–906.

Super, D. E. (1990). A life-span, life-space approach to career development. In D. Brown & L. Brooks (Eds.), *Career choice and development: Applying contemporary theories to practice* (2d ed., pp. 197–261). San Francisco: Jossey-Bass.

Super, D. E., Osborne, W. L., Walsh, D. J., & Brown, S. D. (1992). Developmental career assessment and counseling: The C-DAC model. *Journal of Counseling and Development, 71,* 74–80.

Temme, L. V. (1975). *Occupation: Meanings and measures.* Washington, DC: Bureau of Social Science Research.

Tenopyr, M. L. (1994). Big five, structural modeling, and item response theory. In G. S. Stokes, M. D. Mumford, & W. A. Owens (Eds.), *Biodata handbook: Theory, research, and use of biographical information in selection and performance prediction* (pp. 519–533). Palo Alto, CA: Davies-Black Publishing.

Treiman, D. J. (1977). *Occupational prestige in comparative perspective.* New York: Academic Press.

U.S. Department of Defense. (1994). *Technical manual for the ASVAB 18/19 career exploration program* (DOD 1304. 12L-ASTPS-TS). Washington, DC: U.S. Government Printing Office.

Van de Ven, A., & Ferry, D. (1980). *Measuring and assessing organizations.* New York: Wiley.

Vondracek, F. W., Lerner, R. M., & Schulenberg, J. E. (1986). *Career development: A life-span developmental approach.* Hillsdale, NJ: Erlbaum.

Weiss, D. J., Dawis, R. V., England, G. W., & Lofquist, L. H. (1967). *Manual for the Minnesota Satisfaction Questionnaire.* Minneapolis: University of Minnesota, Industrial Relations Center.

Weitz, J. (1952). A neglected concept in the study of job satisfaction. *Personnel Psychology, 5,* 201–205.

Westbrook, B. W., Buck, R. W., Jr., Wynne, D. C., & Sanford, E. (1994). Career maturity in adolescence: Reliability and validity of self-ratings of abilities by gender and ethnicity. *Journal of Career Assessment, 2,* 125–161.

CHAPTER FIFTEEN

Assessment and Counseling for Career Mastery

John O. Crites
Crites Career Consultants

WHAT DOES THE convergence of career theory and practice mean? What are the links between career theory and practice? How can these be articulated within some comprehensible schema for both theorists and practitioners that makes sense to clients? These are central questions for the fields of vocational psychology and career counseling if their viability and usefulness are to persist. There are many different ways in which these questions can be answered. This chapter proposes only one approach to translating career theory into practice and informing theory through practice. Based upon the scientist-practitioner model of counseling/career psychology, it proposes that each theorist be a practitioner and that each practitioner be a theorist. There are some theorists who practice and there are some practitioners who theorize, but for many, theory and practice remain separate. Ultimately, though, the convergence of career theory and practice depends on counseling/career psychologists who must theorize as well as practice and practice as well as theorize. Pepinsky and Pepinsky (1954) discussed the "hypothetical client" and Hewer (1963) asked "what is more practical than a good theory?" So there is a precedence in the field of counseling/career psychology for attempting an integration of theory and practice. The goal now, of this book in general and this chapter in particular as it relates to the concept of career mastery, is to build on these historical antecedents as a foundation for the convergence of career theory and practice.

This chapter specifically addresses the integration of theory and practice as they relate to the concept of career mastery, a new rubric but a relatively old idea. It was born of consultation in corporate America and career development theory for adults (Crites, 1976). It has become current with Levinson's (1992) book, *Career Mastery*, and Crites' (1992) publication of the *Career Mastery Inventory,* which dates back to the *Career Adjustment and Development Inventory* in 1982, developed at Lawrence Livermore Laboratories and refined in an Ohio State University project on "A Diagnostic Taxonomy of Adult Career Development Problems" (Campbell et al., 1979).

The focus of the discussion that follows is on how this concept of career mastery can be translated from theory, through assessment, to successful career adjustment counseling with adults who have made a career choice and are in the job marketplace. Sometimes theory precedes practice, and, other times, practice, including assessment, precedes theory. This chapter presents an integration of theory and practice, focusing on the links between the two, which can be exemplified by a case study of an adult in career adjustment counseling. First, I will present a theoretical discussion of links; then I will provide a psychometric plan for assessment of the salient variables in adult career adjustment; and, finally, I will present a case study of an adult client who went through a counseling process that integrated career theory with measurement and counseling strategy/technique.

ARTICULATION OF
CAREER THEORY INTO PRACTICE

The first link between career theory and practice is articulation between the so-called theory-language and data-language levels used in philosophy of science and psychology (Marx, 1963). The theory-language level is conceptual. It can derive from a variety of sources, both formal and informal. Examples of formal theory-language include mathematical specification of relationships among variables (Estes, 1959) and hypothetical-deductive models of learning (Hull et al., 1940). In contrast, informal theory-language often comes from field observations (e.g., Roe, 1953), case studies, or armchair speculation. Concepts are generated logically or mathematically and then related to the data-language level. The latter is empirical. Data may be qualitative or quantitative, depending on the nature of the investigation. Qualitative data may be $N = 1$ studies, or *ipsative* (intraindividual) Q-sorts, or simply case analyses of clients in counseling. Quantitative data are expressed somehow in numbers, however rudimentary, such as counting or classification base rates, or in statistical terms, such as mean differences or correlation coefficients. Whether qualitative or quantitative, these sources define the data-language level. The problem in converging career theory with practice is to relate the theory-language level to the data–language level. How can this be accomplished?

There are basically four modes for articulating the relationship between the theory-language and data-language levels, as shown in Figure 1: *model, deductive, functional,* and *inductive* (Marx, 1963; Crites, 1969). These modes are defined by the direction of inferences they specify between the two levels. In the model approach,

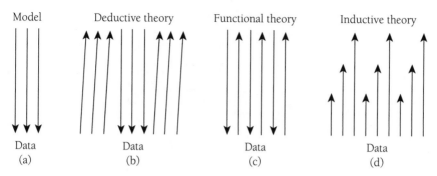

Model   Deductive theory   Functional theory   Inductive theory

Data   Data   Data   Data
(a)   (b)   (c)   (d)

FIGURE 1   Four Modes of Theory Construction

From *Theories in Contemporary Psychology* (p. 14), by M. H. Marx, 1963, New York: Macmillan. Copyright 1963 by M. H. Marx. Reprinted by permission.

the direction is one-way—from the theory-language level to the data-language level. These modes are wholly conceptual, not based on data. Their virtue is that they precisely specify variables and their interrelationships and that they can be tested on the data–language level, given appropriate operational definitions and measurement methods. An example in vocational psychology is Crites' (1978) model of vocational maturity. It parallels Wherry's (1984) statistical model for hierarchical factor analysis, which delineates three types of factors in the hierarchy: general, group, and specific variables. When this statistical model was fitted to the variables measured by the *Career Maturity Inventory*, the hierarchy shown in Figure 2 was derived. It conforms exactly to theoretical and statistical expectations. If it had not, then the structure would have been different, and there would have been no solution from the hierarchical factor analysis. Thus, in model testing, the relationship between the theory-language level and data-language level is unidirectional and exact—either the model fits or it does not.

The *deductive* mode of relating the theory-language and data-language levels usually begins with a set of already established empirical laws, then proceeds to deductions of testable hypotheses from theorems and postulates, which are investigated in research. The process is iterated with extrapolations from the new data and so forth, as shown in Figure 1. It is critical to this mode that the new data are different than the old, otherwise the research is simply a replication. It is difficult to find examples of deductive theories in vocational psychology. Perhaps the closest approximation is Bordin's (1943) theory of interests as dynamic phenomena. The work adjustment theory of Dawis, England, and Lofquist (1964) might be included, but it is more an enumeration of declarative statements than it is inferences deduced from postulates. A truly deductive theory, as an articulation between the theory-language and data-language levels, must conform to the hypothetical syllogism "if —, and if —, then —.", in which the middle term relates the other two to each other.

240

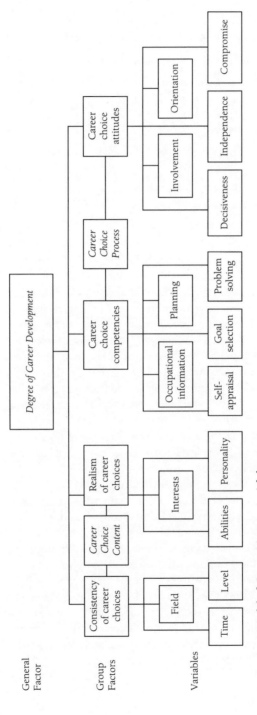

FIGURE 2 A Model of Career Maturity in Adolescence

As shown in Figure 1, the functional mode for relating the theory- and data-language levels moves from hypotheses to data and back again, until an internal consistency of interrelated concepts emerges. This process not only yields an empirical base but also has considerable subsumptive value. The latter has two aspects: "First, it requires of a theory that it account for what is already known about the phenomena of interest; and second, it requires that it be consistent with any new data which become available" (Crites, 1969, p. 625). Clearly, the exemplar of this approach in vocational psychology is Holland's theory of vocational choice. Holland (1959) started with hypotheses, tested them on the empirical level, returned to the theory level, and then made further predictions to the data level. It is noteworthy that Holland "linked" the two levels by operationalizing the concepts in his theory with the *Self-Directed Search*, a necessary condition for converging career theory and practice. What distinguishes his approach from the deductive mode is that although his theory has internal consistency, it was not formulated using the combinatory rules of syllogistic reasoning.

Finally, the inductive mode of articulation between the theory-language and data-language levels proceeds from the empirical level by enumeration (Figure 1). That is, there is little or no attempt to relate statements to each other. The statements are simply summaries of data expressed in words. Thus, Stefflre (1966) titled his inductive theory of vocational development, "Ten Propositions in Search of a Theory." Similarly, Super (1953), in his theory of vocational development, listed a number of statements that covered a variety of empirically verified phenomena but which were essentially unrelated. Darley and Hagenah (1955, p. 101) commented that his theory "embraces primarily in descriptive terms a great range of factors—genetic, endocrine, maturational, sociological, and personality—as determinants of the behavior with which we are concerned." They criticized Super's theory for having only minimal predictive value for generating hypotheses for testing, a criticism that can generally be made of the inductive mode of articulating the relationship between the theory-language and data-language levels.

To conclude, Crites (1969) comments,

> Which of these modes of theory construction will prove to be the best is difficult to say. Perhaps the question should not even be posed, since the several approaches to theorizing may be suited to different purposes, depending upon their relationship to the nature of the research which is being conducted on vocational behavior and development. If the research is experimental and laboratory-based, then the model and deductive modes may be the most appropriate.... If the research is exploratory in the field, however, theorizing of the inductive and functional types may be more useful. These modes are more open-ended and allow for the formulation of hypotheses which are less formal and more tentative.... If and when research in vocational psychology becomes more experimental, there will probably be a shift in the modes of theory construction which are most widely used, from the less to the more formal. But even then, inductive theorizing will have its place in opening up new lines of inquiry and codifying existing empirical knowledge. (pp. 613–614)

RESEARCH ON THE CONVERGENCE
OF CAREER THEORY AND PRACTICE

Articulation between the theory-language and data-language levels necessitates empirical research in all modes of relationship between the two, whether qualitative or quantitative. The term *research* is a generic one that applies to a wide range of studies, depending on what the purpose of the investigation is. Edwards and Cronbach (1952) and Edwards (1954) have provided a meaningful classification of the types of research that can be pursued. In the discussion that follows, these are defined and explicated as exemplified by the construction and development of the *Career Mastery Inventory* (CMAS), an assessment instrument designed for the career adjustment counseling of adults in the job marketplace. The CMAS was developed from a program of research on vocational maturity initiated in the 1960s (Crites, 1961, 1966) and which continues to the present. It was conceived to supplement and extend the measurement of career development in adolescents by the *Career Maturity Inventory* (CMI) into the adult years. In other words, the CMI measures attitudes and competencies essential to realistic decision making in adolescence, whereas the CMAS assesses behaviors and coping mechanisms necessary for maximal success and satisfaction in the world of work.

The four types of research that Edwards and Cronbach (1952) and Edwards (1954) have classified are as follows (Crites, 1969, p. 586):

■ *Survey research:* to discover relevant variables for more systematic study and to establish the parameters of known variables

■ *Technique research:* to develop methods, whether test or nontest, for making observations that are quantifiable

■ *Theoretical (critical) research:* to test hypotheses that have been deduced from theories or formatted to account for empirical laws

■ *Applied research:* to determine what course of action should be taken

In the conceptualization and construction of the CMAS, each of these types of research was conducted in a sequence from survey to technique, through theoretical, ending with applied. Thus, a program of research was designed that cumulatively would either establish the usefulness of the CMAS for career adjustment counseling with adults or not. The intent throughout this research was to relate theoretical concepts (Crites, 1976) to the measurement procedures being explored.

SURVEY RESEARCH ON
THE CAREER MASTERY INVENTORY

The CMAS was originally conceived as a measure of career development in early adulthood (Crites, 1976). The first survey research on it was conducted at Lawrence

Livermore Laboratories, under the direction of Marlys Hanson, in 1975. The purpose of the research, which was largely qualitative, was to identify variables as criteria for the effectiveness of an in-house program of career development for staff personnel ranging from Ph.D. scientists to administrators. This survey research, also based on tryouts of preliminary inventory forms (an iterative process), resulted in an instrument called the *Career Adjustment and Development Inventory* (CADI). In what eventually evolved into the CMAS, the CADI was used in a variety of settings—industrial, higher education, Joint Training Partnership (JTPA) programs, and individual career adjustment counseling. It has also been used as the CADI and the CMAS by the Arkansas Rehabilitation and Training Center to orient people with disabilities and physical handicaps to potential career adjustment problems that they might encounter on the job. Survey reports from these programs have been uniformly positive, the best qualitative evidence being that they use the CMAS in their programs. But these results may be only anecdotal. For a counselor in adult career adjustment counseling with a client, psychometric evidence on the CMAS is essential. This is technique research.

Technique Research on the Career Mastery Inventory

This type of research on the CMAS follows the APA Standards for Educational and Psychological Tests.

Norms.   Subsequent to the initial survey research at Lawrence Livermore Laboratories in 1975, the CADI was administered in commercial, manufacturing, and scientific establishments across stratified *convenience* (nonrandom) samples of employees. However, there were consistent (statistically nonsignificant) findings among them. The different constituencies did not differ. It was assumed that they were, within chance fluctuations, from the same populations. Normatively, in contrast to interest inventories, there were no significant (.05 alpha) gender differences on the CMAS. The CMAS is equally applicable to both men and women. Evidently, they have similar experiences in the work environment and react to them in similar ways, that is, in behaviors and attitudes. Occupational (organizational) level also does not appear to be a differentiating variable on the CMAS. The behaviors and attitudes, as well as coping mechanisms measured by CMAS, appear to be uniformly applicable to employees in an organization. Generalization of these results to other groups, for example, ethnic and racial minorities, and students, supports the results from the initial standardization of the CMAS. Thus, the norms, based on over 5,000 cases, and the findings from stratified organizational analyses lend support to the applicability of the CMAS to a general population of adults (Super & Crites, 1962).

Reliability.   In classical psychometric theory, there are only two indices of the reliability of measurement: *test-retest* and *internal consistency*. Without engaging in the arguments for or against either of these, suffice it to say that neither applies to measures of career development (CMI or CMAS) because maturation variance is confounded in the computational formulas for each. If a maturational variable, such as career development (CMI, CMAS), is being measured, then the maturational variance is part of the test-retest error variance. To extract this variance, which is the essence of career development, it is important to recognize that career development inventories, whether the CMI or CMAS, are not that unreliable (Crites, 1978). In fact, the test-retest reliability for the *Career Maturity Inventory* increased from .72 to .81 when the correction for maturational variance was made. The test-retest reliabilities for the CMAS, over intervals varying from two weeks to four to six months, are in the .70 to .75 range. The initial internal consistencies for the CADI were disappointing for some subscales in Part 1, Behaviors and Attitudes. They ranged as low as the .50s. The total score internal consistency, based upon a summation of all 90 items in Part 1, was an acceptable .85. But since the design of the CADI was to provide subscale scores for profile analysis, revisions were made to increase the subscale internal consistencies and score ceilings. This was accomplished by extending the CADI unidirectional five-point Likert scale to a bipolar scale in the present edition of the CMAS. With this emendation, the internal consistencies of the CMAS subscales increased to the mid .70s.

Scoring. A unique feature of the CMAS is that it can be either machine scored (scanned) or hand scored. The respondent records his or her responses on a top answer sheet, which is scannable for generating a group profile (means and standard deviations) for an organizational profile. These responses are transcribed on a bottom sheet, with a carbon transfer, which then can be scored in approximately 10 minutes by individuals in adult career adjustment counseling or participants in career development seminars or workshops. The feedback of scores from the CMAS is almost immediate, and they can be integrated into the program with the CMAS *User's Guide,* which interprets the scores and gives illustrative examples from case studies. Combining the individual interpretation of CMAS scores with the organizational profile provides a comprehensive summary of how the individual is progressing in his or her career and what the benchmarks are for the organization to encourage and enhance employee career development.

Validity. Crites (1976) specified two criteria for any measure of adult career development: career success and satisfaction. In several studies cited in the CMAS *Sourcebook* (Crites, 1993), the results confirm that the CMAS is significantly related to both these criteria. The total score on Part 1 of the CMAS is correlated .50 with the *Hoppock Job Satisfaction Blank* (HJSB). The subscales correlate in the .30s and .40s with the HJSB, the lower *r*s being expected because the subscales have fewer items. Analyses of the relationship between the CMAS and criteria of career success (i.e., performance appraisals and supervisors' ratings) indicate that those employees who have higher evaluations also have higher CMAS scores on all subscales. Thus, there is criterion-related validity for the CMAS as a measure of adult career development. But in addition, there is supportive evidence of the CMAS's construct validity. Four independent studies cited in the CMAS *Sourcebook* (Crites, 1993) have identified *time/task sequences* in adult career development as measured by the CMAS. Evidently, there are three periods within the *establishment stage*, defined by Super (1957), which start with occupational entry and merge into the *maintenance stage* at midlife. The first period might be characterized as *initial establishment*, involving the time/task sequence of, as measured by the CMAS, Organizational Adaptability and Position Performance. The *intermediate establishment* period embraces Work Attitudes and Habits and Co-worker Relationships, the latter being one of the most critical career developmental tasks of adult career development. The *last establishment* period encompasses the time/task sequence of Advancement and Career Choice and Plans, looking forward to the maintenance stage.

Theoretical Research on the Career Mastery Inventory

The principal findings that have emerged from research on the CMAS are very similar to those on the CMI. Both inventories fit a hierarchical model of the relationship between the theory-language and data-language levels for theory construction (Marx, 1963). Several articles have verified the *model fitting* for the *Career Maturity Inventory*, and there are results that support model fitting for the CMAS as a measure of adult career development (CMAS *Sourcebook*; Crites, 1993). Other modes of theory construction may be viable alternatives to model building, but the latter has a control that the others do not. Either the model fits, following Wherry's (1984) hierarchical factor analytic solution (i.e., the "back solution"), or it does not. The other modes of theory construction are open to alternative interpretations. The model method is not. Since the CMI and the CMAS fit their hierarchical models, there are no alternative interpretations of data on them. There may be other interpretations of other data, which do fit a hierarchical model, but these data are not prescribed by a model approach to the relationship between the theory-language and data-language levels. Figure 3 shows a hierarchical model of career mastery in the establishment stage of career development.

Applied Research on the Career Mastery Inventory

The CMAS *Sourcebook* (Crites, 1993) reports several studies that have used the CMAS in applied organizational settings, three of which are summarized here. In a needs analysis of a manufacturing company's management group, Zinser (1988, p. ii) concluded that the *Career Adjustment and Development Inventories*

> uncovered specific developmental needs of both the individuals and the groups. More importantly, the use of the CADI [CMAS] provides a more comprehensive analysis of the critical career behaviors of the establishment stage, and goes beyond the simple measurement of the amount of career activities in the organization.

Zinser (1988, p. 62) also conducted a program evaluation, eliciting participants' reactions to the CADI (CMAS) in his study. He summarized his findings as follows:

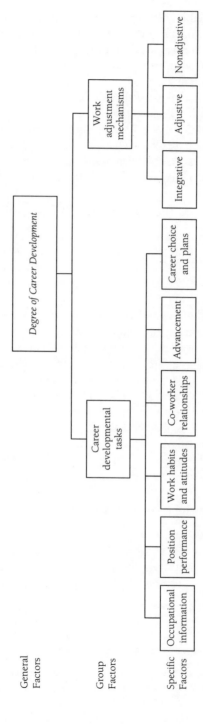

FIGURE 3   A Hierarchical Model of Career Mastery in the Establishment Stage of Career Development

"The results of the group evaluation were comparable to the feedback Crites received using a reactionnaire (in Campbell et. al., 1979). In his sample, 79% agreed that the statements made sense. Another 75% reported that the CADI were relevant to them."

Thus, Zinser (1988) found that not only was the CADI (CMAS) useful for organizational need analysis but also that those who took the inventory reported it was credible.

The CMAS has also been used as a pretest-posttest measure to assess "gains" on such programs as *Managing Toward Career Excellence* (MTCE; Merman & Clark, 1985). The units in MTCE were cross-classified with the CMAS scales, and there was a high degree of agreement between the program and the inventory. In fact, all of the sections in MTCE were matched with the CMAS, although they had been developed independently. Five studies were conducted of hypothesized "gains" on the MTCE, as measured by the CMAS, and the results were uniformly positive.

Similarly, a program evaluation of organizational effectiveness training conducted by Monsanto Corporation and reported in *Workplace Basics: The Essential Skills Employers Want* (Carneval, Gainer, & Meltzer, 1990) found the following gains from pretest-posttest analyses of the CMAS:

- Enhanced job satisfaction, performance, and success
- Behaviors that enabled employees and the organization to grow
- Greater self-control in terms of meeting personal, professional, and social needs
- Evidence that people had knowledge of what they wanted from the organization and how they could obtain it

It was concluded that the CMAS was useful and relevant for evaluation of the Monsanto Organizational Effectiveness Training program.

COUNSELING FOR CAREER MASTERY: A CASE STUDY

To give an example of counseling for career mastery, consider the case of Tom, a real person whose name has been changed. Highly trained in computer science (he has a master's degree), with eight years experience and tenure with the same firm, Tom nevertheless felt less successful and satisfied in his career than he wanted to—he felt thwarted in accomplishing his career goals and experienced increasing anxiety about his future. He came for career adjustment counseling in a quandary about what to do. He took a battery of aptitude and interest surveys, all of which indicated that he was in the best career field for him. When he took the *Career Mastery Inventory*, however, it became apparent that his problem was in accomplishing certain career developmental tasks. As his CMAS profile in Figure 4 indicates, his

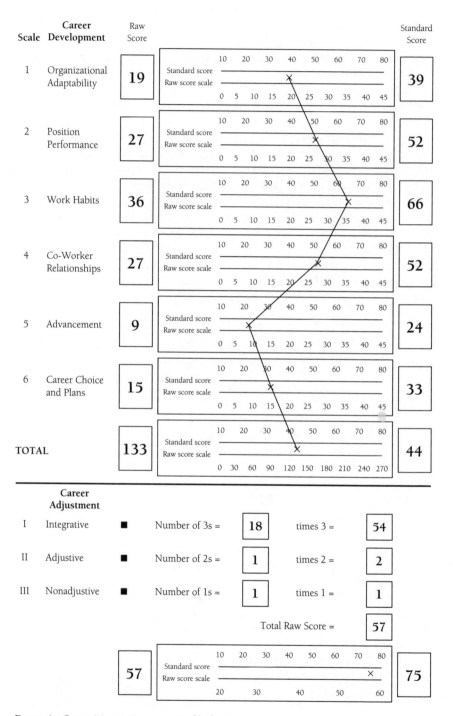

FIGURE 4 *Career Mastery Inventory* Profile for Tom

career adjustment mechanisms were high quality. Clearly, how he coped with conflictual situations in his career was not a problem, nor was his mastery of Position Performance, Work Habits and Attitudes, and Co-Worker Relationships career development tasks—all his standard scores on these scales were at 50 (average) or above. But on the Organizational Adaptability, Advancement, and Career Choice and Plans scales, his scores were considerably below average. Why?

Tom's career adjustment counseling focused on answers to this question. He said he spent most of his time during the past eight years on special projects, which he found not only increasingly repetitive and boring but also essentially a dead end for his career advancement. He wanted to move in a different direction but was uncertain how to do so. He had not talked with his supervisor nor explored other career options in the organization. When he did so, at the suggestion of his counselor, he found that an alternative career track within the firm was administration, which offered higher levels of responsibility and remuneration. He arranged to transfer into administration, where he has been more successful and satisfied and has experienced considerably less anxiety about attaining his career goals. Upon retaking the *Career Mastery Inventory*, his scores on Organizational Adaptability, Advancement, and Career Choice and Plans were well above average. He had mastered these tasks and furthered his career development toward increased success and satisfaction during the Establishment Stage. He was also better positioned to enter and progress in the career stages that follow midlife.

REFERENCES

Bordin, E. S. (1943). A theory of vocational interests as dynamic phenomena. *Educational and Psychological Measurement, 3,* 49–65.

Campbell, R. E., Cellini, J. V., Shaltry, P. E., Long, A. E., Pinkos, D., & Crites, J. O. (1979). *A diagnostic taxonomy of adult career problems.* Columbus: Ohio State University, National Center for Research in Vocational Education.

Carneval, A. P., Gainer, L. J., & Meltzer, A. S. (1990). *Workplace basics: The essential skills employers want.* San Francisco: Jossey-Bass.

Crites, J. O. (1961). A model for the measurement of vocational maturity. *Journal of Counseling Psychology, 8,* 255–259.

Crites, J. O. (1966). *Programmatic research on vocational development.* Unpublished manuscript, University of Iowa, Iowa City.

Crites, J. O. (1969). *Vocational psychology.* New York: McGraw-Hill.

Crites, J. O. (1976). A comprehensive model of career development in early adulthood. *Journal of Vocational Behavior, 9,* 105–118.

Crites, J. O. (1978). *Career Maturity Inventory theory and research handbook.* Monterey, CA: CTB/McGraw-Hill.

Crites, J. O. (1992). *Career Mastery Inventory.* Boulder, CO: Crites Career Consultants.

Crites, J. O. (1993). *Career Mastery Inventory Sourcebook.* Boulder, CO: Crites Career Consultants.

Darley, J. G., & Hagenah, T. (1955). *Vocational interest measurement.* Minneapolis: University of Minnesota Press.

Dawis, R. V., England, G. W., & Lofquist, L. H. (1964). *Minnesota studies in vocational rehabilitation: XV. A theory of work adjustment.* Minneapolis: University of Minnesota, Industrial Relations Center.

Edwards, A. L. (1954). Experiments: Their planning and execution. In G. Lindzey (Ed.), *Handbook of social psychology* (Vol. 1, pp. 259–288). Cambridge, MA: Addison-Wesley.

Edwards, A. L., & Cronbach, L. J. (1952). Experimental design for research in psychotherapy. *Journal of Clinical Psychology, 8,* 51–59.

Estes, W. K. (1959). Component and pattern models with Markovian interpretations. In R. R. Bush & W. K. Estes (Eds.), *Studies in mathematical learning theory* (pp. 9–52). Stanford, CA: Stanford University Press.

Hewer, V. H. (1963). What do theories of vocational choice mean to a counselor? *Journal of Counseling Psychology, 10,* 118–125.

Holland, J. L. (1959). A theory of vocational choice. *Journal of Counseling Psychology, 6,* 35–44.

Hull, C. L., Hovland, C. I., Ross, R. T., Hall, M., Perkins, D. T., & Fitch, F. B. (1940). *Mathematico-deductive theory of role learning.* New Haven, CT: Yale University Press.

Levinson, H. (1992). *Career mastery.* San Francisco: Berrett-Koehler.

Marx, M. H. (Ed.). (1963). *Theories in contemporary psychology.* New York: Macmillan.

Merman, S., & Clark, A. (1985). *Managing toward career excellence.* Denver: PMG.

Pepinsky, H. B., & Pepinsky, P. N. (1954). *Counseling: Theory and practice.* New York: Ronald.

Roe, A. (1953). *The making of a scientist.* New York: Dodd, Mead.

Stefflre, B. (1966). Vocational development: Ten propositions in search of a theory. *Personnel and Guidance Journal, 44,* 611–616.

Super, D. E. (1953). A theory of vocational development. *American Psychologist, 8,* 185–190.

Super, D. E. (1957). *The psychology of careers.* New York: Harper & Row.

Super, D. E., & Crites, J. O. (1962). *Appraising vocational fitness.* (Rev. ed.). New York: Harper & Row.

Wherry, R. J., Sr. (1984). *Contributions to correlational analysis.* Orlando, FL: Academic Press.

Zinser, R. W. (1988). *A pilot test of the Career Adjustment and Development Inventory as a career needs analysis technique.* Kalamazoo: Western Michigan University.

CHAPTER SIXTEEN

Linking Interest Assessment and Personality Theory

An Example of Convergence Between Practice and Theory[*]

Fred H. Borgen
Iowa State University

Lenore W. Harmon
University of Illinois at Urbana-Champaign

MANY WRITERS HAVE commented that practice can and should inform theory. Furthermore, these same writers have encouraged practitioners to work in collaboration with researchers to use practice knowledge to improve theory. Unfortunately, there are few actual precedents for this type of theory-practice integration in the fields of vocational psychology and career intervention. In this chapter, we trace the historical and contemporary status of one outstanding example of practice informing theory and the benefits of practice-theory integration. The example comes from the domain of interest measurement, in particular, the line of work initiated by E. K. Strong, Jr. (1929), that now includes the 1994 edition of the *Strong Interest Inventory (Strong)*. The specific example of theory-practice linkage presented in this chapter concentrates on the convergence between occupational interest measurement and personality models and how this convergence has contributed to personality theory and improved the practice of career intervention.

---

[*]A portion of this chapter is based on a chapter by Harmon, Hansen, Borgen, and Hammer (1994), which appeared in the *Strong Interest Inventory Applications and Technical Guide.*(See Credits section for permission information.)

Gelso and Fassinger (1992) observed that "counseling psychology has not made full or sufficient use of personality and developmental psychology in its theory, research, and practice" (p. 278). Interest measurement has been a cornerstone of counseling psychology, and the *Strong* is one of the field's most respected assessment instruments. In this chapter, we describe how the 1994 *Strong* incorporated new Personal Style Scales, bringing an expanded role for personality dimensions to the *Strong*. We begin with some theoretical observations and empirical generalizations that suggest linkages between interests and personality. Then we will present the four Personal Style Scales that were added to the 1994 *Strong* to further advance the reciprocal interaction between interest measurement and personality theory, thereby enhancing the practice of career intervention (Harmon, Hansen, Borgen, & Hammer, 1994).

INTEREST AND PERSONALITY LINKAGES

Given that E. K. Strong, Jr., was not a theorist but a persistent empiricist, it is ironic that we are writing about theory and the *Strong*. The broad history of interest measurement shows the reciprocal give-and-take of empiricism, theory, and practical assessment instruments. Hansen (1984) observed,

> Although some authors...have suggested that theories should be developed prior to test construction, the more usual chronology has been to use results of empirical techniques to develop a theory, and, then, to return to empirical techniques again to clarify, refine, and expand the theory. (p.101)

Although Strong himself eschewed theory (Rounds & Dawis, 1979), others have brought theory to Strong's interest inventory. Perhaps most notable was the action Campbell and Holland (1972) took in merging Holland's theory and Strong's empiricism. Holland's six RIASEC themes thus became an important organizing principle for the *Strong*.

Contemporary insights suggest personality affects work behavior in many ways (Hogan, 1991; Lowman, 1991; Spokane, 1991). The links between personality and work are today especially evident in the major influence of Holland's (1966, 1973, 1976, 1985a) theoretical model in vocational psychology. Holland's earliest formulations had especially explicit personality linkages. In his first version of the *Vocational Preference Inventory* (1958), the six scales that were later to become the RIASEC scales (Holland, 1985b) originally had names with a distinct personality flavor. With the current RIASEC names displayed here in parentheses, Holland's original scales were Physical Activity (Realistic), Intellectual (Investigative), Emotionality (Artistic), Responsibility (Social), Verbal Activity (Enterprising), and Conformity (Conventional).

It is informative to read Holland's definitive (1976) review and see how closely his RIASEC model draws from early factor analyses that identified the dimensions of interests. (See Hansen, 1984; Dawis, 1991; and Rounds, 1995, for similar reviews of this literature and for coverage of later research.) Much of this historical work, based on factor analyses, revealed combinations of vocational interest and personality factors. In constructing their influential personality-based vocational theories, Roe (1956) and Holland (1976) drew heavily from these early factor-analytic studies. Centrally important was the extensive factor analysis conducted by Guilford, Christensen, Bond, and Sutton (1954), who used a variety of interest and personality scales that they constructed to test specific hypotheses. Their study yielded seven vocational interest factors that are closely related to Roe's and Holland's taxonomies. Although Guilford and his colleagues reported a factor for outdoor work, their remaining six vocational interest factors replicate those in prior studies and are direct precursors to Holland's (1985a) current RIASEC scales: Mechanical, Scientific, Aesthetic Expression, Social Welfare, Business, and Clerical.

The study by Guilford et al. (1954) is frequently cited for its identification of vocational interest factors, yet it also produced numerous factors with a distinct personality flavor. Guilford and his colleagues made it clear that they considered interests and personality to be closely linked motivational variables, and their study included hypotheses and measures of both personality and interest variables. Among the personality dimensions suggested by their results were sociability, responsibility, conformity, need for diversion (play), need for attention, aggression, orderliness versus disorderliness, and adventure versus security. Guilford and his colleagues did not discuss these personality results with the clarity or emphasis that they gave to the vocational interest factors, so it is understandable that these results have had a weaker influence in current work.

One personality theme that recurs throughout the interest measurement literature is orientation to people (Dawis, 1991; Hansen, 1984; Holland, 1976; Jackson, 1977; Roe, 1956; Rounds, 1995). People orientation has frequently emerged in factor-analytic studies, from the very earliest by Thurstone (1931) and Strong (1943) to a more recent study by Rounds and Dawis (1979). Such interpersonal orientation seems to range from the Guilford sociability factor to the aggression factor. Facets within this general extroverted theme include the warmth and nurturance of Holland's Social type on the one hand, and the dominance and persuasiveness of the Enterprising type on the other. The *Strong* has long had an Introversion-Extroversion scale (Hansen & Campbell, 1985); as will be evident later in this chapter, the 1994 *Strong* replaced this scale with two people-oriented Personal Style Scales: Work Style and Leadership.

Holland views his RIASEC types as both vocational types and personality types. For example, in his manual for the *Vocational Preference Inventory*, he presents adjectives that describe each type. People-oriented adjectives, such as *sociable* and *extroverted*, are salient for the adjacent Social and Enterprising types. Although similar in their general liking for people, the two types are distinguished by more warmth for the Social type and more dominance and risk taking for the Enterprising type. Enterprising types "are similar to Social high scorers, but more apt to be

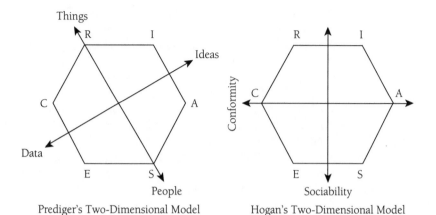

FIGURE 1   Prediger's and Hogan's Two-Dimensional Models
for Holland's Hexagonal Model of RIASEC Types

Note. R = Realistic, I = Investigative, A = Artistic, S = Social, E = Enterprising, and C = Conventional.

persuasive than helpful" (Holland, 1985b, p. 7). Other RIASEC types, on opposite sides of the hexagon from the Social and Enterprising types, do not relish interaction with people. Realistic types are characterized by Holland as having low social interests and poor interpersonal skills. Investigative types are seen as shy, reserved, and unsociable. Curiously, Artistic types are seen not only as sensitive and emotional but also as introverted. Linking Artistic types with introversion seems to be an error, especially given that on the hexagon Artistic types are adjacent to Social types, who are characterized by extraversion.

The discovery by Cole, Whitney, and Holland (1971) that the six RIASEC scales might be organized in a hexagon gave major thrust to theorizing about interests and personality. Theorists placed two dimensional coordinates on the hexagon and gave personality-like meaning to these posited dimensions. At least one of these dimensions typically involves orientation to people. The most prominent example is Prediger's (1982) assertion that People/Things and Data/Ideas are the two bipolar dimensions that structure the hexagon and explain the work tasks underlying the RIASEC dimensions. Prediger's model is displayed in the left portion of Figure 1.

Hogan (1983) presented an alternative two-dimensional interpretation of the RIASEC hexagon, arguing that the best two interpretive dimensions are sociability and conformity, as displayed in the right portion of Figure 1. While Hogan's sociability is similar in content to Prediger's People pole of the People/Things dimensions, Hogan and Prediger differ in how they think this dimension cuts across the hexagon. Hogan views sociability as equally linked to the Enterprising and the Social types, but Prediger places the People pole directly on the Social type. One step in testing these competing models was Rounds and Tracey's (1993) structural analysis of the RIASEC configuration; they concluded that neither the Hogan nor the Prediger model was superior. Rounds and Tracey suggested that each model has something to offer: Prediger's model has value for classifying occupations, and Hogan's model bridges the personality and interest domains and links with Holland's theoretical notions on personality.

Often these attributions about latent dimensions in the hexagon are left as abstractions to be debated by theorists. When they are used in counseling practice, however, one is asked to make a series of assumptions to estimate the personality implications of particular interest scores or configurations. Thus, if one follows Prediger's model, one could say that a person high on Social interests is also likely to prefer working with people over working with things. However, if one opts for Hogan's theoretical model, one would make somewhat different attributions. In Hogan's model, a person high on either Social or Enterprising interests would be seen as preferring to work with people. An alternative to this guesswork for the counselor would be to have a scale that more directly measures a person's preference for working with people. This has been accomplished in the 1994 *Strong* with the addition of the Work Style scale and the Leadership Style scale.

If Holland's RIASEC dimensions are related to personality, then Holland's "Big Six" dimensions should be related in some ways to the five-factor model of personality (Borgen, 1986; Digman, 1990). Holland and his colleagues have conducted several analyses of these relationships (Costa, McCrae, & Holland, 1984; Gottfredson, Jones, & Holland, 1993; Holland, Johnston, & Asana, 1994). Thus far, it appears that the strongest correlations involve positive relationships for Extraversion with Enterprising and Social types, and Openness to Experience with Investigative and Artistic types, and a negative relationship for Neuroticism with the Enterprising type.

Spokane (1991) advocated an increased use of personality measures in career counseling:

> Several general measures of personality may be useful in career interventions. Indeed, the overlap between career development and personality may be substantial, and counselors increasingly view career counseling as life and personal style counseling with a career focus, in which a wide range of life issues and concerns are discussed. (p. 140)

Lowman (1991) presented one of the more comprehensive current reviews of the role of personality in work. A theme of his book is the importance in career assessment of integrating different domains: abilities, interests, and personality. He suggested that career-relevant personality dimensions meriting attention include achievement orientation, introversion-extraversion, ascendance-dominance and need for power, emotional stability-neuroticism, and masculinity-femininity. Many of Lowman's suggested variables have been present historically in various ways on the *Strong;* several of them are also represented in the new Personal Style Scales of Work Style, Learning Style, and Leadership Style in the 1994 *Strong*.

THE PERSONAL STYLE SCALES

Although there is a long history of peripheral emphasis on personality dispositions in the *Strong,* especially its organization around Holland's six types, the 1994 *Strong* introduces an explicit attention to personality in the form of Personal Style Scales. The Personal Style Scales are modes of addressing education, work, or living, whereas other vocational interest scales on the *Strong* deal with more specific occupational content. This distinction is one of relative emphasis, however, because there is natural conceptual and empirical overlap between the dispositional variables of personality and interests. People often express their personalities through their occupational preferences.

Measuring preferences for and comfort with broad styles of living and working, these scales complement the traditional vocational interest scales that measure preferences for more specific aspects of the work itself. The four Personal Style Scales are Work Style, Learning Environment, Leadership Style, and Risk Taking/ Adventure. The Personal Style Scales can help individuals explore how they go about learning, working, playing, or living in general.

The Personal Style Scales have many of the features of the General Occupational Themes and Basic Interest Scales. They have standard scores based on the General Reference Sample of 18,951 women and men. On the *Strong* Profile, they also are reported using box-and-whisker graphs to show separate distributions for women and men; boxes show the middle 50% and whiskers show the middle 80% of scores for each gender. A distinguishing characteristic of the Personal Style Scales, however, is that they are construed as bipolar scales, with a distinctive style (or preference) associated with both the left and the right pole of each scale. The characteristics of the left and right poles for each scale are summarized in Table 1.

Because the mean of these scales is 50 for general groups of people, scores that differ substantially from 50 (either above or below) typify one of the poles of that style. Thus, scores of 45 and below identify the left pole of the scales, and scores of 55 and above identify the right pole. More extreme scores (40 and below or 60 and above) even more clearly identify that particular style. Scores in the midrange (46–54) occur for people with no predominant preference for one style or the other; they probably have a mix of preferences for that style or no strong preferences for a particular one.

Work Style Scale

The Work Style scale distinguishes individuals who prefer to work with people from those who prefer working with ideas, data, or things. Those who prefer to work with people endorse *Strong* items that represent people-oriented occupations and activities, including some items that refer to relating to others as helpers. The item "Can smooth out tangles and disagreements between people" clearly differentiates those who prefer to work with people from those who prefer to work alone.

TABLE 1 Personal Style Scales and Their Poles

Personal Style Scale	Left Pole	Right Pole
Work Style	Works with Ideas/Data/Things	Works with People
Learning Environment	Practical	Academic
Leadership Style	Leads by Example	Directs Others
Risk Taking/Adventure	Plays It Safe	Takes Chances

From *Applications and Technical Guide for the Strong Interest Inventory* (p.156), by L. Harmon, J. Hansen, F. Borgen, and A. Hammer, 1994, Stanford, CA: Stanford University Press. Copyright 1994 by Stanford University Press. Reprinted with permission.

However, items that imply contact with others without directly involving a helping function (e.g., "Raising money for charity" and "Planning a large party") also identify the Works with People pole of the scale. Those who prefer working alone (with ideas, data, or things), in contrast, endorse items in those particular domains. They like scientific and technical activities, see themselves as having mechanical ingenuity, and would prefer being a lighthouse keeper to being a headwaiter/hostess.

The Work Style scale is clearly and symmetrically joined to the RIASEC scales, falling as a bipolar axis across the hexagon, as shown in Figure 2. The Works with People pole links strongly to the Enterprising and Social themes. The Works with Ideas/Data/Things pole ties to the Realistic and Investigative themes. Thus, the Work Style scale is an important, broad dimension that bridge four of the RIASEC scales.

Students who score toward the Works with People pole are often found in major fields such as education, journalism, business, and social sciences, although their mean scores are only moderately high. Students who prefer to work with ideas, data, or things, in contrast, are often found in the physical sciences, machine trades, engineering, biological sciences, computer and information sciences, and mathematics. These students' scores indicate a preference for working with ideas, data, or things and, as such, are distinctly different from the mean of 50 for all people in the norm group.

Scores can be used to help individuals determine whether they are more inclined to work with people or with ideas, data, or things. Interpretation of this scale can explain problems of adjustment when an individual is uncomfortable in a specific work setting.

It would be a mistake to assume that people should choose their occupations based on the Work Style scale. It may be just as productive to explore occupations of interest to the individual in relationship to the type of work settings offered within the occupation. Some social workers, for instance, may have research positions that put them in little contact with people. Likewise, some physicists may find themselves working with great numbers of people in educational or public information

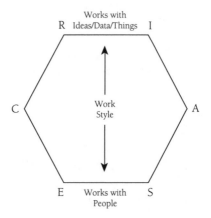

FIGURE 2   Relationship of Work Style to the Pattern of Hexagon Themes

From *Applications and Technical Guide for the Strong Interest Inventory* (p.157), by L. Harmon, J. Hansen, F. Borgen, and A. Hammer, 1994, Stanford, CA: Stanford University Press. Copyright 1994 by Stanford University Press. Reprinted with permission.

settings. Admittedly, such positions are rare, but they are worth discussing with clients whose Work Style scale scores do not seem to fit their vocational interests.

Learning Environment Scale

The Learning Environment scale differentiates people who prefer academic learning environments from those who prefer more practically oriented, hands-on learning situations. People who prefer to learn in academic settings express cultural, verbal, and research interests as well as an interest in teaching itself. People who prefer to learn in more practical settings express interests in clerical, technical, and physical activities. This scale reflects whether an individual is more comfortable in a practical or an academic learning setting. However, this scale does not indicate whether the person will succeed in one setting or the other.

The Learning Environment scale correlates most strongly with the Artistic theme, reflecting the scale's central cultural and verbal content. Because of the Learning Environment scale's research content, it also correlates moderately with the Investigative theme.

There are large average differences in the Learning Environment scale across educational majors. Those scoring toward the academic pole include students with majors with a verbal, cultural/artistic, or research emphasis: language/literature, history, journalism, physical sciences, and social sciences. Those scoring toward the practical pole include students in such areas as the machine trades, vocational technical majors, business (clerical), law enforcement, and agriculture.

The Learning Environment scale may be helpful to individuals who are exploring educational options. Scores of 55 and above typify individuals in occupations that require a great deal of academic preparation and individuals who have achieved a doctoral degree. Scores of 45 and below are common for individuals in many occupations that require practical training of limited duration (e.g., high school or technical training). Within occupations, the range of scores on this scale is fairly large, from about .66 to 1.2 standard deviations. Early evidence suggests that scores below 50 may occur often for college students. In three college samples used for reliability studies, means ranged from 40 to 47, all toward the practical pole.

An individual's score on the Learning Environment scale should not be used to restrict occupational choice. Rather, it is useful for a broadly focused exploration of preferences for learning environments. For instance, the medical field offers occupations requiring various types of training, from courses that last less than a year to advanced medical training requiring many years of academic work.

Leadership Style Scale

The Leadership Style scale is a new Personal Style Scale that, on one pole, reflects a preference for meeting, directing, persuading, and leading other people. People who score toward the Directs Others pole enjoy moving readily and gregariously into interpersonal settings and like to take initiative and take charge in an occupational setting. People who score toward the opposite pole, Leads by Example, are not comfortable taking charge of others. They prefer to do a task themselves rather than direct others to do it. They may lead by example rather than by giving directions.

The Leadership Style scale is highly correlated with the Introversion-Extraversion scale, which appeared in the 1985 *Strong* but has been removed from the 1994 version. People who score toward the Directs Others pole of the Leadership Style scale are likely to show preferences for the general Enterprising Theme and, specifically, the Enterprising Basic Interest Scales of Public Speaking, Law/Politics, and Organizational Management. People who score toward the Leads by Example pole are disinterested in being persuasive or being in charge of others and tend to have little interest in these domains.

Students scoring toward the Directs Others pole of the Leadership Style scale are likely to major in areas such as journalism, social science, law, and history. Likewise, students scoring toward the Leads by Example pole are likely to major in fields such as machine trades, physical sciences, mathematics, biological sciences, and agriculture.

The Leadership Style scale can be particularly helpful in considering people's preferred leadership role within occupational settings, especially settings not typified by people scoring near either the left or right pole on this scale. These settings include those within the Realistic, Investigative, and Conventional themes that are not correlated with the Leadership Style scale. Thus, if someone with interests in one of these areas has a Leadership Style scale score above 55, that person might consider the special roles she or he could play within the occupation. For example, very few physicists have scores above 55 on the Leadership Style scale, yet those who do are likely to play especially valuable roles within the profession. Likewise, because few physicists have a preference for working with people, a physicist with both a directive leadership style and a people-oriented work style would be quite rare and would be expected to show an interpersonal style atypical for physicists. This atypical physicist might play complementary roles that are helpful to colleagues and the physics profession itself.

Risk Taking/Adventure Scale

The content of the Risk Taking/Adventure scale is a mix of physically risky activities, such as auto racing, and other more general items about risk taking and adventure. This scale was first developed by David Campbell and his colleagues in 1968, so considerable experience and lore have developed about its implications and counseling use (Campbell, 1971; Douce & Hansen, 1988; Hansen, 1992; Hansen & Campbell, 1985). Until the 1994 revision, the scale was called Adventure and appeared with the Realistic Basic Interest Scales. It has now been renamed and moved to the Personal Style Scales section of the Profile.

Primary sources on the construct validity of the Risk Taking/Adventure scale, as outlined below, are research studies by Douce and Hansen (1988, 1990) and Cronin (1995). Risk Taking/Adventure scores toward the Takes Chances pole tend to correlate significantly with other measures for which a high score indicates a willingness to (a) take physical and social risks, (b) act spontaneously and playfully, and (c) seek novel sensations and thrills. People who score toward the Takes Chances pole also tend to be socially dominant, extroverted, and independent and to enjoy being at center stage in group activities, especially athletics, politics, and public speaking. People who score near the Plays It Safe pole of the Risk Taking/ Adventure scale generally avoid physical harm and social risks, act cautiously and prudently, and try to protect their personal safety (Douce & Hansen, 1988, 1990).

Hansen (1992) indicated that the best way to interpret this scale for clients is to first suggest several hypotheses explaining why people score toward one or the other pole, and then suggest that clients consider how these possibilities best fit their knowledge of themselves. This approach works especially well with individuals who score at the Plays It Safe pole because their physical safety holds paramount importance for them yet they see themselves as psychological risk takers in most other aspects of their lives.

Scores on the Takes Chances pole often reflect a daring and reckless youthful exuberance that moderates toward more caution with increasing age. There are, of course, within any age group, large individual differences in dispositions to play it safe versus take chances. But there also is an overall life span trend for adults to move with time toward a more cautious, play it safe approach to life, especially with regard to physical risks and challenges. Many people over 30, however, will continue to be undaunted by risky and daring challenges and will seek ways to satisfy their need for adventurous stimulation.

Some people, for example, those who partake in hang gliding, score toward the Takes Chances pole because they relish physical risk taking. Occupations that incorporate physical risk taking include paramedics, police officers, and jet fighter pilots. People who bungee jump, ski the steepest slopes, race high-powered cars, rappel mountains, and use lethal weapons are the prototypic physical risk takers. Other people for whom physical activity and potential risk is a central part of their Realistic Theme job, such as electricians, carpenters, and auto mechanics, also fall toward the Takes Chances pole of the scale.

For some people, the Risk Taking/Adventure Takes Chances pole is expressed through a carefree embrace of physically challenging activities such as athletics, outdoor treks, or travel; for others, it is expressed by more general risk taking, such as pursuing nontraditional careers or selling on a commission. For yet others, such scores may reveal a comfort with risking work and personal choices, even when success and satisfaction cannot be guaranteed.

Scores on the Plays It Safe pole of Risk Taking/Adventure may indicate an aversion to trying new activities without careful planning and as many guarantees as possible. The change process of counseling and the rehearsal of new modes of behavior can be especially challenging for such clients. Hansen (1992) recommended that counseling tactics might include special preparation and role-playing to address these clients' fear of failing. They may need special encouragement to take initial steps, such as returning to school or beginning a new job or course of study. With initial success, self-efficacy will increase, and increasing accomplishments can be undertaken with yet more growth in confidence.

Relationship of Personal Styles to RIASEC Themes

The relationships of the four Personal Styles Scales to the six RIASEC General Occupational Themes evince strong and fascinating relationships across the two types of scales, which might be anticipated because Holland's (1985a) theory of occupational types is also a personality theory. It is important to note that the pattern of relationships is very similar for men and women. The relationships between the RIASEC Scales and the Personal Style Scales can be summarized as follows:

- High Realistic Theme interest—works with ideas/data/things work style; takes chances risk taking/adventure style
- High Investigative Theme interest—works with ideas/data/things work style; academic learning environment
- High Artistic Theme interest—academic learning environment; directs others leadership style
- High Social Theme interest—works with people work style; directs others leadership style

■ High Enterprising Theme interest—works with people work style; directs others Leadership Style

■ High Conventional Theme interest—no clear relationship to Personal Style Scales

One of the most revealing patterns of correlations in Table 2 is for the Work Style scale. Not only are the linkages for women and men very similar but two RIASEC scales are also distinctly associated with the left pole of Work Style and two are clearly associated with the right pole. Realistic types and Investigative types prefer working with ideas, data, and things; Social types and Enterprising types prefer working with people.

These linkages are shown schematically in Figure 2, in which the Work Style scale forms a superordinate axis that cuts across the RIASEC hexagon. This configuration should then be compared with the predictions from Hogan's (1983) and Prediger's (1982) models, as displayed in Figure 1. The results fit Hogan's model rather than Prediger's. Hogan's model, which closely follows Holland's (1985a) constructs, argues that a sociability orientation, or people dimension, should underlie the hexagon, just as the correlations for the Work Style scale suggest.

The strength and clarity of these relationships for Work Style and the hexagon surprised us because they emerged somewhat by serendipity as we pursued a loosely focused theoretical agenda. The Work Style scale was constructed empirically using contrasting groups of respondents to the *Strong*. Six items were added to the *Strong*, which ask the respondent to indicate preferences between all pairwise combinations of four work foci: data, ideas, things, and people—the anchors for the two poles in Prediger's (1982) two-dimensional scheme for the hexagon. From the responses in the 1994 norm group (n = 18,951), it was possible to identify individuals who consistently preferred one of the options over all the others. These individuals were collected into two groups, those who consistently preferred people (n = 6,681) and those who consistently preferred one of the other three options (n = 5,574). Then using the same empirical method as is used for constructing Occupational Scales, 51 items that differentiated the two groups were identified for the scale.

Thus, the Work Style scale is a bipolar contrast of preference for people versus preference for data, ideas, or things. This is somewhat different from Prediger's two-dimensional model that contrasts people and things on one dimension and data and ideas on a second dimension. Consequently, a caveat with these results is that the test of Prediger's model is not set up precisely as his model would specify. It would be possible to use the same empirical strategy with *Strong* data to create scales for Prediger's People/Things and Data/Ideas dimension. This could be a productive undertaking that could more precisely address Prediger's model.

A final caution about the intercorrelations of Personal Styles and Holland RIASEC themes in Table 2 is that there is substantial item overlap across the two sets of scales. Thus, some of these correlations are likely inflated for theoretical purposes,

TABLE 2 Correlations Between the Personal Style Scales and the General Occupational Themes for Women and Men

| | Personal Style and Gender | | | | | | | |
| General Occupational Theme | Work Style | | Learning Environment | | Leadership Style | | Risk Taking/ Adventure | |
	F	M	F	M	F	M	F	M
Realistic	-39	-33	05	-11	-05	-07	44	41
Investigative	-46	-38	41	40	03	04	30	26
Artistic	11	21	65	70	35	33	30	15
Social	64	62	09	25	37	47	04	12
Enterprising	60	57	01	04	50	51	18	24
Conventional	07	10	-31	-07	-01	13	-09	02

Note. General Reference Sample of 9,467 women, 9,484 men; decimals omitted.
From *Applications and Technical Guide for the Strong Interest Inventory* (p.164), by L. Harmon, J. Hansen, F. Borgen, and A. Hammer, 1994, Stanford, CA: Stanford University Press. Copyright 1994 by Stanford University Press. Reprinted with permission.

although they do reflect the structure of the relationships among *Strong* scales and how they are likely to be related in counseling use.

The four dimensions introduced to the *Strong* by the Personal Style Scales are not seen as comprehensively covering the potential domain of personal style. The actual four dimensions arose out of serendipity and empirical results rather than from an initial systematic intent to introduce such scales. Future revisions of the *Strong* may well contain additional dimensions of personal style as future revisers more systematically examine the possibilities for building additional scales. The systematic approach to build additional scales that will be helpful for career, leisure, and lifestyle planning would begin by asking the question, What are the dimensions of personal style that can be measured by the kinds of items traditionally used in the *Strong?*

CONCLUSIONS

The significant contributions of interest measurement practice and research to personality theory and career intervention clearly demonstrate the productive results of continual interchange between practice and theory. The practitioner-scientist model displayed by E. K. Strong, Jr., and his followers has led to many important advances within personality theory in general and vocational personality theory in particular. The new Personal Style Scales for the 1994 *Strong* continue the tradition of practice-theory linkages grounded in both rigorous empiricism and clinical insight.

REFERENCES

Borgen, F. H. (1986). New approaches to the assessment of interests. In W. B. Walsh & S. H. Osipow (Eds.), *Advances in vocational psychology: Vol. 1. The assessment of interests* (pp. 83–125). Hillsdale, NJ: Erlbaum.

Campbell, D. P. (1971). *Handbook for the Strong Vocational Interest Blank.* Stanford, CA: Stanford University Press.

Campbell, D. P., & Holland, J. L. (1972). Applying Holland's theory to Strong's data. *Journal of Vocational Behavior, 2,* 353–376.

Cole, N. S., Whitney, D. R., & Holland, J. L. (1971). A spatial configuration of occupations. *Journal of Vocational Behavior, 1,* 1–9.

Costa, P. T., Jr., McCrae, R. R., & Holland, J. L. (1984). Personality and vocational interests in an adult sample. *Journal of Applied Psychology, 69,* 390–400.

Cronin, C. (1995). Construct validation of the Strong Interest Inventory Adventure scale using the Sensation Seeking scale among female college students. *Measurement and Evaluation in Counseling and Development, 28,* 3–8.

Dawis, R. V. (1991). Vocational interests, values, and preferences. In M. D. Dunnette & L. M. Hough (Eds.), *Handbook of industrial and organizational psychology.* (2d ed., Vol. 2, pp. 833–871). Palo Alto, CA: Davies-Black Publishing.

Digman, J. M. (1990). Personality structure: Emergence of the five-factor model. *Annual Review of Psychology, 41,* 417–440.

Douce, L. A., & Hansen, J. C. (1988). Examination of the construct validity of the SVIB-SCII Adventure scale for college women. *Measurement and Evaluation in Counseling and Development, 20,* 171–174.

Douce, L. A., & Hansen, J. C. (1990). Willingness to take risks and college women's career choice. *Journal of Vocational Behavior, 36,* 258–273.

Gelso, C. J., & Fassinger, R. E. (1992). Personality, development, and counseling psychology: Depth, ambivalence, and actualization. *Journal of Counseling Psychology, 39,* 275–298.

Gottfredson, G. D., Jones, E. M., & Holland, J. L. (1993). Personality and vocational interests: The relation of Holland's six interest dimensions to five robust dimensions of personality. *Journal of Counseling Psychology, 40,* 518–524.

Guilford, J. P., Christensen, P. R., Bond, N. A., Jr., & Sutton, M. A. (1954). A factor analysis study of human interests. *Psychological Monographs, 68* (No. 4).

Hansen, J. C. (1984). The measurement of vocational interests: Issues and future directions. In S. D. Brown & R. W. Lent (Eds.), *Handbook of counseling psychology* (pp. 99–136). New York: Wiley.

Hansen, J. C. (1992). *User's guide for the Strong Interest Inventory* (Rev. ed.). Stanford, CA: Stanford University Press.

Hansen, J. C., & Campbell, D. P. (1985). *Manual for the Strong Interest Inventory* (4th ed.). Stanford, CA: Stanford University Press.

Harmon, L. W., Hansen, J. C., Borgen, F. H., & Hammer, A. L. (1994). *Applications and technical guide for the Strong Interest Inventory.* Stanford, CA: Stanford University Press.

Hogan, R. T. (1983). A socioanalytic theory of personality. In M. Page (Ed.), *Nebraska Symposium on Motivation, 1982: Current Personality Theory and Research* (pp. 55–89). Lincoln: University of Nebraska Press.

Hogan, R. T. (1991). Personality and personality measurement. In M. D. Dunnette & L. M. Hough (Eds.), *Handbook of industrial and organizational psychology.* (2d ed., Vol. 2, pp. 873–919). Palo Alto, CA: Davies-Black Publishing.

Holland, J. L. (1958). A personality inventory employing occupational titles. *Journal of Applied Psychology, 42,* 336–342.

Holland, J. L. (1966). *The psychology of vocational choice.* Waltham, MA: Blaisdell.

Holland, J. L. (1973). *Making vocational choice: A theory of careers.* Englewood Cliffs, NJ: Prentice Hall.

Holland, J. L. (1976). Vocational preferences. In M. D. Dunnette (Ed.), *Handbook of industrial and organizational psychology* (pp. 521–570). Chicago: Rand McNally.

Holland, J. L. (1985a). *Making vocational choices: A theory of vocational personalities and work environments* (2d ed.). Englewood Cliffs, NJ: Prentice Hall.

Holland, J. L. (1985b). *Vocational Preference Inventory professional manual.* Odessa, FL: Psychological Assessment Resources.

Holland, J. L., Johnston, J. A., & Asama, N. F. (1994). More evidence for the relationship between Holland's personality types and personality variables. *Journal of Career Assessment, 2,* 331–340.

Jackson, D. N. (1977). *Jackson Vocational Interest Survey manual.* Port Huron, MI: Research Psychologists Press.

Lowman, R. L. (1991). *The clinical practice of career assessment: Interests, abilities, and personality.* Washington, DC: American Psychological Association.

Prediger, D. J. (1982). Dimensions underlying Holland's hexagon: Missing links between interests and occupations? *Journal of Vocational Behavior, 20,* 259–287.

Roe, A. (1956). *The psychology of occupations.* New York: Wiley.

Rounds, J. B. (1995). Vocational interests: Evaluating structural hypotheses. In D. Lubinski & R. V. Dawis (Eds.), *Assessing individual differences in human behavior: New concepts, methods, and findings.* Palo Alto, CA: Davies-Black Publishing.

Rounds, J., & Dawis, R. V. (1979). Factor analysis of Strong Vocational Interest Blank items. *Journal of Applied Psychology, 64,* 132–143.

Rounds, J., & Tracey, T. J. (1993). Prediger's dimensional representation of Holland's RIASEC circumplex. *Journal of Applied Psychology, 78,* 875–890.

Spokane, A. R. (1991). *Career intervention.* Englewood Cliffs, NJ: Prentice Hall.

Strong, E. K., Jr. (1929). Diagnostic value of the Vocational Interest Test. *Educational Record, 10,* 66–73.

Strong, E. K., Jr. (1943). *Vocational interests of men and women.* Stanford, CA: Stanford University Press.

Thurstone, L. L. (1931). A multiple factor study of vocational interests. *Personnel Journal, 3,* 198–205.

CHAPTER SEVENTEEN

Career Counseling Theory
Problems and Prospects

W. Bruce Walsh
Ohio State University

I N SOME RESPECTS career theory informs counselors about what to do, yet not necessarily how to implement what needs to be done. The how-to category rests heavily on each career counselor's sensitivity, wisdom, and talent. Career development theories have not been well applied to career counseling practice. If active researchers have difficulty making sense of the connections between career theory and research, how can we expect career counselors to effectively use research to guide interventions? Stated differently, what research agenda would facilitate the translation of the science of career theory into the practice of career counseling? Conversely, what practice agenda would facilitate the translation of practice into theory?

Thus, this chapter addresses the perceived gap between career counseling research and practice. Within this context, two questions will be addressed: What research agenda can produce knowledge that is useful to practitioners in working with their clients? and How can practice inform research and theory? Career counseling research should yield information useful to practicing career counselors. In this chapter, it is proposed that the idiographic model, the Big Five, and practical intelligence are examples of research agendas that may facilitate the translation of career theory and research into practice. These three constructs appear to be meaningful methods for organizing human behavior along practical and useful dimensions. This chapter further discusses what practice agenda would facilitate the translation of the practice of career counseling into career theory and research. How can practice make theory and research more user friendly to practitioners? Until recently, only the work of Crites (1981) has provided theoretical guidance for career interventions. More recent contributions provide additional conceptual direction from assessment through intervention to evaluation; yet this research further begs the question, Can we develop and benefit from a unified theory of career counseling? The second section of this chapter discusses the practice agenda by describing some potential principles that could possibly be useful in devising a unified theory for counseling career clients.

RESEARCH AGENDA

All theories of career development tend to adopt, either implicitly or explicitly, a trait-oriented approach to comprehending career choice and implementation: Holland's *personality types*, Super's *self-concept implementation in work*, work adjustment theory's *work personality*, social learning theories' use of *self-observed generalizations*, and Bordin's *psychoanalytic motives and drives* (Osipow, 1990). Each theory of career development primarily addresses prediction, based on traditional positivist assumptions. Research designs and measures are determined prior to the researcher's exposure to a life domain, and prediction is the most important outcome. There is no question that the positivist perspective has been a dominant and productive worldview in career development research during the 20th century. The quest for prediction and control have resulted in a very solid data base.

Idiographic Model

Nevertheless, there is another theoretical model (Walsh, Craik, & Price, 1992; Wicker, 1992) that merits some attention. It may be described as idiographic, interpretative, emergent, and social constructionist in orientation. This model focuses on the way in which socially situated individuals interpret their current and past circumstances or actions. This model departs most from traditional positivist assumptions and is perhaps the most skeptical about the possibility of prediction. A primary aim of this model is to gain an in-depth understanding of persons using idiographic methods and to communicate that understanding. Prediction and control are less likely outcomes of this research. Research designs and measures are not determined prior to the researcher's exposure to a given life domain. Instead, they are formulated as the researcher encounters the events to be understood. In this paradigm, conceptual and theoretical development is regarded as a continually evolving process, and qualitative research methods are frequently used because of their flexibility and sensitivity.

This may be a fresh perspective for pursuing career theory, research, and practice that needs to be considered. People and environments are not logically independent of one another in the real world (Campbell, 1986). However, in many respects, career theorists and researchers tend to investigate the person and the environment as independent variables. As noted by Altman and Rogoff (1987), person and context coexist and jointly define one another and contribute to the meaning and nature of a holistic event. It then makes sense that the idiographic holistic approach may help us greatly in our efforts to learn more about the career counseling process as well as its desired outcomes.

The Big Five Dimensions of Personality

A second research agenda that may facilitate the translation of existing career theories into the practice of career counseling deals with the Big Five personality dimensions. Personality theorists seem to be developing a consensus that there are five overarching personality factors, termed the Big Five (John, 1990; McCrae & John, 1992): Extraversion, Agreeableness, Conscientiousness (will to achieve), Neuroticism, and Openness to Experience. Whether or not the five-factor model of personality is universal remains an open question. However, the research reviewed by Buss (1991) demonstrated the robustness of the five-factor model across time, contexts, cultures, and data sources. Buss (1991) argued that personality traits such as Extraversion, Agreeableness, and Conscientiousness are very important psychological dimensions of our social adaptive landscape. They provide information for answering important life questions and would seem to help individuals to actively shape their careers through the processes of evoking, restructuring, and manipulating features of their environments. Examples of adaptive relevant life-career questions include the following: Who is high or low in the social hierarchy? Who is likely to rise in the future? Who will make a good member of my coalition? Who possesses the resources that I need? Who will be a good cooperator and reciprocator? Who might do me harm? Whom can I trust? Who will betray my trust? Few of the major approaches to career theory draw upon the five-factor model of personality. One exception is Holland's (1992) framework, in which research has demonstrated some meaningful relationships between the Big Five personality factors and the RIASEC personality types. A study by Costa, McCrae, and Holland (1984) investigated the relations between the six vocational personality scales of the *Self-Directed Search* (SDS; Holland, 1985a) and three scales of the *NEO* (Neuroticism-Extraversion-Openness) *Inventory* (McCrae & Costa, 1983), which was a forerunner of the five-factor *NEO Personality Inventory* (NEO-PI; Costa & McCrae, 1985).

A study of 394 adults revealed that Investigative and Artistic SDS scores had moderate, positive correlations with the NEO Openness scores and that Social and Enterprising SDS scores had moderate, positive correlations with NEO Extraversion scores. In a more recent study, Gottfredson, Jones, and Holland (1993) extended the earlier inquiries by reporting on the relations between the five-factor personality theory, as defined by the NEO-PI (Costa & McCrae, 1985), and vocational personality, as defined by the *Vocational Preference Inventory* (VPI; Holland, 1985b). In a sample of 479 male and 246 female U.S. Navy trainees, the Social and Enterprising vocational preferences were positively correlated with Extraversion; Investigative and Artistic preferences had a positive correlation with Openness; and Conventional preferences correlated with Conscientiousness. Finally, a study by Holland, Johnston, and Asma (1994) replicated the correlation patterns between the *Self-Directed Search*, the *Vocational Preference Inventory*, and the *NEO Personality Inventory* observed in earlier investigations. This study used a sample of 175 men and 123 women who participated in a series of career workshops for displaced farmers, shoe workers, and unemployed and employed workers. Given these findings, the obvious question is whether career theory should pay more attention to the Big Five adaptive dimensions of human action. Stated differently, these adaptive dimensions of human action might facilitate the translation of career theory into practice.

Practical Intelligence

A third research agenda that might facilitate the translation of career theory into practice deserves mention. Why is prediction of job performance by intelligence tests modest, or at least more modest than is prediction of academic performance? Sternberg and Wagner (1993), along with others, suggest two important reasons. First, academic and practical problems have different characteristics. Second, academic and practical intelligence have different characteristics.

Sternberg and Wagner (1993) indicated that academic problems tend to be formulated by other people, are fairly well defined, and are complete with regard to the information needed to solve them. Furthermore, they usually possess only a single correct answer, frequently possess only a single method of obtaining the correct answer, and have little or no intrinsic interest. Practical problems, in contrast, tend to require problem recognition and formulation, be ill-defined, require information seeking, possess multiple acceptable solutions, allow multiple paths to solutions, be embedded in and require prior everyday experience, and require motivation and personal involvement.

Sternberg and Wagner (1993) also believed that academic and practical intelligence differ in kind. In academic intelligence, the relevant knowledge is of content and rules and is formal and out in the open. It is learned primarily by reading and listening and is highly valued in the schools. In contrast, in practical intelligence, the relevant knowledge is of norms, and the knowledge is informal and often tacit. It is knowledge about, rather than of, a discipline. It is learned primarily by observation and modeling. People at the top of the scale are often called shrewd.

Sternberg and Wagner (1993) believed that the key to practical intelligence is what Michael Polanyi has called *tacit knowledge*, the practical know-how one needs for success on the job. Often it is not openly expressed or stated, and it usually is not taught directly. Tacit knowledge can refer to management of oneself, other people, or tasks. It can be either local and short-term or global and long-term. It is applied toward adapting to a job and other contexts. Evidence indicates that tacit knowledge predicts job performance moderately well, correlating about .3 to .5 with measures such as rated prestige of business or institution, salary, performance appraisal ratings, number of publications, and the like.

Again, the obvious question is whether the constructs of practical intelligence and tacit knowledge may facilitate the translation and integration of career theory and practice.

PRACTICE AGENDA

From a different perspective, what practice agenda would facilitate the translation of the practice of career counseling into career research and theory? Until the past few years, only the work of Crites (1981) has provided theoretical guidance for career interventions (Hackett, 1993). Fortunately, more recent contributions by Spokane (1991), Brown and Brooks (1991), Sharf (1992), and Walsh and Osipow (1990 & 1994) provide some conceptual direction from assessment through intervention to evaluation. These works on career counseling models hold promise for stimulating more sophisticated approaches to career assessment and intervention, yet they further beg the question, Can we learn from psychotherapy?

Some Basic Assumptions

In March 1988, Ernest Beier, author of the *Silent Language of Psychotherapy* (1966 & 1984) and a widely recognized therapist, stated some basic assumptions toward a unified theory of psychotherapy. He described some principles that could possibly be useful to devise a unified theory of therapeutic processes.

First, all psychotherapeutic models assume that the therapist-client exchanges lead to a significant change in the client's behavior and attitude. Beier noted that this assumption, obvious as it appears, is actually based on a very complex belief system. The belief system is expressed differently in various psychotherapeutic models. But, in the end, all models aim at a better life.

The second assumption noted by Beier that underlies the therapeutic process is that changes in behavior caused by psychological interventions occur through the arousal of uncertainty. The therapist makes a response that fosters exploratory behavior or new ways of thinking. It is the unexpected response in a beneficial, warm climate that permits clients to explore unhappy certainties. For that moment, clients can afford to become uncertain and, consequently, explore new ideas and choices.

The third principle of the therapeutic process for Beier is that therapists remain disengaged from their clients. They are neither lovers, friends, nor family. They are getting paid for their services. Beier noted that whatever the model, on some level of this relationship, the therapist will always stay disengaged. To Beier, this meant that the therapist stays disengaged from the emotional demands of the client's messages. In this context, the therapist will not do the things that a friend, lover, or family member might. For example, the therapist will not join the client in hating his or her father. According to Beier, the expert therapist will understand the client's demands yet stay disengaged.

A fourth assumption for Beier is that all forms of treatment, that is, all psychotherapeutic models, involve information gathering. Clients have experienced uncertainty in their vulnerable area of life and chosen not to gather further information. According to Beier, in the psychotherapeutic situation, clients are given the opportunity to explore new responses and to gather information.

Finally, Beier suggested that in all psychotherapeutic models, it is in one form or another the disengagement process, the unexpected response in a beneficial climate, and information gathering that appear responsible for the client's therapeutic gains.

The following basic assumptions or principles considered by Beier might be useful for moving toward a unified theory of career counseling.

One assumption is that all career counseling models assume that the exchanges between counselors and clients lead to significant change in clients' career behavior and attitudes. Similar to Beier's assumption, obvious as it appears, a client's career attitude and behavior are complex and expressed differently in various career counseling models. In any event, all career counseling models lead to career decision making and a better life.

A second assumption is that the quality of the counseling relationship is a central contributor to the career counseling process. Its significance generalizes across theoretical schools, theory-specific concepts, and a diversity of measurement procedures (Beutler, Machado, & Neufeldt, 1994). The evidence clearly indicates that counselor empathy, respect, and genuineness tend to be associated with positive client benefit. Studies consistently show that a positive association exists between quality of the counseling relationship and subsequent counseling benefit (Beutler, Machado, & Neufeldt, 1994). It makes good sense that these findings would hold for models of career counseling.

A third assumption is that career counseling involves a working alliance between the counselor and the client. This alliance is not a counselor quality but rather a set of processes that depend on both the counselor and client. Bordin (1975) conceptualized the working alliance as consisting of three parts: (a) an emotional bond between the participants, (b) an agreement about the goals of counseling, and (c) an agreement about the tasks of the work involved.

A fourth assumption is that counselors perceived to be expert, attractive, and trustworthy contribute to positive client benefit in career counseling. Evidence (Heppner & Heesacker, 1983; McNeil, May, & Lee, 1987; Zamosttny, Corrigan, & Eggert, 1981) demonstrated a moderate to strong relationship between perceived expertness, attractiveness, and trustworthiness and satisfaction with counseling. LaCrosse (1980) found that perceived expertness, attractiveness, and trustworthiness at the beginning and end of counseling were strongly correlated with the achievement of precounseling goals. McNeil, May, and Lee (1987) further found that premature counseling terminators viewed their counselors as less expert, attractive, and trustworthy than did successful terminators and that client's satisfaction with counseling and perceptions of counselor's expertness, attractiveness, and trustworthiness were more positive for persisters than for premature terminators. This research, from all indications, appears to be relevant for models of career counseling.

A fifth assumption is that all models of career counseling involve information gathering. Any information about individuals or their environments that contributes to understanding career behavior, attitudes, and emotions must be considered in the career assessment process (Walsh & Betz, 1990). Self-report interview data, test data, behavioral data, perceptions of others, and any other relevant information need to be considered.

The sixth assumption is that all career counseling models involve a learning process—cognitive, behavioral, and affective learning. The learning process leads to changes in career cognitions, career behavior, and career emotions.

A seventh and final assumption is that the career decision-making process involves compromise. In stating this assumption, I view career as one of a number of life domains (e.g., marriage, children, extended family, friends, health, and leisure). Clients develop plans for achieving these goals in their domain. Environments offer affordances—functional utilities or action possibilities offered by the physical or social environment (Gibson, 1979; Walsh, Craik, & Price, 1992). These action possibilities may or may not coincide with the client's goals and plans. Thus, as noted by Pervin (1992) and Gibson (1979), client-environment career transactions involve the interplay among multiple goals and multiple paths for goal enactment. On the client side, we have routes, or plans, through which these goals may be achieved. On the environment side, we have affordances, or action possibilities, offered by the physical or social or occupational environment. These action possibilities may or may not be congruent with the client's goals and plans. It is important to note that multiple goals tend to be involved with multiple affordances, and the environment may provide for action possibilities congruent with some plans but not with others (Gibson, 1979; Pervin, 1992; Walsh, Craik, & Price, 1992). Viewed in this context, it would be a rare person who would not sooner or later have to compromise some aspects of his or her career goals.

I have described some of the principles that could possibly be useful to devise a unified theory of career counseling. I realize that we are strictly at the beginning of such an enterprise, but the time seems right to begin constructing.

SUMMARY

In conclusion, my hope about psychotherapy, similar to Goldfried's (1980), is that one day we might be able to have a working conference directed toward developing the field of career counseling. In this hypothetical conference, the participants would include practicing career counselors of varying theoretical persuasions who would be willing to sit down and outline intervention strategies. Such a dialogue would ultimately need to include the direct observation of what actually occurs in the process of career counseling. These career counselors would not be asked to give up their own particular orientation but to take steps to work toward some consensus. Also present at this conference would be individuals who have been involved in career counseling research. Their task would be to guide the discussion in such a way that the strategies outlined can be operationalized and put to empirical tests.

REFERENCES

Altman, I., & Rogoff, B. (1987). Worldviews in psychology: Trait, interactional, organismic, and transactional perspectives. In D. Stokols & I. Altman (Eds.), *Handbook of Environmental Psychology, 1,* 1–40. New York: Wiley.

Beier, E. G. (1988). Toward a unified theory of psychotherapy: Some basic assumptions. *Clinicians Research Digest (Supplemental bulletin), 5,* 1–4.

Beutler, L. E., Machado, P. P. P., & Neufeldt, S. A. (1994). Therapist variables. In A. E. Bergin & S. L. Garfield (Eds.), *Handbook of psychotherapy and behavior change* (pp. 229–269). New York: Wiley.

Bordin, E. S. (1975). The generalizability of the psychoanalytic concept of the working alliance. *Psychotherapy: Theory, Research, and Practice, 16,* 252–260.

Brown, D., & Brooks, L. (1985). Career counseling as a mental health intervention. *Professional Psychology, 16,* 860–867.

Brown, D., & Brooks, L. (1991). *Career counseling techniques.* Boston: Allyn & Bacon.

Buss, D. M. (1991). Evolutionary personality psychology. In M. Rosenweig & L. Porter (Eds.), *The Annual Review of Psychology* (Vol. 49, pp. 459–493). Palo Alto, CA: Annual Reviews and Company.

Campbell, A. (1986). The streets and violence. In A. Campbell & J. Gibbs (Eds.), *Violent transactions: The limits of personality* (pp. 115–131). New York: Basil Blackwell.

Costa, P. T., Jr., McCrae, R. R., & Holland, J. L. (1984). Personality and vocational interests in an adult sample. *Journal of Applied Psychology, 69,* 390–400.

Costa, P. T., Jr., & McCrae, R. R. (1985). *The NEO Personality Inventory.* Odessa, FL: Psychological Assessment Resources.

Crites, J. O. (1981). *Career counseling: Models, methods, and materials.* New York: McGraw-Hill.

Gibson, J. (1979). *The ecologic approach to visual perception.* Boston: Houghton Mifflin.

Goldfried, M. R. (1980). Toward delineation of therapeutic change principles. *American Psychologist, 35,* 991–999.

Gottfredson, G. D., Jones, E. M., & Holland, J. L. (1993). Personality and vocational interests: The relation of Holland's six interest dimensions to five robust dimensions of personality. *Journal of Counseling Psychology, 40,* 518–524.

Hackett, G. (1993). Career counseling and psychotherapy: False dichotomies and recommended remedies. *Journal of Career Assessment, 1,* 105–117.

Heppner, P. P., & Heesacker, M. (1983). Perceived counselor characteristics, client expectations, and client satisfaction with counseling. *Journal of Counseling Psychology, 30,* 31–39.

Holland, J. L. (1985a). *Manual for the Self-Directed Search*. Odessa, FL: Psychological Assessment Resources.

Holland, J. L. (1985b). *Manual for the Vocational Preference Inventory*. Odessa, FL: Psychological Assessment Resources.

Holland, J. L. (1992). *Making vocational choices: A theory of vocational personalities and work environments*. Odessa, FL: Psychological Assessment Resources.

Holland, J. L., Johnston, J. A., & Asma, N. F. (1994). More evidence for the relationship between Holland's personality types and personality variables. *Journal of Career Assessment, 2,* 331–340.

John, O. P. (1990). The Big Five factor taxonomy: Dimensions of personality in the natural language and in questionnaires. In L. Pervin (Ed.), *Handbook of Personality Theory and Research* (pp. 66–97). New York: Guilford.

LaCrosse, M. B. (1980). Perceived counselor social influence and counseling outcomes. *Journal of Counseling Psychology, 27,* 320–327.

McCrae, R. R., & Costa, P. T., Jr. (1983). Joint factors in self-reports and ratings: Neuroticism, extraversion, and openness to experience. *Personality and Individual Differences, 4,* 245–255.

McCrae, R. R., & John, O. P. (1992). An introduction to the five factor model and its applications. *Journal of Personality, 52,* 175–215.

McNeil, B. W., May, R. J., & Lee, V. E. (1987). Perceptions of counselor source characteristics by premature and successful terminators. *Journal of Counseling Psychology, 34,* 86–89.

Osipow, S. H. (1990). Convergence in theories of career choice and development: Review and prospect. *Journal of Vocational Behavior, 36,* 122–131.

Pervin, L. (1992). Transversing the individual environment landscape: A personal odyssey. In W. B. Walsh, K. Craik, and R. Price (Eds.), *Person-environment psychology: Models and perspectives* (pp. 71–88). Hillsdale, NJ: Erlbaum.

Savickas, M. L., & Lent, R. W. (Eds.). (1994). *Convergence in career development theories: Implications for theory and practice*. Palo Alto, CA: Davies-Black Publishing.

Sharf, R. S. (1992). *Applying career development theory to counseling*. Pacific Grove, CA: Brooks/Cole.

Spokane, A. R. (1991). *Career intervention*. Englewood Cliffs, NJ: Prentice Hall.

Sternberg, R. J., & Wagner, R. K. (1993). The egocentric view of intelligence and performance is wrong. *Current Directions in Psychological Science, 2,* 1–5.

Walsh, W. B., & Betz, N. E. (1990). *Tests and assessment*. Englewood Cliffs, NJ: Prentice Hall.

Walsh, W. B., & Osipow, S. H. (Eds.). (1990). *Career counseling*. Hillsdale, NJ: Erlbaum.

Walsh, W. B., Craik, K., & Price, R. (1992). Person-environment psychology: A summary and commentary. In W. B. Walsh, K. Craik, & R. Price (Eds.), *Person-environment psychology: Models and perspectives* (pp. 243–269). Hillsdale, NJ: Erlbaum.

Walsh, W. B., & Osipow, S. H. (Eds.). (1994). *Career counseling for women*. Hillsdale, NJ: Erlbaum.

Wicker, A. W. (1992). Making sense of environments. In W. B. Walsh, K. H. Craik, & R. H. Price (Eds.), *Person-environment psychology: Models and perspectives* (pp. 157–192). Hillsdale, NJ: Erlbaum.

Zamosttny, K. P., Corrigan, J. D., & Eggert, M. A. (1981). Replication and extension of social influence process in counseling: A field study. *Journal of Counseling Psychology, 28,* 481–489.

CHAPTER EIGHTEEN

Addressing Diversity in the Process of Career Assessment

Linda Mezydlo Subich
University of Akron

I N A 1992 "Centennial Feature" in the *Journal of Counseling Psychology*, René Dawis wrote,

> ...one issue connected with individual differences psychology seems likely to overshadow all other future concerns, and that issue is cultural pluralism (or cultural diversity)...a related issue is how to transcend ethnocentrism, or how to develop cultural empathy. (p. 17)

Yet Richardson (1993) recently pointed out that "the theoretical and research literature in vocational psychology-career development is notably oriented toward the White middle class" (p. 426). Society is rapidly becoming more diverse, and vocational psychologists must ensure that career theories and practices keep pace with this transformation. This challenge guided the preparation of this chapter on issues of diversity in career assessment. Career assessment practices must keep pace with changes in the workforce and society.

Fully integrating an appreciation of diversity into the practice of career assessment requires revealing and rejecting models and methods of assessment that assume the cultural uniformity of clients. In the past, career theories, tests, and other assessment techniques sometimes have been constructed from an author's cultural or sociopolitical vantage point with little serious acknowledgment by the author, or, perhaps more often, recognition by users, of the limitations this places on generalizability; reflected implicitly, then, in the content and organization of many of these models and methods are the particular worldviews and assumptions of their authors. Further, researchers and practitioners alike appeared to assume that if a theory or technique was found to be relevant and valid for one client group, it also would be relevant and valid for other groups; so despite the fact that these models and methods often were validated and normed only for limited client samples, they often were applied to a broad range of clients. Consequently, vocational psychology has given rise to an array of models and methods for career and vocational counseling and assessment that seems to address every manner of individual difference (e.g., interests, abilities, values, developmental stage), yet often comparatively little is known about the relevance of these assessment models and methods beyond White, middle-class, college-educated individuals.

Therefore, more must be done in the future than has been done in the past to ensure that the diversity of clients' personal and contextual characteristics are *explicitly* recognized and *actively* addressed in both the construction and application of models and methods of career assessment. Dawis (1992) noted the importance in any type of assessment of considering within-group differences, diverse dimensions of the person, and multiple methods of measurement. Authors such as Fouad (1993) and Worell and Remer (1992) have urged attention to the client's environmental conditions. As career assessments are revised, clearly there is a need to go beyond the traditional interest and ability assessments commonly employed in career counseling and to consider idiographic, qualitative, and other approaches to assessing multiple aspects of both people and their situations.

The remainder of this chapter is focused on suggestions drawn from a number of areas as to how models and methods of career assessment may be updated to meet the challenges posed by a changing society. Specifically addressed are the contribution of multicultural theory and counseling practice to career assessment, the influence of feminist theory and practice on career assessment, the adequacy of instrumentation, and the significance of literature on idiographic and qualitative approaches to career assessment.

MODEL ISSUES

Calls to revise the career assessment process are not new. In 1990, Healy argued for the need to "reform" career appraisals to meet more effectively the needs of clients. He defined career appraisal as "a process intended to help people identify, gather, and interpret information for pursuing viable career options" (p. 214), and he outlined what he saw as a traditional approach to this process as well as a more desirable alternative approach.

Healy pointed out that although the process of career appraisal has been refined extensively since Parsons' (1909) time, its basic structure has changed little. According to Healy, clients often are still cast in a dependent role, contextual factors often are still deemphasized, and the focus during the process often remains on choice to the exclusion of implementation issues.

These structural elements are apparent when one reviews the presentation of career assessment in recent career counseling texts. Authors of such texts continue to emphasize the counselor's role in career assessment as that of a diagnostician who uses assessment data to conceptualize the client and to guide him or her in making an appropriate choice (Sharf, 1992). In their chapters on the use of tests in career counseling, they highlight technical descriptions of commonly used instruments (e.g., the *Strong Interest Inventory*, the *General Aptitude Test Battery*) rather than other broader aspects (e.g., environmental assessments, measures of career barriers) of career assessment (Zunker, 1990). In one text (Isaacson & Brown, 1993), the authors actually noted Healy's (1990) points regarding the need to "reform" career appraisals but then devoted much of the rest of their chapter to describing specific instruments and discussing the career assessment process primarily in terms of the counselor's role and responsibilities. It seems the basic structural elements of the traditional career assessment model identified by Healy are difficult for even informed authors to sidestep completely.

The traditional career appraisal model described by Healy assumes a hierarchical relationship in which the counselor directs the client to focus on intrapsychic characteristics in the interest of uncovering information that the client will then use to make a "good" choice for him or herself, with little explicit consideration of environmental barriers to implementation or adjustment. Such an approach probably works best when both parties share individualistic, Western values and have had similar life experiences; the counselor's assumptions about what to assess and how to do the assessment are then more likely to be "on target," to use Leong's (1993) term. In a more diverse society, however, such an approach to the process of career assessment is likely to be effective less consistently.

As an alternative to the traditional approach, Healy (1990) advocated the importance for the future of collaborating with clients, empowering them to take an active role in their vocational development, explicitly recognizing contextual issues, and following through with clients to help them implement action plans. Since 1990, other authors (e.g., Brown & Brooks, 1991; Mastie, 1994) have echoed Healy's call and endorsed career assessment strategies consistent with his suggestions for accomplishing such "reform."

Upon examination, these suggestions for "reforming" the career appraisal process seem to address a number of issues relevant to the increasing diversity of our society and thus may provide process guidelines for attending to diversity in career appraisal. Specifically, Healy's "reformed" career appraisal requires the vocational counselor to work as a partner with the client and to utilize the client's worldview and life experiences to structure the form and content of the appraisal process. It also does not assume a client's sense of personal agency but rather aims to empower clients who may feel they have little power in other life arenas. In general, it has the flexibility needed both for work with a diverse clientele and for managing counselor and client differences. Interestingly, as Healy himself noted, this type of appraisal process bears a strong resemblance to the client-centered model of assessment described by Patterson and Watkins (1982).

Healy's (1990) calls for collaborative appraisal relationships, greater awareness of contextual issues, and more attention to implementation issues have also been discussed in the literature focusing on multicultural and gender issues. Recent contributors to these discussions (e.g., Bowman, 1993; Forrest & Brooks, 1993; Fouad, 1993; Leong, 1993; Worell & Remer, 1992) have emphasized the importance of cultural and environmental context in career counseling and assessment and called for the empowerment of clients. These authors' writings provide additional guidance about how the traditional career assessment approach may be changed specifically to attend more effectively to clients' diversity.

Fouad's (1993) emphasis on the importance of culturally relevant assessment processes strongly implies the need for more collaborative client-counselor relationships. Bowman's (1993) literature review on career intervention strategies also supports this need; she documented recommendations in the literature that counselors emphasize client-generated information in counseling. Finally, Leong's (1993) discussion of appropriate career counseling process and goals argues strongly for the importance of collaborating with the client to set and decide how to realize career assessment goals; otherwise, career counseling process or goals may be ethnocentric and inappropriate. Further, all of these authors recognize the value of attending to the social and cultural context of the client, noting that, in many cases, exploring family variables, socioeconomic status, or environmental barriers may be more important than exploring a client's personal interests or abilities.

Feminist therapists, too, emphasize empowering clients, forming a collaborative partnership with them in therapy, attending to their context, and acting as their partner and advocate in implementing changes. Forrest and Brooks (1993) suggested a career assessment model in which the counselor and client work as partners from the point of selecting an assessment strategy to the interpretation of the information gathered. They, as well as Worell and Remer (1992), also highlighted the importance of assessing contextual variables, especially social and political barriers to a client's career development (e.g., institutional sexism or racism, lack of role models, occupational discrimination). Finally, feminist approaches to therapy typically stress the importance of including strategies to bring about change in the client's life, and this may include an advocacy role for the counselor as the client makes an effort to implement the plan derived from vocational assessment (Worell & Remer, 1992).

The work of feminist and culturally sensitive authors, then, lends support to Healy's (1990) suggestions for a "reformed" career appraisal model. As did Healy, they suggest that career assessment should be collaborative, and they assume that relevant and useful assessment can be accomplished by neither the counselor nor the client alone; such a collaborative, rather than diagnostic, stance helps to ensure career assessment processes and goals acceptable to and relevant for the client. They also recommend that discussion of assessment goals and how to achieve them be done with awareness of the client's and counselor's backgrounds, especially if there are differences in their backgrounds, values, or experiences. Similarly, they also support raising clients' awareness that they have important contributions to make to the career assessment process and its content and that the counselor will actively support the realization of their goals. Finally, significant attention directed routinely to the assessment of contextual variables, along with more traditional variables such as interests and abilities, is advocated by Healy as well as by authors writing on gender and multicultural issues. The revised model of career assessment that emerges from these writings incorporates sensitivity to diversity at every step.

METHOD ISSUES

Revision of the traditional approach to the process of career assessment is only part of what must be done to "reform" current practice. Concomitantly, the actual assessment methods used must change as well. Four method areas are discussed herein: psychometric considerations, contextual assessment, acculturation, and qualitative assessment.

Psychometric Concerns

The specific techniques and instruments used in career assessment need reform. The foci, designs, and construction technologies of assessment tools often do not fully acknowledge or incorporate information about individual differences. Recent critiques of vocational instrumentation from a multicultural perspective may illustrate some of the issues and problems.

Fouad (1993), for example, examined a number of issues relevant to cross-cultural vocational assessment, one of which is the adequacy of our instrumentation. She discussed concerns about the functional and conceptual equivalence across groups of behaviors examined or constructs and language used, the appropriateness of the language in which the test is presented, test biases, and the adequacy of norms provided for interpreting test results. Each of these issues has relevance for the question of whether current instrumentation addresses diversity as well as it might, but the issue of norm and criterion group composition is the present focus. Fouad stated it is axiomatic that assessors be aware of the norms available for a test, but it is open to question whether this axiom is applied regularly by those who do career assessment.

As an example, I use one of the most respected and valued career assessment tools—the *Strong Interest Inventory* * (*Strong*; Hansen & Campbell, 1985); because it is so well respected, it serves as a potent illustration. Surveys indicate consistently that the *Strong* is widely used and very highly regarded (e.g., Watkins, Campbell,

---

* A revised 1994 version of the *Strong Interest Inventory* is now available; this discussion and the issues raised in it are based on the previous edition of the instrument.

& McGregor, 1988), and yet serious questions have been raised as to its validity when used with diverse populations. In particular, the Occupational Scales (OSs), which are attractive to counselor and client alike because they provide guidance regarding the fit of the client's interests with those of satisfied persons actually working in the occupations listed, suffer from a lack of information regarding the racial or ethnic makeup of their reference groups. The *Strong* manual (Hansen & Campbell, 1985) details gender, education, and employment setting characteristics of the OSs reference groups but not race or ethnicity. It is therefore impossible for a practitioner to determine for him or herself the adequacy of these reference groups for evaluating the similarity of a client's interest pattern to those of specific occupational incumbents; for example, what does a "dissimilar" score on the occupation of systems analyst mean for an African-American client if the reference group sample is primarily European American? The individual may share interests with these systems analysts, but whether these shared interests necessarily translate into the same kind of job satisfaction as expressed by the reference group members is uncertain.

Moreover, the research literature presented in the *Strong* manual (Hansen & Campbell, 1985) provides little assurance that the practitioner need not be concerned about the client's race or ethnicity; only two studies that investigated racial differences in the predictive validity of OS scores are detailed. One study sampled White and African-American National Merit scholars and was published in 1973; the other sampled White and African-American vocational students and was published in 1964. Carter and Swanson (1990), in their review of the literature on the validity of the *Strong* with African Americans, voiced similar concerns. They noted the knowledge gap in this area and concluded that "little evidence exists for the psychometric validity of the *Strong* with Blacks" (p. 206).

Despite the aforementioned lack of information on criterion group race/ethnicity and the forcefully stated concerns regarding the validity of the *Strong*, counseling psychologists frequently use it in the career assessment process (Watkins et al., 1988) and justly laud it as an example of one of the best constructed and most useful tools available for interest assessment. It is not, however, without its flaws, and it is to these that the vocational assessor who aims to be sensitive to individual diversity must attend. Perhaps all too often the assessor's professional knowledge of what psychometric information "should be" available and considered prior to applying an assessment tool does not inform his or her practice. Reputation, stature, or easy availability of a tool may all contribute to failure to verify the instrument's psychometric adequacy in a particular case. The *Strong* is perhaps the best (but certainly not the only!) example of this problem, precisely because it is such a well-respected tool; the *Strong* is a generally sound and useful instrument when used with many individuals. It should be used cautiously, however, with some individuals due to the lack of information on its validity for members of diverse groups.

Thus, it seems essential to remain vigilant and critical in evaluating even "standard" vocational instrumentation; unless explicit knowledge of the uniform applicability of an instrument is possessed, such knowledge must not be assumed. With the recognition that the labor force and society are becoming more diverse comes the mandate to reexamine even tried-and-true instruments to determine whether they are as useful and valid for various new majority client groups as they have been in the past.

The 1994 revision of the *Strong* has, in fact, been sensitive in both construction and examination with regard to race and ethnicity. At the 1994 American Counseling Association convention, Allen Hammer reported that the revised *Strong* includes information about race and ethnicity of occupational group respondents and that preliminary analyses by Nadya Fouad indicated few item and scale differences among White, Asian, African, Hispanic, and Native Americans.

Contextual Assessment

Another aspect of career assessment that may benefit from reformation is the lack of attention typically paid to developing, validating, and using standardized instruments or procedures to assess environmental or contextual variables relevant to a client's vocational concerns. The scarcity of such measures or methods was addressed by Ward and Bingham (1993). Although the assessment interview is certainly one way to obtain information about the client's environmental context, Ward and Bingham (1993) presented the *Multicultural Career Counseling Checklist* for counselors and the *Career Checklist* for clients as examples of how this information might be gathered routinely and in standard fashion.

The former checklist serves, among other things, to heighten the counselor's awareness of cultural, political, societal, and familial variables relevant to the client's concerns. The latter tool serves to stimulate the client's thinking about various factors, including contextual ones, that may be important to consider in the career counseling process. Checklist items cover topics such as the relation of race and ethnicity to the client's occupational choice and the relevance of religious values and family responsibilities to career-related decisions. The routine use of checklists or surveys such as those presented by Ward and Bingham (1993) could help to ensure that there is more consistent counselor attention and sensitivity to contextual factors during assessment.

Environmental barriers are contextual variables often not addressed explicitly in career assessments but are very relevant to the vocational behavior of members of "minority" groups. One method to assess environmental barriers is Swanson and Tokar's (1991) *Career Barriers Scale*. This scale assesses a person's perceptions of the internal and external barriers she or he may face in job or career plans. It taps a broad range of barriers that are thought to cluster into social/interpersonal, attitudinal, and interactional areas. Individual items address, for example, barriers related to economic concerns, family obligations, and discrimination due to gender, race, ethnicity, age, sexual orientation, or disability. Examination of a client's perception of the overall level of barriers she or he faces, the barriers perceived in each of the three general areas, and even responses given to specific items may be instructive in the counseling process.

In their discussion of a feminist approach to vocational counseling and assessment, Worell and Remer (1992) also addressed the importance of career barriers. They specifically identified a client's experiences with sexism and occupational discrimination as potential barriers to that client's career development. The assessment techniques they suggested to obtain information about these areas of a client's experiences seem easily generalizable and relevant to other types of barriers (e.g., racism, heterosexism, socioeconomic status) as well.

For example, Worell and Remer suggested that counselors and clients examine client life events and their relation to career choices with the *Personal Career Development Chart* (PCDC); one could also use some variation of the lifeline approach Goldman (1990) described. More specifically, the PCDC requires clients to recall developmental and career-related events that occurred at various points in their lives. The events in these two areas are then examined for linkages and evidence of potential causal effects of gender-role socialization or sexism on subsequent vocational attitudes and behavior. Again, although Worell and Remer focused on the gender-related aspects of the life events documented by the client and the manner in which they may have impeded or otherwise affected the client's career development, life events certainly could be analyzed in terms of race, sexual orientation, or socioeconomic status as well.

Worell and Remer also proposed the use of gender-role and power analysis to assess (and address) environmental barriers. They suggested gender-role analysis to help raise a client's awareness of how societal gender-role expectations affect choices. In gender-role analysis, clients identify societal messages related to gender (e.g., "A woman can rely on her spouse to provide for her financial needs") and examine their positive and negative consequences (e.g., this may mean less pressure to achieve but inferior status in the relationship). They can then distinguish self-talk used to support the messages, eventually decide what changes in the messages are desired (e.g., "A woman should be able to provide for her own financial needs") and their implications (e.g., status may improve but stress may increase), and, finally, plan and implement change. Similarly, through power analysis with the counselor, clients examine the types of power available to them and the power differentials present in society and determine how gender-role stereotyping and institutionalized sexism affect their use of power. This leads to action strategies to obtain a better balance of power. Once again, both of these assessment/action strategies could easily be adapted to identify environmental barriers related to racism or sexism.

Acculturation

Just as assessing a client's gender-role socialization may aid in understanding his or her occupational choices so too, may assessing a client's level of acculturation or stage of identity development contribute important information regarding the role of these factors in his or her vocational behavior. Research continues to grow and instruments continue to be developed in these areas; authors such as Arbona (1990), Leong (1993), Croteau and Hedstrom (1993), Darou (1987), and Ward and Bingham (1993) have discussed issues of acculturation and identity development in relation to the vocational behavior of persons diverse in their race, ethnicity, and sexual orientation.

Recognition and assessment of an individual's level of acculturation or stage of identity development exemplifies the essence of counselor attention to individual diversity; attention *only* to race or ethnicity or gender or sexual orientation as categories in which to place a person is insufficient to fully appreciate individual differences. Leong's (1993) example of the Japanese-American woman with "a Madonna T-shirt and Calvin Klein jeans" illustrates vividly the interaction of race and gender with acculturation level. Acculturation and identity information have implications for both the career assessment process and the interpretation and application of data derived from it.

Qualitative Methods

A solution to many of the abovementioned problems with and shortcomings of career assessment methods may be to follow (finally) Goldman's (1990) recommendations regarding the utility of qualitative methods. He has long championed such methods of assessment as they have the potential for infinite flexibility to meet the needs of diverse clients. Goldman (1990, 1992) noted that these methods allow for the active participation of the client in the assessment, provide a holistic view of the person, are effective in both group and individual contexts, and can be modified to fit the language or educational or cultural background of the person; they also do not require the assemblage of norm or reference groups because data are interpreted in an idiographic fashion.

Qualitative methods may be used to assess traditional vocational variables such as interests, values, and abilities as well as less traditional variables such as socialization, barriers, and cultural orientation. Goldman (1990, 1992) outlined methods such as card sorts, lifelines, and work samples as ways to assess interests, values, and abilities, respectively. Forrest and Brooks (1993) suggested sentence completions to assess gender-role socialization and sociopolitical barriers; for example, having a woman complete the sentence stems "Since I am a woman, I am required to _____; I am allowed to be _____" provides information on her perceptions of the roles and barriers present in her life. Similarly, Forrest and Brooks noted that exploring daydreams that have been discouraged or encouraged by significant persons in the client's life may provide important information about contextual barriers. In an investigation of a variety of methods to assess individualist versus collectivist cultural orientations, Triandis, McCusker, and Hui (1990) described how persons' responses to the sentence stem "I am _____" could be evaluated to determine their relation to social entities (e.g., family, religion) indicative of a collectivist cultural orientation. Although intended as a research tool, this method seems applicable to assessment of cultural variables germane to a career context as well.

Qualitative methods of career assessment are also congruent with the specifications for transforming the process of career assessment discussed previously. These methods not only allow for the flexible gathering of extensive information about a client but they also complement an assessment process that emphasizes the importance of a collaborative relationship between client and counselor, client empowerment, and the awareness of contextual issues. As an addition to one's assessment repertoire, these techniques may also help facilitate attention to individual diversity.

SUMMARY

American society is indeed changing and becoming more diverse, and the practice of career assessment must keep pace with these changes. It has been suggested in this chapter that increased sensitivity to and awareness of diversity may be critical to transforming the traditional model and methods of career assessment. The field's traditional reliance on objective measurement and the knowledge it produces may be complemented by empathic assessment strategies that lead to greater understanding of the individual client. Guidance in how to accomplish this task may be obtained from extant literature focusing on gender and multicultural issues, from the work of Goldman (1990, 1992) and Healy (1990) who proposed alternative assessment paradigms, as well as from other literature not examined in this chapter; for example, Super's (1980) presentation of the career rainbow, applications of self-efficacy theory to career counseling (Betz, 1992), Russell and Eby's (1993) review of assessment strategies relevant to business and management, and Savickas' (1995) narrative approach to career assessment also may facilitate more sensitive career assessment. This literature offers new perspectives on the career assessment process, identifies additional variables that may be important to assess, and provides suggestions for how to accomplish assessment of these variables.

In any attempt to revise the traditional career assessment model and methods, it is also important to examine critically the basic worldview assumptions that undergird them. Authors bring to their work a set of assumptions about career development based on their experiences and socialization, and to the extent that these assumptions are not relevant to particular clients, related practice guidelines also may not be relevant. For example, the importance of future orientation may be one such assumption that needs to be reexamined. For individuals in some life situations (e.g., persons caught in the cycle of poverty, those who witness random violence every day), a future orientation as it is traditionally understood in career psychology may not be reasonable or adaptive. Also, in some cultures (e.g., Native

American), future orientation is not as prominent of a force as it is in Western cultures. Which of our career assessment paradigms or techniques is capable of facilitating occupational choice or development with such persons? Which is compatible with a client's assumption of a present orientation? Although the literatures focusing on gender and multicultural issues cited previously acknowledge social and cultural differences in future orientation, even these literatures only indirectly address this worldview assumption in their specific recommendations for vocational assessment practice. This is but one example (e.g., others might include the assumptions of personal control and equal opportunity within the societal system) to illustrate that attention to diversity in persons' worldview assumptions may be the biggest challenge to be met in "reforming" career assessment.

Finally, many of the career assessment transformations suggested in this chapter imply that counselors must extend their role beyond the office. Healy's career appraisal model includes the recommendation that counselors follow through and aid their clients to implement the plans derived from assessment processes. Similarly, authors focusing on gender and multicultural issues urge counselors to assume public and personal advocacy roles with clients; such roles may lead to lobbying efforts to change social or educational programs or to efforts on behalf of an individual attempting to enroll in college. In the future, career counselors' appraisal responsibilities may extend beyond the role of gathering and interpreting information with clients to acting on this information with clients to facilitate their career development.

In summary, careful and thoughtful examination of available literature appears to provide some beginning direction for increasing the sensitivity to diversity of our traditional career assessment model and methods. Literatures outside the customary vocational realm may be especially useful, and attempts to use perspectives other than traditional Western ones may be even more important. In all cases, what is needed are creative and integrative thinkers to delve into and critically examine the literature, to step outside their own assumptions about "normal" or "healthy" behavior, and then to translate their ideas into practice. By investigating, adapting, and adopting models and methods suggested in these literatures, increasing our sensitivity to and understanding of varied life experiences and worldviews, and building upon these efforts with the energy and innovation that vocational psychology has so successfully brought to bear in the past, the challenges of a changing society may be met successfully.

REFERENCES

Arbona, C. (1990). Career counseling research and Hispanics: A review of the literature. *The Counseling Psychologist, 18,* 300–323.

Betz, N. E. (1992). Counseling uses of career self-efficacy theory. *Career Development Quarterly, 41,* 22–26.

Bowman, S. L. (1993). Career intervention strategies for ethnic minorities. *Career Development Quarterly, 42,* 14–25.

Brown, D., & Brooks, L. (1991). *Career counseling techniques.* Boston: Allyn & Bacon.

Carter, R. T., & Swanson, J. L. (1990). The validity of the Strong Interest Inventory with Black Americans: A review of the literature. *Journal of Vocational Behavior, 36,* 195–209.

Croteau, J. M., & Hedstrom, S. M. (1993). Integrating commonality and difference: The key to career counseling with lesbian women and gay men. *Career Development Quarterly, 41,* 201–209.

Darou, W. G. (1987). Counselling and the northern native. *Canadian Journal of Counselling, 21,* 33–41.

Dawis, R. V. (1992). The individual differences tradition in counseling psychology. *Journal of Counseling Psychology, 39,* 7–19.

Forrest, L., & Brooks, L. (1993). Feminism and career assessment. *Journal of Career Assessment, 1,* 233–245.

Fouad, N. A. (1993). Cross-cultural vocational assessment. *Career Development Quarterly, 42,* 4–13.

Goldman, L. (1990). Qualitative assessment. *The Counseling Psychologist, 18,* 205–213.

Goldman, L. (1992). Qualitative assessment: An approach for counselors. *Journal of Counseling and Development, 70,* 616–621.

Hammer, A. L. (1994, April). *The 1994 Revised Strong Interest Inventory: Integrating tradition and innovation.* Presentation at the 1994 American Counseling Association Convention, Minneapolis.

Hansen, J. C., & Campbell, D. P. (1985). *Manual for the SVIB-SCII* (4th ed.). Palo Alto, CA: Consulting Psychologists Press.

Harmon, L. W., Hansen, J. C., Borgen, F. H., & Hammer, A. L. (1994). *Applications and technical guide for the Strong Interest Inventory.* Palo Alto, CA: Consulting Psychologists Press.

Healy, C. C. (1990). Reforming career appraisals to meet the needs of clients in the 1990s. *The Counseling Psychologist, 18,* 214–226.

Isaacson, L. E., & Brown, D. (1993). *Career information, career counseling, and career development* (5th ed.). Boston: Allyn & Bacon.

Leong, F. T. L. (1993). The career counseling process with racial-ethnic minorities: The case of Asian Americans. *Career Development Quarterly, 42,* 26–40.

Mastie, M. M. (1994). Using assessment instruments in career counseling: Career assessment as compass, credential, process, and empowerment. In J. T. Kapes, M. M. Mastie, & E. A. Whitfield (Eds.), *A counselor's guide to career assessment instruments* (pp. 31–40). Alexandria, VA: NCDA.

Parsons, F. (1909). *Choosing a vocation.* Boston: Houghton Mifflin.

Patterson, C. H., & Watkins, C. E., Jr. (1982). Some essentials of a client-centered approach to assessment. *Measurement and Evaluation in Guidance, 15,* 103–106.

Richardson, M. S. (1993). Work in people's lives: A location for counseling psychologists. *Journal of Counseling Psychology, 40,* 425–433.

Russell, J. E. A., & Eby, L. T. (1993). Career assessment strategies for women in management. *Journal of Career Assessment, 1,* 267–293.

Savickas, M. L. (1995). Examining the personal meaning of inventoried interests during career counseling. *Journal of Career Assessment, 3*(2).

Sharf, R. S. (1992). *Applying career development theory to counseling.* Pacific Grove, CA: Brooks/ Cole.

Super, D. E. (1980). A life-span, life-space approach to career development. *Journal of Vocational Behavior, 16,* 282–298.

Swanson, J. L., & Tokar, D. M. (1991). College students' perceptions of barriers to career development. *Journal of Vocational Behavior, 38,* 92–106.

Triandis, H. C., McCusker, C., & Hui, C. H. (1990). Multimethod probes of individualism and collectivism. *Journal of Personality and Social Psychology, 59,* 1006–1020.

Ward, C. M., & Bingham, R. P. (1993). Career assessment of ethnic minority women. *Journal of Career Assessment, 1,* 246–257.

Watkins, C. E., Campbell, V. L., & McGregor, P. (1988). Counseling psychologists' uses of and opinions about psychological tests: A contemporary perspective. *The Counseling Psychologist, 16,* 476–486.

Worell, J., & Remer, P. (1992). *Feminist perspectives in therapy.* Chichester, UK: Wiley.

Zunker, V. G. (1990). *Career counseling: Applied concepts of life planning* (3d ed.). Pacific Grove, CA: Brooks/Cole.

CHAPTER NINETEEN

Practical Applications of Career Counseling with Ethnic Minority Women

Rosie Phillips Bingham
University of Memphis

Connie M. Ward
Georgia State University

NUMEROUS WRITERS HAVE called for changes in the career counseling theories and techniques used with ethnic minority women (Gainor & Forrest, 1991; Saveri, 1991; Ward & Bingham, 1995). The authors have noted the need for the changes because demographics in the work world will alter the complexion of the workforce. Fouad and Bingham (in press) indicated that the population of the United States is more racially and ethnically diverse at this point in time than it has ever been in recorded history. We have seen many forecasts for the employed population for the year 2000 and beyond. Each report cites statistics that suggest that the increase in the percentage of workers from ethnic/racial minority workers will greatly outdistance the percentage of growth for White workers. Among those just entering the workforce, women and minorities will constitute the large majority. Saveri (1991) reported that the rate of participation in the workforce for Whites is expected to grow about 17% by the year 2005, whereas the rates of participation for minority groups will equal about 27% during that same period of time. We can also anticipate different demographics at the high school and college levels. Generally, the U.S. Department of Labor reports indicate that Hispanic and Asian increases in the college population will reach a rate as high as 75% and the rate of increase for African Americans will be about 32%. Still, the reports state that high school dropout rates will continue to be high for Hispanics and African Americans.

Bingham and Ward (1994), Ward and Bingham (1993), and Fouad and Bingham (1995), maintained that data such as these demand an examination of career counseling methods and their effectiveness with ethnic minority clients. Helms (1994) and Meyers, Haggins, and Speight (1994) have even stated that the very theories on which career counseling has traditionally been based are inadequate for counseling with ethnic minorities. Helms (1994) maintained that salient racial factors were not a part of the theoretical conceptualizations as the theories were conceived. She indicated that the theories could potentially be very different if socioracial issues were considered.

In each of these publications, the authors concluded that traditional counseling was not adequate to meet the needs of women of color. They have proposed methods, models, and materials for more effective intervention strategies with ethnic minority women (see Helms, 1994, & Meyers et al., 1994, for complete details).

In this chapter, we will present a brief overview of intervention strategies that can be used with ethnic minority women as outlined by Ward and Bingham (1993), Bingham and Ward (1994), and Fouad and Bingham (1995), followed by an explanation of how to apply their models and methods in an actual counseling case.

OVERVIEW

Bingham and Ward (1994) have presented a method for career counseling with ethnic minority women that was designed to change the mindset of counselors as they began to intervene with their clients. Bingham and Ward believed that it was time for counselors to begin to apply the information from the multicultural literature to the career counseling process. They indicated that it was vital for counselors to begin considering the variety of worldviews that are held by the clients who seek help. Ward and Bingham (1993) also thought it essential for counselors to consider issues such as racial identity development, high school experiences, and family factors. They asserted that it was important to immediately involve clients in expanding and exploring their conceptions of the career counseling process. Clients were invited to think about many of the same things that counselors needed to consider. To facilitate the change in intervention strategies, Ward and Bingham constructed two instruments and one schematic that counselors and clients may find useful: the *Multicultural Career Counseling Checklist* (MCCC), the *Career Counseling Checklist* (CCC), and the Career Decision Tree instrument (CDT). Each of these are included as appendixes at the end of this chapter and will be described below. Also described will be a career counseling model devised by Fouad and Bingham (1995), which extends the Ward and Bingham (1993) work.

Multicultural Career Counseling Checklist

It is tempting to conclude that one can divide the career counseling process into an assessment and an intervention phase. In fact, the counselor must continually assess the client, the counselor, and the process before, during, and after counseling takes place. Before counseling begins, the counselor must prepare for the client. To facilitate preparation, counselors can use the *Multicultural Career Counseling Checklist* (MCCC; see Appendix A). The MCCC has an opening paragraph that asks the counselor to identify the racial/ethnic identity of the client and the counselor. It is important for counselors to begin immediately pondering notions of their own racial/ethnic identity and that of their clients to identify critical factors that could influence the particular career counseling interaction in question.

The MCCC is divided into three general steps: (a) counselor preparation, (b) exploration and assessment, and (c) negotiation and working consensus. The first step is designed to encourage the counselor to think through and review the minimum multicultural counseling competencies (Sue, Arrendondo, & McDavis, 1992; Sue et al., 1982). Other items for the counselor to think about include knowledge about the racial/ethnic group to which the client may belong. The MCCC asks about knowledge such as the client's worldview, history, local sociopolitical issues, and stereotypes. In the preparation step, counselors must also think about their own worldviews and racial identity development.

If counselors do this initial thinking and planning, then they are more likely to gather information that can assess the degree to which ethnic and racial factors may influence the career decision-making process of the client. It is important to remember that clients may not come into the therapy process having thought through or even heard of matters like racial identity development. It is the counselor's responsibility to think about such matters and ensure their appropriate place in the counseling process.

The next step on the MCCC involves exploration and assessment to help the counselor clarify the actual career questions that the client might have. Of the 15 statements included in this step, six specifically mention family. Numerous authors, including Fouad (1994) and Martin and Farris (1994), have discussed the important role of the family in the lives of ethnic minority women. If what they espouse is true, then it is essential for the client and counselor to explore family factors. Otherwise, the counselor may unknowingly miss information that could be vital to the client's decision-making process. It may even be important to include one or more of the client's family members in the career counseling sessions or homework assignments.

Other statements in the exploration step encourage the counselor to explore the client's perception of the influence of ethnic/racial factors and how they may limit career choices. Gainor and Forrest (1991) maintained that African-American women avoid certain careers because they fear the influence of sexism and racism. The MCCC cautions counselors to understand that the perceptions could easily be grounded in reality.

The third step, negotiation and working consensus, invites a more collaborative working relationship between client and counselor. The two participants need to agree on counseling goals and, to some extent, the counseling process. The 20 statements under this step call attention to the need for research-based assessment instruments and nontraditional interventions. The statements look at such things as the client's self-efficacy and gender issues.

Career Counseling Checklist

An instrument that can be used for precounseling preparation is the *Career Counseling Checklist* (CCC; see Appendix B). The CCC serves as an assessment instrument for the counselor. The opening statement on the CCC explains to the client that the statements are "designed to help you think more thoroughly about your career concerns and to help your assessment counselor understand you better." The statement sets the stage for the client to understand that the counseling process is a dynamic interaction in which counselor and client must be active participants. The CCC, which was initially developed by Ward and Tate (1990) and subsequently modified by Ward and Bingham (1993), contains 42 statements concerning the client's knowledge about the world of work; the influence of age, race, gender, disability, and so on; and client self-confidence in the decision-making process. Consistent with the important role of the family in the career decision-making process for many ethnic minority groups, the CCC includes materials regarding the role of the family. Additionally, there are statements that are useful in helping the counselor narrow and focus the client's concern and questions in the potentially vast area of vocational psychology.

Decision Tree

After completing both the MCCC and the CCC, the counselor will be in a position to determine whether the client is seeking personal or career counseling. Stabb and Cogdal (1990) have maintained that some members of ethnic minority groups will seek career counseling, when, in fact, they are really looking for psychological counseling. Ward and Bingham (1993) described a Decision Tree to help the counselor find a pathway for determining what the client actually needs (personal or career counseling) and then the initial steps the counselor must take to ensure that the client receives the most effective service.

The Decision Tree (see Appendix C) is a brief schematic that shows the counselor the decision points that might be necessary in the career counseling process. For example, the first decision is to determine whether the client is actually seeking career or personal counseling. If the client needs personal counseling, then the therapist will provide a referral and terminate career counseling. If the counselor discovers that career counseling is needed, the schematic indicates that the next counselor decision is whether to proceed with traditional career counseling or to explore ethnic and cultural issues. The Decision Tree can help the counselor raise appropriate questions from the beginning of counseling on through termination.

CULTURALLY APPROPRIATE
CAREER COUNSELING MODEL

Fouad and Bingham (1995) expanded the work of Ward and Bingham (1993) and Bingham and Ward (1994) by proposing a culturally appropriate career counseling model. The model may be especially important in light of the review of career counseling models conducted by Fouad and Bingham (1995). Their review indicated that the main theories did not mention cultural factors and that others often only gave cursory attention to the matter. An exception is the work of Spokane (1991).

The model may also speak to some of the concerns raised by Helms (1994) and Meyers et al. (1994). Helms maintained that the major theorists did not include salient racial factors in their initial theoretical conceptualizations. Meyers et al. (1994) stated that all of the theories are suboptimal because they generally reflect one worldview and are not "inclusive of most of the world's population." It may be that a culturally appropriate career counseling model would allow counselors to be more inclusive and considerate of worldviews that differ from their own.

Fouad and Bingham (1995) proposed the following seven-step model:

- Step 1. Establish rapport/culturally appropriate relationship
- Step 2. Identify career issues
- Step 3. Assess impact of cultural variables
- Step 4. Set counseling goals
- Step 5. Make culturally appropriate counseling interventions
- Step 6. Make decision
- Step 7. Implementation and follow-up

Step 1 makes it clear that for many ethnic minority groups, the relationship may be more important than the assessment or the intervention. The counselor must learn from the client the type of relationship that will lead to effective counseling. Clients can be excellent cultural informants and teachers. Sue and Sue (1990), Fouad (1993), and Leong (1993) described potentially effective counseling relationships with various ethnic minorities. In addition, if counselors attend to the verbal and nonverbal actions and reactions of the client, they are likely to be able to determine some of the behaviors with which the client is comfortable. Martin and Farris (1994) indicated that counselors must note how Native American clients attend or maintain eye contact in counseling. Counselors' reciprocal behaviors will enhance or deter the relationship. The relationship could be facilitated by a discussion of ethnic/racial information at the outset of counseling. The CCC lets the client know immediately that racial, ethnic, and cultural information is welcome in the therapeutic interchange. Clients can determine the extent to which they are ready to reveal relevant cultural information.

At step 2, identification of career issues, the counselor must thoroughly consider and investigate issues of worldview as discussed by Sue and Sue (1990). Sue and Sue's model helps the counselor to more easily assess external barriers to career decision making. These authors posit a four-component model that identifies internal versus external locus of control and internal versus external locus of responsibility. Sue and Sue maintained that it is highly appropriate for White males, in particular, to believe that they can have control of the events that affect their career decisions and implementation. Furthermore, it is reasonable for White males to believe that they are also responsible for the success or failure of their career decisions. Ethnic minorities may be more adversely affected by factors such as sexism, racism, discrimination, poverty, and inadequacy. Given these factors, it may be quite appropriate for an ethnic minority female to hold a worldview in which she feels an internal sense of responsibility for her career but understands that there are numerous external events controlling and influencing her career decisions. The career counselor must aid the client in the search for what these external factors might be.

Step 3 directs the counselor to more carefully assess the influence of cultural variables. A cultural graphic submodel hypothesized the relationship between such variables as biological factors, family matters, gender, ethnic/racial group, and dominant group influences. According to the submodel, the interaction is dynamic and can reflect inter- and intragroup variations. It indicated that individuals are born with a core that includes biological and personality traits. Gender begins to influence children even before they are born. Because people are born into families, the family members significantly influence the vocational decision-making process of the children in them. It is easy to see that culture shapes gender roles and families and that they, in turn, shape culture. The instruments that we described herein take these factors into consideration. There are several items on the MCCC and the CCC that ask questions about gender issues and family matters. However, because these instruments and schematics may not actually be recording protocols, counselors must keep the data in mind and probe appropriately in the clinical interview based on the information obtained from the instruments. The instruments are checklists that facilitate the thinking processes of the client and the counselor. It is likely that counselors will not have the MCCC in front of them as the client is interviewed. That is why the counselor's mindset is so critical. It is this mindset that aids the counselor in formulating appropriate questions and statements for the client as the interview session proceeds.

The same can be said for relations between ethnic/racial groupings and the dominant group. Counselors are reminded to give special attention to matters of worldview and racial identity development. Of course, it will also behoove the counselor to be aware of structural barriers that are derived from the dominant group area. Fitzgerald and Betz (1994) provided a fuller discussion of structural barriers that is quite relevant for this portion of any assessment with ethnic/racial minority individuals. If step 3 is followed carefully, the counselor should have a better sense of how cultural variables influence career decisions.

At this point, a fairly complete assessment will have been conducted, and the therapist and client are ready for step 4 in the culturally appropriate career counseling model—setting counseling goals. Perhaps the most important point to remember in this step is that the goal setting is a collaborative venture between client and counselor. It would be inappropriate to merely set goals based on the agency's philosophy or the theoretical models that Helms (1994) maintained were conceived without consideration of important racial factors.

The goals will lead to culturally appropriate counseling interventions, step 5 in this model. Although one might not usually invite family members into career counseling sessions, it is one of the recommendations made by Bowman (1993) for use with some ethnic/racial groups. We have found the recommendation useful in our practice of vocational psychology. By implication, such a process means that career counseling will not follow the common "test them and tell them" procedure. The intervention could last over four or more sessions. Some authors have even suggested that to provide effective and culturally appropriate interventions, the counselor may need to visit a client's home. It is likely that one needs to consider a variety of factors before making such a decision, including client age, familial attitudes, and customs regarding counseling.

Other recommendations for vocational counseling include group interventions, conversing in the client's native language, using interpreters, and involving other community members. Whatever intervention is used, the decision must be made jointly with the client, and it must fit the client's comfort level. That comfort level may be greatly influenced by variables such as culture and family.

If the intervention includes the administration of an interest inventory or another structured instrument, the counselor should ensure that the measure is appropriate for the ethnic/racial group in question. To help ensure the appropriateness of an instrument, the counselor can read the manual to determine what it says about the instrument's use, validity, and reliability with this particular clientele. If there is little or no research with this ethnic group, then the counselor should proceed with care. It may be that, at this point, the counselor may need to turn to Leong and Leung's (1994) notion of *creative uncertainty*. In other words, the counselor may need to use the instrument in a novel way that is appropriate or create another intervention that will elicit the same information.

According to Fouad and Bingham (1995), if the first five steps have been successfully completed, the client is ready to make a decision, step 6. Counseling may approach an end, or other issues may have arisen that cause the client to want to cycle back through the process. This point in the model is a sensitive one for counselors and clients because they may be tempted to end counseling prematurely.

The counselor must continue to be vigilant about cultural issues that might cause the client to make a decision merely to reassure the counselor that she or he has done a good job. Some clients may believe that if they do not reach a conclusion, they or the counselor have somehow failed. Therefore, it is important for the counselor to continue to be aware and to let the client know that it is appropriate to go through the cycle as often as is necessary. It may even be useful at this point to discuss the model with the client in order to help the client feel comfortable with the entire intervention.

When the client and counselor arrive at step 7, implementation and follow-up, the process is more fully in the hands of the client. The counselor's main responsibility is to refer the client to the resources, people, and agencies that will aid her in the implementation step. Also, the counselor must tell the client that it is OK to return to the counseling process as the need arises.

Although the culturally appropriate career counseling model has not been formally researched, it does flow from the practical work being done by Ward, Fouad, and Bingham, and perhaps others. To provide a clearer example of how career counseling can follow this model, in the next section we describe a typical career counseling intervention with an ethnic/racial minority client.

THE CASE OF CARLY

The case of Carly illustrates the use of the previously mentioned tools in career counseling. (Client and counselor names are fictitious.) Carly is a 26-year-old woman who checked African American and Asian as her race on the demographic data sheet. Carly is single and has an older brother, aged 36, two older sisters, aged 35 and 30, and a younger brother, aged 22. She has a B.S. degree with a double major in biology and sociology. Her father is 58 and retired from the army; her mother is 55 and working in real estate. Carly is employed full time as a lab technician and recently enrolled in college for five hours of classes, including sociology.

Carly is from a middle-class military family that valued economic success, and her siblings work in professional jobs in medicine, business, and academics. Carly felt stuck in the technician job that she has had for the last three years. She graduated with honors from college and took the technician job as a temporary measure because she was engaged to be married to someone in the military and was waiting to find out where they would live before concentrating on her career. The relationship ended abruptly, and Carly went back to school to try to get her career on track.

Carly was referred to Cheryl for career counseling. Cheryl is a 30-year-old White female counselor who has some experience working with African-American and Asian clients. She has attended three workshops on multicultural counseling and has done some reading in the area, and she has a few other biracial clients. Cheryl was working through stage 5 of White racial identity development* and was aware that she held an Eurocentric worldview at the time she began to work with Carly.

Client Preparation

It is important for the client to begin to think about the career counseling process. We believe that there are numerous factors that individuals may or may not consider that might influence career decisions. To begin to raise those issues, Cheryl gave the CCC to Carly. On it, Carly marked the following items as "true" for herself:

1. I feel obligated to do what others want me to do; and their expectations conflict with my own desires.
3. I am afraid of making a serious mistake in my career choice.
11. I lack knowledge about myself and what I have to offer the world of work.
18. I have great difficulty making most decisions about my life.
24. I am afraid of making mistakes.
28. My orientation to career is very different from that of the members of my family.
31. My race may greatly influence my career choice.
33. I have some career-related daydreams that I do not share with many people.
38. I have undergone a change in my life which necessitates a change in my career plans.

The stage was now set for Cheryl to begin to understand how these items fit into an entire process for her client.

Preparation for Counseling

The counselor may begin to prepare for the counseling session by using the MCCC. The preparation involves a mental process of answering questions about the client that can either be done by the counselor before the actual meeting (if the counselor has demographic information about the client) or during the session. After several uses of the MCCC, the counselor will more automatically integrate the items into preparation for a client.

The first area of counselor preparation is cultural sensitivity, as evidenced by familiarity with the minimum cross-cultural counseling competencies (Sue et al., 1982) and the updated standards (Sue et al., 1992). Cheryl had a copy of the updated cross-cultural counseling competencies and she had attended workshops

---

*See Sabnani, Ponterotto, and Borodovsky (1991) for a discussion of three models of White racial identity development that begin with Whites at stage 1, lacking awareness of themselves as racial beings, and goes through stage 5, which is marked by a culturally transcendent view and respect for other cultural groups.

on cross-cultural and multicultural counseling. She was mindful of the fact that the workshops she attended did not require her to submit her counseling techniques to critique. She believed that she had good basic training and was now working to sharpen her ability to understand subtle nuances in her cross-cultural interactions. The CCC helped Cheryl attend to more of those matters. Having Carly complete the CCC allowed her to express a range of her concerns and suggested to Carly that racial or cultural information would be acknowledged, valued, and respected.

Being knowledgeable about cultural groups is the second component outlined by Bingham and Ward (1994). A certain amount of knowledge of cultural and racial groups is needed to begin initial work with clients. While Cheryl had exposure to African-American and Asian culture, she did not know how these two cultures might interact in one family or how this interaction played itself out in Carly's family. Carly had checked both African American and Asian on the demographic checklist. Because the demographic checklist did not provide space for designating biracial or multiracial, she could not make assumptions about Carly's racial or ethnic identity. While some biracial or multiracial individuals will designate one racial identification, especially those with African-American heritage, in either a forced or willing choice, Carly designated both, even though the instructions asked for only one. Cheryl, therefore, had a cue that both of Carly's racial identities were important to her.

The demographic checklist did not allow Cheryl to know which Asian cultural group Carly identified with. Leong and Leung (1994) noted that there are many Asian cultural groups and that each group is unique. Cheryl noted that because she did not have additional information on the demographic checklist, Carly's Asian designation could mean many things. Cheryl was aware of tension between some African-American and Asian-American groups. Cheryl had also learned from her few biracial clients. Some reported conflicts as they tried to find a group with which they felt totally comfortable. Others were uneasy when forced to choose a single ethnicity or when categorized strictly based on appearances. Certainly, Cheryl found herself dealing with the same struggle. She sometimes wondered whether it would just be easier to encourage her client to choose one identity or the other. She knew she did not have any experiences in her life that prepared her to have empathy for that conflict. Cheryl realized that she would have to let Carly tell her about her ethnic/racial identification. Making assumptions at this point could prove to be disastrous.

Cheryl had made an effort to understand and respect different cultures. She was aware of some of the general stereotypes held about Carly's ethnic groups. One of Cheryl's strong traits was her honesty. She knew that she still wrestled with some stereotypes about young African-American males. She still had some fears of them, born of personal experience and perhaps media or other dominant group portraits of them. On the rare occasion that she counseled a minority male, she was conflicted because her fears made her feel guilty. That knowledge helped Cheryl to remember to withhold her assumptions and learn from her client.

Each new client will reveal information that will allow counselors to determine which of their knowledge and experiences pertain in each situation. Counselors can prepare for this by being aware of their own worldview and how it was shaped, where they are in their own racial identity development, and how their socioeconomic status and political views may shape their ability to work with some groups. Cheryl was aware that she has a Eurocentric worldview and therefore sought out experiences that would allow her to understand other worldviews. She was mindful of her interest in competitiveness based on individual accomplishments. She found that her participation and work in the women's community had strengthened her interest and trust in cooperative ventures. Although Cheryl saw herself working through stage 5 of White racial identity development, she knew that in this society she had the benefits of privileges that were based on her race, socioeconomic status, and whatever status afforded her by marrying a White male. She sometimes had to remind herself that things she took for granted were considered major accomplishments by others. She learned that many of her clients depended totally on themselves and often did not have parental backing or other economic security.

Cheryl considered herself a feminist and had learned to be open to the range of ideas brought to counseling by her female clients. She was careful to let them explain how they viewed their gender in relation to the concerns they brought to counseling. She still caught herself assuming that every woman who comes for counseling or consultation is concerned about gender issues. Although Carly did not check the item related to gender issues on the CCC, Cheryl made a note to ask Carly about gender issues when it seemed appropriate. Cheryl wanted to ask Carly about these issues anyway because she found some ethnic minority female clients put ethnicity or race before gender issues. She wondered if that was a duality conflict for these women. That was another area where she needed to be sensitive.

Finally, Cheryl wondered what had made Carly seek counseling at this time. Carly marked the item indicating a change in her life necessitated a change in her career plans. Because Carly had already indicated this item on the CCC, Cheryl felt invited to ask her about it. Cheryl knew that confronting ethnic minority clients had been difficult for her. She was also concerned about providing a balance between being an active counselor and being intrusive. At this point, Cheryl was aware that Carly potentially needed help with both career and personal issues.

Cheryl made a mental note to think about her client within the context of the Career Decision Tree. She was aware that making a clear-cut decision about whether the counseling should focus on career or personal issues was premature at that point. She just reminded herself that the Decision Tree encourages her to look at racial and ethnic material as it relates to the client's career or personal issues.

Culturally Appropriate Career Counseling Model

Step 1: Establish rapport/culturally appropriate relationship. Cheryl had now gone through the counselor preparation part of the MCCC. Bingham and Ward's (1994) model of career counseling with ethnic minority women includes (a) counselor preparation, (b) exploration and assessment of client variables, (c) negotiation and working consensus, and (d) intervention and follow-up. The first three steps correspond to areas on the MCCC. Cheryl had mentally completed those steps and was now ready to proceed through the steps of the career counseling process with multicultural competencies listed by Fouad and Bingham (1995). These steps are illustrated below.

Fouad and Bingham stated that "it is critical to establish a culturally appropriate relationship with the client, which as the term implies, may differ across cultures" (p. 348). Culturally appropriate relationships set the context for a working consensus and diffuse the mistrust with which a client may approach counseling. The core conditions that help establish a relationship based on empathy apply to career counseling. Ivey, Ivey, and Simek-Morgan (1993) outlined a three-stage model of multicultural empathy in which counselors (a) listen to and observe clients' comments, learning how they wish to be related to; (b) respond to clients' main worlds and constructs, using basic attending skills; and (c) check out statements with clients.

Cheryl and Carly began their relationship by discussing what brought Carly to counseling, what were Carly's expectations for counseling with Cheryl, and how counseling could be affected by the differences in their races. At first, Carly was surprised that Cheryl would bring up the racial issue, but she was pleased that she did. Carly volunteered that she had always had difficulty with demographic questionnaires because she felt like she had to choose one or the other ethnic/racial designation. She explained that her father is African American and her mother is Japanese. Carly asked Cheryl about her racial identification. She also asked Cheryl if she had counseled with other biracial clients and if she knew anything about the concerns of biracial or multiracial people.

Cheryl listened to Carly's questions about her experience with biracial clients and felt incompetent. She began to think that perhaps she should not be working with clients from different cultures. Then she remembered that she did better with clients when she was honest with herself and them. Cheryl told Carly that she did not understand what it was like to be caught between cultures, but she was willing to listen to her and learn from her. Cheryl did understand that people are typically forced to choose one race or the other in terms of their identity. She wondered if Carly felt the pressure to choose from within herself, from the African-American or the Asian-American community, or from the dominant society. Carly seemed pleased that she could talk about these things with Cheryl, because being biracial sometimes made her feel special and sometimes caused problems.

Cheryl hypothesized that Carly struggled with balancing African, Asian, and European worldviews. Cheryl could only wonder what that balance might look like to Carly and if or how she might want that balance to change.

Carly was able to tell Cheryl that she came to career counseling because she had broken up with her fiancé. She felt she had put her career goals on hold while she waited for him to work through his "commitment jitters." She now felt in a hurry to decide because she had wasted precious time. That information told Cheryl that Carly want some concrete information to come quickly of their work together. She knew that insight without results might not be enough for this client.

Cheryl and Carly established an effective initial working relationship. Although Carly had not been in counseling before, she felt Cheryl was inviting her to bring all of her issues into the career counseling session. Cheryl knew that the counseling relationship was at the beginning stages.

Step 2: Identify career issues.   After completing the CCC, Carly and Cheryl saw that Carly's career issues were in the following areas: (a) differences in her own and her family's expectations for a career, (b) lack of confidence or trust in herself and her decision-making skills, (c) lack of knowledge about herself and the world of work as well as about how college experiences related to the workworld, (d) questions about how her race would influence her career choice, and (e) reactions to a life transition.

Carly explained that she was a good student and had done well in all her classes in high school and college. She felt she was pushed to pursue math and science as a woman because she excelled in these subjects. She acknowledged that she preferred the "model minority" stereotype often applied to Asian students to the negative academic stereotypes often associated with African-American students. Cheryl thought those comments might indicate something about the racial identity status of Carly (see Helms, 1994). Carly might be in stage 2, where she was accepting stereotypes held by the dominant culture.

Carly said she chose to major in sociology because she was interested in the ideas of "groupness" and "belongingness." She explained that her parents had expected her to go to medical school like her oldest sister. Carly saw college as an opportunity to explore some personal issues in addition to preparing for a career. She thought her parents believed majoring in sociology diverted her attention from medicine.

Further into the session, Carly revealed that she is a published poet. She published poetry under another name, Nakata Jones. Her poetry spoke of her struggle to live in two worlds and her ambivalence about committing to either. There were themes of dichotomies, yin and yang, duality, invisibility, and specialness in her poetry. Carly told Cheryl that what she really wanted to do was to pursue a doctorate in sociology while minoring in creative writing. Carly was relieved that Cheryl thought that was a realistic goal.

Step 3: Assess impact of cultural variables.   Fouad and Bingham (in press) assert that it is important to more fully assess the impact of cultural variables on career issues. Cheryl was able to help Carly see how her struggle with two cultures was mirrored by her double major in college and her goals of obtaining a doctorate in sociology and making a living from her writing. Carly felt her parents would find her goals acceptable because they included a doctorate degree. Cheryl was aware that the support of Carly's family meant a great deal to her. Carly had strong interests in sociology and felt the doctorate would be a good compromise because she planned to teach at a liberal arts college, where the academic environment would provide a creative incubator for her writing.

Cheryl asked Carly if her parents would be proud of her if they knew she was a published poet. Carly felt being a published poet was easy and did not think her parents would consider it a big deal. She knew her parents were proud of her sisters and brother, and she wanted them to be proud of her. She did not think her dream of going to a writer's colony six weeks out of the year would make them proud. She believed her parents would see the six-week excursions as frivolous and not something that would help her to earn more money.

Although Carly liked science, she did not want to enter the field of medicine. She wanted to make people think and reflect. Carly acknowledged that through her poetry she felt she could voice ideas that she could not express in everyday life. She liked the idea of writing because no one in her family was in the field. It was all her own and she would not have to compete with any of them.

Step 4: Set counseling goals. It was clear that Carly was decided about earning a doctorate in sociology. Her questions revolved around graduate programs, subsequent job opportunities, and informing her parents about her decision. Cheryl and Carly established the following career goals: (a) gathering relevant career data about graduate schools, college teaching jobs, alternative career options available to people with the pursuit of doctorates, and graduate sociology programs that allowed nontraditional projects; (b) developing a time line; (c) preparing for the *Graduate Record Examination;* and (d) discussing her new goal with her parents.

Although Cheryl might have suggested Carly share her poetry with her parents, Cheryl knew that Carly had gone to great lengths to conceal that part of her life from her family. Too much discussion in this area might not have respected Carly's personal struggle with her racial identification. Disclosing her secret to her parents might have elicited guilt and concern on their part and feelings from Carly that she had let them down. Carly's compromise goal—the doctorate in sociology—had something for her parents and something for herself. It was a pragmatic approach to a very complex problem.

Sue and Sue (1990) described four conditions to which a culturally different client might be exposed: appropriate process-appropriate goals (AP–AG), appropriate process-inappropriate goals (AP–IG), inappropriate process-appropriate goals (IP–AG), and inappropriate process-inappropriate goals (IP–IG). Leong (1993) applied this model to the cross-cultural career counseling of Asians. He labeled the AP–AG quadrant the *on-target counselor,* the AP–IG quadrant *the good-hearted bumbler,* the IP–AG quadrant the *barking up the wrong tree counselor,* and the IP–IG counselor the *miss by a mile counselor.* Leong (1993) believed inappropriate goals might include career choices based on self-actualization rather than a pragmatic approach. Cheryl's approach with Carly seems to be an effective balance between appropriate process and appropriate goals.

Step 5: Make culturally appropriate counseling interventions.   Although Carly had a plan she was comfortable with, Cheryl knew that Carly lacked confidence in herself and her decision making from items marked on the CCC. On further exploration, Cheryl found that Carly had not lacked confidence in her abilities until her first serious romance. Her fiancé had not been as studious or as ambitious as she, and she had found herself minimizing her accomplishments. She characterized her former fiancé as very "laid back." Carly had thought herself very much in love with him and had taken the first job (lab technician) that came along while waiting to be married. He had gone on several overseas assignments with the military, and the marriage was postponed several times. Later, Carly found out that he had been unfaithful. She wondered what she had done wrong. Cheryl was able to help Carly see that her fiancé's unfaithfulness had little to do with her and indicated his own lack of readiness for marriage.

Although focusing on this relationship may not seem appropriate for a career counselor, the intent was to discover elements that undermined Carly's confidence and then develop strategies to help increase her confidence. Such interventions must be culturally appropriate. It was clear that family was quite important to Carly. Cheryl hypothesized that any effective intervention needed to include a focus on significant relationships. Carly's relationship with her fiancé had risen to the importance of family. Since the relationship had direct bearing on her career decisions, it was reasonable for the problem-solving strategies to include dimensions of that relationship.

The following interventions were initiated: (a) enrolling in a women's support group, (b) identifying other biracial individuals or contacting the local affiliate of an association focusing on biracial families, (c) taking a graduate course in sociology, (d) taking a *Graduate Record Examination* (GRE) preparation class, (e) talking to a female sociology professor she admires, and (g) joining a literary group to gain support and nurture her writing. These interventions aimed at building up Carly's confidence and her ability to make decisions and achieve her goals. It was mutually decided that Carly would join a women's support group because she felt isolated. She lacked a place to check out her ideas and get validation for them. Carly and Cheryl agreed that this could help her build some confidence in her own ideas, learn to give support to others, and find a place where she belonged. Because Carly seemed to believe that no one would understand her struggle, Cheryl encouraged her to seek out the Biracial Families Support Network. Cheryl knew that Carly brought long-term issues about her racial identity to career counseling, and she knew that while the racial issues influenced Carly's career decision, Carly would continue to sort these issues out, even after she made her preliminary career decisions. The biracial network would give Carly support and guidance in that area.

Cheryl encouraged Carly to take a graduate course in sociology because she had been away from school for three years. Her performance in the class could tell her whether she was ready to confront work on a doctorate or whether she would need to revisit her career decision. The class would also get her back to thinking about research questions for doctoral work. Taking a graduate class would perhaps allow her to meet some of the professors in the department, learn about research specialties, identify professors who would write letters of recommendation, and find role models for the type of academic life she wanted to lead.

Carly knew taking a GRE preparation course would boost her chances of scoring high enough to be accepted into a doctoral program and help her to rebuild her confidence about her academic skills. Cheryl wanted to support Carly in both her writing and her struggle to make peace with her identity. She suggested that Carly join a literary group and continue to write rather than put the writing and publishing off until after obtaining her graduate degree.

Step 6: Make decision.   Carly used her time with Cheryl to firm up her goals. She had Cheryl's reassurance that her goals were realistic. It seemed to help her to have someone there who thought she could do it. Carly was able to see that her goal was attainable after she looked at the information for taking the GRE and talked to a favorite sociology professor. The professor gave her the names of graduate programs that seemed to fit Carly's interest in the theoretical as well as her creative side.

Step 7: Implementation and follow-up.   Carly followed up on all the suggested interventions for building her confidence. She especially liked the biracial support group she found. It was good for her to see others struggling to make sense of the challenge of being biracial. Since the group was comprised of younger and older individuals, she could see people at different stages of their development making a variety of choices. That was good for Carly because she had always felt there was one "right" way to be biracial. She found through participating in the group there was no right or wrong way.

Carly finished a GRE preparation class and is busy talking to professors about letters of recommendations. She contacted the writer's colony and discovered that there are scholarships for deserving writers. She might not have to wait until her graduate studies are concluded to take advantage of the opportunity. Carly is now researching financial aid for graduate school. She hopes her parents will help financially, yet she wants to take responsibility for her education. She has saved money from her published poetry for that purpose.

As may be apparent by the time the counselor and client have arrived at step 7, Carly had assumed most of the responsibility for the counseling intervention. As the model indicated, the counselor's primary charge at that point is to refer the client to the appropriate people and places so that the client can implement the intervention. Finally, Cheryl encouraged Carly to return to counseling if she had additional questions and to let her know how graduate school was going. She was careful to explain again the counseling model to Carly so that she understood that it would be quite reasonable for her to return to the counselor if the need arose.

SUMMARY

The model and illustration described herein provide the reader with one method for conducting a career counseling intervention. The case is a real example that was altered to hide the identities of the client and the counselor. It is clear that the instruments do have some shortcomings. For example, the CCC does not account for biracial individuals in particular. Counselors might want to have a demographic data sheet that addresses the issue. In the culturally appropriate career counseling model, there is not a clear delineation of how to determine the size of the concentric circles in step 3 (see Fouad & Bingham, 1995). However, regardless of the shortcomings, the authors believe that career counselors can use the material to begin to expand their counseling interventions so that multicultural information is included and used in ways that make the interventions more effective and successful. We encourage counselors to modify the process to fit into their own systems for doing career counseling with ethnic minority women. We further recommend that the models and instruments be researched so that they can be strengthened. And, finally, we strongly recommend that training programs begin to incorporate the multicultural literature into vocational psychology courses.

REFERENCES

Bingham, R. P., & Ward, C. M. (1994). Career counseling with ethnic minority women. In W. B. Walsh & S. H. Osipow (Eds.), *Career counseling with women* (pp. 165–195). Hillsdale, NJ: Erlbaum.

Bowman, S. L. (1993). Career intervention strategies for ethnic minorities. *Career Development Quarterly, 42*, 14–25.

Fitzgerald, L., & Betz, N. E. (1994). Career development in cultural context: The role of gender, race, class, and sexual orientation. In M. L. Savickas & R. W. Lent (Eds.), *Convergence in career development theories: Implications for science and practice* (103–117). Palo Alto, CA: Davies-Black Publishing.

Fouad, N. A. (1993). Cross-cultural vocational assessment. *Career Development Quarterly, 42*, 4–13.

Fouad, N. A. (1994). Career assessment with Latinos/Hispanics. *Journal of Career Assessment, 2*, 226–239.

Fouad, N. A., & Bingham R. P. (1995). Career counseling with racial/ethnic minorities. In W. B. Walsh & S. H. Osipow (Eds.), *Handbook of vocational psychology* (2d ed.). Hillsdale, NJ: Erlbaum.

Gainor, K., & Forrest, L. (1991). African-American women's self-concept: Implications for career decisions and career counseling. *Career Development Quarterly, 39*, 261–272.

Helms, J. E. (1994). Racial identity and career assessment. *Journal of Career Assessment, 2*, 199–209.

Ivey, A. E., Ivey, M. B., & Simek-Morgan, L. (1993). *Counseling and psychotherapy: A multicultural perspective*. Boston: Allyn & Bacon.

Leong, F. T. L. (1993). The career counseling process with racial/ethnic minorities: The case of Asian Americans. *Career Development Quarterly, 42,* 26–40.

Leong, F. T. L., & Leung, S. A. (1994). Career assessment with Asian-Americans. *Journal of Career Assessment, 2,* 240–257.

Martin, W. E., & Farris, K. K. (1994). A cultural and contextual decision path approach to career assessment with Native Americans: A psychological perspective. *Journal of Career Assessment, 2,* 258–275.

Meyers, L. J., Haggins, K. L., & Speight, S. (1994). Optimal theory and career assessment: Towards an inclusive, global perspective. *Journal of Career Assessment, 2,* 289–303.

Sabnani, H. B., Ponterotto, J. G., & Borodovsky, L. G. (1991). White racial identity development and cross-cultural training: A stage model. *The Counseling Psychologist, 19,* 76–102.

Saveri, A. (1991). The realignment of workers and work in the 1990s. In J. M. Kummerow (Ed.), *New directions in career planning and the workplace: Practical strategies for counselors* (pp. 117–154). Palo Alto, CA: Davies-Black Publishing.

Spokane, A. (1991). *Career intervention.* Englewood Cliffs, NJ: Prentice Hall.

Stabb, S., & Cogdal, P. (1990, April). *Needs assessment and the perception of help in a multicultural college population.* Paper presented at the annual meeting of the American College Personnel Association, St. Louis.

Sue, D. W., Arrendondo, P., & McDavis, R. J. (1992). Multicultural counseling competencies and standards: A call to the profession. *Journal of Multicultural Counseling and Development, 20,* 64–88.

Sue, D. W., Bernier, J. E., Durran, A., Feinbert, L., Pedersen, P., Smith, E., & Vasquez-Nuttal, E. (1982). Cross-cultural counseling competencies. *The Counseling Psychologist, 10,* 45–52.

Sue, D. W., & Sue, D. (1990). *Counseling the culturally different: Theory and practice* (2d ed.). New York: Wiley.

Ward, C. M., & Bingham, R. P. (1993). Career assessment of ethnic minority women. *Journal of Career Assessment, 1,* 246–257.

Ward, C. M., & Tate, G. (1990). *Career Counseling Checklist.* Atlanta: Georgia State University, Counseling Center.

APPENDIX A

Multicultural Career Counseling Checklist

If you have a client of a different ethnicity/race than yours, you may wish to use this checklist as you begin to do the career assessment with your client.

The following statements are designed to help you think more thoroughly about the racially or ethnically different client to whom you are about to provide career counseling. Check all the statements that apply.

My racial/ethnic identity_____

My client's racial/ethnic identity_____

I. Counselor Preparation

❏   1. I am familiar with minimum cross-cultural counseling competencies.
❏   2. I am aware of my client's cultural identification.
❏   3. I understand and respect my client's culture.
❏   4. I am aware of my own worldview and how it was shaped.
❏   5. I am aware of how my SES influences my ability to empathize with this client.
❏   6. I am aware of how my political views influence my counseling with a client from this ethnic group.
❏   7. I have had counseling or other life experiences with different racial/ethnic groups.
❏   8. I have information about this client's ethnic group's history, local sociopolitical issues, and her attitudes toward seeking help.
❏   9. I know many of the strengths of this client's ethnic group.
❏   10. I know where I am in my racial identity development.
❏   11. I know the general stereotypes held about my client's ethnic group.
❏   12. I am comfortable confronting ethnic minority clients.
❏   13. I am aware of the importance that the interaction of gender and race/ethnicity has in my client's life.

II. Exploration and Assessment

❏   1. I understand this client's career questions.
❏   2. I understand how the client's career questions may be complicated with issues of finance, family, and academics.
❏   3. The client is presenting racial and/or cultural information with the career questions.
❏   4. I am aware of the career limitations or obstacles the client associates with her race or culture.
❏   5. I understand what the client's perceived limitations are.
❏   6. I know the client's perception of her family's ethnocultural identification.
❏   7. I am aware of the client's perception of her family's support for her career.
❏   8. I know which career the client believes her family wants her to pursue.
❏   9. I know whether the client's family's support is important to her.
❏   10. I believe that familial obligations are dictating the client's career choices.
❏   11. I know the extent of exposure to career information and role models the client had in high school and beyond.
❏   12. I understand the impact that high school experiences (positive or negative) have had on the client's confidence.
❏   13. I am aware of the client's perception of her competence, ability, and self-efficacy.

❏   14. I believe the client avoids certain work environments because of fears of sexism or racism.

❏   15. I know the client's stage of racial identity development.

III. Negotiation and Working Consensus

❏   1. I understand the type of career counseling help the client is seeking (career choice, supplement of family income, professional career, etc.).

❏   2. The client and I have agreed on the goals for career counseling.

❏   3. I know how this client's role as a woman in her family influences her career choices.

❏   4. I am aware of the client's perception of the woman's work role in her family and in her culture.

❏   5. I am aware of the client's understanding of the role of children in her career plans.

❏   6. I am aware of the extent of exposure to a variety of career role models the client has had.

❏   7. I understand the culturally based career conflicts that are generated by exposure to more careers and role models.

❏   8. I know the client's career aspirations.

❏   9. I am aware of the level of confidence the client has in her ability to obtain her aspirations.

❏   10. I know the client understands the relationship between type of work and educational level.

❏   11. I am aware of the negative and/or self-defeating thoughts that are obstacles to the client's aspirations and expectations.

❏   12. I know if the client and I need to renegotiate her goals as appropriate after exploring cultural and family issues.

❏   13. I know the client understands the career exploration process.

❏   14. I am aware of the client's expectations about the career counseling process.

❏   15. I know when it is appropriate to use a traditional career assessment instrument with a client from this ethnic group.

❏   16. I know which instrument to use with this client.

❏   17. I am aware of the research support for using the selected instrument with clients of this ethnicity.

❏   18. I am aware of nontraditional instruments that might be more appropriate for use with clients from this ethnic group.

❏   19. I am aware of nontraditional approaches to using traditional instruments with clients from this ethnic group.

❏   20. I am aware of the career strengths the client associates with her race or culture.

APPENDIX B

Career Counseling Checklist

The following statements are designed to help you think more thoroughly about your career concerns and to help your assessment counselor understand you better. Please try to answer them as honestly as possible. Check all of the items that are **true** for you.

❑   1.   I feel obligated to do what others want me to do, and these expectations conflict with my own desires.

❑   2.   I have lots of interests, but I do not know how to narrow them down.

❑   3.   I am afraid of making a serious mistake with my career choice.

❑   4.   I do not feel confident that I know in which areas my true interests lie.

❑   5.   I feel uneasy with the responsibility for making a good career choice.

❑   6.   I lack information about my skills, interests, needs, and values with regard to my career choice.

❑   7.   My physical ability may greatly influence my career choice.

❑   8.   I lack knowledge about the world of work and what it has to offer me.

❑   9.   I know what I want my career to be, but it doesn't feel like a realistic goal.

❑   10.   I feel I am the only one who does not have a career plan.

❑   11.   I lack knowledge about myself and what I have to offer the world of work.

❑   12.   I do not really know what is required from a career for me to feel satisfied.

❑   13.   I feel that problems in my personal life are hindering me from making a good career decision.

❑   14.   My ethnicity may influence my career choice.

❑   15.   No matter how much information I have about a career, I keep going back and forth and cannot make up my mind.

❑   16.   I tend to be a person who gives us easily.

❑   17.   I believe that I am largely to blame for the lack of success I feel in making a career decision.

❑   18.   I have great difficulty making most decisions about my life.

❑   19.   My age may influence my career choice.

❑   20.   I expect my career decision to take care of most of the boredom and emptiness that I feel.

❑   21.   I have difficulty making commitments.

❑   22.   I don't have any idea of what I want in life, who I am, or what's important to me.

❑   23.   I have difficulty completing things.

❑   24.   I am afraid of making mistakes.

❑   25.   Religious values may greatly influence my career choice.

❑ 26. At this point, I am thinking more about finding a job than about choosing a career.

❑ 27. Family responsibilities will probably limit my career ambitions.

❑ 28. My orientation to career is very different from that of the members of my family.

❑ 29. I have worked on a job that taught me some things about what I want or do not want in a career, but I still feel lost.

❑ 30. Some classes in school are much easier for me than others, but I don't know how to use this information.

❑ 31. My race may greatly influence my career choice.

❑ 32. My long-term goals are more firm than my short-term goals.

❑ 33. I have some career-related daydreams that I do not share with many people.

❑ 34. I have been unable to see a connection between my college work and a possible career.

❑ 35. I have made a career choice with which I am comfortable, but I need specific assistance in finding a job.

❑ 37. My gender may influence my career choice.

❑ 38. I have undergone a change in my life, which necessitates a change in my career plans.

❑ 39. My fantasy is that there is one perfect job for me, if I can find it.

❑ 40. I have been out of the world of work for a period of time and I need to redefine my career choice.

❑ 41. Making a great deal of money is an important career goal for me, but I am unsure as to how I might reach it.

❑ 42. My immigration status may influence my career choice.

APPENDIX C

The Decision Tree

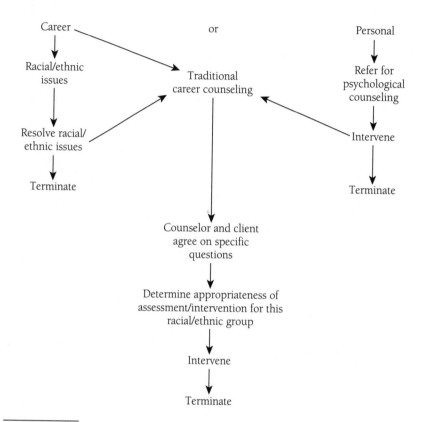

CHAPTER TWENTY

Prudence and Career Assessment

Making Our Implicit Assumptions Explicit[*]

Naomi M. Meara
University of Notre Dame

Oｆｔｅｎ ａｓ ｃｏｕｎｓｅｌｏｒｓ or counseling psychologists, we are se-
duced into believing that we do not set agenda for clients or others who consult with
us. We say we want clients to explore and find their way. Sometimes we realize this
is not the case when we read the work of Betz and Fitzgerald (1987), Brooks and
Forrest (1994), or Bingham and Ward (1994) or the concerns raised by Subich and
by Bingham and Ward (this volume), which assert that the procedures and
measuring instruments of career assessment must be more sensitive to the needs of
women and racial and ethnic minorities and take into account the environments in
which these clients find themselves, environments that are often not optimally
hospitable to their personal or vocational development. But I think we state the case
and then often leave it at that. We do not make explicitly clear the processes we value
implicitly and the fact that we believe our clients must value and enact these
processes if they are to make sound choices and achieve satisfaction. I submit that
we believe these implicit assumptions, whatever the gender, ethnic makeup, or
socioeconomic status of our clients. I argue further that these beliefs may not be
relevant to many whom we are trying to serve. In forming my thoughts about what
some of these implicit evaluative assumptions are, I was greatly influenced by the
writings of Haslam and Baron (1994) and recommend their work.

---

[*]This chapter is based on discussant comments prepared for Session IV, Innovations in Career
Assessment, May 6, 1994, of the conference Toward the Convergence of Career Theory and Practice.

315

IMPLICIT EVALUATIVE RULES OR NORMS

An obvious evaluative rule or norm for career theory and practice is that it is future oriented. We ask clients to be planful and self-regulating, to think through the consequences of their choices, and to be restrained, not impulsive. In terms of careers, from initial considerations to retirement and beyond, we emphasize that it is important to pursue long-term goals, exercise good judgment in the face of uncertainty, and concentrate on overcoming impulsive or short-sighted choices (Haslam & Baron, 1994). Or, in a word (Haslam and Baron's word), to be prudent. Prudence, as you know, refers to practical wisdom, and those who are prudent have goals and reasoned plans for accomplishing them. Improved awareness of gender differences or environmental constraints on women and minorities does not change these values or lessen our belief in the virtue of prudence. Most of us think that future orientation and planfulness are intelligent, virtuous behaviors when it comes to career choice, self-assessment, midlife change, or retirement. We also think that such behaviors are important in many other aspects of our lives. In addition to being future oriented, we are normative and prescriptive—not about what our clients ought to decide but about how they ought to decide it. In our judgment, they need to plan and set goals and understand the long-term results of contemporary choices, such as reduced job opportunities or other negative consequences many have experienced because they lack training in mathematics or other critical skills. Whether we collaborate, assess qualitatively, or advocate in the public arena for more occupational choices, we are normative and perspective.

For instance, an ideal or norm for which many strive is gender equity; when we describe what the world is like, we conclude it often falls short of that ideal, so we prescribe to parents, teachers, researchers, therapists, and others what to do about it. For example, we insist that our counseling relationships be more collaborative. Although these norms and prescriptions may be appropriate, it is no less important to be fully aware of them as we go about our work. If we look closely at ourselves, as psychologists we advocate such prudent, planful thinking as effective, regardless of domain; we value it in educational achievement, daily problem solving, and character development. Whether we all engage in such prudent behavior is another matter. We surely prescribe it, however, for clients, students, and others.

WHAT ABOUT THE FUTURE?

If I am correct, these implicit assumptions, although popular among counselors and career specialists, are not the coin of the realm in contemporary life. The prospects do not seem promising for many individuals (adults as well as the young who are part of the so-called Generation X) to develop prudent, planful thinking. It is truly frightening that many perceive—and perhaps correctly—that there is no future for them, so the prudence and planfulness we value are simply not relevant. For others who try to be planful, the future seems uncertain. The security of the traditional verities (e.g., work hard, become educated, develop loyalty to an employer) is gone. College-educated individuals are unemployed; individuals with 25 years of excellent service are finding themselves unemployed through layoffs and firings. For many, seeing the connection between current interest or skill development and their future selves is difficult. Haslam and Baron (1994) stated that it is important to have altruism toward the person you will become. That is why we encourage individuals not to smoke, to eat nutritious food, to take high school mathematics, and the like. Yet we must reflect on the possibility that we are presenting—and not always clearly—a set of future-oriented implicit assumptions about careers that might have little meaning for many people.

I think we need to do several things if we are to be successful with career interventions and assessments for those who do not share these values or are unable to realize them. First, we need to make explicit our beliefs and strategies for constructing a future. Second, we need to develop systematic programs (group interventions, if you will) for students, teachers, parents, community leaders, and others. We need to train individuals to think about their futures in planful, prudent ways, and we need to help teachers, parents, and others provide such training for their students and their children. Third, through influencing public policy, we need to help provide others with futures that are worth aspiring toward and achieving. All three of these ideas: (a) making our assumptions explicit, (b) training individuals to be planful and prudent, and (c) influencing public policy, which are designed with the goal of seeing that reasonable, attractive futures exist, are important first steps in providing a context in which to make career assessment more useful and applicable to what is occurring in our culture. I use these thoughts, in the present context, to discuss the six previous chapters in this volume.

INNOVATIONS FOR CAREER ASSESSMENT

In their chapter, Borgen and Harmon's work sets an appropriate tone of caution in using the new Personal Style Scales of the *Strong Interest Inventory*. The cautionary tone is repeated, in particular, when interpreting gender differences, and careful use of same-sex norms is recommended. I believe, therefore, that they may have already considered most, if not all, of my reflections on their work. In reading their careful empirical work, I was not able to discern with precision the theoretical links being posited between personality and interests, and at this stage in the development of the Personal Style Scales, I am unclear about their utility for counseling practice. But as noted above, I think Borgen and Harmon are appropriately cautious on this latter point. In fairness, the tradition of interest measurement developed by E. K. Strong is empirical, not theoretical. It is the authors themselves, however, who raise the prospect of theoretical links between personality and interests and hint at a theoretical context for the development of these scales. I encourage the authors to do more with the ideas of theory that they introduce and be candidly explicit in the manual (Harmon, Hansen, Borgen, & Hammer, 1994) about the proposed theoretical links and the usefulness of the scales, as they are currently, for the practitioner. However, if John Holland (1994) is correct and no one reads test manuals, the usefulness of this suggestion may be limited.

Again, as Borgen and Harmon (this volume) note (but the issue cannot be stressed too much), only the Risk Taking/Adventure scale has a history; the other three (work, leadership, and learning environment) were created for this revision "so amplification of their meaning and interpretation can be expected from future research and counseling use." It seems to me that although the scales are clearly ready for inclusion as research, their use in counseling is more problematic. I have several reasons for raising my concern, which I think may be alleviated with further explanations. For example, I am not exactly sure into what context, if any, these scales conceptually fit. What is the central idea here about the relationship of personality and interest? What is the internal coherence of this package of four scales? If internal coherence is not important, then that needs to be explained. In addition, I am unclear as to what they tell the client that the Holland hexagon or Occupational Scales do not. For example, the discussions about interesting patterns of scales and how they can be applied to counseling strike me as somewhat vague. I would encourage the authors to be more specific here.

Finally, some specifics of how the scales may be applied raise concerns for me. In terms of the Work Styles scale, I find the ways this scale relates to the Holland hexagon (i.e., Realistic and Investigative types like working with data, ideas, and things and Enterprising and Social types like working with people) of interest for research and for elaborating on the intrinsic meaning of the scale. I am concerned, however, that the higher status jobs and those that are considered "masculine" (by reputation and by the percentage of males who hold them), for example, physicist, chemist, and mathematician, are at the data pole, and the lower status, lower paying, more "feminine" jobs, for example, child care worker, social worker, and high school counselor, are at the people pole. Although the authors are cautious about this, I remain concerned that women, in particular, because of their scores, may continue to be encouraged to seek or view themselves as suited for (cf. e.g., Chalk, Meara, & Day, 1994) lower status, lower-paying occupations rather than those with higher prestige and salaries.

Although I do not have interpretation concerns with respect to gender on the Learning Environment scale, I do have status concerns, as educational accomplishment was the metric used to derive the scale. The Leadership Style scale is less troublesome for me, as concerns of gender and status are less salient. I do, however, think we need to look at the unidimensionality of this scale (having interest in taking charge versus not having interest in taking charge), in particular, as it applies to some minority group members. Patricia Hill Collins, an African-American social scientist, wrote a compelling essay, "Toward an Afrocentrist Feminist

Epistemology" (Collins, 1991, pp. 201–220) in which she stated that knowledge validation from this perspective is more of a collaborative effort in which dialogue and empathy are important components. Those who support this perspective might have very different ideas about leadership that would not be tapped by this scale. Also, it is well to remember that the ability to be accepted by others when taking charge can often depend on accidents of birth, such as gender and ethnicity; those who have learned this might be more reticent to declare their interest in taking charge than those for whom leadership is less problematic. The Risk-Taking/ Adventure scale seems to cover a multitude of activities from physical risk to financial risk to independence and autonomy, but it does have much more empirical history behind it. The utility of the scale may be more a description of present behavior than a prediction about future behavior.

In summary, this is carefully done, carefully documented empirical work in the fine tradition of the *Strong*. Research with the four scales as they now stand bodes to be beneficial for the career assessment enterprise in general and for the *Strong* in particular. As the scales are used, I hope there will be more discussion about the theoretical and practical concerns I have raised.

BEYOND MULTICULTURAL AWARENESS

An important aspect of competent theorizing and proficient practice in career counseling is understanding multiculturalism. In particular, it seems important to go beyond a set of vague or amorphous ideas and reflect upon several issues. These include thinking about how "taken-for-granted" middle-class achievement values affect the workplace and interact with workers who do not share this perspective. In addition, sound, integrative career interventions with those who do not share these taken-for-granted perspectives—and, in fact, might take strong exception to them—must be developed and tested. To get beyond a surface understanding of multiculturalism requires prudent reflection and thoughfully derived and empirically based interventions.

Reflection

I favor much of what Subich writes in her chapter; she has integrated a number of strands in the literature that point out the need for more emphasis on individual differences and different methodologies in career assessment. Thanks to the work of many, we have made progress in this arena, and this progress has probably sensitized us all to majority as well as minority concerns. There are two suggestions I have for the Subich chapter. First, I would like her to consider some of what she suggests in light of my earlier comments, particularly my thoughts about (a) training individuals to be planful and (b) encouraging professionals to influence public policy in a way that might provide better future prospects for the young, particularly for those youth who are different from most career counselors or who do not share or are unable to implement the values of the upwardly mobile middle class.

In regard to the first suggestion, I hope that we can all be aware of both the reasonableness and the potential problems inherent in the future-oriented model I describe. Although focus on the future is important, we don't want to frighten individuals from taking a chance in the present or paralyze them into believing that current mistakes or bad decisions doom one's future. Also, we must realize that as sound as prudence might be in charting a career and assessing one's progress and satisfactions, the kind of thinking I am advocating is a Eurocentered middle-class value. Ironically, it seems to be a value that large segments of the middle class are either abandoning or finding difficult to implement. That is why we need to be explicit about this future-oriented value so our intentions are clear and our efforts are not patronizing. For some individuals, certain choices (e.g., having a child) often affect the controllability of other future plans; all choices have restrictions. To advise clients to think otherwise would be foolhardy.

In regard to my second comment, that career development specialists work to influence public policy, this is more easily said than done. As others before me have pointed out, the personal needs of many represent political problems or inequities in our culture; the personal is political. In addition, if we have learned nothing else in psychology in the last 50 years, it is that the professional issues are political ones as well. Thus, it can be self-defeating for clients if counselors attempt to empower individuals who have no power outside of their offices or clinics. To put it another way, we cannot do enough in the interview room to empower those who are not empowered by their culture. Sensitivity to cultural context or constraints and skill training for the future (as important as these ideas may be) are not ultimately helpful if the context does not provide opportunities for developing that future or using those skills.

The time seems right for those interested in vocational issues to be more active in the public sector, the public interest sections of the American Psychological Association (APA), the Division of Counseling Psychology of the APA, the American Counseling Association, and other organizations. Many psychologists and career specialists have influence with the government agencies and private corporations where they consult and where they can raise these issues. But as I noted previously, this is easier said than done. To me there is no clear strategy or plan; and local efforts to improve the future in our own schools and communities are probably as important as anything we can do nationally.

My other general suggestion about the Subich chapter is that more specificity is required. For example, she does not state exactly what she thinks should be done about her suggestions. Once we have assessed environmental barriers to occupational achievement, what should we do about them? It has been very well documented that such barriers exist (e.g., Betz, 1994), yet now what is to be done about their existence? It seems that it is not enough to simply help clients become aware of these obstacles.

Although these issues have been raised before, they are still salient. Many writers and practitioners have attended to these issues in theorizing, commentary, and empirical work (cf. e.g., Bingham & Ward, 1994; Ward & Bingham, 1993). As Subich herself notes, the 1994 revision of the *Strong* demonstrates that measurement specialists have been sensitive to what she has addressed herein. Yet more attention is needed and more programs of research and practical interventions must be developed. Stating the problems in however elegant a fashion is only the first step.

Intervention

The Bingham and Ward chapter (this volume) is integrative and specific and thus may be said to add continuity and substance to Subich's ideas. Use of the methods Bingham and Ward suggest provides a means for client and counselor alike to make explicit the many implicit assumptions they may have with respect to race, ethnicity, gender, and the world of work. The processes and model they espouse enable both counselor and client to examine their global assumptions with regard to being in counseling where the race, ethnicity, and gender of the participants, as well as their specific views about each other, are salient. Their integrative approach, which combines the work of Bingham and Ward (1994), Fouad and Bingham (1995), and Ward and Bingham (1993), is a service to scientist-practitioners as well as potential clients. Their work provides a sensible blueprint, neither too flexible nor too rigid, for counselors. It also provides clear, sensible directions for research. Components of the model can be empirically tested; components also provide clear links to constructs (e.g., racial identity, family expectations) thought to be important for career decision, satisfaction, and adjustment of ethnic/racial minority women.

The structure that the model provides for practice and research needs no elaboration here; application of the model for practice is well illustrated in the case example. The authors are to be commended for the explanation of what they are about, the development of specific assessment aides (e.g., the *Multicultural Career Counseling Checklist*), and the illustration of what they espouse. The illustration clears up some misgivings one might have, for example, when reading about the Decision Tree, that the authors may be making too sharp a distinction between personal and career counseling when many authors (cf. e.g., Hackett, 1993; Krumboltz, 1993) do not favor such a distinction. The case example demonstrates that such decision making is not overemphasized, although it is a stage in the counseling model. Lastly, the case study illustration provides a model for multiple intervention strategies that are more group and family oriented, thus focusing on a strength of many ethnic/racial minorities: their emphasis on the collective as opposed to the individual.

Although these features of the Bingham and Ward chapter are explicit and compelling, what these authors imply may have a more profound impact than the cogent model they have carefully delineated. First of all, the fact that counselor and client both prepare (with the assistance of the Bingham and Ward, 1994, and Ward and Bingham, 1993, *Multicultural Career Counseling Checklist* and the *Career Counseling Checklist*) provides a model of prudence and planfulness. Rather than. telling the client what to do, the counselor provides prudent, planful parallel activities for counselor and client alike. In addition, as the authors explain, a major purpose of this exercise, and everything else they espouse, is to *change the counselor's mind-set*. In theorizing or teaching about counseling, often even in practicum training or collegial supervision, we focus on client change. Seldom do we focus on counselor change; in particular, we do not focus on the importance of a counselor changing across the course of counseling. If psychology, counseling psychology, and career counseling (either through research or practice) are to serve competently an ethnically and racially diverse society, these disciplines and professions must change their theoretical perspective, methods of empirical investigation, and procedures of practice. As Bingham and Ward imply in their chapter, understanding the worldview of the client not only causes the counselor to reflect on his or her own worldview but to change it as well. Although the authors do not make this implication explicit, it is the changing of worldview—about the world of work and those in it—that is needed. Such change will eventually happen (with or without psychology's help). As the demographics of the workforce continue to change, employers and employees will do what is necessary to accommodate each other. I believe these tasks would be easier if psychology and other disciplines would intervene in the manner implied by Bingham, Ward, and others. For instance, as Quintana (1995) observes in reacting to Smart and Smart's (1995) suggestion that Hispanic clients learn English, why not suggest counselors learn Spanish?

Another example of implied change is in the explicit wording of steps 1 and 3 of the culturally appropriate career counseling model. In step 1, the goal is to "establish a culturally appropriate relationship." Perhaps the knowledge, reflection, and sensitivity needed to accomplish this step should be applied when counseling majority clients as well. The focus on culture seems appropriate whatever the race, ethnicity, or gender of the counseling participants. It seems appropriate that everyone be aware of his or her stage of racial identity and other issues raised by the checklists. One could argue that no small portion of the ethnic and racial conflict that exist in the United States today is due to ignorance regarding these matters. It would also seem helpful as well for clients to be aware of how large a part gender, race, and ethnicity play in what "can be taken for granted" in establishing rapport between White counselors and clients.

The goal of step 3 is to assess the impact of cultural variables. As far as this step is concerned, many majority clients (and, unfortunately, perhaps some counselors as well) are unaware of the advantage that being a member of the majority gives them. Collaborating with clients to assess the impact of cultural variables on career domains and satisfaction could be instructive. Lastly, the demographics of the future workforce might make it prudent for career counselors to explore with their majority clients how they will respond to supervisors and more rapidly advancing peers whose gender, race, and ethnicity, or even prior socioeconomic status, may be quite different from their own. In addition, majority students or clients need to prepare for the prospect that in a specific work group, company, or corporation, their ethnicity, racial group, or gender may be in the minority.

Bingham and Ward present an explicit, prudent, collaborative plan for career assessments and intervention with ethnic/racial minority women. They integrate the multicultural literature into their scheme and provide a case example that demonstrates how their methods and models can be applied as well as multiple intervention strategies to address many facets of the client's concern. We have much to learn from this developing thoughtful approach. Most importantly, the work has implications for the science and practice of career psychology well beyond its contribution to the career counseling of ethnic minority women.

Specificity and Appropriate Application

Practitioners have to be practical above all else. No matter how sophisticated and well versed they are in the science and theory of their work, sooner or later they have to do something concrete and enable clients to do the same. Often the problems clients bring to counselors and which the counselors in turn bring to vocational researchers are specific and applied. Practitioners expect a prudent reciprocal interchange with scientists, a conversation that demonstrates that researchers have incorporated into their theories specific practical concerns that confront the career counselor daily.

Career Attitudes and Strategies.   Gottfredson receives high marks for being very specific about his goals for his chapter, that is, illustrating the usefulness of multiple career theories for specific practical problems or issues (e.g., career choice, satisfaction, or attainment). As perhaps inevitable with such ambitious goals, he disappoints somewhat in their achievement; in particular, he presents incomplete information regarding theories or perspectives with which he disagrees. In places the chapter strikes me as a more of a brief for his point of view rather than what his introduction and history of careful scholarship promise, an open-minded and thorough presentation of all perspectives or a simple, dispassionate, straightforward argument for his perspective. Although he affirms that each perspective is to be admired and appears useful for understanding some problems "despite the disparagement each perspective sometimes receives from those plugging another perspective," I think that he could be more affirming of the positive features of other viewpoints.

He brings an important and often neglected issue to the discussion when he writes of individuals who have a general disposition to be satisfied or dissatisfied. From a practical standpoint, he could elaborate on this contribution by suggesting how counselors and clients, whom he suggests should not devote much time to searching for the roots of such dispositions in assessing person-job mismatches, should deal with this information.

I think many of Gottfredson's major points are well taken, and his views are shared by many. I think he is correct in assuming that it is not realistic to think that any one theory can explain everything but that in the aggregate we should be able to explain a lot that is relevant for practice. A major premise of his work is that a "fruitful approach to the practice of counseling may be to use applicable partial theories to gain the best grasp on particular problems." Given the state of our knowledge in counseling, this is a premise that may have merit, but I do not think, nor do I think he thinks, we should let it stand without carefully examining it. On the positive side, the premise enables us to take problems from practice back to theory. Such a strategy can enrich both endeavors and is probably not implemented with nearly enough frequency. On the negative side, exclusive use of such a strategy could lead to "cookbook" interventions as well as segmented, incomplete, or incoherent views of clients and their concerns and a further split between theory and practice. These latter results are clearly not his intention, nor would they necessarily eventuate if his specific ideas were implemented; nevertheless, there exists the potential for such negative outcomes.

He is enthusiastic about his point of view. I understand and appreciate that. I think he would be more persuasive, however, if he better explained his own points and elaborated his criticisms with more specificity and with concrete examples of how others fall short rather than the more general claims that the views of others are misguided or that they misunderstand a theoretical perspective he favors.

I applaud the specificity of some of the things he writes; for example, he is very clear in his summary of certain salient variables, such as the characteristics of environments that produce better performance. I am less satisfied with how fixed he believes personality variables are, or at least with how fixed he seems to believe certain characteristics are, characteristics that he terms *personality variables* (e.g., ability, commitment, and self-discipline). Surely, the last two can be learned, unlearned, and modified. This observation may be more a comment on my own biases than a legitimate criticism of his point of view.

A major contribution of his chapter is the *Career Attitudes and Strategies Inventory* (CASI). This career assessment instrument provides a concrete means of assessing multiple aspects of career status that are important in providing sound career interventions. In my judgment, his chapter would have been strengthened if he focused on this instrument by providing more information about it and by explicitly elaborating on the links between the concepts he believes need to be measured and the scales the CASI provides to measure these constructs. I think such a strategy could integrate in a positive and productive way many of the important ideas in his chapter.

Gottfredson writes to the theme of this volume, that is, the linking of theory and practice, although I might argue that some of the things that he talks about (e.g., general dispositions, reward contingencies) are more ideas or constructs, albeit important constructs to the enterprise of career choices and satisfactions, than theories about vocational behavior. As he himself notes, he enumerates far too many constructs to be useful for either counselors or clients, but he does propose a way to address important constructs through the use of the CASI. This instrument may tap relevant questions for many clients. Readers can gain from what he has to say and from a more thorough explanation of his major premise, better explanations of the linkages between relevant variables and the CASI, and, finally, more complete conceptual and statistical information about the instrument itself.

Career Mastery. Crites' chapter provides an example of the linking of theory and practice and reviews means for linking the language of theory and the language of data. His discussion provides a narrative of the process and demonstrates the time it takes to conduct programmatic research that has relevance for practice. His treatment illustrates the schisms between science and practice. Practical problems often cannot wait for careful science, and even applied research is frequently only suggestive of practical action. Crites (cf. e.g., 1981) for some time now has been explicit about the necessity of repairing such schisms; in particular, he has advocated for and demonstrated how theory and "hardheaded" empiricism can usefully guide practice. In addition, Crites (cf. e.g., Fitzgerald & Crites, 1980) has been sensitive to the practical nuances of the career development of women and the implications of such nuances for theory building, accurate assessment, competent counseling, and problems of career prediction in general.

In his chapter in this handbook, Crites firmly establishes his arguments within the historical scientist-practitioner traditions of counseling psychology more broadly and career psychology in particular. This history is often neglected, and we neglect it at our peril. For example, in career work (be it science or practice), I believe (and other authors concur, cf. e.g., Bingham & Ward 1990; Walsh, this volume; Osipow, 1990) we will never appropriately encompass multicultural and other pluralistic concerns if we do not systematically apply practice to theory and research. Crites makes an important contribution in focusing on the career success and satisfaction of adults. There is not enough work in this important area as the complexities of the current economy and the changing workforce indicate we need to know more about this population. As the opportunities in the workplace continue to change, more focus is needed on the work satisfaction of adults who have already made initial, if not subsequent career choices, and are thus "placed." The career mastery concept as well as its multivariate measurement via the *Career Mastery Inventory* (CMAS) could become, as Crites proposes, a significant linkage for researchers and practitioners. As the case example demonstrates, they could also be very helpful for the workers and the organizations that employ them.

Crites informs the reader that the instrument itself dates back to the *Career Adjustment and Development Inventory* (CADI) and that the conceptual and theoretical thinking that produced it is "developed from a *program* of research on vocational maturity initiated in the 1960s." Specifically, he states that the CMAS is designed to "supplement and extend" to adults the "measurement of career development in adolescence" as operationalized by the *Career Maturity Inventory* (CMI).

A major concern I have with Crites' presentation is that he does not articulate as well as he surely can the construct of career mastery and its precise linkages to the concept of vocational maturity and the two other inventories, that is, the CADI and the CMI. He misses an important opportunity to model explicitly what he is advocating and has advocated throughout his career: the clear linkage of theory, research, and application. He does define career mastery and give us some information about the programmatic nature of what he has done and how it links to prior work. But from my perspective, the chapter lacks the thoroughness and clarity that have characterized his work and that we have come to expect from him. The literature review is selective and, if a reader does not already know some of the work and where to find out about it, the references are not as helpful as they might be. The historical references are complete, but the contemporary ones are not. For example, references to the many studies that have used the CMI or more contemporary treatments of career maturity in the vocational literature (cf. e.g., Spokane, 1991) are missing. Zytowski (1978) registered a similar concern with respect to the information in the CMI manual. The concerns that I have may be rectified in the *CMAS Sourcebook* (1993) and elsewhere. If not, I would ask him to consider a more complete presentation of his ideas in other publication outlets.

In summary, this is important work that I hope will continue. I also hope that explicit linkages will be made to other pivotal career constructs. I can think of no one more qualified than Crites to carefully explicate the nomological net that contains the construct of career mastery and its conceptual, empirical, and practical relationships. He is a good choice as well to fit this net within the broader picture of developments in the field, historical and contemporary. Finally, since he so clearly addresses the theme of the book, perhaps he can be forgiven for not explicating and elaborating on the meaning of career mastery as much as I would like.

Reciprocity and Levels of Integration

The Walsh chapter presents several ideas for bridging research and practice in career psychology. I think there is much merit in all of the ideas he presents, but I will confine my remarks to those ideas that I think could have the largest positive influence on the convergence of research and practice. He suggests what might be termed reciprocal approaches to building bridges, namely, looking at how science can inform practice and how practice can inform science. He is to be commended for presenting this balance and for the specificity and applicability of his ideas. His overarching theme seems to be a more sophisticated integration of theory into both the research and the practice endeavors.

His first suggestion, implementing a more idiographic research approach (Walsh, Craik, & Price, 1992), is one easily recognized by practitioners. Counselors operate in the fashion Walsh describes. They gather information about a client; they then form hypotheses about salient issues that brought the client to counseling and interventions that might prove effective in addressing these issues. In addition, leading methodologists in counseling psychology (cf. e.g., Hoshmand, 1989; Howard, 1986; Howard, 1991; Howard & Conway, 1986a, 1986b; Howard, Maerlender, Myers, & Curtin, 1992) have been writing about methodologies that could implement systematically what counselors already do and the specific idiographic approach Walsh espouses. While these methodological approaches have been applied to the research endeavor of so-called personal counseling, they have been used less frequently in career counseling. Below, I raise some concerns and make a suggestion with respect to the conference Walsh proposes; however, there is one suggestion regarding the conference that seems appropriate to mention here. Perhaps the research portion of the conference could be limited to alternative methodologies (alternative to those governed by logical positivism) applied to the issues raised by practitioners.

Walsh's suggestion with respect to the conceptualization and application of the Big Five critical personality traits (McCrae & John, 1992) to career research deserves wider consideration than even he suggests. It seems that the content he proposes for research could be included in the education and training of counseling psychologists, career researchers, and career counselors as part of their assessment sequence in either the personality segment, the vocational segment, or both. A thorough grounding in this view could more closely relate career research and practice to basic psychological theory and science. In addition, individuals who receive this training are those who eventually make career commitments primarily to science, primarily to practice, or some combination. They are in classes and seminars together and thus can learn and discuss information designed to bridge the science-practice gap before their daily work activities make the opportunities for bridge building less available.

The treatment of practical intelligence makes explicit much of the tacit knowledge about career success. The characteristics of practical intelligence are very similar to the prior discussion of prudence in this chapter. Because career research and practice have always had an applied emphasis, the construct of practical intelligence is particularly promising for building science-practice bridges. As part of their daily routines, practitioners model practical intelligence for clients and so I think would be very receptive to a research agenda that focuses on its antecedents, consequents, and component parts.

I agree with Walsh's practice agenda and his work adds to the understanding recently endorsed by many (Hackett, 1993; Krumboltz, 1993; Meara & Patton, 1994) of the parallels between, and the difficulties in separating, personal and career counseling. I support the ideas contained in the hypothetical conference he proposes. There are several cautions that I think need to be raised if such a conference is to engage scientists and practitioners in the meaningful dialogue that is necessary to achieve some of the conference's goals. I think we need to realize that the culture of scientists and the culture of practitioners are very different from one another. For example, as Meara and Schmidt (1991) noted, research is a public activity; counseling a private one. Researchers like to "announce" or in some other way disseminate what they are doing; counselors, on the other hand, are concerned with confidentiality. What this means for a conference is that the researchers, who are accustomed to announcing, can dominate the conversation, and the practitioners, who are accustomed to listening, may be more passive. As Osipow notes and as Walsh stresses in their chapters, we need more ideas from practice to guide science. To implement the idea of practice informing science, the conference must be structured so that practitioner ideas and methods receive complete and detailed attention. Also, as stated above, the researchers' portion of the conference should be dominated by applying alternate research methodologies to what the practitioners present. Some such structure is needed to keep the conference from business as usual, that is, the scientists guiding practice more from theory or "dust-bowl empiricism" rather than experience.

Walsh presents useful ideas for bridging the gap between science and practice, for making theory and practice more useful to each other, and for advancing the field and helping clients. All concerned can benefit if we use practical intelligence and prudence in implementing what he has to say.

SUMMARY

The authors of these chapters offer us many ideas that deserve the attention and reflective capacities of those interested in advancing the theoretical and practical frontiers of career psychology. The careful work of Borgen and Harmon continues the fine empirical tradition of the *Strong*, arguably one of the most helpful career assessment instruments in psychometric history. Subich reminds us of the cautions we need to observe in generalizing assessment results to diverse populations, and Bingham and Ward present a thoughtful, detailed invention (with appropriate assessment aides) for career counseling with ethnic minority women. Gottfredson has taken an important step in linking a number of important career variables to an instrument that could provide heuristic and concrete measures of them, and Crites continues work on the development and assessment of an important construct: career mastery. Finally, Walsh provides us with sensible suggestions for how science and practice can mutually inform each other and advance the field, both theoretically and practically.

The theorizing and empirical work of these researchers will continue to have significant practical applications for many clients as they plan their careers and assess their current occupational situations with a view toward their futures. This will prove to be especially true when this work is applied and interpreted by skilled practitioners who understand the implicit assumptions of vocational research and who can integrate that knowledge with a clear understanding of the needs of their clients and the realities of the worlds in which their clients live.

Despite my quibbles, I appreciate the opportunity to comment on this fine work and to present my comments in the context of prudence. I have done so in the hope that this context may help us consider the implicit assumptions of what these authors and other career specialists are advocating. I have concentrated specifically on the assumption of prudence and planfulness, but there are many others we need to consider as we examine the messages we professionals are sending to clients and the general public. Empirical work must attend to detail (and Borgen, Harmon, Gottfredson, and Crites have always done that), conceptual ideas and specific interventions must relate to culture (and Subich, Bingham, and Ward have attended to that), and, ultimately, if career theory is to be meaningful, science and practice need to remain linked (and Walsh has provided agendas for that). In integrating theory and practice, we must be ever careful not to get too far from our data when we intervene in the lives of others. I congratulate the authors for their products. They are indeed planful scholars whose work can help us be more reflective and prudent scientist-practitioners.

REFERENCES

Betz, N. E. (1994). Basic issues and concepts in career counseling for women. In W. B. Walsh & S. H. Osipow (Eds.), *Career counseling for women* (pp. 1–41). Hillsdale, NJ: Erlbaum.

Betz, N. E., & Fitzgerald, L. F. (1987). *The career psychology of women.* New York: Academic Press.

Bingham, R. P., & Ward, C. M. (1994). Career counseling with ethnic minority women. In W. B. Walsh & S. H. Osipow (Eds.), *Career counseling for women* (pp. 165–195). Hillsdale, NJ: Erlbaum.

Brooks, L., & Forrest, L. (1994). Feminism and career counseling. In W. B. Walsh & S. H. Osipow (Eds.). *Career counseling for women* (pp. 87–134). Hillsdale, NJ: Erlbaum.

Chalk, L. M., Meara, N. M., & Day, J. D. (1994). Possible selves and occupational choices. *Journal of Career Assessment, 2,* 364–383.

Collins, P. H. (1991). *Black feminist thought: Knowledge, consciousness, and the politics of empowerment.* New York: Routledge.

Crites, J. O. (1981). *Career counseling: Models, methods and materials.* New York: McGraw-Hill.

Crites, J. O. (1993). *Career Mastery Inventory sourcebook.* Boulder, CO: Crites Career Consultants.

Fitzgerald, L. F., & Crites, J. O. (1980). Toward a career theory of women: What do we know and what do we need to know? *Journal of Counseling Psychology, 27,* 44–62.

Fouad, N. A., & Bingham, R. P. (1995). Career counseling with racial/ethnic minorities. In W. B. Walsh & S. H. Osipow (Eds.), *Handbook of vocational psychology,* (2d ed.) (pp.331–366). Hillsdale, NJ: Erlbaum.

Hackett, G. (1993). Career counseling and psychotherapy: False dichotomies and recommended remedies. *Journal of Career Assessment, 1,* 105–117.

Harmon, L. W., Hansen, J. C., Borgen, F. H., & Hammer, A. L. (1994). *Strong Interest Inventory: Applications and technical guide.* Palo Alto, CA: Consulting Psychologists Press.

Haslam, N., & Baron, J. (1994). Intelligence, personality, and prudence. In R. J. Sternberg & P. Ruzgis (Eds.), *Personality and intelligence* (pp. 32–58). Cambridge, U.K.: Cambridge University Press.

Holland, J. L. (1994, May). *The integration of career theory and practice.* Keynote address presented at career conference, Toward the convergence of career theory and practice, Columbus, OH.

Hoshmand, L. T. (1989). Alternate research paradigms: A review and teaching proposal. *The Counseling Psychologist, 17,* 3–80.

Howard, G. S. (1986). *Dare we develop a human science?* Notre Dame: Academic Publications.

Howard, G. S. (1991). Culture tales: A narrative approach to thinking, cross-cultural psychology and psychotherapy. *American Psychologist, 46,* 188–197.

Howard, G. S., & Conway, C. G. (1986a). Can there be an empirical science of volitional action? *American Psychologist, 41,* 1241–1251.

Howard, G. S., & Conway, C. G. (1986b). The next steps toward a science of agency. *American Psychologist, 42,* 1034–1035.

Howard, G. S., Maerlender, A. C., Myers, P. R., & Curtin, T. D. (1992). In stories we trust: Studies of the validity of autobiographies. *Journal of Counseling Psychology, 39,* 398–405.

Krumboltz, J. D. (1993). Integrating career and personal counseling. *Career Development Quarterly, 42,* 143–148.

McCrae, R. R., & John, O. P. (1992). An introduction to the five factor model and its applications. *Journal of Personality, 52,* 175–215.

Meara, N. M., & Patton, M. J. (1994). Contributions of the working alliance in the practice of career counseling. *Career Development Quarterly, 43,* 161–177.

Meara, N. M., & Schmidt, L. D. (1991). The ethics of researching counseling/psychotherapy processes. In C. E. Watkins & L. J. Schneider (Eds.), *Research in counseling* (pp. 237–259). Hillsdale, NJ: Erlbaum.

Osipow, S. H. (1990). Convergence in theories of career choice and development: Review and prospect. *Journal of Vocational Behavior, 36,* 122–131.

Quintana, S. M. (1995). Acculturative stress: Latino immigrants and the counseling profession. *The Counseling Psychologist, 23,* 68–73.

Smart, J. F., & Smart, D. W. (1995). Acculturative stress: The experience of the Hispanic immigrant. *The Counseling Psychologist, 23,* 25–42.

Spokane, A. R. (1991). *Career intervention.* Boston: Allyn & Bacon.

Walsh, W. B., Craik, K., & Price, R. (1992). Person-environment psychology: A summary and commentary. In W. B. Walsh, K. Craik, and R. Price (Eds.), *Person-environment psychology: Models and perspectives* (pp. 243–269). Hillsdale, NJ: Erlbaum.

Ward, C. M., & Bingham, R. P. (1993). Career assessment of ethnic minority women. *Journal of Career Assessment, 1,* 246–257.

Zytowski, D. G. (1978). Review of the career maturity inventory. In O. K. Buros (Ed.), *8th Mental measurements yearbook* (pp. 1565–1567). Highland Park, NJ: Gryphon Press.

PART FOUR

INNOVATIONS IN CAREER COUNSELING

THE FOUR CHAPTERS in Part 4 concentrate on criticisms of and new directions for the contemporary practice of career intervention. In Chapter 21, Leong attributes the surface problems in theory-practice integration to deep structure. He identifies the structure's underlying factors as boundaries, cultures, and complexities. After describing the problems caused by boundaries, he proposes that one way to transcend boundaries is to begin a systematic program of integration that is problem based rather than discipline based or theory based. Culture, the second factor in Leong's analysis of deep structure, involves a shared set of values and beliefs. Leong proposes that vocational psychology and career counseling are separate cultures and that the attendant culture differences promote the gap between theory/research and practice. Moreover, clients come from their own cultures, which explains, in part, why the work of career counselors is not perceived as useful by a large segment of the population in the United States. Leong identifies the third deeper factor in the contemporary split between theory and practice as the lack of complexity in career theories. Revision must include nonlinear, systematic interactions. Leong offers three simple yet sagacious strategies for addressing these three factors and healing the rift between theory and practice. He asks researchers and practitioners to remain in contact with each other, communicate, and collaborate.

In Chapter 22, Richardson builds on her prior argument that career psychologists reposition themselves to focus on the role of work in people's lives and considers the implications for career counseling practitioners of this shift in focus from career to work. Following an analysis of false splits between normal and pathological functioning and the location of the vocational self in the occupational structure, she suggests that career counseling be reconceptualized as counseling/psychotherapy with a specialty in work, jobs, and career. She bolsters this proposal by explaining that it would (a) place emphasis on the counseling process rather than career content, (b) eschew distinctions concerning health and psychopathology and instead view people from a developmental and contextual frame, (c) focus on the centrality of work in people's lives, and (d) reduce the middle-class bias implicit in career by acknowledging both jobs and careers. She closes by recommending a future agenda for the practice of counseling/psychotherapy with a specialty in work, jobs, and career.

In Chapter 23, Young and Valach propose action theory as a postmodern alternative for practice in the field of career counseling because action theory addresses the need for greater convergence of theory and practice. They discuss how postmodernism has contributed to the call for addressing the disjunction between career theory and practice. Founded on a constructionist epistemology, action theory responds to this call with a conceptual framework for several alternatives to career theory and contemporary practice, including narrative, hermeneutic, and ecology models for clarifying the work that counselors and clients do together. They then discuss the constructionist epistemology on which action theory rests and provide some explication of the concepts of action relevant to career counseling, including the place of interpretation and narrative, the role of emotions, and the joint action of client and counselor in career counseling. Following the action-theoretical perspective, career research, theory, and practice are closely related, allowing easy transition from one to the other. Moreover, the counselor's conceptions of the client become more accessible to research because they are part of the theory itself.

In the final chapter in this section, Collin assumes the task of discussant for the three chapters in this section. She integrates the common elements in the chapters by considering the nature of practice and the relationships between theorists/researchers, practitioners, and their clients. She then discusses the nature of contexts and why the changing context of career services demands that counselors innovate their models and methods. Clients are having new experiences that are not amenable to traditional theoretical analysis and their problems are not amenable to traditional solutions. She proposes a broader and more radical approach to prompting the collaboration between researchers and practitioners. In particular, she presents a model for "reflective practice" and action research that create a "virtuous circle"—in contrast to a vicious circle—of ambidirectional relationships between researchers/theorists, practitioners, and clients—all of whom live in a changing context.

CHAPTER TWENTY-ONE

Challenges to Career Counseling
Boundaries, Cultures, and Complexity

Frederick T. L. Leong
Ohio State University

THE PROBLEMS THAT face the fields of vocational psychology and career counseling are quite numerous. Each one of us, if asked, could produce our own list. Let me propose that these and other problems, if we can borrow from Chomsky's (1965) work on psycholinguistics, are surface structures. I believe that there are some factors that underlie these surface structure problems. These underlying factors, like those in Chomsky's (1965) transformational grammar, are deep structures that require a closer look in order for us to identify them. I believe that there are several deep structures underlying the problems facing the fields of vocational psychology and career counseling. The challenges facing the field lie in these deep structures. In this chapter, I will discuss three of them: boundaries, cultures, and complexity. The chapter concludes with some strategies that address these challenges.

BOUNDARIES

In discussing the challenge of boundaries, I would like to begin with a poem by Robert Frost, "The Mending Wall" (Lathem, 1969, pp. 33–34):

"Something there is that doesn't love a wall,
That sends the frozen-ground-swell under it
And spills the upper boulders in the sun,
And makes gaps even two can pass abreast....
There where it is we do not need the wall:

He is all pine and I am apple orchard.
My apple trees will never get across
And eat the cones under his pines, I tell him.
He only says, 'Good fences make good neighbors.'

Spring is the mischief in me, and I wonder
If I could put a notion in his head:
'Why do they make good neighbors? Isn't it
Where there are cows? But here there are no cows.
Before I built a wall I'd ask to know
What I was walling in or walling out,
And to whom I was like to give offense.
Something there is that doesn't love a wall,
That wants it down.'

He moves in darkness as it seems to me,
Not of woods only and the shade of trees.
He will not go behind his father's saying,
And he likes having thought of it so well
He says again, 'Good fences make good neighbors.' "

Origins and Functions of Boundaries

An examination of the origins and functions of boundaries reveal that they are usually developed to protect, keep outgroup members out, define territory, and minimize conflict. Boundaries, whether they be theoretical, disciplinary, or cultural, serve to provide a comfortable place for like-minded, same sex, same race, or same social class individuals to socialize and interact. These benefits usually have costs. The costs include the disadvantages of groupthink (Janis, 1982). Schneider (1987) warned of the stagnation and organizational decline that often results from the Attraction-Selection-Attrition (ASA) cycle. Through this ASA cycle, a group, an organization, or a scientific discipline becomes more and more homogenous in terms of its ideas, outlook, and values, so that eventually there is no growth in that unit.

I do not mean to imply that counselors need to lead a revolution to remove all boundaries. Like Frost, I am only suggesting that fences are necessary when there are cows and also when there are no cows: "Before I built a wall I'd ask to know / What I was walling in or walling out." Fences keep strangers and intruders out, but they also keep friends out. To meet this challenge of boundaries, it is essential that vocational psychologists and career counselors examine their boundaries to determine how much of the wall between them is really necessary and how much of the wall is simply a refusal to go "behind our fathers sayings" and the safety and certainty provided by that wall.

Although it is not quite that simple, I believe that it is creation and maintenance of racial boundaries, both in our country and elsewhere in the world, that have created much conflict and unnecessary suffering. It is the creation and maintenance of rigid ethnic and cultural boundaries that have contributed to the recent problems in Bosnia and Rwanda. Although it is always useful to keep an eye on all the boundaries that we inhabit, for our present purpose, I propose that it is the rigid boundaries between the science of vocational psychology and the practice of career counseling that is most in need of examination. The two fields are separated by a wall, a wall that divides two cultures. On the one hand, most vocational psychologists are members of the Counseling Psychology Division in the American Psychological Association, whereas most career counselors are members of the National Career Development Association in the American Counseling Association. Members of these two groups, or cultures, attend different conferences, read different journals (the *Journal of Counseling Psychology* and *Journal of Vocational Behavior* for the former and *Career Development Quarterly* and *Journal of Counseling and Development* for the latter) and exist in different environments (academia for the former and community agencies or private practice for the latter).

It is no accident that the most popular and most successful career counseling models, as exemplified by Holland's model, tend to be created by creative individuals in boundary-spanning roles. Research from industrial and organizational psychology tells us that boundary-spanning roles are particularly stressful because they involve serving two masters who may not always agree with each other. Yet it is precisely in the intersections between areas that creative solutions often arise. Holland (1994) began developing his hexagonal model precisely because the *Dictionary of Occupational Titles* was too massive and overwhelming for him to use with his clients. It is quite unlikely that a career counselor with no theoretical interests would have developed an alternative occupational classification system. It is equally unlikely that a theoretician (e.g., Anne Roe) would have developed a system that is as practical and user friendly as Holland's.

Problems Created by Boundaries

Boundaries provide a sense of coherence, yet they also prevent integration. In the narrowness of our bounded reality, we feel safe and competent, yet sometimes we also do a disservice to our clients. Besides the boundaries separating theorists and practitioners, the rigid boundaries between different theoretical orientations among both theorists and practitioners often create additional problems for clients. Consider the following quote from a patient who recently posted these observations in an E-mail network focused on psychiatry and abnormal psychology. The quote is not directly related to career counseling and vocational psychology; however, the message is relevant:

> Thanks for posting that very sane and succinct statement of a multifactoral perspective on the etiology of and treatment interventions for mental illness. As a person on the consumer side of mental health care, I think that this is very important. Although all disciplines have their follies, this division of the mental health field into various intransigent camps organized around one unicausal model or another has always made the field look particularly primitive. The intransigence of the various groups of theorists

and practitioners often does direct harm to patients, in my experience. Persons with mental health problems are frequently very frightened, and prominent among their presenting symptoms is often an inability to focus, concentrate, or think clearly. In the still-stigmatized act of reaching out for care, the patient is already doing enough. Having to take sides within the mental health field between practitioners who are deeply divided and often quite hostile to forms of treatment other than their own is really asking way too much. But many, many patients are put in that position. And, frankly, many practitioners act in a manner that indicates such hostility toward and fear of other kinds of practitioners that I can only describe it as pathological behavior.... In the real world, not only are different forms of treatment better suited to different types of conditions but this also even varies from patient to patient. The best practitioners I have had were ones that had a multicausal approach to treatment or at least had strong ties to other practitioners in subdivisions of mental health other than their own.

Another major boundary problem is created by the fact that most vocational psychologists are trained within the field of counseling psychology. In a recent paper, Osipow (1993) commented on the disciplinary provincialism evident in our field. Although there are exceptions, counseling psychologists, and this includes vocational psychologists, tend not to use or keep informed about the theoretical developments in other areas of psychology. The boundaries that define us as vocational psychologists also serve to limit us from opportunities for synergistic integration with other areas of psychology, sociology, and anthropology. Let me just cite one example of this problem of boundary-induced myopia. If one were to examine the major areas of psychology that deal with human problems, it will become readily apparent that fields such as clinical psychology, school psychology, and community psychology recognize the importance of prevention as an important alternative to remedial intervention. Yet despite its direct relevance for vocational psychology, the area of prevention has been relatively ignored by our field. Surely, the prevention of vocational and career problems needs to occupy a major position in our theoretical efforts and intervention programs. For me, the absence of such a concerted effort only reveals the severity of our boundary problem.

Let me end my observations about boundaries with an example from medical school education. For many, many generations, medical students were taught the basic disciplines that formed the foundations of their practice—anatomy, physiology, biochemistry, and so on. Yet, throughout this wonderful training, there were few opportunities to integrate the knowledge from these basic disciplines into a meaningful whole to aid the medical student in facing his or her central concern, namely, the patient. Over a decade ago, some medical schools, when faced with the rigidities of the disciplinary approach to medical education, found the courage to ask what it is that they were "walling in or walling out." These institutions began exploring the use of a problem-based learning approach in medical education. Instead of memorizing massive amounts of information from each of the basic disciplines, medical students were given real-life problems presented by patients and were told to learn all they could about the problem, its etiology, manifestation, course, outcome, and recommended treatment. To give you an idea of the success of this problem-based learning approach to medical education, I would like to share a few numbers from a recent medline search I conducted on this topic. From 1975 to 1979, there were two articles related to problem-based learning. From 1980 to 1985, there were eight articles. From 1986 to 1990, the number of articles was 24, and from 1991 to 1994, the number of articles jumped to 94.

Clearly, there is a need to transcend some of our boundaries and begin a systematic program of integration that is problem based rather than discipline based or theory based. As Charcot has aptly observed so long ago, "Theory is good, but it has never stopped anything from existing." It is time that our respective groups begin addressing existing problems with a spirit of collaboration.

CULTURES

Moving onto the second deep structure, let me quote from Ruth Benedict's (1934) classic book, *Patterns of Culture,* and her observations about the central role of culture, or what she refers to as *customs,* in human behavior. The quote, while quite sexist in its use of the language of the time, nevertheless contains some very important insights.

> No man ever looks at the world with pristine eyes. He sees it edited by a definite set of customs and institutions and ways of thinking. Even in his philosophical probings he cannot go behind these stereotypes; his very concepts of the true and the false will still have reference to his particular traditional customs.... From the moment of his birth the customs into which he is born shape his experience and behaviour. By the time he can talk, he is the little creature of his culture, and by the time he is grown and able to take part in its activities, its habits are his habits, its beliefs his beliefs, its impossibilities his impossibilities. Every child that is born into his group will share them with him, and no child born into one on the opposite side of the globe can ever achieve the thousandth part. There is no social problem it is more incumbent upon us to understand than this of the role of custom. Until we are intelligent as to its laws and varieties, the main complicating facts of human life must remain unintelligible. (pp. 2–3)

On one hand, it is quite discouraging that Benedict's observation about the centrality of culture to our full understanding of human behavior has gone relatively unheeded in mainstream psychology. On the other hand, there has been a confluence of several factors, including the changing demographics in U.S. society, that make such a position no longer tenable, and the current decade is ripe for those of us who have always tried to echo Benedict's observations. For the current purpose, I would like to use Brislin's (1990) definition of culture:

> Culture refers to the widely shared ideals, values, formation and uses of categories, assumptions about life, and goal-directed activities that become unconsciously or subconsciously accepted as "right" and "correct" by people who identify themselves as members of a society.... (p. 11)

With this definition in mind, I would like to point out that I am referring to two levels of culture. On the first level, our disciplines of counseling psychology, vocational psychology, or career counseling are each in and of themselves a separate culture, with their own shared set of values, beliefs, and goals. On the second level, I am referring to the culture of participants in the career counseling enterprise, namely, the researchers, counselors, clients, and test publishers.

Regarding the first level of culture that we are using in the current discussion, the major implication is that we need to examine the various groups and disciplines involved in the career counseling enterprise as cultural institutions. As cultural institutions, these groups and disciplines possess specific beliefs about what is the right and wrong way of doing things. To the extent that each discipline is a separate culture and has its own set of boundaries, then the problems created by boundaries that have been discussed above also apply here. My proposition is that just as it is valuable to study the psychology of scientists in order to understand the science of psychology, it is equally valuable to examine the social and cultural psychology associated with the career counseling enterprise. For example, surely it is no accident that counseling psychology's primary focus on initial career choice as a central problem from the wide spectrum of vocational psychology issues seems to parallel the fact that most counseling psychologists with vocational psychology interests are located in colleges and universities. Furthermore, much of the research that informs career counseling practice seems to be funded by agencies that have vested interests in this group of American youth (e.g., the American College Testing Service). Is it any wonder, then, that other groups have begun questioning why we have ignored the noncollege-bound youths?

Regarding the second level of culture, namely, the culture of our clients, as Fitzgerald and Betz (1994) have pointed out, we have provided primarily lip service to culture as a major moderator in both our theories and our practice. Besides recognizing that our specialties and our disciplines are cultural institutions, it is also time that we recognize that all of our clients are cultural beings, as Helms (1994) has so aptly stated in the title of her latest book, *A Race Is a Nice Thing to Have*.

Space does not permit us to provide a detailed exposition of all the ways in which culture may serve as a moderating variable in the career counseling enterprise. Such information is readily available elsewhere (e.g., Fitzgerald & Betz, 1994; Leong, 1995). Let me instead relate a story that illustrates what I believe will be an increasing trend, namely, a gradual shift in all spheres of the American experience from ethnocentrism to cultural enlightenment. As most of you know, Dunnette and his colleagues at the University of Minnesota recently prepared a second edition of their classic *Handbook of Industrial and Organizational Psychology*. The second edition of the Handbook was originally going to consist of three massive volumes, with each volume ranging from 700 to 1,000 pages. Within this scheme, Dunnette had originally asked Triandis, an eminent cross-cultural psychologist, to prepare a chapter on cross-cultural issues in industrial and organizational psy-chology for the third volume. Let us stop and think about this for a moment: 40 chapters and close to 2,500 pages on how industrial and organizational psychology is carried out in the United States and one chapter or approximately 60 pages on how the rest of the world goes about doing industrial and organizational psychology. To his credit, Dunnette (see preface to Triandis, Dunnette, & Hough, 1994) recognized his own "naive decision" and decided to publish a fourth volume devoted to cross-cultural issues in industrial and organizational psychology. It is time that we as vocational psychologists and career counselors also recognize our own shortsightedness and ethnocentrism.

Keeping with the psycholinguistic theme (Chomsky, 1965) with which I began this chapter, let me refer to the Whorfian (1956) hypothesis, which maintains that language influences thought. You all have probably heard the story that whereas Americans in the United States have only a few terms to describe snow, the Inuits have over a dozen terms to describe it. Just as language influences thought, let me formalize Benedict's observation and propose a "cultural hypothesis," namely, that culture influences behavior. Surely, the role of the family is qualitatively different for a culture such as can be found in China, where there are over 35 unique terms for members of the extended family in comparison to the White European culture that has only a few unique terms for relatives. The challenge for vocational psychology and career counseling is how to incorporate this cultural hypothesis into its theories and practice.

To summarize, the work of career counselors and vocational psychologists will continue to have relevance to only a small portion of our population until and unless they begin to recognize that clients and potential clients are cultural beings and that they too, as psychologists and counselors, are cultural beings that also belong to cultural institutions that both guide and limit their effectiveness. If what I am describing does not seem to be making sense, pause for a moment and ponder how you would, if you could, explain what water is to a goldfish. In some sense, your culture is to you what water is to the goldfish: You are both constantly surrounded by it but rarely give it much thought. More than 30 years ago, Wrenn (1962) ably discussed the dangers of culturally encapsulated counselors, but it is sometimes useful to revisit these issues (e.g., see Wrenn, 1985).

COMPLEXITY

As a person who believes in crossing boundaries and transcending our "customary ways" in the way that Ruth Benedict conceptualized customs, I bring to you some ideas from the emerging science of complexity. My final proposition is that our dominant paradigms limit us because they are based on simple nondynamic and reductionistic models of human behavior. What I would like to offer has been referred to as "Visions of the Whole" (Waldrop, 1992). It is time to recognize that different disciplines and specialties, like the proverbial blind men of Hindustan, have held on too long to parts of the elephant with the assumption that they, and only they, have a true picture of the beast. The next quote, which is about complexity, appears in Waldrop's (1992) book, *Complexity: The Emerging Science on the Edge of Order and Chaos:*

> Finally, every one of these complex, self-organizing, adaptive systems possesses a kind of dynamism that makes them qualitatively different from static objects such as computer chips or snowflakes, which are merely complicated. Complex systems are more spontaneous, more disorderly, more alive than that.

A large part of counselors' disillusionment with career theories is that the theories based on reductionistic science too often fail to capture the richness and complexity of clients' lives. Career theories, in seeking after the academic holy grail of internal validity, have too often ignored the complexity of external or ecological validity. Women and ethnic minority groups have long lamented that the dominant career theories do not capture the totality of their experiences. They repeatedly report that the work environment and the larger society that surrounds them is one in which race matters, culture matters, and gender matters. Theories proposing that career choice and advancement are solely a function of effort and ability are not only naive; they are also wrong. Counselors are not dealing with simple static states but, instead, complex adaptive systems. Those who doubt this argument need only review a few issues of the scholarly journal to see how much of variance the theoretical models account for.

The third challenge facing career psychology and career counseling is to develop new models based on a complexity paradigm. The emerging science of complexity is represented in books such as Waldrop's (1992) *Complexity: The Emerging Science at the Edge of Order and Chaos* and other books such as Lewin's (1994) *Complexity: Life at the Edge of Chaos,* Glick's (1987) *Chaos: Making a New Science,* and Zohar's (1991) *The Quantum Self.* The underlying message within this science of complexity, although there is no one theory, is that researchers are often dealing with complex adaptive systems.

These complex adaptive systems are characterized by a number of features. Typically a complex system is composed of a large number of independent or semi-independent components, which we shall call *agents:* From the point of modeling, it may be necessary to treat the agents as diverse, or they may be similar and treatable as essentially identical. The dynamical behavior of the agents, their interactions with each other, is typically highly nonlinear, for example, the essential features that the environment in which the agents exist are normally determined in large part by their actions and states of other agents. Therefore, it is not possible to understand the system by superimposing the properties of individual components as this system may display emergent macroscopic features not readily predictable from the structure and character of the interactions of the individual agents. Simmons (1993) pointed out that the attributes of complex adaptive systems include the fact that they are often:

- Nonlinear
- Multivariate
- Nonequilibrium
- Open
- Multiple equilibria
- Pattern forming
- Information processing
- Adapting
- Evolving
- Coevolving
- Self-organizing
- Consisting of rugged landscapes

Our theories fail to take into account these emergent and self-organizing properties in complex adaptive systems. All too often our practice and the theories that guide them are based on simple models that are linear, univariate, single equilibrium, and static (e.g., you make a career choice in college and live happily ever after). Vocational psychologists and career counselors need to integrate the science of complexity into their theory and practice—not because it is the latest scientific fad or quick fix but because it more accurately reflects the nature of the phenomena with which they deal. Staying with the status quo of linear reductionistic science would be akin to the young man kneeling under the street lamp looking for his keys. When asked by the police officer where he had lost them, he pointed over to the grassy knoll. The police officer asked, "Then why are you looking under the lamp?" The young man replied, "Because this is where the light is."

Many who write about this new emerging science of complexity discuss large adaptive systems such as star systems, organizations, or even economies, but I would like to propose that each individual is in and of him or herself a complex adaptive system. In a paper I recently presented at the Teachers College Winter Roundtable on Cross-Cultural Counseling and Psychotherapy (Leong, 1994), I proposed an integrative model of cross-cultural counseling based on notions of complexity and on the three components within the Kluckhohn and Murray personality framework. They had observed many, many years ago that the individual personality consists of three interacting components: the universal, the group, and the individual unique elements. In my integrative model, I have proposed that these elements interact in a dynamic, nonlinear, multivariate, open fashion. Furthermore, the client as a complex, adaptive system also engages in a coevolving process with the counselor, another complex adaptive system comprised of the three elements: the universal, group, and individual aspects. I have also argued in that paper that counseling models based on only one of these elements, if presumed to be static, are too limited and doomed to capture only a small portion of the variance in a counseling relationship.

STRATEGIES FOR ADDRESSING THE CHALLENGES

In an important article that delineates the different cultures of science versus practice in psychology, Gelso (1985) has accurately identified the conflicting values of rigor for the scientists and relevance for the practitioner. In applying career theories to career counseling practice, the fundamental challenge is to make the practice of career counseling more scientifically rigorous and the science of vocational psychology more clinically relevant. In this chapter, I have identified three main challenges that serve as obstacles to the integration of career theory and practice: boundaries, cultures, and complexity. I would like to propose three strategies that are important if we are to face these challenges and overcome the obstacles: contact, communication, and collaboration.

Contact

First, given the boundaries that separate the scientists and the practitioners, the primary strategy would be to increase and facilitate regular contact between the two groups. Without this contact, the two groups will remain isolated from each other and continue to seek solutions to only half of the problem. Practitioners would continue to deal with the relevant counseling issues of the day without regard to the empirical foundations of the theories being used. Scientists would continue to pursue the holy grail of internal validity and rigorous causal inference without much progress on external or ecological validity. Regular contact is necessary for both groups to become familiar with the complexity of each other's cultures and the ultimate need for integration.

Communications

Indeed, contact is the prerequisite for the second strategy, communication. Respect and appreciation of each other's issues and concerns can only come about with communication. Although communication may seem like a simplistic solution, there is a great deal more involved than just talking to each other, just as racism can never be eliminated merely by having Whites, African Americans, Asians, Hispanics, and Native Americans talk to each other. Yet without contact and communication, not much progress will be made. Communication is important in identifying the ways in which each side is bounded by its own culture, its competing set of values and reward systems, and its language. Communication is necessary to identify ways to transcend differences in values and language. For example, how can scientists be more clinically relevant in their research and still maintain their allegiance to the scientific method? How can career counselors be more rigorous in evaluating their interventions and still serve their clients given the slow pace of science?

Collaboration

With contact and communication as the foundation, we come to the third strategy, collaboration. If researchers and counselors can spend time together learning about each other's concerns and exploring how they can transcend their boundaries and overcome the centrifugal forces of their respective cultures, they are then ready to attempt an integration of the science and practice of career psychology. This, of course, requires collaboration that would ultimately yield the joint product. The numerous collaborative projects would produce career counseling models that are both clinically relevant and scientifically rigorous.

Although many counselors and psychologists, due to territorial, turf, or guild issues, resent being compared to physicians, I would like to do so anyway. My point is that an integration of career theory and practice would eventually look like the field of medicine. Few of us would support the channeling of public funds for medical research that does not address relevant clinical problems. Even fewer of us would go to physicians who did not keep up with the latest scientific developments and advances in their specialties. The success of modern medicine in society is due in large part to the seamless integration of science and practice within that profession. For example, Ohio State University's Medical School has researchers who conduct multimillion dollar research projects on cancer. They share the same office space and serve on multidisciplinary teams with frontline physicians who treat the cancer patients. The physicians support the research because the effectiveness of their future treatments depends on it. Furthermore, the researchers who alternate back and forth between their laboratories and the consulting rooms respect the physicians and the complex issues presented to them by patients on a daily basis. The regular contact, communication, and collaboration between scientists and physicians build mutual respect for each other's perspectives and a greater appreciation of the challenges in each other's culture.

In the field of career counseling, what we need are the structural mechanisms for the same regular contact, communication, and collaboration between scientists and practitioners that has made medicine the successful science and profession that it is. We may not have teaching hospitals in medical schools with major research grants, but just about every university has a career counseling service or a counseling center. In those centers, we can begin to foster the regular contact, communication, and collaboration between researchers and practitioners. Of course, such changes would occur only if enough counselors and researchers accept this vision of how to integrate career theory and practice. This, of course, would require us to "go behind our father's saying."

I would like to end with another story: Gretchen Alexander was a courageous woman who refused to allow her blindness to limit her life experiences. She mastered archery, golf, softball, sailing, and water skiing as well as a number of other activities her sighted friends had yet to learn. When she spoke to a group of high school students about her achievements, one student asked if there was anything she wouldn't try. She answered, "I've decided never to try skydiving...it would scare the heck out of my dog." I hope that we have the same courage to face our challenges as Gretchen Alexander had in facing hers.

REFERENCES

Benedict, R. (1934). *Patterns of culture*. New York: Houghton Mifflin.

Brislin, R. (1990). *Applied cross-cultural psychology*. Beverly Hills, CA: SAGE.

Chomsky, N. (1965). *Aspects of the theory of syntax*. Cambridge, MA: MIT Press.

Fitzgerald, L. F., & Betz, N. E. (1994). Career development in cultural context: The role of gender, race, class, and sexual orientation. In M. L. Savickas & R. W. Lent (Eds.), *Convergence in career development theories* (pp. 103–117). Palo Alto, CA: Davies-Black Publishing.

Gelso, C. (1985). Rigor, relevance, and counseling research: On the need to maintain our course between Scylla and Charybdis. *Journal of Counseling and Development, 63,* 551–553.

Glick, J. (1987). *Chaos: Making of a new science*. New York: Viking Penguin.

Helms, J. (1994). *A Race is a Nice Thing to Have*. Kansas City, MO: Content Communications.

Holland, J. L. (1994). Separate but unequal is better. In M. L. Savickas & R. W. Lent (Eds.), *Convergence in career development theories: Implications for science and practice* (pp. 45–51). Palo Alto, CA: Davies-Black Publishing.

Janis, I. L. (1982). *Groupthink*. (2d ed.). Boston: Houghton Mifflin.

Lathem, E. C. (1969). *The poetry of Robert Frost*. New York: Holt, Rinehart & Winston.

Leong, F. T. L. (1994, February). *An integrative model for analyzing cross-cultural counseling relationships*. Paper presented at the Annual Teachers College Winter Roundtable on Cross-Cultural Counseling and Psychotherapy, Teachers College, Columbia University, New York.

Leong, F. T. L. (Ed.). (1995). *Career development and vocational behavior of racial and ethnic minorities*. Hillsdale, NJ: Erlbaum.

Lewin, R. (1994). *Complexity: Life at the edge of chaos*. New York: Macmillan.

Osipow, S. H. (1993, August). *Toward mainstreaming the study of career psychology: Overcoming the Rodney Dangerfield effect*. Paper presented at the Third International Symposium on Career Development, International Association of Applied Psychology, University of Toronto, Ottawa, Canada.

Schneider, B. (1987). The people make the place. *Personnel Psychology, 40,* 437–453.

Simmons, L. M. (1993, November). *Complex adaptive systems: Metaphors and models for prevention?* Paper presented at the Center for Substance Abuse Conference on Prevention and Complexity, Baltimore.

Triandis, H. C., Dunnette, M. D., & Hough, L. M. (1994). Preface: *Handbook of Industrial and Organizational Psychology. Vol. 4.* (2d ed.). Palo Alto, CA: Davies-Black Publishing.

Waldrop, M. M. (1992). *Complexity: The emerging science at the edge of order and chaos.* New York: Simon & Schuster.

Whorf, B. L. (1956). *Language, thought, and reality.* New York: Wiley.

Wrenn, C. G. (1962). The culturally encapsulated counselor. *Harvard Education Review, 32,* 444–449.

Wrenn, C. G. (1985). Afterword: The culturally encapsulated counselor revisited. In P. Pedersen (Ed.), *Handbook of cross-cultural counseling and therapy* (pp. 323–329). Westport, CT: Greenwood Press.

Zohar, D. (1991). *The quantum self: Human nature and consciousness defined by the new physics.* New York: Morrow, William and Company.

CHAPTER TWENTY-TWO

From Career Counseling
to Counseling/Psychotherapy
and Work, Jobs, and Career

Mary Sue Richardson
New York University

IN A RECENT article on work in people's lives (Richardson, 1993), I argued that a focus on work rather than career was more appropriate and useful and that it was time to move beyond the theoretical confines of the domain of career development. This line of thinking was developed primarily from the perspective of research and theory. The idea was that research and theory in career development would be much improved if the locus of inquiry was shifted to work. Implicit in that article, as in much of the theoretical and research literature in psychology, is the assumption that theory and research should then somehow be of value to practitioners and that theory and/or research easily translates into implications for practice. Upon closer scrutiny, this assumption appears to be both naive and simplistic. In fact, the relations between theory and practice can be quite conflicting and problematic.

Numerous writers have examined the complex interconnections between research and practice, both in general and in relation to specific areas of inquiry and professional practice such as career development (Hoshmond & Polkinghorne, 1992; Young & Collin, 1992). Much of the current debate revolves around issues of methodology and epistemology and the conflicts between a frequently positivist conception of science and the appropriateness or applicability of theory and research that derives from such a position for practitioners in the human services (Howard, 1985; Koch, 1981; Smith, 1991). It is not the purpose here to review this literature but rather to emphasize that the connections between theory or research and practice are frequently more complex or conflicted than would be expected. The recommendation to shift from career to work represents a fundamental shift, both in the focus for theory development and in the generation of research. To address what this might mean for practice requires that the question be considered from the perspective of practice rather than from the perspective of theory and research. The position here is that implications for practice can best be addressed within the context of practice, taking into account the current issues, controversies, and variations in practice.

To put the matter more simply, this chapter can be read as a response to one of my students who recently told me that as far as she was concerned, my article on work in people's lives was very interesting but not at all relevant to her. She explained that she wants to be a career counselor, thinks there is a need for career counseling, and thought my paper had nothing to say to her with respect to her future practice. Her position, although it could be considered overly simplistic, underlines the frequent gap between theory and practice from the viewpoint of practitioners and the problem of translating theory into practice implications when the context of practice is ignored. What I hope to do in this chapter is to con-sider a shift from career to work from a practice perspective and, in so doing, explore the kinds of shifts this might imply for practice.

THE CURRENT CONTEXT
OF CAREER COUNSELING

Any review of the current career counseling literature reveals a persistent, ongoing, and vocal debate regarding career counseling and personal counseling, with numerous attempts to distinguish these practices, describe their similarities and differences, and, in most cases, attempt to resolve these differences. Most of these attempts to integrate or resolve the differences between the two practices are based on a more holistic understanding of the person that militates against isolating one life role from other roles. Writers following this line of thinking propose terms such as *life design* or *life role counseling* (Brown, 1988; Savickas, 1993), call for simply combining the practices without proposing a new name for such practice (Betz & Corning, 1993), or suggest that these two practices be considered as the ends of a continuum rather than as dichotomies (Super, 1993; Blustein & Spengler, 1995). In this endeavor, Blustein and Spengler have developed the most comprehensive framework to date, drawing on social constructionist thought, systems theory, relational theory, problem-oriented brief psychotherapy, and the importance of context to develop a conceptualization of a domain-sensitive approach to counsel-ing. In this counseling model, the two practices are integrated within a framework that is sensitive to the domain in which problems occur, that is, career or noncareer, and the counselor is capable of intervening across domains as needed.

A second subtheme in the efforts to integrate practices is the acknowledgment of similarities in the process of both personal and career counseling as they are traditionally conceived (Betz & Corning, 1993; Spokane, 1991; Rounds & Tracey,

1990). Savickas (1993), for example, points out that career development theories are not a sufficient basis for career counseling practice and calls for the development of career counseling theory. Others such as Meara and Patton (1994) apply constructs from clinical theory such as the working alliance to career counseling. Although these efforts are valuable, they are superseded by those whose ideas imply a more full-scale integration of theories across career and psychotherapy modalities (Betz & Corning, 1993; Blustein & Spengler, 1995).

A further problem of language and discourse has been noted (Haverkamp & Moore, l993; Krumboltz, 1993; Savickas, 1993). To continue to talk about career and personal counseling, even if one is attempting to integrate these practices, is to continue the separate and dichotomous discourse that has contributed to the problem of a "wall of words," so evocatively described by Savickas (1993, p. 212).

Finally, there are significant historical and social structural barriers to resolving the differences between career and personal counseling. These barriers noted by Subich (1993) include the structure of training and education in which, for example, practica frequently are distinguished in terms of career and personal counseling, and the structure of practice in which service delivery systems separate out career and personal counseling. This context and these forces continue to support a perception of career and personal counseling as separate or different practices in the minds of both practitioners and the consumers of such services.

Recent research documents the split between career counseling and personal counseling in the minds of practitioners. For example, in an examination of the professional aspirations of counseling psychology graduate students, a multidimensional scaling method revealed not only that students are more interested in the general realm of counseling and psychotherapy than in vocationally related work such as career counseling but also that these two domains of professional practice are negatively related (Fitzgerald & Osipow, 1988). Thus, the dichotomous nature of these two practices, in turn, structures the professional identity of future practitioners in the field, which, in turn, constitutes a further barrier to integration.

The debate regarding personal and career counseling, then, is one striking feature of the current career counseling literature and is the context of practice from which the implications of a shift from career to work will be addressed. What I would like to contribute to this debate in this chapter is one analysis of why it is so difficult to integrate these practices. This analysis, which is somewhat similar to the ideas developed by Hackett (1993) regarding false dichotomies, traces the split between career and personal counseling to a series of false splits in conceptions of self and personality that occurred in the history of psychology, counseling psychology, and career counseling. These false splits have pervaded and deeply structured current practice modalities and our thinking about these modalities. In particular, these splits have structured the disjunction between career and personal counseling. In this chapter, I will refer not to personal counseling but to the broader enterprise of counseling and psychotherapy, which is a more general reference for personal counseling. Thus, the disjunction addressed will be that between career counseling and counseling and psychotherapy. The implications of a shift from career to work for practice will be addressed more fruitfully if these false splits can first be resolved.

Following an analysis of the problem, I will propose a new location for the practice of career counseling, as opposed to an integration of career and personal counseling. I hope this new location will enable the field to move beyond dichotomous and separate discourses regarding personal and career counseling.

FALSE SPLITS:
THE PROBLEM OF CAREER COUNSELING

The first false split to be considered is that between normal and pathological personality functioning so well described by Gelso and Fassinger (1992). Once it was accepted that there could be a split between normal and pathological, the normal was considered the appropriate territory for counseling interventions and, in particular, for counseling in relation to vocation and career, and personality or the self in its wholeness and complexity was ignored. Obviously, it was not only counseling psychology that was affected by this false split. The existence of abnormal psychology, with its associated diagnostic categories, attests to the split in psychology as a whole.

This first false split between normal and pathological was followed by a further split of the person or self into domains of functioning. If one could split off the normal from the pathological, why not also split off aspects of the self and the self in the world? An outgrowth of this split was the practice of vocational guidance and counseling that considered the person or self in relation to the occupational domain.

A third and final split was to locate this vocational self in the occupational structure with the concomitant change in terminology from vocation to career (Super, 1957, 1969). Thus, the concept of career split the vocational self even further from any central organizing self by considering it more fully in relation to the occupational structure.

These splits into domains of functioning and the view of the vocational self considered in relation to the occupational structure mirrored the splits between public and private worlds that developed in the 20th century and which were reflected throughout the social sciences (Kanter, 1977; Parson & Bales, 1955; Smelser, 1980). Accordingly, it is essential to understand these false splits between career development theory and career counseling practice and the more person-focused theory and practice of counseling and psychotherapy as part and parcel of this phenomenon throughout the social sciences and contemporary social structure.

The considerable literature in career counseling regarding efforts to bridge the gap that developed between career and personal counseling can essentially be conceived of as efforts to heal these false splits. What I hope to do in this chapter is to contribute to these efforts.

TOWARD A HEALING OF FALSE SPLITS

Normal Versus Pathological

The first split to be addressed is that between the normal and the pathological. This split is found in such ideas as counseling is for normal people, psychotherapy addresses psychopathology, or counselors focus on resources rather than deficits in personality functioning. It is also the split and imbalance mirrored in the complexity of diagnostic manuals generated by a medical model of psychological functioning. This model has generated a highly developed capacity to perceive and develop discourse regarding psychological symptomatology and illness. In contrast, there is a relative paucity of professional discourse relevant to the healthy personality or to healthy components of personality (Gelso & Fassinger, 1992).

In an attempt to move beyond this split and imbalance, I would like to propose a perspective for understanding personality functioning that, for want of a better term, I will call an empathic and contextual one.

The Empathic Perspective.   By *empathic* I am referring to a venerable and rich tradition in counseling, psychotherapy, and psychoanalytic literature—from Rogers (1951, 1980) through Kohut (1959) to current psychoanalytic formulations regarding empathy (Basch, 1983; Feiner & Kiersky, 1994; Hayes, 1994; Lichtenberg, Bornstein, & Silver, 1984). This literature has elucidated the value of the attempt to understand another person from that person's subjective point of view regarding his or her experience in the world. Empathic understanding seeks to avoid the imposition of preexisting categories of thought, including diagnostic labels, metapsychological constructs, or any other a priori categories that might interfere with understanding. To listen empathically is to enable the fullest possible symbolic expression of the meanings of experience generated by the person who is the focus of understanding—in this case, the client.

To elaborate further on what is meant here by an empathic perspective, current literature in psychoanalysis is relevant. The investigation of the interpersonal dynamics in a therapeutic situation is, perhaps, most richly developed in this domain. In this literature, there is increasing recognition of what has been called intersubjectivity by writers such as Aron (1992), Atwood and Stolorow (1984), Benjamin (1990), Hoffman (1991), and Stolorow (1991). While the construct of intersubjectivity may differ as it is developed by different theorists, it essentially connotes that the meanings of experience, in fact, the experience itself, is not so much discovered as coconstructed by the partners in a therapeutic dialogue. As such, the idea that a person can know another's reality or experience without in some way "contaminating" it with his or her own subjective experience, ways of relating, and approaches to organizing experience and interactions with others is naive. I have placed quotation marks around the word *contaminating* to indicate the point of view of some (Aron, 1992; Hoffman, 1991; Gill, 1983) that it is important to keep the client's experience at the center of inquiry without undue or unwanted influence by the therapist. Others (Atwood & Stolorow, 1984; Stolorow, 1991) are more accepting of the mutual coconstruction of the counseling process and the client narrative and consider empathy to be a process for understanding the client in counseling and psychotherapy that inevitably is fully colored by and contextualized in the interpersonal (i.e., intersubjective) interaction that occurs between the client and the counselor or therapist.

In this intersubjective empathic process, I would propose that categories of normality and pathology are more frequently barriers to therapeutic understanding and progress than facilitative, whether these categories are used by the client or the counselor. Although I have no evidence to cite in support of this belief, it is open to empirical scrutiny and would be a valuable and interesting line of investigation to pursue. At the very least, it seems legitimate at this point to propose that the complexity of human behavior is dangerously oversimplified by most conceptions of the normal and the pathological and that therapeutic work with people of all types and dispositions will be enhanced if the split between normal and pathological recedes in importance.

This position does not seek to deny that there may be cases and circumstances in which considerations of and categories of normality and pathology are both useful and helpful. Rather, it seeks to enlarge our capacity to understand the meanings of behavior, including symptomatic behavior beyond these categories. From this perspective, for example, a migraine headache, frequently considered a psychosomatic symptom, is viewed as the best possible way a person might have for dealing with what otherwise would be a situation of overwhelming rage and/or fear. Similarly, a sexual enactment that some might consider perverse can be seen as a way to maintain some level of personality integration in the face of overwhelming affect (McDougall, 1985), and bulimia can be seen as a creative and constructive attempt by the mind to forestall a psychic disaster, what Hamburg (1989) refers to as a falling together as opposed to a falling apart.

The Contextual Perspective. The *contextual* component of this perspective is a further elaboration of intersubjectivity. It refers to an understanding of people's behavior as fully embedded in the context of their lives. Stolorow and Atwood (1992) have best articulated this perspective in their analysis of the myth of the isolated mind, a myth that has affected both psychological and psychoanalytic theory and practice. In contrast to this myth, they consider the private experience of human beings to be at all times intimately connected to both the natural (biological) and the social world. For example, a personal and subjective experience of individuality requires a particular sustaining intersubjective context. From this point of view, notions of individual normalcy and pathology also become suspect. Disordered behaviors result from disordered contexts rather than residing in the person. For example, a depressive mood can be seen as a function of a misattuned, uncaring, abusive, or otherwise damaging interpersonal environment, as opposed to being considered a symptom of a depressive illness. An interesting example of the interpersonal contextualization of depression for women is provided in the analysis of depression as loss of self and voice (Jack, 1991).

The contribution of the current context to experience is, in fact, a cornerstone of current thinking regarding the experience of transference in psychoanalysis or psychoanalytically oriented psychotherapy, namely, that any transference feeling or reaction (or countertransference, for that matter) is both a product of the past interpersonal experience of the person in therapy and of the interpersonal and intersubjective experience of the two participants in the current therapeutic dyad (Gill, 1982, 1984; Hoffman, 1991). The power of this interpersonal context to affect and change behavior, including deeply structured components of personality, as in psychoanalytic psychotherapy, is elucidated within models of therapeutic change from Loewald (1960) to more contemporary theorists and clinicians (Slavin & Kriegman, 1992; Stern, 1994; Stolorow, Brandschaft, & Atwood, 1987).

Finally, a clinical perspective characterized by an empathic and contextual understanding dovetails very nicely with current interactional developmental theory, which also attends to the extent to which self, personality, and behavior are shaped along diverse developmental lines and trajectories by the proximate and distal social environment (Bornstein & Bruner, 1989; Bronfenbrenner, 1988; Galatzer-Levy & Cohler, 1993).

Splits of the Person

The second split to be considered is the split of the person or the self into component parts. Although it is true that contexts and environments differ in what they require of people and that aspects of self-functioning are affected by contexts and environments in a multitude of ways, a person also is a dynamic whole who brings to any situation or setting both the unique characteristics and behavioral capacities that might be required by the setting as well as his or her own set of central and personally identifying characteristics. To think otherwise would be, in fact, to reify a kind of multiple personality mentality and to impoverish self-experience in relation to any domain. What a person brings to a work setting or situation may differ over time as well as reflect a more encompassing sense of self-identity. To conceive that it is possible to split a person into domains of functioning is to do a disservice to the clinical and theoretical phenomenon with which counselors work and to advances in understandings of self-phenomena.

Current clinical thinking, in fact, does conceive of multiple selves as well as a central or integrated identity. The range of clinical positions regarding the self can best be seen in Mitchell's (1991) synthetic analysis of the dialectic tension between a coherent and integrated central organizing self versus multiple and emerging selves, with optimal functioning considered to be some kind of balance or creative tension between these poles. One might argue that the tension is between who we are, who we have been, and who we are in the process of becoming—all of which rests on an assumption of continued growth and development through the life span.

From the perspective of postmodernism, the whole question of self and subjectivity, whether it be multiple, or integrated and unitary, is problematic (Flax, 1990; Gergen, 1985; Nicholson, 1990). Postmodernism questions the extent to which any self or subjective experience is a social construction or, more radically, a reflection of the power hierarchies in which people live. This problematizing of self-experience adds yet another wrinkle to any consideration of self or selves.

What is important here is to acknowledge the centrality of self-experience in our theory and in our professional practice with respect to work and career yet move beyond the idea that aspects of self-experience can be considered independent of the whole constellation of self and to locate practice in these domains within the rich and provocative context of contemporary clinical thinking about the self. These ideas are essentially an elaboration of the need to move toward a more holistic conception of the person as developed by writers such as Betz and Corning (1993) and Hackett (1993).

Split Between the Public and Private

Finally, following the split into domains of functioning, a practice that locates work solely in the occupational structure under the rubric of career mirrors the split between public (i.e., career) and private (i.e., personal) in the contemporary social structure. Such a split potentially alienates people from the work they might do in other arenas of their lives; denies the existence of privilege in which some people have opportunities for productive careers while others in our social structure do not; denies changes occurring in our occupational structure in which opportunities for even middle-class and professional lifetime careers have diminished; and promulgates values of self-enhancement and individual achievement at the expense of what I consider to be the more humane and communally oriented values associated with the notion of work (Richardson, 1993). It also fosters an over-identification of persons or selves with their social roles rather than, as in Le's (1993) analysis, considering work to be a personal function through which self or parts of self are expressed in any number of domains. To bring the locus of work out of the occupational structure and to locate it in people's lives—in the wholeness and multiplicity of their self-experience in relation to the roles and structures of their lives but not identified with these roles and structures—would promote the healing of these false splits.

A NEW LOCATION
FOR CAREER COUNSELING

It is my contention that a resolution of these false splits enables a relocation of career counseling within which a shift from career to work takes on a more variegated and multifaceted coloration. The first step in such a relocation is to assert a central belief in the value and importance of work in people's lives as a basic and essential human function and activity. This is a belief that can be traced back to Freud and has been foundational to the practice of career counseling (Wrenn, 1964).

Although this is a belief that has long provided a basis for the study of career development and the practice of career counseling, it is one that demands the renewed attention of researchers, theoreticians, and practitioners. Savickas (1993) suggests that the meaning of work in the 21st century may have more to do with self-development as opposed to a 20th century career ethic. Exploration of the meanings and value of work among all different kinds of people is a critical research agenda for the future. Certainly, these meanings will differ according to differing locations in the social structure such as gender, race, and class. Such an exploration can be conducted from multiple epistemological and theoretical perspectives, including the more recent hermeneutical approaches so well delineated by Savickas (1993), as well as from the perspectives of traditional developmental and clinical theory. In this, the rich literature of vocational psychology that has a venerable history of theory and research relevant to work in the occupational structure has a special contribution to make.

To give several examples here, the research on career decision making (Phillips & Blustein, 1994; Walsh & Osipow, 1988) or identity development and career development (Blustein, Devenis, & Kidney, 1989; Savickas, 1985; Vondracek, 1992) represents lines of inquiry from a more positivistic tradition of research that can provide important information to practitioners about how people make choices in the occupational structure and how these socially situated choices are, for some at least, an important fulcrum for identity development. What I am trying to suggest here is that the meaning of work is a large domain within which there is room for many points of view, both new and old.

The second step is to retire the label of career counseling and refer to this practice as counseling/psychotherapy and work, jobs, and careers. There are several significant features of this label and its related conceptualization. First of all, by placing counseling/psychotherapy first, it fully acknowledges and draws upon the diversity and value of the many theoretical orientations that have been developed to enable people to improve their lives and that are included under any general category of counseling and psychotherapy. It also assumes that across this wide spectrum of theoretical orientations there are people who would identify their practice or part of their practice with this label. If work is indeed such a significant part of people's lives, it is, or should be or could be, a significant focus within and across all kinds of practice and models of intervention. There is absolutely no reason why people interested in and committed to the importance of work in people's lives should be limited to any single theoretical or clinical perspective regarding therapeutic change. Nor is there any reason why people with a specialty in work, jobs, and career might not also have other specialities, for example, sexual abuse and family therapy. Use of the generic term *counseling/psychotherapy* enables practitioners to fill in their own orientations as qualifiers of or as substitutes for the generic label, for example, psychoanalytic psychotherapy and work, jobs, and careers; or cognitive–behavioral therapy and work, jobs, and careers; or educational (learning-based) counseling and work, jobs, and careers.

A second feature of this label is that it is not meant to imply an exclusive focus on work, jobs, or career in counseling/psychotherapy but rather that these aspects of people's lives are included within the practice of counseling/psychotherapy. Work, jobs, and career could or should be integral to both the processes and outcomes of therapeutic intervention. Thus, the *and* in this title essentially refers to a practice that is inclusive of work, jobs, and career.

A third feature of this label is that I have deliberately used both terms, *counseling* and *psychotherapy,* to attempt to communicate a perspective that does not split people into healthy or sick, normal or pathological, but rather that views people from a more holistic empathic and contextual frame of understanding. Issues of work, jobs, and career are critical throughout this frame of understanding.

A fourth significant feature is that I have used all three terms—*work, jobs,* and *career*—to acknowledge that, although work itself is central regardless of location or context, jobs and careers do provide an important context for much of the work in our society. This is not to say that these are the only or even the most important work contexts for many people but that to ignore the occupational structure as a setting for much societal work—and most especially paid work—would be as limiting and unhelpful as to confound work and career. Both jobs and career are included to avoid the middle-class bias implicit in career. The significance of including both of these terms will be further elucidated in the concluding section of this chapter.

A FUTURE AGENDA FOR THE PRACTICE OF COUNSELING/PSYCHOTHERAPY

Obviously, I think that there are many useful outcomes of relocating career counseling fully within and across the professional enterprise of counseling and psychotherapy. This relocation is applicable to all theories of intervention and does not presuppose to consider a priori any method of intervention better or more useful than any other. By putting the model of intervention first, it opens up this practice to a wide range of practitioners. Conversely, it does not limit a practitioner who is particularly interested in issues of work, jobs, and career to any one theory or model of therapeutic intervention. Further, it is expected that practitioners who operate out of diverse models may well have some different contributions to make concerning the role of work in people's lives, the relations between working and other aspects of self-functioning, and the ways in which work, jobs, and career interface with and are involved in the therapeutic effort to improve lives.

Although up to this point I have primarily focused on the problem of career counseling, which, to my mind has become overidentified with and trapped in the occupational structure, it is striking that a very different problem is embedded in the diverse models of intervention incorporated in the current enterprise of counseling and psychotherapy. This problem is the extent to which work, jobs, and career are ignored (Lowman, 1993). Whereas career counseling has seemed too much embedded in the social structure, counseling and psychotherapy, for the most part, are blind to these aspects of the social structure. Blustein and Spengler (in press) and Lowman (1993) have provided current reviews of the neglect of work-related issues and outcomes in the psychotherapy literature.

What is of particular interest here is the extent to which ignoring work and work-related issues in the enterprise of counseling and psychotherapy may function to help maintain the blindness of our theories and models of therapeutic intervention to socially structured inequities such as gender, race, and class. These inequities have powerful effects on the opportunities and resources available through work in the occupational structure. Not attending to the significance of work and work-related issues as central to therapeutic practice may essentially insulate practitioners from these uncomfortable realities.

The blindness referred to here is that which has been analyzed by Sandra Harding (1991), among others, in her considerations of gender, race, and class in the social sciences. It is not just that counseling and psychotherapy needs to be open to and available to diversely located social groups. It is that our theories and models of intervention need to be transformed by an analysis of gender, race, and class. How can a model of intervention designed to improve lives that are actually lived in radically different—both privileged and oppressed—social conditions not take account of these factors in how these lives and the processes of change are conceived? Certainly, the rich and extensive literature on feminist counseling and therapy (Enns, 1992) and the emerging work in cross-cultural counseling and therapy (Atkinson, Morten, & Sue, 1993; Altman,1993) do address these issues. However, it appears to me that a practice of counseling/psychotherapy and work, jobs, and careers is ideally situated to consider the effects of privilege and inequity, as these are so centrally embedded in the occupational structure. Such a practice may provide a valuable perspective from which to develop a more adequate understanding of socially located personality development and socially responsive models and theories of intervention. In other words, attention to issues of work, jobs, and career in efforts to improve people's lives through counseling/psycho-therapy necessarily requires a consideration of people in their social locations and has the potential for opening up the wide range of intervention models to increased social consciousness.

I gratefully acknowledge the assistance of the students in my seminar on Research in Vocational Development, spring 1994, who helped to articulate the ideas in this chapter.

REFERENCES

Altman, N. (1993). Psychoanalysis and the urban poor. *Psychoanalytic Dialogues, 3,* 29–49.
Atkinson, D. R., Morten, G., & Sue, D. W. (1993). *Counseling American minorities: A cross-cultural perspective* (4th ed.). Madison, WI: Brown and Benchmark.

Aron, L. (1992). Interpretation as expression of the analyst's subjectivity. *Psychoanalytic Dialogues, 2,* 475–507.

Atwood, G., & Stolorow, R. (1984). *Structures of subjectivity: Explorations in psychoanalytic phenomenology.* Hillsdale, NJ: Analytic Press.

Basch, M. F. (1983). Empathic understanding: A review of the concept and some theoretical considerations. *Journal of the American Psychoanalytic Association, 31,* 101–126.

Benjamin, J. (1990). An outline of intersubjectivity: The development of recognition. *Psychoanalytic Psychology, 7,* 33–46.

Betz, N. E., & Corning, A. F. (1993). The inseparability of "career" and "personal" counseling. *Career Development Quarterly, 42,* 137–142.

Blustein, D. L., Devenis, L. E., & Kidney, B. A. (1989). Relationship between the identity formation process and career development. *Journal of Counseling Psychology, 2,* 196–202.

Blustein, D. L., & Spengler, P. M. (1995). Personal adjustment: Career counseling and psychotherapy. In W. B. Walsh & S. H. Osipow (Eds.), *Handbook of Vocational Psychology* (2d ed., pp. 295–329). Hillsdale, NJ: Erlbaum.

Bornstein, M. H., & Bruner, J. S. (1989). *Interaction in human development.* Hillsdale, NJ: Erlbaum.

Bronfenbrenner, U. (1988). Interacting systems in human development. Research paradigms: Present and future. In N. Bolger, A. Caspi, G. Bowney, & M. Moorehouse (Eds.), *Persons in context: Developmental processes* (pp. 25–49). Cambridge, UK: Cambridge University Press.

Brown, D. (1988). *Life planning workshop for high school students.* Chapel Hill: University of North Carolina.

Enns, C. Z. (1992). Towards integrating feminist psychotherapy and feminist philosophy. *Professional Psychology: Research and Practice, 23,* 453–466.

Feiner, K., & Kiersky, S. (1994). Empathy: A common ground. *Psychoanalytic Dialogues, 4,* 425–440.

Fitzgerald, L. F., & Osipow, S. H. (1988). We have seen the future, but is it us? The vocational aspirations of graduate students in counseling psychology. *Professional Psychology: Research and Practice, 19,* 575–583.

Flax, J. (1990). *Thinking fragments: Psychoanalysis, feminism, and postmodernism in the contemporary west.* Berkeley: University of California Press.

Galatzer-Levy, R. M., & Cohler, B. J. (1993). *The essential other: A developmental psychology of the self.* New York: Basic Books.

Gelso, C. J., & Fassinger, R. E. (1992). Personality, development, and counseling psychology: Depth, ambivalence, and actualization. *Journal of Counseling Psychology, 39,* 275–298.

Gergen, K. J. (1985). The social constructionist movement in modern psychology. *American Psychologist, 40,* 266–275.

Gill, M. M. (1982). *Analysis of transference.* Vol. 1. Madison, CT: International Universities Press.

Gill, M. (1983). The interpersonal paradigm and the degree of the therapist's involvement. *Contemporary Psychoanalysis, 1,* 200–237.

Gill, M. (1984). Psychoanalysis and psychotherapy: A revision. *International Review of Psychoanalysis, 11,* 161–179.

Hackett, G. (1993). Career counseling and psychotherapy: False dichotomies and recommended remedies. *Journal of Career Assessment, 1,* 105–117.

Hamburg, M. (1989). Bulimia: The construction of a symptom. *Journal of the American Academy of Psychoanalysis, 17,* 131–140.

Harding, S. (1991). *Whose science? Whose knowledge? Thinking from women's lives.* Ithaca, NY: Cornell University Press.

Havercamp, B. E., & Moore, D. (1993). The career-personal dichotomy: Perceptual reality, practical illusion, and workplace integration. *Career Development Quarterly, 42,* 154–160.

Hayes, G. E. (1994). Empathy: A conceptual and clinical deconstruction. *Psychoanalytic Dialogues, 4,* 409–424.

Hoffman, I. Z. (1991). Discussion: Toward a social constructivist view of the psychoanalytic situation. *Psychoanalytic Dialogues, 1,* 74–105.

Hoshmond, L. T., & Polkinghorne, D. E. (1992). Redefining the science-practice relationship and professional training. *American Psychologist, 47,* 55–66.

Howard, G. S. (1985). Can research in the human sciences become more relevant to practice? *Journal of Counseling and Development, 63,* 539–44.

Jack, D. C. (1991). *Silencing the self: Women and depression.* Cambridge, MA: Harvard University Press.

Kanter, R. M. (1977). *Work and family in the United States: A critical review and agenda for research and policy.* New York: Russell Sage.

Koch, S. (1981). The nature and limits of psychological knowledge: Lessons of a century qua "science." *American Psychologist, 36,* 257–269.

Kohut, H. (1959). Introspection, empathy, and psychoanalysis: An examination of the relationship between mode of observation and theory. *Journal of the American Psychoanalytic Association, 7,* 459–483.

Krumboltz, J. (1993). Integrating career and personal counseling. *Career Development Quarterly, 42,* 143–148.

Le, C. (1993). *The American dream: From cultural restraint to individual freedom.* Unpublished manuscript. New York University, Counseling Psychology Program.

Lichtenberg, J., Bornstein, M., & Silver, D. (Eds.). (1984). *Empathy I.* Hillsdale, NJ: Analytic Press.

Loewald, H. (1960). On the therapeutic action of psychoanalysis. *International Journal of Psychoanalysis, 58,* 463–472.

Lowman, R. L. (1993). *Counseling and psychotherapy of work dysfunction.* Washington, DC: American Psychological Association.

McDougall, J. (1985). *Theatres of the mind: Illusion and truth on the psychoanalytic stage.* New York: Basic Books.

Meara, N. M., & Patton, M. J. (1994). Contribution of the working alliance in the practice of career counseling. *Career Development Quarterly, 43,* 161–178

Mitchell, S. A. (1991). Contemporary perspectives on self: Toward an integration. *Psychoanalytic Dialogues, 1,* 121–148.

Nicholson, L. J. (Ed.). (1990). *Feminism/postmodernism.* New York: Routledge.

Parson, T., & Bales, R. F. (1955). *Family, socialization and interaction process.* New York: Free Press.

Phillips, S. D., & Blustein, D. L. (1994). Readiness for career choices: Planning, exploring, and deciding. *Career Development Quarterly, 43,* 63–83.

Richardson, M. S. (1993). Work in people's lives: A location for counseling psychologists. *Journal of Counseling Psychology, 40,* 425–433.

Rogers, C. R. (1951). *Client-centered therapy*. Boston: Houghton Mifflin.

Rogers, C. R. (1980). *A way of being*. Boston: Houghton Mifflin.

Rounds, J. B., & Tracey, T. J. (1990). From trait and factor to person-environment fit counseling: Theory and process. In W.B. Walsh & S.H. Osipow (Eds.), *Career counseling: Contemporary topics in vocational psychology* (pp. 1–44). Hillsdale, NJ: Erlbaum.

Savickas, M. L. (1985). Identity in vocational development. *Journal of Vocational Behavior, 27*, 329–337.

Savickas, M. L. (1993). Career counseling in the postmodern era. *Journal of Cognitive Psychotherapy: An International Quarterly, 7*, 205–215.

Slavin, M. O., & Kriegman, D. (1992). *The adaptive design of the human psyche: Psychoanalysis, evolutionary biology, and the therapeutic process*. New York: Guilford Press.

Smelser, N. J. (1980). Issues in the study of work and love in adulthood. In N. J. Smelser and H. E. Erickson (Eds.), *Themes of work and love in adulthood* (pp. 1–26). Cambridge, MA: Harvard University Press.

Smith, M. B. (1991). Psychology and the decline of positivism. In R. Jessor (Ed.), *Perspectives on behavioral science: The Colorado lectures* (pp. 53–69). Boulder, CO: Westview.

Spokane, A. R. (1991). *Career and intervention*. Englewood Cliffs, NJ: Prentice Hall.

Stern, S. (1994). Needed relationships and repeated relationships: An integrated relational perspective. *Psychoanalytic Dialogues, 4*, 317–345.

Stolorow, R. D. (1991). The intersubjective context of intrapsychic experience: A decade of psychoanalytic inquiry, *Psychoanalytic Inquiry, 11*, 171–184.

Stolorow, R. D., & Atwood, G. E. (1992). *Contexts of being: The intersubjective foundations of psychological life*. Hillsdale, NJ: Analytic Press.

Stolorow, R., Brandschaft, B., & Atwood, G. (1987). *Psychoanalytic treatment*. Hillsdale, NJ: Analytic Press.

Subich, L. (1993). How personal is career counseling? *The Career Development Quarterly, 42*, 129–131.

Super, D. E. (1957). *The psychology of careers*. New York: Harper.

Super, D. E. (1969). Vocational development theory: Persons, positions, and processes. *The Counseling Psychologist, 1*, 2–9.

Super, D. E. (1993). The two faces of counseling: Or is it three? *Career Development Quarterly, 42*, 132–142.

Vondracek, F. W. (1992). The construct of identity and its use in career theory and research. *Career Development Quarterly, 41*, 130–144.

Walsh, W. B., & Osipow, S. H. (Eds.). (1988). *Career decision-making*. Hillsdale, NJ: Erlbaum.

Wrenn, C. G. (1964). Human values and work in American life. In H. Borow (Ed.), *Man in a world at work* (pp. 24–44). Boston: Houghton Mifflin.

Young, R. A., & Collin, A. (Eds.). (1992). *Interpreting career: Hermeneutic studies of lives in context*. Westport, CT: Praeger/Greenwood.

CHAPTER TWENTY-THREE

Interpretation and Action in Career Counseling

Richard A. Young
University of British Columbia

Lasislav Valach
University of Berne, Switzerland

THE FOCUS OF this handbook, the integration of career theory and practice, provides an important frame of reference for what follows in this chapter. It suggests that career theory and practice could benefit from a better fit, to use a vocational metaphor, or that recent developments suggest that greater integration is being realized. Clearly, this handbook not only reports on but indeed also fosters the convergence between career theory and counseling.

A classical conception of the relation of theory to practice is that theories are developed, empirically tested and refined, and then applied to practice. This conception has been found wanting not only because of the general difficulty of moving between theory and practice and the different purposes many researchers and practitioners have for theories but also because there are several perspectives of career theory and practice that are not always referred to univocally. Four of these perspectives are represented along two continua in Figure 1, the theory-practice continuum and the ordinary experience-formal interventions continuum.

The first quadrant of Figure 1 refers to the many career development theories, of which Super's and Holland's are preeminent. Similarly, there are many career intervention programs and procedures used by practitioners that are represented by the fourth quadrant. Some of these represent efforts to translate career theories directly into operational terms. Others are based more specifically on theories of intervention and counseling, represented in quadrant 2. Walsh and Osipow's (1990) edited text on career counseling represents a number of these theories that serve to mediate between the findings of career theory and research and the work

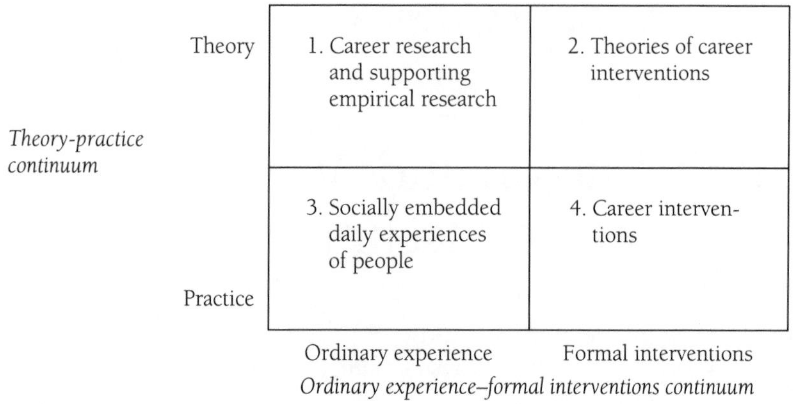

	Theory	1. Career research and supporting empirical research	2. Theories of career interventions
Theory-practice continuum			
	Practice	3. Socially embedded daily experiences of people	4. Career interventions

Ordinary experience   Formal interventions
Ordinary experience–formal interventions continuum

FIGURE 1   Perspectives of Career Psychology on Two Axes

of the practitioner. Notwithstanding the efforts represented in quadrant 2, Spokane (1991) noted that counselors, in their efforts to translate theory into practice, lose much of the sophistication and complexity that theories can offer. Some practitioners have found that career theories and research are of limited value to career counseling practice (Manuele-Adkins, 1992; Rosenbaum, 1989). Citing evidence of Morrow-Bradley and Elliot (1986), Polkinghorne (1992) argues even more pointedly that practitioners in psychology are guided by personal experience and professional consultation rather than by the academy's research findings. Many counselors and practitioners rely on the everyday socially embedded experience of their clients to inform their practice, which is represented in quadrant 3. The thesis of this chapter is to suggest that in looking to the third quadrant as the basis for theory and practice, convergence between career theory and practice will be facilitated. The thesis is based on the assumption that career is a "practice" construct in that it addresses how people construct and resolve problems in their daily lives. It is not primarily a theoretical construct. As a "practice" construct, career does not have a precise meaning; rather, as most counselors know, it is used in meaningful ways, it is given meaning, and it creates meaning.

The search for greater convergence of career theory and practice is precipitated, at least in part, by the rise of postmodernism. Career as an area of theory, research, and practice has a position in both the modernist and postmodernist camps. But to follow Polkinghorne's (1992) argument, as domains of practice, career and other areas of psychology are the basis for the challenge to the modernist program in psychology.

Savickas (1995) identified a number of approaches to career development and counseling, which he labeled as postmodern approaches. Included among these are an emphasis on narrative (Cochran, 1990; Savickas, 1989), context (Vondracek, Lerner, & Schulenberg, 1986), and the social character of career (Young, Valach,

Dillabough, Dover, & Matthes, 1994). Polkinghorne (1992) casts a wider net in the identification of postmodern approaches in psychology. He suggested that the psychology of practice is the template for a postmodern psychology because it is built more on the actual interactions between practitioners and clients and less on the discovered general laws of behavior.

Narrative, hermeneutics, constructionism, and action represent recent shifts to postmodernism that offer counselors and clients approaches that are conceptually and practically useful in understanding career counseling and clarifying the work that counselors and clients do together. Although differences exist among them, the essential themes of these approaches is their concern with the development of meaning in social interaction, the involvement of intersubjectivity, the place of context, and the construction of career. All of these themes are critical to career counseling and are closely associated with the third quadrant of Figure 1.

These approaches—narrative, ecological, hermeneutical, and constructionist— have coalesced in an action theoretical approach (Valach, 1990; Young, Valach, Dillabough, Dover, & Matthes, 1994). Although the relevance of an action theoretical perspective for career conceptualization and analysis was recently argued (Polkinghorne, 1990; Valach, 1990), the full utilization of this approach for career counseling is yet to be achieved in theoretical and practical terms. In this chapter, we will discuss the constructionist epistemology on which this approach is based, provide some explication of the concepts of action relevant to career counseling, including the place of interpretation and narrative, the role of emotions, and the joint action of client and counselor in career counseling.

Constructionism

The approach advocated here relies initially on a distinction Super (1969) made between a psychology of occupations and a psychology of careers. The latter is situated "in the person" and is based on phenomenological experience. Super's (1969) point is that *career* is grounded in the meaning of one's experience. It is based on Husserl's (1931) phenomenology as a philosophy of experience and the meaning of that experience. The link between phenomenology and constructionism is that the meaning or sense one makes of experience reflects and is reflected in one's construct system. A person brings to any event or action a construct system reflective of his or her experiences and history. What constructionism tells us is that people use a variety of constructs to organize and explain their own and others' behavior. Career is one such construct. The meaning we attach to career is constructed through social, historical, and cultural relationships and processes. More important, however, is the task of situating the career construct among the range of possible constructs. Constructs account for a variety of behavior. As these become increasingly complex domains, superordinate constructs such as narrative (Sarbin, 1986), lifestyle (Giddens, 1991), flow of experience (Csikszentmihalyi, 1990), project (Karlsson, 1992), and career are required. Whether people use or are even aware of the term *career* itself is in one sense peripheral to the position put forward here. They may use other constructs. What is important is that we construct social meaning not only within the frame of present and moment-to-moment action but also broadly within the longer frame of one's life. As a superordinate construct, career allows for actions to be connected; accommodates roles and relationships in ecological settings; accounts for effort, goals, plans, and consequences; accommodates internal states such as emotion; and has feedback and feedforward characteristics. Thus, career is a common form of meaning people use to interpret their behavior. As a construct subsumed by career, career development refers to the process that people intentionally engage in to acquire social meaning within the frame of their lives.

Intentional action is another common construct people use to make sense of their behavior (Valach, Cranach, & Kalbermatten, 1988; Wegner, Vallacher, & Dizadji, 1989). As constructs, action and career share a number of the characteristics delineated above, including ecological validity, feedback and feedforward capabilities, and the accommodation of internal states and goals, plans, and consequences. Career has the advantage of linking actions. Linking actions in emergent social systems have already been undertaken, particularly to the structural properties of a social system (Giddens, 1991). However, linking actions with career have not been described. Career and action, then, are interrelated constructs through which people make sense of their lives and the events in their lives acquire meaning.

This constructionist epistemology leads away from two mainstays of vocational psychology—the *person,* as represented by relatively stable traits, and the *environment*, as represented by the characteristics of occupations. It also shifts the focus from efforts to determine characteristics of the external world or the individual psyche that may be related to careers. Rather, attention is given to the process of constructing career through action, which has both practical and symbolic characteristics. The construction process involves discourse, which itself can be considered a career action, and language. Moreover, career can be represented in narrative form, which, as Mancuso (1993) pointed out, involves inference, causality, and consciousness. Career can be considered an overarching construct that serves to frame and organize the complex pattern of intentional actions over longer segments of life.

BASIC CONCEPTS IN ACTION THEORY

Action is the central construct in the approach to career counseling proposed herein. It relies on concepts derived from an action theoretical view in which intentional, goal-directed actions used by agents are conceptualized and analyzed as oriented toward ends and processes (Bullock, 1991; Cranach, Kalbermatten, Indermuehle, & Gugler, 1982). At one level, goal-directed action is represented consciously and, as such, is used by most people as a framework to understand their own and others' behavior. Thus, it is a self-organizing or self-active system.

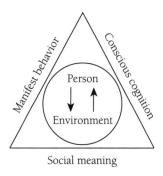

Social meaning

FIGURE 2   Perspectives of Action

Adapted from "The Psychology of Goal-Directed Action" by M. von Cranach, 1982, in *The Analysis of Action: Recent Theoretical and Empirical Advances*, p. 49, edited by M. von Cranach and P. Harré. Copyright 1982 by Cambridge University Press. Reprinted with the permission of Cambridge University Press.

Goal-directed action is central to both career development and counseling psychology. Egan (1994), whose skilled helper model is foundational to much of counseling practice, has identified action, by which he means doing something based on the counseling intervention, as characteristic of the later stages of the counseling process. In Egan's view, action is mainly understood as a consequence of counseling, not as an ongoing process. In contrast, action in this chapter is also understood explicitly as representing the ongoing process of career counseling and as an interpretive construct.

Career development is equally concerned with the person's choice of and action toward goals. Borgen (1991) suggested that all the major career approaches share a belief in active human agency through cognitive processes. The specific characteristics that link action theory, cognition, and social processes in the study of career are discussed herein. Like action, career can also be considered an interpretive construct. Thus, as will be argued, a theory of goal-directed action has heuristic value for the theoretical, conceptual, and methodological issues in the study of career and in counseling practice, thus facilitating the convergence of career theory and practice.

Based on the constructionist epistemology described earlier, we are able to turn to the role of action within career and career counseling. Action is the basis for the construction process, that is, it is through engaging in practical and symbolic action that career and other constructs are formed. Action includes the action of discourse, which is so much a part of counseling and career development. The primacy of action, as Cranach (1992) pointed out, is based on the notion of the self-active system that characterizes higher living systems. As such, the goal-directed actions of these systems are a highly developed form of directed behavior.

Goal-directed action, which involves the person acting in a given situation, can be considered from three perspectives: manifest behavior, conscious cognitions, and social meaning (Cranach, Kalbermatten, Indermuehle, & Gugler, 1982). Figure 2 illustrates these three perspectives of action. Manifest behavior refers to the

Social meaning

FIGURE 3   Perspectives of Action in Career Counseling

Adapted from "The Psychology of Goal-Directed Action" by M. von Cranach, 1982, in *The Analysis of Action: Recent Theoretical and Empirical Advances*, p. 49, edited by M. von Cranach and P. Harré. Copyright 1982 by Cambridge University Press. Reprinted with the permission of Cambridge University Press.

explicit course of a career-relevant action, for example, an application for a job. Conscious cognitions that accompany the observable behavior refer to the thoughts and feelings that the person has while the action occurs. The manifest behavior is related to the conscious cognitions, both as a result of bringing certain cognitions into consciousness and by being influenced by the cognitions. The conscious cognitions are also influenced by social meaning, which represents the meaning of the action to the self and others, and accounts for the influence of society and culture in cognitions and action. These perspectives pertain equally to individual action, group action, and career.

The uniqueness of the action theoretical approach is its efforts to link and make explicit the three perspectives of action. Other recent approaches based on the constructionist epistemology emphasize one or the other perspective, but it is important to recognize the close links among these perspectives. For example, narrative approaches to the study of career (Cochran, 1990) concentrate on the social meaning dimension, whereas the cognitive aspects are delineated by researchers such as Betz and Hackett (1987) and Lent and Hackett (1987).

The same three perspectives apply to career counseling, which, as noted earlier, can be understood as action. The actions, as they apply to career counseling, are illustrated in Figure 3. In this case, the manifest behavior is the observable discourse between the client and the counselor. Both client and counselor have thoughts and feelings about the discourse as it is occurring (conscious cognitions), which serve to steer and direct the action. Finally, both the client and the counselor are subject to the context in which social meaning is made by them and others about this counseling interaction. It is important to note that these are perspectives, that is, ways of viewing action; they are not distinct and separable parts of action that exist independently.

Career-relevant action and the action of career counseling can be considered as subordinate constructs in which career is the superordinate construct. A superordinate construct is one that is used to organize other constructs. As a superordinate construct, career involves (a) a goal or goals, (b) a sequence of events or actions, (c) internal states, including cognitions and emotions, (d) predisposing factors, and (e) a pattern of some type. Action, including the action of career counseling, as a subordinate construct involves (a) context, (b) a goal or goals, (c) social meaning, (d) internal states, and (e) observable behavior. The distance between career as a superordinate construct and action as a subordinate construct may be sufficiently great in a client's or a counselor's experience to render career as a less than helpful construct in career counseling. "Project" or career step may serve as midrange constructs between action and career.

Interpretation in Career Counseling

In career counseling, as in career and action generally, interpretation occurs as part of the interpersonal communication process and is an important part of knowledge and emotion processing. Thus, the cognitive processes involved in career counseling are based on social meaning. In particular situations, interpretation and meaning making, which have been discussed recently regarding career (e.g., Cochran, 1990; Collin & Young, 1986, 1992; Sloan, 1987), are central to the approach that we propose. Collin and Young (1992) identified several characteristics of interpretation in career counseling, including the major role of language, narrative, and meaning, and its context-dependent, relative, and perspectival features. Each is closely connected to human action, which is the subject of career counseling.

Some important assumptions about interpretation included in an action theoretical perspective are, first, people interpret their own and others' behavior as actions, that is, for the most part, behavior is seen as intentional and goal directed; second, people frequently interpret ongoing action as part of some superordinate process such as career; and third, people frequently reinterpret their past actions and career in terms of their present action, and possibly career, thus establishing the relevance of career and similar constructs.

Career counselors need to be cognizant that people not only interpret but also plan their behavior in terms of social meaning. Moreover, social structures develop as a result of individuals pursuing tasks with meaning in mind. As is well recognized, a chain of events does not make up a career, just as a series of movements does not make up an action. But interpretation has to be understood as meaning that works forward as well as backward in time. Moreover, interpretation does not reflect only what happens outside of counseling; it also involves the manifest behavior, cognitions, and social meaning of the counseling itself. Thus, interpretation is an inherent part of the career development process.

As noted earlier, interpretation involves language and narrative. Narrative has recently emerged as having an important and explicit role in career counseling (Cochran, 1990). Narrative has been proposed as a means of making sense of life (Bruner, 1986; Sarbin, 1986; Russell, Broek, Adams, Rosenberger, & Essig, 1993). As Russell et al. (1993) noted, the construction of coherent narratives in counseling allows clients to see their life histories differently. It also allows clients to adopt novel perspectives and confront the future differently. Narrative also accommodates the role of chance and fate in people's lives, which has recently become an area of interest in career psychology.

Narrative represents an attempt to gain coherence and continuity. As Atkinson (1987) noted, "A coherent narrative holds persuasive power in making sense out of unrelated events" (p. 149). The emphasis on "making sense" is one key to this phrase. However, "unrelated events" represents only a portion of the events that narrative is used to make sense of. Narrative has feedforward as well as feedback functions and serves to construct intentional, goal-directed actions and make them possible.

There is an important connection between narrative and action. One might think of narratives as a special form of talk that people use to justify and render their actions intelligible to themselves and to one another. As sequences of actions and events are "narrativized," people construct career, and career contributes to the content of an account that justifies and renders action intelligible and makes future actions possible. Russell et al. (1993) also argue that narrative serves to both represent and make sense of daily events and the longer life history.

In suggesting that action pertains to interpretation and meaning, external events are not ignored. As agents engaged in meaningful actions, people rely on this meaning to set, steer, and control their actions and integrate them into higher-order entities such as group action or career. The latter are equipped with features similar to goal-directed action, which includes the basic concepts for a discourse on human processes.

Shotter (1993) asserted that just as we do not live in theories, we do not live wholly in narratives. Rather, we live by taking practical and symbolic action in our daily lives. Some actions may appear, and even be experienced as, disjointed and unrelated but have practical meaning in their own particular contexts. Counselors are to be cautioned against helping or expecting clients to seek a single thematic representation or grand career theme for their lives without giving due attention to the particularities of context.

Short-Term Action and Long-Term Career

Counselors frequently work with clients whose decisions involve existential, teleological, and other issues that are not readily dealt with in utilitarian decision-making approaches. Career is a significant frame in which these broader issues can be addressed without losing perspective on the action in which they are likely to occur. This capability of action is further enhanced by the distinction drawn between the cognitive cognitions that accompany action and its social meaning. Both these characteristics of the action theory perspective allow us to consider both action (short-term) and career (long-term) that involve historical and cultural components as well as actual discourse. Further, the traditional cognitive approaches do not allow for the mapping out of the experience of decision making in social situations that are related to career.

Although a goal-directed conceptualization is not new to career thinking (Borgen, 1991), this chapter adds to the identification of these constructs by presenting a system of organization in which short-term action, for example, applying for university entrance, is a systemic part of the long-term career process seen in action terms. Further, we point out that such goal-directed systems comprise not only individual but also joint actions and processes. In conceptualizing action in systemic terms, we overcome the duality of person (active) and environment (sociostructural) influence. In addition, social meaning and representation are at the base of our conceptualization, just as they provide the cognitive framework for individuals themselves.

Notwithstanding the proposition that career represents a socially constructed meaning system, career processes must also be addressed from other perspectives as well. Action theory proposes not only a social meaning perspective but also a perspective of the concepts (constructs) of manifest processes and those of internal knowledge, information, and emotion processing. Cognitive processes at the individual level and communication at the group level are representative of the latter. However, neither this conceptualization nor the methods used here, such as systematic observation and gathering data on cognitive processes, are independent of social meaning.

Role of Emotions

Emotion has not been adequately addressed in vocational psychology and career development. Two major texts in the field, one addressing career theories (Osipow, 1983), the other career addressing counseling (Walsh & Osipow, 1990), do not index it. This gap exists notwithstanding the central place that emotion plays in the everyday lives of most people. In action theory, career is not considered from a dualistic or rationalistic perspective in which emotion and cognition are separated or in which cognition is seen as the basis for means-ends reasoning about career. In dualistic and rationalistic perspectives, dealing with emotion seems to have been neglected. It is precisely because of the neglect of this topic in the career literature that we address it here, not because it stands separately from cognition, action, or career. One must be aware of emotion at every level of understanding of action and career.

Emotions are not processes that just happen to us. As Averill and Nunley (1992) note, "Emotions are constructions in much the same sense that language is a construction.... Exactly how [our] capacities [for emotion] are realized is a function of social and individual development. In the final analysis, we are the artificers of our own emotions" (p. xii). A career is deeply and essentially connected with emotions. The setting of challenging but realistic long-term plans are directly related to happiness, a very strong emotion. Purpose and direction are fundamental to happiness (Emmons, 1986; Ryff, 1989). Similarly, as we have seen in our study of parent-adolescent career conversations as one of the first career-related joint actions (Young et al., 1994), emotions and emotional well-being are among the primary purposes, operating principles, and basis for evaluation of these conversations. They are also a source of much positive and negative emotions.

Several aspects of career and action establish a clear place for emotion and allow for the role it plays to be accessed. First, conscious cognitions, which include emotions and emotion processing, are identified as one of the perspectives of action and career. The intention here is not to separate cognition from action arbitrarily, nor emotion from cognition. People construct and experience these in concert, and it is in this way that action-theoretical researchers study them. A cognitively based self-efficacy approach to career (Lent, Brown, & Hackett, 1994) can only be enhanced by explicit attention to emotions. From the counselor's perspective, among the salient emotions associated with career-relevant actions are fear of deciding too early or too late, or of making the "wrong" decision, liking or disliking certain activities, pleasing and displeasing others, sadness and anticipation about changes, joy about one's own and jealously about others' achievements, and fatigue with difficult, repetitive, or frustrating tasks. Emotions occur in specific actions and broadly within career in diffuse ways. They also serve as an important energizing function for individual and group action.

Second, career addresses practical activities in which people attempt to create meaningful links between what is demanded in a situation and what is available (Shotter, 1993). It is precisely in these situations that emotions constitute part of conscious cognitions. At the simplest level, as Boesch (1991) noted, success or failure experienced in action is associated with feelings of satisfaction or dissatisfaction, which contribute to the construction of the action and are subsequently accessed in further performances of the action. In a group action, such as a parent and adolescent discussing career, the role of emotion is made more complex by the attribution of emotion to the other for example, "My father is disappointed with my decision," notwithstanding whether or how that emotion is actually verbalized by the father. It is further complicated by the role of emotion in conversation (argument) generally and the awareness of individuals that they can strengthen or weaken their positions by appealing or not appealing to emotions.

Finally, Bruner (1986) argued that the connection among action, cognition, and emotion achieve "integration within a cultural system" (p. 117). Career is one dimension of the cultural system that provides a means of integrating emotion, cognition, and action. In this chapter, we have maintained a connection between action and career based on the latter as a superordinate and long-term construct that links actions. If emotion is a constituent part of action, how much more relevant is it for a construct like career? From a constructionist perspective, the emotions associated with career are determined by culturally based beliefs and values. Inasmuch as career is a significant cultural construct, it is also significant for the construction of emotion, if only to circumscribe a particular place for it. In turn, as Averill and Nunley (1988) pointed out with regard to emotion generally, people's emotional reactions to career "serve to reinforce the very beliefs and values by which they are determined" (p. 80).

Joint Action

Joint action is another construct from action theory that has particular relevance for career counseling. In the counseling psychology literature, career has been conceptualized as involving intrapersonal processes—whether as decision making, interests, traits, abilities, or cognitions. This, of course, has been one of the impediments in the convergence of career theory and practice, that is, the difficulty of moving from theories that address intrapersonal processes to practice that is essentially interpersonal. Shotter (1980) introduced the notion of joint action as a third category of activities that lies between human actions (what I, as a human agent, do) and external events (what happens to me outside my agency; see also Shotter, 1993, pp. 3–4).

Although socially embedded, some career actions are solitary, for example, writing an examination. However, a great many career actions occur between people, for example, the discussions that parents and adolescents have about career (Young, Friesen, & Pearson, 1988; Young et al., 1994). Career counseling itself is a particularly good example of joint action, but it also can be about the joint action of the client and some other person.

Joint action is a pertinent construct for cases in which the participants act spontaneously, as is the case in career counseling. Although both the counselor and client come to counseling with their own goals and are intentional throughout, the conversation is not directed solely by those intentions. Nor is the conversation about something that already exists. Joint intention and goals have to be developed by the counselor and client. As many career counselors know from direct experience, career and action emerge as the client and counselor engage in dialogue. They coconstruct action and career, and the action within the counseling forms and sustains career.

As individual action is identified with individual knowledge processing and energizing, so group action is identified with group knowledge processing and energizing. The energizing function of emotion, discussed earlier in this chapter, also applies to joint action.

A greater understanding of the dialogic action of career in general and of career counseling specifically offers the possibility of greater convergence of theory and practice by making the quadrant boundaries shown in Figure 1 more permeable.

SUMMARY:
SALIENT POINTS FOR COUNSELING PRACTICE

Four salient points raised in this chapter address the greater integration of theory and practice. First, counseling itself is career-relevant action, like other career-relevant actions in which the client participates. As action, counseling can be understood from the perspective of manifest behavior, conscious cognitions, and social meaning. Frequently, career counseling deals with some amalgam of behavior, cognitions, and meaning, as experienced or anticipated outside of counseling itself. It is unlikely that manifest behavior outside of the counseling session has a large, singular role in the counseling process about career. However, understanding and interpretation of conscious cognitions and social meaning play substantial parts in career counseling. Recent efforts such as narrative (Ochberg, 1988; White & Epston, 1990), cognitive (Neimeyer, 1988), and other forms of counseling represent illustrations of these perspectives in practice. Thus, manifest behavior, at least as recounted by the client, cognitive processes, including emotion that frequently has been the missing piece in career counseling, and social meaning, as perspectives of action, provide a framework for use in counseling about action and career. In addition, these same perspectives can be used in career counseling research.

Second, the emphasis on cognitive processes and social meaning highlights the characteristics of interpretive career counseling identified by Collin and Young (1992). Interpretive career counseling emphasizes language and discourse. The words and sentences used in career counseling are not only talk about career, they are also individual and joint action that actually construct career. Interpretive career counseling is also context dependent, relativistic, and perspectival.

Third, in addition to the individual action of the client and counselor, career counseling can be considered as joint action. One reason for the lack of integration of theory and practice is that career as a group, particularly a dyadic, system has not conceptualized (Rosenbaum, 1989). Career counseling has largely reflected an intrapersonal perspective that focused on traits and abilities. An action theoretical perspective is based on a systemic approach: One's career-relevant action and one's career are in fact or imply joint action between or among relevant parties. One potentially relevant party is the counselor. Together the client and counselor produce new action in counseling that could not have been produced by either alone. Counselors can also help clients realize the extent to which career is a system in addition to an intrapersonal process.

As part of the career system, self and others, for example, family members, co-workers, and counselors, can be seen as agents. The action of these others, frequently offered through help, guidance, advice, or counseling, is "interpreted" by the person through communication and negotiation. But it is more than the unidirectional influence of others. An adolescent girl, for example, may recognize the parts that others play in her career, what their conceptions are, what she wants to do, and how she can help to create an adequate structure for joint action that can support her goals. Furthermore, her parent may be seen as restrictive and uninformed about the possibilities and interests of the adolescent. Although the parent's own conception of his or her role in this career is one of emotional support, the only supportive strategies the parent uses in reaction to the adolescent are advice giving and questioning her judgment. As counselors well know, this type of incident is often the subject of counseling.

Finally, in an action approach, career research, theory, and practice are closely related, allowing easy transition from one to the other. It employs everyday constructs based on social meaning and experience and provides a framework to understand the part others play in one's career. The counselor's conceptions, those of other participants, and the social representation of these processes become relevant and accessible ingredients of the study of career because they are part of the theory itself.

This work was supported in part by a grant from the Social Sciences and Humanities Research Council of Canada to the first author.

REFERENCES

Averill, J. R., & Nunley, E. P. (1988). Grief as an emotion and as a disease: A social-constructionist perspective. *Journal of Social Issues, 44,* 79–85.

Averill, J. R., & Nunley, E. P. (1992). *Voyages of the heart: Living an emotionally creative life.* New York: Free Press.

Atkinson, R. (1987). The development of purpose in adolescence: Insights from the narrative perspective. *Adolescent Psychiatry, 14,* 149–161.

Betz, N. E., & Hackett, G. (1987). Concept of agency in educational and career development. *Journal of Counseling Psychology, 34,* 299–308.

Boesch, E. E. (1991). *Symbolic action theory and cultural psychology.* Berlin: Springer-Verlag.

Borgen, F. H. (1991). Megatrends and milestones in vocational behavior: A 20-year counseling psychology retrospective. *Journal of Vocational Behavior, 39,* 263–290.

Bruner, J. (1986). *Actual minds, possible worlds.* Cambridge, MA: Harvard University Press.

Bullock, M. (Ed.). (1991). *The development of intentional action: Cognitive, motivational and interactive processes.* Basel, Switzerland: Karger.

Cochran, L. (1990). *The sense of vocation: A study of career and life development.* Albany: State University of New York Press.

Collin, A., & Young, R. A. (1986). New directions for theories of career. *Human Relations, 39,* 837–853.

Collin, A., & Young, R. A. (1992). Constructing career through narrative and context: An interpretive perspective. In R. A. Young & A. Collin (Eds.), *Interpreting career: Hermeneutical studies of lives in context* (pp. 1–12). Westport, CT: Praeger.

Cranach, M. von. (1982). The psychological study of goal-directed action: Basic issues. In M. von Cranach & R. Harré (Eds.), *The analysis of action: Recent theoretical and empirical advances* (pp. 35–73). Cambridge, UK: Cambridge University Press.

Cranach, M. von. (1992). The multi-level organization of action and knowledge. In M. von Cranach, W. Doise, & G. Mugny (Eds.), *Social representations and the social bases of knowledge.* Swiss Monographs in Psychology (Vol. 1, pp. 10–22). Berne, Switzerland: Huber.

Cranach, M. von, Kalbermatten, U., Indermuehle, K., & Gugler, B. (1982). *Goal-directed action* (M. Turton, Trans.). London: Academic Press.

Csikszentmihalyi, M. (1990). *Flow: The psychology of optimal experience.* New York: HarperCollins.

Egan, G. (1994). *The skilled helper: A problem-management approach to helping* (5th ed.). Pacific Grove, CA: Brooks/Cole.

Emmons, R. A. (1986). Personal strivings: An approach to personality and subjective well-being. *Journal of Personality and Social Psychology, 50,* 1211–1215.

Giddens, A. (1991). Modernity and self-identity. Cambridge, UK: Polity Press.

Husserl, E. (1931). *Ideas: General introduction to pure phenomenology.* (W. R. B. Gibson, Trans.). London: George Allen & Unwin. (Original work published 1913)

Karlsson, G. (1992). The grounding of psychological research in a phenomenological epistemology. *Theory and Psychology, 2,* 403–429.

Lent, R. W., Brown, S. D., & Hackett, G. (1994). Toward a unifying social cognitive theory of career and academic interest, choice, and performance. *Journal of Vocational Behavior, 45,* 79–122.

Lent, R. W., & Hackett, G. (1987). Career self-efficacy: Empirical status and future directions [Monograph]. *Journal of Vocational Behavior, 30,* 347–382.

Mancuso, J. (1993). *Constructionism, personal construct psychology and narrative.* Manuscript submitted for publication.

Manuele-Adkins, C. (1992). Career counseling is personal counseling. *Career Development Quarterly, 40,* 313–323.

Morrow-Bradley, C., & Elliot, R. (1986). Utilization of psychotherapy research by practicing psychotherapists. *American Psychologist, 41,* 188–206.

Neimeyer, G. J. (1988). Cognitive integration and differentiation in vocational behavior. *The Counseling Psychologist, 16,* 440–475.

Ochberg, R. (1988). Life stories and the psychosocial construction of careers. In D. McAdams & R. Ochberg (Eds.), *Psychobiography and life narratives* (pp. 173–204). Durham, NC: Duke University Press.

Osipow, S. H. (1983). *Theories of career development* (3d ed.). Englewood Cliffs, NJ: Prentice Hall.

Polkinghorne, D. (1990). Action theory approaches to career research. In R. A. Young & W. A. Borgen (Eds.), *Methodological approaches to the study of career* (pp. 87–106). New York: Praeger.

Polkinghorne, D. E. (1992). Postmodern epistemology of practice. In S. Kvale (Ed.), *Psychology and postmodernism: Inquiries in social constructionism* (pp. 146–165). London: Sage.

Rosenbaum, J. E. (1989). Organization career systems and employee misperceptions. In M. B. Arthur, D. T. Hall, & B. S. Lawrence (Eds.), *Handbook of career theory* (pp. 329–353). Cambridge, UK: Cambridge University Press.

Russell, R. L., Broek, P. van den, Adams, S., Rosenberger, K., & Essig, T. (1993). Analyzing narratives in psychotherapy: A formal framework and empirical analyses. *Journal of Narrative and Life History, 3,* 337–360.

Ryff, C. D. (1989). Happiness is everything, or is it? Explorations on the meaning of psychological well-being. *Journal of Personality and Social Psychology, 57,* 1069–1081.

Sarbin, T. R. (Ed.). (1986). Narrative psychology: The stories nature of human conduct. New York: Praeger.

Savickas, M. L. (1989). Career-style assessment and counseling. In T. Sweeney (Ed.), *Adlerian counseling: A practical approach for a new decade* (3d ed., pp. 289–320). Muncie, IN: Accelerated Development Press.

Savickas, M. L. (1995). Current theoretical issues in vocational psychology: Convergence, divergence, and schism. In W. B. Walsh, & S. H. Osipow (Eds.), *Handbook of vocational psychology* (2ed., pp. 1–34). Hillsdale, NJ: Erlbaum.

Shotter, J. (1980). Action, joint action, and intentionality. In M. Brenner (Ed.), *The structure of action* (pp. 28–65). Oxford: Blackwell.

Shotter, J. (1993). *Cultural politics of everyday life: Social constructionism, rhetoric and knowing of the third kind.* Buckingham, UK: Open University Press.

Sloan, T. S. (1987). *Deciding: Self-deception in life choices.* London: Methuen.

Spokane, A. R. (1991). *Career intervention.* Englewood Cliffs, NJ: Prentice Hall.

Super, D. E. (1969). Vocational development theory: Persons, positions and processes. *The Counseling Psychologist, 1,* 2–9.

Valach, L. (1990). A theory of goal-directed action in career research. In R. A. Young & W. A. Borgen (Eds.), *Methodological approaches to the study of career* (pp. 107–126). New York: Praeger.

Valach, L., Cranach, M. von, & Kalbermatten, U. (1988). Social meaning in the observation of goal directed action. *Semiotica, 71,* 243–259.

Vondracek, F. W., Lerner, R. M., & Schulenberg, J. E. (1986). *Career development: A life-span developmental approach.* Hillsdale, NJ: Erlbaum.

Walsh, W. B., & Osipow, S. H. (Eds.). (1990). *Career counseling: Contemporary topics in vocational psychology.* Hillsdale, NJ: Erlbaum.

Wegner, D. M., Vallacher, R. R., & Dizadji, D. (1989). Do alcoholics know what they're doing? Identifications of the act of drinking. *Basic and Applied Social Psychology, 10,* 197–210.

White, M., & Epston, D. (1990). *Narrative means to therapeutic ends.* New York: W. W. Norton.

Young, R. A., Friesen, J. D., & Pearson, H. M. (1988). Activities and interpersonal relations as dimensions of parental behavior in the career development of adolescents. *Youth and Society, 20,* 29–45.

Young, R. A., Valach, L., Dillabough, J., Dover, C., & Matthes, G. (1994). Career research from an action perspective: The self-confrontation procedure. *Career Development Quarterly, 43,* 185–196.

CHAPTER TWENTY-FOUR

New Relationships Between Researchers, Theorists, and Practitioners

A Response to the Changing Context of Career

Audrey Collin
De Montfort University, Leicester, England

With rapid and significant upheavals in its context, the concept and experience of career are changing in ways that present new challenges to career counselors. Some of these have been explored in this volume, and Leong, Richardson, and Young and Valach have discussed significant ways to respond to them. In this chapter, I shall attempt not only to pull some of these ideas together but also to take them further and argue that the changing context of career calls for a reversal in the traditional relationships between career theorists, researchers, and counselors.

The three preceding chapters address the need for innovations in counseling from different perspectives and with different foci. From the point of view of researchers and theoreticians, Young and Valach examine the relevance of action theory for the theoretical framework and microlevel practice of career counselors. Richardson, from a professional practice orientation, proposes a major innovation at the level of the profession itself and its underpinning discipline. Leong's chapter takes a wider focus and overlays the other two by indicating the need to address the boundaries, cultures, and complexity in both the world of clients and that of the institutional arrangements for counseling. This chapter will examine, from yet another perspective, the relationships between researchers/theorists, practitioners, and their clients.

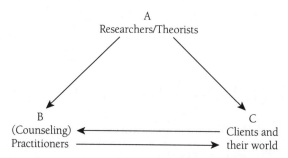

FIGURE 1   The Traditional Relationships Between Researchers/Theorists, Practitioners, and Their Clients

The starting point of my argument is shown in Figure 1, which depicts a traditional view of these relationships. Researchers and theorists, who in a closer examination of my argument would perhaps need to be disaggregated, have been expected to develop scientific knowledge through research and to disseminate it. For their part, practitioners have been expected to find this knowledge useful and to apply it in their work with their clients.

I shall start to question the nature of these relationships by referring to the field of management and organizations, not usually associated with that of counseling. However, managers and organizations also play major roles in the field of career, so that here I shall not only be introducing a new perspective to the discussion but also perhaps initiating some resonance of ideas between these fields.

The chapter will proceed first by outlining my particular perspective and, from it, considering the nature of context and that of practice, and then considering the relationships between researchers/theorists, practitioners, and their clients. It moves on to discuss the changing context of career and its implications for counseling practice. In light of this, the chapter concludes by suggesting the need for a reversal in the vicious circle in the traditional relationships between researchers/theorists, career counselors, and their clients.

The perspective of this chapter derives from my work in a business school, where I teach various kinds of practicing managers who are taking postgraduate, postexperience courses in management. In terms of Figure 1, they are practitioners, and my role is to introduce them to researchers/theorists, with the ultimate goal that they improve their practice as managers. To do this, we need to understand what organizing and managing are. However, as Watson (1994) demonstrates, this is not such a straightforward task as might be supposed. Researchers/theorists have generated considerable knowledge about organizations and management, but it is often decontextualised knowledge, which managers/practitioners have difficulty applying. Less attention has been paid to the processes of organizing and managing and understanding how managers actually practice.

Moreover, the context of organizations is changing profoundly and rapidly, teetering "on the edge of chaos" (Leong, this volume). Managers' assumptions are being challenged and their practices are perforce having to change, but it takes time to construct and disseminate new and appropriate theories. Like counselors (Harmon, 1994), they therefore often find little relevance in management theories but rely on their own "personal theories," in which there is "a mixing of principle and pragmatism, a blending of the normative and the analytical" (Watson, 1994, p. 168), or they resort to fashionable nostrums (such as Peters & Waterman, 1982). As students, however, they are ambivalent because they believe they ought to *know* theories, if only to gain their qualifications. To address their dilemma, I encourage them to focus on their practice and how they conceptualize it.

The main body of management and organization theory—and often the thinking of managers themselves—is informed by the positivist philosophy, which emphasizes rational and technocratic approaches (Alvesson & Willmott, 1992). However, there are other approaches for students to be aware of that challenge this orthodox view. Seeing the world as essentially ambiguous, Weick (1979) regards organizing as a continuous process of meaning-making. Organizations are, therefore, according to Weick, constantly in the making, continuously transforming: "The idea of process implies impermanence...organizations keep falling apart and... require chronic rebuilding. Processes continually need to be reaccomplished" (p. 44).

The social-constructionist perspective, informed by a contextualist epistemology (Pepper, 1942), emphasizes that humans are meaning-seeking and meaning-making. This draws attention to the nature of managing as an interpretive activity. Managers' practice is informed and shaped by their interpretive frameworks, one element of which may be the work of researchers/theorists. As Watson (1994) writes in concluding his "search" for management,

> Management is essentially a human social craft. It requires the ability to interpret the thoughts and wants of others—be these employees, customers, competitors or whatever—and the facility to shape meanings, values and human commitments. (p. 223)

The theories of organizations and management have also been arrived at through their authors' interpretive activity. As my students try to apply them to their practice, I encourage them recognize and challenge both their own and others' assumptions and to develop a critical awareness of their managing—to reflect on the changing context in which they work and the needs of their daily practice in response to it.

From this social-constructionist perspective, it will be seen that both managers and counselors are engaged in ongoing interpreting, as Young and Valach point out (this volume). Therefore, although I approach the task of addressing the topic of innovations in career counseling with some humility, I also do so with a degree of confidence. Just as I have found valuable applications for my work with managers in the various chapters in this handbook, so I believe that my particular perspective may also offer career theorists and counselors new insights.

THE NATURE OF CONTEXT

In this section, I shall examine the nature of context and its implications for practice from the perspective of managing and organizing. I shall then return to the context of career later in the chapter.

The concept of *context*, to be examined shortly, represents a social-constructionist approach to the relationships between an organization and its wider field. It can be contrasted with an orthodox positivist approach, which construes the organization as surrounded by an external world, or *environment*, from the objective reality of which emanate various influences on the organization. Management literature has for the last 20 years or so focused on the influence of change on organizations in this environment and has disseminated theories intended to facilitate the effective "management of change." In the social-constructionist view, however, the relationship between theory and practice is more problematic.

The Causal Texture of the Environment

The orthodox understanding of the environment has been broadened by the work of Emery and Trist (1981). This work traces the increasing degree of interconnectedness between the systems within the organization's environment (the "causal texture of the environment") and identifies four "ideal types" of causal texture which "form a series in which the degree of causal texturing is increased, in a new and significant way" (p. 250). The series starts, according to Emery and Trist (1981), with the "simplest type" of environmental texture, the "placid, randomized environment" where "goals and noxiants...are relatively unchanging in themselves and randomly distributed." The appropriate response here, say Emery and Trist, is one of trial and error: "There is no distinction between tactics and strategy" (pp. 250–251). The second step for Emery and Trist is that of the "placid, clustered environment," where goals and noxiants are no longer randomly distributed but clustered together in the organization's environment. Now the organization critically needs knowledge of its environment for survival, and so it needs "strategy as distinct from tactics." The third level of causal texturing, according to Emery and Trist, is the "disturbed-reactive environment." The characteristic of this is the existence of a number of similar organizations, each of which has to take account of the others: tactics, operations (a campaign calculating others' actions and reactions and devizing counteractions), and strategy.

Emery and Trist's fourth step must now be more widely understood and experienced than when they first published their ideas. The responses of organizations in step 3, having produced an effect analogous to that of a "company of soldiers marching in step over a bridge," create the "turbulent fields" of step 4: "dynamic processes...arise from the field itself.... The 'ground' is in motion" (p. 253). This increases the area of "relevant uncertainty" for organizations so that the consequences of their actions become increasingly unpredictable and, as Emery and Trist (1981) point out, "do not necessarily fall off with distance, but may at any point be amplified beyond all expectation; similarly, lines of action that are strongly pursued may find themselves attenuated by emergent field forces" (p. 254).

Emery and Trist propose that the appropriate response to turbulent fields is to take a form "that is essentially different from the hierarchically structured forms to which we are accustomed" (p. 257).

This recognition of the increasing complexity of the environment, and of the consequent need for managers to take into account the interests of other parties (p. 259), highlights how today's practitioners have to grapple with a shifting reality. This reinforces the definition of managing as an ongoing interpretive activity in which there may be little scope for the direct application of theory.

Emery and Trist (1981, but first published 1965) recognized that this "new set of values" will not develop overnight and noted that it was believed that it could take 10 to 15 years for new values to permeate an organization and at least a generation to permeate a whole society: "One may ask if this is fast enough, given the rate at which type 4 environments are becoming salient. A compelling task for social scientists is to direct more research on to these problems" (pp. 259–260).

The outcomes they envisaged are by no means evident in the organizational field today. Nevertheless, their analysis could still be fruitfully applied to the field of career and the development of career theory. It is their turbulent fields that Leong (this volume) refers to, and the proposals made by both Leong and Richardson (this volume) could perhaps be interpreted in terms of institutionalization.

The Social Construction of Context

A social-constructionist view of context is very different from a positivist view of environment. Context is socially constructed, the organization's context being constructed by its members from their perspectives. Weick, an influential writer on sense-making in organizations who is also interested in careers in the new forms of self-designing organizations (Weick & Berlinger, 1989), and whose work will again be referred to in the next section, suggests that "people create the environments which then impose on them" (Welick, 1979, p. 135). Further, he writes: "Investigators who study organizations often separate environments from organizations and argue that things happen between these distinct entities.... But [this view] excludes the possibility that people *invent* rather than discover part of what they think they see" (p. 166).

This recognition that the organization produces enacted environments has important implications for its response to that environment and, once again, raises the issue of how practitioners make use of theory.

The concept of structuration (Giddens, 1976) offers a further interpretation of context and recalls the concept of appreciative systems that will also be referred to in the next section. According to Giddens (1976), society and its structures are constituted or produced by human agency "by the active doings of subjects" (p. 160), and, reciprocally, their action is constituted structurally. Social structures provide not only the conditions for human agency but are also produced by it; they are, therefore, both enabling and constraining. Barley (1989) discusses some of the implications of this for career.

Formative Contexts

Unger's concept of *formative contexts*, influenced by critical legal theory, adds a political dimension to social construction. For him, "everything in society is frozen or fluid politics" (in Blackler, 1992, p. 279). The temporary mechanisms put in place to resolve societal tensions and conflicts become supported by institutional and technological arrangements and are taken up by various power groups. "The resulting 'formative context' provides a set of pragmatic but unreflective routines" (Blackler, 1992, p. 279). These rules and routines become taken for granted and appear natural; individuals find meaning in them and thereby reaffirm their context:

> Through the roles they enact, people behave as if their social worlds are coherent, intelligible and defensible; the biased, indeed arbitrary, nature of the terms upon which different interests have come to be understood are overlooked and social practices assume a "false necessity." (Blackler, 1992, p. 280)

Metaphors for Context

The social-constructionist interpretation of the relationship between an organization and its wider field leads on to the recognition that the organization is an inherent part of that field; that which constitutes the field also constitutes the organization. The organization is a node of meaning within its context. This interpretation reframes our understanding of how contextual changes— demographic, technological, ideological, or any other—also bring about changes in the organization. It can be expressed through the metaphor of the web: Human beings are animals "suspended in webs of significance…[they themselves have] spun" (Geertz, 1973, p. 5). Influenced by an edition of the *Journal of Management Studies* (1990) devoted to the texture of organizing, I have also used the metaphor of a tapestry to convey this interpretation of organizational context. The organization is constituted of the very warp and weft threads that make up its context. They may vary in texture or color throughout the tapestry, so producing pattern, whether intentionally fashioned or random. As I have written elsewhere (Collin, 1994a), "The tapestry itself inheres in the whole, not its parts" (p. 31). To regard the organization as a separate entity "would be like taking the tapestry to bits: We would be left with threads" (p. 31).

In conclusion, the adoption of this understanding of context reinforces the view that the practitioner is an interpreter and maker of meaning who, rather than receiving theory, engages actively with it, interpreting it according to the needs of practice situations. This interpretive activity increases as the practitioner tries to respond to the changing context. I shall now turn to examine in closer detail the nature of practice.

THE NATURE OF PRACTICE

In Britain, a discussion of management practice among those committed to the orthodox paradigm would probably deal with the nature of managers' competencies and the various competency frameworks that have been designed for use in appraisal, training, and development (see Collin, 1994b). However, espousing a social-constructionist approach, I shall draw on the work of two theorists who closely examine processes of relevance to both managers and counselors. The first (Weick, 1979) does not directly address practice as such but offers concepts with which to examine it; the second (Schon, 1983) addresses professional practice directly.

Insights from Weick

Weick (1979), whose work was referred to earlier, views organizing as a process of, first, attending to "ecological change" (p. 130) in the "stream of experience," then of interpreting it because it is "ambiguous, uncertain, equivocal," and arriving at a "workable degree of certainty" (p. 6). The process, according to Weick, "can be thought of as a set of recipes for connecting episodes of social interaction in an orderly manner" (p. 45) and comprises enactment, selection, and retention. *Enactment* is the bracketing of changes in the stream of experience for further attention. Sense then has to be made of these equivocalities. Weick expresses his "recipe for sense-making" as "How can I know what I think until I see what I say?" (p. 133). *Selection* is the imposition of a set of interpretations on the bracketed portions in order to reduce their equivocality and to connect events within the stream in an orderly manner, and *retention* is the storage of these interpreted segments for future application.

Weick here is concerned solely with a social psychology of organizing, but I believe that his views have relevance for other interpretive processes, such as managing and counseling. Indeed, he himself applies the notion of the retrospective sense-making of selection to career.

This, however, appears to conflict with Young and Valach's view of career from their action theory perspective (this volume). For them, career is "an overarching construct that serves to frame and organize the complex pattern of intentional actions over longer segments of life." Moreover, they are also proposing, in contrast to Weick, that career has both feedback and feedforward characteristics. This difference of view may lie in the differing perspectives of those who are doing the interpreting. For individuals, perhaps "agents who dream new dreams" (Sullivan, 1984, p. 148), career may have both retrospective *and* prospective meaning, as Young and Valach are suggesting, whereas for the external observer of the individual's life, it may have meaning only retrospectively (see also Freeman, 1984; Polkinghorne, 1990). The significance of these differences for counseling merits further consideration.

I have already drawn attention to the interpretive nature of practice. Whether in managing or counseling, practice is far more than the application of theory and technical knowledge or the exercise of technical skills, or even interpersonal skills, although these are indeed important. Weick gives us concepts with which to understand it better. Practitioners, as well as their clients and researchers/theorists, are engaged in the enactment of reality, in selection, and retention. The relationships between them are mediated by their interpretive frameworks, as Figure 2 will later set out.

The three previous chapters in this volume illustrate Weick's selection and retention. For example, Young and Valach see career as a superordinate construct used by counselors to help their clients construct coherent narratives and thus see their life history differently. Richardson's proposal to reconceptualize career counseling would lead to changes in practice that would appear likely to enhance the choice and relevance inherent in selection. Leong's statement of the need for problem rather than discipline- or theory-based approaches to career counseling is drawing attention to the process of retention.

Insights from Schon

Schon's (1983) focus on practice has direct relevance for both my students and the argument of this chapter. He derived his understanding of the *reflective practitioner* from detailed case studies of practice in various professional fields: managing and psychotherapy, as well as architecture, town planning, and others. Many of the situations that such practitioners (and certainly managers and counselors) address are complex and uncertain, and, as Schon puts it, "there is a problem in finding the problem" (p. 129). Some practitioners are reflective and proceed, Schon suggests, through "reflection-in-action," that is, by engaging in a "reflective conversation with a unique and uncertain, situation" (p. 130). The reflective practitioner steps into the situation, reframes it, experiments with it to identify the consequences and implications of this frame, listens to the situation's backtalk and, if necessary, reframes again: "The process spirals through stages of appreciation, action, and reappreciation" (p. 132). There are clear echoes here of Weick's bracketing, selection, and retention. Schon pulls out the phases of this process from the close analysis of his case studies, thereby allowing us to see practice in slow motion and offering valuable insights into the way in which practitioners work.

He points to practitioners' very active and instrumental approach to theory. When they confront a new situation, says Schon, their "*repertoire* of examples, images, understandings, and actions" (p. 138) enables them to see it as both familiar *and* unique. Hypothesizing about its potential for transformation (p. 166) on the basis of their repertoires, they step into the situation and impose their own order on it, reframe and experiment with it. Practitioners, says Schon (1983), are trying to adapt it to their frame "through a web of moves, discovered consequences, implications, appreciations, and further moves" (p. 131). However, these moves "also produce unintended changes which give the situation new meanings. The situation talks back, the practitioner listens, and...reframes the situation once again" (pp. 131–132).

As Weick (1979) also asks, "How can I know what I think until I hear what I say?" (p. 134). The construction of narratives in counseling that "allows clients to see their life history differently" (Young & Valach, this volume) could be seen in these terms.

Schon relates how practitioners must listen to the situation's backtalk and be willing to enter into new confusions and uncertainties (p. 164). This calls for "a kind of double vision": The practitioner must both pursue the rationale of the frame adopted and be prepared to break it open in order to make new sense of his or her transaction with the situation and eventually arrive "at a deeper and broader coherence of artifact and idea" (p. 164). As "choices become more committing... moves, more nearly irreversible," and the risk of uncertainty increases, writes Schon (1983), the practitioner (manager and counselor) must avoid the "temptation to treat the view as the reality" (p. 164).

Schon believes that practitioners work with an overarching theory and appreciative system. The latter term is used by Vickers (in Checkland, 1981, p. 263), who argues that our readinesses to see and value people, things, and situations in one way rather than another are organized into an appreciative system that both conditions and is modified by new experience. Schon stresses that the constancy of the overarching theory and appreciative system that the practitioner brings to a situation otherwise in flux is important. If there were a sudden shift here during the practitioner's experiment, writes Schon (1983), "inquiry would no longer have the character of a reflective conversation. It would become a series of disconnected episodes" (p. 272).

Reflective practitioners, according to Schon (1983), try "to discover the limits of [their] expertise through reflective conversation with the client" (pp. 295–296). They are not dependent on established theories but construct a new theory of the unique case. They do not limit themselves to a concern about means on the basis of some prior agreement about ends. They do not keep ends and means separate but define them interactively as they frame a problematic situation. They do not "separate thinking from doing, ratiocinating [their] way to a decision which [they] must later convert to action." Schon (1983) writes further that

> because [their] experimenting is a kind of action, implementation is built into [their] inquiry. Thus reflection-in-action can proceed, even in situations of uncertainty or uniqueness, because it is not bound by the dichotomies of Technical Rationality. (pp. 68–69)

Through these processes, practitioners generate both objective knowledge (that can be disconfirmed) and personal knowledge, which is bounded by their "commitments to [their] appreciative system and overarching theory" (Schon, 1983, p. 166). Schon recognizes that this is at odds with orthodox, scientific values and is "compelling only to members of a community of inquiry who share these commitments" (p. 166). Different professional communities of inquiry have different appreciative systems that lead to differing approaches to the same situation. Fragmentation in the counseling community, the existence of different appreciative systems, is highlighted as dysfunctional by both Leong (this volume) and Richardson (this volume). Schon (1983), however, asserts that inquirers have the "little-understood ability to enter into one another's appreciative systems and to make reciprocal translations from one to another" (p. 273). What significance has this for the counseling field?

Schon's analysis lays bare some of the interpretive activity of practice, revealing something of practitioners' use of theory. This and Weick's work enable us to look more closely at the relationships between practitioners and researchers/theorists, and practitioners and clients, in the fields of both managing and counseling.

THE RELATIONSHIP BETWEEN
PRACTITIONERS AND RESEARCHERS/THEORISTS

The work of Schon and Weick enlarges our understanding of the role of theory in practice. This role can be inferred in the interpretations that practitioners select to filter the bracketed portion of the stream of experience, to generate, as Weick (1979) puts it, "answers to the question 'What's going on here?'" (p. 175). It is also implied in the hypothesizing, repertoires, and appreciative systems in Schon's reflective practice. However, the nature of this role is problematic, for many theories do not address the issues with which practitioners have to grapple. This is, in part, because, in a changing context, theory must inevitably lag behind the realities with which practitioners deal. It is also because many theorists operate according to what Schon (1983) calls the "traditional epistemology of practice":

> Whenever a professional claims to "know," in the sense of technical expert, he [or she] imposes his categories, theories, and techniques on the situation.... He [or she] ignores, explains away, or controls those features of the situation, including the human beings within it, which do not fit his [or her] knowledge-in-practice. (p. 345)

The theorist assumes the role of expert and, hence, exercises an institutionally reinforced pattern of unilateral control; this is implied in Figure 1.

Moreover, undertaken within the positivist paradigm, much conventional research and theory in both management and career is designed to achieve scientific rigor and is thereby often too refined for practical application in the field. Hence, in Weick's (1979) words, "selection occurs in the sense that many of the possible meanings that are tried simply fail, either because they are not useful or because the present data are inconsistent with them" (p. 175). Through the process of retention, practitioners overlay these theories with the experiential knowledge of their application and store them away for future use. This is an active and interpretive rather than a passive and formulaic use of theory. Young and Valach (this volume) acknowledge this in the case of counselors who, "in their effort to translate theory into practice, lose much of the sophistication and complexity that theories can offer."

Practitioners, therefore, do not draw directly upon the output from theorists and researchers in their practice. Their relationship is mediated by their respective interpretive frameworks. During their initial professional training, practitioners may have been more open to theory (or, in Schon's terms, more able to enter into and make reciprocal translations of the other's appreciative system) than Leong (this volume) and Richardson (this volume) appear to believe they are when they eventually practice. By that stage, they are using theories instrumentally as a resource rather than a revelation, filtered through their interpretive frameworks and overlaid with the experience of practice. The idea that "a theory is constructed through its use," that "the meaning of theory changes as it is used," is, according to Savickas (1994, p. 240), a powerful one.

Furthermore, there are differently constituted knowledges: propositional, relational, practical, and tacit. In general, theorists and practitioners are working in different currencies as well as in different directions. In a positivist approach, greater respect is accorded to propositional than to practical or relational knowledge. Or as Schon (1983) writes, "the more basic and general the knowledge, the higher the status of its producer" (p. 24). It is therefore assumed that, as Figure 1 depicts, the direction of flow is from researchers/theorists to practitioners, who will then apply the knowledge to clients. This is evident in the contrast Schon makes between the traditional epistemology of practice, which is noted above, and reflective practice.

It also has to be acknowledged that, like managers, practitioners (and their clients) develop their own theories (Watson, 1994), which will play their part in selection and retention. We certainly know that managers' *espoused theories* differ from their *theories-in-use* (Argyris & Schon, 1974).

All this suggests the need to question the commonly assumed status/power relationship between theorist and practitioner. It is the practitioner who in the process of selection chooses whether to use a particular theory and in what way, and who, in overlaying it with experiential knowledge in the process of retention, is modifying it for further use. Such adaptation and modification may be regretted by purists as sullying the rigor that researchers/theorists have struggled to attain. It is, nevertheless, essential to the interpretive process, whether of manager or counselor, both in times of stability and, even more so, in times of change.

I conclude from this that, although Leong's general and Richardson's specific proposals concerning the disciplinary and professional divisions within the overall field are valuable, they would perhaps make little difference to the traditional relationship between theorist and practitioner. Having next considered the implications of the changing context of career, I shall argue the need for a radical change in this relationship.

THE RELATIONSHIP BETWEEN PRACTITIONERS AND CLIENTS

Counselors and their clients also engage in selection and retention in their relationship. However, in contrast to the theorist-counselor relationship based on Schon's traditional epistemology of practice noted earlier, the counselor may well be engaging in reflective practice with the client. Here, technical expertise is "embedded in a context of meanings" so that practitioners' actions may have different meanings for their clients than they had intended and they have to seek to understand what these might be. According to Schon (1983), they are aware of "an obligation to make [their] own understandings accessible" to their clients, which means that they often need to reflect anew on what they know. They try "to discover the limits of [their] expertise through reflective conversation with the client" (Schon, 1983, pp. 295–296). Just as reflective practice takes the form of a "reflective conversation with the situation" (Schon, 1983), so the practitioner's relationship with clients also takes the form of a reflective conversation. Moreover, Schon suggests, the competent client also acts like a reflective practitioner; together they engage in a reflective contract.

These aspects of reflective practice have much in common with counseling that is premised on empathy (Richardson, this volume). According to Young and Valach (this volume), counseling represents joint action, dialogue, and coconstruction: "Together the client and counselor produce new action in counseling which could not have been produced by either alone." Client-oriented practitioners seek the opportunity to facilitate the client's construction of an emancipatory narrative, so that practice for such a counselor is praxis (Habermas, 1974) for the client. Many counselors could therefore be seen as reflective practitioners. However, as Richardson points out, although counseling may be a two-way process, there is still a disparity in power between the two parties and a "blindness of our theories and models of intervention to [the] socially-structured inequities" of gender, race, and class; career counseling has been trapped in the occupational structure. Leong, too, notes the "shortsightedness and ethnocentrism" of practitioners in this field and urges them to recognize their clients as cultural beings. In the terms of Schon and Weick, this blindness is present in the appreciative systems, selection, and retention processes. The reflective practitioner, however, according to Schon, can, as a participant in a larger societal conversation, change social reality.

I shall return to this larger vision of practice at the end of the chapter. Meanwhile, we can now update Figure 1 to indicate how these relationships, whether in managing or counseling, are mediated by these interpretive processes.

Figure 2 shows the traditional relationships between researchers/theorists, practitioners, and practitioners' clients as primarily unidirectional but mediated by the interpretive processes (IP) of enactment, selection, retention, and reflective practice (RP). Counseling, however, is represented as a two-way process, since, given its underpinning values and professional ethos, the counselor is often a reflective practitioner, although not necessarily fully so, nor conscious of Schon's concept. To be complete, the model should also have incorporated implementation and feedback. One of the frustrations for practitioners in the present climate is having implementation constrained or directed by outside forces, such as government policies. I have not, however, extended my argument that far.

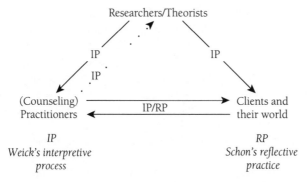

FIGURE 2   An Expanded View of the Traditional Relationships Between
          Researchers/Theorists, Practitioners, and Clients (The Vicious Circle)

THE CHANGING CONTEXT OF CAREER

The Role of Context in Career Theory

Attention to environment, as defined earlier in this chapter, introduces significant challenges to positivist social science. For example, in laboratory experiments, the environment is controlled and maintained, supposedly in a neutral state that will not affect the subject. To give recognition to the subject's environment is to introduce a multiplicity of uncontrollable variables into the experimental situation, some of which may influence the subject in subtle ways. Context, in this circumstance, has no meaning, or little useful meaning. In much research, therefore, individuals have been largely decontextualized.

The study and theory of the phenomenon of career has largely been undertaken within the orthodox mode of social science. Nevertheless, the relationship between individual and work environment is central to the concept of career so that, of necessity, the nature of that environment—of the individual and of the relationship between them—have been matters of concern to all the major career theorists (e.g., Arthur, Hall, & Lawrence, 1989; Savickas & Lent, 1994; and, for a British context, Watts, Super, & Kidd, 1981). However, the environment of the individual's career has also been construed as objective and separate from the individual. Considerable energy has been invested in identifying, measuring, and matching characteristics of individuals and their environments to inform theory and counseling practice.

By the time that Collin and Young (1986) were criticizing the decontexualized manner in which career was construed, the field had begun to change dramatically with the developmental contextual approach (Vondracek, Lerner, & Schulenberg, 1986). Vondracek, Lerner, and Schulenberg, however, deliberately eschewed what they refer to as a pure form of Pepper's contextualism (1942), believing a merger of organicism and contextualism to be a more appropriate underpinning of their approach. Nevertheless, the espousal of the career equivalent of the organizational *tapestry* is increasingly reported (e.g., Arthur, Hall, & Lawrence, 1989; Blustein, 1994; Young & Collin, 1992; see also Savickas, 1994, p. 238). Richardson (this volume) refers to a "contextual perspective" that recognizes "behavior as fully embedded in the intersubjective context of people's lives." These developments are supported by others in the social sciences generally, with, for example, the emergence of "societal psychology," which quotes among its key propositions that "[o]ntologically the individual and the collectivity are inseparable" (Jahoda, 1986, in Himmelweit, 1990, p. 23).

However, despite the greater recognition of both the environment and context of career in research and theory, some of their significant characteristics (class, gender, race) still remain disregarded, as both Leong and Richardson have pointed out in this volume.

Changes in the Organizational Context of Career

Just as the context of organizations has become turbulent, so also has the context of career, which has perhaps also experienced Emery and Trist's (1981) four steps of causal texturing. In many industrialized countries, the very availability of work has become a major issue, and this is now increasingly the case for previously secure middle-class people. There are many other significant changes concerning individuals as well as organizations and communities in the various threads of the tapestry that is the context of career: social, cultural, economic, demographic, political, and ideological. These are addressed in previous chapters by both Leong and Richardson, who allude to changing conceptions of self (see also Blustein, 1994). Here, however, I shall focus on organizational change because it is this with which I have the greatest familiarity.

Today's organizations are increasingly different from the bureaucratic structures in which the modern concept of career took root (Kanter, 1989; Savickas, 1993). Two postmodern forms (Reed & Hughes, 1992) that have emerged during the 1980s are the reengineered organization (Hammer & Champy, 1993) and the learning organization (Pedler, Burgoyne, & Boydell, 1991; Senge, 1990). The latter, for example, tends to be flatter and more flexible than traditional forms, often with an enabling, tentative, and experimental structure with temporary boundaries, scaffolding (Pedler, Burgoyne, & Boydell, 1991). It is committed to multiskilling, teamworking, participation, continuous improvement, the empowerment of employees (through, e.g., information technology), flexibility in rewards, "double-loop learning" (Argyris & Schon, 1978), a learning climate, and self-development opportunities for all.

These new self-designing organizations have considerable implications for the nature of career and call for appropriate "career improvisation" (Weick & Berlinger, 1989). Their flatness and strong lateral emphasis do not provide scope for the traditional onward and upward career, nor for the differentiation of roles and statuses, and the clustering of skills that have hitherto provided differential rewards, prestige, and esteem, publicly observable and honored. Rather, tasks, jobs, and roles change according to circumstances, and individuals with them. The flexibility that organizations need in order to adapt to changing circumstances thwarts the individual's future orientation. Where structures are temporary and experimental, individuals find it difficult to discern a visible stable future pathway and are unsure where to invest, what steps to take, and what the appropriate timetables are.

The new organizational cultures do not encourage the individualistic, future goal-oriented approach—the "values of self-enhancement and individual achievement" (Richardson, this volume)—that has typically motivated in traditional careers. Perhaps the need for affiliation will become more important than the needs for achievement and power (McClelland, 1961). The increasing emphasis on team membership, moreover, makes it difficult to attribute tasks or specific outcomes to individual team members, further robbing them of the opportunity to be rewarded for being distinctive. Here group identity may be more important than that of the individual, and synergy more than individual prowess. Emphasis on continuous improvement and employee development for all further lessens the scope of individual distinctions. These new organizations, therefore, may not favor or reinforce elites for whom hitherto the concept of career has been applicable.

Although many of these changes undoubtedly threaten the traditional form of career, they simultaneously offer new and exciting prospects. The flexibility may well appeal to those who from choice or necessity want to live more flexible lives. It may generate new, unheard of possibilities that challenge and stimulate and perhaps unlock previously unrecognized potentials. The erosion of former boundaries of various kinds and commitment to employee development may benefit those for whom Leong and Richardson have expressed concern. Certainly, it could be inferred that there will be greater scope in such organizations for women's values and modes of operation (Marshall, 1989).

These organizational changes are undoubtedly bringing about changes in individuals' careers. As part of the wider and dramatically changing tapestry of the context of career, they raise questions about its very future (Collin, 1993). Whether construed as environmental or contextual, these changes are starting to demand appropriate responses from counselors. According to Weick (1979), there may be fewer and fewer theories that they will be able to employ directly in their process of selection; they may need to carry out more iteration in their experimenting; and they may find the backtalk more difficult to understand (Schon, 1983). The next section will explore some of the implications of this.

The Challenge of the Changing Context to Career Counselors

The changing context presents counselors with novel and challenging issues. Their clients are having new experiences that are not amenable to traditional analysis and problems that are not amenable to traditional solutions. They face new threats and opportunities and, as in management, the outcomes of research come too late and may not be relevant or specific enough (see Savickas & Lent, 1994). Moreover, like managers, they will also themselves be affected by changes in the tapestry of their context and may have experiences that parallel those of some of their clients, such as insecure employment contracts, increasing pressures, and changing and sometimes alien values. As Harmon (1994) explains, "we are in an economic time.... Today, more than ever before, we are asked to show that we spend both our research and practice efforts wisely" (p. 233). In their field, as in many others, government through social, employment, and education policies sets targets or otherwise constrains what counselors can achieve in significant ways. In terms of Unger's "formative contexts," they may be increasingly aware of "false necessity" for themselves and their clients. The notion of empowerment may indeed at times seem hollow.

The nature of the relationships between researchers/theorists, career practitioners, and their clients, therefore, which is already complex (see Savickas & Lent, 1994), may also have to change radically. When their activities, experiences, and interrelationships are construed as part of their wider and changing context, as part of complex adaptive systems, then, as Leong suggests, they can be seen as verging on the edge of chaos, where stability and creativity coexist and stagnation and anarchy battle it out. If this is so, it would suggest that the proposals of the previous three chapters are, although valuable, not sufficiently bold.

The imagination of the debate on converging career development theories (Savickas & Lent, 1994) was clearly caught by Krumboltz's metaphor of mapmaking to represent theory construction. Discussing the state of the field, Krumboltz (1994) suggests that "we need to draw a different map.... We need to see ourselves as career cartographers" (p. 16). Extending this metaphor, Subich and Taylor (1994) suggest that "the counselor is analogous to a travel agent who consults a map to help clients reach their destinations as happily, pragmatically, or efficiently as possible" (p. 172). What is needed, in their view, is for theorists, researchers, and practitioners to collaborate in order "to identify and operationalize the elements of the routes on our map" (p. 174). They acknowledge, however, that practitioners may well greet this metaphor coolly and may question "whether current theories and research are able to inform practice and whether practice is ever allowed to inform theory" (p. 174).

The notion of mapmaking and mapreading, I suggest, does not capture the activities in which researchers, theorists, and practitioners—whether managers or counselors—now have to engage in today's "turbulent fields"—if those, indeed, represent what faces us. They are themselves an inherent part of their changing context, and their ground is in motion (Emery & Trist, 1981). Turbulence may not be universal; there are perhaps many residual parts of the old world for which a map will continue to be a guide. However, it is the uncertainty and unpredictability with which we are having to learn to deal. When crossing a previously well-known area that is now lurching and shifting and opening up before our feet, we need to be able to keep our balance and a cool head, a combination of conceptual and practical skills that are perhaps not yet well developed. Maps will be of little value now. In Harmon's (1994) words, "what we hope to do may require us to adopt new ways of thinking and conceptualizing reality" (p. 229).

As already seen, Emery and Trist propose that organizations need to develop new values in order to survive in "turbulent fields" by taking into consideration the needs of other organizations. They are aware that this will take time. The very occurrences of two recent conferences addressing these issues is testimony to the fact that those working in the field of career are not prepared to let the grass grow under their feet. As the views of Subich and Taylor (1994), noted above, suggest, the need for collaboration is well recognized. As, in many respects, an outsider, I am going to propose a broader and more radical approach, one which I have been grasping for in my own work with managers and which I am beginning to discern more clearly as I write this chapter.

RESPONDING TO CONTEXTUAL CHANGES— INNOVATIONS IN CAREER COUNSELING

Reversing the Flow:
From Vicious to Virtuous Circle

I am arguing for a reversal of the traditional flow of influence and of the hierarchy of ideas that now reveals itself as a vicious circle. Although, as I have suggested, it is practitioners who are making judgments about the value of theories through Weick's (1979) selection and retention and implementing their judgments in the real-life situation with their clients, they are nevertheless cast in inferior and dependent roles (Schon's traditional epistemology). As Schon (1983) points out, the personal knowledge they generate through practice is not valued. As represented in Figure 2, researchers/theorists exert much greater influence on practitioners and research respondents than vice versa (see Harmon, 1994; Savickas, 1994). This unidirectional flow of influence creates a vicious circle because there is no, or only a little, leverage to make changes in the external world and thereby change the situation of the practitioner's clients. Because their knowledge—even where relevant for their clients' needs—is not deemed rigorous or valid, practitioners have little influence for change. Researchers/theorists have rigorous and valid knowledge, but it is often not relevant. More research or converging theories cannot break the circle, which is self-reinforcing.

The three previous chapters in this handbook make valuable proposals. The action theory that Young and Valach argue for would, when operationalized, offer counselors concrete steps to take (see Valach, 1990). Richardson's proposals could ensure a sounder disciplinary footing for practice. Leong offers the "vision thing," the significance of which few managers since the pronouncements of Peters and Waterman (1982) would doubt. These proposals, however, are still largely reinforcing the direction of the current flow of activity and influence. We need to break the present loop, to reverse the flow and convert the vicious to a virtuous circle appropriate for the present changing world. To start this process, I suggest that practitioners and researchers/theorists should become reflective practitioners (Schon, 1983).

Practitioners and Clients, Researchers, and Theorists as Reflective Practitioners

The key figure is the practitioner, whether manager or counselor. It is here that the changing nature of the terrain is immediately felt, here that it has to be negotiated, and here that moral actions have to be taken. The traditional processes of research and theorizing make researchers/theorists generally too distant from the action to offer anything but echoes of a former or passing world. The virtuous circle sees the practitioner researching in the practice situation, the researcher/theorist learning from and with the practitioner/researcher who is learning from and with the client. This newly configured force field will generate energy that can be directed into and bring about changes within the wider society.

Many counselors are already reflective practitioners and as such, according to Schon, are already researchers in the practice context. I am arguing that their changing context demands that those who do not yet do so should practice reflectively. They should be encouraged to do so and be given recognition, respect, and support for doing so. All counselors should also be encouraged to extend their practice research consciously and deliberately and through it enrich and refine their own personal theories (Watson, 1994). For this, they need to learn and practice appropriate research skills, such as action research skills, so that they can meet the changing needs of their clients. From this, they could come to regard their clients as coresearchers (see Reason & Rowan, 1981; Reason, 1988). The competent client, Schon (1983) suggests, also acts like a reflective practitioner; together they will engage in a reflective contract.

With training in research skills and support to develop the changed attitudes and confidence necessary to accommodate a more equal power relationship with researchers/theorists, the enlarged scope of their practice would be reinforced by the virtuous circle. As practitioners/researchers in the world of practice, they would be empowered to feed back to the researchers/theorists in academia and their voices would be heard. The issues they would raise could be communicated to policymakers and thus have a chance of being acted on.

This reversal to create the virtuous circle would have a particularly dramatic impact on the researchers/theorists. In abandoning their traditional epistemology of practice for reflective practice (Schon, 1983), they would be changing their role in the circle and the nature of their power derived from the place of theory in the hierarchy of knowledge (with some aspects of it lessened, others increased). By becoming reflective practitioners, too, they would engage in a "reflective conversation with the situation" and their new clients—both practitioners and research respondents. Many could then also find themselves drawn to research approaches that would be compatible with their reflective practice: interpretive, collaborative approaches (e.g., Reason & Rowan, 1981; Young & Collin, 1992). This would offer an emancipatory experience for their respondents (Sullivan, 1984). These changes, although divesting researchers/theorists of their traditional power as experts, would accord them the more subtle influence of facilitator of the practitioners' research and possibly teacher of research skills.

At the same time, this reversal would give them a new role and source of power. Benefiting from close contact with practitioners/researchers, they could feed this grounded knowledge into their more detached longer-term theory construction. They would also have the current and grounded knowledge that policymakers should be ready to listen to, in contrast to what now happens; in the words of Harmon (1994), "they are simply not addressing the problems of most interest to either policy-makers or the public" (p. 231). They would now be able to report on what practitioners/researchers are conveying of their clients' everyday experiences. This enlarges the researchers/theorists' role, giving them what many clearly yearn for (Harmon, 1994; Leong, this volume; Richardson, this volume)—the ability to play a transformational rather than merely a transactional role in society. The concrete and timely evidence they would be able to adduce could persuade policymakers to confront some of the "false necessities" of society (Unger, 1987, in Blackler, 1992) and introduce changes that would be emancipatory. As Schon (1983) writes, professionals are "participants in a larger societal conversation; when they play their parts well, they help that conversation to become a reflective one (p. 346). When they act upon the ideas they develop about society's problems as they engage in social life, they "change social reality" (p. 347). He goes on to say that "[w]e are in the problematic situation that we seek to describe and change, and when we act on it, we act on ourselves. We engage in a continuing conversation with the larger societal situation of which we are a part...we also elicit 'back-talk,' which takes the form of unanticipated meanings, problems, and dilemmas" (p. 347).

These far-reaching proposals would also affect upon educational institutions, which would have to develop the attitudes, skills, and material to educate and train researchers/theorists and practitioners/researchers in more appropriate ways. Should these proposals also lead to emancipatory changes in the world of the client, then there could also be new and greater demands for education. Changes in the context of individual careers will reverberate throughout the whole tapestry.

The model, therefore, needs to be further elaborated, as it is in Figure 3.

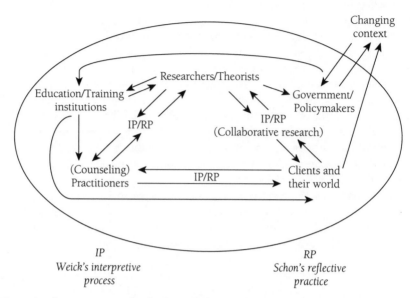

FIGURE 3   The Virtuous Circle of Relationships Between Researchers/Theorists,
           Practitioner/Researchers, and Clients in a Changing Context

CONCLUSIONS

This examination of the nature of practice within a changing context has led to the
proposal for the need to reverse the present vicious circle of relationships between
researchers/theorists, practitioners, and clients. The resulting virtuous circle gives
each of them a new and enlarged role and a wider sphere of influence. Although
these changes would undoubtedly challenge the existing sites of power, they would
also be empowering: Practice will become praxis for all. Schon (1983) puts it this
way: "The unique and uncertain situation comes to be understood through the
attempts to change it, and changed through the attempt to understand it" (p. 132).

There are many questions raised by this proposal that I have not addressed.
Where would one start to reverse the present flow? Who would do so? What are the
arguments against? What would it cost? The threats are not just those from vested
interests; there is the real danger, too, of apathy and inertia. However, the virtuous
circle offers something to all parties, many of whom already recognize that, without
some dramatic changes, career theory may become increasingly sterile and counseling impotent. With the commitment of the powerful networks represented in the
conferences that inspired the book *Convergence in Career Development Theories*
(Savickas and Lent, 1994) and this handbook—and the spirit of Gretchen Alexander
(Leong, in this volume)—there is a chance of success.

REFERENCES

Alvesson, M., & Willmott, H. (1992). *Critical management studies.* London: Sage.

Argyris, C., & Schon, D. A. (1974). *Theory in practice.* San Francisco: Jossey-Bass.

Argyris, C., & Schon, D. A. (1978). *Organizational learning: A theory of action perspective.* Reading, MA: Addison-Wesley.

Arthur, M. B., Hall, D. T., & Lawrence, B. S. (Ed.). (1989). *Handbook of career theory.* Cambridge, UK: Cambridge University Press.

Barley, S. R. (1989). Careers, identities, and institutions: The legacy of the Chicago School of Sociology. In M. B. Arthur, D. T. Hall, B. S. Lawrence (Eds.), *Handbook of career theory* (pp. 41–65). Cambridge, UK: Cambridge University Press.

Blackler, F. (1992). Formative contexts and activity systems: Postmodern approaches to the management of change. In M. Reed & M. Hughes (Eds.), *Rethinking organization: New directions in organization theory and analysis* (pp. 273–294). London: Sage.

Blustein, D. L. (1994). "Who am I?": The question of self and identity in career development. In M. L. Savickas & R. W. Lent (Eds.), *Convergence in career development theories: Implications for science and practice* (pp. 139–154). Palo Alto, CA: Davies-Black Publishing.

Checkland, P. (1981). *Systems thinking, systems practice.* Chichester, UK: Wiley.

Collin, A. (1993, July). The future of career. In the symposium on *The future of career: Death or transfiguration?,* De Montfort University, Leicester, England.

Collin, A. (1994a). Human resource management in context. In I. J. Beardwell & L. Holden (Eds.), *Human resource management: A contemporary perspective* (pp. 28–66). London: Pitman.

Collin, A. (1994b). Learning and development. In I. J. Beardwell & L. Holden (Eds.), *Human resource management: A contemporary perspective* (pp. 271–334). London: Pitman.

Collin, A., & Young, R. A. (1986). New directions for theories of career. *Human Relations, 39,* 837–853.

Collin, A., & Young, R. A. (1992). Constructing career through narrative and context. In R. A. Young & A. Collin (Eds.), *Interpreting career: Hermeneutical studies of lives in context* (pp. 1–12). Westport, CT: Praeger.

Emery, F. E., & Trist, E. L. (1981). The causal texture of organizational environments. In F. E. Emery (Ed.), *Systems thinking,* Vol. I (pp. 245–263). Harmondsworth, UK: Penguin.

Freeman, M. (1984). History, narrative, and life span developmental knowledge. *Human Development, 27,* 1–19.

Geertz, C. (1973). *The interpretation of cultures.* New York: Basic Books.

Giddens, A. (1976). *New rules of sociological method.* London: Hutchinson.

Habermas, J. (1974). *Theory and practice.* London: Heinemann.

Hammer, M., & Champy, J. (1993). *Reengineering the corporation: A manifesto for business revolution.* New York: Harper Business.

Harmon, L. W. (1994). Frustrations, daydreams, and realities of theoretical convergence. In M. L. Savickas & R. W. Lent (Eds.), *Convergence in career development theories: Implications for science and practice* (pp. 225–34). Palo Alto, CA: Davies-Black Publishing.

Himmelweit, H. T. (1990). Societal psychology: Implications and scope. In H. T. Himmelweit & G. Gaskell, *Societal psychology* (pp. 17–45). Newbury Park, CA: Sage.

Jahoda, M. (1986). Small selves in small groups. *British Journal of Social Psychology, 25,* 253–254.

Journal of Management Studies. (1990). 27(6), 573–649.

Kanter, R. M. (1989). Careers and the wealth of nations: A macro-perspective on the structure and implications of career forms. In M. B. Arthur, D. T. Hall, & B. S. Lawrence (Eds.), *Handbook of career theory* (pp. 506–521). Cambridge, UK: Cambridge University Press.

Krumboltz, J. D. (1994). Improving career development theory from a social learning perspective. In M. L. Savickas & R. W. Lent (Eds.), *Convergence in career development theories: Implications for science and practice* (pp. 9–31). Palo Alto, CA: Davies-Black Publishing.

Marshall, J. (1989). Revisioning career concepts: A feminist invitation. In M. B. Arthur, D. T. Hall, & B. S. Lawrence (Eds.), *Handbook of career theory* (pp. 275–291). Cambridge, UK: Cambridge University Press.

McClelland, D. C. (1961). *The achieving society.* New York: Van Nostrand.

Pedler, M., Burgoyne, J., & Boydell, T. (1991). *The learning company: A strategy for sustainable development.* London: McGraw-Hill

Pepper, S. C. (1942). *World hypotheses: A study in evidence.* Berkeley: University of California Press.

Peters, T. J., & Waterman, R. H., Jr. (1982). *In search of excellence.* New York: HarperCollins.

Polkinghorne, D. E. (1990). Action theory approaches to career research. In R. A. Young & W. A. Borgen, *Methodological approaches to the study of career* (pp. 87–105). New York: Praeger.

Reason, P. (Ed.). (1988). *Human inquiry in action: Developments in new paradigm research.* London: Sage.

Reason, P., & Rowan, J. (Eds.). (1981). *Human inquiry: A sourcebook of new paradigm research.* Chichester, UK: Wiley.

Reed, M., & Hughes, M. (Eds.). (1992). *Rethinking organization: New directions in organization theory and analysis.* London: Sage.

Savickas, M. L. (1993, July). *Fracture lines in career counselling.* Paper presented at the symposium on *The future of career: Death or transfiguration?,* De Montfort University, Leicester, England.

Savickas, M. L. (1994). Convergence prompts theory renovation, research unification, and practice coherence. In M. L. Savickas & R. W. Lent (Eds.), *Convergence in career development theories: Implications for science and practice* (pp. 235–257). Palo Alto, CA: Davies-Black Publishing.

Savickas, M. L., & Lent, R. W. (Eds.). (1994). *Convergence in career development theories: Implications for science and practice.* Palo Alto, CA: Davies-Black Publishing.

Schon, D. A. (1983). *The reflective practitioner: How professionals think in action.* New York: Basic Books.

Senge, P. (1990). *The fifth discipline: The art and practice of the learning organization.* London: Century.

Subich, L. M., & Taylor, K. M. (1994). Emerging directions of social learning theory. In M. L. Savickas & R. W. Lent (Eds.), *Convergence in career development theories: Implications for science and practice* (pp. 167–175). Palo Alto, CA: Davies-Black Publishing.

Sullivan, E. V . (1984). *A Critical psychology: Interpretation of the personal world.* New York: Plenum.

Unger, R. M. (1987). *False necessity*. Cambridge, UK: Cambridge University Press.

Valach, L. (1990). A theory of goal-directed action in career research. In R. A. Young & W. A. Borgen, *Methodological approaches to the study of career* (pp. 107–126). New York: Praeger.

Vickers, G. (1968). *Value systems and social process*. London: Tavistock Publications.

Vondracek, F. W., Lerner, R. M., & Schulenberg, J. E. (1986). *Career development: A life-span developmental approach*. Hillsdale, NJ: Erlbaum.

Watson, T. J. (1994). *In search of management: Culture, chaos and control in managerial work*. London: Routledge.

Watts, A. G., Super, D. E., & Kidd, J. M. (Eds.). (1981). *Career development in Britain: Some contributions to theory and practice*. Cambridge, UK: Hobson's Press.

Weick, K. E. (1979). *The social psychology of organizing*. New York: Random House.

Weick, K. E., & Berlinger, L. R. (1989). Career improvisation in self-designing organizations. In M. B. Arthur, D. T. Hall, & B. S. Lawrence (Eds.), *Handbook of career theory* (pp. 313–328), Cambridge, UK: Cambridge University Press.

Young, R. A., & Collin, A. (Eds.). (1992). *Interpreting career: Hermeneutical studies of lives in context*. Westport, CT: Praeger.

PART FIVE

CLOSING
COMMENTS

THE THREE CHAPTERS in the final section of this handbook each reflect on and underscore the most important ideas discussed in this volume. In the opening chapter of this section, Osipow highlights ideas from the preceding chapters that he wishes to underscore. He begins by contrasting the abstract ideals of theory with the concrete tasks of practice. From this analysis, he argues that contemporary career theory was not designed to provide operational procedures to use in career intervention. Theories, according to Osipow, do not specify diagnostic procedures and intervention practices. Given this conclusion, he wonders if counselors expect too much from career theory. Then he asks readers to reflect on the question, What is career counseling? Following his own answer to this question, he focuses on the artificial separation of careers from their owners that is promulgated by distinguishing career and personal counseling. Osipow concludes by encouraging practitioners to be more active in theory construction and more willing to communicate and collaborate with researchers in turning theory into practice.

In Chapter 26, Myers analyzes this handbook's chapters to determine if the authors believe that the gulf between career theory and practice is a problem. He concludes that most of the authors seem convinced that a problem exists and that the goal of converging practice and theory is both worthy and attainable. A few authors display no particular concern about the gulf in that they have found ways to integrate theory and practice that work for them. Myers concludes that the handbook, as a whole, makes a convincing case that the lack of convergence in career theory and practice is a significant problem, one that is likely to endure into the foreseeable future. This handbook's major contribution, according to Myers, is its examination of the varying levels of dissatisfaction about the lack of convergence and the varying explanations for the source of the theory-practice rift and how to resolve it.

In the closing chapter, Walsh and Savickas report the results of a survey completed by participants at the conference that inspired this handbook. The conference participants, including the chapter authors, responded to questions about how career theory and research influence their practice as well as questions concerning their critiques of career counseling research. Walsh and Savickas go on to restate and emphasize the suggestions offered by this volume's chapter authors for better integrating career practice, theory, and research.

CHAPTER TWENTY-FIVE

Does Career Theory Guide Practice or Does Career Practice Guide Theory?

Samuel H. Osipow
Ohio State University

ONE OF THE things I really enjoy about specializing in the career psychology field is its dynamic nature. Ideas about career theory and practice change and continue to change rapidly, sometimes in ways that can seem chaotic. Change often implies growth that requires one to stretch one's skills and knowledge to keep up. One of my colleagues suggested, perhaps facetiously, perhaps not, that knowledge of chaos theory might be a useful guide to career theories of every stripe. That suggestion may be taken more seriously than it might first appear.

WHAT IS CAREER COUNSELING?

Those readers who are familiar with the book *Convergence in Career Development Theories* (Savickas & Lent, 1994) already know that a major point was that career development theory is not the same as career counseling theory.

Thus, as I reflected on this topic, one of the first thoughts I had was to ask, What is career counseling?

What would I hope this enterprise would produce? Probably in an optimistic way, I had hoped I might "see" a career counseling theory, or "touch" one, so that I could return to my class in career development and parade it before my students. Naturally, I did not expect to be fully satisfied. After all, describing theory is an elusive business, understanding and describing practice is even more elusive, and clearly connecting the two is extremely difficult for many good reasons. One reason for this difficulty is that practice is a very concrete activity, while theory building is an abstract endeavor. Theory is not usually designed to provide operational procedures to use in career interventions.

A major problem we face in connecting theory to practice is the considerable difficulty of doing research on career interventions. This difficulty exists for many reasons, not the least of which is our failure to adequately describe the career interventions under study in a clear and concrete way. What counseling practices do we expect to grow out of our career development theories? Do we expect those theories to advise us about diagnostic process and diagnostic categories of career problems and issues? Or do we expect the theories to tell us the prognosis for treatment of these problems and issues? Or should they explain the etiology of the development of the problems and issues? Do we expect the career development theories to guide our process efforts? Do we expect the theories to instruct us about the shape and execution of counseling procedures? Finally, do we expect the theories to help us evaluate the outcomes of counseling?

If we, as practitioners, expect the above products from career development theory, we are likely to be sadly disappointed. It is important to recall that career development theory proponents generally have sought to apply theory to career counseling only as an afterthought. The overwhelming majority of our career-related research deals with topics that focus on the career development choices. Very little of this research deals directly with issues involved with providing career-related services to clients who need them or to better understanding the process of career counseling.

As was pointed out by Herr, Lucas, and Gottfredson (this volume), we probably need segmented minitheories to deal with sets of career events and career objectives. At the same time, it is unrealistic and unreasonable for practitioners to expect theory to guide their activities at a micro level.

Another one of the problems with research, theory, and practice in career development and counseling might at least be the result of ambiguity in how we practice when counseling about careers and the identification of our goals. To help myself think this ambiguity through, I then made a list of all the things I thought might qualify as career counseling or contribute to its success:

- Interviewing clients about careers and career plans
- Helping clients of all ages learn about themselves
- Helping clients explore occupations
- Helping clients develop occupational skills
- Helping clients develop occupational decision-making skills
- Helping clients acquire information about the world of work
- Helping clients make career-related choices
- Helping clients with career adjustment problems
- Helping clients deal with the interface between work and family
- Helping clients implement career decisions

HOW COUNSELORS HELP PEOPLE

At that point, I stopped listing career counseling examples, realizing I could generate a very lengthy list, and began to think about *how* career professionals help people deal with career issues. Career counseling goals and outcomes, as opposed to counseling methods, address a different set of issues, all surrounding the concern of how career counseling can help. Confounding the methods with outcomes serves only to cloud our efforts to understand career counseling.

What do we mean by "helping?" With respect to both issues noted above, that is, defining career counseling practice and describing how we do it, I hoped we would get some clues from the chapters in this handbook. I remembered that at the career theory convergence conference held in 1992 (Savickas & Lent, 1994), it was generally agreed that career development theories are not the same as career counseling theories. Swanson and Chartrand, both in this volume, but especially Krumboltz (this volume) remind us that career theory and career counseling theory are not the same thing. Krumboltz presents an interesting model in which career development theory serves as a general basis for the creation of a more specialized theory, with career counseling as its target. Krumboltz's chapter represents precisely the kind of thinking I had hoped for: A theory whose scope involves more than career development. Unfortunately, our tendency to lapse into thinking and talking as though career development theory is the same as career counseling theory was evident many times during the conference that inspired this work. We must etch that difference in stone and plant it in front of us.

Before Krumboltz's chapter, I was prepared to state the heresy that there is no career counseling theory. However, his point that trait-and-factor theory was created in a different time to deal with a set of problems that are different from those faced now is well taken and fits with Swanson's views (this volume) and, in a way, with those of Holland (this volume), who have asserted or implied that trait-and-factor theory is career counseling theory. However, in practice, I do not believe we had a career counseling theory until Krumboltz proposed his model, and even then the final judgment must be reserved.

A third major problem in conducting basic research in career counseling designed to facilitate theory development is the difficulty gaining access to the counseling workplace. Counselors are either defensive or too busy or concerned about client privacy at the expense of openness to research. Certainly, conducting research in a field setting is sometimes intrusive to practicing, forcing practitioners to change their normal style. Unfortunately, the result of this barrier to research is an inadequate research base. Most of the research on career counseling fails to meet criteria set forth by Oliver (1979) or Fretz (1981), describing what constitutes good field research in counseling. They each proposed an extensive list of guidelines that should be met in order for good research to be conducted. Examples of these guidelines include training counselors to apply the same or similar procedures, selecting clients appropriately, assigning different treatment groups randomly, using more than just a few counselors, and using reliable and widely used outcome measures. There are some exceptions in which investigators have met many or most of these guidelines. Two examples exist in the research conducted by Spokane and Fretz (1993) and Barak, Golan, and Fisher (1988). Those investigators used numerous counselors, tried to control the intervention, and used many established outcome measures.

CAREER INTERVENTIONS

One must ask how we can increase our science base for career counseling without access to counseling situations in which the interventions need to be somewhat controlled with carefully defined client concerns and identifiable and well-described interventions with clients whose important personal and career attributes are identified.

Many other important points are raised in this handbook. It was generally implied, but not made explicit, that career counseling is but one example of career interventions. We should really be using the term *interventions,* as Spokane (1991) has suggested. If we do not do so, we run the risk of confusing theory and practice so badly that we will have virtually no chance to succeed in our task of integrating theory and practice.

We know that careers are not segmented from their owners. Careers interact with personality, affect, and family life. Career counseling, as many have previously indicated (e.g., Hackett, 1993), usually gives short shrift to the counseling process, just as the counseling process has not been overly concerned with career counseling issues. What must be remembered is that counseling is counseling: It may, at times, focus on the career part and at other times focus on the personal part of the process. Just to illustrate how troublesome this separation can be, I recall a career case in which the client, who sought counseling to redirect her career after a series of job losses that led to severe financial difficulties, revealed that her career problems existed in the context of difficult relations with male supervisors, a history of abuse in childhood, and a long-standing pattern of depression. Is this a career counseling or psychotherapy case? Which of the client needs require attention first?

Fortunately, as Richardson (this volume), Lent (this volume), as well as others have implied and as stated earlier, counseling is counseling. We may be starting to recognize that counseling should not be segmented by hyphenated topics. I agree with Lent when she, along with many others, states that there is no career counseling, only counseling—and furthermore, that this counseling is a mixture of procedures and experiences involving the examination of subjective experience, focusing on affect at times, at other times on cognitions, and, in toto, dealing with our relationships with others, with objects, with information, and with who knows what else. An anecdote drawn from my early professional experience as a counselor illustrates how clients may perceive our arbitrary divisions of their worries and concerns. To secure an appointment, clients were asked to indicate whether their problem was a career one, an educational one, or a personal one. If they said a personal problem, they were seen almost immediately. Otherwise, their names were put on a waiting list. What were we telling them? To their credit, the students quickly learned to indicate they had "personal problems," reckoning that they could see a counselor earlier than otherwise and then deal with whatever issues were important to them. Maybe they were smarter about counseling than were we professionals. Borgen (1991) has suggested that career counseling is what counseling psychologists do best, and this observation has especially interesting implications in the context of the intermixture of personal and career counseling that is becoming increasingly popular today. Because of our training in both career counseling and psychotherapy, counseling psychologists may be uniquely qualified to help a broad spectrum of adults with their life problems.

In our difficulty of applying theory to practice, counseling psychologists are not alone. Consider psychotherapy theory and personality theory. Personality theory is analogous to the practice of psychotherapy in the same way that career development theory relates to career counseling practice. Furthermore, it must be remembered that the theory underlying psychotherapy has a far longer history than does career development theory, yet, even with that history, the connection is not nearly as well developed as would be desirable. We must thus temper our optimism about the readiness of career counseling practice to adopt career development theory as a guide.

This handbook has identified at least one additional challenge to the career development and career counseling professions. Arbona (this volume) has pointed out that everybody has a career but that some of them are not very attractive, particularly the options available for ethnic and racial minorities who live in poverty. This statement reflects a very sad state of affairs. What is needed is to increase the attractiveness of the career prospects of poor people, admittedly a very difficult task in the current transitional labor market situation, that is, the movement of labor to a postindustrial employment situation. It is necessary to develop solutions to employment for the postindustrial age. Furthermore, we still do not have a good grasp of how to apply career theory to understand the career behavior of racial and ethnic minorities, though we are getting there (see Leong, in press). Before we can practice effectively from a theoretical base, an empirical data base must be developed describing ethnic/racial minority career behaviors and problems.

CONCLUSION

In conclusion, the point I would like to make most strongly comes in the form of an admonishment to both theorists/researchers *and* practitioners. To those practitioners who think that theory doesn't inform you in your practice, I have some advice: Be less passive about applying theory. Don't wait for the theorists to do all the work for you. You are smart enough to extrapolate from theory to practical applications. In addition, in order for the academicians among us to do relevant research and develop cogent theories, you need to let us study what you do, how you do it, with whom you do your work, and the outcomes you experience. How can we study counseling if we don't have access to the process and procedures? How can we develop connections between career theory and practice without the help of our colleagues in practice. Please collaborate with us.

To my academic colleagues, let me share with you a criticism that I hear from practitioners. The composition of the panels from the conference that inspired this book provide a good example of why practitioners are alienated from theory. Where are the practitioners as panelists? There are too few practitioners who are heard. Most of the practitioners who were on the panel practice only part time. Academics must reach out and include practitioners in their thinking and research. If I had my way, I would match each researcher/theorists with a practitioner so they could learn from each other. I have had the extremely good fortune to be collaborating with just such a person in Mary Lynne Musgrove for the past year, a practitioner par excellence, from whom I have learned much. The moral? One I have stated before (Osipow, 1990; Osipow & Fitzgerald, 1996): Remember, practice informs science; science informs practice. Again: Practice informs science; science informs practice. Put that slogan on your wall.

Perhaps some academician among us can develop an effective career theory with clear implications for practice and some practitioner among us can continue to refine the application of that theory to counseling process. We need to talk to each other (à la Jepson, this volume)—maybe at times continuously but certainly at least occasionally—so that each of us can continue to do his or her distinctive work.

REFERENCES

Barak, A., Golan, E., & Fisher, W. A. (1988). Effects of counselor gender and gender-role orientation on client career choice traditionality. *Journal of Counseling Psychology, 35,* 287–293.

Borgen, F. H. (1991). Megatrends and milestones in vocational behavior: A 20-year counseling psychology perspective. *Journal of Vocational Behavior, 39,* 263–290.

Fretz, B. R. (1981). Evaluating the effectiveness of career interventions. *Journal of Counseling Psychology, 28,* 77–90.

Hackett, G. (1993). Counseling and psychotherapy: False dichotomies and recommended remedies. *Journal of Career Assessment, 2,* 105–117.

Leong, F. (Ed.). (in press). *Career development and vocational behavior of racial and ethnic minorities.* Hillsdale, NJ: Erlbaum.

Oliver, L. W. (1979). Outcome measurement in career counseling research. *Journal of Counseling Psychology, 26,* 217–226.

Osipow, S. H. (1990). Careers: Research and personal, or how I think an individual's personal and career life intertwine—A personal example. *The Counseling Psychologist, 18,* 338–347.

Osipow, S. H., & Fitzgerald, L. F. (1996). *Theories of career development* (4th ed.). Boston: Allyn & Bacon.

Savickas, M. L., & Lent, R. W. (Eds.). (1994). *Convergence in career development theories: Implications for science and practice.* Palo Alto, CA: Davies-Black Publishing.

Spokane, A. R. (1991). *Career intervention.* Boston: Allyn & Bacon.

Spokane, A. R., & Fretz, B. R. (1993). Forty cases: A framework for studying the effects of career counseling on career and personal adjustment. *Journal of Career Assessment, 2,* 118–129.

CHAPTER TWENTY-SIX

Convergence
of Theory and Practice
Is There Still a Problem?

Roger A. Myers
Columbia University

KNOWING ABOUT MY penchant for football—especially Ohio State football—the editors of this volume (both Ohioans) requested that I review several chapters of this handbook and comment as I saw fit. Their request of me was to "read and react."

Football buffs will recognize "read and react" as one of several defensive strategies employed in the game. As I understand it, the strategy requires an overall sense of the opponent's game plan, sufficient patience to forestall premature commitment, heightened sagacity in picking up important cues, and, finally, aggressive action in pursuit of one's goals (i.e., thwarting one's opponent). Although I am in no mood to thwart, or even identify, an opponent among the distinguished contributors to this handbook, I pursue this metaphor if only to rekindle memories of place, of sunny Saturday afternoons at Ohio Stadium and the importance of scholarly achievements at Ohio State University in matters with which this handbook is concerned.

THE GAME PLAN

The editors of this handbook—Mark L. Savickas and W. Bruce Walsh—offered as apologia for its creation the fact that attendees at a conference on the convergence of career development theories (see Savickas & Walsh, 1994) "strongly agreed that the time was right for a national dialogue on the integration of theory and research in vocational psychology with the practice of career counseling and education"

(p. 415). From such an assertion, one can infer the existence of a problem, a problem of such consequence that the Vocational Special Interest Group of the Division of Counseling Psychology of the American Psychological Association resolved to do something about it. Nearly everyone agrees that there are "gulfs" between career theory and research on the one shore and between counseling practice and social policy on the other (Lent & Savickas, 1994; Osipow, this volume). Given the history of applied psychology, or applied anything, this insight can hardly be labeled as a heuristic breakthrough. But there are other insights. It is generally true that theorists do not practice and practitioners do not theorize. Some say that researchers and practitioners enjoy the same avoidant relationship (Osipow, this volume). Unabashed idealists, such as the leadership of the American Association of Applied and Preventive Psychology, for example, call for the end of all practice that is not based solidly on research. Others argue that no research or theorizing should proceed without there first being clearly discernible implications for practice.

Such concerns are the designated stigmata of the disease that bedevils those of us who devote our energies to influencing or understanding the careers of others. However, one must ask if the stigmata are real or merely apparent. Worst yet, is it possible to identify the signs and attribute to them the wrong cause? Could it be that regardless of the diagnostic accuracy applied, nothing can be done to cure the patient?

From my "read and react" posture, I concluded that the game plan of those contributing to this volume was to render judgments about whether the lack of convergence between theory and practice is still a problem and, if it is, whether or not a remedy could be found.

PATIENCE TO FORESTALL EARLY COMMITMENT

The venerable John Holland certainly believes that the problem still exists and laid the blame on the differing means of communication favored by theorists/researchers and by practitioners. As has been his career-long habit, Holland provides some simple and elegant solutions for solving the problem. Herr (this volume) and Harmon (this volume) agree that the problem exists and suggest that convergence was inhibited largely because current theories are not adequate to meet the newly emerging challenges of life at work. Arbona (this volume) and Subich (this volume) see the problem as resulting from the fact that career theories are not sufficiently attentive to the practice-relevant realities of traditionally underserved groups. Leong (this volume) and Richardson (this volume) believe that there is a problem and point the blame at the fact that the entire enterprise is too narrowly conceived. Richardson also joined Young (this volume) in suggesting that a new epistemology is upon us and extant theories have not been constructed to incorporate that fact. On this point, Holland disagrees.

Gottfredson (this volume) goes to considerable length to illustrate how relevant existing theories and research are to enduring career issues but recognizes that the problem is still salient because practitioners are not well informed about this relevance. Krumboltz (this volume) sees the lack of convergence as a result of counselor passivity, that is, counselors' reluctance to take prescriptive action with clients, even when adequate research and theory exist.

Reading these chapters could leave one reasonably convinced that the problem continues to trouble many concerned people and that the goal of convergence remains one that is both worthy and unattained. However, there are other voices.

OTHER CUES AND GOAL-DIRECTED ACTIONS

It should not escape notice that, rather than dwelling on the inadequacies of the researchers and the theorists, both Gottfredson and Krumboltz suggest that the shortcomings of the practitioners—and, by implication, those who train the practitioners—might play a role in the lack-of-convergence drama. Other authors (Borgen, this volume; Chartrand, this volume; Lent, this volume; Savickas, this volume; Swanson, this volume) display no particular concern for the "gulfs" and present thoughtful contributions that seemed to illustrate that, for all the fuss about lack of convergence, things are moving along rather nicely in *their* theory shops. There are varying levels of dissatisfaction about the lack of convergence between career theory and practice and varying explanations for it. It is well understood that theorists and practitioners—though both groups care about careers—come from different cultures, worship different heroes, communicate in different formats, and are incumbents of different occupations. Don't take my word for it; check your nearest Occupations Finder.

LATE HITS

Pressing this puerile, gender-biased metaphor to its limit, I am emboldened to write about matters not *of* this handbook but evoked by it.

The first of these is that many of the contributors to this volume seem overly impressed with the drastic changes being experienced in the world of work. Most of us have read Handy's (1990) dire predictions about the Shamrock Organization—consisting of the professional, managerial *core*, the *contractual fringe*, and the *flexible labor force* of low-wage workers "of whom little is expected and to whom little is given" (p. 99). Handy also described "the Federal Organization," with its decentralized structure and its low profile center, and "the Triple I Organization," in which intelligence, information, and ideas are the key ingredients. Most of us are pleased by the heady wine of futurism. Yet all of us know that the world of work and the nature of paid activity do not change as rapidly as some journalists would have us believe.

Who among us has not uttered, or at least nodded in assent to, "We are training people today for occupations that will not exist when the training is finished"? Who has not offered or endorsed the statement, "By the time you graduate, occupations will exist that were not conceived of when you started"?

There are many stabilizing influences that keep work behavior from being altered in such drastic ways. One is the comprehensive system of legal entitlements spread so widely throughout our society. In the state where I live, 37 different occupations are licensed or certified by laws, and most such laws define a scope of practice. Hundreds of occupations and millions of positions are defined by contractual labor relations agreements. The building trades change slowly despite technological advances. Personal service occupations—including career counseling—resist change, even when the elders in the fields plead and cajole (e.g., Krumboltz, this volume).

My point is that, while keeping one eye on the horizon, we are better advised to stay focused on the stability of work, the constancy of work motives, the enduring relationships between individual personalities and occupational environments, and the persistent centrality of work in the lives of humans. Let the Sunday supplement writers alert the world to the sea of changes that are about to engulf us if we don't watch out.

Not long ago, it was announced that the chief executive officer of a major U.S. corporation had arranged compensation for himself in excess of $6 million for the year. In that year, he had decreased the corporation's losses by eliminating 30,000 jobs. It is not the size of the reward that troubles me (but if you like being troubled by such matters, see Bok, 1993) so much as the behavior being rewarded. With increasing frequency, corporations are viewing the elimination of jobs as the main vehicle for increasing profitability. In the current fervor to reduce our taxes, local, state, and federal governments are tidying up their ledgers by reducing their workforces. Because our economy continues to grow, people continue to find work. More people are employed today than ever before, and the U.S. unemployment rate is acceptably low. So what's the problem?

The problem, as I see it, is the rapid erosion of the psychological bond between employee and employer. The accustomed mutual dependence between worker and employing organization is being seriously weakened. Studies of employee commitment to their organizations show a continuous downward trend. Organizations, public as well as private, no longer behave as if they have an obligation to create satisfying and challenging careers for their employees.

It seems to me that there are serious changes taking place in the opportunity structure of our society. These changes, although economically driven, are primarily psychological in nature. Let us hope that career theorists and career practitioners can help prepare our clientele to face them.

REFERENCES

Bok, D. (1993). *The cost of talent.* New York: Free Press.

Handy, C. (1990). *The age of unreason.* Boston: Harvard Business School Press.

Lent, R. W., & Savickas, M. L. (1994). Is convergence a viable agenda for career psychology? In M. L. Savickas & R. W. Lent (Eds.), *Convergence in career development theories: Implications for science and practice* (pp. 259–271). Palo Alto, CA: Davies-Black Publishing.

Savickas, M. L., & Lent, R. W. (Eds.). (1994). *Convergence in career development theories: Implications for science and practice.* Palo Alto, CA: Davies-Black Publishing.

Savickas, M. L., & Walsh, W. B. (Eds.). (1994). *Toward the convergence of career theory and practice.* [Brochure]. Department of Psychology, Ohio State University, Columbus.

CHAPTER TWENTY-SEVEN

Integrating Career Theory and Practice

Recommendations and Strategies

W. Bruce Walsh
Ohio State University

Mark L. Savickas
Northeastern Ohio Universities College of Medicine

IN THE FINAL chapter of this handbook, we look to the authors who have contributed to this volume for ideas that can further the integration of career practice and theory. We want to underscore important ideas that they offer about how theory informs practice and how practice informs theory. In particular, we summarize the recommendations that they have articulated and the strategies that they have described in reflecting on and responding to the five central questions posed in Chapter 1:

- How can we increase the cohesiveness between practitioners and researchers?
- How can career theories be renovated to address the majority of individuals in society?
- What are the best prospects for building clearer connections between practice and theory?
- How can practice inform theory?
- What type of research can produce knowledge that is useful to practitioners in realistically addressing the complexities presented by diverse clients in various clinical situations?

In responding to these questions, the authors have offered eight distinct recommendations, with accompanying action strategies, for strengthening the union between career practice and theory.

IMPROVE COMMUNICATION AMONG PRACTITIONERS, THEORISTS, AND RESEARCHERS

The most frequently stated recommendation for improving the linkages between theory and practice focused on something that practitioners and researchers both need to do, namely, make a concerted effort to communicate with each other, continually and candidly. Lucas points out the irony that, after they complete the same graduate school curriculum, counseling psychologists who choose academic and those who choose practice paths become so different from each other that they no longer talk to each other. She urges more collegial involvement in which academicians and practitioners draw on their scientist-practitioner roots.

The very basis of the scientist-practitioner model assumes that the two activities of practice and research are mutually informative. However, it has not always worked that way (Goldfried, 1993). Career theorists and researchers have traditionally paid relatively little attention to enhancing the practice of career intervention, while, at the same time, career counselors have invested relatively little effort in contributing to the development of career theory and the improvement of career research. Although both groups offer several cogent explanations for their inattention to the issues of the other group, the fact remains that further integration of practice and theory requires more communication and interaction between practitioners and researchers.

In scientific inquiry, a distinction must be made between the context of discovery and the context of verification. Discovery of many important phenomena would, from all indications, seem more likely to occur in career counseling practice. Thus, practicing career counselors have the potential to offer their research-oriented colleagues significant hypotheses in need of investigation and to provide contexts and participants with which to examine these hypotheses. Because of the uncontrolled and potentially biased processes that produce practitioners' discoveries and hypotheses, the new insights must be verified under the controlled conditions mandated by research paradigms. From this perspective, practice provides the greater possibility for discovery, whereas research involves the confirmation of these discoveries. Together, discovery and verification propel development for the field of career counseling.

Collin points out, however, that participants in the current situation do not acknowledge the importance of this interaction. There is no question that practitioners who use research are the very ones who make the most important judgments about the adequacy of theories, yet these practitioners are "cast in inferior and dependent roles." Theorists and researchers exert unidirectional influence on practitioners. She characterizes this unidirectional flow of information as a "vicious circle" and then contrasts it with a "virtuous circle" in which practitioners adopt a new role and position of influence by continually interacting with theorists and researchers. Ideas to address the assumed split in theory and practice require more collaboration on theory building and research by teams of theorists and practitioners. Given the current "vicious circle," it seems appropriate that Osipow asks academicians to "reach out and include practitioners in their thinking and research."

Toward this end, Holland suggests a number of ways that the interaction and communication among practitioners, researchers, and theorists could be improved. He suggests that career journals establish practitioner sections or forums devoted to articles about career theory and practice written by practitioners. Lucas recommends that these articles suggest ways to accomplish successful treatment in particular situations. Holland further suggests that changes in convention formats might also help. He urges program planners to explore convention venues for interaction within and between small groups composed of equal numbers of practitioners and researchers. This may be a first step in implementing Osipow's suggestion that academicians take the lead in creating teams of researchers and practitioners to learn from each other. Whatever we try, Holland asserts, should involve more face-to-face interaction and discussion.

Arranging opportunities for face-to-face communication, in and of itself, however, would be insufficient because the two groups will bring different languages to the encounters. Relating the two languages of practice and theory is itself a longstanding problem, one that Crites clearly describes. Language differences may, in part, explain why practitioners and researchers rarely communicate directly with each other. As Crites and Herr both observe, theorists tend to communicate in abstract words and concentrate on generalizable concepts, whereas practitioners tend to communicate in concrete words and concentrate on the contextualized particulars of an individual client's situation. Herr suggests that practitioners are less interested in the conceptual language of research and more interested in an understandable language that describes their work. In contrast, Crites writes, researchers seem more interested in decontextualized, abstract principles that are widely generalizable.

Jepsen approaches the language problem with the metaphor of clubs. He likens the segregation of theorists from practitioners to membership in two distinct clubs. The two groups employ different languages and rhetoric forms that make mutual understanding very difficult. He further notes that the metaphors of clubs, language, and rhetoric should assist in constructing promising topics for the dialogue between theory and practice. One way to begin such dialogue might be to ask practitioners to articulate for researchers and theorists the practical goals and intended outcomes that accurately represent their practices.

Leong deals with communication problems by first identifying three obstacles that block communication, namely, boundaries, cultures, and complexity. Then he suggests three strategies with which to confront these obstacles: contact, communication, and collaboration. According to Leong, the first strategy would be to increase and facilitate the contact between scientists and practitioners. Without this contact, argues Leong, the two groups will remain isolated from each other with their different conferences and journals and seek solutions to only the problems that concern them. Similar to Holland, Krumboltz, and Arbona, Leong emphasizes the critical importance of increased communication. An understanding of each other's issues and concerns can only come about with communication. The third strategy suggested is collaboration. If researchers and practitioners can spend time together learning about each other's concerns, they are then ready to attempt an integration of the science and practice of career psychology.

Myers accurately and dramatically describes the current status of communication among researchers and practitioners: "theorists and practitioners—though both groups care about careers—come from different cultures, worship different heroes, communicate in different formats, and are incumbents of different occupations." Without striving to increase direct communication between the two "occupations," the field will not advance the integration of career practice and theory.

INCREASE THE APPLICATION
OF EXISTING THEORY AND RESEARCH

A second recommendation articulated by the authors in this handbook implicitly argues that the theory-practice link can be strengthened if practitioners and theorists increase their attention to applying existing theory to practice and research. For example, Osipow enjoins practitioners to invest more of their own effort in applying theories and research to practice and not wait for theorists to do it. In this regard, Harmon explains that practice changes much more quickly than theory. Thus, practitioners must always go beyond existing theory in their work. They must use theory to the extent possible but then use their intuition and clinical knowledge to guide them where theory leaves off. She urges practitioners to use theory to the extent it applies to their clients, knowing that it will lag behind the problems clients present.

Several chapter authors offer specific suggestions for increasing the applicability of existing theory to practice. Swanson suggests that the link between trait-and-factor theory and person-environment fit counseling exemplifies the convergence of theory and practice, as illustrated by the continued value of the model and methods and by the flexibility and adaptability they continue to offer. She suggests that perhaps the most immediate need for theoretical revision is the clear and explicit inclusion of variables such as gender, race, and ethnicity. Despite the fact that career counseling has been steeped in the tradition of individual differences, some of these fundamental differences variables have often been overlooked, yet they remain critical given the diversity of clients requesting career counseling. A second direction in which both theory and practice may be modified is in the realm of process variables in career counseling. Swanson notes that although person-environment counseling has been criticized for its inattention to the client-counselor relationship, it still offers a useful strategy for investigating the therapeutic relationship through the concept of person-environment correspondence. Finally, Swanson concludes that, taken together, trait-and-factor theory and person-environment counseling offer a useful framework for addressing the kind of questions that require attention in the theory and practice of career counseling. For example, what counseling techniques and conditions will produce what types of results with what types of clients?

In discussing implications for practice and science from a person-centered perspective, Lent seems to agree with Swanson when she asserts that career counselors have often neglected relationship factors in favor of delivering information. If the two dimensions of counseling deal with communication and relationship, then the communication dimension has been disproportionately emphasized. Similar to Swanson's advocacy for the utility of the trait-and-factor model for studying the relationship dimension in career counseling, Lent cogently argues that the person-centered model offers a valuable paradigm with which to study the therapeutic relationship within career counseling. Another emerging strategy noted by Lent, one with implications for vocational science and practice, is to use the plethora of alternative research paradigms, including discovery-oriented psychotherapy research. Person-centered theory in the career counseling field may be enhanced through such research methods. Finally, Lent notes that person-centered theory may be useful to practitioners in four ways. First, person-centered theory protects against inaccurate diagnosis and incorrect application of special technologies by defining the goal of the assessment phase as understanding the client's worldview. Second, it clarifies at which point on the psychological helping continuum a particular intervention lies by separating occupational information and experiential counseling. Third, it focuses on perspective taking, a particularly important step in assisting the diverse population that continues to request career counseling. Fourth, it is consistent with methods of data gathering, such that practitioners may more comfortably take on the researcher role in their everyday work.

Jepsen examines the issue of applying existing developmental models of vocational behavior to the practice of career counseling. He suggests that converting developmental theories to a story form could facilitate practice applications. Such stories may be validated by counselors who will certainly offer modifications and elaborations. He also comments that the publication and discussion of more career counseling cases would certainly strengthen the theory-practice link, especially if the case presentations focus primarily on counseling rather than development. Jepsen urges practitioners to use qualitative or naturalistic methods to collect behavioral data about their practice experiences and then offer this information to theorists. Practitioners, unlike theorists and researchers, have access to unique data that may be more coherently assessed using idiographic, qualitative methods.

Qualitative data is rich in hypothesis generation potential; it also has the potential to identify lacunas in theory.

As an example of an effort to better apply existing theory to practice, Vandiver and Bowman propose a revision of Linda Gottfredson's theory of occupational aspirations, resulting in a more effective translation of the theory into practice. They note that Gottfredson's theory of circumscription and compromise provides a new perspective from which to comprehend the development of occupational aspirations. Their revision of Gottfredson's theory offers more flexibility in understanding how the dimensions of sex type, prestige, and interest interact to explain the unique career choices and compromises each individual makes. Using the revision of Gottfredson's theory, counselors can incorporate a broader base of information into their assessment and counseling practices.

An innovative idea for applying existing theory to practice is offered by Gati when he suggests that computerized career guidance systems may serve as laboratories for this work. Not only does he explain a mechanism by which existing theories can be tested for applicability; he actually illustrates how resolving problems and dilemmas in designing computer-assisted career guidance systems (CACGS) furthers the integration of decision theory with the practice of career intervention. Then he suggests and shows how practice can drive the improvement of theory.

The strategies offered by the authors of this handbook for moving toward the goal of better applying career theory to the practice of career intervention provide clear direction for the future. Moreover, they offer an initial agenda for dialogue and collaboration between practitioners and academicians, once communication among the groups is firmly established. The goal of better applying existing theories to practice seems to be widely endorsed, especially by adherents of each individual theory, who see the potential benefits in improved use of their preferred theory. In contrast, a related recommendation attracts fewer supporters. It deals with converging theories as a means of making them more applicable to practice.

USE FRAMEWORKS THAT LINK PRACTICE TO THEORY

Individual theories focus on particular problems; each one has a circumscribed range of convenient application. By systematically linking the theories based on their range of convenience, practitioners may be able to better apply the theories to individual cases. Gottfredson shows how this can be done by introducing a general purpose framework that uses subtheories as specific engines for specific problems. As a starting point, he notes that this framework serves as a reminder that vocational outcomes are functions of both persons and environments. The framework rests on five main ideas—career status, satisfaction, attainment, direction of activity, and work performance—and is supported by four secondary concepts—environmental competence, personal resources, life circumstances, and congruence. Gottfredson presents this framework and follows it by using a map that shows how multiple partial theories may fit together into a comprehensive model of career status. Gottfredson explains that the selective use of partial theories tailored for specific career problems requires sound measures of the theoretical constructs that can be practically applied. Two such instruments are the *Position Classification Inventory* (Gottfredson & Holland, 1991) to assess person-job match and the *Career Attitudes and Strategies Inventory* (Holland & Gottfredson, 1994) to assess geographic barriers and interpersonal abuse.

Savickas shares Gottfredson's preference for a technical eclecticism rooted in a systematic linking of specific theories to particular career problems. He provides a framework intended to link theory and practice. His framework casts the career theories into a structural model that accounts for the major dimensions of work in people's lives, describes the measurement techniques associated with each unit in the model, and identifies the career intervention that best expresses each theory in action. Savickas then explains how distinct presenting problems are best approached by using certain theories, measures, and interventions. Following the framework and its associated Decision Tree may be a way that counselors can become even more systematic and eclectic in rigorously applying pertinent theory to particular clients. Savickas hopes that the framework can be used to stimulate and facilitate research on career intervention, especially following Lucas' suggestion of constructing minimodels for subpopulations of clients and, in so doing, advance a science of practice. A related recommendation articulated by several authors requires going well beyond converging existing theories to improve their applicability to practice; this recommendation focuses on construction of new theories.

CONSTRUCT CAREER COUNSELING THEORIES

Whereas many participants in the two "convergence conferences" that inspired this and a previous book thought that theory-practice integration projects should concentrate on improving the applicability and use of existing theory, others thought that a need existed for construction of new theories. In the main, those who called for new theories argued that existing theories deal with vocational development, not career counseling. From this viewpoint, practitioners might benefit from collaborating with theorists in constructing theories of career counseling. Swanson's chapter in this handbook can be read as a creative and insightful response to this call. She articulates the difference between the trait-and-factor theory of vocational choice and adjustment and the person-environment counseling model and methods. After drawing this important distinction, she describes how the theory of vocational behavior has informed the theory of career intervention and seems to urge a more reciprocal interaction between the two in the future. To use Collin's term, Swanson appears to call for establishing a *virtuous circle* among adherents to the Minnesota point of view.

Rather than dealing with existing theoretical approaches, Walsh offers a blueprint for constructing a career counseling theory by discussing principles that could structure a unified theory of counseling career. He lists several principles inspired by work in the psychotherapy literature that deal with a unified theory of therapeutic process. For example, one principle suggests that all career counseling models assume that the exchanges between counselors and clients lead to significant change in a client's career behavior and attitudes. A second assumption is that the quality of the counseling relationship is a central contributor to the career counseling process. A third assumption is that all models of career counseling involve information gathering. A fourth assumption is that all career counseling models involve cognitive, behavioral, and affective learning. Finally, a fifth assumption is that career decision making hinges on compromise. Taken together, these principles could form the nucleus of a career counseling theory.

Krumboltz and Chartrand, two authors who stress learning conceptions of vocational behavior, both offer new theories of career counseling in this handbook. Krumboltz, in publishing, for the first time, a learning theory of career counseling, discusses learning as the focus of counseling. He suggests the use of assessment instruments to stimulate new learning, the application of more educational interventions, the selection of learning outcomes as criteria of success, and the reduction of distinctions between career and personal counseling. Helping clients create more satisfying lives for themselves is a general goal shared by many helping professions. Krumboltz hopes that practitioners who use his new learning theory will no longer be matchmakers but instead will generate learning experiences for their clients that address a wide array of personal as well as career issues. To Krumboltz, the general goal of the career counselor is to promote positive learning. For the career development profession, the practical implications involve the task of career counseling becoming a national priority, professional career counselors assuming a leadership role, and counseling becoming more central to the mission of schools of education. According to Krumboltz, conceiving of career counseling as a learning experience puts it as one of the central educational goals of the nation. Under a learning theory, career counseling becomes central to the educational enterprise. Counselors can be viewed as educators responsible for tailoring learning experiences to accomplish cognitive, emotional, and behavioral goals.

Chartrand, in presenting for the first time her theory of sociocognitive career counseling, notes that theories of career development and adjustment were created to explain vocational behavior, whereas models of career counseling are created to guide practice. In general, the major theories have done a fairly good job of mapping out theoretical networks that explain vocational behavior. However, these theories, Chartrand observes, do not answer many of the questions that arise in counseling practice. Theories of career development were not devised to address how clients view their problems or how they view counseling. Theory sometimes remains several steps removed from the applied goal of changing behavior. Chartrand explains that, in practice, counselors seek to address specific client problems, whereas theorists seek to explain universal behavior. Each serves a very different purpose, and consolidating them, Chartrand argues, would ignore their critical difference. A more viable option than consolidation is the construction of career counseling models that incorporate and complement theories of vocational development. In that context, Chartrand constructs a sociocognitive-interactional model for career counseling as an initial effort to complement the sociocognitive theory of vocational development. The social cognitive component addresses the counseling content and the interpersonal component addresses interpersonal functioning, both in terms of individual style and the dynamic counseling process.

Bingham and Ward give a precis of a third new career counseling theory (Ward & Bingham, 1993; Bingham & Ward, 1994; and Fouad & Bingham, 1995), the culturally appropriate career counseling model. The counseling process model that they have developed in collaboration with Fouad consists of seven steps:

1. Establish a culturally appropriate relationship
2. Identify career issues
3. Assess the influence of cultural variables
4. Set counseling goals
5. Implement culturally appropriate interventions
6. Support client decisional processes
7. Ensure that the client implements plans and the counselor follows up with client

Bingham and Ward describe each step in the model and illustrate the model with a case example.

Clearly, the contributions proffered in this volume by Swanson, Krumboltz, Chartrand, Bingham, and Ward presage a new direction in the career field, one with the goal of better integrating career theory and practice. The specific strategies that they explain and model present innovative ideas that open a new domain with special opportunities for practitioner-theorist communication and collaboration, especially with regard to clinical case studies.

CONDUCT RESEARCH BASED IN CLINICAL CASES

Collaboration on developing theories of career counseling will certainly require clinical research involving studies that examine the theories as they pertain to particular clients in unique situations. Harmon urges researchers to approach this work inductively from the problems that practitioners routinely encounter. This would help them focus theory development on the more difficult career problems such as chronic indecisiveness, job dissatisfaction, feelings of hopelessness about getting a job, and discouragement concerning changing jobs. Harmon counsels theorists to recognize, from cases described by practitioners, that many contemporary career problems are beyond the individual's control and may actually rest within a larger set of problems in modern living.

Lucas suggests a practitioner-scientist model in order to increase the clinical relevance of career research and strengthen the natural relationship that exists between practitioners and researchers. In this discussion, she uses Holland's Social and Investigative personality types to consider practical ways to prompt practitioners to convert their clinical questions into research projects. She further suggests that in addition to describing individual cases that scientists and practitioners develop—from case-based research—models or minitheories should consist of treatment protocols for frequently encountered career problems in specific populations. According to Lucas, such a scientist-practitioner or a practitioner-scientist engagement allows both parties to make unique contributions to theory-practice integration. Lucas notes that, although current research methodology cannot address fully the nature of the career counseling process, practitioners' involvement in case research would help them to refine their own counseling hypotheses. Recognizing one's own biases and thinking more objectively can both function as crucial checks on one's work. This perspective may even reveal the need to attend to new issues that arise in clinical practice as modern society transforms itself into a form that affirms multiculturalism.

FOCUS INTEGRATION PROJECTS
ON THE CULTURAL CONTEXTS OF CAREERS

Modern career theories were constructed for an industrial culture that requires hierarchical organizations and rewards individual achievement. These theories, using the dictates of 20th century science, emphasize decontextualized abstract principles and universal generalizability. Contemporary theory construction and renovation, according to Herr, must increasingly become contextualized and particular, especially in understanding and explaining the behaviors, problems, and situations brought to career counseling by increasingly diverse groups of clients. Furthermore, Collin points out that the career field requires innovation from perspectives that attend to context because the context of career has become turbulent, with the work environment changing rapidly to meet needs of information society.

Arbona suggests that the field needs to reformulate its questions regarding the relationship between ethnic/racial group membership and vocational development, paying closer attention to issues of social class and access to education. To date, qualitative studies suggest that Hispanic college students and graduates may not be all that different from their White counterparts regarding career-related variables. Other qualitative studies suggest that low-income Hispanic collegebound high school students are similar to their mainstream counterparts in various aspects of vocational development. However, Arbona asks, Is it possible to expand career theories so that they apply to poor, uneducated Hispanics? Or do we need to develop new theories that may relate to the life experiences of these groups? According to Arbona, attending to the needs of poor, uneducated Hispanic children and youth will take more than expanding existing theories of vocational behavior. She suggests that it may require the field to move from the study of careers to the study of work in people's lives so that theory and practice may focus on work at all levels of the educational and prestige scales. Or it may require that the field shift its attention from career choice to cognitive and academic development.

Subich attends to issues of diversity as she seeks to improve the translation of theory into practice by investigating the uniformity myth that is implicit within modern career assessment models, measures, and materials. She invites readers to more fully integrate an appreciation of individual uniqueness into the practice of career assessment. In considering future directions, she recommends attention to psychometric concerns, contextual assessment, acculturation, and qualitative assessment. In terms of psychometric concerns, she notes that specific instruments used in career assessment would benefit from review and revision. The construction technologies of these assessment tools often do not fully acknowledge information about individual differences. In contextual assessment, Subich sees the need for more standardized instruments to measure environmental or contextual variables relevant to a client's career concerns. For example, environmental barriers are a contextual factor that is often ignored in career assessments, yet it is very relevant to the vocational behavior of members of minority groups. Just as contextual assessment may aid in the understanding of occupational choice, so too may assessing a client's level of acculturation or stage of identity development contribute important information regarding the role of these individual differences factors in vocational behavior. Subich explains that recognition and assessment of an individual's level of acculturation or stage of identity development exemplifies the essence of counselor attention to individual difference variables. Finally, Subich underscores the need to use more qualitative-oriented procedures and idiographic interpretations in assessing contextual and acculturation career variables.

Bingham and Ward demonstrate how attention to issues related to diversity can strengthen the integration of career theory and practice. Toward this end, Bingham and Ward describe three instruments that they have developed to assist counselors in the assessment and treatment process with ethnic minority women. The *Multicultural Career Counseling Checklist* (Ward & Bingham, 1993) focuses on issues of racial and ethnic identity. The *Career Counseling Checklist* (Ward & Bingham, 1993) assesses the client's knowledge about the world of work, self-confidence, and the client variables of age, race, gender, and disability. The Decision Tree assessment focuses on whether to emphasize personal or career concerns with a client. These instruments are best used within a culturally appropriate career counseling model such as the one developed and described by Bingham and Ward (this volume). In addition to using insights from scholarship on multiculturalism to advance theory-practice integration, the literature on constructivist and feminist praxis provides ideas for furthering practice-theory integration.

RECONSIDER ASSUMPTIONS
THAT SEPARATE PRACTICE FROM THEORY

The transformation from an industrial society to an information society has recently prompted a reexamination of the assumptions on which modern career theories rest. Part of this reexamination includes particular attention to linkages between theory and practice. For example, Meara suggests that the field become more in touch with the assumptions of industrial society, on which career counseling is built. She draws attention to two assumptions in particular. First, career theory and practice assume that individuals are oriented toward the future. Theorists and practitioners emphasize long-term goals, ranging over the whole life span. Second, theory and practice are normative and prescriptive about how clients ought to decide, preferring that they be rational. Nevertheless, Meara wonders if the values of rationality and future orientation are still the "coin of the realm in contemporary life." If not, then those among us who see no future for themselves are not well served by career planning theories or services. Collin shares Meara's point of view and applies it to organizations and the context of work. Collin argues that the new learning and self-designing organizations, which fit the needs of the information age, require new views of career, especially views that go beyond the concentration on individualistic, future-oriented goals.

Richardson also suggests that we need to reexamine our assumptions and then reconceptualize career counseling to resolve the false splits between theory, research, and practice. The first step in the reconceptualization process is to assert a central belief in the value and importance of work in people's lives as a basic and essential human function and activity. The second step, according to Richardson, is to retire the label *career counseling* and refer to this practice as counseling and psychotherapy with a specialty in work, jobs, and careers. Richardson uses both terms, *counseling* and *psychotherapy,* in order to emphasize the counseling process rather than career content, to reduce the distinction between healthy and sick or normal and pathological, and to further suggest that people be viewed from developmental and contextual perspectives. Richardson uses all three terms—*work, jobs,* and *career*—to acknowledge that although work itself is the central concern regardless of location or context, jobs and careers do provide an important context for much work in our society.

Young and Valach draw on constructivist epistemology in suggesting four points that could contribute to greater integration of theory and practice. First, counseling itself is career-relevant action, like other career-relevant actions in which the client participates. As action, the authors note, counseling can be understood from the perspective of manifest behavior, conscious cognitions, and social meaning. These same perspectives can be used in career counseling research. Second, the emphasis on cognitive processes and social learning highlights the characteristics of interpretative career counseling. Interpretation in career counseling emphasizes language and discourse. The words and sentences used are not only talk about career, they are also both individual and joint action that actually construct career. Third, in addition to the individual action of the client and counselor, career counseling can be considered as joint action. Together the client and counselor produce new action in counseling, which could not have been produced by either alone. Finally, in an action approach, career research, theory, and practice closely interrelate, allowing easy transition from one to the other.

As the field reconsiders its assumptions and incorporates insights from constructivist and feminist scholarship, it must not lose sight of its most useful and culturally appropriate knowledge. Myers counsels practitioners and academicians to keep our best knowledge, "to stay focused on the stability of work, the constancy of work motives, and the enduring relationships between individual personalities and occupational environments, and the persistent centrality of work in the lives of humans." As new knowledge emerges concerning the integration of career theory and research, it must be transmitted to the next generation of practitioners, theorists, and researchers.

CHANGE TRAINING TO STRENGTHEN THEORY-PRACTICE INTEGRATION

Although academicians have escaped the attention of many involved in projects to improve linkages between theory and practice, Harmon focuses her attention squarely on them in asking professors to value the practice ambitions of their students as much as they value their students' research ambitions. Moreover, she urges professors to be creative in having students think about the theoretical implications of their practice as well as in helping students to reframe practice as basis for theoretical innovation and development. And she gives some very practical advice for improving the theory-practice nexus when she asks professors to encourage their students to evaluate clinical interventions for their thesis and dissertation research. Savickas agrees with Harmon that more evaluation and clinical research is needed. He asserts that most current research focuses on questions of "what can we know and how can we know." The integration of theory and practice will be better served by research that focuses on questions about "what should counselors do, how do counselors know what works, and can counselors do it better." Walsh actually suggests a research agenda that may produce knowledge that is useful to practitioners in working with clients, an agenda exemplified by research that concentrates on idiographic models, the Big Five, and practical intelligence. Collin goes a step further than Harmon, Savickas, and Walsh when she implies that academicians, in her model of a virtuous circle, should relinquish their traditional power as producers and purveyors of knowledge and become facilitators of practitioners' research and teachers of research design.

Fostering an appreciation for linkages between career theory and practice may require the revision of graduate school curricula pertaining to vocational psychology and career counseling. One direction worth exploring is to devise a course, or at least a segment of one, that is based in case studies. Early in this century, American pragmatists advised researchers that theory should begin with practice, not abstractions. Following this sage counsel, professors could generate theoretical issues from clinical cases in increasing depth. Theory would remain a cornerstone of the graduate curriculum, yet the clinical case would be the starting point for each discussion. In this way, the theory enterprise would start with student questions, not faculty lectures. Students, given greater responsibility for their own learning, would be expected to identify the theoretical concepts that they need to know for their practice. Accepting this responsibility for generating theory from their own cases would stand students in good stead for their careers as practitioner-scientists.

CONCLUSION

This chapter has highlighted eight recommendations, articulated by the authors in this handbook, for strengthening the union between career practice and theory. The major recommendations for a project that would more completely integrate career practice and theory call for improving communication among theorists and practitioners so that they can collaborate in better applying existing theories, devising frameworks that systematize the simultaneous application of multiple theories, and constructing career counseling models. Furthermore, the recommendations include testing the revised and newly developed theories by clinical research based in case studies that attend to the full range of career concerns presented by clients living in diverse contexts and experiencing the turbulent transformations caused by the conversion from an industrial society to an information-intensive one. As these goals are met, academicians must also seek to innovate their vocational psychology and career counseling curricula to account for and further strengthen the integration between career theory and practice.

REFERENCES

Bingham, R. P., & Ward, C. M. (1994). Career counseling with ethnic minority women. In W. B. Walsh & S. H. Osipow (Eds.), *Career counseling with women* (pp. 165–195). Hillsdale, NJ: Erlbaum.

Fouad, N. A., & Bingham, R. P. (1995). Career counseling with racial and ethnic minorities. In W. B. Walsh & S. H. Osipow (Eds.), *Handbook of vocational psychology: Theory, research, and practice* (2ed., pp. 331–366). Hillsdale, NJ: Erlbaum.

Goldfried, M. R. (1993). Implementation research for the practicing therapist: An unfulfilled promise? *Clinical Research Digest, Supplement 10,* 1–5.

Gottfredson, G. D., & Holland, J. L. (1991). *Position Classification Inventory: Professional manual.* Odessa, FL: Psychological Assessment Resources.

Holland, J. L., & Gottfredson, G. D. (1994). *Career Attitudes and Strategies Inventory: An inventory for understanding adult careers.* Odessa, FL: Psychological Assessment Resources.

Ward, C. M., & Bingham, R. P. (1993). Career assessment of ethnic minority women. *Journal of Career Assessment, 1,* 246–257.

Contributors

Toward the Convergence of Career Theory and Practice Conference participants are pictured left to right as follows: (front row) J. Krumboltz, J. Holland, E. Lent, S. Bowman, B. Vandiver, H. Tinsley, L. Subich, D. Tinsley, J. Chartrand, A. Collin;(second row) F. Borgen, J. Swanson, S. Osipow, C. Arbona, D. Jepsen, E. Herr, R. Myers, G. Gottfredson, W. Walsh, L. Harmon, N. Meara, R. Bingham, N. Betz, M. Richardson, C. Ward, M. Savickas, I. Gati, R. Young. Authors not pictured: M. Lucas, J. Crites, F. Leong, and L. Valach.

Consuelo Arbona, Ph.D., is a member of the Educational Psychology Department faculty of the University of Houston. Her areas of interest are cross-cultural psychology and career and vocational counseling with an emphasis on Hispanic populations. Her research has examined issues related to the measurement of acculturation and ethnic identity and the career and educational development of Hispanic and other minority students. She serves on the editorial board of the *Career Development Quarterly*.

Rosie Phillips Bingham, Ph.D., is currently assistant vice president of student affairs/ student development at the University of Memphis, where she is an adjunct professor in the College of Education and the Department of Psychology. She has written and presented extensively on the topics of multicultural and career counseling. She has served on the editorial boards of the *Journal of Counseling and Development* and *The Counseling Psychologist*, and she currently serves on the editorial board of the *Journal of Career Assessment*.

Fred H. Borgen, Ph.D., is professor of psychology at Iowa State University, where he previously directed the Counseling Psychology Program. He earned his Ph.D. in psychology at the University of Minnesota, where he worked with David Campbell in the 1960s to develop the Basic Interest Scales of the *Strong Interest Inventory (Strong)*. He was one of the developers of the 1994 revision of the *Strong*. His research focus is on vocational assessment and theory.

Sharon L. Bowman, Ph.D., is an associate professor in the Department of Counseling Psychology and Guidance Services at Ball State University in Muncie, Indiana, where she is also the director of doctoral training. Her research focuses on career development and multicultural issues, particularly for African Americans, women, and gay, lesbian, and bisexual people. She is also interested in the issue of women's identity development. She serves on the editorial board of the *Journal of Vocational Behavior*.

Judy M. Chartrand, Ph.D., is currently an assistant professor in the Department of Psychology at Virginia Commonwealth University, where she teaches career development and counseling practice. Her research areas include the study of career decision making, person-environment fit theories, and the career development of at-risk populations. She has coauthored grant projects designed to enhance career planning by older adults, inner city adolescents, and female offenders. She currently serves on editorial boards for the *Journal of Counseling Psychology* and the *Journal of Vocational Behavior*.

Audrey Collin, Ph.D., is reader in organizational behavior in the Department of Human Resource Management at De Montfort University, Leicester, England. She previously worked in personnel management and then in social research. She carried out a study of midcareer change, which generated several publications. Her study also influenced her current interest in developments in career research and theory. Some of these interests focus on the nature of practice and have led to a number of publications in the management field.

John O. Crites, Ph.D., is president of Crites Career Consultants in Boulder, Colorado. He is author of *Vocational Psychology: The Study of Vocational Behavior and Development* and *Career Counseling: Models, Methods, and Materials*, and coauthor, with D. E. Super, of *Appraising Vocational Fitness*. He has constructed and developed the *Career Maturity Inventory* and the *Career Mastery Inventory*. Dr. Crites served as president of the Counseling Psychology Division in the American Psychological Association and received the Eminent Career Award from the National Career Development Association and the Walter F. Storey Award from the American Society for Training and Development. He was also previously a professor of counseling psychology at the University of Iowa, the University of Maryland, Kent State University, and Northwestern University. He is currently field testing a revision of the *Career Maturity Inventory*.

Itamar Gati, Ph.D., is professor of education and psychology at the Hebrew University of Jerusalem. His research program focuses on the processes involved in making career decisions and on facilitating such decision making through computer-assisted career guidance systems. He headed the development teams for three such systems in Israel.

Gary D. Gottfredson, Ph.D., is president of Gottfredson Associates, Inc., a psychological research and development corporation he founded after reviewing his profile on the *Career*

Attitudes and Strategies Inventory and the *Position Classification Inventory* for the prospective job of "research entrepreneur" (the first-listed occupation in the Daydreams section of his *Self-Directed Search*). His research involves improving measurement and evaluation practices for drug abuse and violence prevention programs, improving the effectiveness of criminal justice and educational programs, and developing tools for assisting people with career plans.

Lenore W. Harmon, Ph.D., is a professor of educational psychology at the University of Illinois in Urbana-Champaign. She served as editor of the *Journal of Vocational Behavior* from 1975 to 1984 the *Journal of Counseling Psychology* from 1988 to 1993. She is a past recipient of the American Psychological Association's Leona Tyler Award for Outstanding Contributions to Counseling Psychology. Her research interests include the career development of women and athletes and the development of interest inventories.

Edwin L. Herr, Ed.D., is distinguished professor of education and associate dean for academic programs and research in the College of Education at Pennsylvania State University. For 24 years, he headed the Department of Counselor Education, Counseling Psychology and Rehabilitation Services at Penn State. He edits the *Journal of Counseling & Development*. His recent books include *Career Guidance and Counseling Through the Life Span: Systematic Approaches (Fourth Edition)*, *Counseling Employment Bound Youth*, and *Handbook for College and University Career Centers*. He has served as president of the American Counseling Association, the National Career Development Association, and the Association for Counselor Education and Supervision, and is currently a member of the board of directors of the International Association for Educational and Vocational Guidance.

John L. Holland, Ph.D., has been a researcher-practitioner and research supervisor and teacher for 45 years. He is best known for *The Self-Directed Search*, a leading interest inventory. In 1994, he received the American Psychological Association's award for Distinguished Professional Contributions.

David A. Jepsen is a professor in the Division of Counselor Education at the University of Iowa, where he has taught courses in vocational psychology, career guidance, and career decision making for more than 20 years. He served as editor of the *Career Development Quarterly* from 1982 to 1988 and was president of the National Career Development Association. The personal processes involved in career decision making and life-span career development are the major topics of his research program. Dr. Jepsen received the Eminent Career Award from the National Career Development Association in 1995.

John D. Krumboltz, Ph.D., is professor of education and psychology at Stanford University. He received a Guggenheim Fellowship and spent one year as a Fellow at the Center for Advanced Studies in the Behavioral Sciences. On three occasions he received the Outstanding Research Award as well as the Distinguished Professional Services Award from the American Personnel and Guidance Association. He coauthored *Changing Children's Behavior* and coedited *Counseling Methods* and *Assessing Career Development*. He developed the social learning theory of career decision making in *Social Learning and Career Decision Making*, which he coedited. Dr. Krumboltz received the American Psychological Association's Leona Tyler Award for Outstanding Contributions to Counseling Psychology in 1990 and the National Career Development Association's Eminent Career Award in 1994.

Ellen B. Lent, Ph.D., is currently an adjunct assistant professor in the Counseling and Personnel Services Department at the University of Maryland at College Park. She was previously a staff psychologist at St. Lawrence Behavioral Medicine Services in Lansing, Michigan, senior staff member at the Michigan State University Counseling Center, assistant dean of student life at Ohio Wesleyan University, and human resource consultant at Control Data Corporation. Her research interests and publications are in the areas of counseling skills, career development, predictors of work satisfaction, and prevention of workplace stress. She is an ad hoc reviewer for the *Career Development Quarterly, Journal of Vocational Behavior,* and *Journal of Mental Health Counseling.* She is a frequent presenter at national and regional conferences on career development and related topics.

Frederick T. L. Leong, Ph.D., is an associate professor of psychology at Ohio State University. He has served on the editorial boards of numerous journals, including the *Journal of Vocational Behavior,* the *Career Development Quarterly,* the *Journal of College Student Personnel,* and the *Journal of Career Assessment.* He has authored or coauthored more than 50 publications in various counseling and psychology journals and 14 book chapters. He coedited *Womanpower: Managing in Times of Demographic Turbulence* and *Asians in the United States: Abstracts of the Psychological and Behavioral Literature, 1967–1991.* He recently completed *Career Development and Vocational Behavior of Racial and Ethnic Minorities.* He is the past recipient of the American Psychological Association's Early Career Scientist/Practitioner Award.

Margaretha S. Lucas, Ph.D., is the training director of predoctoral psychology interns at the Counseling Center and assistant professor in the Counseling and Personnel Services Department at the University of Maryland in College Park. Her research has focused on personality characteristics of students who are unclear about their career choices, career issues of minority students, personal aspects of career counseling, and comparisons between career and noncareer help seekers at counseling centers. She has presented her research at national and international conferences and she serves on the editorial board of the *Career Development Quarterly.*

Naomi M. Meara, Ph.D., is a professor of psychology at the University of Notre Dame. With Michael J. Patton, she coauthored *Psychoanalytic Counseling* and "Working Alliance in Career Counseling." She has collaborated with Linda M. Chalk and Jeanne D. Day on papers applying the paradigm of "possible selves" to the career choices of women and to career counseling. She is past president of the American Psychological Association's Counseling Psychology Division and is currently a fellow of the American Psychological Association, the American Psychological Society, and the American Association of State Psychology Boards.

Roger A. Myers, Ph.D., is Richard March Hoe professor of psychology and education at Teachers College at Columbia University, where he has also served as director of training in counseling psychology, chair of the Psychology Department, and director of the Division of Psychology and Education. He has directed a counseling center at the University of North Dakota and has been a consultant on career issues to Peru, Kenya, Uganda, Tanzania, Turkey, Kuwait, and Iran. He helped construct *The Career Development Inventory* and *The Adult Career Concerns Inventory* and coedited *Behavior Change* and the second edition of *Counseling from Profiles.* In addition to the Hoe professorship, he received an Honorable Mention for Outstanding Research from the American Personnel and Guidance Association and the

American Psychological Association's Leona Tyler Award for Outstanding Contributions to Counseling Psychology.

Samuel H. Osipow, Ph.D., is professor of psychology at Ohio State University in Columbus. He has been a faculty member at Ohio State since 1967 and served as chair of the Psychology Department from 1973 to 1986. He is the author of *Theories of Career Development*, coeditor of the *Handbook of Vocational Behavior*, the founding editor of the *Journal of Vocational Behavior*, past editor of the *Journal of Counsel-ing Psychology*, and currently serves as the editor of *Applied and Preventive Psychology*. He is also the coauthor of the *Career Decision Scale* and *The Occupational Stress Inventory*. Dr. Osipow has received the American Psychological Association's Leona Tyler Award for Outstanding Contributions to Counseling Psychology.

Mary Sue Richardson, Ph.D., is currently a professor in the Department of Applied Psychology in the School of Education at New York University, where she directs the Counseling Psychology Doctoral Program. She has served on the editorial boards of the *Journal of Counseling Psychology* and the *Psychology of Women Quarterly*. Her publications have been on topics that relate to work and vocational psychology, women's development, feminist theory and research, and psychoanalytic psychotherapy.

Mark L. Savickas, Ph.D., is professor and chair in the Behavioral Sciences Department at the Northeastern Ohio Universities College of Medicine and adjunct professor of counseling at Kent State University. He edits the *Career Development Quarterly* and currently serves on editorial boards for the *Journal of Counseling Psychology, Journal of Vocational Behavior*, and *Journal of Career Assessment*. With R. W. Lent, he coedited *Convergence in Career Development Theories*. He serves as U.S. national correspondent for the International Association for Educational and Vocational Guidance and chairs the Career Psychology Special Interest Group in the Organizational Psychology Division of the International Association for Applied Psychology. In 1994, he received the American Psychological Association's John L. Holland Award for Outstanding Achievement in Career and Personality Research.

Linda Mezydlo Subich, Ph.D., is a professor in the Department of Psychology at the University of Akron, where she teaches in the Counseling Psychology Doctoral Program. Her professional interests include vocational psychology theory and research, with special emphasis on issues relevant to women and members of minority groups. Her publications and presentations have encompassed topics of career choice and development, self-efficacy theory, and counseling process. She is associate editor of the *Career Development Quarterly* and serves on the editorial boards of the *Journal of Vocational Behavior* and the *Journal of Counseling Psychology*.

Jane L. Swanson, Ph.D., is an associate professor of psychology at Southern Illinois University. She has served as associate editor of the *Journal of Vocational Behavior* and on the editorial boards of the *Journal of Counseling Psychology* and the *Career Development Quarterly*. Her research focuses on career assessment and interest measurement, perceptions of career-related barriers, and women's career development.

Lasislav Valach, D. Phil., is a research psychologist in the Department of Psychiatry at the University of Berne in Switzerland. He has worked on several research projects dealing with the issues of goal-directed action, group action, and career for more than two decades, as well as on health psychology research. He has coauthored chapters in *Methodological Approaches to the Study of Career* and *Representation of Health, Illness and Handicap*. He also coauthored several articles on social dimensions of goal-directed action, coping with various illnesses, and self-confrontation procedure in parent-adolescent career conversations from an action perspective. He has served as a board member for the European Health Psychology Society and is active in the Society for Cultural Psychology and in the Swiss Society for Psycho-Social Medicine.

Beverly J. Vandiver, Ph.D., is an assistant professor of counseling psychology at Pennsylvania State University. She was previously a staff psychologist and assistant professor at the University of Notre Dame. She has focused on the cultural em-powerment of minority students as a way to facilitate their academic achievement and career development. Her research interests are in the areas of multicultural psychology and career development.

W. Bruce Walsh, Ph.D., is a professor in the Department of Psychology at Ohio State University, where he has served as coordinator of the Counseling Psychology Program for the past seven years. Dr. Walsh is the founder and charter editor of the *Journal of Career Assessment*. He coauthored *Tests and Assessments* and *Tests and Measurements* and coedited *Career Counseling for Women, Career Counseling, The Handbook of Vocational Psychology*, and *Person-Environment Psychology*. He has also served on the editorial boards for the *Journal of Counseling Psychology*, the *Journal of Vocational Behavior*, the *Journal of Professional Psychology*, and the *Journal of College Student Development*.

Connie M. Ward, Ph.D., is a counseling psychologist and associate professor in the counseling center at Georgia State University (GSU). She also serves as the director of the Career Development Center, where she consults with government and social service agencies. She holds a joint appointment in GSU's Department of Counseling and Psychological Services. As a licensed psychologist in the state of Georgia, Dr. Ward conducts a private practice of psychotherapy and vocational psychology. She is presently performing research on the *Career Checklist* and examining the roles of ethnicity and gender as they relate to career counseling.

Richard A. Young, Ed.D., is professor of counseling psychology at the University of British Columbia. He coedited *Methodological Approaches to the Study of Career* and *Interpreting Career: Hermenuetical Studies of Lives in Context*. Dr. Young is a registered psychologist in British Columbia and a director of the College of Psychologists of British Columbia. He is also vice chair of the Counseling Psychology Section of the Canadian Psychological Association. In addition to his interest in constructionist, contextual, and action perspectives on career, he and his colleagues continue to research family influences on career development. He is currently on the editorial boards of the *Canadian Journal of Counselling*, the *Career Development Quarterly*, and the *European Journal of Education*.

Credits

Acknowledgment is made to the following authors and publishers for their kind permission to reprint material from copyrighted sources.

Chapter Seven

Page 97 From *Career Counseling: Models, Methods, and Materials* (pp. 49, 52) by J. O. Crites, 1981, New York: McGraw-Hill. Copyright 1981 by McGraw-Hill. Reprinted by permission.

Chapter Eight

Page 111 From "Person-Centered Career Counseling" by J. D. Bozarth and R. Fisher in *Career Counseling: Contemporary Topics in Vocational Psychology,* W. B. Walsh and S. H. Osipow, Eds (1990), Hillsdale, NJ: Erlbaum. Copyright 1990 by Lawrence Erlbaum Associates, Inc. Reprinted by permission.

Chapter Sixteen

Pages 251–264 Modified and reproduced by special permission of the Publisher, Consulting Psychologists Press, Inc., Palo Alto, California 94303 from *Strong Interest Inventory Applications and Technical Guide* by Lenore Harmon, Jo-Ida Hansen, Fred Borgen, and Allen Hammer. Copyright 1944 by the Board of Trustees of the Leland Stanford Junior University. Exclusively distributed by Consulting Psychologists Press, Inc. All rights reserved. Further reproduction is prohibited without the Publisher's written consent.

Chapter Twenty-one

Pages 333–334 From *The Poetry of Robert Frost* edited by Edward Connery Lathem. Copyright 1958 by Robert Frost. Copyright 1967 by Lesley Frost Ballantine. Copyright 1930, 1939, 1969 by Henry Holt and Co., Inc. Reprinted by permission of Henry Holt and Co., Inc.

Page 337 From *Patterns of Culture* by Ruth Benedict. Copyright 1934 by Ruth Benedict, renewed 1961 by Ruth Valentine. Reprinted by permission of Houghton Mifflin Co. All rights reserved.

Index